Same-Sex Desire in the English Renaissance

A Sourcebook of Texts, 1470–1650

Edited by Kenneth Borris

Routledge
Taylor & Francis Group
New York   London

First published in 2004 by
Routledge
711 Third Avenue, New York, NY 10017

Published in Great Britain by
Routledge
2 Park Square, Milton Park, Abingdon, Oxfordshire OX14 4RN

First issued in paperback 2014

Routledge is an imprint of the Taylor and Francis Group, an informa business

Cataloging-in-Publication Data is available from the Library of Congress.

ISBN 13: 978-1-138-87953-9 (pbk)
ISBN 13: 978-0-8153-3626-6 (hbk)

To Luigi Mirando
"because it is he, because it is myself"

Contents

Illustrations

Acknowledgments

Raymond Waddington, editor of Garland Studies in the Renaissance, enthusiastically supported my initial proposal for this book, and Matthew Byrnie, my subsequent editor at Routledge, ensured publication. Faith Wallis generously translated various lengthy Latin texts, never before accessible in English, that much enhance understanding of the history of sexuality and sexual subjectivities. I further thank Konrad Eisenbichler, Anne Lake Prescott, Dorota Dutsch, Mawy Bouchard, Nicola Martino, and Keira Travis for other substantial translations or related assistance. Eisenbichler told me of Laudomia Forteguerri's love sonnets to women, provided a prepublication copy of his essay on her, and authorized the reprinting of his translations of her poems. Patricia Parker told me of Thomas Hill's physiognomical comments on cinaedi, which appear in my entry for his main source, Bartolommeo della Rocca or Cocles. Christopher Frey and his wife Renata typed transcriptions of some English sources. Bruce Smith and Joan Cadden provided some very kind assistance, and Stephen Orgel encouraged me during a dinner in Montreal. Winfried Schleiner provided early counsel on medical sources. As I was completing this manuscript in the summer of 2002, Valerie Traub helpfully supplied the publisher's proofs for her *Renaissance of Lesbianism in Early Modern England* so that I could take some account of her important work. Publishers and holders of copyright acknowledged in the permissions for illustrations and texts were wonderfully cooperative. Fellowships at the Centre for Reformation and Renaissance Studies at Victoria University in the University of Toronto were invaluable, and I am much indebted to the librarians and research collections there and at the Thomas Fisher and Robarts Libraries at the University of Toronto; the McLennan, Blacker-Wood, and Osler Libraries at McGill University; the Biblioteca Nazionale Marciana, Venice; and the Newberry Library, Chicago. My work was facilitated by a Standard Research Grant from the Social Sciences and Humanities Research Council of Canada, and a McGill University Humanities Research Grant. I am most thankful to Luigi Mirando.

Notes on Editorial Practice and Using This Handbook

In editing the selections included in this anthology, I have sought to produce texts that can both constitute a standardized, coherently readable volume, and yet remain authoritative even for most scholarly purposes. So I adjust the diverse presentational styles of the sources according to reader-friendly norms throughout, yet in modest ways that do not affect the content. Though modernizing punctuation and spelling (including proper names), and normalizing usage of u, v, i, and j, I retain old forms such as "saith." I regularize the spelling of archaic words in accord with the *Oxford English Dictionary*, and retain italics only when they accord with modern norms of particular emphasis. Where appropriate, I silently rationalize paragraphing, formerly sometimes erratic or interminable, according to current practice. However, I retain former uses of capital letters to emphasize particular words, and the original subject-verb agreement. Many early modern texts have marginal headings, references, and glosses; I note those that appear significant for the context. For each of the readings, I state my textual source and any further editorial information relevant to its particular treatment here, in a note attached to its general title heading the excerpt.

Notes on Use

For cross references to further related information in the General Introduction, chapter introductions, or sections of chapters (such as author entries), I state the relevant section title or author's name with a preceding asterisk. "*Leone Ebreo" indicates this volume includes an entry for that author, where related information appears. "*Law" likewise refers to that chapter's introduction.

For the quick location of anthologized entries, I provide, in addition to the Contents, an alphabetical index of anthologized authors or headings with the corresponding page numbers. Otherwise, the introductions for chapters, providing a concentrated survey of material related to their topic, supersede an index.

For the organization of each chapter, I provide an introduction to its topic followed by a series of related readings ordered chronologically. Author entries appear in order of date of birth.

For bibliographical references, I cite primary and secondary sources relevant to the topic of each chapter within its notes. Because of the diversity of subjects addressed in the chapters, and thus of citations, a cumulative bibliography for this volume would have been unwieldy. Instead, the notes for each chapter furnish a bibliographical survey germane to the topic.

For economy in reference to ancient Greek and Roman texts, I always silently use the Loeb bilingual edition unless otherwise stated. However, some older English translations in that series bowdlerize homoerotic comment, and so readers relying on English should check other translations of such passages. I give titles of ancient texts in English, but when citing or introducing early modern texts, I give the original title to indicate the language of initial publication (including Latin), with an English translation.

For biblical quotations, I use the King James Bible unless otherwise stated in context.

For general biographical and other information in introductions for author entries, I summarize widely reported or otherwise obvious material without attribution. I note such sources only when they provide unique or obscure information. Some particularly useful reference works are *The Dictionary of National Biography* for Britain (soon to be updated), *The Dictionary of Literary Biography*, *The Dictionary of Scientific Biography*, *The Oxford Classical Dictionary* (third edition), *The Oxford Encyclopedia of the Reformation*, *The Encyclopedia of the Renaissance*, and *Contemporaries of Erasmus*.

General Introduction

As the Renaissance sought to renovate the cultural accomplishments of Greek and Roman antiquity, it also renewed awareness of the ancients' common homoerotic practices and aspirations. The reputed same-sex amours of such prestigious figures as Sappho, Socrates, Alexander the Great, Julius Caesar, and Virgil became widely publicized. Hence Christopher Marlowe (1564–1593) observed, "The mightiest kings have had their minions" and "not kings only, but the wisest men."[1] Gutenberg's invention of movable type around 1450 newly facilitated the mechanical reproduction of texts, so that, despite the ensuing development of restrictions on print media, writings and images could circulate much more readily, including those that challenged sexual and other orthodoxies. Same-sex bedsharing was ordinary in early modern culture, and though it was to some extent regulated by an expected etiquette of appropriate intimacy, such situations would have encouraged the development and exploration of homoerotic interests. Virgil's Second Eclogue traditionally said to express his own ardent desire for handsome young Alexis was standard reading for Renaissance schoolboys throughout Europe. Inspired by classical ideals of physical beauty embodied in surviving sculptures, the visual arts cultivated a new esthetic of anatomically realistic and sensuous human corporeality, with much androgynous or muscular male nudity, sometimes directly treating homophile or homoerotic subjects. Such cultural conditions would support Mario DiGangi's view that "the 'homosocial' and the 'homoerotic' . . . overlapped to a greater extent, and with less attendant anxiety, in the early modern period than would later be possible under a modern regime of sexuality."[2]

Yet others would urge we may too readily underestimate former anxieties about female and male homoeroticism, as Alan Bray and Bruce R. Smith have shown for the latter in England.[3] Same-sex sexual behaviors were officially demeaned or stigmatized, in some cases capital offenses, and often represented as especially grievous sins. After discussing incest, John Bishop (fl. 1577) demands, "What so abominable lust of man can I rehearse, that worse remaineth not still untold? I would have been ashamed to have declared, if that the Apostle had not written it before me [marginal gloss: Romans 1], that men against nature do filthily abuse men, and women, women."[4] As at present, attitudes ranged from rabid condemnations through disgust and scorn to neutrality, sympathy, acceptance, delighted indulgence, and enthusiastic advocacy, all in complex social interplay. But the former ascendancy of what most would now

1

consider fundamentalist, ultraconservative, morally narrow-minded interpretations of Christianity ensured that adverse views were much more influential and oppressive, with all the costs for homophiles that entailed. Moreover, the former more rigidly prescriptive gender hierarchy acutely devalued females and thus also anyone who assumed a sexual role associated with his or her opposite sex. While the early modern social status of female homoeroticism seems somewhat ambiguous (*Theology, *Law, *Brantôme), sexual relations between males could not have occurred in forms that, as Digangi has proposed, were generally considered socially normative or orderly.[5] When compared to official norms, positive understanding of male-male sex could only constitute dissent, not orthodoxy, and such desire was subject to various modes of repression (*Theology, *Law). Especially for males, homoerotic possibilities or behaviors, however favorably conceived by those involved or their sympathetic associates, were always vulnerable to sodomitical reinscription by others, through gossip, insults, or formal denunciations, and hence were at least incipiently—in the Vatican's present archaism—an ostensible "objective disorder." As Western homophobia substantially emerged from traditions of orthodox Christianity, so the missionaries who arrived in China and Japan in the sixteenth century immediately sought to counter the social currency of male-male sex by inculcating antisodomitical prejudices.[6]

The heightened religious, moral, and legal prescriptive zeal of the Reformation and Counter-Reformation exacerbated the European predicament of same-sex erotics, and effects of that repression and its antecedents continue. To rationalize denying male homosexuals any constitutional freedom to practice "sodomy," and thus uphold all state laws criminalizing oral and anal sex between males, the 1986 majority decision of the United States Supreme Court in *Bowers* v. *Hardwick* invoked the statutory prohibition of buggery by the English parliament in its session of 1533–34.[7] Based on much earlier legal and theological anathemas, the terminology and attitudes of that statute are Levitical and Pauline, like its Edwardine, Elizabethan, and colonial American successors, and resultant indictments.[8] Only now, as of June 26, 2003, has the Supreme Court overturned *Bowers* v. *Hardwick* and the related precedents, in *Lawrence* v. *Texas*. But that decision was split, and this anciently rooted "culture war," as one of the opposing Justices called it, continues.

The cultural paradoxes produced by the dissonances of early modern representations of same-sex eros, whether between males or females, would not only have constrained and confused homophiles, but would also have afforded opportunities for strategic evasions. They could shelter transgressive desires and practices under, for example, norms of patronage or approved ideals of intensely committed friendship that included bedsharing, or oppose classical precedence to theological anathemas.

Insofar as spatial constraints allow, I have sought to provide a combined multidisciplinary handbook and anthology of readings for both female and male same-sex erotics during the time generally known as the Renaissance, and focusing on England. The readings sample and document the remarkable diversities of early modern perspectives on the varieties of homoeroticism; introductions for these texts vary in scale according to their explanatory needs. I have also selected the readings to survey some intellectual disciplines or discursive domains significant at this point in the recovery of early modern sexual history. Corresponding chapters gather related texts: Theology, Law, Medicine, Astrology, Physiognomics, Encyclopedias and Reference Works, Prodigious Monstrosities, Love and Friendship, The Sapphic Renaissance, Erotica. Besides assembling excerpts that collectively afford a convenient provisional overview of the engagements of its discursive field with homoeroticism, each chapter has its own summary introduction citing further primary and secondary sources. Rather than reprinting texts now readily available in reliable recent editions or at least well known to English readers interested in this subject, such as certain writings of Marlowe, Shakespeare (1564–1616), Richard Barnfield (1574–1626?), and Katherine Philips (1632–1664), I have chosen those that are not, unless the content seems insufficiently represented otherwise.

While particularly addressing England, I include readings originally written in other European vernaculars or Latin whether or not English translations were issued during the period, for these, especially Latin texts, were also to varying extents available and potentially influential there,[9] or at least represent viewpoints independently possible, as in the case of *Laudomia Forteguerri (1515–1555?). Not only the more educated or well-traveled classes were affected, for the concepts and attitudes could be diffused in English writings, such as those of homophobic theologian *Andrew Willet (1562–1621), or in oral exchanges, as between literate and illiterate sodomites. Since males formerly had much more social, educational, and sexual latitude than females, particularly masculine same-sex sexual contacts would have cross-fertilized conceptions about those behaviors across social strata. While acknowledging England's dynamic relations with continental homoerotic conditions, I can further provide some introduction to the latter, and offer, as Valerie Traub recommends, "a thick associational field" for inquiry.[10] As the Renaissance across Europe began and ended later as the distance from Italy increased, so I draw Italian readings mainly from the quattrocento and cinquecento, but English ones from the sixteenth to mid-seventeenth centuries. Sexual history should not isolate Britain like the pre-Columbian Americas.

My inclusive rather than narrowly regional approach also follows from treating female as well as male same-sex erotics. Their social expression and development evince a relative structural asymmetry produced by different gendered constraints and options assigned to masculine and feminine roles. Though vastly smaller than we would wish, the documentary remains of early modern homoerotic relations among males nonetheless far exceed those for females, centrally because the social privileges of patriarchy and the phallus itself ensured that masculine homosociality and sexual deviance had much greater public scope and recognition. Relative exclusion of females from education and public life ensured that both writing and publication were predominantly male. Although I have sought to include Renaissance feminine writers who treat amorous interplay between females, few currently known representations within my normative temporal bounds are not male-mediated. Two main exceptions are *Forteguerri and possibly the *anonymous poem on female amity in a Maitland manuscript. In England an efflorescence of publications impinging upon female homo-eroticism by such women as Philips, Aphra Behn (1640?–1689), and Delarivier Manley (1663?–1724) occurred after 1650. Their absence here bespeaks prior feminine discretion in treating such topics, which evolved, in Harriette Andreadis' phrase, "a language of erotic ellipsis."[11] However fanciful and reductive, the masculine accounts enable us to explore discursive and social conditions of erotics between females, and assess what they confronted in seeking to define themselves. Since the range of not only early modern English but also European sources on this topic is as yet very narrow, broadly comparative surveys and analyses are necessary to ensure some provisionally helpful sampling of comment.

In framing this volume, I have also sought to address currently central debates, gaps, and difficulties in the historiography of homoeroticism. The controversy between essentialists and social constructionists, who stress the impact of changing historical factors, now widely appears passé, and as Smith observed in 1991, intermediate positions are advisable (9–18). In ancient Rome, for instance, it is clear some men were sexually "more interested" in males than females, "or even . . . exclusively,"[12] so that the history of such persons is lengthy indeed, hence also that of distinctive sexual self-identifications and corresponding categories prior to the terminological and conceptual advent of "homosexuality."

For current investigation of sexual history prior to the nineteenth century, at least, the central controversies appear to revolve around what I will call "the acts paradigm." Sexual acts and sexual identities are not equivalent, and the distinction between them is useful from any viewpoint. However, pressing a historiographically absolute interpretation of that distinction, advocates of the acts paradigm assume anyone (or sometimes almost everyone) who engaged in same-sex sexual practices prior to some particular time in the proximate past could experience them only as disconnected *acts*, in ways divorced from any felt distinctive sense of a homoerotic disposition, subjectivity, or identity. Such perceived affiliations would have been inconceivable to former same-sex lovers and anyone else, in this view, and so experience of sexual relations would have been very fluid. That would have tended to preclude formation of homoerotic fellowships or prototypical subcultures. Perceptible same-sex sexual preferences and consequent self-recognitions only became possible, then, through medical and psychological development beginning in the nineteenth or sometimes eighteenth century (or, as in some accounts such as Bray's, around 1650–1700). The current predominantly binary view of human sexual potential, whereby people are for the most part presumed either homosexual or heterosexual, is thus a recent construction with little or no substantive prehistory, as if it is a new, unprecedented departure from prior norms. Hence I call historiographers of homosexuality who promote the acts paradigm "recent constructionists."[13] Likewise, it has been fashionable to claim that even interiority and subjectivity themselves in Western culture arose only in Shakespeare's time,[14] in which case emergence of specific sexual sensibilities would seem inevitably recent.

On the other hand, both essentialists and moderate constructionists reject the acts paradigm to various extents. While arguing the historical development of same-sex sexual subjectivities and subcultures has been an extended and complex process, the latter would stress that premodern experiences and perceptions of love between females or males do not correspond to sexual orientations and identities in our current sense, but involve significant cultural differences. The origins of interiorities in general have been backdated far before Shakespeare.[15]

Although the basic recent-constructionist claim that "before the modern era sexual deviance could be predicated only of acts, not of persons or identities," is often advanced on Michel Foucault's authority, David M. Halperin recently argues this is not only "a misreading of Foucault," but also "heedless of European history" and "a bogus theoretical doctrine."[16] Halperin's evidence includes a story in the *Decameron* of Giovanni Boccaccio (1313–1375) connecting "the performance of sodomitical acts [between males] with a deviant sexual taste and a deviant sexual subjectivity," so that "sexual acts" could indeed be deemed "related to sexual dispositions, desires, or subjectivities." For Boccaccio's character Pietro di Vinciolo, "his sexual preference for [male] youths is a settled feature of his character and a significant fact about his social identity as a moral and sexual agent" (40–41). While stressing this should not be understood "as a sexual identity, or a sexual orientation in the modern sense," Halperin argues that sexual acts and identities in European culture were not strictly separate prior to the nineteenth century, so that sexual historians must, in effect, "inquire into the construction of sexual identities before the emergence of sexual orientations." "We need to find ways of asking how different historical cultures fashioned different sorts of links between sexual acts, on the one hand, and sexual tastes, styles, dispositions, characters, gender presentations, and forms of subjectivity, on the other" (42–44). Many examples could be added: a similar tale by Gerolamo Morlino (c. 1500), the account of Porcellio by *Matteo Bandello (1485–1561), the elaboration of Orphic homoerotic advocacy by *Angelo Poliziano (1454–1494), and analogous writings by Marlowe and Barnfield among others.[17]

Various other scholars have qualified, questioned, or rejected the acts paradigm. Doubting "whether the distinction between sexual acts and identities can be used to divide premodernity from the modern," Louise Fradenburg and Carla Freccero seek to promote "new thinking" that would avoid taking that distinction's salience and putative political utility for granted, and avoid imposing such a "schematic" structure on the complex relations between past and present.[18] Demonstrating some limited continuity in sexual history, Valerie Traub has shown that ancient medical associations of tribadism with pseudophallic enlargement of the clitoris produced an at least early modern "anatomical essentialism" contributing to present conceptions of female sexual identities (ch. 5). For Smith, Marlowe "introduces us to the possibility of a homosexual subjectivity" in late sixteenth-century England (223), while Gregory W. Bredbeck finds such awarenesses represented in the poetry of Barnfield and Shakespeare.[19] Formative changes in homosexual identity were "gradual and highly uneven," Alan Sinfield argues, so that "there may have been in early modern Europe, especially in aristocratic circles, coteries where something like our concept of the same-sex-oriented individual developed."[20] Mark D. Jordan shows "the idea that same-sex pleasure constitutes an identity of some kind is clearly the work of medieval theology, not of nineteenth-century forensic medicine," and other medievalists such as Allen J. Frantzen have come to similar conclusions.[21] Unlike Halperin, Bernadette J. Brooten backdates the concept of homosexuality and lifelong erotic orientations to antiquity, and so, to some extent, does Amy Richlin.[22]

Joseph Cady has initiated a controversial line of inquiry into early modern male homoeroticism that, whatever the pros and cons of his formulation, affords much as yet unrealized potential for advancement of knowledge about the antecedents of our current sex/gender system, and the former implications of sex differences for perceived sexual dispositions.[23] To appreciate how this is so, we may compare the five-part typology of the European development of male homosexuality proposed by Halperin first in 2000 and again in 2002: (1) male effeminacy, not in all cases implying sex with males; (2) pederasty or "active" sodomy, involving penetration of a subordinate male; (3) friendship or male love; (4) passivity or inversion, again not necessarily implying sex with males; (5) homosexuality.[24] Allowing for some transhistorical continuities, so that inversion has clear precedents such as the ancient cinaedus, Halperin argues these five discursive traditions overlap to some extent, yet each have distinct features. The nineteenth-century identification and description of "homosexuality" as such, he stresses, marked an important shift from the four earlier "prehomosexual" conceptions in various ways. Two of those proposed differences are particularly important for my brief comparison. In one sense, Halperin says, homosexuality newly removes "polarization of identities and roles (active/passive, insertive/receptive, masculine/feminine, or man/boy)," because the prior categories, he assumes, all polarized them. And in another sense, he claims, homosexuality newly focuses on "same-sex sexual object choice in and of itself" to define "sexual and social difference" (133–34). Of course, the extent to which Halperin's five acknowledged social representations actually reflect the former realities of male sexual and other homosocialities is debatable. At least two more models might be added: "pathic" or "passive" sodomy (male availability for sexual penetration), which had its own distinctive development comprising ancient medical texts among others, and differs from Halperin's fourth category in being a specifically sexual disposition; and *amor Socraticus*, a philosophical elaboration of male homoeroticism.[25]

However, in 1992 Cady had established the existence of a significantly different premodern discursive tradition of male same-sex love that cuts across many of Halperin's distinctions between his five categories as well as the two I have added. In some ways (not all, I would stress) it anticipates homosexuality in particular. As Cady does, we may denominate this further paradigm "masculine love," probably its most common formulation throughout Europe, though it also has broadly synonymous or correlative variants such as "virile love," "male venery," "love of males," "male-mingled love," and so forth. Thoroughly androcentric, such early modern usages assume the subject is male (never a female who loves males) and typically denote particular or general male-male relations involving sex in some sense, often implying personal affinity for that. (I have encountered a few cases where it seems to mean overriding attraction and emotional bonding between males that is not sexually consummated.) Since "masculine love" is both nonpolarized and focuses on same-sex sexual object choice (though only male-male, not also between females), it anticipates these two features that Halperin's scheme reserves for homosexuality alone. In these two ways, he proposes, homosexuality "translates same-sex sexual relations into the register of sameness and mutuality," so that they "no longer necessarily imply" structural asymmetries between partners, and it becomes "possible" for them "to bond with one another not on the basis of their difference but on the basis of their sameness, their identity of desire," enabling "companionate, romantic, and mutual . . . love" (133). Yet such amorous same-sex relations were clearly anticipated by the model of masculine love. And in any case, I would emphasize, they were indeed both conceivable and practiced among males and among females in many ways prior to the nineteenth-century advent of "homosexuality" (*Love and Friendship, *Theodor Zwinger).

Masculine love even somewhat anticipated our homosexuality/heterosexuality opposition, for it implied a binary contrast with "feminine love."[26] Again assuming the subject is male, the latter expression conventionally denominated amorous male-female relations or such affective and sexual affinities. (Although Traub sometimes uses "feminine love" to mean love between women, this is, as she has confirmed to me, a pragmatic usage that neither assumes nor implies any historical basis for the expression; no early modern instances have yet been adduced.) This bipartite tradition of masculine love/feminine love was international, just as Cady's examples include English, French, Italian, and Swiss instances in both vernacular languages and Neolatin. For examples specifically opposing "feminine love" to more or less amorous relations between males, I would add *Leone Ebreo (fl. 1460–1521) and *Antonio Rocco (1586–1652).

Although commentators on the history of sexuality have taken little account of masculine love to date, the temporal, geographical, and linguistic range of Cady's examples establishes the broad European vitality of this discursive tradition, and shows that many more can be found.[27] In this volume I provide new instances in writings of *Niccolò Leonico Tomeo (1456–1531), *Ebreo, Lodovico Ricchieri (1469–1525), Philemon Holland (1552–1637), *Willet, *Robert Burton (1577–1640), *Rocco, and *Johannes Thuilius (c. 1590–1630).[28] So definitive was the expression "masculine love" for considerations of sex between males that it is focal for entries treating that subject in the major reference works of Ricchieri and *Theodor Zwinger (1533–1588). They would have further reinforced its terminological currency (*Encyclopedias and Reference Works).

Though the historical significance of masculine love/feminine love will be much debated, and my interpretation differs from Cady's, it constituted an important and distinct early modern means of conceptualizing the possibilities of amorous relations, and necessitates at least some revision of our existing historiographies of homosexuality/heterosexuality. Whether used pejoratively or not, masculine love implies some recognition of an alternate type of erotic pursuit and commitment (exclusive or otherwise), and thus a good deal of potential conscious agency for male same-sex lovers. Also, the implied conceptual formulation of this former terminology sidesteps the horrific divine curse focused in "sodomy" and its cognates.

In addition, whereas it has been recently fashionable to assume that binary analysis of human sexual potential derives from modern notions of sexuality, and would formerly have been unthinkable, prior notions of masculine love show such categorizations had a much more lengthy and complex development. In subsequent readings, *Ebreo, *Marsilio Ficino (1433–1499), and *Agnolo Firenzuola (1493–1543) all suppose that some males are distinctively characterized by particular erotic and/or affective affinities with males rather than females. In his widely read *Dialoghi d'amore* (Dialogues on Love), Ebreo thus distinguishes between those who pursue "masculine love" and those who pursue "feminine love," and assumes these different amorous inclinations are innately predetermined by the astrological conditions of birth. In *De amore* (On Love), a text also widely known throughout early modern Europe, Ficino uses a somewhat comparable analytic model without those specific terms, as in his chapter heading "Whence Comes Love for Males, Whence for Females," in which he assumes the lover is male (Speech VI, ch. 14). Probably because he is awkwardly concerned to advocate his own powerful homoerotic impulses while forbidding them any sexual consummation, his account here is not logically consistent. Nevertheless, Ficino clearly identifies a type of male who strongly tends to pursue love of males in a "heavenly" way, contrary to other males, whose love is corporeal, sexual, and directed toward women or boys. Despite seeming to claim that those corporeal lovers may pursue sex with either gender indiscriminately, as an effect of the chances of personal association, he contrarily states that some males are astrologically predisposed to seek same-sex sexual love. Firenzuola, on the other hand, devises a model that is yet closer to modern binarism and applies it also to women, so that he distinguishes three types of persons according to their typically preferred mode of amorous conjunction: with the opposite sex, or with the same sex, either between males or between females. Each mode may be sexually consummated or not; for same-sex lovers to do so, he claims, is morally despicable. These three writers provide little explanation for their distinctions based on the typical gender of the chosen beloved, as if such categories were readily recognized and understood. They do not have to justify or explain that recognition.

The formerly usual applications of masculine love/feminine love further evince how much the androcentric biases of early modern culture pressed eros between females to the periphery of any official recognition. And yet, much as social ideals of masculine friendship tended to produce parallel effects among women (*Love and Friendship), the male-male commitments acknowledged by masculine love/feminine love would have tended to stimulate such recognitions between females too. As Halperin observes that his four prehomosexual paradigms crucially depend on notions of gender, whereas the denominations homosexuality/heterosexuality are not gender-specific (134–35), so masculine love/feminine love seems in that way, among others, prehomosexual. But it nonetheless seems a main historical precursor of our present homosexual/heterosexual categories. Smith has questioned whether love between males in early modern England was as inherently intergenerational and status-inflected as sometimes assumed (75–76), and masculine love accommodates equalizing impulses, which would have been also suggested by certain prestigious archetypes of male lovers, such as Harmodius and Aristogiton, and corroborated by some social observations of Aristotle and Cicero that were well-known at least in educated circles during the Renaissance.[29]

In any case, whatever our theoretical affinities, we should acknowledge the difficulties of generalizing legitimately about the former characteristics and possibilities of male and female homoerotic attitudes and behaviors. As Craig Williams cautions, even the voices of ancient Roman cinaedi, tribades, and same-sex couples (sometimes married), with their potentially distinctive and dissident insights, cannot now be heard except through impersonations within writings that largely bespeak the dominant sexual ideologies, so that we are reduced to imagining such alternate views through extrapolations (4, 127, 153–59). Early modern social, legal, and theological repression together with restrictions on printed media ensured that, whatever circulated orally or in manuscript, relatively little positive or "insider" representation of same-sex sexual relations has survived. Insofar as those involved tended to keep their views and experiences private or within circles of initiates or privileged sympathizers, how can we justly reconstruct such a history of deliberate occlusion? We should vigorously question the adequacy of evidence adduced for big generalizations claiming to define "the former limits" of homoerotic awareness, perspectives, and interactions, and the chronological "turning points" in their development.

Consideration of *Nüshu* or Women's Script in Southern Hunan, China, clarifies some historiographical difficulties of assessing the former possibilities of sexual subjectivities and subcultures. Officially "discovered" only in 1954, it amounted to a linguistic code of women's community as a resistant subculture distinguished from men, very few of whom could read any of it.[30] Although *Nüshu* originated as far back as the eleventh century in local legends, it was virtually eradicated in the cultural revolution starting in 1966. Inscrutable beyond circles of its adepts, this feminine resource provided a vibrant means of developing and communicating gynocentric perspectives. If it had died out before the twentieth century, there would now almost certainly be no record or knowledge that this fully developed language and body of writings had ever existed.

Pursued in predominantly adverse religious, legal, and social conditions, early modern male and female same-sex sexual interests would have fostered ways of communicating, advocating, and fulfilling those desires while yet excluding outsiders, such as significant glances, sign language of many kinds, selective choice of addressees for openly prohomoerotic speech, and avoidance of recording such views except in ambiguous formulations.[31] Smith proposes that Latin partly constituted a "private language of male sexual desire—of homosexual desire in particular" (84). The extents to which these and other coded mutualities would have produced sexual coteries, networks, undergrounds, and prototypical or nascent subcultures would have depended on many changing factors of place and time, including size of local population and degree of legal and unofficial harrassments. Besides convergences of shared erotic desires and conventionalizations of meeting places or circles of introduction, decisive factors in the formation of homoerotic subcultures include a more or less hostile cultural context; Christian condemnation of same-sex sexual behaviors, combined with complementary endeavors to enforce that legally, provided such stimulus. As Andreadis observes, the relative spatial restrictions of females would have circumscribed the public possibilities of their erotic associations, aside from the exceptional milieus of courts, and, I would add, prostitution (182n.31). The unusually extensive antisodomitical investigative records of Renaissance Florence show it afforded "a profusion" of male homoerotic networks linked with "certain locations" and "circles of sodomite friends," both "well documented." By some they were called "an *arte* (corporation) or even 'sects,' perhaps implying a clandestine organization and specialized skill or knowhow."[32] According to Mary Bly, between 1607 and 1608 the Whitefriars theater in London focused several overlapping communities or fellowships "characterized by a sympathetic awareness of homoerotic desire" now documented by the "queer puns" of its distinctive repertory (6–7). A boys' company known as the King's Revels, who cross-dressed for female roles, acted these plays.

Reconstruction of sexual undergrounds anywhere in early modern Europe is nonetheless difficult. Extant documents concerning same-sex eros in the period were mostly produced by outsiders who were in many cases more or less hostile: those whom its enthusiasts, cautious of gossip, interference, and official or unofficial reprisals, would have sought to exclude from substantial knowledge of their views and doings. The relatively uninformed and biased testimony of outsiders has very limited value for investigating even such basic questions as whether or not same-sex sexual subcultures and subjectivities existed, and to what extent.

However, we can break the vicious circle of defining early modern same-sex lovers solely or largely according to their persecutors by focusing on the far fewer verbal or visual artefacts of the time that represent homoerotic attractions favorably or sympathetically. Such evidence provides only provisional indications of insiders' ideological resources and agencies, for usually we cannot now establish the creator actually had same-sex sexual contacts. But the expression of a more or less prohomoerotic viewpoint documents such potentials or possibilities in the period, including particular approaches, strategies, and arguments that were then conceivable. Particularly important are texts that formalize same-sex sexual advocacy, for these evince considerable scope for deliberate homoerotic agency, self-identification, and commitment (Borris, 238–44). No doubt some defensive writings circulated privately in manuscript, never published and now lost. We are most likely to find relevant material in verbal or visual expressions of creative imagination. Stressing the importance of literary or poetic discourse for the historiography of homoeroticism, Smith argues that, relative to moral, legal, medical, and, I would add, theological discourses, literariness opens up the imaginative dimensions of sexual experience and desire, in ways that are far less dogmatic than provocative, and articulated in fictional codes affording some possible expressive emancipation from official ideals and constraints (15–29). Prohomoerotic creations are as much to be found in the visual arts (*Erotica). Caravaggio (1573–1610) depicts a fey young John the Baptist winsomely flaunting himself with exposed genitals on a fur rug while fondling a ram with phallic horns (Museo Capitolino, Rome). Such verbal or visual remains now offer us the most direct possibilities of insight into former same-sex affective and erotic awareness.

In the case of masculine love, both ancient and "modern" writings held to promote it, or formal verbal defenses, certainly circulated in Europe from at least the later fifteenth century both in manuscript and print (*Love and Friendship, *Erotica). Rather then explicitly urging prohomoerotic arguments and mapping same-sex sexual undergrounds, such early modern texts tend to proceed at least somewhat discreetly in fictional formats through symbols, epitomes, and indirections. Since same-sex sexual behaviors were subject to official and unofficial anathemas and constraints, including the death penalty, felt social pressures ensured the realities of consummation ordinarily left few substantial testimonies to their positive expressions.[33] The favorable writings and their visual counterparts would have arisen from those realities to some extent (whether directly or indirectly), sought to engage and reinforce them, and now constitute our prime sources for reconstructing the conditions and experience of insiders at least in literate or more or less privileged circles. Remarks of outsiders help confirm both masculine love's social currency and its rejections by official religion, morality, and law. In 1622 lawyer and antiquarian Sir Simonds D'Ewes (1602–1650) observed in his private coded diary that the "sin of sodomy," generally referring to sex between males in his context, was so "frequent" in London that he expected only a special divine dispensation would avert retribution as for Sodom.[34] English and continental writers make similar remarks earlier. *Henri Estienne (1528–1598) affirms that, though many Frenchmen advocated such sodomy in the late fifteenth century, it had become even more current in his own time.

Assessing the former possibilities of "sapphism," as we may call it, presents yet more difficulties due to the social subordination and consequent relative silencing of women in general.[35] And early modern feminine homoeroticism was fraught with paradoxes because of the cultural privilege of phallic penetration and ejaculation. What counted as transgressive sexual acts between females could thus be variously construed from different viewpoints to an extent much beyond the possibilities for males (*Theology, *Law, *Medicine, *Brantôme). Andreadis thus posits potential ambiguities of genital focus and erotic recognition among female partners (104–5), while Traub explores the bizarre trope of their "impossible love" and the paradoxical "femme-femme" erotics of "chaste feminine love" (278, chs. 4, 6, 7). Nevertheless, as they and Elizabeth Wahl have shown, there is enough early modern reportage of genital and other modes of erotic interaction between women to establish considerable social currency, concern, and interest.[36] Noting "the appearance of explicitly female same-sex literary subject matter" in Englishwomen's writings of the later seventeenth century, Andreadis rightly concludes this "certainly suggests the existence of contemporary female networks" (95–96). Yet I would question her further conclusion, based on Mary McIntosh's and Bray's accounts of early modern male homoeroticism, that 1650 likewise marks for females "a major break with the past and a movement into new forms of erotic and sexual understanding" (16, 51–52, 98–96). To me such chronological parallelism seems improbable, for "women are regulated *differently* than men" (Traub, 31). Also, as women at that time were becoming far less inhibited about publishing and about dealing with sexual matters in print, so their public literary turn to addressing sapphism is causally overdetermined, and more likely a function of those changes rather than some dramatic shift in female homoerotic consciousness and networking themselves.

We can take some comparative bearings from outsiders here, for earlier publications of males, particularly *Firenzuola, *Pontus de Tyard (1521/2–1605), *Pierre de Ronsard (1524–1585), *Brantôme (1540?–1614), and *John Donne (1572–1631), evince considerable sixteenth-century awareness of women with strong homoerotic commitments or interests. These were unlikely to be somehow possible in France, but not across the channel. And sixteenth-century Frenchwomen apparently did not publish on this topic either. The newly sapphic publications of Englishwomen after 1650 to some extent indicate attitudes and social realities that had also been current at least in sixteenth-century England, but had not, due to the felt constraints of female writing and publishing at that time, been recorded by women in sufficient quantity for us now to have textual traces of their views. Backtracking somewhat, and rightly allowing for developmental discontinuities in sexual history, Andreadis concedes that "certain behaviors, both physical and verbal, that may seem to us similar to what we are accustomed to defining as 'lesbian' may have been a tacitly accepted cultural element in certain segments of [English] society" before "the late sixteenth century" (23). Others locate such behaviors in the Middle Ages (cf. Sautman and Sheingorn). If, as Traub argues, female homoeroticism tended not to attract stigma unless perceived to violate feminine gender roles or reproductive expectations (chs. 4, 6, 7), it may have long enjoyed much scope if discreetly encrypted. But as in the case of Katherina Hetzeldorfer in 1477, indiscretion could bring execution for "female sodomy" in various continental jurisdictions.[37]

An internationally comparative approach best clarifies the possibilities of same-sex sexual advocacy, awareness, and interactions in any early modern European state. Although that could, if not conducted with appropriate tact, possibly distort understanding of conditions there, in this field narrowly regional considerations are bound to be misleading. Since extant records evince major gaps in evidence from both male and female insiders, we can gain some provisionally useful sense of the potential extent of prohomoerotic thinking only by surveying as many available samples as possible, so as to map the conceivable scope of this early modern discursive field. While Shakespeare, Marlowe, and Barnfield furnish an atypically rich cluster of English texts favoring masculine love around 1600, for example, even that is insufficient to define the possible range of such perspectives in England at the time. Certain classical texts contributed much to the prohomoerotic repertoire throughout Renaissance Europe, and so we would need to consider their reception, and also that of such "modern" texts in the continental vernaculars, which could cross borders in their original languages and sometimes translations, whether in print, manuscript, or oral comment. For example, Ben Jonson (1573?–1637) based his comedy *Epicoene* (1609) on *Il marescalco* by *Pietro Aretino (1492–1556), a play sympathetic to masculine love. Besides clarifying the potential scope of prohomoerotic discourse and questions of direct and indirect influence, the vernacular writings can now also illustrate how elements of ancient Greek and Roman texts could be appropriated in the Renaissance for same-sex sexual advocacy, independently or through traditional filiations. Allowance for such factors is particularly important in considering the situations of populous cities. Relevant local conditions could also include foreign trade or tourism; proximity of universities or similar institutions, or substantial numbers of graduates, which would expand linguistic and textual resources; and concentrations of expatriates. To assess the *possibilities and rationales* of prohomoerotic conceptions in Renaissance urban and literate contexts, at least, our inquiries should be informed by comparative study of sources advocating or portraying sexual resistance and dissidence. By reconstituting this discursive repertoire, we clarify the former possibilities, options, conventions, strategies, and models of prohomoerotic standpoints, and turn from the history of repression to that of emancipation and enjoyment.

Not only does a shortage of insiders' testimony produce major difficulties in assessing the possibilities of early modern same-sex sexual sensibilities and interactions, but also little research was done prior to 1980, so that much evidence remains still undiscovered, unconsidered, unpublicized, or unavailable even in secondary English reportage. Since early modern attitudes toward homoerotic behaviors varied exceedingly as I stressed at the outset, anyone can cite facts or anecdotes that appear to demonstrate some sweeping generalization that yet other ones would contradict. Foucault's epochal divisions of history geared to shifts in modes of thought, Sinfield observes, are "vulnerable to almost any scrap of empirical evidence showing ideas occurring at the 'wrong' time" (13). As the documentary remains of early modern homoeroticism are scattered and fragmentary, its study requires piecing together evidence across many texts and disciplines, with as yet few specialized guides to particular discursive aspects of the field, or multidisciplinary surveys, and so we can readily err due to inadvertent gaps in our knowledge.

Advocating a version of the acts paradigm that assumes a gestation of homoerotic self-recognition somewhat less prolonged than in others, Bray proposes sexual acts between males finally begot same-sex sexual identities around 1650 to 1700. Hence he adduces William Browne's comment when charged with a sexual offense involving another male in 1726: "I think there is no crime in making what use I please of my own body." For Bray this marks a decisive shift in sexual consciousness, for it would have been much more difficult to conceive "in Jacobean England," he supposes, and would not have been recorded or understood before (113–14). Yet such defenses of supposed sexual transgressions had already been cited, rejected, and inadvertently publicized centuries before, by St. Thomas Aquinas (1224/5–1274) when analyzing sins of lust in the *Summa theologica* (*Theology). Also, Bray's major claim that Englishmen could have no conscious awareness of same-sex sexual affinities before the mid-seventeenth century largely depends on his interpretation of English legal evidence. But "Bray's emphasis on legal records skews the extent to which his arguments reflect sexual practice" and the actual "construction of a sodomitical subject" (Bly. 22, 143). Even the English legal data do not support Bray's conclusions, I would add, for he does not take into account that, relative to continental conditions, there were great inadvertent difficulties in prosecuting sodomy in England because of special restrictions there on investigative torture in virtually all criminal cases (*Law). As Smith observes somewhat critically in his context, studies in this field have often assumed that "it was not until the eighteenth century . . . that gender entered the ontological picture and males who enjoyed sex with other males, the passive partners at least, began to speak, act, and sometimes dress like women" (76). Yet there are many documented cases of male homoerotic effeminacy and transvestism far earlier (figure 7).[38] A touchstone of much recent sexual historiography has been the principle, widely attributed to Foucault, that the Renaissance deemed a sodomite's sex acts part of the general fallen potential of human beings to commit sinful actions, hence not individuated, nor a possible ground of any distinctive identity.[39] But different persons were thought temperamentally predisposed to different sins, including sodomy, as Jordan has shown (*Theology), and the former sciences offered anatomical and other essentialist interpretations of both male and female same-sex sexual inclinations and behaviors (*Medicine, *Astrology, *Physiognomy).

Straightforward periodizations of early modern homoeroticism are especially dubious, for they all too conveniently satisfy temptations to find master narratives with clear transitions in the erratic plenitudes of history.[40] Some temporal turning point, whether 1650, 1700, 1750, or 1850, is said to mark radical change, and we are told what males or females who had sex with their own gender could and could not conceive of themselves before that. Much of this involves projecting the acts paradigm into the past and interpreting some selected historical evidence accordingly, whereas its causality may be overdetermined, or it may not be fully representative, either because other evidence could be contradictory, or we have lost too much historical context to be capable of reasonably determining its significance. Although the molly houses that seem to have arisen in London circa 1700 are often used to produce sharply periodizing narratives, for example, "it is not safe to conclude that the mollies signal a decisive stage in western ideas of sexuality," Sinfield advises, for "we should not suppose that . . . model was the only one in circulation," just as "an elaborate social structure should entertain diverse sexual schema" (38).

While the nineteenth-century promulgation of "homosexuality" no doubt reflected significant cultural changes in views of homoerotic relations, we need more nuanced, empirically patient, inductive, and provisional ideas of the social construction of sex differences than the acts paradigm enables, just as perceptions of same-sex sexual desires, practices, and corresponding sexual subjectivities have had a complex and historically extensive development. Although I propose no watersheds of sexual history in the fourteenth through seventeenth centuries, since the evidence for that is insufficient, sexual attitudes would have shifted significantly as Greek and Roman texts were recovered, gained status, and circulated more widely through print, and many of them would have helped authorize homoerotic affiliations and commitments. However, little research has yet been done on the Renaissance reception of prohomoerotic classical materials. With the exception of Plato (*Ficino), it is still unclear how the relevant Greek texts were mediated in their much more accessible Neolatin translations and commentaries. Meanwhile, social conditions also seem to have shifted adversely after around 1500 due to the sexually regulatory impacts of newly virulent syphilis, the Reformation, the Counter-Reformation, and increasing state power. In any case, sexual history involves many discontinuities, so that positing some definitive point of departure inaugurating more or less continuous development, like advocates of the acts paradigm or sharp periodizations, is inappropriate. Awareness, interpretation, and pursuit of personal homoerotic interests probably varied according to factors such as social rank, education, familial circumstances, contacts, and size of local population. And just as feminist social history allows for the impact of female heads of state in enhancing protofeminist insight and agency during their reigns, rulers and eminent nobles who were reputedly sodomites, such as King Henri III of France and King James I of England, likely had similar effects on homoerotic experience, at least indirectly.

Since sexual historians to date have addressed medicine, astrology, and physiognomics much less than other disciplines such as law, these former sciences have particular importance for probing the archaeology of homosexuality at this point. Largely based on ancient treatises deemed authoritative, they furnished Renaissance options for conceiving of particular sexual inclinations that could be more or less exclusive, so that the possibilities of illicit sexual desire were not simply undifferentiated debauchery, as Bray and other "recent constructionists" claim (25), but from some viewpoints intensively categorized. Moreover, these inclinations were often deemed innate, hence essential, transhistorical, and to varying extents predetermined in life, so that certain arrays of stars and planets, for example, supposedly instilled particular homoerotic dispositions at birth. Those kinds of explanations would only have first developed in the speculative milieu of the ancient sciences because the sexual behaviors involved already seemed engrained commitments of particular persons anyway, so that deterministic rationalizations of these human phenomena appeared to make sense and were invented accordingly. Nevertheless, we are often told that, as Smith puts it, "the structures of knowledge that impinged on what we would now call 'homosexuality' did not ask a man who had sexual relations with another man to think of himself as fundamentally different than his peers" (11). But the *pseudo-Aristotelian *Problems* had proposed that many men who enjoyed receptive anal intercourse exclusively or otherwise were indeed different in their fundaments. And other essentialist interpretations of sex differences applied to their insertive counterparts and, as Traub and Brooten have shown, to tribades.

Renaissance sexual essentialisms and determinisms further contributed to the agencies and ideological latitude of male and female same-sex lovers. Whereas theologians claimed they were "sinning against nature," willfully contravening a general God-given code of sexual morality and thus damnably abominable, sodomites and tribades could argue that same-sex attractions and sexual behaviors were temperamentally inscribed in certain persons from birth, and hence appropriate to their individual natures. Such claims much predated the Renaissance, for the bishop of Paris condemned them in 1275 (*Theology). Debates in our own time about the extent to which homosexuality results from innate factors or from environment had been to some extent anticipated in commentaries on inversions of sex and gender at least as early as Parmenides and the ancient Hippocratic medical corpus (*Medicine). Since same-sex erotics are in any case justified by an individual's moral right to have free and consensual choice in such a personal and private matter, I address former sexual essentialisms and determinisms not because I have some ethical or political investment in either side of the nature/nurture debate, but because of their historical importance for early modern concepts and etiologies of sex differences, and their subversive implications for orthodox theology and sexual morality of that time.

Although former scientific discourses contributed to the prehomosexual possibilities of perceiving same-sex sexual affiliations and dispositions, such perceptions had come to be so culturally diffused that they had many other potential popular and learned bases, including, for example, literary and philosophical traditions of same-sex love and friendship. In Plato's once widely cited fable assigned to the speaker Aristophanes in the *Symposium* (189C–93E), as humans were originally three types of double beings, male-female, male-male, and female-female, but were divided by gods jealous of their power, so love then became the desire and pursuit of the lost whole. Descendants of the androgynes amorously seek an opposite-sex counterpart, but those from the others seek the same. Although some have claimed no one in antiquity could have thought this fable proposed distinct categories of same- and opposite-sex sexual preference that recognizably characterized specific persons (cf. Borris, 247n.27, Halperin 68–71), it could certainly be understood that way in the Renaissance, as in *Firenzuola's published comment. And this fable was widely adduced as an explanatory context for same-sex desire and love, sexual or otherwise, as by *Ficino, *Ronsard, Étienne Jodelle (1532–1573), *Donne, and probably Shakespeare.[41] Firenzuola contextually insists on Plato's high authority, and this myth provided one further potential counterweight to Christian dogmas of sex and gender. Whereas Genesis offered an exclusively heteroerotic model of originary humanity to our creationist early modern forebears, Plato's Aristophanes appeared to provide one not only including male and female same-sex love of equal value at the source, but also in a way focal for the lives and particular affective and erotic inclinations of such lovers, just as he argues that eros impels all to seek the completion of their counterparts. This favorable myth is deployed most of all in Renaissance literary contexts, with their relative freedom to explore human desires beyond official norms. And yet they indicate how ready indeed such recourses could be in the inward poetics of personal amorous desire.

Against prejudicial assumptions of heterosexual "universality" and "naturalness" such as those that were officially enshrined in *Bowers* v. *Hardwick* until 2003, and still remain in force in many ways through much of contemporary society, we can expose the arbitrariness and cruelties of former normative regimes from which current homophobia emerged. Premodern notions of sex differences were fraught with repugnant misogynies, contradictions, and absurdities perpetuated in the conceptual genealogy of homosexuality. But the sexual resistance and dissidence of our sodomitical, sapphic, and tribadic ancestors attest to the lively wonders of human diversity. "A body is always revolutionary," Pier Paolo Pasolini observes, "because it represents what cannot be codified."[42] By manifesting realities of amorous desire and exchange definitively contrary to official codes, the bodily conjunctions of sodomy, in Aquinas's sense targeting intercourse between males and between females, demonstrated with the force of scandal the failure of those codes to be commensurate with humanity.

Note on Terminology

Usage of terms in this field is vexed and necessarily pragmatic.[43] From its initial Italian glimmerings to its protracted seventeenth-century demise in northern Europe, the distinctive endeavor to revive ancient Greek and Roman culture designated "the Renaissance" was a major factor in the cultural conditions of homoeroticism. Though whether women had a Renaissance has been questioned, erotics between them arguably did, mainly because of Sappho's recovery. In contexts not requiring the intellectually historical resonance of antique revival, I use the more socially historical expression "early modern" instead. Sexual taxonomies for early modern culture should avoid major anachronisms that impute present conceptions of sex and erotic affinities to the past. Except when discussing recent times, I avoid the medical-psychological vocabulary of "sexuality," "heterosexuality," and "homosexuality" that developed in the nineteenth century, as well as currently popular counterparts such as "gay." Although "lesbian" has been used at least since the Middle Ages to designate sexual love between females (Brooten, 5, 337), and *Brantôme indicates that it had some currency in the Renaissance, such usage was relatively rare, and so even that word now seems too fraught with modern and postmodern connotations to be helpful here.

Other recent sexually expressive coinages have a relatively neutral conceptual content that enables pragmatic early modern applications, as if in implicit quotation marks, and so I use "heteroerotic," "homoerotic," and "homophile" accordingly. I also use "homophobia." Some have denied it could exist prior to the nineteenth-century identification of homosexuality as such: Before that, they assume, same-sex sexual relations supposedly consisted in acts alone, without recognition of related personalities or selfhoods. However, virulent hateful reactions specifically against male and female homoeroticism and its practitioners have a much longer history.[44] Describing Sodom's destruction with vicious gusto in *Les semaines*, Guillaume Du Bartas (1554–1590) invents ingenious horrors for its male same-sex lovers. Not only those who commit such sins deserve this dire fate, he urges, but also everyone who would pity or extenuate it.[45] The anonymous *Legend of Orpheus and Euridice* published at London in 1597 attacks Orpheus for originating and proselytizing intergenerational masculine love. As he used his musical virtuosity to promote it, so the poem ends not only with his body mangled, but also with his hands dismembered.[46] I use "homophobia" in a provisional and heuristic way, assuming that such early modern reactions were much more motivated by consciously antisodomitical fears and presumptions. Usage of this term strategically bears witness to Western homophobia's deep roots in the past, and most of all in the vagaries of Judaeo-Christian tradition.

Whereas early modern sources often use "active" and "passive," or equivalents, for denoting sexual roles, in my own comment I prefer the more neutral descriptive terms "insertive" and "receptive," partly to mark the difference of former usage. A sexual partner is never passive unless inert.

Some other terms for female and male same-sex sexual relations and their agents that were either used in the period or particularly reflect its conditions remain much more useful for present commentators on sexual history. In Renaissance Europe, "tribade" was the single most well-known word pertaining to a female who obtained genital pleasure with other females. Though not so forcefully pejorative as "sodomite," its usage in many contexts condemning such persons and sexual behaviors invested it with adverse connotations from antiquity onward. Andreadis cautions that many women-loving women would not have identified themselves and their sexual behaviors in this way deemed transgressive, but would have evasively constructed "an erotics of unnaming" (2–3). Yet women less obedient to patriarchy could have appropriated the term for resistive deployments, privately and otherwise. It attested that female homoerotic desires and practices have their own ancient lineage and tradition, including Sappho, who was sometimes called a tribade, and could thus support cultural relativism. Although "tribade" sometimes designated the more assertive or supposedly masculine partner, and "tribadic" sex either rubbing or pseudophallic penetration, both could also have wider applications (Traub, 211). Unless my context indicates otherwise, I use the term in a general sense incorporating various possible sexual roles and acts of female couples. By avoiding such broader usage of "tribade," we would occlude its possibilities of resistive and relativistic usage. Whereas Traub sharply distinguishes nonpenetrative erotic relations of apparently "chaste" feminine friends ("femme-femme" in her terms) from definitively "unnatural" tribadism (231), I do not, for these categories interpenetrated (*Love and Friendship). Traub reserves "sapphism" for the eighteenth-century transformation of erotics between women resulting from consolidated "domestic heterosexuality" (222, 323). However, although I know of no Renaissance usage of the word to designate female homoeroticism, it aptly reflects Sappho's powerful revival and her predominant linkage at that time, from at least the early sixteenth century, with sexual love between females (*The Sapphic Renaissance). While evoking the positive potential of her precedent, this term also bears witness to negative standpoints insofar as some denigrated the poet's reputed homoeroticism. I use "tribade," "sapphic," and their cognates to express these diverse (not synonymous) attitudes and associations, and, as with "sodomites" for males, to acknowledge oppression.

I use "sodomy" and its cognates primarily for sexual relations between males, unless my context indicates broadened or more restricted application through, for example, the addition of an adjective, as in "anal sodomy." Restriction particularly occurs in discussion of English law, which addressed homoeroticism by focusing on sodomy in the technical sense of male-male anal intercourse (*Law). A complex word with a varied and potentially contradictory scope, "sodomy" had polemical extensions optionally censuring any kind of extramarital or nonprocreative and thus "illicit" sex, including tribadism and bestiality, and could also comprise heresy and treason (*Theology). Hence Foucault goes so far as to say sodomy was "an utterly confused category."[47] However, "of all the many images of [male] homosexuality the English Renaissance affords, one above all recurs over and over again: the catastrophe that overwhelmed the cities of Sodom and Gomorrah at the hands of an angry God. Even when not the ostensible subject, it seems never to be far from the mind of the writer when homosexuality is mentioned" (Bray, 28). Just as Sodom's destruction was the dominant social image of male-male sex in the Renaissance, "sodom(y)" maintained that recognizable core significance.[48] Besides thus reflecting cultural conditions, my usage registers the particular early modern stigma that could readily attach to male homoerotic desire and sexual behaviors, and its roots in religious ideology. Although "sodomy" in this derogatory sense could specifically focus on anal intercourse between males, masculine homoeroticism in general was often subsumed in sodomy or termed "sodomitical" or "tending to sodomy." Even in England, some men were accused of sodomy, convicted, and executed without any claim or proof of anal penetration, as in the *Castlehaven scandal.

I also use "cinaedus," which had become an English loanword (though absent from the *Oxford English Dictionary*).[49] Anciently a complex word (Craig Williams, 75–78), it most often means "catamite" or "pathic" in Renaissance Neolatin usage. In my own commentary it denotes males who sometimes or always assume a receptive and hence supposedly "feminine" role in sex with their own gender, whether or not they also have heteroerotic relations. As its sense can sometimes be complex or ambiguous (perhaps involving male effeminacy but not homoeroticism, e.g.), so the translations of Latin and Neolatin sources in this anthology render "cinaedus" as English in all cases.

When sources use "boy" or equivalents (such as *puer*) in treating masculine love, the implied age can be highly ambiguous. In a morally censorious sense, "boy" could apply to a man in his late twenties (Smith, 193–96), yet could also be used as an endearment well beyond late adolescence. Renaissance culture was

Latinate, and Roman boyhood could extend to around twenty, while *puer* could "refer to a man's sexual object regardless of his . . . actual age" (Craig Williams, 73, 77). It is often assumed that substantial age difference particularly characterized early modern sexual love between males. However, insofar as sodomites did seek adolescent male partners, that actually paralleled much heteroerotic marital and extramarital practice. Upon first marrying, John Milton (1608–1674) was thirty-four, his bride seventeen. Donne was eleven years his adolescent bride's senior.

CHAPTER 1

Theology

> The failure of many Christian churches to speak intelligently, much
> less prophetically, about sexuality brings discredit on the whole of
> their preaching. The churches could begin to repent of their failure by
> examining honestly the paradoxes embedded in their long traditions
> of moral teaching on sexuality.
> —Mark D. Jordan, *The Invention of Sodomy*[1]

Early modern oppression of same-sex erotics was mainly based on perceived
Judaeo-Christian tradition. The chief biblical text alleged to condemn sexual
relations between males was Sodom's destruction in Genesis 19. As *Andrew
Willet (1562–1621) explains in his synoptic commentary on Genesis first published in 1608, it seemed "the most fearful" of "God's judgments . . . in scripture," because of the "strange punishment," its "suddenness," the supposedly
"perpetual monuments thereof to this day" at the Dead Sea, and its prefigura-
tion of infernal "everlasting fire and perdition" according to Jude 6–7.[2] Hence
masculine love could appear a most dire sin that, if not socially condemned and
punished, could call down the wrath of God upon an entire populace. Leviticus 18:22 and 20:13 seemed to confirm that reading of Genesis: If a man lies
with mankind as with woman, both have committed abomination and must be
killed (20:13). St. Paul's epistles were adduced to locate condemnation in the New
Testament: Romans 1:26–27, 1 Corinthians 6:9–10, and 1 Timothy 1:9–10. Early
modern commentators on these passages sound not unlike Antonio de Corro
(1527–1591) on Romans 1:26–27: "horrible vices," "most shameful and filthy
lusts," "the use that nature abhorreth," "defiled themselves with all filthiness,"
"my whole mind and body shudders," "terrible judgments of the sovereign God,"
"everlasting destruction."[3] This Pauline context was often interpreted to forbid
couplings of females as well.[4] In "the judgment of God . . . they which commit
such things are worthy of death," the apostle claims in concluding that chapter, and so he could seem to approve civil executions or everlasting damnation
(1:31). Although some other biblical passages were also used for the Christian
elaboration of homophobia (*St. Peter Canisius), these were the fundamental
pretexts and, despite the Bible's apt decline in authority and readership, they
still resonate culturally today.

Yet in view of its length, the Bible contains remarkably few comments that
have been adversely applied to same-sex sexual love, and the relevance of most
is dubious. Recent scholarship indicates that "at least until the Babylonian exile

in 586 B.C., the Hebrews had no prohibition against homosexuality."[5] And if the proscriptions of Leviticus were binding, not only would sex in general, even marital, be a defilement, and menstruating females "unclean" for seven days, as well as everything and everyone they touched (15:16–30), but we would also have to prohibit clothes mixing linen and wool (20:19). Current Christian apologists for oppression of homosexuals ignore such absurdities in claiming, as they often do, Levitical authorization. Yet even the homophobic account of homosexuality in the first *New Catholic Encyclopedia* questions whether Genesis 19 really applies to sex between males.[6] Most biblical scholars now consider the Pauline epistles to Timothy spurious, and Paul's diction in the other contexts does not indisputably pertain to sex between males or between females (Greenberg, 210–17). The only biblical text that can possibly be interpreted to condemn the latter, Romans 1:26, is so ambiguous in the original Greek that it has been variously understood since patristic times, and applied instead, for example, to "unnatural" copulations of opposite sexes.[7] Although Bernadette J. Brooten learnedly concludes that Paul does condemn male and female homoeroticism there, she argues he should have no authority on that point, for his position "reflects and helps to maintain a gender asymmetry based on female subordination" (302). In any case, also "worthy of death" in Paul's view are backbiters, boasters, and disobedient children (Rom. 1:30–32). As represented in the Gospels, Jesus himself had no particular interest in condemning sexual love between males or females, for he makes no such comment. John is called "the disciple whom Jesus loved," who "leaned" upon Jesus's "bosom" (John 13:23, 21:20).

Nevertheless, in the development of orthodox Christian theology sexual legitimacy quickly became restricted to procreative acts within opposite-sex marriage, and even these readily became sinful if undertaken immoderately for sensual pleasure, for example, or in postures deemed inappropriate.[8] Whereas the ancient Roman world had accommodated both male and female same-sex marriages, the sons of the first Christian Roman emperor, Constantine, outlawed conjugal unions between males, at least, in 342 (Greenberg, 228–29; Brooten). At its patristic doctrinal foundations, Christianity evinces a strong antisexual bias resulting from ascetic trends of later classical thought and from biblical texts that condemn even heteroerotic conjugal sex, such as Luke 20:35–36 and Revelation 14:3–4.[9] The latter claims the redeemed will be those "not defiled with women; for they are virgins." Paul urges "*it is* good for a man not to touch a woman," but "it is better to marry than to burn" lustfully (1 Cor. 7:1, 9). At least nominally because virginity had greater sanctity than marriage (spousal and familial ties allegedly impaired devotion to God), celibacy became an official obligation of Roman Catholic clergy beginning in the eleventh century, even though it had not been required by the early church and was often violated. Breaching celibate vows compounded lust with sacrilege. Amid deep religious suspicion of heteroerotic sex, same-sex varieties could not escape greater stigma. Though apparently ignored by some churchmen, especially in the case of females, the latter behaviors appeared abhorrent to more punitive figures such as St. Peter Damian (1007?–1072), as some major patristic authorities and the prevalent biblical interpretation demanded.[10] Against objections that Jesus had never condemned sodomy, some medieval theologians retorted he had no need to, for on the night of his birth, they claimed, God had exterminated all sodomites.[11]

The religiously mandated condemnation of same-sex sexual love increased in the later Middle Ages (Greenberg, 272–98), and early modern Roman Catholicism and Protestantism concurred on that, despite their other doctrinal antagonisms. However, joint abomination made charges of such sexual practices, usually targeting males, a preferred weapon for both in their polemics against the rival faith's alleged corruptions of doctrine and life. While some Catholics claimed that the Reformers *Jean Calvin (1509–1564) and Théodore de Bèze (1519–1605) were sodomites, for example,[12] Protestants exploited their opponents' long-standing policy of clerical celibacy, and consequently expansive history of both opposite- and same-sex violations of that vow. Privation from heteroerotic contacts tends to foster same-sex desire, or attract those so inclined, and Catholic celibacy especially thus affected monasteries and nunneries (Greenberg, 283–92; Brown).

Protestant anti-Catholic propaganda strongly associated homoerotic transgressions with Roman Catholicism and its clergy for centuries. In *The Acts of English Votaries* (1560), the English Reformed bishop John Bale (1495–1563) fulminates, "what Sodomites and Devils they are, that have all this time condemned Christian marriage instituted of God, . . . leading their lives in unspeakable fleshly filthiness." "Rome hath been so sinful a sink and pernicious puddle, as hath all the world infected by the Sodometrous vow of their simulate chastity."[13] Appropriating St. Paul's claim that God abandoned the pagans to so-called unnatural lusts on account of their idolatry (Romans 1), Protestant polemicists urged that Roman Catholic images and clerical celibacy had been jointly condemned by apostolic prophecy. Hence Bale exclaims: "They, . . . leaving the natural use of women (saith S. Paul), have burnt in their own lusts one to another, that man with man, that is to say monk with monk, nun with nun, friar with friar, and priest with priest, wrought filthiness (Rom. 1), besides that they did with boys, bitches, and apes with other beasts, yea the holiest fathers of them. If ye spell 'Roma' backward, ye shall find it love in this prodigious kind, for it is preposterous amor, a love out of order or a love against kind" (Second Part, sigs. A7ᵇ–8ª). Often expressed in less unsubtle ways, these accusations were tantamount to Protestant articles of faith and widely parroted.

By rejecting Catholic clerical celibacy, Protestants raised the prestige of marriage even though, like Martin Luther (1483–1546) and Calvin, they typically denied its sacramentality. Since Protestant attacks on celibacy's practical viability insisted that controlling sexual desire is enormously difficult, they also made marriage seem much more obligatory for the positive recuperation of eros, and rendered the single condition more suspect and problematic. The Reformation's aims included redefining the personal, social, and spiritual role of sex: Not only was marriage newly valorized against celibacy, but Calvin and others also sought to regulate sexual activity through socially disciplinary programs, courts, and other institutions (cf. Weisner-Hanks, ch. 2).

However, Protestant criticism and sexually regulatory measures provoked Catholic internal reforms, especially after the accession of Pope Paul III in 1534 (cf. Weisner-Hanks, ch. 3). As the diverse religious groups competitively strove to propagate "correct" beliefs, they publicized definition of authorized marital and sexual conduct to discourage and vilify contrary behaviors. They sought to enforce these strictures through ecclesiastical or secular courts and otherwise, with much local and national variation. Even denial of the mortal sinfulness of fornication (meaning extramarital, nonadulterous, male-female intercourse in the vagina) could bring indictment in Catholic church courts (Weisner-Hanks, 111, 123–24). How much more dangerous it was, then, publicly to contest condemnation of same-sex sexual relations. Restrictive or "puritanical" views of sex broadly typified religious reformers throughout early modern Europe, whether Catholic, Protestant, or eastern Orthodox (Weisner-Hanks, 134).

The Christian anathema upon homogenital acts depended partly on theological notions of the significance of reproduction and marriage. My use of the past tense for summarizing these ideas is tactically optimistic, for they still have considerable influence even on civil laws in many parts of the world. As God created humankind, so the genitals and sexual capacities of his creatures had a particular God-given purpose that restricted their proper use to a single end: generation that echoed and perpetuated the Creator's creative act to multiply his children. To use these capacities for nonprocreative ends thus sinfully violated divine will. Moreover, Christian procreation was the divinely appointed means to propagate the faithful and expand God's church to his greater glory, both on earth and in the afterlife.[14] But these rationales would still be dubious, to say the least, even if their theistic assumptions were accepted. Aside from the question of nocturnal emissions, sperm and ova vastly outnumber actual conceptions. Also, contraception would be abominable, and so would marriages in which one partner were sterile, or the wife otherwise incapable of giving birth successfully. And what of clerical celibacy? Nevertheless, voluntary nonprocreative sexual acts, including masturbation, coitus interruptus, and other types of artificial contraception, thus appeared profoundly sinful transgressions against a divinely ordained natural order, and deliberate couplings of the same sex seemed particularly flagrant travesties of that order's generative norms and purposes.

Such same-sex behaviors also appeared to travesty the Christian institution of marriage. Protestants and Catholics agreed that marriage was God's divinely authorized context for sex and procreation, thus providing the very cornerstone of human social order. Addressing the seventh commandment, against adultery, the continental Reformer Heinrich Bullinger (1504–1575) defines marriage as a divine ordinance approving oneness of flesh "for the holy keeping of honorable wedlock, and for the true sanctifying of the body, against adulteries, wandering lusts, and all incontinency." Through this consensual commonalty of man and woman, "honesty and chastity may flourish among good men, and children may be brought up in the fear of the Lord." As for those "entangled in the very same sin" as "the detestable Sodomites," "those filthy men," "fire shall destroy both them and theirs: and they themselves shall forever burn in hell."[15] The Elizabethan Church of England authorized official homilies to be read in rotation in churches, as vehicles for inculcating approved doctrine and morality, and the homily "Of the State of Matrimony" insists marriage is God's means for "bridling the corrupt inclinations of the flesh" against "all whoredom and uncleanness," so that "the Church of God and his kingdom might by this kind of life be conserved and enlarged" through godly procreation.[16] The Roman Catholic catechism of *Canisius (1521–1597) says much the same, while further stressing matrimony's Catholic sacramentality as a particular means of divine grace.

Moreover, the Pauline epistles link the maritally authorized union of flesh with ecclesiastical union with Christ, sanctification of the body as a godly temple, and the participation of Christians in Christ's mystical body. Through becoming conjugally one flesh, Paul assumes, a man and woman become a counterpart of Christ and the church (Eph. 5:22–33). The "body is the temple of the Holy Ghost," "not for fornication but for the Lord," in which God should be glorified. And a Christian's body is one of Christ's "members," incorporated in his inclusive or mystical body. So "fornication" would conjoin God's bodily temple and Christ's greater body to a "harlot" as "one body" and "one flesh": "God forbid," cries Paul.[17] This context urging Christian sexual discipline was understood to include condemnation of same-sex lovers, particularly male: the "effeminate," and "abusers of themselves with mankind," or, in the Geneva Bible (1560), "buggerers" (1 Cor. 6:9–20).[18] These interlocked ideas about marriage, the body, appropriate sexual behavior, and Christ's relation to the church would have tended to make same-sex physical unions seem deeply alien, ecclesiastically contaminating, and perversely anti-Christian. Much of the visceral repugnance evinced by many religious commentators of the past and their lay disciples probably stems from these notions in conjunction with the Bible's supposedly antisodomitical texts and the related teleological restrictions on the sexual usage of genitals.

At once nonprocreative, extramarital, and same-sexed despite the presumed divine ordinances of sexual love instituted in the originary couple according to Genesis, Adam and Eve, homogenital interactions could well appear a triply sinful species of lust deserving especial admonitory stigma, hence to be named through paradoxical refusal of naming, as "the sin so grievous it could not be named." Although most often referring to sex between males, this circumlocution sometimes applied yet more vehemently to females (Brown, 19–20). Sins, including those of lust, had different degrees of gravity. In early modern rigorist (as opposed to laxist) Catholic analysis of sexual morality, even heteroerotic vaginal coitus between married partners was seriously sinful, if too motivated by desire for pleasure rather than for procreation. Laxists were relatively relaxed about options for marital sex so long as there was no ultimate intent to impair generation. However, Catholic theologians commonly classified even heteroerotic extramarital "fornication" as a mortal rather than venial sin that, if not confessed, could damn the sinner. While viewing marital sex much like Catholic laxists, Protestant theologians too condemned extramarital sex, so that *Thomas Wilson (1563–1622) declares "it deserveth Hell fire, 1 Cor. 6:9."[19]

Deliberately nonprocreative sexual acts were deemed much more heinous, much more difficult to forgive, for despite some variations of definition, such sex was commonly said to sin further against nature.[20] According to St. Thomas Aquinas (1224/5–1274), for example, "the plan of nature comes from God, and therefore a violation of this plan, as by unnatural sins, is an affront to God." Not only masturbation, homogenital behaviors, and bestiality are unnatural in his view, but also opposite-sex conjunctions "if the natural style of intercourse is not observed, as regards the proper organ [i.e., vagina] or according to other rather beastly and monstrous techniques."[21] In rigorist views, which partly depended on Aquinas, even conjugal coitus in the vagina could constitute a type of "sin against nature" if undertaken in postures other than the "missionary position"— worst of all from the wife's rear or with her on top—for these were thought to impair impregnation and introduce a degree of variety that promoted pleasure-seeking, while the latter pose seemed to violate "natural" masculine supremacy.[22]

But in the theological evaluation of the various sexual possibilities that could be deemed "unnatural" or incommensurate with human reproduction, sex between males tended to inspire the most immediate punitive horror aside from bestiality, partly on account of the conventional association of sodomites with Sodom's destruction. Another factor was the almost wholly masculine discursive gendering of theology itself, so that sexual doctrines were driven by patriarchal assumptions and anxieties. Defined as a "defect of nature," females did not appear to matter so much as the so-called superior sex, sexually or socially (*Medicine). Male theologians would have tended to feel their masculine status and sexual discipline most radically challenged by a mode of love in which a male assumes and enjoys a receptive, thus supposedly "feminine," role in sex with another male, or, even more alarming, can alternate conventional gender roles. These homoerotic possibilities threatened the gender hierarchy—male topping female—deemed essential to the natural order.

After Thomism's resurgence in the late fifteenth century, Aquinas became the central theologian of early modern Roman Catholicism, and his analysis of sins of lust in the *Summa theologiae* defines "intercourse (*concubitum*) . . . with a person of the same sex, male with male and female with female," as the specific type of sexual sin against nature that is sodomy, and the worst sin of lust, in his view, except bestiality, for "sodomy . . . does not observe the due sex."[23] Since the possibilities of sex between males and between females differ substantially, not so much any particular act is at issue here as the sexual homology of gender, and it is that which most defines "sodomy" in this case. Aquinas's analyses of virtues and vices became widely diffused in Christian tradition, and his writings directly influenced some Reformers, including Luther, Martin Bucer (1491–1551), and Pietro Martire Vermigli (1499–1562).[24] Nevertheless, "sodomy" could also be used much more broadly to censure, for example, any kind of extramarital or nonprocreative and thus supposedly illicit sex, including heteroerotic anal intercourse and bestiality, and even heresy or treason (Greenberg, 274–79; Jordan, 161–63). It could thus further function as a polemical trope for alleged violation of nature, or for culpably dissolute transgression. But since Sodom's holocaust was the dominant early modern social image of sexual love between males, that remained the core meaning of "sodomy," charged with a horror seemingly authorized by the Word of God (*General Introduction, "Note on Terminology"). "Sodomy" could apply also to female same-sex couplings, although they were sometimes viewed more leniently (Brown, 12–13). Subsequent excerpts of various early modern theological texts include such homoerotically focused usages of "sodomy" and its cognates. The common Protestant and Catholic classification of sex between males (and sometimes between females) as one of the four "crying sins," those most demanding divine retribution as *Canisius explains, further establishes its much greater opprobrium relative to other sexual sins except for bestiality.

Many appear to have considered anal intercourse between males the paradigmatic act of sodomy, yet other male homoerotic sexual practices were variously subsumed in that model or deemed sodomitical. Although the early modern status and currency of male-male fellatio are still unclear, at least some moralists found it yet more shocking than such anal intercourse, apparently because the former act appeared genitally to degrade "the most noble" bodily part, the head, and thus willfully invert rightful corporeal hierarchy as well.[25] Sex between females was more diversely construed, so that, though sometimes considered sodomy, as Aquinas maintained, it could otherwise constitute fornication or "pollution," not any kind of so-called unnatural or sodomitical sin. Or it could become sodomy, some claimed, if a penetrative instrument were used, or if, as they fancied, one partner had a pseudophallic clitoris (Brown, 13–19). And yet, just as masculine authorities conceived sex in a penetrative way, some considered nonpenetrative sex between female partners a species of masturbation.

Although much recent commentary on sexual history assumes that former theological understandings of sin precluded the formation and apprehension of same-sex sexual subjectivities, not only did other intellectual disciplines and sexual dissidence have contrary cultural effects (*General Introduction), but also early modern religious thought was itself more complex. Since all human sin ostensibly stemmed from original sin, Alan Bray supposes everyone was deemed to share equally in that undifferentiated potential, and thus equally also in lust or debauchery and its sodomitical possibilities. As sinful acts reflecting such a general debility, he concludes, same-sex couplings provided no basis for any perceptions of personally distinctive sexual affiliations or notions of self.[26] For much the same reasons David F. Greenberg declares that "someone who wanted to engage in sodomy but did not do so was no sodomite and someone who had done so but had stopped was one no longer. The category was defined by the act, not the person" (278). Yet according to Catholic moral theologian Jean Benedicti (1573–1662), for example, even a male who masturbated while just fantasizing about another male had thus committed sodomy (Weisner-Hanks, 110). Same-sex sexual behaviors were not deemed simply a matter of *acts*, but also entailed sodomitical inner conditions, and hence distinctive interiorities.

Sins themselves were not considered equal in type or gravity, as if all on the same level, and thus somehow equivalent or merely general, but were carefully distinguished and classified, so that different sinners were characterized by distinctive patterns and psychologies of sin. And theologians recognized that different persons have different kinds, proportions, and intensities of appetites and desires, as *Calvin's commentary on 1 Corinthians 6:11 shows. Some could thus conceivably tend to sodomy far more than others. Likewise, involvement in a sin could conceivably proceed far beyond specific, discrete acts or transgressions. Repetition was held to produce habituation and a psychology distinctive to that type of sinning, or the sinner's characterization, at least in part, by a particular "vice" or habit of sin: a more or less confirmed disposition of mind and behavior. Sin constituted deviation from the only human identity thought rightful or authentic for Christians, which required regenerate conformation to the divine image in which humankind was supposedly created, thus reversing the effects of the Fall. Yet, though perversely inhuman by definition, according to the standards imputed to prelapsarian nature, certain vices, or tendencies thereto, with their associated affinities, perspectives, and behaviors, nonetheless marked the distinctive temperaments of specific persons. Cited by many moral theologians, Aristotle's *Nicomachean Ethics* not only observes such personal variations, and in relation to some practices of sex between males, but also suggests that personally compelling reasons of natural disposition or upbringing could be responsible (7.5.1–9).

By providing grounds for defining sexual nonconformists, the theological attempt to define an erotically prescriptive model of human identity inadvertently demarcated individual deviations and their personal significance. Medieval theological definition of "sodomy" and thus "the sodomite," Mark D. Jordan has shown, already evinced "the idea of an identity built around the genital configuration of one's sexual partners" or "same-sex pleasure," with, for example, a "sodomitic anatomy and physiology, personal history, and secret community." Hence "the invention of the homosexual may well have relied on the already familiar category of the sodomite"—a same-sex sexual identity, of a sort, dating from the Middle Ages (163–64).

Allegations of grievous sin could exert much mental and social pressure on early modern males and females who had homogenital relations. The bitterness of religious controversies at the time indicates how powerful indeed its Christian ideologies could be. Throughout Europe, considerably more than half the texts printed in the sixteenth century were religious (Weisner-Hanks, 71).

Some basic texts of the Reformed English church indicate the extent to which those who persisted in an alleged sin, and hence practitioners of sodomitical or tribadic lust, were theologically threatened, and the graver the sin, the greater the threat. That church's central doctrinal statement was the Thirty-nine Articles (1563), and according to Article 29, when "the wicked" consume "the sacrament of the body and blood of Christ" in communion, they do so only "to their destruction."[27] Read several times annually in churches, the "Commination against Sinners" in the Elizabethan *Book of Common Prayer*, introduced in 1559, insists "the wrath of God in the days of vengeance" will fall upon "obstinate sinners" to fling them, accursed, "into the fire everlasting, which is prepared for the devil and his angels." All must abjure their sins and humbly repent.[28] Likewise repeatedly read to congregations, the Elizabethan official homily "Of Whoredom and Uncleanness" threatens all those who engage in illicit sex with hellfire and damnation in "that utter darkness, where weeping and gnashing of teeth shall be." Although discreetly avoiding any particular discussion of same-sex sexual behaviors, no doubt to avoid advertising their delightful possibilities to naive churchgoers of all ages throughout England, it cites St. Paul on heaven's exclusion of both "softlings" (usually referring to effeminate males and masturbators in exegetical tradition) and "sodomites" (1 Cor. 6:9–10).[29] Just as "sodomite" could readily denote a male who had sex with other males in some sense, in this homiletic context it parallels "abusers of themselves with mankind" (the usual correlative expression, which presumes the abusers are male, in former English translations of that Pauline passage); or "buggerers," as in the Geneva Bible. Even aside from English law, other theological texts could be presumed to have established the far greater perceived gravity of sodomy versus most other sexual sins such as heteroerotic fornication.

Turning to the interpretation of the New Testament most authoritative and widely disseminated in England from around 1549 to at least 1580, we find sex between males broadly condemned, and apparently between females also. The Roman Catholic moderate reformer Erasmus (1467?–1536) had sought to elucidate all its books, except for Revelation, in his Latin *Paraphrases*, and the last queen of Henry VIII, Catherine Parr, sponsored an English translation involving Mary Tudor. The Edwardine and Elizabethan *Injunctions* (1547, 1559) obliged all parish churches to provide this version of at least the *Paraphrases* on the Acts and Gospels for public consultation, and all the less theologically qualified clergy to study Erasmus's text.[30] Despite his humanist appreciation of classical culture, Erasmus's brief comment on Romans 1:26–27 amplifies Paul's censures traditionally applied to male homogenital behaviors and often their female counterparts. In the quasi-official translation by Miles Coverdale (1488–1568), his diction is damning:

> God being displeased [by the pagans' idolatry] suffered them to run forth head-long into all filthy and beastly lusts. Insomuch that not only the men, but also their women forgetting their kind, changed the natural use of woman's body into that, which is against nature, therein doubtless following the men, which leaving (as I said) the natural use of women, burnt in foul and abominable lusts, one of them upon another, so that the male upon his like committed detestable uncleanness. And after they had by such villainous ways done injury and spite to God, reward was given unto them meet for such madness.[31]

The marginal gloss observes, "Sodometry and other vices in men given over to their own lusts." These are "horrible sins," "filthy uncleanness," "shameful villainy" (fol. 3ª). The wording broadly includes various kinds of male homogenital acts, whether penetrative or not (abominable *lusts,* one of them upon another), and stresses the sexual homology of gender (the male upon his like) as a definitively abominable factor. Following such male examples, females might imitate nonprocreative sexual practices, but with males; or more likely, on account of the context's particular anxiety about like "upon . . . like," pursue sex with each other. On 1 Corinthians 6:7–10 and its exclusion of "weaklings" and "abusers of themselves with mankind" from "the inheritance of the kingdom of heaven" (quoting the Great Bible), Coverdale's Erasmus interprets these sexual offenders as "weaklings, which growing out of man's kind live after an horrible kind of bodily lust" (perhaps masturbators, but more likely cinaedi here), and "such as instead of women abuse men" (fols. 57ᵇ–58ª). Linking sodomy with "the burning of Sodom and Gomorrah," the Index addresses it under the heading "Sodometry," followed by the heading "Sodom." The former entry cites the fore-going comment on Romans 1:26–27 that broadly condemns sexual interactions between males. These in general are clearly anathema in this text privileged within England, not in any sense to be considered normative, orderly, or authorized. Though relatively ambiguous in treating female sexual behaviours, as if these are less troubling or require more tact, the context denounces those presumed "against nature" or contrary to "kind."

Nevertheless, early modern same-sex lovers could variously contest homophobic religious orthodoxy with considerable critical self-possession, like Porcellio in a following story by *Matteo Bandello (1485–1561), or Antonio Vignali (1500/01–1559) and *Antonio Rocco (1586–1652) in their dialogues advocating male-male sex. Although the Bible's former cultural influence was formidable, some passages could be appropriated for homophile inspiration or support. As "the soul of Jonathan was knit with the soul of David, and Jonathan loved him as his own soul," when they had to part, "they kissed one another and wept . . . until David exceeded" (1 Sam. 18:1, 21:42). When Jonathan died, David declared "thy love to me was wonderful, passing the love of women"

(2 Sam. 1:26). Christopher Marlowe (1564–1593) reportedly adduced Jesus's special love for his disciple John, who "leaned" upon his "bosom" (John 13:23, 21:20), to claim Jesus practiced sodomy.[32] Female same-sex lovers could have appropriated these models, transposing genders, or Ruth's devotion to her mother-in-law Naomi, pledging to remain with her even to death (Ruth 1:16–17). Or some might learnedly insist on the exegetical tradition in which Romans 1:26 did not address sex between females. The poet Richard Barnfield (1574–1626?) even uses the love of Solomon and his betrothed in the Song of Songs, formerly thought to allegorize Christ's relationship with the church or faithful soul, to express homoerotic love for Ganymede.[33] The Bible has always been open to heterodox interpretations, including homophile ones. According to *Thomas Wilson (1563–1622) libertines might flippantly say, "the more we sin, the more God is glorified in pardoning it."[34]

Other alternatives for contesting official Christian homophobia included culturally relativist deployment of pagan sexual diversities that the Renaissance could render prestigious; or recourse to the sciences, or to libertinous or Lucretian-Epicurean dismissals of judgmental divine providence; or downright irreligion. Ironically, Aquinas's very procedure whereby he states and rejects possible objections to his position ensured that his condemnation of so-called sexual sins advertised contrary arguments that could be developed for homoerotic advocacy:

1. "It is either a slight sin, or none at all, for a person to use a part of the body for a different use than that to which it is directed by nature (say, for instance, one chose to walk on his hands)."
2. "A seminal discharge is, according to Aristotle, from a surplus to nourishment. No sin is present in the discharge of other superfluities, consequently not in that of sexual activity."
3. "A person can lawfully do what he likes with what belongs to him. But in the sexual act a man does but use what is his own, except perhaps with adultery or rape. Therefore there is nothing wrong in venery and looseness there will not be sinful."
4. "The more a sin is against charity the worse it is. Now adultery and seduction and rape harms our neighbour, whereas unnatural sin injures nobody else, and accordingly is not the worst form of lust."[35]

Countering orthodox notions of "sins against nature," such arguments as these and others in Aquinas's text were thus certainly conceivable at least from the thirteenth century onward.

The ancients' moral philosophy and sciences afforded further means of homoerotic advocacy by allowing for the sex differences of individuals. If dispositions toward same-sex desire and even specific sexual roles and acts are inborn in particular persons, as Greek and Roman *medicine, *astrology, and *physiognomy proposed, then such behaviors accord with those individuals' natures rather than being simply "unnatural," and claims of moral responsibility become problematized, as Aristotle's formerly well-known *Nicomachean Ethics* acknowledges (7.5.1–9). Such ideas were forcefully circulating from at least the thirteenth century onward, for in 1277 the bishop of Paris, Étienne Tempier (c. 1210–1279), condemned the proposition that "the sin against nature, in particular the abuse in the course of coitus, although it is against the nature of the species, is not, however, against the nature of the individual." Shortly beforehand, Roger Bacon (c. 1219–c. 1292) had noted the expulsion of "many" theologians and theological students from Paris due to "sodomitical corruption."[36] Despite condemning sodomy, the Roman Catholic theologian and ethicist Martin Le Maistre (1432–1481) conceded that "sodomitic inclinations may be due to sickness or to defective physical qualities."[37]

Official Christian sexual morality was more radically sidestepped or challenged through the diverse types of "godlessness," unbelief, libertinism, skepticism, free-thinking, and irreligion subsumed in the early modern bugbear of "atheism." These could involve popular and intellectual traditions of rejecting the Bible's authority; decrying its contradictions; denying providence, creation of the world, the soul's immortality, and the Last Judgment; and asserting that religion was humanly invented for purposes of political control.[38] Moral theologians had long claimed spiritual despair and related doubt of rewards in afterlife were major causes of allegedly excessive or improper pursuits of sexual pleasure, as in Aquinas's account of lust, citing Ephesians 4:19, or in the apocryphal Wisdom of Solomon 2.[39] When denouncing intemperance, including lust and sodomy, the encyclopedic *Academie françoise* of Pierre de La Primaudaye (1545/6–1619?) explains, "If death brought with it an end of all sense and feeling, and an utter abolishing of the soul, as well to men as to beasts, intemperate folks should seem to gain much during their lifetime, and to have good cause to wax old, even to melt in their foul and filthy pleasures." Yet as "the soul dieth not with the body," he maintains, "the just shall shine as the Sun in the kingdom of God, and the wicked shall be cast headlong into everlasting fire, where shall be weeping and gnashing of teeth."[40] Entailing acute divergence from reigning Christian sexual orthodoxy, early modern pursuit of same-sex sexual liaisons would have tended to promote crises of conscience and alienation from conventional religion and theism, especially for males, since condemnation of such behaviors was usually much stronger and more wide-spread for them than for females. Sodomy had long been associated with atheism, heresy, or at least religious instability. Marlowe's reputation for being both a sodomite and atheist at least exemplifies social expectations of such a linkage,[41] and so does the prosecution's attack on the earl of *Castlehaven in 1631. In Italy, twenty-two-year-old Francesco Calcagno was charged with sodomy and related atheistic blasphemy in 1550.[42] In his journal for 1646, John Winthrop (1588–1649), first governor of the colony of Massachusetts Bay, records a similar investigation there that resulted in William Plain's execution:

> One Plain of Guilford being discovered to have used some unclean practices, upon examination and testimony, it was found that, being a married man, he had committed sodomy with two persons in England, and that he had corrupted a great part of the youth of Guilford by masturbations, which he had committed and provoked others to the like above a hundred times; and to some who questioned the lawfulness of such a filthy practice, he did insinuate seeds of atheism, questioning whether there were a God and co. The magistrates and elders (so many as were at hand) did all agree that he ought to die, and gave divers reasons from the word of God. And indeed it was *horrendum facinus* [a horrendous crime], and he a monster in human shape, exceeding all human rules and examples that ever had been heard of, and it tended to the frustrating of the ordinance of marriage and the hindering the generation of mankind.[43]

Whether through rejections or personal adaptations of Christianity and its sexual doctrines, early modern male and female same-sex lovers had many means to justify their different modes of love and resist heteroerotic hegemony. After St. Bernardino of Siena (1380–1444) attacked sodomy in his preaching, "four irate sodomites almost succeeded in their plot to beat Bernardino with clubs" (Mormando, 6). The late-fifteenth-century Florentine ascendancy of the Dominican friar Girolamo Savonarola (1452–1498), now being considered for sainthood, brought a severe, religiously motivated attack on masculine love, in partial fulfillment of his demand for "a law that is without mercy, . . . that such persons be stoned and burned." And yet this provoked concerted resistance to his regime from sodomites and their sympathizers.[44] Records of the Sicilian Inquisition document prosecutions of sexual heretics who verbally asserted that anal intercourse between males is not sinful, but natural, just, and holy.[45] The accomplishments of homoerotic advocacy in early modern Europe are now most eloquently focused for us in surviving homophile visual images and writings ranging from evocations of such attractions, to the rarer more formalized defenses issued despite prospects of censorship or other official and unofficial sanctions (*General Introduction, *Love and Friendship, *Erotica).

Matteo Bandello (1485–1561)

In 1554 this friar and bishop published a story presenting a sodomite, Porcellio, who recognizes his own sexual preference for young males, and considers it so central to his own distinctive nature that he rejects Christian claims that such sex is against nature. Born in the Piedmont village of Castelnuovo Scrivia, Matteo Bandello studied at the University of Pavia, became a Dominican friar, and pursued literary interests while serving as a secretary and courtier in the suites of noble families including the Bentivoglio, Gonzaga, and Fregoso. Disturbed by the Franco-Spanish wars in Italy, he moved to France, and became bishop of Agen from 1550 to 1555 through the Fregoso family's patronage. His writings include a relatively amoral compilation of 214 prose tales, *Le novelle*, analogous to the *Decameron* of Giovanni Boccaccio (1313–1375). The initial three-part edition with Porcellio's story was first published in 1554 and the four-part enlargement in 1573.

The preeminent exemplar of its genre written in the cinquecento, Bandello's *Novelle* was selectively translated, adapted, and moralized by Pierre Boaistuau (1517–1566) and François de Belleforest (1530–1583) as the *Histoires tragiques*, which appeared in installments between 1559 and 1582. The similarly modified English selections by William Painter (1540?–1594) and Sir Geoffrey Fenton (1539?–1608) were first printed, respectively, in 1566 and 1567: Painter working from both Bandello and his French interpreters, Fenton from the latter alone.[46] The French version was rendered into Spanish in 1589. Many writers throughout Europe drew on Bandello's *Novelle* or its redactions; English adaptations include *Romeo and Juliet* (1595) by Shakespeare (1564–1616) and *The Duchess of Malfi* (1612/13) by John Webster (1580?–1625?). Shunned by the didactic early modern translators, the tale of Porcellio was only accessible to Italians and Italianists, but would nonetheless have had considerable currency.

Bandello dates the dedication and telling of this story between 1513 and 1515, and emphasizes that Porcellio (otherwise known as Pietro or Gianantonio Pandoni) was an actual person who flourished in the quattrocento.[47] Even if this anecdote were wholly fictitious, it would nonetheless reflect, document, and further disseminate attitudes current by at least Bandello's time that not only enabled the establishment of same-sex sexual subjectivities, but also considerable homoerotic agency and critical self-possession. A much earlier tale by Boccaccio has similar implications (*General Introduction).

From Porcellio's viewpoint, restrictive Christian conceptions of "natural sex" are ridiculous. When the confessor repeatedly demands if Porcellio has committed "the sin against nature," each time Porcellio protests his innocence, mocking antisodomitical ideology through feigned incomprehension. Only when the frustrated confessor abandons the elliptical rhetoric of such "sin" and specifically states "you are a thousand times more eager for boys than goats are for salt," does Porcellio claim to understand him, for Porcellio says, "to amuse myself with boys is more natural to me than eating or drinking to man." This is not any incidental homoeroticism, for the narrator stresses Porcellio's sexual tastes are so much for males that his marriage resulted from strong social and economic pressures, and did not change his sexual behavior. In rejecting orthodox sexual ideology, Porcellio advances a rival concept of nature that assumes sex between males can be deeply natural for some persons. Even when threatened on his supposed deathbed with everlasting hellfire if he does not repent and abjure his sodomy, Porcellio maintains and advocates his type of homoerotic commitment.

This bishop's depiction of Porcellio is surprisingly nonjudgmental. Bandello introduces each tale with a dedicatory letter addressing its origins, circumstances, and implications. The letter introducing Porcellio's story may at first appear to uphold religious orthodoxy, for it warns that a vice can become an incorrigibly engrained habit, and presents Porcellio as an example. Hence this sodomite's assertions of personally natural homoeroticism may seem subjected to a standard theological rejoinder: his claimed "homoerotic nature" is just a habitual vice to which he is prone, that has culpably supplanted his proper humanity. But Bandello's dedications are often alibis or excuses for including material that could otherwise seem too scandalous, and his treatment of Porcellio's case readily counters the tale's ostensibly censorious introduction. To illustrate its putative moral, Bandello did not have to tell a story about sodomy, still less one about an unrepentant sodomite who contests orthodoxy in a way that makes us laugh at a conventionally respectable ecclesiastic. Not only orthodox notions of "sin against nature" become risible. After Porcellio swallows the eucharist without repentance and his confessor realizes that, the latter laments having thus thrust Christ into the inner "furnace" of a sodomite. Porcellio's demand for a bucket of water to save Christ from this fire ridicules pious superstitions and theological speculations in general. Although Porcellio's community then shuns him, so that the tale implicitly urges discretion upon all sodomites, and although the narrator claims we may suppose Porcellio finally died a beast's death, the sodomite nevertheless recovers his health, so that Bandello pointedly avoids providing an exemplum of divine retribution. He introduces and ends Porcellio's story with the proverb, "the wolf sheds his coat, but not his vice." Since being a wolf is natural for a wolf, the proverb can not only complement the dedication's halfhearted orthodox moralizing, but also Porcellio's position.

Male same-sex sexual subjectivity was sufficiently familiar, Bandello could assume, that its opposition to sexual orthodoxy could underwrite readily intelligible jokes. By insisting on the historical authenticity of the narrative, the dedication and story also proclaim the actuality of Porcellio's kind of standpoint. Although Bandello's sodomite undergoes homophobic social and psychological pressures (to marry, change sexually, repent or burn in hell, conform at least outwardly to the mores of his community or else be ostracized), he subjects sexual orthodoxy and authority to his carnivalesque laughter, upending their restrictive world according to the tutelage of his felt desire. He wins insofar as others come to share his laughter.

The Tale of Porcellio[48] (1554)

To the very honorable Signor Cesare Fieramosca, Lieutenant of the most illustrious Signor Prospero Colonna.

In Lombardy we have a proverb cited very often, that the wolf sheds his coat, but not his vice. And since proverbs are expressions commonly approved, they must most often be true; so when a man is seen to be grown old in a habit, whether it be good or ill, it may commonly be held certain that he will die therein. A man of worth may sin, and sin for some time, but, not being inured to evil, he realizes his error with the aid of God's mercy, and repenting, returns to the right way. Again, depraved and wicked men, who have become hardened in wrongdoing, are sometimes seen to do good and virtuous acts, but don't persevere long in them; indeed, they soon return to their evil living. When by long and frequent practice a man has made a habit of something, it is difficult to stop. Not long ago this matter was discussed at the house of the most noble Signor Galeazzo Sforza, Lord of Pesaro, who was then at Milan, and in the presence of the most illustrious Lady Ginevra Bentivoglia, his consort. When the talk turned to an old man who, having had a mistress more than twenty years, refused to renounce her on his deathbed, the honorable Messer Paolo Taeggio, Doctor of Laws, related an extraordinary circumstance that occurred in Milan, which made all who heard it marvel infinitely. Certainly the case is worthy of wonder and pity, and were it not mingled with things sacred, it would also be exceedingly laughable. To augment my stories I thought I should write it down and dedicate it to you, knowing as I do that you will find it remarkable, you who are exceedingly punctilious in things sacred, as I have other times found. May it please you also to have our pleasant friend Gian Tommaso Tucca read it, recalling to him the story of Il Rammarro, which you yourself wrote when you were with the men at arms at Finale in the Ferrarese. Farewell.

Porcellio of Rome amuses himself by making a fool of the friar who confesses him.

When in company, Messer Dionisio Corio, a gentleman of this city of high consideration and ancient family, would readily divert the gathering with some story or other. He was a very good speaker and always had some fine matter at hand. When Signor Alfonso Visconti celebrated his marriage with the Lady Antonia Gonzaga, I, being among those invited, recall that he related, amongst other stories, a case that happened in Milan, and since it relates to what you were discussing, I will repeat it. You must know, then, that Francesco Sforza, who acquired the Duchy of Milan by force of arms, was in military things a man without doubt comparable to any illustrious ancient Roman. And although he was unlettered, having been reared from his tenderest years by the victorious captain Sforza Attendolo, his father, nevertheless he still loved learned men of whatever kind and gave them great stipends.

Among many whom he thus entertained at Milan and elsewhere was one Porcellio, a Roman poet, who, though born and bred at Naples, assiduously sought to be considered a Roman. He was a very good poet for those times, when the literary arts, which had been buried so many hundreds of years, began to be revived and gain new refinement. Whoever would wish to see some of Porcellio's work can go to the former palace of the famous

Count Gasparo Vimercato, where, in the salons and chambers, beneath various paintings, many of his epigrams on divers subjects appear, which display his lively wit. But his excellence in letters and the lustre of his muse were far surpassed by the many and enormous vices which abounded in him. One of the most signal was that the flesh of young goats always pleased him far more than whatever other food might be given him, and so it was his supreme delight to go in overshoes through the dry.[49] Anyway, to reduce the ill opinion in which he was commonly held at court, more than for any desire he himself had, and moreover urged by Duke Francesco, who wanted him to adopt other diet, he espoused a widow aged twenty-eight, whom the duke approved for him and who had a good dowry. The lady, who was very well-bred, soon saw that her husband disliked going on ship through the wet[50]; but, being a good-natured woman and hoping that he would in time change his habits, she resigned herself as best she might, praying God all day long that he would enlighten her husband and turn him from so abominable a sin.

Presently Porcellio fell most grievously sick, with such loss of sleep and appetite that the doctors had little hope of the poor man's life, for he was nearer seventy than sixty and grown very feeble. Seeing this, his wife strove with a thousand excellent arguments to induce him to confess, and he listened to her, but then said he would not. Seeing she wearied herself in vain, she sent to Duke Francesco, humbly begging him for the love of God to send some person of authority who would persuade Porcellio, grievously sick as he was, to have some care of his soul, so he might not die like a dog without the sacraments of the Church. The duke, hearing the pious petition of this good woman and affectionate wife, sent to the Convent delle Grazie of the Friars of St. Dominic, which was then newly built, and called upon Fra Giacomo da Sesti, an old man of very holy life, to perform this task.

The holy man, hearing the duke's will, went straight to Porcellio's house, where, telling the lady how he came by the prince's command to visit and confess her husband, he was received by her with the utmost reverence. Then, after she had sat him down, she proceeded fully to acquaint him with the depravity of her husband's life, imploring him with tears in her eyes to do his utmost to amend her spouse. The friar shrugged his shoulders and had little wish for the task, but replied that, not to fail of his duty, he would do everything he could.

Accordingly, anxious to save a soul which was in the devil's grasp according to the wife, he entered Porcellio's chamber and said, "The peace of God be upon this house and upon all that live here!" So saying, he went to the bed and softly greeted the sick man, who feigned pleasure to see him. Then, in conversation, the friar told Porcellio that he had been sent by the duke's most excellent lordship, and why, with many good words, discreetly exhorting him to confess, for his confessor was ready to hear him at whatever time would be convenient.

Porcellio, after thanking the duke for his courtesy and the friar for his pains, replied that he would confess then and there. Whereupon, all having departed the chamber, the holy friar began with the utmost diligence to do his office, and coming to the sins of the flesh, asked him moderately if he had ever sinned against nature.

At this question, Porcellio, collecting himself, considered the friar with amazement. Then, as if he were scandalized, "Sir," said he, "this is a strange question to ask me. What do you speak of? Never in my life have I sinned against nature."

The priest, ashamed to have put such a question to him, passed to other things, using every means in his power so that the sick man should confess himself thoroughly. Then, seeing that Porcellio had nothing else to say, he assigned him such penance as seemed fit and gave him absolution, concluding that the wife must be grossly mistaken. After giving a pious exhortation, the friar said, being about to take his leave, "Messer Porcellio, I will come tomorrow to visit you, and if you remember anything else, I will hear you. Afterward, your parish priest shall come and give you the holy sacrament of the Eucharist, so that, having taken the salutary viaticum, you may be ready to do whatever shall please our Redeemer, the Lord Jesus Christ, in whose hands abides our life and our death."

"As you wish," replied Porcellio, "for I will do whatsoever you shall command me."

The good father blessed him with the sign of the holy cross and left the bedroom.

The wife came to meet him and asked if her husband was resolved to sin no more against nature. The holy friar replied, "Madam, you may understand that, when we hear the confession of anyone, whoever he may be and whether he be whole or sick, we do our whole duty, and none should seek to know what the penitent said; nor should we, who are deputized by our superiors to hear confessions, in any way disclose anything told us. If we were to reveal a confession we would deserve to be put to death. But so much I will and may presently say to you, that you are grossly mistaken in the strange opinion you have of your husband. He (praised be God!) in no way has that filthy vice which you declared to me, indeed he is very far from it."

Whereupon the good woman, who well knew how the case stood, said, crying pitifully, "Dear father, I am in no way mistaken, nor do I deceive myself. It is my wretched husband who deceives himself and is ashamed to tell this great sin. Believe me, who knows, he is more wrapped up in it than a chick becomes in tow. For mercy's sake, father, come speak with him again and ignore what he says, for I assure you he has told you a lie."

"It is well, madam," answered the good friar. "I shall return tomorrow to have him take the sacrament, and if it be as you say, I will do what I should." So saying, he took leave of the lady and returned to his convent.

Next morning, he came to the sick man and, after exchanging greetings, said to him, "My son, I am come back so you may this morning receive Our Savior, as every true Christian should. But, before doing so, the communicant must, insofar as human frailty allows, prepare his mind for the worthy harboring of such a guest; hence it behooves him to have entirely confessed himself of all his sins and to conceal nothing whatsoever from the priest. You told me yesterday that you had nothing other to say to me, but I am credibly advised that for shame you have kept silent about a sin which is in you. This serves no purpose, for, if you had crucified Christ and heartily repented and confessed yourself, he still abides there, nailed upon the cross, with open arms, and is always ready—if you but will it—to pardon you. Wherefore, my son, tell me freely your every sin and just as you thought no shame to commit it, even so do not be ashamed to confess it. Are you before the judge of the criminal court, that you should tremble for your life? Fear not, but tell me all as it stands."

"Father," replied Porcellio, "I thoroughly confessed myself yesterday, and I answered the sheer truth to all the questions you put to me. Nevertheless, if you have any doubt, speak and I will quickly resolve you of it."

Thereupon the friar, full of intense zeal for the sinner's welfare, said to him, "Son, it has been affirmed to me that you are guilty of the sin against nature, and I am even told you are an especially great offender in this way. If it be so, you should tell me and repent of so abominable a vice, steadfastly determining never again to commit it. If you confess yourself thereof, I will absolve you. Otherwise you will go into Lucifer's mouth, amongst the insupportable torments of hell."

Porcellio appeared somewhat provoked at these words and answered as in choler, "Sir, to me it seems you are not yourself, for what you have said to me is not true, and whoever claims I am guilty of the sin against nature doesn't know what he's talking about. Indeed he lies. In this matter you should credit me and not others. None knows my own affairs better than myself."

The holy father, hearing this and knowing that a confessor should credit the penitent with what he says in his own favor as well as against himself, replied, "Son, I have done my duty, according as God of his goodness inspires me. You would do well to send for the priest of the parish to bring you the sacrament of the altar, for I told him of your need as I came here, and he awaits."

Accordingly, they sent for the priest, and the wife, seeing that the friar had stayed a good while with the sick man, and understanding, as well, that the parish priest was coming, concluded that her husband had confessed everything. While they awaited the Sacrament, the holy friar talked of pious things with Porcellio, who presently said to him, "I do not know, nor do I wish to know, who has defamed me to you by accusing me of the sin against nature, which was never in me. May God pardon him!" Here Porcellio began affirming to the friar with oaths that he'd been lied to, and called all the saints of heaven to bear witness to his own innocence, corroborating his words with the most solemn adjurations in the world.

The good father, seeing him near death, could not imagine that he said otherwise than the truth. The parish priest being come, poor Porcellio received the holy sacrament and to all appearances showed great contrition, at which his wife exceedingly rejoiced, thinking to have saved her husband's soul. Accordingly, the friar presently taking leave, the lady accompanied him to the door, thanking him heartily for the pious office he had done her husband and begging him to pray God that Porcellio might remain in that mind and return no more to his vomit. The friar mildly rebuked her, saying "Madam, you are too obstinate and sin in deeming ill of your husband touching that of which he is not guilty, and in impeaching him, as you do, of so shameful a vice. This is not well, nor should one do thus."

Hearing this, the lady stopped the friar, who would eagerly have left the house, and said, "Father, I would not have you leave displeased with me, for I have done nothing to merit that, and still less would I have my husband die like a beast. Even if he had, as he has until this present, lived worse than animals without reason, I would nonetheless, if it be possible, have him die as all good Christians should. That which I told you of him, you must not think that I said for jealousy or some slight suspicion of him, for I would not commit myself so lightly. But I have seen all with these two eyes, nor (alas!) am I alone in this. All in the house will bear witness to it. As if I had not a hundred times decried what he did! And I assure you he would not have ventured to deny it in my presence. So, my father, disregard any denial he may make, but, for God's sake, return to his chamber and see to it that you pluck him from the devil's clutches."

The holy man was aghast at this, and, returning to Porcellio, said to him, "Alas, son, I know not what to think of you. You have denied to me that you committed the sin against nature, with which you are more burdened than as if you had Milan Cathedral on your shoulders, and yet I am assured that you are a thousand times more eager for boys than goats are for salt."

Whereupon Porcellio shook his head, and said as loudly as he might, "Ho, ho, reverend father, you didn't know how to question me. To amuse myself with boys is more natural to me than eating and drinking to man, and you asked me if I sinned against nature! Just go, go away—you don't know what a good tidbit is."

Stricken all aghast with this diabolical and stunning speech, the holy friar shrugged his shoulders, and looking upon Porcellio awhile with horror and amazement as he were some frightful monster, said, sighing, "Woe is me, Lord God, I have let Christ be cast into a fiery furnace."[51]

With that he departed, and meeting the lady, as he went, said to her, "Madam, I have done what I might."

Meanwhile Porcellio called loudly for his wife, who ran to her husband's chamber, whereupon that ribald and wicked man told her, "Wife, fetch me a bucket of water and don't delay." She asked what he wanted with it, and he replied, "I am eager to quench the fire about Christ, for that jackass of a friar tells me I have cast him into a furnace."

Porcellio told her all that had happened, at which she was grieved nearly to death.

He presently began to convalesce and regained his health. But the thing becoming publicly known at court and around Milan, everyone pointed scornfully at him, so that he had to stay within his house, and we may suppose that, just as had lived like a beast, even so he died the death of one. To conclude, then, it may well be said that the wolf sheds his coat, but not his vice.

Andrea Alciato (1492–1550)

Originator of the Renaissance vogue for emblems, Andrea Alciato produced two that denigrate male homoeroticism and attest to the far-reaching cultural influence of its theological proscriptions. One of these may further condemn tribadism. The only child of a successful merchant and mother of noble descent, he studied Greek and Latin in Milan, his probable birthplace, then law at the universities of Pavia, Bologna, and Ferrara between 1507 and 1516, finally gaining a doctorate. By introducing humanist principles to study of law, he became a Renaissance legal celebrity, and his lucrative professorships ranged through both French and Italian universities. Besides authoring many legal treatises and some philological works, he produced the seminal book of European emblematics, first published in 1531. According to Alciato's generic model, not quite realized in that unauthorized first edition, an emblem consists of a mutually interactive motto, symbolic picture, and epigram that together constitute a tripartite verbal-visual whole. Including the French, Italian, Spanish, and German translations of Alciato's Latin collection, its sixteenth- and seventeenth-century editions exceeded two hundred, and it quickly inspired a host of imitations across Europe.

In Emblem 4, *In Deo laetandum* (Joy Is Found in God), Alciato reinterprets the Ganymede myth to rebuke sexual love between males, especially intergenerational, and urge devotion to God (figure 1). Otherwise, this myth could readily support masculine love and culturally relativist critiques of orthodox sexual ideology. The chief Greco-Roman god's pursuit of Ganymede epitomized the

Fig. 1 *In Deo laetandum*, from Andrea Alciato, *Emblemata* (Lyons, 1551). By permission of the Thomas Fisher Rare Books Library, University of Toronto.

Renaissance collision between ancient homoerotic mores and Christian sexual orthodoxy. According to the epigram, as I translate it somewhat freely,

> The pictured Trojan boy is borne above,
> Soaring through stars on Jove as an eagle.
> But who'd think Jove touched by a boyish love,
> So what was old Homer's ground for this fable?
> Believe he who enjoys God's mind and truth
> Is depicted by this enraptured youth.

The Greek inscription above Ganymede, "to delight in counsels," glosses his name in accord with Xenophon's Socrates, who claims Ganymede gained apotheosis only through spiritual merits, an interpretation furthered in medieval and early modern allegoresis.[52] Imaging human flight beyond the earth, the picture insists on the gap between the weighty terrestrial flesh and the transcendental godly soul, and implies that sex between males constitutes an earthbound travesty of spiritual ascent. The barking dog may signify impotent worldly calumny or base attitudes surmounted. Subsequent emblematists produced emblems of Ganymede modeled on Alciato's; Francis Thynne (1545?–1608) inveighs against "impure minds whom unclean lusts defile / Against the rightful course of nature's kind."[53]

Besides the emblems printed in 1531 (including Ganymede), Alciato produced many more, and a further emblem bearing on homoeroticism, Emblem 80, was first published in 1546: *Adversus naturam peccantes* (Those Sinning against Nature, figure 2). The epigram proclaims, in my English rendering,

> Shocking to say, but fouler yet in deed,
> To defecate on one's own dinner plate.
> So transgressors of law that God decreed
> Defile themselves as they fornicate.[54]

Unlike the 1621 version reproduced here, the picture in the 1546 edition shows a bearded man seated at stool in an urban setting, fully clothed except for his breeches pushed down his thighs, revealing his posterior. In his French edition of 1549, Barthélemy Aneau (1505?–1561) makes the emblem bluntly antisodomitical, entitling it *Contre les bougres* (Against Buggerers).[55] However, despite Alciato's fundamental moral intention, concerns about the decorum of his analysis here often led to its elimination from editions of his emblems, or to its deposit at their physical rear end, often unnumbered, unpaginated, and un-indexed, presumably to avoid possible censorship or to ease its purgation if desired.[56]

Even in editions that included this emblem, none provided an illustration after 1546 until the 1621 Paduan *editio optima* supervised by the German scholar Johannes Thuilius (c. 1590–1630). Apparently unaware of the 1546 image, he commissioned the new design reprinted here: "Let there be a bed—on all sides closed with curtains—and beside it, let there be a naked man who unburdens his belly into a golden vessel. Close by him, let there stand on a table an earthenware

Aduerſus naturam peccantes.

EMBLEMA LXXX:

T VRPE quidem diĉtu , ſed & eſt res.improba faĉtu ,
Excipiat ſiquis chœnice ventris onus .
Menſuram , legisque modum hoc excedere ſanĉtæ eſt ,
Quale ſit inceſto pollui adulterio.

Fig. 2 *Adversus naturam peccantes*, from Andrea Alciato, *Emblemata* (Padua, 1621). By permission of the Rare Books and Manuscript Library, Columbia University.

pitcher and a goblet made of glass. . . . Yet what goes on in the screened-off bed, . . . I am anxious to spare chaste eyes and—in doing so—minds."[57] As the picture situates the curtained bed directly behind the man defecating in a misappropriated vessel, so it substitutes a putative symbolic epitome for the occluded sexual possibilities. Both the epigram and the 1621 edition's picture focus on excrementally defiling a vessel properly used for an opposite purpose and orifice: the ingestion of food. This alleged analogy renders so-called sins against nature polemically repulsive; the reversal of purpose corresponds to the orthodox claim that such sexual behaviors are *contrary* to nature. The vessel corresponds to the body itself as a container or *vas* potentially subject to licit or illicit sexual use, and that was a standard metaphor of orthodox moral theology. The due measure of Alciato's choenix figures supposed standards providentially prescribed for the gratification of sexual appetites. A specious argument by false analogy, the emblem epitomizes irrational confusions of early modern sexual orthodoxy and its polemics: The experience of so-called unnatural sexual acts is not like defecating in a choenix.

Many editions of Alciato's emblems included commentaries on their allusive contexts and meanings. In Thuilius's following account of the excremental emblem, he notes that ancient antecedents of the food-dish / chamber-pot analogy target incest, but argues that Alciato appropriated it especially to condemn masculine love. Although Alciato's polemic could be applied to any type of sex deemed "against nature," including various such heteroerotic acts and tribadism, the emblem foregrounds perceived transgression that is anal, and that was primarily associated with "the vice of Sodom" and male homoeroticism. Through his distorted claims that the Romans condemned this, Thuilius, like the encyclopedist *Theodor Zwinger (1533–1588), inadvertently demonstrates the deep anxieties that antique sexual mores provoked in view of Christian orthodoxy.

Johannes Thuilius's Commentary on Emblem 80, "Those Sinning against Nature" [58] *(1621)*

. . . I am ready to wager that when he devised this emblem, Alciato was thinking of Martial's epigram about Bassa: "The burden of your bowels, Bassa, you do not blush to unload into a golden vessel—how I pity it!— and you drink from one of glass. And so it costs you more to shit."[59] And that Alciato turned it against that infamy of masculine love (*masculae Veneris*), a comparison which the epigraph also points to reasonably well. For what is more like a hysteron proteron,[60] and what other abuse is more offensive, than to deposit one's stool in a golden vessel, and then drink from a vessel of glass or earthenware? Such a deplorable [sexual] switching of vessels against nature is likewise against nature (for this is the term which many jurists give to this sin). This is my opinion about this Emblem, to which I have accommodated this picture. As for the rest, it is for the reader to judge. . . . [Thuilius dissects the epigram and explains its relation to condemning incest.]

Be that as it may, masculine love (*mascula Venus*), for some unknown reason, takes precedence over all other monstrous crimes by its sheer enormity; proof being the Sodomite cities, overthrown by God with fire and sulphur (Genesis 19). And thus we also see that the death penalty is prescribed for those who are tainted by the filth of this impious deed (*Authentica*, "That none should lust against nature," and "Of those who lust against nature").[61] The *Lex Scantinia* is directed against this, and upholds the principle that sex with boys is impious and the lust of catamites a preposterous abomination, by the heavy punishment it metes out to those who sleep with them, as Laetus says in his work on Roman laws.[62] The emperors Constantius and Constans ordered these people to be put to the sword, when in their rescript they wrote: "When a man marries a woman in order to lie as men do [i.e., together sexually] . . . , what can be desired, when a sex forgets its place? When the crime is something which yields no profit? When the sex act (*Venus*) is changed into another form? When love is sought and not seen? We command that the laws take action, and arm themselves with the sword of vengeance, that those infamous people who are or shall be found guilty may be handed over to a particularly suitable punishment" (*l. cum uir 31 C. ad L. Iul de adult.*).[63]

Nor is the punishment reduced even if the crime was committed with the consent and volition of both the catamite who submits, and of the man who sleeps with him. For thus the triumvir Caius Fescenninus threw C. Cornelius into a state prison—a man who had been granted a military pension for valiant service in arms, and who in recognition of his virtue had been named four times by the generals to the rank of senior centurion of his legion—because he had illicit relations with a free-born youth. He appealed to the tribunes, not to deny the crime, but to declare that he was willing to pledge that the youth had openly and publicly been accustomed to profit from his body, but [the tribunes] refused to accept his surety. And so Cornelius was forced to die in prison. And their decision was perfectly just, [namely] that it was not possible for any reason to excuse this wicked deed of males with males (*masculorum nefas*), for what is forbidden by nature, law and custom ought not to be perpetrated even upon one who consents. Again, Cominus, tribune of the people, served a summons to the military tribune M. Laetorius Mergus that his adjutant officer had accused him of illicit sexual activity (*stuprum*). Mergus did not stand trial, and committed suicide. Also the general C. Marius pronounced in favour of Plotius, who killed C. Lusius, the military tribune and the son of [Marius'] own sister, because [Lusius] had dared to accost [Plotius] for immoral purposes.[64] Ulpian testifies that a man who has played the role of a woman is to be removed by the praetor from the bench.[65] We have it on Plato's authority that King Laius of Thebes decreed a ghastly punishment for those who were guilty of emasculation or perversions against nature, [namely] execution by burning.[66]

O laws, where are you now? Why does sin get off scot-free? Why do these pederasts (to borrow a phrase from Ausonius) trample beneath their shameless foot the majesty of sacred decency?[67] In the *Laws*, chapter 8, Plato solemnly [declares]: "In my view, one should abstain from males, for those who make use of them intentionally kill the human race, sowing upon stone what can never put down roots there."[68] [Marginal gloss: "Plato on masculine love (*venerem masculam*)."] Maximus of Tyre writes in a similar vein: "Union with a male body is iniquitous, and the congress sterile. Why do you consign seeds to the rocks? Why do you plow gravel? Transfer this source of delight to nature itself, and look to agriculture, to rejoice in pleasures which bear fruit, lest future ages should perish for want of seed."[69] But one can find so many men these days who subject this feeble and defenseless age to their lust, to be depopulated and polluted. The magnitude of the crime makes it impossible to describe in full. You could call men of this type—and not without reason—impious, and parricides,[70] who are not content with the sex which God gave them, but must use it for sexual pleasure in an irreligious and insolent manner. With these men, such things are treated as trivial, and almost honorable. Is it any wonder that we hear the female sex complaining? Recently I heard this with my own ears: a prostitute was gravely spinning thread she had purchased with her paltry earnings, and a beardless youth came by, who asked her why she had changed her line of work in favour of linen and wool? She replied without hesitation: "We owe this to you catamites, who have done us out of our profits." The bystanders responded with much raucous laughter.

What shall I say of these men, who indulge what is not so much an abominable lust as a form of insanity? It is revolting to speak about. But nonetheless one must speak of it, because it happens. I speak of those men whose monstrous lust and execrable madness spares no one. With what words, or with what indignation shall I pursue so great a crime? The magnitude of the wickedness surpasses the power of speech. Let us examine another monstrosity. The emperor Nero tried to turn the boy Sporus into a woman by castrating him, and he added to this a dowry, a bridal veil, and a wedding celebrated with great ostentation. What else? He publicly took him as his wife. So someone cracked this clever joke: "It would have gone well for humanity had Nero's father Domitius had such a wife."[71]

Tradition relates that at one time amongst the Gauls this evil of backdoor sex (*posticae Veneris*) raged with such intensity that it was sanctioned by a wicked law to the effect that no one could take a wife who had not first performed the functions of a wife. It is very much otherwise in our Germany, which although it has a reputation amongst other nations for being drunken, filthy, mistrustful and proud (Alexander the Great reproached it for this last vice), has at least never been accused of this wicked lust. And rightly so, for so great is the turpitude of this deed, so indecent is it, that death is preferably to carrying out[72] such an act, as Paulus responds in *l. isti quidem 8ff. de eo quod metus causa*.[73] [Marginal gloss: "Sodomitical enormity (*Sodomia enormitas*)."]

But I shall say no more about this wicked crime, on account of which the wrath of God came down upon the children of unbelief, and through which that very society which ought to exist between God and ourselves is violated, and by which that very nature which He created is polluted, for merely to mention it befouls the page. Nonetheless it may be found in Julius Clarus, book 5, in the section entitled *Sodomia*; in Jacobus Menochius, Book 2, *De arbit. iudic. cent. 3 casu 285;* and in Caelius Rhodiginus, Book 15, chs. 9 and 10.[74]

Jean Calvin (1509–1564)

This leading Reformer's commentaries on the judgment of Sodom in Genesis, on Romans 1:24–31, and on 1 Corinthians 6:9–11 evince an abhorrence for sexual love between males typical of many early modern theologians, whether Protestant or Roman Catholic, and would have further reinforced that view. Born in middle-class circumstances at Noyon in Picardy, Calvin studied mostly at Paris after 1523, vacillating between theology and law due to paternal insistence on the latter, and meanwhile gravitated toward Protestantism. When a friend was investigated by the Inquisition in 1533, Calvin fled from Paris to Basel. His *Institutio Christianae religionis* (Institution of Christian Religion), a central compendium of Reformed doctrine, was first published there in 1536, then revised and expanded. After ecclesiastical appointments in Geneva and Strasbourg, where he married in 1540, he led the Genevan Reformed Church from 1541 onward. There he promulgated a new religious discipline involving a consistory to regulate private life, including sexual conduct, according to standards supposedly authorized by the Bible, and using Inquisitorial methods of enforcement. A significant number of Genevans resisted Calvin's disciplinary measures. On doctrinal grounds Jérome Bolsec (c. 1524–1584) and Sébastien Castellion (1515–1563), later an important advocate of religious toleration, were exiled, and Michael Servetus (1509/11–1553) was burned at the stake in 1553. Calvin's voluminous writings include theological and polemical treatises besides the *Institutio* and commentaries. Most of these were translated into various vernacular languages. Through his publications and leadership of the Genevan church, one of the most prestigious models of emergent Protestantism, he became one of the most influential figures in early modern Europe. The following commentaries reprint each biblical chapter before Calvin's analysis; I retain the most relevant verses.

Commentary upon the First Book of Moses Called Genesis[75] *(c. 1550)*

From Chapter Nineteen

[Discussing Genesis 18, Calvin declares "Sodom was full of all filthy corruptions and abominations"; but "the next chapter following expresseth the most filthy crime which reigned in Sodom" (i.e., sex between males). He invokes Ezekiel 16:49–50 to claim it arose from lechery, plenty, pride, and cruelty. "Therefore, if so be we do abhor this extreme outrage, we must embrace temperance and sobriety." In Genesis 19, God sends two angelic visitors disguised as young men to test Sodom. Lot hospitably provides them dinner and lodging in his home.]

4 But before they went to bed, the men of the city, even the men of Sodom, compassed the house round about, from the young to the old, all the people from all quarters.

5 Who crying unto Lot, said unto him, "Where are the men which came to thee this night? Bring them out unto us that we may know them." . . .

24 Then the Lord rained upon Sodom and upon Gomorrah brimstone and fire from the Lord out of heaven.

25 And overthrew those cities and all the plain, and all the inhabitants of the cities, and that which grew upon the earth. . . .

4 *But before they went to bed:* Here in one wicked fact Moses setteth forth a lively image of Sodom. For hereby it doth evidently appear what a devilish consent was among them to all wickedness, in that they all conspired together to commit such horrible and detestable filthiness. How great their wickedness was, it doth hereby appear in that, as it were with an army, they beseige the house of Lot. How blind and beastly is their lust insomuch that like brute beasts, void of all shame, they run to and fro? How great is their fierceness and cruelty in threatening so shamefully the holy father, and in assaying all extremities. Hereby also we gather that they were not infected with one vice alone, but also that they were fallen to all boldness of sinning, insomuch that they were devoid of all shame. And Ezekiel (as we have said already) doth notably declare from what beginnings and entrances of evils they fell to extreme filthiness (16:49–50). Hereunto also pertaineth the saying of Paul, how that God punisheth the ungodliness of men when he giveth them over into so great blindness that they fall into divers lusts and defile their bodies (Rom. 1:24–28). But whenas shame being set aside, the reins are loosed to lust, filthy and beastly barbarousness must needs by and by follow, and divers kinds of wickednesses must of necessity be therewithal mingled that there may be more than a deformed confusion.

Wherefore, if so be the vengeance of God fell upon the Sodomites, insomuch that being blinded with outrage they gave themselves to all kind of wickedness, we shall be scarce more favorably dealt withal, whose impiety is by so much the less excusable, by how much the truth of God is more plainly revealed unto us. *From the young to the old:* Moses concealeth many things which the reader may call to mind of himself: as this, that he maketh no mention by whom the multitude was stirred up. For it is very likely that there were certain provokers: but notwithstanding, we hereby perceive how willing and ready they were to commit wickedness, who, as it were with a watchword, came by and by together. It also showeth that there was no manner of shame left in them: because neither gravity restrained the old men, nor that modesty the young men, which became that age. To be short, he meaneth that all care of honesty was abolished and that the order of nature was perverted, when he saith that from the young to the old they came together from the furthest parts of the city [marginal gloss: "Both young and old in Sodom were defiled"].

5 *Where are the men:* Although they minded filthily to abuse the guests to preposterous[76] lust, yet notwithstanding, in words they pretend another thing. For as if Lot had offended in receiving strange men into the city, wherein he himself dwelt but as a foreigner, they command them to be brought forth before them. Some expound this word *Know* to have to do carnally, and so the Greek interpreters have translated it. But I think that this word was put in another sense, as if they should say, "We will know what manner of guests thou hast brought into our City." For the Scripture is wont modestly to note by this word a matter of shame. Therefore the Sodomites would have spoken more filthily of their detestable lying with those men; but to cover their wickedness, they quarrel with the holy man proudly, in that he durst presume to receive unknown men . . .[77]

And this is without all doubt, that although the Sodomites professed not in plain words what a filthy desire they had, yet notwithstanding, Lot was fully certified of the same by their daily wickedness. If any man affirm it to be very absurd that the whole people should require two men to commit fornication with them, I answer that, because they imagined by custom and use that the same vice was lawful for them, a few setting the matter abroach, the whole multitude was stirred up. Even as it cometh to pass where there is not any difference made between right and wrong. . . .

24 *Then the Lord rained upon Sodom:* Moses here very briefly toucheth the destruction of Sodom and of the other cities. The grievousness of the matter required a larger treatise, yea, a tragical discourse. But Moses simply, according to his manner, reciting the judgment of God, those things which he could not vehemently enough express with words, he leaveth to the consideration of the readers. Therefore it is our part to have a full consideration of that horrible vengeance, the which seeing it happened not without the wonderful shaking of heaven and earth, we ought to be afraid at the only naming of it, and therefore mention is so oftentimes made of the same in the Scriptures. And the Lord would not have those cities to be swallowed up with an earthquake only; but to the end he might make a more notable example of his judgment, he cast fire and brimstone from heaven. . . . Moses commendeth here unto us the extraordinary work of God, to the end we may know that Sodom was not destroyed without a manifest miracle. . . . God doth always work by the hand of his son, and by so horrible an example of vengeance I doubt not but that the son bore rule. . . . And whereas it was always wont

to be demanded out of this place, what the infants deserved, which were destroyed together with their parents, the answer is easy to be made: that mankind is in the hand of God, insomuch that he appointeth to destruction whom he will, and upon whom he will he showeth mercy. Also we ought to submit unto his secret judgment whatsoever we cannot comprehend within the compass of our understanding and reach. Last of all, all that seed was accursed and execrable, insomuch that of right he spared not the least.[78]

Commentary upon the Epistle of St. Paul to the Romans[79] *(c. 1550)*

From Chapter One

24 . . . God gave them up to their hearts' lusts, unto uncleanness, to defile their own bodies between themselves.

25 Which turned the truth of God unto a lie, and worshipped and served the creature above the creator, which is blessed forever, Amen.

26 For this cause God gave them up unto vile affections: for even their women did change the natural use into that which is against nature.

27 And likewise also the men left the natural use of the women and burned in their lust one toward another, and man with man wrought filthiness, and received in themselves such recompense of their error as was meet.

28 For as they regarded not to know God, even so God delivered them up unto a reprobate mind, to do those things which are not convenient [i.e., morally suitable].

29 Being full of unrighteousness, fornication, wickedness, covetousness, maliciousness, full of envy, of murder, of debate, of deceit, taking all things in evil part, whisperers. . . .

31 Which men though they knew the Law of God, how that they which commit such things are worthy of death, yet not only do the same but also favor them that do them. . . .

26 *For this cause God gave them up:* As though he had interposed a Parenthesis, he returneth unto that which he had begun before, concerning the revengement of the Lord. And he bringeth the first example in the horrible sin of preposterous lust.[80] Whereby appeareth they were not only given over to beastly lusts, but also became worse than beasts when they overthrew the whole order of nature. Secondly, he reckoneth a great Catalogue of vices which have both been extant in all ages, and at that time reigned everywhere most licentiously. Neither hindereth this one whit that everyone was not laden with such a heap of vices. For in reproving the general corruption of men, it is sufficient if everyone be compelled to acknowledge some mole or blemish.

Thus therefore it is to be taken that Paul doth here briefly touch those vices which both were common in all ages, and also were specially to be seen in that age. For it is marvelous how common that filthiness was, which the brute beasts abhor; as for the other vices they were vulgar.[81] Secondly, that he reciteth such a Catalogue of vices as all mankind is comprehended in it. For although all men be not murderers, or thieves, or adulterers, yet there is no man that is not found to be polluted with some vice. *unto vile affections:* He calleth those vile affections which even in the opinion of men are most vile or shameful and serve to the dishonor of God. . . .

28 . . . *To do those things which are not convenient:* Because hitherto he hath mentioned only that one execrable example,[82] which though it were common amongst many, yet it was not common unto all, he beginneth to reckon such vices as no man could be found to be free of. For albeit (as it is said) they appear not all at once in every one, yet all men know themselves to be guilty of some of them, that every man for his own part might be reproved of manifest pravity [i.e., corruption]. First of all, whereas he calleth them *not convenient*, understand that they abhorred from all judgment of reason, and were far from the duties of men. For he declareth the tokens of a confounded mind, that without all difference men addicted themselves to those vices which common sense ought to have refused. . . .

Commentary upon St. Paul's Epistles to the Corinthians[83] *(c. 1550)*

[Calvin quotes 1 Corinthians 6:9–11 before commenting. In 1 Corinthians 6:13–20 St. Paul argues "the body is not for fornication but for the Lord," for "your bodies are the members of Christ." He who fornicates "sinneth against his body," "the temple of the Holy Ghost" for glorifying God.]

9 Do ye not remember how that the unrighteous shall not inherit the kingdom of God? Be not deceived: for neither fornicators, neither worshippers of Images, neither whoremongers, neither weaklings, neither abusers of themselves with mankind.

10 Neither thieves, neither the covetous, neither drunkards, neither cursed speakers, neither pillers [i.e., plunderers] shall inherit the kingdom of God.

11 And such were ye verily, but ye are washed: ye are sanctified, ye are justified, by the name of the Lord Jesus, and by the spirit of our God.

9 . . . *Be not deceived:* Taking occasion of one vice, he speaketh of many, and I think that he hath principally noted those vices which were among the Corinthians. He noteth the venerious and filthy lusts of the Corinthians by three terms, which filthy lusts all histories testify reigned among them and abounded too generally. . . . *For neither fornicators:* In what fornicators differ from adulterers, it is well enough known. By weaklings I understand those which although they do not commonly give themselves to lust, yet notwithstanding they do bewray their impudency by unchaste

and bawdy talk, by effeminate gesture, by their apparel, and by other delights. The fourth,[84] of all the rest, is most detestable, being the very same monstrous filthiness which hath been too usual in Greece [marginal gloss: "Sodomites"]. . . . And to the end his speech might be of the greater force, he saith *Be not deceived.* By which words he admonisheth them not to deceive themselves by vain hope, as commonly men are wont, in extenuating their sins, to inure themselves to the contempt of God. Therefore there is no poison more pernicious than those delights which confirm us in our sins. Let us then eschew the vices of wicked men not only as the alluring enticements of Mermaids but also as the deadly stinging of Satan, when they turn the judgment of God and the reprehensions of sins unto a jest. . . .

11 *And such were ye:* . . . We must not construe that they all are so bound up in one faggot [i.e., bundle], as though all these vices were in every one of them; but only his purpose is to show that no man is free from these evils until he be born again by the spirit. For we must thus account that the seed of all evils is included in the nature of man: and that other vices do reign and appear in others even as the Lord declareth the wickedness by the fruits of the flesh. Even so Paul in the first Chapter of his Epistle to the Romans gathereth many kinds of wickednesses and vices which spring from the ignorance of God, and from that ingratitude whereof he had made all the unbelievers guilty. Not that any one infidel is infected with those vices in general, but because all men are subject unto them and there is no man pure from them all. For he which is not an adulterer sinneth in some other kind of sin. . . . Before such time as we be reformed of God, one is given to cruelty, another to falsehood, another to filthy lusts, and another to deceit and fraud. Insomuch that there is none in whom there is not some show of common corruption, and we are every one of us by the inward and secret affection of the mind subject to all diseases in part, were it not that the Lord doth inwardly repress them lest they should openly burst forth. Therefore the simple sense is that before the grace of regeneration some of the Corinthians were covetous, some were adulterers, some robbers, some weaklings, and some cursed speakers; but now being delivered by Christ, they have left off to be such. And this is the purpose of the Apostle, to humble them by the commemoration of their former state and also to stir them up to reknowledge the grace of God toward them. For the greater that the misery is known to be, from whence we are delivered by the goodness of God, so much the more the bounty of his grace doth shine. . . . The purpose of the Apostle in this place is nothing else than to amplify the grace of God with many titles, which hath delivered us from the bondage of sin, that we might thereby learn how greatly we ought to abhor all things which provoke the wrath and vengeance of God against us. . . .

St. Peter Canisius (1521–1597)

For early modern Catholics, this Jesuit's famous catechism first published in 1555, the *Summa doctrinae Christianae*, was a central means of defining the varieties of sin allegedly involved in sexual love between males. The catechist does not explicitly mention female possibilities, perhaps because, having been composed in Latin, his text was primarily intended for masculine personal instruction. Not only were there at least two hundred editions in twelve languages during Canisius's life, but it was used for centuries thereafter. Originally from Nijmegen in the Low Countries, he studied at the University of Cologne from 1536. Whereas his father, a wealthy burgomaster, wanted him to marry and study law, he became Germany's first Jesuit in 1541 and a priest in 1546. As preacher, theologian, administrator, and founder of Jesuit colleges, he energetically fortified German Catholicism against insurgent Protestantism. Written at the request of Ferdinand, the younger brother and German deputy of the Holy Roman Emperor Charles V, the catechism was quickly enlarged after the first edition, and abridged in two versions designed for children and adolescents. In 1925 Canisius was canonized and declared a Doctor of the Church.

The catechism seeks to codify Roman Catholic orthodoxy so as to proselytize the faith and strengthen its grip on believers' minds. In treating sexual issues, it stresses that only sex sanctified by marriage, a sacrament for Catholics, is divinely authorized; reflecting the union of Christ and the Church, matrimonial sex propagates the latter to the glory of God and enables the spouses to avoid fornication.[85] The possibilities of extramarital sex are sinful to varying extents, we are told, and the sixth commandment, against adultery, also forbids "fornication, . . . all unlawful copulation, and unclean voluptuousness" (81). Referring also to bestiality here, but still clearly directed against a male lying with a male as with a woman (following Leviticus 18:22 and 20:13), and thus especially censuring "the liers with mankind" (319), sodomy is not only a sin against nature, Canisius advises, but also specifically one of the biblical "crying sins," as the English Protestant legal authority *Sir Edward Coke (1552–1634) similarly observes, and thus a most heinous sin deserving death. Unrepentant sodomites, especially those who defend sodomy or deny its sinfulness, further sin against the Holy Ghost—a crime God almost never pardons, the catechism maintains—and almost certainly incur damnation. Moreover, anyone knowing of another's sodomy who does not rebuke or punish it is guilty of "alien sin." Such sins are "those which, although they be wrought and accomplished by the hands and deeds of other men, yet they are worthily imputed unto us and do make our consciences guilty of damnation in the sight of God." There are nine ways of committing them: "by counsel, by commanding, by consent, by provocation, by praise or flattery, by silence, by winking or Indulgence, by participation in the fault, and by wicked defending or maintaining the same" (296–98). Canisius's delineation of the categories of sin clarifies the daunting theological predicament of early modern sodomites.

A Sum of Christian Doctrine[86] *(1555)*

Of the Seven Deadly Sins

5. WHAT IS LECHERY, AND WHAT MANNER OF OFFSPRING DOTH IT ENGENDER?
Lechery is an inordinate appetite of unclean and libidinous pleasure.
And it bringeth forth blindness of mind, inconsideration, inconstancy,
headlongness, love of himself, hatred of God, too much desire of this
life, a horror of death and future Judgment, and desperation of eternal
felicity.

Against this sin which maketh the wise mad and causeth men to become in manner beasts (3 Kings [i.e., 1 Kings] 11:1, Ecclus. 19:2), thus
writeth S. Paul: "Fly fornication. Every sin whatsoever a man doth is without the body, but he that doth fornicate sinneth against his own body"
(1 Cor. 6:18). And in another place thus: "Fornication and all uncleaness,
or avarice, let it not so much as be named among you, as becometh Saints;
or filthiness or foolish talk or scurrility, being to no purpose; but rather
giving of thanks" (Eph. 5:3–4). And it is a wonderful thing that Christians are not marvelously ashamed, who do pollute themselves with filthy
lust in the sight of God and his Angels, whereas they have consecrated in
Baptism their bodies and members as pure temples to the holy Ghost and
to Christ our Lord (1 Cor. 3:16). Hereupon again saith S. Paul: "Know
you not that your members are the temple of the Holy Ghost which is in
you, whom you have of God, and you are not your own?" (1 Cor. 6:19).
Then again: "Know you not that your bodies are the members of Christ?
Taking therefore the members of Christ, shall I make them the members
of an harlot?" (1 Cor. 6:15). And finally he concludeth in this sort: "For
you are bought with a great price. Glorify and bear God in your body" (1
Cor. 6:20). "For fornicators and advouterors, God will judge" (Heb. 13:4,
1 Cor. 6:9, Eph. 5:5, Gal. 5:19–21, Rev. 21:8)....

Of Sins against the Holy Ghost

1. WHAT IS A SIN AGAINST THE HOLY GHOST?
It is maliciously and contemptuously to reject the grace and liberality
of God being offered, which grace certes[87] is peculiarly attributed to the
Holy Ghost, as to the fountain of all goodness. And this is to sin without
any remedy or redress: insomuch that, according to the speech of Christ,
for such and so great a sin no forgiveness is obtained either in this world
or in the world to come (Matt. 12:31, Mark 3:28–29, Luke 12:10).[88] For
after this manner Almighty God dealeth with us, that he giveth neither
grace upon earth nor glory in Heaven to any other but unto those only
which, having once known sin do detest it, and setting before their eyes
that which is good, do make choice of a righteous course of life. But from
these sins far is banished both detestation of sin, and the choice also of
that good which were to be followed; and that moreover is clean rejected

whereby the Holy Ghost doth use of his singular grace to withdraw a man from sin. And for this reason they which are fettered with such kind of sins do either never get the grace of God or seldom and very hardly. For these sins are not committed of human imbecility and frailty . . . , nor yet of ignorance, . . . but that which is far worse without comparison, these sins are committed of malice and obstinacy of mind. . . .

2. HOW MANY SINS ARE THERE AGAINST THE HOLY GHOST?

There are of that kind accounted six, and their names commonly used are these: Presumption of the mercy of God, or of the impunity of sin; Desperation; Oppugning of the known truth; Envying of brotherly charity; Obstinacy; and impenitency. But more plainly and significantly they may be thus numbered. 1. Confidently to abuse the mercy of God. 2. Utterly to despair of the grace of God, or of his [i.e., the sinner's] own salvation. 3. Rebelliously to oppugn the truth of religion against his own conscience. 4. Vehemently to be moved with a settled Envy because of the increase of salvation and virtue in his brother. 5. With an obstinate mind to persist wittingly in a fault. 6. Without purpose of amendment, never to make an end of a lewd and perverse kind of life. . . .

8. WHEN IS A SIN OF IMPENITENCY COMMITTED?

When a man without any end or measure of his sins, which truly he should wash away by wholesome Penance, resolveth moreover that never he will do any Penance at all. Of this kind of persons, who are such desperate and pitiful sinners and so will remain, both their life and their death is most abominable. Forasmuch as, if not in words, yet in deed they seem to say: "We have entered into league with death, and with hell we have made a pact" (Isa. 28:15, 3:8–9, Ps. 51:3–7, Prov. 2:14). . . .

Thus much concerning the sins against the Holy Ghost, which are doubtless most grievous, and which Almighty God either never or very hardly doth pardon. For which cause, we ought often to guard ourselves and to confirm others against the same. . . . Now therefore let us come to those sins which are also not a little heinous, and are wont to be called sins that Cry unto Heaven.

Of Sins That Cry unto Heaven

1. WHAT SINS ARE THOSE THAT ARE SAID TO CRY UNTO HEAVEN?

Those which notably above others are known to have a manifest and exceeding wickedness, and do singularly purchase to those which commit them God's indignation and vengeance. Of this sort there are four numbered in holy scripture, to wit, willful Murder (Gen. 4:10); Sodomy (Gen. 18:20); Oppression of the Poor (Exod. 22:23); and defrauding the Laboring man's hire (Deut. 24:15; James 5.4). . . .

3. AND WHAT IS EXTANT IN HOLY SCRIPTURE TOUCHING THE SIN OF SODOM AND
THE PUNISHMENTS THEREOF?

The men of Sodom, saith the scripture, "were very naught, and sinners before God too too much" (Gen. 13:13). This horrible and abominable sin S. Peter and S. Paul do reprove (2 Pet. 2:6; Rom. 1:24, 1 Tim. 1:10, Eph. 5:5, Judg. 19:22, 20:46); yea nature herself doth abhor. And the scripture also doth declare the greatness of so foul a wickedness in these words: "The cry of the Sodomites and the Gomorreans is multiplied, and their sin is aggravated too too much" (Gen. 18:20). For which cause the Angels do speak thus unto the just man Lot, who did greatly abhor from the outrageous filthiness of the Sodomites (2 Pet. 2:6): "We will destroy this place, because the cry of them hath increased before our Lord, who hath sent us to destroy them. Therefore our Lord rained down upon Sodom and Gomorrah brimstone and fire from our Lord out of heaven, and overthrew those Cities and all the Country about" (Gen. 19:13, Wis. 10:6, Deut. 29:23, Jude 1:7, Gen. 13:10). Neither doth the scripture leave untouched the causes which moved the Sodomites and may also move others to this so grievous a sin. For thus we read in Ezekiel: "Behold this was the iniquity of Sodom thy sister: Pride, fullness of bread, and abundance, and the idleness of her and her daughters: and they did not stretch their hand to the needy and poor" (16:49).

And of this vice, which can never be sufficiently detested, are they guilty who do not fear to break the law of God, yea and the law of nature written in Leviticus, which is this: *Cum masculo non commiscearis coitu foemineo, quia abominatio est. Cum omni pecore non coibis, nec maculaberis cumeo* (Lev. 18:22–23, Deut. 27:21).[89] Which sin if it be committed, we are admonished in the same place, that the very earth is polluted with such horrible and abominable lusts, and that God's wrath is very much provoked against the people, and that the crime is to be punished with death (Lev. 20:13, 15, Exod. 22:19, Joel 3:3). For which cause S. Paul doth not once only rebuke the liers with mankind (1 Cor. 6:19, Rom. 1:24, 1 Tim. 1:10, Gal. 5:10–11). And he condemneth also unclean and effeminate persons, of which one was Onan son of Judas, who could not escape the present revenge of God, for that he sinned against his own body, and worse than any beast would violate the honesty and order of nature (Gen. 38:9). . . .

Henri Estienne (1528–1598)

According to Henri Estienne's loyally French Protestant *Apologie pour Hérodote*, sodomy is a primarily Italian vice and an endemic evil of Catholic religion, but has greatly spread due to his countrymen's increased travels in Italy and Turkey. A scion of the important Estienne humanist publishing house, this distinguished Hellenist and scholar-publisher inherited the Genevan branch from his father Robert in 1559. Along with a Latin edition of Herodotus, Henri's popular *Apologie* was published in 1566 and many further editions quickly followed. The ostensible argument of the *Apologie* is that, however unbelievable the stories of ancient Herodotus may seem, they must be historically genuine because recent events are even stranger. Estienne uses this theme for caustic satire of his own time expressed through scandalous anecdotes, especially about Roman Catholicism. Urging the traditional notion that human history evinces a decline of the ages, he argues that, despite Christianity, human vices have only become progressively worse since the ancients. Hence he compares three successive periods: antiquity; the "last" or "former" age *circa* 1490, using preachings from that time by Olivier Maillard (1430–1502), Michel Menot (1440?–1518) and Gabriel of Barletta (fl. 1480) to define its moral condition; and "this day," Estienne's own time. Herodotus records no folly so strange, Estienne concludes, as the persecution and martyring of Reformers for opposing religious abuses.[90] Neither priest nor theologian, he indicates how exercised indeed early modern laity could be about religious issues. Although Estienne's superb classical learning could potentially have conduced some relativistic acceptance of same-sex sexual love, he instead promotes homophobic religious ideology in its Protestant variant.

Aside from advocating Protestantism, Estienne's avowed purpose in the *Apologie* is to show "the frowardness and corruption of our nature, or the sleights of Satan, . . . how he lies in ambush for us at every corner." So "every . . . report of such heinous and horrible crimes should be so many alarms . . . to stir us up . . . to ply [God] more effectually by humble and hearty prayer, that he would not leave us to ourselves, nor let loose the reins to our unruly and disordered affections, but bridle and keep them in compass, and ever take us into his holy protection" (60; cf. 14–15). And "the reason why the godly do not pour themselves forth into pleasure and let loose the reins to their lusts is because they have the fear of God continually before their eyes," as "the good child feareth to offend his father for the love he beareth him" (61).

Since the late fifteenth century, Estienne claims, sex between males has become much more current among Frenchmen, and he ascribes that to growing travel in Italy and Turkey, where it has long been institutionalized as a way of life, he says, and interpreted as a mere peccadillo by most. Although he allows "many Christians" of Maillard's and Menot's time in France were "so blinded and besotted" with sodomy that they were "not ashamed to defend it" (and thus had considerable confidence and agency in conceptualizing their sexual difference), Estienne nonetheless insists that Maillard did not speak of it "as . . . a thing whereof men made a trade and occupation," whereas his contemporary Barletta, "having to deal with Italians," condemned it "often" (33). Instead, of course, Maillard could simply have been more circumspect or less homophobic. However, besides inadvertently attesting to the sexually relativistic and tolerationist effects of enhanced European acquaintance with other cultures, Estienne's remarks implicitly broach possibilities of early modern male homoerotic sexual tourism. When recounting a visit to Venice, renowned for its numerous courtesans, Thomas Coryate (1577?–1617) openly acknowledges the heteroerotic counterpart.[91] Considering female same-sex love, Estienne seems particularly exercised by the assumption of supposedly masculine prerogatives of dress, occupation, and marriage.

Apology for Herodotus[92] *(1566)*

Chapter 10: How That the Foresaid Preachers [Maillard, Menot, and Gabriel of Barletta] Have Left Sundry Vices Untouched and Uncensured

. . . As for sodomy, I am easily drawn to believe that the former Preachers were very sparing in speaking thereof, lest they should open a gap to men's curiosity which is naturally exorbitant in this kind. The more knaves are the Priests, who in their auricular confession (as they call it) stir the minds and awake the spirits of their confessionists by their interrogatories, occasioning them to muse upon such matters and to feed their fancies with such facts as otherwise they would never have dreamed of. For mine own part I confess that for this very reason I have had much ado to persuade myself that swinish Sodomites and beastly buggerers should be executed publicly. True it is, sundry weighty reasons may be alleged on both sides, but I hold me to that which I see practiced in well ordered cities. Furthermore, the reason which moves me to think that sodomy was not then[93] (in all probability) so common as at this day is for that there was not such resort into those countries where it is made a trade and occupation as at this present.[94] For proof hereof if we consider who those Frenchmen be that give themselves to such horrible and hellish sins, we shall find that most of them have been in Italy or Turkey, or (not to go out of France to seek them) have frequented their company, at leastwise have familiarly conversed with their scholars. For albeit Athenaeus tell us in his thirteenth book (which I remember I have read elsewhere under the name of Hermippus) that the Celts in his time, notwithstanding they had fairer women than other Barbarians, were addicted to this sin,[95] yet (God be thanked) before we could speak so good Italian in France, there was (almost) no speech of this villainy, as I have heard of divers old folks. And verily it is more pardonable in Italians than in Frenchmen (if pardonable in any) seeing that they (who for the most part call it but peccadillo) are nearer their sanctities who do not only give a license for it by way of permission, but a precedent also by way of example, as hereafter shall be showed. Notwithstanding the words wherewith we express such devilish and damnable dealing, being borrowed from the Italian tongue, are a pregnant proof that France learned all the villainy it hath of them, though it were hard to say from what particular place. For this is a common song in Italy, current in every man's mouth: "For these four things Siena looks so high, / For towers, for bells, for whores, for buggery (*bardasse*)." But Master

Pasquin sheweth plainly in sundry of his Satires that notwithstanding that proverb, Rome in regard of the [fourth] particular ought to go before Siena, as where he saith, "Sed Roma[e] puero non licet esse mihi."[96] And were it but only for the reason I have now alleged, he cannot endure (and surely not without cause) that Rome should be deprived of this honor. . . .

Chapter 13: Of Sodomy and the Sin against Nature, Committed at This Day [97]
Moreover, if there were nothing else but such swinish Sodomy as is committed at this day, might we not justly term this age the paragon of abominable wickedness? The heathen (I confess) were much addicted to this vice, but can it be showed that it was ever accounted among Christians as a virtue? Yet some in these days have not only accounted it a virtue but also written in commendation of it and published their writings in print to the view of the world. For we may not forget how that Giovanni della Casa, a Florentine and Archbishop of Benevento, writ a book in Italian rhyme wherein he sings forth a thousand praises in commendation of this sin which good Christians cannot so much as think of without horror, calling it (among other epithets which he giveth it) *a heavenly work*. This book was printed at Venice by one Troianus Nanus as they who copied it out do testify.[98] The author of which worthy work was the man to whom I dedicated certain of my Latin verses whilst I was at Venice. But I protest I committed that fault before I knew him to be such a monster. And when I was advertised thereof, it was past recall and recovery. But to return to this so foul and infamous a sin. Is it not great pity that gentlemen, who before they travelled into Italy abhorred the very naming of it, should after they have continued there a time, delight themselves not only in talking and discoursing, but in practicing and professing it as a thing which they have learned in a happy time? As for those who through bad custom have only kept the Italian phrase there commonly spoken (though borrowed from such wicked villainy), they have (I grant) some colorable excuse. But what can the rest allege for themselves? Yet I dare not affirm that all who are tainted with this sin learned it in Italy or Turkey: for our M. Maillard[99] was never there and yet he made profession of it. So that he, who like a great Sorbonnical doctor caused so many silly souls to fry a faggot[100] against all right and reason, equity and conscience, was the man whom the Judges might justly have burned, not as a Lutheran (as they then called them) or an obstinate Gospeller, but as a Sodomitical buggerer.

But I were much to blame if I should forget Peter Lewis (or rather Aloisius, for he was called in Italian Pietro Aloisio) son to Pope Paul the third. This Prince of Sodom, Duke of Parma and Placentia, that he might not degenerate from the Popish progeny (whence he was descended) was so addicted to this horrible and hellish sin and so carried away with the burning thereof, that he did not only forget the judgments of God and the provident care he should have had of his good name (at least with such as make no conscience to give themselves to such villainy). Nay (which is more), he did not only forget that he was a man, but even the daily danger of death itself, whereof brute beasts do stand in fear. For not content to satiate his lawless lust with innumerable persons of all sorts, sexes and degrees, he went a wooing at the last to a young man called Cosmus Cherius, then Bishop of Fano, and perceiving that he could not otherwise have his pleasure of him and work him to his will, he caused his men to hold him. Shortly after which fact, he received the reward due to such monsters.[101] And as he had led a wicked and shameful life, so they made for him so infamous and villainous an Epitaph that the Reader had need of a pomander in his pocket, or some preservative, lest his stomach should rise at the reading thereof.

Concerning bestiality, or the sin against nature (which was ever more common among shepherds than others) who so list to make inquiry into the examples of later times shall find as great store of them as of the rest. But if any desire examples of fresher memory, let him go to the Italian soldiers of the camp that would have beleaguered Lyons, during the civil wars, and ask them what they did with their goats. Notwithstanding an accident happened in our time far more strange than any that can be alleged in this kind, of a woman burned at Toulouse (about seven and twenty years ago) for prostituting herself to a dog, which was also burned with her for company: which I account a most strange fact considering her sex. Now this sin I call *the sin against nature*, having respect rather to the common use and phrase of speech than to the proper signification of the word, according to which Sodomy is as well a sin against nature as bestiality. But not to enter into a warfare of words, let this suffice that brute beasts do condemn us herein.[102]

Now albeit the former example be very strange, yet we have here another far more strange (though not altogether so wicked) committed about thirty years ago by a maid born at Fountaines (between Blois and Rommarantin), who having disguised herself like a man served as an hostler at an Inn in the suburbs of Foy for the space of seven years, and afterwards married a maid of the town, with whom she companied for the space of two years or thereabout, attempting much, but effecting nothing. After which time her cousinage and knavery in counterfeiting the office of a husband being discovered, she was apprehended, and having confessed the fact, was burned. By which examples we see that our Age may well boast that (notwithstanding the vices of former times) it hath some proper and peculiar to itself. For this fact of hers hath nothing common with that which was practiced by those famous strumpets who in old time were called *Tribades*.[103]

Andrew Willet (1562–1621)

Discussing Leviticus 18:22 and 20:13, and Romans 1:26–27, Andrew Willet's synoptic Protestant commentaries amplify perceived biblical condemnations of male and female same-sex love, while surveying the views of prior commentators. Son of a notary who later became a priest, Willet was born at Ely in 1562 and entered Cambridge University in 1577, first at Peterhouse and then Christ's College. After obtaining his B.A. in 1580 and M.A. in 1584, he took holy orders in the Church of England in 1585. In order to marry, he resigned his academic fellowship at Christ's, held since 1583, in 1588. He fathered eighteen children. Further studies yielded his B.D. in 1591 and D.D. in 1601. Besides holding various church livings, mainly at Barley in Hertfordshire, he became chaplain-in-ordinary and tutor to Prince Henry, eldest son of King James I, but was later jailed for one month for opposing Prince Charles's ultimately unsuccessful attempt to marry the Spanish king's daughter. Despite Willet's prolific religious publications, reputation for great learning, and dedicated advocacy of the English church against Roman Catholicism and Puritanism, he never received a bishopric.

Hexapla in Leviticum, a Sixfold Commentary[104] *(1631)*

Question 27: Against Lying with the Male, v. 22

[On Lev. 18:22: "Thou shalt not lie with mankind as with womankind: it *is* abomination."]

1. These are the sins which reigned among the Heathen as a reward of their Idolatry, as the Apostle showeth (Rom. 1:24), which was familiar among the Greeks, even the wisest of them, as Solon, Socrates, Zeno, Minos, Rhadamanthys.[105] And the Romans, their Emperors were given to this filthiness: Nero, Vespasian, Caligula, Trajan, Vitellius, Julius Caesar, Augustus, and most of all Hadrian the Emperor, who made Antinous, his Minion, a god, and instituted a temple, sacrifices, and priests unto him, of whom a city and country in Egypt was so called.

2. And in Scripture are set forth examples in this kind to be abhorred: this unnatural sin was punished in the Sodomites with fire and brimstone; and, as Chrysostom[106] saith it caused gehenna, hell-fire, to be before the time.[107] This the Hebrews understand to have been the sporting of Ishmael with Isaac. And Rupertus[108] taketh this to be the evil report of Joseph's brethren, which he brought to his Father (Gen. 37:2). This was that exercise of effeminate young men, which wicked Jason obtained leave of Antiochus to set up (2 Macc. 4:9–13), which Saint Jude calleth to go after other flesh (Jude 1:7). And it is the sin for the which specially the Lord will plead with his people in the valley of Jehosaphat, for giving the child for an harlot (Joel 3:1–3). In the Old Testament it is punished with death (Lev. 20:13); and in the New, those such as lie with the Male, called Buggerers, are shut out of the kingdom of heaven (1 Cor. 6:9).

3. The causes of this unnatural sin are not, as Tostatus[109] suggesteth, by reason of sickness which changeth the complexion and inclineth the mind; nor by the nature of the place, but these rather. 1. Abundance of idleness. 2. Fullness of bread, which are set down to have been the causes of the sin of Sodom (Ezek. 16:49). 3. Custom from the youth, as in Sodom they compassed the city from the young to the old. 4. The refusing of God's ordinance, which is Matrimony, appointed for a remedy against fornication (1 Cor. 7:2): whereupon the Monasteries in England, when they were dissolved, were found to have been defiled this way. 5. The greatest cause is God's Justice, who punisheth Idolatry with this wicked fruit, giving such over to vile lusts to defile their bodies among themselves (Rom. 1:24), as is evident to be seen in the old Pagan Idolaters and the Pseudo-Christian Idolaters of these times.[110]

4. Unto this kind of unnatural lust may be referred other the like, as they which are called by the Apostle effeminate persons and seed-spillers, such as were Er and Onan, whom the Lord did slay for this uncleanness (Gen. 38:7–10). And some men's lust was so far enraged that they did not forbear to act such filthiness with the very Idols and statues, Pliny.[111] Add hereunto, as among the Gentiles, men with men burned in lust, so the women also among themselves were defiled as the Apostle showeth (Rom. 1:26). Such was Sappho, who abused five of her Maids to unnatural lust, Ravisius.[112] And as men with men, women with women; so Men with Women may sin against nature, in abusing the natural organs to unnatural ends. But these things are fitter to be left to men's understanding than expressed in writing.

Question 11: Against the Abominable Sodomitical Sin, v. 13
[On Lev. 20:13, "If a man also lie with mankind as lieth with a woman, both of them have committed an abomination: they shall surely be put to death; their blood *shall be* upon them."]

1. How grievous this unnatural sin is, appeareth by the word of aggravation here used: that whereas incest with the daughter-in-law is called *tebhel*, "confusion"; with the mother and daughter, v. 14, *zimmah*, "wickedness"; this is called *tognebhah*, "abomination," in Latin called *nefas*, of the which *ne fari liceat*, it is not lawful to speak. Or as Varro deriveth it, as though such were *ne farre digni*, not worthy to eat bread.[113] In the other sins before named, violence is offered to Marriage, as in Adultery; or to Affinity, as in Incest: but here, infamy is offered to the whole human nature, Tostatus.

2. This sin was punished in the Sodomites with fire from Heaven, and accordingly by the Law of Theodosius and Arcadius, such Sodomites were adjudged to the fire, though by the usual Caesarean and Imperial Law they died by the sword.[114] Among the Athenians he which defiled the

male was put to death, and the party abused was barred from all office, Aeschines.[115] In the Council of Vienna, the Templars, as being guilty of this sin, were decreed to be burned, Petrus Crinitus.[116] Among the Romans, it was lawful for him that was attempted to that abuse, to kill him that made the assault, as C. Lucius did, as Tully saith of him: the honest young man had rather do dangerously, than suffer shamefully.[117] And Pausanias complaining to Philip, King of Macedon, of the indignity offered unto him by one Attalus, and being by him scorned, revenged himself upon him and slew him.[118]

Lorinus[119] here also telleth us how that Pius V, and before him, Leo X, decreed all such filthy persons to be delivered up to the secular power to be punished; and, if they were Clergymen, to be degraded. It seemeth then, that such uncleanness was usual in Rome, and much practiced, that it needed to be beaten down by such Canons. And so Mantuan their Poet saith it was, as those Verses shew: "Sanctus ager scurris, venerabilis ara Cinaedis, / Servit honorandae divum, Gan[y]medibus aedes."[120] I forbear to English them: a modest pen is ashamed to write what they are not ashamed to practice. Neither was this a fault in the vulgar sort: some of their Popes have not been without touch herein, as Julius II who abused two noble youths, sent to him to be instructed from the French Queen, and Sixtus IV, before him, gave a licence to two Cardinals and their families, in the hot months, to do that which was uncomely. Paulus III bare with his son Petrus Aloisius that abused that way a young man, one Cosmas Cherias. Julius III gave the like liberty to Peter Mendosa, a Cardinal. Some of these were since Leo X. See hereof what Master Bale writeth in his Book *Acta Romanorum Pontificum*, and worthy Bishop Jewel, *Defense of the Apology*.[121] Yea, John Casa, Archbishop of Beneventum, was not ashamed to write Verses in commendation of this unnatural sin,[122] so that it is true which Borrhaeus[123] saith here: "Under the reign of the Beast, you may find some which by public writing dare defend this wickedness." It seemeth, then, that small reformation followed in Rome, upon those Decrees of the said Popes. The abounding of this vice in Italy maketh it seem probable which Suidas[124] writeth (whom herein Lorinus refuseth), that this vice began in Italy, in those latter times, who in time of War thought it lawful, in the absence of their Wives, to use that filthy remedy. But the true cause hereof Bernard well delivereth in his time: "Take away out of the Church honorable Marriage, do you not fill it with concubine keepers, incestuous persons, and abusers of the Male," *Cantic. Serm. 66*.[125]

4. Tostatus here moveth a needless question, Whether the Agent or Patient offend more in this unnatural sin, and he resolveth for the latter: because the other doth only wrong Nature; the other doth wrong also the sex. And Lorinus thereunto consenteth. But the contrary rather is true

because it is more to be an actor of evil than a sufferer, and both of them do sin against Nature and their kind. Yea, the patient may be sometime blameless if he be forced, according to the analogy of that Law of the forced Maid (Deut. 22:25). And thus was it practiced in the Athenian State, which punished the Agent more than the Patient, whereof mention is made before.[126]

Hexapla, a Sixfold Commentary upon the Most Divine Epistle to the Romans[127] *(1611)*

Question 67: Of the Unnatural Sins of the Heathen

[On Romans 1:26–27, already quoted to introduce *Calvin's comment.]

V. 26. *For this cause God gave them up, etc.* 1. Aretius[128] taketh this to be but a further explanation of that which the Apostle had spoken of before: but it is . . . an exaggeration rather, and amplification, for it is more to be given over unto passions, than unto the lusts of the heart. For they differ in three things. 1. The passion here signifieth a settled disease of the mind, which could not be removed, whereas the lust of the heart was not yet perfected, Faius.[129] 2. By the lust is signified their unclean desires, but here the Apostle also speaketh of their unclean acts, Pareus.[130] 3. And before the Apostle touched such uncleanness, as defiled the body: but now they are given over unto such vile affections as also defile the mind, depraving it of the use of reason, Tolet.[131]

2. How the women did change the natural use, may seem strange: Theophylact[132] thinketh it was some obscene thing, that is not to be uttered. Lyranus,[133] so also Tolet, and before them Ambrose and Anselm, understand it of the commixtion of women among themselves, as the men were defiled between themselves. But rather here the natural use is to be referred unto the organ and instrument of generation: when the women did prostitute themselves, the men exercising preposterous and sterilous venery, Osiander;[134] or they companied with men, as Sodomites, Pareus; and as Augustine saith, when the males abused that part of the body in the female, which was not appointed for generation; so the Syrian translator, they used the thing both which was not of nature, and co.[135]

3. So likewise the men with men wrought filthiness: Actively in forcing upon others unnatural acts of uncleanness; and passively, in suffering others to do it. This was the sin of Sodom, for the which they were destroyed. Socrates is noted among the Philosophers for masculine venery, which Plato condemneth.[136] And the Apostle may seem to have special relation here unto the abominable uncleanness of the Romans, and specially Nero, who was a monstrous beast for such sins against nature, Pareus. Chrysostom here elegantly showeth how, whereas by God's ordinance, in lawful copulation by marriage, two became one flesh, both sexes were joined together in one; by this Sodomitical uncleanness, the same flesh is

divided into two, the men with men working uncleanness with women, and so serve instead of two sexes. . . .[137]

Question 70: What It Is to Be Delivered Up to a Reprobate Mind

[Addressing Romans 1:28: "And even as they did not like to retain God in *their* knowledge, God gave them over to a reprobate mind, to do those things which are not convenient."]

3 . . . This word "reprobate" is rather here taken actively: for a mind void of all judgment, Beza,[138] which taketh good for evil, and evil for good, Isa. 5:20. Bucer.[139] Which pravity [i.e., corruption] of mind cometh not by one or two evil acts, but by a continual custom to evil when it is grown into an habit: like as the taste that is corrupted taketh sweet things for bitter, Lyranus. So the Gentiles were not delivered over to this reprobate mind all at once, but by divers degrees: first they were given up to their heart's lusts, v. 24, then to vile affections, v. 26, last of all to a reprobate sense, to such an evil habit, that they could do nothing but evil, Faius.

4. This pravity of the mind is here described. 1. By the subject, in the very mind, not in the sense, as the Latin translator: the word is νοῦς, which signifieth the very judgment and understanding, both theoretical, and practical, they err both in their judgment and conscience: as the Apostle saith, their minds and consciences are defiled (Titus 1:15). 2. The material part wherein this reprobate disposition of the mind consisteth is more distinctly showed where the Apostle imputeth to the Gentiles vanity of mind, their judgment and understanding was corrupt, then their cogitations were darkness, their reason and thoughts were obscured, and their hearts were hardened (Eph. 4:18): that is, their wills and affections. 3. The causes are expressed. The meritorious cause is their rejecting of God: they regarded not to know God, they rejected God and he rejecteth them. Where there is a fit allusion in the words: for it is said of them they approved not to know God, so they are delivered up into a reprobate mind, Pareus. The efficient cause, not of their reprobate mind, but of giving them up to a reprobate mind, is God, who as a just judge doth deliver them to this punishment, Gryneus.[140] 4. Then follow the effects of their reprobate mind, to do things not convenient, that which was forbidden both by divine and human laws, Haymo. . . .[141]

Thomas Wilson (1563–1622)

Analyzing sexual lusts in his *Commentary on Romans* of 1614, this Puritan divine especially condemns buggery (meaning "uncleanness with beasts" in his usage) and sodomy. Broadly defined as "uncleanness between them of one sex," the latter includes a variety of sexual possibilities, not just anally penetrative intercourse as in the contemporaneous English legal definition of the act as a capital crime. Born in the county of Durham, Wilson studied at Queen's College,

Oxford, obtaining his B.A. in 1583 to 1584 and his M.A. in 1586. He married, had a large family, and, for most of his life, was a rector at Canterbury Cathedral. Though *A Christian Dictionary* was Wilson's most ambitious and popular work, the *Commentary* was reprinted in 1627 and 1653.

Commentary upon the Most Divine Epistle of St. Paul to the Romans [142] *(1614)*

Romans, Chapter One, Verses 26–27

"For this cause, God gave them up to vile affections: for even their Women did change their natural use into that which is against Nature: and likewise also the men left the natural use of women and burned in lust one toward another."

Timotheus. What doth this Text contain in it, for drift, order, and matter?

Silas. The Apostle, to the end he may better clear and free from exception and reproach the Justice of God in punishing the Gentiles, and more thoroughly beat down and tame their pride and overweening (a main stop and enemy to the Justifying grace of Christ), he now so toucheth their punishment as that their shameful uncleanness (not to be named but with detestation) is withal more particularly and fully laid out, yet with much modesty, most foul and unhonest things being uttered in seemly and honest terms. In which he describeth their more than beastly impurity. First, by the moving and meritorious cause thereof in the first term of the text, *For this cause:* that is, for their Idolatry sake, because they changed the most glorious God contumeliously [i.e., insolently] into an Idol. Secondly, the chief agent or working cause is mentioned: *God delivered them.* This God doth not as an evil author enticing to sin, but as a righteous judge punishing most justly sin by sin, Idolatry with impurity and uncleanness. As a Judge doth commit and give up a malefactor to be tormented by the Executioner, so God delivereth Idol-servers to be tormented by Satan and their own lusts. . . .

Timotheus. It is now fit time to slide into our Text and to consider the thing itself whereunto they were delivered. What is it called and what is meant by it?

Silas. The thing is affections vile or shameful, and dishonorable affections: which importeth not only burning and flames of lusts and whatsoever is forbid, unhonest, and loathsome to chaste ears, meant before by uncleanness and lusts of their own hearts, Verse 24. But most filthy acts, both actively which they committed toward others, and passively which they suffered themselves from others. And as their punishment is generally expressed in this word, so more particularly in the next, which declare the monstrous impurity of both sexes, both Women and Men in the act of generation, going against natural course ordained of God for propagation and increase of mankind.

Timotheus. What do ye call the natural use of man and woman?

Silas. The use of their bodies for generation, which is according to the order that God hath set in Nature. This order is that our kind should be continued by generation, and the order hath three parts. First, that man be joined to a woman. Secondly, that one man be joined to one woman. Thirdly, that one man and one woman be lawfully joined. . . .

Timotheus. What Lusts are against this order?

Silas. Some are inordinate only, some also unnatural and beastly.

Timotheus. What sins do ye refer to inordinate lusts?

Silas. Fornication, Whoredom, Adultery, Incest, Rape or forcing, Polygamy, or having more wives than one at once. This was the sin of the Fathers,[143] for it was against God's ordinance; yet it was their secret sin, because in those times it was not noted as a fault, or so judged to be.

Timotheus. What sins refer ye to unnatural lusts?

Silas. Buggery, which is an uncleanness with beasts; Sodometry, which is an uncleanness between them of one sex.

Timotheus. Why is it called Sodometry?

Silas. Because the Sodomites are the first we read to have committed this sin. Also they were outrageous in the committing of it. Gen. 19:4–7, and co. . . .

Romans, Chapter One, Verse 31

"Which men, though they knew the Law of God, how that they which commit such things are worthy of death, not only do them, but favor them that do them."

Timotheus. . . . What death are they worthy of, which do such things against the Law of God, imprinted first in man's mind, then written in Tables of Stone?

Silas. Both natural death, violent death, and death eternal; this eternal death standeth in a separation from God and in a sense of painful torments in body and soul. It is to be suffered in Hell: a Prison, a Lake, a place of darkness, a depth, in the company of the Devil, wicked Angels, and Reprobate men, and forever without end, infinitely without measure.

Timotheus. How is this pain and smart of this death shadowed out in Scripture?

Silas. By the similitude of fire and Brimstone; the effects of this pain be weeping, howling, and gnashing of teeth. This pain shall endure as long as God endureth, even everlastingly. . . .

Thomas Beard (?–1632)

Thomas Beard's *Theater of God's Judgments* loosely associates sexual love between males with cross-dressing, effeminacy, allegedly Roman Catholic corruption, atheism, luxury, bestiality, and general monstrosity. An outspoken Puritan divine and Doctor of Divinity, Beard was master of Huntington hospital and grammar school, where he taught Oliver Cromwell (1599–1658), and regularly preached in the town. He married, had children, and, in 1630, became a justice of the peace. Originally published in 1597 and republished in several editions, the last in the late 1640s, the *Theater* was Beard's first and most popular book. His few other writings, such as *Antichrist the Pope of Rome* (1625), are primarily anti-Catholic. By collecting allegedly historical examples under various categories in *The Theater*, he sought to show that God assuredly punishes transgressors of various types, thus vindicating the faithful. Although the title page claims this book was "translated out of French and augmented by more than three hundred Examples, by Th. Beard," no French original seems to have been identified. The first to address the violent death of the reputedly sodomitical Christopher Marlowe (1564–1593) in print, Beard links atheism with sensual pleasure-seeking in Book I, Chapter 25, "Of Epicures and Atheists," adduces Marlowe as a wicked atheist, and treats his death as a sign of divine judgment, so that all like Marlowe should either repent or be destroyed. I reprint Beard's chapter on effeminacy and sodomites, which follows condemnations of prostitution, adultery, illicit divorce, and incest. Using a common early modern strategy of homophobic vilification, he collapses distinctions so that sex between males and diverse other condemned social phenomena all become grossly self-indulgent sinful godlessness deserving death and damnation. The resultant morass of guilt by association astutely avoids conceding grounds of special argument to prohomoerotic standpoints.

The Theater of God's Judgments[144] *(1597)*

Book I, Chapter 32: Of Effeminate Persons, Sodomites, and Other Suchlike Monsters

Sardanapalus, king of Assyria, was so lascivious and effeminate that to the end to set forth his beauty, he shamed not to paint his face with ointments and to attire his body with the habits and ornaments of women, and on that manner to sit and lie continually amongst whores, and with them to commit all manner of filthiness and villainy.[145] Wherefore, being thought unworthy to bear rule over men, first Arbaces his lieutenant rebelled, then the Medes and Babylonians revolted and jointly made war on him until they vanquished and put him to flight. And in his flight he returned to a tower in his palace, which (moved with grief and despair) he set on fire and was consumed therein.

Suchlike was the impudent lasciviousness of two unworthy Emperors, Commodus and Elagabalus, who laying aside all Imperial gravity, showed themselves oftentimes publicly in woman's attire: an act as in nature monstrous, so very dishonest and ignominious. But like as these cursed monsters ran too much out of frame in their unbridled lusts and affections, so there wanted not many that hastened and emboldened themselves to conspire their destruction, as unworthy in their judgments to enjoy the benefit of this light. Wherefore to one of them poison was ministered, and when that would take no effect, strangling came in the room thereof, and brought him to his end; the other was slain in a jakes where he hid himself, and his body (drawn like carrion through the streets) found no better sepulcher but the dunghill.[146]

Touching those abominable wretches of Sodom and Gomorrah (Genesis 19), which gave themselves over with all violence, and without all shame and measure, to their infamous lusts, polluting their bodies with unnatural sins, God sent upon them an unnatural rain, not of water, but of fire and brimstone, to burn and consume them that were so hot and fervent in their cursed vices. So that they were quite rooted and raked out of the earth, and their cities and habitations destroyed; yea, and the very soil that bore them made desolate and fruitless, and all this by fire whose smoke ascended like the smoke of a furnace. Yea, and in sign of a further curse for to be a witness and a mark of this terrible judgment, the earth and face of that country continueth still parched and withered; and as Josephus saith, whereas before it was a most plentiful and fertile soil, and as it were an earthly paradise bedecked with five gallant cities, now it lieth desert, inhabitable,[147] and barren, yielding fruit in show, but such as being touched turneth to cinders.[148] In a word, the wrath of God is so notoriously and fearfully manifested therein, that when the Holy Ghost would strike a terror into the most wicked, he threateneth them with this like punishment, saying, "The Lord will rain on each wicked one / Fire, snares, and brimstone, for his portion" (Ps. 11:6).

Howbeit this maketh not but that still there are too many such monsters in the world, so mightily is it corrupted and depraved. Neither is it any marvel, seeing that divers bishops of Rome, that take upon them to be Christ's vicars and Peter's successors, are infected with this filthy contagion. As namely Pope Julius the third, whose custom was to promote none to Ecclesiastical livings save only his buggerers: among whom was one Innocent, whom this holy father (contrary to the Suffrages of the whole college) would needs make Cardinal. Nay, the unsatiable and monstrous lust of this beastly and stinking goat was so extraordinary that he could not abstain from many Cardinals themselves. John de la Casa, a Florentine by birth, and by office Archbishop of Benevento, and Dean of his Apostatical chamber, was his Legate and Intelligence in all the Venetian signiories: a man equal or rather worse than himself, and such a one as whose memory ought to be accursed of all posterity, for that detestable book which he composed in commendation and praise of Sodomy, and was so shameless, nay rather possessed with some devilish and unclean spirit, as to divulgate it to the view of the world. Here you may see (poor souls) the holiness of those whom you so much reverence, and on whom you build your belief and religion. You see their brave and excellent virtues, and of what esteem their laws and ordinances ought to be among you. Now touching the end that this holy father made, it is declared in the former book among the rank of Atheists, where we placed him.[149] And albeit that he and suchlike villains please their own humors with their abominations and approve and clear themselves therein, yet are they rewarded by death, not only by the law of God, but also by the law Julia. . . .[150]

It is not for nothing that the law of God forbiddeth to lie with a beast and denounceth death against them that commit this foul sin.[151] For there have been such monsters in the world at some times, as we read in Caelius and Volaterranus[152] of one Crathes a shepherd, that accompanied carnally with a she-goat. But the Buck, finding him sleeping, offended and provoked with this strange action, ran at him so furiously with his horns that he left him dead upon the ground. God, that opened an ass' mouth to reprove the madness of the false Prophet Balaam, and sent lions to kill the strange inhabitants of Samaria, employed also this buck about his service in executing just vengeance on a wicked varlet.[153]

CHAPTER 2

Law

If out of a thousand sodomites the authorities punish even one
well, all of them experience fear. Although their crimes may not be
completely prevented, they may in part be contained.
—Office of the Night, Florence, 1436[1]

Most of the readings in this section deal with the legal conditions of homoeroticism in early modern England, and they are best understood comparatively, in their broader European and colonial contexts. That approach newly clarifies aspects of the English situation that have seemed perplexing, such as the surprisingly low incidence of prosecution there, and its significance for sexual history. Biblical and late–imperial Roman precedents underlie Renaissance criminalizations of same-sex sexual acts. Abominating any man who lies "with mankind as he lieth with a woman," Leviticus 20:13 enjoins death; lacking any Levitical anathema of the feminine counterpart, persecutors of sapphism invoked St. Paul's ambiguous censure of women who "change the natural use into that which is against nature" (Rom. 1:26). Although Renaissance legal authorities claimed that Roman legislation broadly criminalizing sex between males originated during the republic, the first Roman laws that did so were issued by Christian emperors in the late empire: Constantine's sons Constantius and Constans in 342; Valentinian II, Theodosius, and Arcadius in 390, first to stipulate the penalty of burning; and Justinian in his code promulgated in 529 and revised in 533, reaffirming capital punishment, supplemented by *novellae* or edicts 77 and 141.[2] The *novellae* provide the first legislative citations of the fate of Sodom to justify prohibition. If overlooked, Justinian claims, these alleged sins against nature likewise provoke God's retribution against society as a whole, causing famines, earthquakes, and plagues.[3]

Revived in the later Middle Ages, Roman law strongly influenced the subsequent development of canon (or ecclesiastical) and secular law in Western Christendom, and Justinian's rhetoric and rationales in addressing *sex between males* remained typical of sodomy laws, prosecutions, and legal commentary throughout Renaissance Europe and its colonies. Although legal condemnation of sex between females lacks Roman precedent, the Italian jurist Cino da Pistoia (1270?–1336/7) imputed that meaning to the imperial *lex foedissimam* of 287, and Bartholomaeus de Saliceto (?–1411) concurred.[4] After having long *been a religious crime* regulated through penances imposed by local clerics, sodomy in its various definitions became increasingly subject to secular statutes from the mid-thirteenth century onward, as in France, Castile, and various self-governing towns in Italy and elsewhere.[5] These continued to assume religious justification, and strictest enforcement tended to correlate with periods of especial religiosity. Legal regulation of perceived sexual transgressions seems to have broadly increased across sixteenth-century Europe with the Reformation and Counter-Reformation, and locally whenever civil administration coalesced with a zealous religious agenda, as in Savonarolan Florence, Calvinist Geneva with its morally judgmental Consistory, and Puritan New England.[6]

Penalties, means and extent of enforcement, liability of female same-sex lovers, and even the particular proscribed and prosecuted homoerotic practices not only varied greatly across early modern Europe but also fluctuated in particular jurisdictions. In accord with God's supposed destruction of Sodom by fire, the mode of capital punishment most commonly stipulated on the continent was live incineration for public warning and entertainment. But other methods were sometimes more expedient, so that in Geneva, for example, drowning conserved valuable wood. Whereas edicts of the Holy Roman Empire in 1510 and 1532 established execution by fire for "unchastity contrary to nature" between two males, two females, or with a beast, Venetian and English sodomy law ignored sex between women, and the latter required hanging.[7] The wording of the relevant legislation typically focused on bestiality together with sodomy as sex between males, in some sense, but could nonetheless have applications to tribadism and heteroerotic anal intercourse on the continent. Prosecutions for the latter were relatively rare, even though, partly for birth control as well as pleasure, it was not uncommon; bestiality cases were most frequent in the country. However, the sexual transgression of sodomy implied male partners so much that it could be difficult to construe otherwise.[8] In an English case of anal sex inflicted on an eleven-year-old girl in 1718, the judges had to debate whether sodomy could be committed by a male with a female.[9]

In England after the parliamentary session of 1533 to 1534 (when masculine love first became subject to any secular law there) and up to around 1700, criminal sex between males was almost exclusively defined and treated as buggery or "sodomy" in the sense of anally penetrative intercourse. It was similarly dealt with through the seventeenth century in the Dutch Republic.[10] But other jurisdictions were variously inclusive. In Florence, it was anal, intercrural, interfemoral, and oral intercourse; incipiently sodomitical and thus prosecuted sexual acts between males included solicitation, kissing, and fondling genitals (Rocke, 91–93). In Venice during the fifteenth century, at least, it was anal, intercrural, or interfemoral; on fellatio, Venetian legal records of the time appear silent, and joint masturbation without physical contact was of little or no legal concern (Ruggiero, 114–15). Under the Spanish royal sodomy edict of 1497, in force, with some modifications, for centuries, males could be convicted of committing "sodomy" together not only for consummated anal intercourse but also for acts closely approximating it. Even "pollutions," not involving coitus, could be severely punished.[11] In Reformed Geneva, all types of sex between males could be prosecuted, but entailed beatings and banishment for lewdness and fornication unless anal penetration occurred, which constituted capital sodomy.[12] The usually draconian penalties across Europe included death, galley service, castration, confiscation of assets, attainder, facial mutilation, imprisonment, exile, public humiliations, whipping, fines, and combinations thereof. Sentences for convicted male same-sex lovers ranged from certain hanging in England for those who had reached the age of discretion (fourteen, there), through gradations of punishments elsewhere, assessed according to the perceived severity of the circumstances. Leniency tended to increase in proportion to a defendant's youth. Other factors being equal, receptive sexual partners were treated more severely than their insertive counterparts in some areas, less in others, such as Venice, and the same in some, as in England. But even when not capital, sentences for adults and older adolescents were usually so harsh that those accused often fled, if they could, before standing trial. Since suspects were routinely tortured in legal investigations of male homoeroticism on the continent, even exoneration or a light sentence could involve terrible anguish, disfigurement, and injuries. Having convicted sixteen-year-old Carlo Bomben for receptive anal sodomy, the Venetian authorities sentenced him to two years of prison and three of exile in consideration of his youth; but investigative torture had already mutilated his genitals and destroyed his left arm (Ruggiero, 125).

In sixteenth- to late-seventeenth-century Europe, prosecution for consensual homogenital behaviors seems to have been least likely in England. Although surviving English court records for this period are incomplete and have yet to be fully investigated, it is clear that sexual relations between women were legally ignored and those between males very rarely prosecuted, usually just in cases involving anal rape of a minor.[13] "During the forty-five years of Queen Elizabeth's reign and the twenty-three years of King James I's reign only six men are recorded as having been indicted for sodomy in the Home County assizes, for example, with only one conviction."[14] However, through much of the Renaissance the best place to be convicted for sexual offenses of masculine love was probably Florence. Although the rigor and numbers of prosecutions varied there, for long periods the investigative process and sentences were exceptionally lenient, exacting relatively light fines that often went unpaid, as if the crime were a minor misdemeanor. Hence it was comparatively easy to discover and convict suspects, so that, even though the population was only about 40,000, around 15,000 men were investigated and over 2,400 convicted between 1432 and 1502 (Rocke, 147). Yet from 1570 to 1630 in Valencia, Barcelona, and Saragossa, where sodomy enforcement was much more severely administered by the Spanish Inquisition, 445 men were tried, of whom 75 were executed and 143 sent to the galleys.[15] In Venice between 1426 and 1500, there were 377 prosecutions, 61 involving boys under fourteen.[16] In the small city of Geneva between 1536 (when it became a Protestant republic) and 1672, fifty-five males were tried, with, among the known capital sentences, one decapitation, two hangings, eleven drownings, and fourteen burnings.[17]

Though early modern legal sanctions against same-sex sexual relations mainly targeted males, some females were nonetheless prosecuted and killed on the continent.[18] However, currently known cases between 1450 and 1700 total less than thirty, and little documentation is extant. In seventy-five Genevan sodomy trials between 1444 and 1789, only one, in 1568, concerns sex between females.[19] Among the colonies of New England, only New Haven specifically addressed that in a sodomy statute (1656),[20] and only one instance of prosecution is known: the case of *Sara Norman (fl. 1639–1654) and Mary Hammon (1633–1705) in Plymouth.

Erotics between females appear to have been somewhat shielded by phallocentric notions of sex and widespread suppositions of feminine inferiority and relative sensual fallibility. Without phallic penetration, what females could do together tended to seem dubiously sexual, at least to many men. Accordingly, even though St. Thomas Aquinas (1224/5–1274) had classified both male and female same-sex sexual copulations as sodomy and sins against nature (*Theology), St. Carlo Borromeo (1538–1584) considered those of women fornication, a much lesser sin of lust, and Luigi Sinistrari (1622–1701) found them sodomitical only if one or both women had an enlarged clitoris enabling penetrative coitus. Otherwise, their sexual acts constituted aggravated "pollution," little worse than masturbation, though even that was deemed a sin against nature (Brown, 16–19). Less appeared socially at stake in sex between females than between males. A woman's role in procreation was so subordinated to a man's that nonreproductive uses of male sexual capacities seemed greater offenses "against nature" than the feminine counterparts (*Medicine). And women tended to be economically and thus sexually dependent on men anyway, whereas males had a degree of social freedom that made masculine love appear more practically threatening to conventional society.

For these and other reasons, when sexual acts between females were not legally ignored, as in early modern England and Venice, European canon and secular law traditionally treated them more leniently than those between males, both through lighter penalties and, at least civilly, far less enforcement. Nevertheless, some authorities urged the equivalence of both in gravity and punishment, and that view, enshrined in the Holy Roman imperial law of 1532, became somewhat more influential in the sixteenth century. Even where local or national legislation did not expressly criminalize tribadism on the continent, it was nonetheless potentially subject to the death penalty, for in continental legal tradition informed by ancient Roman precedent, leading jurists' opinions had possible legal force in states beyond their own.[21] When confronted with confessed tribadism in the Genevan republic in 1568, the jurist Germain Colladon's recommendation of capital punishment cited the imperial law of 1532.[22] Among early modern legal commentators who address the subject, the Spaniard

Antonio Gómez (1501–?) and the Italian Prospero Farinacci (1554–1618) distinguish a range of transgressions, recommending death for penetration with a dildo, whereas the former's compatriot Gregorio López (1496/7–1560) mandates death with no distinctions. Through penetration enabled artificially or, as some male authorities strangely fancied, by clitoral hypertrophy, women might appear to appropriate power and privileges socially reserved for males. Tribades were especially persecuted for penetration and cohabiting as in male-female marriage, it seems, for the currently known cases resulting in execution often involve those behaviors.[23]

After centuries of ecclesiastical regulation in England, male homogenital relations there were first addressed by secular law when a statute against "buggery" was enacted in the parliamentary session of 1533 to 1534 during the reign of King Henry VIII, partly to assert royal prerogative against the papacy. Except for probably inadvertent decriminalization in the reign of Queen Mary, anal intercourse between males thus became a long-standing statutory felony or capital crime punished by hanging (*English Sodomy Statutes).[24] Nevertheless, almost invariably in both theory and practice, any other kind of male homoerotic interaction was subsequently exempt from English secular prosecution until around 1700. In a corollary of much European masculine thought about tribadism, conditioned by the imputed privilege of phallic vaginal penetration, only full coitus between males that substituted the anus for the vagina appeared a same-sex sexual transgression of such manifest gravity, as an extreme act of carnal knowledge "against nature," that it demanded formal proscription, prosecution, and execution under English law as it was typically understood. This likely resulted from strict construction, in accord with Reformed biblical hermeneutics, of Leviticus 18:22 and 20:13 (if a man lies with a man *as with* a woman, both shall be put to death).[25] In effect, the English state took the Levitical law as its source and warrant for the way in which sex between males would become subject to statutory criminalization there.

That implicit basis of the English sodomy law further accounts for its exclusion of female homoeroticism, which Leviticus ignores. Moreover, Traub observes the "gendered logic of penetration and physical position" in early modern English legal commentary on sodomy: "Locked into a position of receptacle, women cannot—in English law—penetrate another woman" (165). As the English legal proscription of homoeroticism according to Leviticus revolves around perceived penetrative abuse of the phallus, I would add, the law's application to sexual behaviors between females was strictly inconceivable.

Yet, having criminalized one sexual expression of male homoeroticism, the crown could proceed more broadly if that were expedient, as in the case of the earl of *Castlehaven (1631), whose conviction for "sodomy" was energetically pursued and narrowly secured even though penetration could not be proven, and the sex between males had only involved consenting adults. This prosecution must have alarmed English sodomites who had assumed they knew their legal status. However, continuing limits of the sodomy law ensured that, in 1817, a man who forced a seven-year-old boy to fellate him and ejaculated in the boy's mouth was exonerated and pardoned on appeal, on the grounds that this did not constitute sodomy.[26]

Nevertheless, sexual love between males had no official or general English civic acceptance, but was contrary to conventional social norms: in effect, a practice of sexual dissidence, however construed by those involved and their sympathizers, not orthodoxy.[27] Of course, viewpoints varied, just as it could be neutrally or favorably represented, most often in literary contexts (*Love and Friendship, *Erotica). But official Christian morality, whether Protestant or Roman Catholic, authoritatively condemned it. Even joint masturbation would at least constitute "unnatural sin" in conventional classifications and could well appear incipiently sodomitical (*Theology). Insofar as the English sodomy law was rooted in such ideas and their presumed biblical precedents, the state assumed that sexual acts between males other than anal coitus, and probably those between females as well, were deplorable corruptions that would incur divine retribution anyway. Such a situation cannot be considered tolerant. Nor one where, in theory if not in practice, the lives of all those who consensually engaged in a main means of sexually consummating masculine love were legally forfeit. Among legal commentators Anthony Fitzherbert (1470–1538) finds "buggery ... the most abominable vice," William Lambarde (1536–1601) "the detestable vice," and Michael Dalton (?–1648?) a "felony" constituting "sin against God, Nature, and the Law."[28]

Many writings of the time manifest the social force of antisodomitical homophobia, and unofficial public and private oppressions supplemented the signal impact of the law. In a private notebook written in the early seventeenth century, Sir Thomas Wilson records that "Sodomy the most detestable and unnatural Sin ... doth much wrong to those that most hate it and never use it; for ... jealous women most and some men also will be apt to think that any man useth it that hath but a boy or a young man to serve him."[29] This wrong would involve consequences of damaged reputation. *Brantôme (1540?–1614) observes that an insult alleging the practice of sodomy or buggery is "most shameful" and socially problematic for a man. Community pressures experienced by male same-sex lovers in fifteenth-century Florence, including vigilante squads during the Savonarolan period, are well documented (Rocke, 80–84, 211–12), and other parts of Europe would not likely have differed much. Sir Simonds D'Ewes (1602–1650) records that a sheet reviling Sir Francis Bacon (1561–1626) for sodomy and demanding his death was anonymously deposited at his London residence.[30] If the tremendous public enthusiasm for tormenting pilloried homophiles in eighteenth-century London is any indication,[31] unofficial beatings probably occurred then and earlier. There was considerably more popular violence in the sixteenth and seventeenth centuries than today, with higher rates of assault and homicide.[32]

Moreover, the legal commentaries of *Sir Edward Coke (1552–1634) as well as records of indictments and trials within England and its American colonies show that, for at least much of society, not only sodomy as the English statute was almost always deemed narrowly to define it, but also male-male sex in general appeared profoundly repugnant. In colonies of New England where Puritan religious zeal could strongly influence laws and their enforcement, a range of "sodomitical uncleannesses" between males was vilified and prosecuted, including, in Plymouth, one couple's "spending seed one upon another" and another couple's "lewd and sodomitical practices tending to sodomy."[33] In New Haven, where the sodomy law of 1656 was especially detailed and comprehensive, six youths were convicted for sexually committing "much wickedness in a filthy corrupting way one with another."[34] Penalties in such lesser cases included flogging, branding, and banishment. In 1642 three ministers of Plymouth wrote thoroughly documented legal and religious opinions for the governor of Massachusetts Bay Colony arguing that, for capital sodomy between males, penetration is not necessary but only body contact, friction, and ejaculation, or even, one insisted, attempts thereof.[35]

With all this English "sodomophobia" targeting male homoeroticism quite broadly, why was masculine love so little prosecuted in England? Even though, with Levitical punctilio, only its anally coital expression had been outlawed there according to the law's usual interpretation, that homogenital act was prosecuted far more often in many continental jurisdictions, whether or not they prosecuted others. Narrowly anal legal definition of sodomy cannot in itself be responsible for the much lower English rate of prosecution. However, England was regulated by its own unique tradition of "common law" supplemented by statutory legislation, whereas continental regimes had a "civil law" system primarily based on Roman law. The norms for conducting criminal proceedings *in general* under English common law inadvertently made prosecution of the crime of sodomy very problematic by continental standards. Hence the remarkable rarity of English prosecution of that offense in this period does not actually demonstrate any uniquely English perceptions of sodomy or male homoeroticism in particular, nor any lower incidence of such sexual relations in English society. That rarity is instead a function of general legal conditions in England at this time, as they affected enforcement of the statute prohibiting sodomy.

Unfortunately, this has not been recognized by prior commentators on the implications of legal evidence for the social and psychological status of male homoeroticism in early modern England, for they have not taken a comparative approach. Randolph Trumbach surmises "there were few prosecutions because there was very little sodomy" there before the eighteenth century; or "sodomy with men was not yet conceived as excluding sex with women," and *hence seemed less offensive.*[36] However, male-female rape was also rarely prosecuted in England, but we would not thus conclude that it was rare.[37] And there is no shortage of evidence that, whether exclusive or not, male same-sex sexual behaviors were recognized and denounced in England and its colonial possessions, and on the continent. Bruce Smith suggests that English sodomy legislation was understood, at least by Coke, to criminalize only "rape of an underaged boy" (51–53). But the statutes clearly make consensual anal sex between males in general a capital offense for anyone at or over the age of discretion (fourteen), and that is how *Coke interpreted them. Alan Bray supposes prosecutions were rare in England because society and even sodomites themselves sedulously avoided recognizing male same-sex sexual behaviors as such, so that, however much practiced, they remained socially diffused and unacknowledged by anyone—even their practitioners. Thus, he concludes, same-sex sexual identities had not yet emerged there (74–76, 92–93). But Englishmen in New England readily perceived links between sodomy and male homoerotic acts such as joint masturbation or bodily friction and prosecuted them accordingly, as the cases just cited and others show. The rarity of prosecution in England could not, *pace* Bray, have arisen from some peculiarly national sexual blindness or refusal of recognition that, as a further consequence, compromised the possibilities of homoerotic self-identification and sexual subjectivities. Finally, in Mario Digangi's view, his own theory that "much early modern homoeroticism" was conventionally considered "normative" or "socially orderly" in England "explains why the laws that did narrowly define sodomy in terms of specific sexual acts were so rarely and selectively deployed" (73). Yet English colonial records document the suppression of male homoeroticism in general as a reprehensible disorder, so that such social attitudes would also have had considerable currency in England. The well-connected D'Ewes, who became a member of parliament, wrote in his coded private diary that "the sin of sodomy" (contextually between males) was "frequent" in London, and in his view such relations constituted a pervasive social disorder that could incur "horrible" divine punishment.[38] Views of male homoeroticism had a wide range, but for many it was deeply implicated in sodomy, hence disorder.

Relative to continental prosecutions, English legal proceedings against sodomy were necessarily rare, I propose, because certain unique characteristics of English common law inadvertently entailed major difficulties of establishing proof in the case of this consensual and ordinarily private sex crime. According to the normative legal interpretation of sodomy in England, once again probably based on a strict construction of Leviticus 18:22 and 20:13, the Crown had to prove the "carnal knowledge" of anal penetration to secure conviction.[39] But since consensual insertive and receptive partners were both equally felons liable to be hung (unless one were beneath fourteen, the age of discretion), neither could be expected voluntarily to incriminate the other. On the continent, these circumstances would not have discouraged the prosecution of any homogenital acts, for under Roman legal tradition prevalent there, torture was commonly used to extract incriminations of others and full confessions of guilt. But the

English legal system virtually prohibited investigative judicial torture (as opposed to punitive torture following conviction).[40] On account of the nature of this particular crime, which would normally occur between two consenting persons in private, lack of recourse to the confessional compulsions of torture was by far the most crucial factor in its low rate of prosecution in England compared to many areas of the continent. In practice, the general investigative limits of English common law ensured that such cases were almost inevitably confined to situations involving a scandalized third-party observer of anal sex willing to send both participants to their deaths, or parental complaint about anal rape of a minor willing to testify against the accused. Otherwise, sex between males could only come before English courts under certain exceptional conditions. As in the cases of *Castlehaven and John Atherton, Bishop of Waterford and Lismore (1598–1640), these involve defendants who became special targets railroaded for exemplary retribution, partly on account of political motives and purposes. But to prosecute Castlehaven for sodomy, the crown was reduced to using a false promise of immunity to trick his adult consensual partner Fitzpatrick into testifying that they had sex, and then wrenching the accepted English legal definition of "sodomy." On that charge the jury's vote to convict, fifteen to twelve, was nevertheless so close that the case demonstrates the great difficulty of securing convictions for consensual sodomy in England on account of its common law system. And none of these cases resulted in further sodomy prosecutions beyond their immediate circumstances.

Yet on the continent, torture readily enabled legal officials zealous in prosecuting sex between males to convict suspects and expand the scope of investigations to pursue and extirpate networks of sodomites. Torture was standard in questioning such suspects in Venice (Ruggiero, 95, 133, 142). Although not legally authorized in Florence, it was nonetheless threatened, with display of instruments, and sometimes used, especially during Savonarola's regime (Rocke, 50, 291n.35). However, various special factors, such as leniency, bounties, guarantees of anonymity for denunciations, and incentives for confession, made the systematic prosecution of sodomites unusually easy there. To secure its many sodomy convictions, the Spanish Inquisition in Barcelona, Valencia, and Saragossa used torture frequently, but in doing so did not differ from the typical practices of continental secular courts.[41]

The periodic flaring of little continental holocausts and the higher levels of enforcement in some areas were not practically possible under English law. That did not result from any deliberate policy of treating sodomites in particular with consideration, nor from, as Bray would have it, some distinctively English inability to "see" sodomy, or to perceive the sodomitical implications of male homoeroticism. The inherent constraints that English legal procedures placed on enforcement for felonies *in general* inadvertently crippled the pursuit of a private crime of mutual consent, where anal penetration normally had to be proven. Under English law, moreover, the accused in a capital case was entitled to trial by jury and could avoid having to testify under oath against himself by citing the right against self-incrimination.[42]

These special conditions in England had enormous impact on the investigation and prosecution of sodomy there, relative to continental practices, and thus profoundly restrict the conclusions about the social and psychological conditions of same-sex love that can now be drawn with any legitimacy from English legal evidence of that time, or from the rarity of English prosecutions.[43] Lack of allowance for these limitations of the extant legal data has obscured the nature and possibilities of early modern homoerotic experience in England, and its relation to European sexual history. In 1642 the governor of the Massachusetts Bay Colony sought guidance from Plymouth's governor, magistrates, and church elders on the means available for extracting a confession in such cases to ensure conviction. Admission of guilt, he was advised, was not to be obtained by legal chicanery or torture.[44]

Though primarily seeking to curb extramarital heteroerotic sex, the parliamentary attempts of religious moralists to criminalize fornication and adultery during the reigns of Elizabeth and her successor James would at least have provided, if they had been successful, some standard means to prosecute same-sex sexual acts other than anal intercourse. Legal records of New England demonstrate what could thus have happened in England itself, for the comprehensive legislation on sexual morality enacted by the Puritan colonies enabled some prosecution of diverse types of sex between males in those small, tightly knit communities, and even a female coupling. However, such broad legislation against perceived sexual immorality never secured sufficient support for parliamentary passage in England except in the Rump Parliament (1648–1653, 1659–1660), was then little enforced, and lapsed in 1660. The advocates of heightened sexual regulation failed partly because the political nation would not brook interference with its common extramarital heteroerotic pursuits. But, in any case, the relative anonymity of large English cities, the low age of discretion, and especially the general restrictions on investigative torture would have continued to obstruct the enforcement of any laws targeting private, consensual sexual acts in England.[45]

English prosecutions of male homoerotic liaisons thus remained rare and concerned only individuals, not groups, until around 1700, when changes in the available means of investigation and prosecution enabled somewhat increased numbers of cases. In Alan Bray's view, this rise in prosecution shows that a specifically homosexual subculture and identity newly emerged at this time in London, as never before, provoking hostility with a clear target that had previously been lacking. Hence homosexual identity, he assumes, dates from around 1650 to 1700 (ch. 4, 117). However, the "molly houses" that he considers the signifiers of the emergence of this identity and subculture were really nothing new insofar as they were specific meeting places for devotees of masculine love. As Bray concedes, brothels, taverns, houses, and public places associated with that had already long existed in London and elsewhere anyway (53–54, 85; cf. Smith, 288n.71). In fifteenth-century Venice, the Council of Ten had identified and restricted various sodomitical rallying points: certain types of shops, gaming parlors, schools, some public places, private dinner parties (Ruggiero, 138–40). In 1492 the Florentine authorities imposed antisodomitical regulations on taverns, inns, gambling houses, public baths, and houses used for sexual rendezvous (Rocke, 203). If aggressive prosecutorial reactions against sodomite networks are evidence of emergent homosexual identity, as Bray assumes (92–93), such identities would have to be continentally backdated before the fifteenth century. Legal persecution had already long been conducted with enormous energy in Venice and Florence, for example. Indications of French male brothels antedate the thirteenth century.[46] For many reasons English society could not have remained wholly isolated from continental developments in male homoerotic agency and awareness until the later seventeenth century. Reconsidered in view of sodomy prosecutions elsewhere, Bray's interpretation of the legal predicament of the London mollies requires dating the efflorescence of male same-sex sexual subjectivities much earlier, not only in continental centers but also in London, one of the largest cities of early modern Europe.

The prosecution of sodomy in Europe had long varied at least somewhat as a function of local religious enthusiasms and legal innovations, and late-seventeenth-century England provides yet another instance. Partly in response to forcefully renewed warnings of imminent divine judgment on a sinful nation, the Society for the Reformation of Manners was founded at London in 1691 to suppress perceived immorality by promoting the enforcement of current civil laws, and declined only around 1730.[47] Effected through sermons and the cultivation of informers who cooperated with the constabulary, their program secured many thousands of prosecutions, mainly for breaking the sabbath and for heteroerotic prostitution, and the general sweep also affected some sodomites. As it was not a reaction specifically against their networks or communities, so the raids on molly houses were very sporadic (1699, 1707, 1726). Meanwhile, English prosecutorial practice had ingeniously overcome the great difficulties of proving felonious sodomy in its narrow statutory sense by developing a much more easily substantiated charge of "assault with intent to commit unnatural crimes" under common law, classified as a misdemeanor and based on the offense of assault.[48] Unfortunately, how and precisely when this came about is as yet obscure. It would be difficult to claim this legal shift somehow marks decisive social or psychological shifts in sexual history, for the actual causes may well be quite different or overdetermined. And there had been many substantial variations in sodomy prosecution throughout Europe for hundreds of years already. In any case, prosecution in England could thus newly proceed even if sexually motivated contact had been consensual and very slight, for both parties need only to have "laid hands" on, hence "assaulted" each other. This further enabled group arrests in the raids on molly houses. Conviction typically entailed a fine, imprisonment, social ostracism, and the potentially fatal man-glings of the pillory. Through the activities of the Society and this new legal device, the virtual impunity of English sodomites relative to their continental fellows ended.

However narrowly or broadly defined and enforced, sodomy legislation throughout Europe marked and monitored sexual bounds, to exert control over same-sex sexual behaviors and denote their official anathema in accord with conventional Christian morality. By legally formalizing condemnation, society could differentiate itself from Sodom and notionally avert that city's terrible fate in accord with precedents set by Justinian himself. In the English House of Commons, bills seeking to regulate morality typically invoked the threat of divine judgment on the land if vices were unpunished,[49] and the attor-ney general invoked Sodom's destruction to demand *Castlehaven's death at his trial in 1631. However, when we compare the possibilities of intervention and enforcement under continental civil law, it is clear that, despite England's sim-ilar criminalization of anal intercourse between males, the distinctive English tradition of common law inadvertently tended to obstruct implementation of that officially mandated persecution. Aside from enabling rare indictments and convictions, the English antisodomy law thus mainly turned out to have socially symbolic functions such as discouraging and restricting male homoeroticism and denoting severe stigma through capital proscription of its sexual expression deemed most flagrant.

English Sodomy Statutes

In England prior to the parliamentary session of 1533 to 1534, when, in the reign of King Henry VIII, legislation made sodomy a statutory felony punishable by hanging, it had not been an offense in common law, nor a secular crime. It had been subject to ecclesiastical jurisdiction, regulated through the confessional, penances, and church courts. Although the latter could sentence death, relin-quishing the convict to the secular power for execution, there seem to have been no such sodomy cases in England. At first requiring renewal by each successive parliament to remain in force, the Henrician law became perpetual in 1540. Since it was originally part of a series of measures to transfer power and judicial authority from the Church of Rome to the English Crown, the law's immedi-ate impetus appears to have been political. Secular jurisdiction over sodomy helped enable the investigation of religious houses for moral offenses, and thus expedited parliamentary approval of their hugely profitable dissolution.

However, as the Henrician statute's aims and implications were not only ecclesiastical, so the first parliament of King Edward VI introduced changes to protect the interests of the propertied classes. It prohibited indictments initiated more than six months after an alleged offense and witnesses who would materi-ally benefit from conviction. Heirs of those convicted regained rights of inheri-tance, not only for goods and lands but also titles, thus eliminating the original statute's additional penalty of attainder or "corruption of blood" (1548). But Queen Mary's first parliament revoked all recently created felonies and treasons to dismantle Henry's legislative program against the Roman Catholic establishment (1553). Sodomy ceased being a secular crime until 1563, when Queen Elizabeth I's second parliament restored and perpetuated the law in its harsher Henrician form, whereupon it remained unamended until the nineteenth century. Only in 1861 was the resultant death penalty for the anal coitus of males abolished; only in 1967 was private homosexual sex between consenting adult males decriminalized in England.[50]

The Henrician law's impact on subsequent English legal history shows its motivations were not just politically circumstantial. It served further purposes that assured long continuance, such as officially stigmatizing sexual love between males by rendering one of its main expressions a felonious capital crime. In prescribing death for this "abominable" vice, it seeks to align the law of England with Leviticus 20:13, which prescribes death for this "abomination," and with divine retribution against Sodom, just as the Elizabethan reinstatement invokes "the high displeasure of almighty God." Partly as a consequence of the Reformation, there was a general trend throughout Europe to promote moral reform legislatively and otherwise, and England was no exception.[51] Even though the sodomy law deprived the accused of "benefit of clergy," it did not specifically target ecclesiastics. Since the reign of King Henry VII, the benefit, which conferred right to trial in an ecclesiastical court and eliminated capital punishment for a first offense in some kinds of felony, had applied to anyone who could read.[52] To maintain secular jurisdiction and treat sodomites with the prescribed rigor, benefit of clergy had to be eliminated, as for a variety of other felonies. In Queen Elizabeth's reign the process of reinstating the sodomy law began with a private members' omnibus bill in the Commons, which sought to revive various lapsed felonies and treasons. Though these were recriminalized by separate acts through interventions of the Privy Council,[53] the private initiative likely indicates some broader appeal of the alleged moral rationale of antisodomy legislation.

25 Henry VIII, Ch. 6[54] (1533–1534)

An Act for the Punishment of the Vice of Buggery

Forasmuch as there is not yet sufficient and condign punishment appointed and limited by the due course of the laws of this realm, for the detestable and abominable vice of buggery committed with mankind or beast. It may therefore please the king's highness, with the assent of his lords spiritual and temporal, and the commons of this present parliament assembled, that it may be enacted by authority of the same, that the same offense be from henceforth adjudged felony, and such order and form of process therein to be used against the offenders, as in cases of felony at the common law. And that the offenders being hereof convict by verdict, confession, or outlawry, shall suffer such pains of death and losses, and penalties of their goods, chattels, debts, lands, tenements, and hereditaments, as felons been accustomed to do according to the order of the common laws of this realm. And that no person offending in any such offense shall be admitted to his clergy. And that justices of peace shall have power and authority within the limits of their commissions and jurisdictions to hear and determine the said offense as they use to do in cases of other felonies. This act to endure till the last day of the next parliament.

2–3 Edward VI, Ch. 29 (1548)

An Act against Sodomy

Forasmuch as there is not at this present time any sufficient and condign punishment by due course of the laws of this realm for the detestable vice of buggery: be it therefore enacted by the assent of the king's highness, the lords spiritual and temporal, and the commons in this present parliament assembled, that all and every offender or offenders in that crime, after the first day of April next ensuing, being thereof convicted or attainted by verdict, confession, outlawry, or otherwise, shall suffer such pains of death, without loss of goods, or lands, or any other commodity, his life only excepted, as felons convicted or attainted of felony been accustomed to do, touching the said pains of death, by the common laws of this realm. And that no such person shall enjoy the privilege or benefit of his or their clergy or sanctuary, and that the justices of peace shall have full power and authority within the limits of their commission and jurisdictions to hear and determine the said offense, touching the said pains of death, as they do and have used to do in cases of felony, saving to the wife and children, the heirs and successors and administrators of the said offender or offenders, and all other persons and bodies politic other than the said offender or offenders, all such right, title, claim, and interest to all and every the said offender or offenders' goods, lands, and hereditaments, as they or any of them might have or ought to have had, if the said offender or offenders had died his or their natural death, or had neither in this case, neither by any other mean, offended any of the king's laws.

Provided that no manner of person be impeached or molested for the said offense by reason of this present act, except the said person be indicted of the said offense within six months next and immediately following the time of committing the same. And that no person be received for witness, or to lay or give evidence against the said offender, as upon whose credit the inquest should inform themself, which person should take any profit or commodity by the death of the said offender, if he were attainted or convicted of the said crime and offense: nor that any such attainder shall make any corruption of blood to the heir or heirs of such offender or offenders.

1 Mary, Ch. 1 (1553)

An Act Repealing Certain Treasons, Felonies, and Praemunire[55]

Forasmuch as the state of every king, ruler, and governor of any realm, dominion, or commonalty standeth and consisteth more assured by the love and favor of the subject toward their sovereign ruler and governor, than in the dread and fear of laws made with rigorous pains, and extreme punishment for not obeying of their sovereign ruler and governor: and laws also justly made for the preservation of the commonweal without extreme punishment or great penalty are more often for the most part obeyed and kept, than laws and statutes made with great and extreme punishments. And in special such laws and statutes so made, whereby not only the ignorant and rude unlearned people, but also learned and expert people, minding honesty, are often and many times trapped and snared, yea, many times for words only without other fact or deed done or perpetrated.

The queen's most excellent majesty, calling to remembrance that many as well honorable and noble persons, as other of good reputation within this her grace's realm of England, have of late (for words only without other opinion, fact, or deed) suffered shameful death, not accustomed to nobles, her highness therefore, of her accustomed clemency and mercy, minding to avoid and put away the occasion and cause of like chances hereafter to ensue (trusting her loving subjects will, for her clemency to them showed, love, serve, and obey her grace the more heartily and faithfully than for dread or fear of pains of body), is contented and pleased that the severity of suchlike extreme, dangerous, and painful laws shall be abolished, annulled, and made frustrate and void. . . .

And be it further ordained and enacted by the authority aforesaid, that all offenses made felony, or limited, or appointed to be within the case of praemunire, by any act or acts of parliament, statute, or statutes, made sithens the first day of the first year of the reign of the late king of famous memory king Henry the eight, not being felony before, nor within the case of praemunire, and also all and every branch, article, and clause mentioned, or in any wise declared in any of the same statutes, concerning the making of any offense or offenses to be felony, or within the case of praemunire, not being felony, nor within the case of praemunire before, and all pains and forfeitures concerning the same, or any of them, shall from henceforth be repealed and utterly void and of none effect.

5 Elizabeth, Ch. 17 (1563)

An Act for the Punishment of the Vice of Buggery

Wherein the parliament begun at London, the third day of November, in the one and twentieth year of the late king of most famous memory, king Henry the eight, and after by prorogation holden at Westminster, in the five and twentieth year of the reign of the said late king, there was one act and statute made, entitled "An act for the punishment of the vice of buggery," whereby the said detestable vice was made felony, as in the said statute more at large it doth and may appear. Forasmuch as the said statute, concerning the punishment of the said crime and offense of buggery, standeth at this present repealed and void, by virtue of the statute of repeal made in the first year of the reign of the late queen Mary: sithens which repeal so had and made, divers evil disposed persons have been the more bold to commit the said most horrible and detestable vice of buggery aforesaid, to the high displeasure of almighty God.

Be it enacted, ordained, and established by the queen our sovereign lady, and by the assent of the lords spiritual and temporal, and the commons of this present parliament assembled, and by the authority of the same, that the said statute before mentioned, made in the five and twentieth year of the said late king Henry the eight, for the punishment of the said detestable vice of buggery, and every branch, clause, article, and sentence therein contained, shall from and after the first day of June next coming, be revived, and from thenceforth shall stand, remain, and be in full force, strength, and effect forever, in such manner, form, and condition as the same statute was at the day of the death of the said late king Henry the eight, the said statute of repeal made in the said first year of the said late queen Mary, or any word general or special therein contained, or any other act or acts, thing or things to the contrary notwithstanding.

Michel Eyquem de Montaigne (1533–1592)

Michel Eyquem de Montaigne's *Journal de voyage* recounting his travels across Europe in 1580 to 1581 contains remarkable anecdotes describing continental legal reactions to female and male same-sex marriages. Biographical information appears in his other entry, in the chapter Love and Friendship. Whereas Montaigne's secretary transcribed the first part of the *Journal* presumably from dictation (including the first excerpt here), Montaigne recorded the rest himself. The text was first published in 1774 from a single manuscript discovered in 1770 and lost during the French Revolution. The Venetian ambassador Antonio Tiepolo independently reports the Roman male marriages in a dispatch of August 2, 1578: "Eleven Portuguese and Spaniards were taken. They were assembled in a church near San Giovanni in Laterano and they were celebrating some of their rites, desecrating the sacred name of matrimony with horrendous and filthy wickedness by marrying one another, uniting themselves as husband and wife. In other circumstances, twenty-seven or more were found together; but this time they were able to capture but the eleven, and they shall go to the flames as they merit."[56]

Travel Journal[57] *(1580–1581)*

Crossing France in September 1580

The next day, we set out after dinner and slept at Vitry-le-François, seven leagues on. It is a small town on the river Marne.... A few days ago there had been a hanging at a nearby place called Montier-en-Der, on this account. Several years before, seven or eight girls around Chaumont-en-Bassigni plotted amongst themselves to dress as males and continue their lives in the world accordingly. Amongst these, one came to Vitry under the name Mary, earning his living as a weaver, a well-behaved young man friendly with everyone. Here he became engaged to a woman still alive; yet because of some disagreement between them, their bargain went no further. After having gone to Montier-en-Der, still earning his living at the said trade, he fell in love with a woman, married her, and they lived together four or five months to her satisfaction, according to what is said. But, having been recognized by someone from Chaumont, and the matter brought to justice, she was condemned to be hung, which she said she'd rather suffer than return to a girl's state, and was hung for the illicit inventions used to supplement the defect of her sex.[58]

Visiting Rome, March 1581

On the eighteenth, the ambassador of Portugal made his obeisance to the pope for the realm of Portugal, on behalf of King Philip—the same ambassador who was here to represent the deceased king, and for the States opposed to King Philip.[59]

Returning from St. Peter's, I met a man who amusingly informed me of two things: that the Portuguese made their obeisance in Passion-week[60]; and then, that this same day the station was at San Giovanni a Porta Latina, in which church certain Portuguese, some years ago, had entered into a strange confraternity. They married one another, male to male, at Mass, with the same ceremonies we use in our marriages, performed their Easter rites together, read the same nuptial gospel together, and then went to bed and lived together. The Roman wits said that, as only the circumstance of marriage renders the other conjunction of male and female legitimate, so to these shrewd people it seemed this other action would become equally right if authorized with the ceremonies and mysteries of the Church. Eight or nine Portuguese of this fine sect were burned.

Franz Hogenberg (c. 1540–c. 1590)

Very few early modern visual depictions of the execution of sodomites are yet known, and two appear in Franz Hogenberg's series of engravings that we may call *Scenes of the Religious and Civil Wars from the History of the Netherlands, France, and England.* Their portrayal of the publicly perceived nature of this kind of occasion is especially valuable. Several generations of the Hogenberg

Fig. 3 Franz Hogenberg, *Execution for Sodomitical Godlessness in the City of Bruges* (1578). Spencer Collection, The New York Public Library, Astor, Lenox, and Tilden Foundations. By permission.

family were artists based in the Netherlands who specialized in printmaking. Franz was born at Mechelen and died at Cologne, apparently a Protestant. Since his oeuvre includes portraits of Queen Elizabeth and other English notables that were reproduced in the Bishops' Bible (1568), he probably visited England.

In Hogenberg's *Scenes* an engraving dated May 18, 1578, shows a lengthy procession of monks being marched out of a monastery in Bruges under armed guard. The title and verses explain that two Franciscans of Calvinist leanings were whipped and then interrogated (probably on account of their Protestantism). But they revealed that many in their order were tainted by sodomy (*Sodomi*). The other monks admitted this (under torture?), and "they were all taken prisoners and led away to the gate for their godlessness."[61] Presumably depicting a result of this, figure 3, dated July 26, 1578, is entitled *Execution for Sodomitical Godlessness in the City of Bruges* (top right). Three monks are about to be burned in a public square while two are being beaten. Underneath, the verses state, "in well-known Bruges in Flanders three Franciscans (*Minnenbroder*) have been burned. Also two others were well beaten with switches and two had to be banished. For they were young and inexperienced and had been seduced by the old ones, so that they unjustly practiced sodomy (*unzuchtt*) upon their bodies." Though

Fig. 4 Franz Hogenberg, *Execution of Sodomitic Criminals in the City of Ghent* (1578). Spencer Collection, The New York Public Library, Astor, Lenox, and Tilden Foundations. By permission.

the circumstances of the monks' trial are as yet unclear, such sentences were carried out by secular authorities. *Minnenbroder* (Franciscans) may be a satiric pun on the word *minne* (which had come to mean debauchery), suggesting "brothers in lust" as opposed to brotherly love. Hogenberg connects sodomy with "godlessness," as was common.

Whereas some prior histories of homoeroticism have already reprinted figure 3 (though without comment), figure 4, entitled *Execution of Sodomitic Criminals in the City of Ghent* (mid-page) and dated June 28, 1578, seems not to have been previously known to sexual history. It shows five monks about to be burned in the foreground and three being beaten in the background. The verses state, "five monks are being burned in Flanders, in the city of Ghent. Four are Franciscans (*Minnenbruder*) and the fifth Augustinian. Also three have been quickly flogged with switches on the market square as they deserve, because of their outrageous sexual offenses (*unzuchtt*) that greatly offended the authorities. That is why the four mendicant orders have now been driven out of Ghent."

No secular cases of sodomy appear in Hogenberg's *Scenes*. The investigations, convictions, and punitive displays in these monastic cases had special topicality for inclusion because they not only afforded titillations of sexual scandal, censure, and public punishment, but also added alleged religious transgression and appealed to Protestant-Catholic rivalries of the time. Although Hogenberg's sodomites are ecclesiastics, his engravings indicate how these public spectacles were managed, while also providing us one contemporary view of the attitudes attendant crowds displayed.

Sir Edward Coke (1552–1634)

By far the most extensive accounts of sodomy in early modern English jurisprudence are Sir Edward Coke's. Born into Norfolk gentry, he was admitted to Trinity College, Cambridge, in 1567, and obtained an M.A. there. To pursue a legal career, he entered the Inner Temple, one of the Inns of Court in London, in 1572, and rapidly advanced through the powerful Lord Burghley's patronage, becoming solicitor general (1592), Speaker of the House of Commons (1593), attorney general (1594), chief justice of the Common Pleas (1606), chief justice of the King's Bench, and privy councillor (both in 1613). But because Coke protested various assertions of royal prerogative, King James I dismissed him from the bench and privy council in 1616, and he later became a leading parliamentary opponent of the Stuarts. After the death of his first wife, a Paston heiress he married in 1582, he wed Lady Elizabeth Hatton, granddaughter of Burghley, in 1598. Partly on that account, Coke and Sir Francis Bacon (1561–1626), reputedly a sodomite himself, were fierce rivals: Bacon had sought to marry Lady Hatton and gain the posts of solicitor general and attorney general. After promoting Coke's unwanted elevation to the King's Bench (which paid less), Bacon helped effect his dismissal in 1616, and Coke helped impeach Bacon in 1621. Coke's chief publications are his thirteen-part *Reports*, largely law reports with comment, for the years 1600 to 1615; his *Book of Entries* of 1614; and the formerly influential four-part *Institutes of the Laws of England*. Whereas the latter's first part was published in 1628, Coke's political conflicts with the monarchy ensured that the rest, along with the final parts of the *Reports* and some further writings, could not be published until parliament intervened in the early 1640s. King Charles I confiscated the former jurist's papers shortly before his death, and some disappeared.

All Coke's substantial treatments of sodomy follow. His account of *Humphrey Stafford's case heads the section "Indictments" from *A Book of Entries* to provide a model for sodomy prosecutions. Coke's most extensive comment appears in *The Third Part of the Institutes of the Laws of England*. In the Proem he states, "We shall first treat of the highest and most heinous crime of High Treason, *Crimen laesa Majestatis;* and of the rest in order, as they are greater and more odious than others."[62] For Coke, high treason, heresy, felony by witchcraft, and murder outrank buggery or sodomy in odium; but sodomy outranks rape, kidnapping a woman, felonious mutilation, burglary, and arson. His citations of Britton, Fleta, and *The Mirror of Justices* appear to document English secular criminalization of sodomy in the Middle Ages, but their claims on this point are spurious (Greenberg, 273n.162). Though *The Third Part* was probably completed no later than 1630, royal suppression postponed its publication until 1644. A further analysis of the offense appears in Coke's *Twelfth Part of the Reports*, whose publication was likewise postponed until 1656. That comment's heading shows it was occasioned around 1607 by the Stafford case: hence its special concerns with intergenerational sodomy and possible analogies with rape. The delays in publication resulted only from Coke's standpoint on the legitimate extent of royal versus parliamentary authority.

As Cynthia Herrrup points out, correcting Bruce Smith, Coke's use of the phrase "knew the said boy carnally" in his sample indictment for sodomy in *The Twelfth Part* and *The Third Part* does not mean that English law, or Coke himself, defined homoerotic sodomy as male rape of *a male minor*, so that anal sex between males was otherwise a legal nonissue (174n.9). Coke just draws on a case he happened to know, that of *Stafford, as a possible example here, and his wording produces some slight unintended local ambiguity. Coke's reputation as a legal authority has collapsed due to his general carelessness as a writer. Nevertheless, *The Third Part* clearly states pederasty "is but a Species of Buggery." In both works buggery is an abominable felony and need only be "mankind with mankind" (not with a minor), or either sex with a beast. Likewise, *Castlehaven's defenses did not include reference to the adulthood of his male sexual partner Fitzpatrick. And the specific grounds for Fitzpatrick's execution included his adult responsibility for his own actions. In *The Third Part*, Coke says, "If the party buggered be within (i.e., younger than) the age of discretion [i.e., fourteen], it is no felony in him, but in the agent only." Coke would not have made this distinction if he thought illegal homoerotic sodomy could only occur between an adult and a minor, or through rape. Although English jurisprudence of this time appears to provide little comment on sodomy aside from Coke's, the legal community could further consult Latin reference works of continental scholars, as Coke would have assumed.

A Book of Entries: Containing Perfect and Approved Precedents [63] *(1614)*

On the Tuesday immediately following the Easter recess within the same term, presentment was made before the Lord King at Westminster in the county of Middlesex, on the oath of twelve jurors, that H. S., knight, lately of London, having not God before his eyes nor respecting the order of nature, but led astray by the instigation of the Devil, on the twelfth of May last year, in the parish of St. Andrew, High Holborn, in the said county of Middlesex, specifically in the house of one M., did with force and with arms assault a certain R. B., a lad of about 16 years of age. And at that time, he did wickedly, and in a manner diabolical, felonious, and contrary to nature, have sexual relations with the same R. B., and did at that time have carnal knowledge of the same R., and did wickedly, and in a manner diabolical, felonious, and contrary to nature, commit and perpetrate with the same R. that detestable and abominable sin of sodomy, which is called in English "buggery" (and is not to be named amongst Christians), to the great displeasure of almighty God, and to the dishonor of the whole human race, against the King's peace, and his crown and dignity, and against the form of the statute published and provided for this case.…

And at another time, namely on the Saturday following the Ascension of our Lord within the same term, the aforementioned H. S. came before the Lord King at Westminster in the custody of the king's Marshall of the Marshalsea, into whose custody he had previously been committed on the aforementioned charge. He who had been committed to the aforementioned Marshall et cetera approached the bar in person. And when asked how he wished to answer the aforesaid charge, he immediately said that he was guilty of none of it. And he placed himself for good or ill upon the judgment of the nation.

Therefore a jury was summoned before the Lord King at Westminster on the Monday following the octave of the Feast of the Holy Trinity next.… And so a day was appointed for the aforesaid H. S., who was in the meantime committed to the custody of the aforesaid Marshall in safe custody, et cetera. On which day the aforementioned H. S., in the custody of the aforesaid Marshall, did appear in person before the Lord King at Westminster. And the aforementioned jury impanelled for this purpose by the Sheriff came in. These [jurors] being chosen, selected and sworn in to declare the truth in the above matter, said under oath that the aforementioned H. S. was guilty *modo et forma* of the aforementioned felony and transgression with which he had been charged in the aforementioned manner, in accordance with the aforementioned indictment brought against him. And [they said] that to the knowledge of the aforementioned jury, [the accused] had no goods or chattels, lands or tenements. And [the accused] was asked if he had anything on his own behalf, or anything to say as to why the Court ought not to proceed to sentencing and execution. And he said nothing which he had not said before. When all this had been examined, and the Court had taken cognizance of all the above, the aforementioned H. S. was condemned to be hung until et cetera.… Easter term, 5 James [I], [1607], Roll 3, among the Pleas of the Crown before the King's Bench.

The Third Part of the Institutes of the Laws of England[64] *(1644, written earlier)*
Chapter 10: Of Buggery, or Sodomy

If any person shall commit buggery with mankind, or beast, by authority of Parliament this offense is adjudged felony without benefit of Clergy. But it is to be known (that I may observe it once for all) that the statute of 25 Henry VIII was repealed by the statute of 1 Mary, whereby all offenses made felony or Praemunire[65] by any Act of Parliament made since 1 Henry VIII were generally repealed, but 25 Henry VIII is revived by 5 Elizabeth.

Buggery is a detestable and abominable sin, amongst Christians not to be named, committed by carnal knowledge against the ordinance of the Creator and order of nature, by mankind with mankind, or with brute beast, or by womankind with brute beast.

Bugeria [sic] is an Italian word, and signifies so much as is before described[66]; *Paederastes* or *Paiderestes* is a Greek word, "Lover of boys," which is but a Species of Buggery, and it was complained of in Parliament that the Lombards had brought into the Realm the shameful sin of Sodomy, that is not to be named, as there it is said.[67] Our ancient Authors do conclude that it deserveth death, the ultimate punishment, though they differ in the manner of punishment. Britton saith that Sodomites and Miscreants shall be burnt, and so were the Sodomites by Almighty God.[68] Fleta saith, those who are guilty of Bestiality and Sodomy should be buried alive[69]; and therewith agreeth the *Mirror*, "for the great abomination," and in another place, he saith "Sodomy is crime of lese-majesty against the celestial King."[70] But (to say it once for all) the judgment in all cases of felony is that the person attainted be hanged by the neck until he or she be dead. But in ancient times in that case, the man was hanged, and the woman was drowned, whereof we have seen examples in the reign of Richard I. And this is the meaning of ancient Franchises granted of *Furca* and *Fossa*, of the Gallows and the Pit, for the hanging upon the one, and drowning in the other, but *Fossa* is taken away and *Furca* remains.

"You shall not lie with a male as with a woman; it is an abomination. And you shall not lie with any beast and defile yourself with it, neither shall any woman give herself to a beast to lie with it; it is a perversion," etc. (Lev. 18:22-23; 1 Tim. 1:10).

The Act of 25 Henry VIII hath adjudged it felony, and therefore the judgment for felony doth now belong to this offense, viz., to be hanged by the neck till he be dead. He that readeth the Preamble of this Act shall find how necessary the reading of our ancient Authors is: the Statute doth take away the benefit of the Clergy from the Delinquent. But now let us peruse the words of the said description of Buggery.

Detestable and abominable. Those just attributes are found in the Act of 25 Henry VIII.

Amongst Christians not to be named. These words are in the usual Indictment of this offense, and are in effect in the Parliament Roll of 50 Edward III . . . [see n.67].

By carnal knowledge, and co. The words of the Indictment be, "against the Creator's ordinance, and against the order of nature, he had sexual relations, and knew the said boy carnally,"[71] and co. So as there must be penetration, that is, *res in re* [i.e., thing in thing], either with mankind, or with beast, but the least penetration maketh it carnal knowledge. See the indictment of Stafford, which was drawn by great advice for committing buggery with a boy, for which he was attainted, and hanged.[72]

The Sodomites came to this abomination by four means: *viz.* by pride, excess of diet, idleness, and contempt of the poor.[73] "The idle man thinks only of food and sex." Both the agent and consentient are felons: and this is consonant to the law of God. "If a man lies with a male as with a woman, both of them have committed an abomination; they shall be put to death" (Lev. 20:13, 1 Cor. 6:[9]). And this accordeth with the ancient Rule of law: those who perpetrate and those who consent are punished with the same punishment.

The emission of semen maketh it not Buggery, but is an evidence in case of buggery of penetration; and so in Rape the words be also "he knew him/her carnally," and therefore there must be penetration, and emission of semen without penetration maketh no Rape. See in the Chapter of Rape. If the party buggered be within the age of discretion, it is no felony in him, but in the agent only. When any offense is felony either by the Common law or by statute, all Accessories both before and after are incidently included.[74] So if any be present, abetting and aiding any to do the act, though the offense be personal, and to be done by one only, as to commit rape, not only he that doth the act is a principal; but also they that be present, abetting and aiding the misdoer, are principals also, which is a proof of the other case of Sodomy.

Or by woman. This is within the Purview of this Act of 25 Henry VIII. For the words be, *if any person*, and co., which extend as well to a woman as to a man; and therefore, if she commit buggery with a beast, she is a person that commits buggery with a beast, to which end this word *person* was used. And the rather, for that somewhat before the making of this Act, a great Lady had committed buggery with a Baboon, and conceived by it, and co.

There be four sins in holy Scripture called "crying sins," whereof this detestable sin is one, expressed in this *Distichon*: "These sins are the voice of lamentation, the voice of blood, the voice of Sodomy, / The voice of the oppressed laborer whose wages are withheld."[75]

The Twelfth Part of the Reports[76] *(1656, written earlier)*

Michaelmas Term, 5 James I [i.e., autumn, 1607]

BUGGERY. NOTE: *BUGARONE*, ITALIAN, IS A BUGGERER, AND *BUGGERARE* IS TO BUGGER, SO BUGGERY COMETH OF THE ITALIAN WORD.

The Letter of the Statute of the 25 Henry VIII, ch. 6: If any person shall commit the detestable sin of Buggery with Mankind, or Beast, and co., it is felony. Which act being repealed by the Statute 1 Mary, is revived and made perpetual by 5 Elizabeth ch. 17. And he shall lose his Clergy.

It appears by the ancient Authorities of Law that this was felony, but they vary in the punishment. For Britton, who writ 5 Edward I ch. 17, saith that Sorcerors, Sodomers, and Heretics shall be burnt. F. N. B. 269A agrees with it. But Fleta, Book I, ch. 35: Apostate Christians, soothsayers, and the like should be drawn[77] and burned (in this he agrees with Britton, those who are guilty of bestiality and sodomy should be buried alive). But in the ancient Book called *The Mirror of Justice*, vouched in Plowden's Commentaries in Fogossa's case,[78] the crime is more high: for there it is called *Crimen laesae Majestatis*, a sin horrible, committed against the King. And this is either against the King Celestial or Terrestrial in three manners: by Heresy, by Buggery, by Sodomy. Note that Sodomy is with Mankind and it is Felony. To make that Offense, penetration must take place, with the emission and spilling of semen, for the Indictment is: "against the Creator's ordinance, and against the order of nature, he had sexual relations, and knew the boy carnally." Every of which ("he had relations, and knew carnally") imply penetration and emission of seed. And so it was held in the case of Stafford, who was attaint in the King's Bench and executed. *Paederastes*, a lover of boys, whereof the Greek word is Παιδεραϛία, Buggery with Boys. *Vide* Parliament Roll 50 Edward III 58: a Lombard did commit the sin that was not to be named. So in Rape there ought to be penetration and emission of Seed, *vide* Stanford, fol. 44.[79] Which Statute makes it felony, he who procures, and co., or receives the Offender, and co., is accessory.

The words of the Statute of Westminster I, ch. 34. If a man ravish a woman, 11 Henry IV, ch. 18. If one aid another to commit Rape, and if he be present, he is principal in the Buggery, *vide* Leviticus 18:22 and [2]0:13, 1 Cor. 6.

The Stafford Scandal (1607)

Published just after Humphrey Stafford was hung for forcible anal sodomy in 1607, an anonymous pamphlet unknown to previous studies of homoeroticism in early modern England summarizes his trial and details his execution, which attracted a "great" throng and "press of people."[80] The case has been known to prior sexual history only from citation of the indictment by *Sir Edward Coke (1552–1634) in his *Book of Entries* and passing references in his other texts as above. The pamphleteer is concerned to portray Stafford's demise as a Christian exemplum of the condemned sinner brought to a "godly end" through repentance: "His true and unexpected contrition in his end made amends for all his former sins of his life, though never so loathsome and unnatural" (sigs. A3[b], C1[b]). We cannot know how accurate this portrayal is. Even the writer acknowledges reports that Stafford attempted suicide. The production of piously edifying narratives about convicted sodomites turning to God at their executions was conventional in England, whether truthful or not, as for the earl of *Castlehaven and his servants Fitzpatrick and Broadway at their deaths, and for John Atherton. We still know nothing of Stafford's prior biography.

I reprint the summary of the trial and conviction. It spectacularly differs from Coke's account: According to the pamphleteer, Stafford raped two youths at once, rather than one as Coke implies. Presumably, the pamphlet gets this right, for it was immediately published and would thus need to report the basic circumstances, no doubt notorious, with reasonable accuracy. Coke likely simplified the case to focus on one youth in order to present a sample indictment that could serve as a paradigm for such cases in general, and he may have wished to avoid sensationalism.

Unfortunately, for the sake of "modesty" the pamphleteer forbears to report the trial and testimony in detail (sig. A3^b). Presumably launched by parental complaint, the case was treated as sodomitical rape. Allegations of "hurt *thereby*" to the youths (implying some anal laceration?) served to indicate some apparent use of force (emphasis mine). Otherwise, they would also have been guilty of sodomy and executed (the age of discretion was fourteen). But did rape really occur? Stafford was outnumbered two to one. How could he control both adolescents at once while allegedly raping one, then the other? Neither Coke nor the pamphleteer mention any accessories. As reported here (correctly or not), Stafford's defense was a denial of responsibility due to drunkenness. Nonetheless, he had more on his mind, for he said at the trial that he had something additional to say in a few days, but was refused that opportunity. When executed, in this account, he further claimed nonconsummation: "I acknowledge that I have deserved death, but yet I could not perform mine intention," for "I could not put it in Execution for drunkenness" (sig. B4^a). But at his death he also reportedly said "the sin his soul then chiefly stood guilty of" was "making...men drunk" (sig. C1^{a-b}), and if so, he rejected Christian sexual orthodoxy to the end.

The Arraignment, Judgment, Confession, and Execution of Humphrey Stafford, Gentleman[81] *(1607)*

> On the eleventh of May, 1607, was indicted at the King's Bench bar at Westminster, before the Reverend Judges there, Humphrey Stafford, Gent., and co., for that he had upon the third of May, in the year of our Lord 1606, unnaturally and feloniously, contrary to the laws of God and the King, used unlawful company with two Boys, and had them carnally known, the one of them named Richard Robinson, the other Nicholas Crosse, the one about the age of seventeen years, the other of thirteen or fourteen years. The place of the fact[82] committed was at the said Humphrey Stafford's lodging, then in the Parish of Saint Andrews in Holborn. To which fact he pleaded not guilty, and for his trial put himself upon God and the Country, whereupon for that day he was returned again unto prison in the King's Bench in Southwark, the place from whence he came, until the eighth of June next following, at which time the said Humphrey Stafford was again called to his further answer.

Being come unto the Bar, his Indictment was again read, whereunto he had before pleaded not guilty, whereupon was presently empanelled a Jury of Gentlemen for his trial. Then were called into the Court his accusers: to wit, the two Boys, Robinson and Crosse, and one of their Father and Mother. Then M. Stafford being before their faces, the Boys were asked whether they knew Master Stafford to be the party whom they meant? They answered yea directly, whereupon an Oath was administered unto those four aforenamed, that they should speak the truth and nothing but the truth. The two boys upon their oaths did directly charge him with the fact, and the particulars thereof: as the time when, the place where, the manner how, the circumstances both precedent and consequent (which here for modesty sake I overpass). The man and the Woman testified only some matters ensuing upon this fact, for confirmation of the truth of the Boys' allegations, showing that the boys had received hurt thereby, and that they were forced to use the help of a Surgeon for their care. Master Stafford denied the fact, affirming and protesting that he was guiltless therein, excusing himself, that if he had offended it was in wine. But the Jury after a little deliberation returned him guilty, whereupon one of the Judges made an exhortation unto him, withal demanding what he could say for himself, wherefore judgment should not be pronounced against him? Whereupon Master Stafford desired three or four days respite before sentence were pronounced: for (said he), I have something to speak, which for some causes unto myself known I cannot now utter. But the honorable bench being not satisfied with that dilatory answer, Judgment was presently pronounced: That he should be conveyed from thence to the place of Execution, there to be hanged till he were quite dead. The sentence pronounced, the prisoner was returned back to the place from whence he came, where he remained until the tenth of the same month of June, being Wednesday following, in which time he disposed himself to Godward, having made his will, and bequeathed his body to be buried in the Church of St. George in Southwark.

The Castlehaven Scandal (1630–1631)

In 1631 the trials of Mervin Touchet (1593–1631), jointly Lord Audley and earl of Castlehaven, and two of his servants, Lawrence Fitzpatrick and Giles Broadway, provided seventeenth-century England's most sensational sex scandal. The earl was charged with committing two acts of sodomy with Fitzpatrick, and acting as an accessory to Broadway's alleged rape of the earl's wife Anne, countess of Castlehaven (1580–1647), all during June 1630. Each offense was a felony, for which the penalty was hanging. After the earl's conviction and execution, Broadway was tried, convicted, and executed for rape, and Fitzpatrick for sodomy. According to testimony, the earl had run his household as a sex circus of voyeurism, group sex, sex between males, corruption of a minor (as we would call it), and alleged rape. The surviving documentary record is exceptionally extensive, though nonetheless incomplete and contradictory. I reprint the passages most relevant to sodomy from one of the most full and accurate published records of the trials, and also a published account of Fitzgerald's execution.[83]

The earl's legal problems began when, in October 1630, his eldest son James Touchet (1612–1684) complained to the Privy Council that his father was projecting his disinheritance in favor of a servant, Henry Skipwith, thus disparaging the family blood and title, and compromising the realm's social order. Skipwith had received munificent gifts, "worth at least £12,000" (Herrup, 38). Not only had the earl allegedly encouraged him and other servants to commit adultery with James's new wife, the earl's step-daughter Elizabeth Brydges (1615–1679), who was only twelve when this began, but had said "he would rather have a Boy of [Skipwith's] begetting than any other."[84] Appearing to be James's son, yet actually Skipwith's, such a child would stand to inherit the earldom, thus disparaging so-called "blood nobility." When the Privy Council launched a formal investigation, household members attested that Skipwith was often the earl's bedmate and also Elizabeth's. Apparently because the earl's lavish favoring of Skipwith and desire for an heir by him appeared sodomitical, both were arrested. The earl's generosity to a previous favorite, John Anktill (?–1638), who had later married the earl's eldest daughter, was also investigated. According to Elizabeth, the earl incited Anktill to rape her mother Anne, was sodomizing Fitzpatrick, and watched Elizabeth and Skipwith have sex "divers times," as did "nine servants of the House" (*State Trials*, 1: 269). Anne herself claimed that, "from the first week of their marriage" in 1624, the earl "had shunned her in favor of prostitutes and male servants" (Herrup, 18), pressured her to have sex with his favorites, and, in 1630, incited her page Broadway to rape her. She repeated rumors of her husband's sodomy with Anktill. However, Broadway claimed he had only attempted the rape, without penetration, and mutually masturbated with the earl, who also "used his Body as the Body of a Woman, but never pierced it, only emitted between his Thighs" (*State Trials*, 1:269). Fitzpatrick likewise admitted sexual relations with the earl while denying penetration. The earl himself denied involvement in any sexual illegality (cf. Herrup, 38–48).

Although the earl was finally charged with committing three alleged felonies (two acts of sodomy with Fitzpatrick, and accessory to rape), the case evinced obvious problems. The sodomy charges did not involve Anktill and Skipwith, even though it was they who had received lavish gifts. Also the evidence for sodomy was inadequate, for there was no proof of penetration, no admission of that from either party involved, and otherwise no witness. And the countess' testimony for her alleged rape by Broadway, with the earl's assistance, was uncorroborated and questionable. Daughter of the fifth earl of Derby, she was a Stanley, one of the most rich and powerful families in England, much beyond the Touchets. Yet she herself testified that the earl had been urging her to copulate with his favorites since they were married six years before (1624). Both Anktill and Skipwith were said to have had her forcibly already, and there were rumors of her adultery and infanticide. Skipwith had openly committed adultery with her daughter Elizabeth since the latter was twelve, abetted by the earl. If the situation had not been to the countess' liking, could she not have fled to her family, or at least sought to extricate Elizabeth, much earlier? Why did she spend six years with the earl, and allow six months to elapse between Broadway's alleged rape and her complaint, while still residing with her husband?

Since evidence for the charges was insufficient, the Crown had to breach various legal conventions to proceed and secure conviction. For example, "wives were not usually allowed to testify against their husbands," and "normal practice was to construe capital felonies," such as sodomy, "narrowly, not broadly" (Herrup, 84). Yet, in this case, the prosecutors and advisory judges dismissed any need to prove penetration to establish fatal sodomitical guilt. Lacking clear proof that the earl was guilty of the specific charges in question as normally understood, the prosecution sought rather to show he was capable of felonious sexual acts (Herrup, 59). Whereas the jury of twenty-seven peers readily convicted him for abetting rape, with just one dissenting vote, his sodomy conviction was secured only after much debate among the jurors, by a tenuous verdict of fifteen to twelve (Herrup, 87). In 1632 the attorney William Drake remarked, "that was made buggery which was never accounted so before" under English law (cit. Herrup, 89). As Sir Richard Hutton (1561?–1639), a judge of common pleas, records in his *Reports*, the panel of judges advised the earl's jury of peers "that Pollution and using of a man upon his Belly Sodomitically without penetration was Buggery by the Statute of 25 Henry VIII," and yet Sir Thomas Richardson, Lord Chief Justice of the Common Pleas, "had been of a contrary opinion." Richardson told Hutton that the judges' opinion was "delivered only upon this case and upon these examinations, . . . but they gave not a general opinion, that may be a rule in other cases, but upon the foulness and abominableness of this fact [i.e., evil deed]. And afterwards the Lords were not unanimously resolved that it was Buggery, but this Point was resolved, that they ought to believe and give credit to the Law as the Judges had declared it. And it seems that they could not give a special Verdict upon this trial, for it never was seen."[85]

The case was in some respects manipulated as a show trial for reasons of state. Not only did the earl allege a familial and domestic conspiracy against him, but he and later even his son James also complained of inappropriate legal procedures and political interference. Ironically, James's complaint about alienated patrimony initiated legal proceedings that made his family notorious and decimated their estates and fortune: As a convicted felon, the earl forfeited his English barony and lands to the crown, including his magnificent estate of Fonthill, leaving James with only the Irish possessions and earldom. King Charles I used the confiscated properties to pay his own debts to courtiers, and that, James later claimed, had motivated his father's prosecution (Herrup, 100–104).

While complex social and political issues converged in this case, the enforcement of orthodox Christian sexual morality, including suppression of sodomy, was central to the framing and presentation of the legal spectacle. Although the earl might not actually have had anal sex with males, evidence from diverse sources indicates his sexual behavior was highly transgressive, and according to the account of Fitzgerald's execution reprinted subsequently, that servant finally repudiated their former denials of anal penetration in his farewell speech before the gallows: "his Lordship had both Buggered him and he his Lordship."[86] Though the earl apparently fathered six children during his first marriage, which probably began before 1612 and ended with his first wife's death between late 1622 and 1624, his second wife testified that within days of their marriage it was clear her husband was much less interested in conjugal intercourse than in sex with male favorites and watching them have sex with her (Herrup, 18). According to her testimony, the earl "would make Skipwith come naked into his Chamber, and delighted in calling up his Servants to show their Privities, and would make her look on, and commended those that had the largest" (*State Trials*, 1: 268). It may be relevant that the sister of the earl's first wife married the reportedly sodomitical Sir Francis Bacon (1561–1626).

Castlehaven's official indictment for sodomy, not included in my copy text of his trial, shows how strongly Christian ideology drove antisodomitical prejudices and legal proceedings:

> Mervin, Lord Audley, not having God before his Eyes, nor respecting the Order of Nature, but moved and seduced by the Instigation of the Devil, the first of June in the ... Mansion House of the said Lord Audley, Did there by Force of Arms upon one Florentius Fitzpatrick, Wickedly, Devilishly, Feloniously, and contrary to Nature, exercise Venery, and the said Florentius Fitzpatrick then and there did Carnally know, and that Detestable and Abominable Sodomitical Sin called Buggery (not to be named among Christians) then and there with the said Florentius Fitzpatrick Devilishly, Feloniously, and contrary to Nature did commit and perpetrate to the great Displeasure of Almighty God and Disgrace of all Mankind, and contrary to the Peace of our said Sovereign Lord the King, his Crown and Dignity, and against the Statute in this Case made and provided, and co. The like Indictment for the same Offense, Committed with the same Person on the Tenth of June ... was also preferred, but not Read against him.[87]

The contemporary force of Christian beliefs further appears in the reports of these sodomites' executions, whether reasonably correct or piously embroidered. When faced with immediate death, they all appeared to atone themselves with Christianity in hope of salvation, including Broadway (who also admitted having nonpenetrative sex with the earl). According to *The Case of Sodomy* (1707/08), a collection of documents on the Castlehaven scandal, the earl was concerned to portray himself as a model of orthodox Protestant piety, despite admitting various (though not technically illegal) debaucheries.[88] We cannot know whether he and his male lovers privately considered their sexual histories of much importance to their God, or if they did, what qualifiers and rationalizations they attached. Insofar as they were at least nominally Christian beforehand, they would also have previously undertaken such inner negotiations about their sexual desires, as in the comments attributed to Fitzpatrick at his execution and reprinted here.

The trials further reflect sectarian and class implications of sodomy as it could be practiced, legally investigated, and prosecuted within aristocratic or otherwise privileged milieus. The earl's flirtations with Roman Catholicism were adduced against him in court to suggest a potentially treasonous and irreligious instability, and Fitzpatrick was Catholic. Needing patronage, Fitzpatrick and Broadway sought to enhance their positions by serving their rich master's desires, but became enmeshed in the maneuvers of higher masters in which they were used for the earl's and their own destruction. Naively expecting that cooperation with the Crown, denial of anal penetration, and apparently a guarantee of immunity from prosecution would save him (Herrup, 49, 90–91), Fitzpatrick testified against his employer, and thereby ironically became not only a scapegoat for sex between males, but also for the death of his noble employer and thus for disloyalty of underlings to the peerage and hence the Crown.

Through these show-trials and executions staged against the violation of official sexual norms, the Crown could publicly demonstrate that there was no impunity for such transgressions at any social level from an earl down to his domestics, thus urging sexual restraint and conformity, or at least fearful discretion. Although successive narratives of the case endued it with different social and political significances through the seventeenth and eighteenth centuries (Herrup, xv, ch. 5), sodomy, in the sense of sex between males, was nonetheless a central factor in its origins, development, and conclusion. Both Skipwith and the earl were jailed soon after the investigation started. Even though the charge of assisting rape was itself enough to ensure the earl's death and readily confirmed by the jury, the Crown went to great lengths to convict the earl also for sodomy: not only descending to inveigle Fitzpatrick with false promises of protection, as seems very probable (Herrup, 49, 90–91), but wrenching prior interpretation of the sodomy statute so much that almost half the jury dissented. The prosecution denounced the earl's sex with males at least as much as the countess' alleged rape, reserving for the former a biblically inspired rhetoric of particular abomination. The earliest printed account of the earl's trial, *The Arraignment and Conviction of Mervin, Lord Audley* (1642), significantly shifts from English to Latin when male deponents address their sex with the earl (even though, in their account, it merely amounted to mutual masturbation with body contact), but not when witnesses discuss the countess' rape or her daughter's adultery.[89] Many clearly considered sexual relations in general between males profoundly taboo, not in any way socially normative or orderly. This newly elastic use of the law against sodomy, whereby, at the whim of the Crown and judiciary, proof of anal penetration seemed no longer essential to establish fatal guilt in masculine love, must have frightened legally informed sodomites throughout England, and was presumably intended to do so. Uxorious and family-oriented by comparison with his father King James I, who was rumored to be a sodomite and extravagantly favored handsome young courtiers (Herrup, 20–21, 33), King Charles I likely seized on Castlehaven as a striking means to proclaim his own contrary principles for the realm's domestic order. Yet, apparently due to a lack of evidence, the chief favorites of the earl's menage, Skipwith and Anktill, were not charged, and under Charles's libidinous son, King Charles II, the earl of Rochester and others could live much like Castlehaven without legal consequences.

The Trial of Mervin, Lord Audley, Earl of Castlehaven, for a Rape and
Sodomy, on the Twenty-fifth of April, 1631, in the Sixth Year of
King Charles the First[90] *(written c. 1631)*

[To inform the jury of peers, the judges first discussed some broad legal issues, including benefit of clergy and technicalities of rape (but not sodomy), the earl was brought forth, and the trial began.]

The Lord High Steward's Speech

My Lord Audley, the King has understood, both by Report and the Verdict of divers Gentlemen of Quality in your own Country, that you stand impeached of sundry Crimes of a most high and heinous nature. And to try whether they be true or not, and that Justice may be done accordingly, his Majesty brings you this day to your Trial, doing herein like the mighty King of Kings in the 18th of Genesis, verses 20, 21, who went down to see whether their Sins were so grievous as the Cry of them: "Because the cry of Sodom and Gomorrah is great, and their Sins be grievous, I will go down (saith the Lord) and see whether they have done altogether according to the Cry of it." And Kings on Earth can have no better Pattern to follow than the King of Heaven; and therefore our Sovereign Lord the King, God's Vicegerent here on Earth, hath commanded that you shall be here tried this day, and to that end hath caused these Peers to be assembled. . . .

[The earl requested legal counsel, was refused, and pleaded not guilty.]

Mr. Attorney Said as Followeth

My Lord Steward, May it please your Grace, there are three Indictments against Mervin Lord Audley: the first for a Rape, the other two for Sodomy. The Person is honorable, the Crimes of which he is indicted dishonorable; which if it fall out to be true (which is to be left to Trial) I dare be bold to say, never Poet invented nor Historian writ of any Deed so foul. And although Suetonius hath curiously set out the Vices of some of the Emperors who had absolute Power, which might make them fearless of all manner of Punishment,[91] and besides were Heathens and knew not God; yet none of these came near this Lord's Crimes. The one is a Crime that, I may speak it to the Honor of our Nation, is of such Variety that we seldom or never knew of the like. But they are all of such a pestilential Nature that, if they be not punished, they will draw from Heaven a heavy Judgment upon this Kingdom. . . .[92]

And first I shall begin with Indictment of Rape. Bracton tells us of King Athelstan's Law before the Conquest: "If the Party were of no chaste Life, but a Whore, yet there may be a Ravishment; but it is a good Plea to say she was his Concubine." In an Indictment of Rape, there is no Time of Prosecution necessary; for *nullum Tempus occurrit Regi*.[93] But in Case of an Appeal of Rape, if the Woman did not prosecute in convenient Time, it will bar her. If a Man take away a Maid by Force and ravish her, and afterwards she give her Consent and marry him, yet it is a Rape.

For the *Crimen Sodomiticum*, our Law had no knowledge of it till the 15th [sic] of Henry VIII, by which Statute it was made Felony. And in this there is no more question, but only whether it be *Crimen Sodomiticum sine Penetratione*.[94] And the Law of 15 [sic] Elizabeth sets it down in general Words, and where the Law doth not distinguish, neither must we. And I know you will be cautious how you will give the least Mitigation to so abominable a Sin which brought such Plagues after it, as we may see in Genesis 17 [sic], Leviticus 18, Judges 19, Romans 1.[95]

But, my Lord, it seemed to me strange at the first, how a Nobleman of his Quality should fall to such abominable Sins. But when I found he had given himself over to Lust, and that *Nemo repente fit pessimus*,[96] and if once Men habit themselves in ill, it is no marvel if they fall into any Sins; and that he was constant to no Religion, but in the Morning he would be a Papist and go to Mass, and in the Afternoon a Protestant and go to a Sermon. When I had considered these Things, I easily conceived and shall be bold to give your Grace a Reason why he became so ill. He believed not God, he had not the Fear of God before his Eyes; he left God, and God left him to his own Wickedness. And what may not a Man run into? What Sin so foul, what Thing so odious, which he dares not adventure?

But I find in him Things beyond all Imagination, for I find his ill Imagination and Intentions bent to have his Wife naught with the wickedest Man that ever I heard of before: for who would not have his Wife virtuous and good, how bad soever himself be? And I find him Bawd to his own Wife. If she loved him, she must love Skipwith (whom he honored above all), and not any honest Love, but in a dishonest Love. And he gives his Reason by Scripture: She was now made subject to him [Gen. 3:16]. And therefore if she did ill at his Command, it was not her Fault but his, and he would answer it. His irregular Bounty toward Skipwith was also remarkable. He lets this Skipwith (whom he calls his Favorite) spend of his Purse £500 per Annum; and if his Wife or Daughter would have any thing, though never so necessary, they must lie with Skipwith and have it from him, and not otherwise; also telling Skipwith and his Daughter in Law, he had rather have a Child by him than any other. But for these things, I had rather they should come forth of the Witnesses' Mouths than from me: and thereupon desired that the Proofs might be read....[97]

[The crown adduced testimony from the earl's steward, wife, step-daughter Elizabeth, Skipwith, and servants including Walter Bigg, Broadway and Fitzpatrick. On John Anktill, Bigg deposed that he reaped large financial benefits while serving as the earl's page. I retain only material directly bearing on sodomy.]

Then Lawrence Fitzpatrick was produced. But before his Examination was read, the Earl desired that neither he nor any other might be allowed Witnesses against him, until he [i.e., the witness] had taken the Oath of Allegiance. This was referred to the Lords the Judges. The Judges resolve against him, that they might be Witnesses unless they were convicted Recusants.[98]

The Examination of Fitzpatrick Was Then Read, . . . Then Again
Confirmed upon Oath

That the Earl had committed Sodomy twice upon his Person. That Henry Skipwith was the special Favorite of my Lord Audley and that he usually lay with him; and that Skipwith said that the Lord Audley made him lie with his own Lady; and that he saw Skipwith in his sight do it, my Lord being present. And that he lay with Blandina in his sight, and four more of the Servants, and afterwards the Earl himself lay with her in their sights....

Fitzpatrick's Second Examination

That the Lord Audley made him lie with him at Fonthill and at Salisbury, and once in the Bed, and emitted between his Thighs but did not penetrate his Body; and that he heard he did so with others.[99] That Skipwith lay with the young Lady often and ordinarily, and that the Earl knew it and encouraged him in it, and wished to have a Boy by him and the young Lady. That Blandina lived half a year in my Lord's House and was a common Whore....[100]

These Testimonies being read, Mr. Attorney pressed things very earnestly and in excellent Method against the Earl.... Then he showed how both the Laws of God and Man were against Sodomy, and cited Leviticus 18 toward the end, that by these Abominations the Land is de-filed, and therefore the Lord doth visit this Land for the Iniquity thereof. And then concludes, that God may remove and take away from us his Plagues, let this wicked Man (saith he) be taken away from amongst us.

Then the Earl (after the Lord Steward had told him he should be heard in his own Defense, with as much Patience as was admitted in his Charge) entered into his own Defense. But the Lord Steward advised him to speak pertinently; whereupon he alleged that he was a weak Man and of ill Memory, and therefore desired that he might not be interrupted. . . .

[In his defense the Earl reportedly argued: 1) his wife was unchaste anyway, as with Broadway by her own admission; 2) the witnesses are incompetent for they are his own wife and servants, and have been suborned by his son in a plot against his life; 3) the charge that he was an accessory to rape, and thus guilty of felony, is questionable because, as Broadway testified, there was no penetration, only emission upon her belly while the Earl held her; 4) allowing testimony of a wife against her husband is questionable. The Lord Steward and judges dismissed these claims.][101]

Then the Lord High Steward desired the Lords the Judges to resolve the Questions which Mr. Attorney in his Charge submitted and referred to their Judgments.

1. Whether it were to be accounted Buggery within the Statute, without Penetration? The Judges resolve that it was; and that the Use of the Body so far as to emit thereupon, makes it so.[102]

2. Whether, it being proved that the Party ravished were of evil Fame and of an unchaste Life, it will amount to Rape? The Judges resolve it to be a Rape though [i.e., even if it were] committed on the Body of a common Strumpet: for it is the enforcing against the Will which makes the Rape, and a common Whore may be ravished against her Will and it is Felony to do it.

3. Whether it is adjudged a Rape when the Woman complaineth not presently? And whether there be a Necessity of Accusation within a convenient time, as within 24 Hours? The Judges resolve that inasmuch as she was forced against her Will and then showed her Dislike, she was not limited to any Time for her Complaint, and that in an Indictment there is no Limitation of Time, but in an Appeal there is.

4. Whether Men of no Worth shall be allowed sufficient Proofs against a Baron, or not? The Judges resolve that any Man is a sufficient Witness in case of Felony. . . .

[Invited by the Lord Steward to say whatever he could further upon his behalf, the earl alleged a conspiracy against him by his wife, eldest son James, and his servants. The Lord Steward requested the jury of peers to deliver their verdict.]

Then the Peers withdrew themselves. And after two Hours Debate and several Advices and Conferences with the Lord Chief Justice, whom they sent for and consulted with four several times, having in that time also sent the Earl of Warwick and Viscount of Dorchester, together with the Lord Chief Justice, to consult with the Lord Steward, at the last they returned to their Places, and then the Lord Steward asked them one by one, beginning at the lowest and so ascending: 1. Whether the said Earl of Castlehaven was Guilty of the Rape whereof he stood indicted, or not? And they all gave him Guilty [sic; actually twenty-six to one]. 2. Whether the said Earl of Castlehaven was Guilty of the Sodomy with which he was charged, or not? And fifteen of the Lords condemned him, and the other eleven [sic; actually twelve] freed him....

[The Lord Steward informed the earl he was found guilty as charged and condemned to be hung as a convicted felon.]

The Lord Steward's Exhortation

Oh think upon your Offenses! Which are so heinous and so horrible that a Christian Man ought scarce to name them, and such as the depraved Nature of Man (which of itself carries a Man to all Sin) abhorreth! And you have not only offended against Nature, but the Rage of a Man's Jealousy! And although you die not for that, that you have abused your own Daughter! And having both Honor and Fortune to leave behind you, you would have had the impious and spurious Offspring of a Harlot to inherit! Both these are horrid Crimes. But my Lord it grieves me to see you stand out against the Truth so apparent, and therefore I will conclude with this Admonition: That God might have taken you away when you were blinded in your Sins, and therefore hope he hath reserved you as a Subject of his Mercy, and as he sends you to see this Day of Shame that you may return unto him, so thereby in a manner he lovingly draws you to him. Therefore spend the remainder of your Time in Tears and Repentance, and this Day's Work, I hope, will be a Correction from many Crimes and Corruptions.

Whereupon at last the Earl descended to a low Petition to the Lords, and very humbly besought them to intercede with his Majesty that he might not suddenly cut him off, but give him Time of Repentance. And then he desired their Lordships' Pardons, in that he had been so great a Stain to Honor and Nobility.[103]

The Trial, Conviction, and Condemnation of Lawrence Fitzpatrick and Giles Broadway[104] (written c. 1631)

On Monday the twenty-seventh of June, 1631, the Marshal of the King's Bench brought Fitzpatrick and Broadway to the Bar, where was a Jury of sufficient and able Wiltshire Men empanelled to go upon and try them....

Fitzpatrick, being asked concerning his Guiltiness or Innocency, demanded who were his Accusers? The Lord Chief Justice answered, "You have accused yourself sufficiently." Fitzpatrick replied that he thought neither the Laws of the Kingdom required, nor was he bound to be, the Destruction of himself. What Evidence he had formerly given was for the

King against the Earl and no further. The Lord Chief Justice replied, it was true, the Law did not oblige any Man to be his own Accuser; yet where his Testimony served to take away anyone's Life and made himself guilty of the same Crime, therein it should serve to cut him off also. Then the Jury demanded of the Court Satisfaction concerning the Words of the Statute, which run, "To charge him alone to be, and accounted a Felon in Law, that committed a Buggery with Man or Beast." (For which Fact the late Earl was only guilty, and had suffered.) The Lord Chief Justice replied that forasmuch as every Accessory to a Felon is a Felon in Law, so [Fitzpatrick] being a voluntary Prostitute when he was not only of Understanding and Years to know the Heinousness of the Sin, but also of Strength to have withstood his Lord, he therefore was so far forth guilty.

Whereupon the Jury found the Bill, and the Sentence of Death was passed on them both; and they were delivered and committed to the Sheriff of Middlesex, who, after he had suffered them to have some Repast at Mr. Hill's in the Palace Yard and Conference with their Friends, carried them to Newgate, where they behaved themselves civilly and religiously.

As soon as they were found Guilty, the Judges of the Court wrote this Letter to the Lord Keeper to prepare him for the King: Right Honorable, May it please your Lordship to be informed that this day Giles Broadway and Lawrence Fitzpatrick were tried ... for the several Offenses of Rape and Buggery ..., and they have received Judgment of Death; but we forbear awarding Execution ... until further Direction from his Majesty. ... Fitzpatrick, who was arraigned for the Buggery, confessed his Examination to be true. But like one very ignorant or rather senseless, would have them true against the Lord Audley and not against himself, which was impossible. He pretended he was promised Security from Danger if he would testify against the Lord Audley, and so sought to raise a Suspicion as if he had been wrought upon to be a Witness to bring the Lord Audley to his End. They were both found guilty to the full Satisfaction of all that were present. And we for our parts thought it to stand with the Honor of common Justice, that seeing their Testimony had been taken to bring a Peer of the Realm to his Death for an Offense as much theirs as his, that they should as well suffer for it as he did, lest any Jealousy should arise about the Truth of the Fact and the Justness of the Proceedings. But ... we have stopped the Execution till his Majesty's further Pleasure be known, to which we humbly submit ourselves and rest at your Lordship's Command, N. Hyde, W. Jones, J. Whitlock, G. Croke.

The King by this means being truly informed how things stood, signified his Pleasure that they should be executed, but to have a Week's time for Repentance.

The Execution of Fitzpatrick and Broadway[105] *(written c. 1631)*

Upon Wednesday the sixth of July they were brought to Tyburn in two several Carts, Fitzpatrick first, and set under the Beam toward Paddington, appropriated (as is said) to and chosen by Romanists. Where when the Executioner had tied the Halter about his Neck, he thus delivered himself: Gentlemen, forasmuch as I am here and as it were upon the Instant to suffer Death, I desire all loving Subjects and Members of the Church of Rome to pray for me.

When no Man for any Thing could be perceived rejoicing at that Motion or signifying a Willingness so to do, he proceeded to a Kind of Prayer to our Savior, his Mother, and the Saints. . . . Then he proceeded with Relation how he had been examined by my Lord Chief Justice touching the Corruptness of my Lord of Castlehaven's Life, wherein he no ways confessed any thing to prejudice the said Earl. That being within three Days after sent for before the Lords of the Council, my Lord Dorset (against whom he did once or twice Envy, yet freely forgave him) had entrapped and ensnared him to his Destruction, for that, saying upon his [i.e., Dorset's] Honor, and speaking it in the Plural Number as the Mouth of the whole Board, that whatsoever [Fitzpatrick] delivered should no ways prejudice himself, [Dorset] thereby got him to declare the Earl guilty of the Sin of Buggery. Wherein himself being a Party was the only Cause he came now to suffer Death, for which his Lordship's Skill and Policy in sifting him, together with Dispensation of his Promise and Oath, [Fitzpatrick] freely forgave him; saying further, the said Lord had done him no Wrong, because [Dorset] therein was but an Instrument to send him out of this World into a better. Then he proceeded to a Kind of Demand of the Company, or rather a Rehearsal of the Earl's denying the Sin at his Death; touching which he desired and wished my Lord had not so spoken (if he did), for it was too true his Lordship had both Buggered him and he his Lordship. That it was true (for some private Discontentment) he bore a little Malice to the Earl and Skipwith, for which he asked God Forgiveness. That Broadway, if he had done anything to the Countess, he did it not out of his own ill or corrupt Nature, but was provoked and persuaded to it by the Earl.

He cleared the young Lord, as never being any Occasion or Means of his Father's Death in hiring or persuading him to give Evidence as he had done. He confessed he had lived an ill Life in that he had delighted in Drinking, Whoring,[106] and all manner of Uncleanness, but now as he was heartily sorry, so he doubted not of Mercy of Almighty God to pardon and forgive him all his Sins, through and for the Merits and Mediation's Sake of Christ Jesus, the Blessed Virgin, and the Saints in Heaven.

That he had fallen or run into these erroneous Sins, and especially that which he came to die for, in Regard and by Reason he had neglected, and not so duly as he should have done, his Repair to his Ghostly Father[107] to make Confessions and take Instructions from him. That after he did make and had his Sins known to the Priest, he was not only sorry for them, but also resolved never to come into my Lord's House again; yet true it was he did, but it was through Frailty, and because he was not furnished of another Place.[108] So turning again to Mr. Broadway and persuading him to embrace the Romish Faith, wherein as he perceived his Labor was in Vain, so the Sheriff and other Persons of Quality willed him to forbear and shut up his Discourse unless he had anything more to say to the purpose. Whereupon praying for the King, Queen, and State, he betook himself to private Prayer, and therein for the most part continued to his Death.

Sarah White Norman (fl. 1639–1654) and Mary Vincent Hammon (1633–1705)

Trial documents naming these women are the only known record of sexual relations between seventeenth-century female English colonists in North America.[109] Sarah White, of whom little is known, married Hugh Norman in 1639. Born in 1642, their daughter Elizabeth drowned in a well in 1648. That year, Mary Vincent, then about fifteen, married Benjamin Hammon, who had arrived from London in 1634. Also in 1648, Mary and Sarah (presumably about a decade older than Mary due to Sarah's much earlier marriage) were prosecuted at Plymouth for "lewd behavior each with other upon a bed." Laws against perceived sexual immorality were much more comprehensive in the Puritan colonies than in England, which had long lacked any standard secular means of prosecuting fornication or "pollutions," as opposed to anally penetrative sodomy between males, and bestiality (*Law). Whereas Mary was only admonished, perhaps because she was younger than sixteen, the local age of discretion, Sarah stood trial. During the time of Sarah's prosecution (1648–1650), her husband deserted his wife and children and returned to England, where he reportedly wasted an inheritance, then lived in debauched poverty. Mary and her husband later had a number of children and she was widowed in 1703.

At the General Court of Our Sovereign Lord the King, Holden at Plymouth Aforesaid, the Sixth of March[110] *(1648)*

> We present the wife of Hugh Norman, and Mary Hammon, both of Yarmouth, for lewd behavior each with other upon a bed. Mary Hammon cleared with admonition.

At the General Court Holden at New Plymouth, the Sixth of March (1649)

> Whereas, at the General Court, holden at Plymouth aforesaid, the 29th of October, 1649, Richard Berry accused Teage Joanes of sodomy and other unclean practises also with Sara, the wife of Hugh Norman, and for that cause the said parties were both bound over to answer at this Court, and

accordingly appeared. The said Richard Berry acknowledged before the Court that he did wrong the aforesaid Teage Joanes in both the aforesaid particulars, and had borne false witness against him upon oath; and for the same the said Richard Berry was sentenced to be whipped at the post, which accordingly was performed.

At the General Court Holden at New Plymouth, the Second of October (1650)

Whereas the wife of Hugh Norman of Yarmouth hath stood presented divers Courts for misdemeanor and lewd behavior with Mary Hammon upon a bed, with divers lascivious speeches by her also spoken, but she could not appear by reason of some hindrances until this Court, the said Court have therefore sentenced her, the said wife of Hugh Norman, for her vild[111] behavior in the aforesaid particulars, to make a public acknowledgment, so far as conveniently may be, of her unchaste behavior, and have also warned her to take heed of such carriages for the future, lest her former carriage come in remembrance against her to make her punishment the greater.

CHAPTER 3

Medicine

Parmenides in his work *On Nature* indicates that effeminate men or pathics may come into being as a result of a circumstance at conception.

—*Caelius Aurelianus, *On Chronic Diseases*

These practices result in some cases from natural disposition, and in others from habit.... When nature is responsible, no one would describe such persons as showing Unrestraint any more than one would apply that term to women because they are passive and not active in sexual intercourse; nor should we class as Unrestraint a morbid state brought about by habitual indulgence.

—Aristotle, *Nicomachean Ethics*[1]

Early modern medical practice included university-educated professionals, deliberate frauds, surgeons trained through apprenticeship, empirics of various types, midwives, local wisewomen, and apothecaries. I will focus on the academic medical tradition, for it venerated ancient Greek and Roman texts that included frank discussions of same-sex sexual behaviors, initiated anatomical research that produced radical reassessments of sex and gender, and left extensive documentary remains. Texts, concepts, and techniques valorized in the university milieu influenced much nonacademic practice. Though rejected by Paracelsus (1493–1541) among others, academic medicine had official prestige and influenced popular culture, partly through indirect oral transmissions. When midwives digitally stimulated the genitalia of female clients thought to suffer from "uterine suffocation" or "hysteria" (supposedly resulting from spoilage of feminine seed through, for example, sexual abstinence), their practice accorded with much learned commentary dating from antiquity, which ignored the possibilities of female-female erotics and tribadism.[2]

The Greek, Roman, and Arabic medical sources known in Renaissance Europe address same-sex sexual behaviors most fully and significantly in considering the possibilities of their congenital causation. The theory of conception derived from the Hippocratic corpus and Galen seeks to account for offspring who do not simply conform to "masculine" and "feminine" types, but constitute variously "feminine males," "masculine females," and hermaphrodites. Contrary to the claim that the father alone provides the seed, a notion controversially ascribed to Aristotle, generation in the Hippocratic-Galenic view results from maternal as well as paternal seed that, in both cases, involves both masculine and feminine principles. Certain combinations of seed thus produce varying degrees of masculinity and feminity, affected also by fetal position in the womb.[3] Allowing for gradations of sex and gender, this theory may suggest a congenital and hence essentialist rationale for homoerotic inversions of sex roles as well. But, as in the Hippocratic *Regimen*, the ancient sources and their followers do not make such sexual implications explicit (*Helkiah Crooke). In a similar tradition that originated in late antiquity, the womb has a series of seven cells in which conception may occur, and the central one produces a hermaphrodite, whereas the three on each side respectively conduce various degrees of masculinity and feminity (*Crooke).[4] Moreover, in the early fifth century *Caelius Aurelianus reports that, according to Parmenides, who flourished circa 450 B.C.E., a certain mingling of parental seed produces offspring innately possessing both "masculine" and "feminine" sexual desires. In any case, Caelius adds, many leading physicians believe that male and female sex-role inversions arise from hereditary causes. The *pseudo-Aristotelian *Problems* assumes that masculine desire to receive anal penetration often arises from an innate condition of the sperm ducts, and *Avicenna (980–1037) debates whether it results from a particular inborn conformation of nerves in the penis and groin. By the later Middle Ages, then, there was already a well-developed medical tradition suggesting that "being a Sodomite might be due to a naturally occurring anatomy or physiology," and so "there is no need to wait for the nineteenth-century 'homosexual' in order to have some same-sex behavior reduced to a medical identity."[5]

As the learned medical community of the Renaissance strongly emphasized knowledge of ancient sources and authorities, so the texts in which these theories appear were familiar in the discipline. An apparently Aristotelian anthology addressing various fields, the *Problems* also had a broad readership beyond medical studies. However, whereas the original treatises of early modern medical writers report the Hippocratic-Galenic theory and its seven-celled counterpart, which involve no direct comment on same-sex sexual affinities, those writers do not, as far as I know, acknowledge the theories of congenital homoeroticism, even to reject them. It seems medical writers could publicly address such notions only in the course of composing a full-scale commentary on the original ancient or Arabic work. Otherwise, secondary reportage amounts to mere mentions of the author, as when *Rodrigo de Castro (1546–1623/9) cites Soranus of Ephesus on tribades (mediated through Caelius Aurelianus). Renaissance medical discourse on same-sex desires and practices appears to have been typically constituted by a paradox of unspeakable knowledge, whereby much of what highly valued ancient sources state on the subject (which would, according to conventional practice in the discipline, be cited often) could not even be restated, let alone further developed, in an independent original work in this field.

Former theories of congenital homoeroticism seem to have occasioned such tact among medical writers because thinking of pagan origin could otherwise appear to challenge Christian orthodoxy—probably a risky move, even if congenial, and contrary to the interests and ambitions of anyone within the privileged medical establishment. Authorities of the profession compelled the eminent surgeon *Ambroise Paré (c. 1510–1590) to excise even some relatively bland material on tribades from one of his books. Whereas medicine sought to provide materialist, "naturalistic" explanations for phenomena in its domain, and respected Greek and Roman medical experts had thus associated certain same-sex sexual behaviors with innate predispositions, according to Christian ideology such acts expressed a willful and grievously culpable corruption of soul, and constituted sins against nature, violations of reproductive sexual ends ordained by God (*Theology). As both religious and medical authors endlessly repeated, the body was to be considered God's own handiwork. But if someone were congenitally disposed to have sex "against nature," questions of determinism would awkwardly confront allegations of moral responsibility, and the "unnatural" act would accord with his or her nature. The extent of medical thinkers' religious conformity on same-sex sexual issues in their own personal sphere would have varied. However, much like their medieval counterparts, their public response, in independent treatises intended for dissemination, seems typically to bespeak an interdiction of silence, not only on possibilities of congenital causes but also on sex between males *tout court*.[6]

Yet medical conventions for comment on homoeroticism varied according to gender, for the discussion of feminine genitalia, unlike accounts of the penis and testicles (let alone mouth and anus), often included some treatment of sex between females, though that still tended to avoid explicit acknowledgment of the implications of any putative congenital factors as such. Thomas Bartholin (1616–1680) on the clitoris exemplifies this early modern discursive convention and its anxious masculine fancies: "In some women it grows as big as the Yard of a man, so that some women abuse the same, and make use thereof in place of a man's Yard, exercising carnal Copulation one with another, and they are termed *Confricatrices*, Rubsters. Which lascivious Practice is said to have been invented by one Philaenis, and Sappho the Greek Poetess is reported to have practiced the same. And of these I conceive the Apostle Paul speaks in the I of Romans 26. And therefore this part is called *Contemptu virorum*, the Contempt of Mankind."[7] On homoerotic usages of male genitals he and his colleagues typically say nothing in such anatomical contexts. This assymetry of female and male homoeroticism in early modern medical discourse reflects the lesser gravity often attributed to sex between females, and the heteroerotic standpoint of the authors, who seek to titillate male readers with revelations of feminine "sexual secrets," so that in this sense medical discourse converged somewhat with erotica.[8] Female contributions to reproduction were less medically valued than male sperm, so that, as Judith Brown observes, the willfully nonprocreative expenditure of the latter appeared the greater scandal. And if females had no seed, as some believed, they could not, unlike male same-sex lovers, undergo the perceived pollution of spilling seed in a wrongful vessel.[9]

Despite the apparent early modern embargo on secondary medical reportage of the ancients' theories of congenital homoeroticism in print, these notions would not have been obscure in the learned medical community and its circles of interlocutors, for the original texts containing these propositions were widely studied. The repertoire of medical knowledge thus afforded some apparently scientific rationales for distinct, inborn sexual dispositions, through which some persons were thought innately characterized by certain exceptional sexual desires and affinities, unlike the majority. These rationales that happened to survive from antiquity (there were probably others) assume that masculine nature should be relatively assertive, hence "active" or insertive, and feminine the contrary, so that nonconforming behavior indicates chronic "illness" or physical malformation. It is nonetheless so definitive for the person that it constitutes his or her nature, different from normative nature but stemming from innate causes, and naturalized in that broader sense. In this context, the Greek and Roman vocabularly of disease and affliction lacks the pathologizing homophobic animus that it would now have, for any "predilection for various kinds of excessive or disgraceful behavior was capable of being called a disease," including immoderate heteroerotic desire.[10] Since these ancient causal analyses of same-sex sexual behaviors depend on an active/passive gender distinction, a male who had sex with males appeared to remain within the expected scope of masculinity so long as he was not penetrated. As far as we know, the homoerotic behaviors that anciently occasioned medical interest, so that identities of sexual deviance were posited for them, involve inversions of the sex roles deemed conventional: male insertive, female receptive. Of course, those who were learned or academically connected enough to encounter these arguments in the Renaissance would also have known the much broader mythic naturalization of sex differences by Plato's Aristophanes in the *Symposium*, classified not by sexual role but by the genders coupled (male/female, male/male, female/female), and hereditary (189C–93E; *General Introduction). As *Pietro d'Abano (1257–1315/16) indicates, Renaissance responses to Greek and Roman medical accounts of homoeroticism would have involved Christian notions of nature and "sins against nature," whether through anachronistic confusions, antipagan reactions, or dissidence.

Aside from issues of causation, academic medicine most affected early modern notions of same-sex desire through momentous redefinitions of gender difference and the female body, resulting mainly from the sixteenth-century renewal of anatomy through human dissections. Although ancient Greek medical writers had identified the clitoris as a specific organ characteristic of feminine genitalia and sexual sensitivity, terminological confusions rendered it obscure to their later European counterparts until sixteenth-century anatomical research enabled its "rediscovery." Despite rival claimants such as Realdo Colombo (1494–1559?), that was often attributed to Gabriele Falloppio (1523?–1562).[11] His published announcement, in a work written about 1550 but not printed until 1561, likens the clitoris to the penis:

> Avicenna, in Book 3, fen 21, close to the end, recalls a certain part situated in a woman's privates, which he calls a "penis" (*virgam*) or *albathara*. Albucasis, in Book 2, chapter 71, calls it a "tumescence" (*tentiginem*), which sometimes increases to such a size that women can have sexual relations with other women as if they were men. The Greeks call this part κλητορίδα [i.e., clitoris], from which comes the obscene verb κλητορίζειν ["to touch lasciviously"]. Our anatomists all but ignore it, and have never assigned a term to it. This little particle is parallel to the male penis....[12]

The early modern medical reemergence of this putatively phallic feminine organ so disrupted the understanding of gender difference that Andreas Vesalius (1514–1564) considered it aberrant, not typical of women. Since female genitals had already been deemed fully correspondent to male ones anyway, an apparently superadded "minipenis" provoked profound reevaluations. All women came to appear in a sense hermaphroditic and, partly as a consequence of the current reassessments of sex and gender, medical writing evinces much interest in hermaphrodites at this time (*Prodigious Monstrosities). The new accounts of feminine genitals acknowledging the clitoris contextualized it in terms of hermaphroditism, supposed feminine potential for labial and clitoral hypertrophy, tribadic sex including penetration with such genital enlargements, and clitoridectomy or nymphotomia as means of controlling such possibilities. This commentary, Katharine Park argues, established a medical paradigm of the "phallic tribade," the penetrative woman who could make love to her own sex and usurp masculine prerogatives, with the quasiphallic configuration of her own genitalia.[13] In thus seeking to account for sexual love between females through presumed feminine genital anomalies conferring special capacities for surrogate manhood, early modern medical discourse tacitly supplemented ancient arguments for innate causation of same-sex sexual behaviors while avoiding any explicit recognition that tribadic dispositions could be congenital, and ignoring the morally heterodox implications (cf. Traub, 213–14). This approach continued into the seventeenth century, as in Bartholin's anatomical handbook (Bartholin, 61–62, 75–77).

According to Valerie Traub, the sixteenth- and seventeenth-century anatomical mapping of the tribadic body "produces and is produced by an anatomical essentialism—the riveting of body part to behavior—that continues to underpin modern discourses of sexuality" and "construction of the homo/hetero divide" (208, 218, 220). While acknowledging this development was based on ancient models, she nonetheless finds it distinctively early modern (217). However, Bernadette J. Brooten insists the precedents for medical linkage of female homoerotic behaviors with a correspondent sexual persona are indeed antique.[14] The implications of premodern medical sources for male homoeroticism are correlative, for they too evince some perceived anatomical and temperamental essentialisms of ancient provenance. However, as Traub remarks on tribades, these "only intermittently and incoherently map on to contemporary understandings" (220).

By upsetting imputed homologies between masculine and feminine genitals, whereby the vagina appeared the inverted feminine counterpart of the penis, anatomical rediscovery of the clitoris also facilitated the recognition that males and females constitute two genitally distinct sexes. According to Aristotle, females are a natural imperfection relative to males, and Galen argues that female genitals are fully correlative to male ones, but remain internal and relatively undeveloped rather than being extruded by the greater heat ascribed to masculine constitution. Hence females can possibly change into males, but never the reverse. Defined by falling short of an Aristotelian-Galenic masculine paradigm of human fulfillment that defined not only bodily but also mental capacities and the extent of rational self-control, the feminine gender appeared inherently inferior, and that prejudice drew further support from various correlative misconceptions such as the menstrual taboo.[15] If genital potential alone were taken into account, as Thomas Laqueur observes, there would thus appear only one, ideally masculine sex, although Park and Joan Cadden rightly caution that medieval and early modern concepts of sex and gender were complex, and assumed significant sex differences.[16] Nevertheless, only in the early 1590s did the "one-sex" Galenic genital theory begin to be challenged in print, apparently first by the anatomist *André du Laurens (1558–1609), and controversy ensued long after.[17] Bartholin still thought the Galenic view worth challenging in the later seventeenth century (61–62). While Galen's position, with its assumptions of feminine imperfection, would have tended to promote both male and female homosocial bonding and thus homoeroticism, it might also have somewhat countered the taboo against same-sex desire. If the genitals are in some sense at one anyway, some might have rationalized, why confine sexual practices to male-female possibilities?[18] On the other hand, the strict subordination of feminity in the one-sex model would likely have further marginalized effeminate males, especially those who enjoyed receptive roles in same-sex love, because they would appear monstrously to reverse the presumption that a male, being "superior," cannot become his "natural inferior," female. Tribades with masculine affinities could have found encouragement in the latent male potential of feminity in this model, yet that nonetheless rendered them ambitious interlopers on the other sex's presumed supremacy. The genital confirmation of sexual dimorphism, which continued to be controversial long into the seventeenth century as Bartholin indicates, redefined males and females, and thus also the cultural implications of same-sex love.

Another new medical factor profoundly affecting the early modern European experience and ramifications of sex in general was the advent of syphilis, or, if it previously existed in Europe as some argue, an especially vicious new type.[19] The French disease, as it was most commonly called, seemed to have originated in Italy in the mid-1490s, where many attributed it to the French army of King Charles VIII besieging Naples, and spread rapidly. Its virulence and gross disfigurements—numerous boils, abcesses, grotesque bodily swellings and putrefactions, and striking disintegration of body parts such as eyes, nose, and genitals—provoked horror. After the spectacular outbreak and initial contagion, the disease weakened somewhat during the course of the sixteenth century according to early modern medical writings. The numerous theories of its origin included a maleficent astrological conjunction, influx from the New World with Columbus, and, as Paracelsus claimed, the copulation of a French leper with a menstruous Neapolitan whore. Marginalized social groups, such as Jews, prostitutes, and women, provided scapegoats. Assuming syphilis came from the New World, Gonzalo Fernández de Oviedo (1478–1557) claimed that God had justly imposed it there to punish the prevalence (in his view) of sodomy, meaning anal intercourse between males, among its peoples.[20] But this homophobic etiology seems not to have gained currency beyond Oviedo's own publications, even though "gonorrhea" had long been falsely etymologized from "Gomorrah," on account of that city's allegedly vain, nonprocreative spilling of seed.[21] Although the French disease was often considered venereal, just as female prostitution was frequently blamed, other means of transmission were posited, such as food, drink, and toilet seats. Often represented as a divine scourge, it thus ostensibly punished sexual or other sins, or heralded the apocalypse, so that this further human suffering was manipulated to serve religious agendas.

Nevertheless, early modern medical publications appear to have long maintained silence on the relations of same-sex sexual behaviors to the French disease. Not only the conventional reluctance to acknowledge such love seems responsible. Medical discussion of this disease homosocially focused on females as alleged agents and vehicles of infection, so that syphilis tended to be conceived in terms of heteroerotic intercourse. Although the disease erupted unpredictably throughout the body, so that sites of contraction were ambiguous, practitioners would have encountered some oral and anal infections in males who evinced some subtle yet not imperceptible relaxation of the anal sphincter. There were continental sodomy investigations, as in Lucca, in which that constituted forensic evidence. Yet the disease continued to be publicly described as if female bodies were its primary site and vehicle, or as if it arose specifically from the vaginal mingling of opposed masculine and feminine principles.[22] Whatever the private beliefs or intentions of medical writers, then, sex between males, and perhaps between females to some extent, would have seemed relatively exempt from the French disease. In a sonnet by the reputedly sodomitical poet

Théophile de Viau (1590–1626), the speaker blames a woman for his venereal infection, and vows, "Dear God, if I survive.../ I'll never fuck anything but ass."[23] Even around 1700, the possibility of contraction in sex between males was still dubious, as *John Marten (fl. 1704–d. 1737) assumes; supposed immunity from this fearsome disease may well have encouraged such sex. In urban centres with substantial concentrations of sodomites, sympathetic or discreet medical practitioners presumably became known among those who could afford to retain medical help for venereal diseases. Assumptions of heteroerotic contraction would have much more readily accommodated female same-sex lovers than sexually penetrated sodomites.

The former demographics of death due to the limits of medical knowledge would have significantly affected the representations, psychology, and rationales of same-sex desires and practices. European infant mortality averaged about 250 deaths per 1,000 live births within the first year, versus under 10 per 1,000 today, and approximately an additional quarter would have died before reaching the age of fifteen.[24] The country was relatively healthy compared with the unsanitary overcrowded cities. London, for example, depended on new arrivals for both population maintainance and growth, for deaths outnumbered births there. The much higher incidence of maternal deaths resulting from pregnancy and childbirth would have increased the possibilities of sexual traumas for children. Early modern theological and medical emphases on the divinely instituted responsibilities of reproductive sex implicitly sought to counter its inherently strong prospects of death and bereavement, which nonprocreative sexual options would not so much incur. Antipathy toward same-sex love was probably driven in part by anxieties about sustaining population and the social structure dependent on reproductive continuance of privileged families.

Pseudo-Aristotle (assembled c. 350 B.C.E.–c. 500 C.E.?)

The physiological discussion of male desire for receptive anal intercourse most widely available in early modern Europe would probably have been a comment in the *Problems*, an ancient Greek text rediscovered around 1300 and attributed to Aristotle. Not only his prestige as "the Philosopher" ensured its currency, but also its constitution as a "book of problems": a genre of natural philosophy that furnished proto-encyclopedias and compendia of curiosities.[25] Although it is an incrementally assembled pseudepigraphic compilation of which the extant text may be a version of the fifth or even sixth century C.E., this text long appeared canonical on account of its incorporation of passages accredited to Aristotle in ancient sources, and his known composition of a lost eponymous work.[26] As a whole, the *Problems* proposes answers to a long series of questions about natural, medical, cultural, and psychological phenomena.

According to a census sampling seven of the many editions of Aristotle's complete works published between 1483 and 1619 (four Latin, one Greek, two bilingual), all but the Latin edition of 1483 include the *Problems*.[27] It appeared in numerous other editions, whether singly or together with other treatises, so that its total sixteenth-century printings in Latin translation alone exceed one hundred.[28] Although texts purporting to be vernacular translations were published in English, French, German, and Italian, at least the English versions are actually a medieval compilation that includes nothing from the ancient pseudo-Aristotelian source.[29] Edwardine statutes of Merton College at Oxford establish the ancient *Problems*' curricular inclusion, at least in the 1540s.[30] From its medieval rediscovery through the seventeenth century, Ann Blair shows (179, 186), it continued to attract commentators such as *Pietro d'Abano (1257–1315/6).

The supposed Aristotle's account of males who seek to be anally penetrated assumes that such an individual either has a specific anatomy in which his own semen discharges into his anus, producing a correspondent sexual desire and mode of release, or has become habituated to enjoying sexual penetration there, partly through prior reception of another's semen in that part. Lustfulness and effeminacy can be ancillary factors. Males who enjoy receptive anal intercourse thus either have an innate bodily structure that renders them sexually intermediate, or an analogous condition becomes their "second nature." In both cases, their exceptional sexual desire expresses a distinctive personal condition inscribed in body and mind either innately or through sexual experience. Comparative study of the treatment of this particular section by Latin and other translators and by commentators has yet to be undertaken; nor do we know whether it also appears in any medieval and Renaissance compilations of problems, nor the extent to which topics of same-sex sexual behaviors were unspeakable in those postclassical versions of the genre. However, Lodovico Ricchieri (1469–1525) fully reports it in his encyclopedic miscellany (*Encyclopedias and Reference Works).

The Problems, 4.26[31] (?before c. 500 C.E.)

Why do some men enjoy sexual intercourse when they play an active part and some when they do not? Is it because for each waste product there is a place into which it naturally secretes, and, when energy is employed, the breath, as it passes out, causes swelling, and expels the waste product; for instance urine passes into the bladder, and desiccated food into the stomach, tears into the eyes, mucus into the nostrils, and blood into the veins? Just in the same way semen passes into the testicles and privates. In those whose passages are not in a natural condition, but either because those leading to the testicles are blocked, as occurs with eunuchs and in other impotent persons, or for some other reason, such moisture flows into the fundament; for it passes in this direction. This is proved by the contraction of this part in intercourse and the wasting of the parts about the fundament. If then a man indulges in sexual intercourse to excess, the semen collects in these parts, so that when desire comes, then that part desires friction in which it is collected. The desire arises partly from food and *partly from imagination.* For when he is excited by anything, the breath races to that part and such waste product flows into its natural place. If, then, it is light or full of breath, when this passes out, the tension ceases without the emission of moisture, as it does sometimes both with boys and adults. [This also occurs] when the moisture dries up. If, however, neither of these results occurs, desire continues until one of them happens. But the naturally effeminate are so circumstanced that little or no secretion occurs in the place in which it occurs with normal persons, but it is secreted in this region.[32] The reason is that such persons are unnaturally constituted; for though they are male this part of them has become maimed.[33] Such maiming produces either complete destruction or a distortion of type. The former is impossible in their case for it would imply their becoming female. So it must involve distortion and an impulse in some direction other than the discharge of semen. So they are unsatisfied, like women; for the moisture is slight and does not force an exit and is quickly chilled. Those with whom the semen travels to the fundament desire to be passive, and those with whom it settles in both places desire to be active and passive in sexual intercourse; in whichever direction it inclines the more, so do their desires. In some cases this state is the result of habit. For men are accustomed to enjoy what they normally do, and to emit semen accordingly. So they desire to do that by which this may occur and so habit tends to become second nature. For this reason those who have not been accustomed to submit to sexual intercourse before puberty but at about that time, because they have recollection of their enjoyment and pleasure is associated with the recollection, because of their habit desire the passive state, as if it were natural, numerous occasions and habit having the same effect as nature. If a man happens to be both lustful and effeminate, this is all the more likely to occur.

Caelius Aurelianus (c. 400 c.e.)

One of the most substantial medical statements on sex between males printed in the Renaissance appears in the ancient Roman physician Caelius Aurelianus's treatise *On Chronic Diseases,* and he defines it partly in relation to tribadism. In Caelius's usage, "tribade" denotes only the more assertive partner. His text is largely based on a second-century Greek treatise of Soranus of Ephesus, no longer extant. Although not unknown in the Middle Ages, as some medieval citations show, Caelius's study became much more accessible in the sixteenth century through print: first at Basel (1529), then Venice (1547) and Lyons (1567, 1569). No further editions followed until after 1700.[34]

The discussion broadly accommodates same-sex sexual acts in general, rather than focusing on any one in particular. Caelius defines so-called "active" tribadism and "passive" male homoeroticism as chronic conditions resulting either from the way male and female seed mixes at conception (a theory he attributes to Parmenides, c. 450 b.c.e.), or from hereditary transmission. Gender determines natural and thus appropriate sexual activity, in his view, in the sense that healthy males are to assume an insertive role and healthy females the reverse. Although he assumes contrary behavior manifests an enduring, personally characteristic "disease of the mind," that lacks any current, specifically homophobic sense, and rather has correlations with other types of supposedly excessive or disgraceful conduct (*Medicine). Caelius's active and passive categories are not necessarily procreative, so that normative masculinity can include insertive or otherwise assertive sexual relations with other males. On treatment of satyriasis, for example, he assumes that boys may well arouse sexually healthy adult males.[35] However, he makes no parallel allowance for the healthiness of passive feminine response to tribades and might assume that sex between females is unhealthy for both partners because it excludes phallic penetration (Brooten, 161–62). Also translated by Caelius, Soranus's treatise on gynecology counsels clitoridectomy for an "oversized" clitoris, because it allegedly conduces a sexually active, phallic role, rejection of sex with men, and feminine disorder. This became common advice in medieval and early modern Arabic and European medical writing on women (Brooten, 162–71). Caelius's categories of sexual analysis reflect anxiety to maintain the sexually penetrative privilege of the phallus and patriarchal control. However, his system establishes both male and female homoeroticism as a sexual category sharply distinguished from heteroeroticism, precisely because he considers same-sex sexual acts distinctively unhealthy—either for the passive partner, if between males, or for both, if between females (Brooten, 162). Though male and female sex-role inversions are contrary to Caelius's normative model of human nature, they evince specific characteristics of such individuals that are intrinsic to their deviant natures, innate, and in that sense natural to them.

On Chronic Diseases[36] *(c. 200 / c. 400* C.E.*)*

4.9 On Effeminate Men or Pathics

People find it hard to believe that effeminate men or pathics really exist.[37] The fact is that, though the practices of such persons are unnatural to human beings, lust overcomes modesty and puts to shameful use parts intended for other functions. That is, in the case of certain individuals, there is no limit to their desire and no hope of satisfying it; and they cannot be content with their own lot, the lot which divine providence had marked out for them in assigning definite functions to the parts of the body. They even adopt the dress, walk, and other characteristics of women. Now this condition is different from a bodily disease; it is rather an affliction of a diseased mind. Indeed, often out of passion and in rare cases out of respect for certain persons to whom they are beholden, these pathics suddenly change their character and for a while try to give proof of their virility. But since they are not aware of their limitations, they are again the victims of excesses, subjecting their virility to too great a strain and consequently involving themselves in worse vices. And it is our opinion that these persons suffer no impairment of sensation. For, as Soranus says, this affliction comes from a corrupt and debased mind. Indeed, the victims of this malady may be compared to the women who are called tribades because they pursue both kinds of love. These women are more eager to lie with women than with men; in fact, they pursue women with almost masculine jealousy, and when they are freed or temporarily relieved of their passion...[38] they rush, as if victims of continual intoxication, to new forms of lust, and, sustained by this disgraceful mode of life, they rejoice in the abuse of their sexual powers. So the pathics, like the tribades, are victims of an affliction of the mind. For there exists no bodily treatment which can be applied to overcome the disease; it is rather the mind that is affected in these disgraceful vices, and it is consequently the mind that must be controlled. For no man has ever overcome bodily lust by playing the woman's sexual role, or gained relief by contact with a penis. In general, the relief of pain and disease is achieved by other means.[39] Thus the account of a cure as given by Clodius obviously refers to a case of ascarides. The latter, as we showed in our chapter on worms, are small worms arising in the parts of the rectum.

Parmenides in his work *On Nature* indicates that effeminate men or pathics may come into being as a result of a circumstance at conception. Since his account is contained in a Greek poem, I shall also give my version in poetry. For I have done my best to compose Latin verses of the same kind, to avoid the commingling of the two languages: "When man and woman mingle the seeds of love that spring from their veins, a formative power maintaining proper proportions molds well-formed bodies from this diverse blood. For if, when the seed is mingled, the forces contained therein clash and do not fuse into one, then cruelly will they plague with double seed the sex of the offspring." Thus Parmenides holds that the seminal fluids are not merely material bodies but possess active principles, and if these fluids mingle in such a way as to form a unified force in the body, they will thereby produce a desire appropriate to the sex of the individual. But if, despite the mingling of the seminal matter, the active principles fail to merge, a desire for both forms of love will harass the offspring.[40]

On the other hand, many leaders of the other sects hold that the condition which we are discussing is an inherited disease, that is to say, is passed on from generation to generation by way of the seed. For this they do not blame nature, since the latter shows us its strict purity by the example of the brute animals, whom philosophers call "nature's mirrors." These physicians place the blame rather on the human race, because, having once incurred the defects, it retains them and cannot rid itself of them by any kind of renovation, and leaves no opportunity for a fresh start...[41] though other diseases, whether hereditary or adventitious, in the great majority of cases become weaker as the body grows older; this is true, for example, of podagera, epilepsy, and mania, which unquestionably become milder in the patient's declining years. The fact is that whatever irritates will produce its strongest effect when the underlying matter offers strong opposition; but, since such opposition fades in the case of old people, disease, like strength, is also blunted. But the affliction under discussion, which produces effeminate men or pathics, is the only one that becomes stronger as the body grows older. It causes a hideous and ever increasing lust. And there is good reason why this takes place. For in other years when the body is still strong and can perform the normal functions of love, the sexual desire [of these persons] assumes a dual aspect, in which the soul is excited sometimes while playing a passive role and sometimes while playing an active role. But in the case of old men who have lost their virile powers, all their sexual desire is turned in the opposite direction and consequently exerts a stronger demand for the feminine role in love. In fact, many infer that this is the reason why boys too are victims of this affliction. For, like old men, they do not possess virile powers; that is, they have not yet attained those powers which have already deserted the aged.

Avicenna or Ibn Sīnā (980–1037)

A central text for European university medical curricula and medical learning in general from the thirteenth to mid-seventeenth centuries, Avicenna's *Canon of Medicine* consecutively discusses males who have receptive anal intercourse, hermaphrodites, and apparently how masculine failure to satisfy a female sexual partner can induce her to embrace homoerotic behaviors. It provided a massive systematic synthesis of Greek, Roman, and Arabic medical knowledge, largely according to Galenic medical paradigms and Aristotelian natural philosophy. Starting with Gerard of Cremona's twelfth-century translation, Latin was the dominant medium of the *Canon*'s medieval and early modern European currency. Between 1500 and 1674, for example, over sixty complete or partial editions were published, and almost all were in Latin, not to speak of the numerous Latin commentaries. Only three editions during those years appeared in another language, Arabic, of which two also gave Latin translations.[42]

Much remains to be done in comparative study of early modern translators' and commentators' representations of the *Canon*'s passages on homoerotic desires and practices. Gerard, whose translation remained the sole published Latin version until the 1520s, did not censor them, and subsequent translators, seeking greater accuracy, probably tended to follow suit. Many editions of the *Canon* included commentaries, and their standpoints vary. In two medieval discussions of these passages that continued to be published in the sixteenth century, Gentile da Foligno (d. 1348) obfuscates their treatment of same-sex love, whereas Jacques Despars (c. 1380–1458) confronts those issues directly but amplifies condemnation, citing Sodom's destruction.[43]

The relevant section of the *Canon* appears in Book III, on illnesses of the body grouped according to organ affected, in fen (or part) 20. This fen and its successor, the penultimate one in Book III, focus on reproduction, and that topic suggests they were among the *Canon*'s better known parts.[44] As in Greek and Roman medical treatises, Avicenna's scope excludes comment on males exclusively insertive in homoerotic anal sex, presumably for much the same reason, that this "active" role remained more readily reconcilable with perceived masculine norms. Despite condemning sexual intercourse with children in general, Avicenna claims coitus with a boy rather than a woman lessens seminal emission; since loss of semen reduced health and longevity according to Aristotle, paedophilia could thus be advantageous.[45] However, Avicenna assumes that at least an adult male who seeks to be anally penetrated has an incurable mental affliction that can only be restrained by punishments. Though he associates such sexual behavior with effeminacy and bad character, his most favored causal explanation posits an interaction between a constitutionally high degree of sexual desire and some physical and perhaps also psychological inability to achieve sexual release through adoption of an insertive role. In his view, such a condition provokes moral indictment for perceived feebleness related to effeminacy, and contrary to masculinity. Although he dismisses an alternative theory positing a unique nervous structure that would foster male desire for anally receptive stimulation, and which would constitute a wholly innate cause, his review of this rationale nonetheless invites consideration of such possibilities, and *Pietro d'Abano (1257–1315/6) exploits it accordingly. In various ways in the *Canon*, male homoerotic receptiveness to anal intercourse appears a phenomenon irremediably arising from a complex of psychological and physical factors specific to persons with such desires. It would not seem a casual matter, then, nor a sequence of disconnected sexual acts that have no implications for personal identity.

Avicenna then considers full physical realization of sexual indeterminacy: hermaphroditism, which turns out to be easier to resolve, ironically, through the expedient of surgical intervention. The sexually penetrable male remains refractory. But the pairing of these chapters implicitly encourages hypotheses of anatomical or physiological causation, as *Pietro again indicates.

Further addressing issues of sex and generation, Avicenna defines the role and means of sexual pleasure in heteroerotic copulation, ignoring the clitoris. Wives sexually unsatisfied by their husbands take lovers; their ambiguous gender and Avicenna's stress on rubbing suggest tribadic possibilities. Relative to his comment on anally receptive males, Avicenna's discourse here is at least morally neutral, though elliptical.

The Canon of Medicine[46] *(c. 1010)*
Book Three, fen 20, tr. 1

CHAPTER 11: THE [MEDICAL] DISADVANTAGES OF SEXUAL INTERCOURSE; DIFFERENT STYLES AND POSITIONS

    ... Sexual intercourse with children is regarded as repugnant by most nations, and is forbidden by the law. In some respects, it is [medically] more harmful, and in some respects less harmful. It is more harmful because in this [kind of intercourse] Nature lacks the powerful movement required to draw out the sperm. In other respects it is less harmful because with a boy, the amount of sperm expelled is not as great as with a woman. And it is accompanied by less of an indication of its presence than [coitus in] the vulva.[47]

CHAPTER 42: CONCERNING "ALUMINATI"[48]

Aluminati is in fact a disease which befalls a man who is accustomed to have other men lie upon him [i.e., who takes a receptive or "passive" sexual role]. He has great sexual desire, and a great deal of sperm which is not moved. His heart is feeble, and his erection is feeble at the root; or else he is now become feeble who was once much given to sexual intercourse. For this reason, he strives after [intercourse], but is incapable of it; or is capable of it only through the power of imagination (*potentia meditatiua*), and therefore he desires to see vigorous sexual intercourse between a couple, and [if] the person with him is nearer (? *propinquior est ille qui est cum eo*), then is his desire stirred up. If he emits sperm when someone is having sexual intercourse with him, or his member becomes erect, then he is bound to satisfy his desire.

There is a certain category (*secta*) of men whose desire is not aroused or stirred unless someone has sexual intercourse with them, and then they experience the pleasure of emitting sperm, whether they actually do so or not. And there is a category of men who do not emit sperm when they engage in sexual intercourse, and in fact these men stoop to sexual union with other men. In truth, these men are debased in soul, malign in nature, evil in their habits, and of a womanly constitution. Sometimes their sexual organs are larger than those of males. You should be aware that apart from this, everything which is said [concerning these men] is without foundation.

The men who try to cure these people are foolish, for the cause of their illness lies in their imagination (*meditatiuum*); it is not natural. The only cure is to break their desire through sadness, hunger, sleeplessness, imprisonment, and flogging.

Some say that the cause of *aluminati* is this: in these people, the nerve of sensation which leads to the penis is divided into two branches, of which the delicate one continues to the root of the penis, while the coarse one bends toward the head of the penis. For this reason, the delicate [nerve] needs to be rubbed vigorously before it will feel anything. Therefore one lies on top of this man, and then he experiences the fulfillment of his desire. But this explanation is far from the truth. The first explanation offered above is more reliable. And some say that [this condition] can be induced by [magical?] knowledge, or by the malign arts[49]; and all of what they relate on this subject has been confirmed.

CHAPTER 43: ABOUT THE HERMAPHRODITE

In a person who is a hermaphrodite, there is neither a male member nor a female one alone. Some of them have both, but one member is rather less visible and weaker, while the opposite is true for the other. There are some in which both members are equal. And it occurs to me that some of these take the active role and some the passive role, but there is little evidence concerning this. Often they are cured by cutting away the less visible member, and then by medical management (*regimen*) of the wound.

CHAPTER 44: THE PHYSICIAN IS EXCUSED FOR TEACHING ABOUT SEXUAL PLEASURE; ABOUT TIGHTENING THE VAGINA (RECEPTRICIS) AND ABOUT WARMING IT

It is not disgraceful for a physician to speak of enlarging the penis and narrowing the vagina, and about [enhancing] the sexual pleasure of women. This is because it touches on the causes by which generation is impeded. For often the small size of the penis is the reason why a woman finds no pleasure in it, for it is different from what she is used to, and so she emits no sperm [i.e., does not have an orgasm], and when no sperm is emitted, there is no child. Sometimes this is why she deserts her husband and seeks out another man. Similarly when the woman is not tight enough, her husband is not properly proportioned to her, nor she to her husband, and there is mutual dissatisfaction. Likewise, sexual pleasure promotes rapid emission of sperm; but women in many cases are slow to emit sperm, and their desire remains unsatisfied, and for this reason there is no pregnancy. These women remain unsatisfied, and for this reason, those who are not supervised will lie beneath whomever[50] they can impose upon, and for this cause they resort to rubbing so that they may achieve what their desire lacks by using what comes between them (*in eo quod est inter eas*).

Pietro d'Abano (1257–1315/16)

The commentary on *pseudo-Aristotle's *Problems* most often published during the Renaissance, Pietro d'Abano's was completed by 1310,[51] and strongly endorses the ancient text's naturalistic approach to explaining why some males enjoy receptive anal intercourse. They thus constitute a sexually distinct group analogous to women and hermaphrodites. This Italian physician, philosopher, and astrologer was born near Padua at Abano, studied first in Padua, and traveled widely, including lengthy residences in Constantinople and Paris. Around 1305 he returned to Padua and taught medicine and philosophy at the university. Besides authoring astrologically inflected works on those subjects, he produced translations, including a Latin version of the pseudo-Aristotelian *Problems* based on a Greek manuscript he acquired in Constantinople. There is no evidence of marriage, but he fathered several sons. Though charged with heresy and acquitted during his life, he was posthumously convicted, disinterred, and burned[52]; his medical renown and reputation as a magician long endured. Many manuscripts of his Latin commentary on the *Problems* survive, and there were eight editions between 1475 and 1582, all published in Italy except for one in Paris (1520).[53]

Pietro's effort to comment in a scientific way on male anal homoeroticism rather than glossing over that part of the *Problems* breaks a conventional silence of contemporary European medicine and natural philosophy on that topic, which was typically referred rather to moral and religious interpretation. Favoring physical explanations for natural phenomena rather than recourse to ostensible divine causes, he was also open to pursuing ideas that could be deemed heretical. By applying the standard techniques of scholarship in his time and martialling respected authorities, he normalizes the subject for scientific inquiry.[54]

His discussion of the supposed Aristotle's comment largely reproduces the principal elements of his source, but with revealing modifications. The source's association of the sexually insertive role with masculinity ensures that, despite the much greater length of Pietro's exposition, males who have sexual relations with their own sex without ever being receptive are of little interest according to the parameters of the discussion, since they adhere to the presumed masculine insertive norm. Pietro's thought on the topic also follows his source's distinction between, on one hand, an innate, physiologically determined male pursuit of receptive anal intercourse, and, on the other, a habitually acquired desire for that, constituting a sexual "second nature." Aristotle himself had commented similarly in the *Nicomachean Ethics* (7.5.3–4). However, Pietro adds various clarifications, so that, toward the end, for example, he notes that his ancient source appears mainly to address penile-anal insertion, whereas there are other means of sodomitical relations, he says, such as rubbing the penis between a boy's thighs. Elaborating on the original's brief comparisons of cinaedi to females, he claims they share the insatiable sexual desire Aristotle ascribes to feminity. In this way too, then, cinaedi are sexually intermediate, with an erotic psychology and physiology markedly different from so-called masculine norms. Rejecting *Avicenna's objections, Pietro further endorses the Greek text's claim that a specific innate bodily structure conduces male desires for receptive anal coitus. According to the Italian, the existence of hermaphrodites, who are yet more anomalous in relation to natural norms, shows there is no reason why the particular sexual desires of cinaedi could not be caused congenitally. He finally observes that *Ptolemy provides an astrological rationale for congenital causation.

Despite Pietro's strong support of his ancient source's assumption that some males innately desire receptive anal intercourse, he nonetheless introduces further censure, including the Christian concept of sodomy. He would have known his position is thus at least somewhat self-contradictory: How can someone have full moral liability for behaving in accord with specific personal characteristics that are distinctively congenital? Pietro's affinities for astrological determinism, which was attacked for compromising free will, moral culpability, and hence Christian orthodoxy (*Astrology), would have ensured his familiarity with such issues. While censure could thus still, in theory, consistently target the habitual variety of cinaedus, as opposed to the congenital type, that would not resolve the ethical problem, for Pietro offers no practical means to distinguish the mode of causation in individual cases. And if the male body's structure is such that receptive anal sex is so enjoyable as to become "second nature" simply through habit, whatever the congenital circumstances, that sexual practice is arguably not "against nature." His final report of a general astrological cause tends further to challenge rationales for affixing personal blame for such sexual behaviors, and his discussion includes no biblical citations. The tenets of the ancient source and Pietro's developments of them variously contradict his gestures of Christian contextualization. Whether he himself was uncertain or was providing a conventional cover for a line of inquiry with deliberately heterodox implications here, his comment challenges prevailing religious notions of sodomy by publicizing and supporting natural explanations. These entail an allowance for males whose anally receptive homoerotic practice expresses a particular, congenitally determined same-sex sexual affiliation.

Commentary on the Problems of Aristotle[55] *(c. 1310)*

> *Translator's note: the lemmata of the text of* **pseudo-Aristotle's "Problems"* *appear as in the English translation reproduced in this anthology (Loeb edition), to facilitate reference.*

> In this chapter, Aristotle poses two questions. The first is, Why do those on whom the sex act is carried out, such as women or those analogous to women, enjoy it and take pleasure in it? Or why do they enjoy coitus whether they are taking the active or the passive role? And this pertains directly to the second question: why do some men take the active and the passive role, and some only the passive?

> *It is because . . . :* Aristotle solves the first problem first, and the second problem second, the second being at *In those whose passages. . . .* The first question is in three parts. In the first part, Aristotle assigns a cause to the first doubtful point, saying that for this reason some men take delight and mutual enjoyment in coitus. In every man, digestion takes place from which he receives some nutriment. The surplus of this nutriment is naturally secreted into a particular location and receptacle, from this nature evacuates it. When retained for some time, it stimulates a windiness, as he says. Expulsion of this kind is caused by exertion and movement. Windiness is provoked, which first induces a swelling in the place through which it passes before it makes its exit. Then, by means of exertion and movement, the surplus is expelled from the place where it was, and cast out of the body, as can be seen in sick people.[56] Hence Avicenna in book 1, fen 1 [of the *Canon*]: Windiness helps in expulsion because it prevents dissolution, and this assists in expulsion, which is what [Avicenna] says. The production of this swelling contributes to enlarging the matter to

be expelled, and because it condenses and compacts the expelled matter laterally, drawing each superfluity into its receptacle; and Aristotle says this when he says *for instance urine.* He says that urine, which is the surplus of the second digestion, is evacuated into the bladder. For the bladder, as was said in the first book [of the *Problems*], is the receptacle of this undigested matter. The surplus of the aliment, that is, of the first digestion,[57] is called "stool," and is removed into the intestines, and retained in their three lower sections, namely the large intestine, colon and rectum. On the other hand, the three upper sections—the duodenum, jejunum and small intestine—retain the pure and nutritious aliment. Tears go into the eyes, whose surplus they are, and are expelled from the eye into the brain. Mucus, the surplus of the first and second ventricles of the brain,[58] is evacuated into the nostrils through the opening called "the sieve" or *alcasim,* which lies under the first ventricle.[59] Likewise blood is carried off into the veins, and so forth. At one time, someone included blood amongst the superfluities, even though it is the most natural of humors, the offspring of nature, whose natural place is in the veins.[60] It should be said that in this context we should take "blood" to mean superfluous melancholy blood, which is mingled with the superfluities of other humors; for menstrual blood or blood which issues from hemorrhoids is not natural blood.[61] We should take "veins" to mean the extremities of the veins, which end at the anus or the nose.[62] We should take the evacuation of this surplus to mean the evacuation of the entire surplus of the third digestion, for example, the insensible transpiration of sweat, so that the surplus of all [the stages of] digestion is covered here.

The same applies to the surplus of sperm which is the principle matter under consideration here. Aristotle says that in the same manner, sperm is secreted into the penis and evacuated with the help of the testicles. These [organs], as it is said, work vigorously to effect this secretion. The cause of delectation and pleasure is the fact that the surplus to be expelled is [in fact] expelled, and in the place where it naturally should be expelled, and in this the harmony of our constitution is preserved, and so forth. It should be noted that of all the forms of evacuation, coitus is the most pleasurable because the sensitive animal virtue[63] is at its most active in [coitus], since its matter passes through the most sensitive members. This [pleasure] is essential, because this act of evacuation is ordained not to preserve the individual, as are the other [kinds of evacuation], but to preserve the species. In the case of the other [acts of evacuation], the opposite is the case. And therefore because of its great necessity and usefulness, it was necessary that the highest degree of delectation be present, lest [coitus] be avoided because of the distaste it inspires. So animals are the more attracted to coitus because of the delight which is experienced in coitus, for delight itself strengthens the [bodily] operations, and makes them more durable and better, as is stated in [Aristotle's] *Ethics*, book 4.[64] The pleasure of receiving the sexual organs is proportionally less than the pleasure of inserting them, because[65] it is by natural and inspirited sense alone, surpassing the other members with its great delectation of desire, as Galen says in *The Usefulness of Parts*, book 4, and Haly [i.e., ibn Ridwan] in his commentary on [Galen's] *Tegni*, the treatise on signs.[66] This is because its desire is not for its own sake alone, but for the sake of the other members, just as coitus is not for the individual, but rather for that of the whole species.

In those [whose passages] . . . : Now he solves the second question, and first he presents a twofold division. He says that in those whose pores or passages are not naturally formed so that they terminate directly at the penis, two things can happen. Either those passages which terminate at the penis are distended by the interposition of matter, which blocks them, just as blindness can occur when viscous humor falls upon the optic nerve— this can be observed in eunuchs, in effeminate men or in eunuchs who lack testicles or who have only small and weak ones, or in those who are so cold and wet that they are reduced to the nature and habits of women— or it can happen in another way, that is, because the pores leading to the tip of the penis are not only blocked and obstructed as above, but because those leading to the tip of the penis are completely blocked, yet somewhat open towards the base of the penis and the anus. In these men, the spermatic moisture converges on the anus; dispersed by movement and rendered subtle by friction, it exits [there]. *This is proved* . . . : He proceeds by declaring the parts of the aforementioned division, so that the solution might be evident. First he deals with those in whom this moisture does not exit in a natural and free manner because they are this way from birth, and in the second place, he deals with this condition or disease in those to whom it has befallen because of an evil habit. The second part is at *Those with whom [the semen travels] to the fundament.* . . . Again, he first unfolds the second part of the aforementioned division, and secondly, the first, at *But the naturally [effeminate].* The first part is divided into three. For first he shows that in these men, spermatic moisture flows into the anus. He says that men of this type cannot emit spermatic moisture to the penis, but [only] to the anus, because when such men engage in coitus there is an accumulation and constriction around the upper end of the penis, and dissolution takes place, and the opening up of those parts which are around the anus, so that what takes place is the opposite to which ought to happen in natural coitus, as is shown in the *second* problem. For this reason, just as in this kind of coitus [i.e., the "natural" type], the spermatic fluid around the anus is forced, as if pressed out by a hand, to go to the penis, so in these men, since everything takes place in the opposite way, this moisture has to be emitted to the anus.

And therefore should someone have an excessive amount of the matter of coitus [i.e., sperm], or perhaps if there is a need for another evacuation, the spermatic matter goes to the region around the anus. For this reason, when the appetite for coitus comes upon him, he desires to expel the spermatic matter by friction and vigorous motion at the place where it accumulates naturally—in accordance with its monstrous[67] nature—and because it naturally accumulates around the anus, he desires that it be expelled from there, and so he craves the motion and friction that will bring this about.

The desire [arises partly] . . . : Since he has mentioned desire, [Aristotle] shows here, in the second place, what causes the desire for such an expulsion. He says that such a motion of desire is caused by two things: namely, food and drink of an inflammatory quality, such as turnips, pastries, the meat of goats, doves and sparrows, new wine and the like—for from these is generated a windy humor which stimulates the spermatic matter to coitus because of its instability; or else sometimes it arises from the practical intelligence or imagination, because the animal imagines the pleasure which perhaps it derived from this act, quite apart from any stimulation from windy spermatic matter. Sometimes it can happen for both reasons. When desire is aroused by either or both of these factors, the windy spirit, excited by friction and motion, converges on the area around the base of the penis, and from there the spermatic moisture flows to the place destined for it in accordance with its confused nature. This moisture is either subtle and watery, as is the case with those men whose passages are wider, or else it is merely windy, but it exits after being rendered subtle by friction, and this is the case with those whose passages are more constricted. It should be noted that as [Aristotle] says in book 3 of *On the Soul*, there are two principles of motion: appetite and intellect.[68] Here one should take "intellect" to mean "fantasy" or "imagination," for motion of this kind does not take place because of intelligence, but because of fantasy, both in many of our species, and in all the other animals in whom there is neither intellect nor reason, but only fantasy. And this is what Aristotle says in his book on the motion of animals: for in animals which move, we observe understanding, fantasy, preference, will and desire, which can nonetheless all be reduced to intellect and appetite, and these two are further subsumed under "the appetible."[69] In considering the principles of motion, there is that which moves, that by which movement takes place, and that which is moved. That which moves is twofold. There is that which is utterly immobile both in itself and in its attributes, so that it is always good, and not sometimes good and sometimes not; this is something which is divine, eternal and worthy of honor. And there is that which is moved by this good, divine and eternal being, and moves for the sake of another good or apparent good, such as the appetible and the intellectual, which is the goal and end of practical operation. That by which motion is accomplished is the instrument or member. That which is moved is the animal itself, the two principles of whose motion he touched on when he said *The desire [arises partly]* etc. In the book on the cause of the movement of animals, [Aristotle] sets out such a hierarchy of movers, so that appropriate passions move instrumental parts, and desire moves the passions, and fantasies move desire—fantasies which are in fact moved by intellect or sensation. Avicenna also sets this out in a very elegant manner at the end of the first [fen of book 1 of the *Canon*, ch. 7], concerning the sixth of the "natural things."[70]

When this passes out. . . : Here, in the third place, [Aristotle] compares those who are thus disposed to certain men who are incapable of emitting sperm in coitus, by showing what additionally happens to them when this moisture exits. He says that when this spermatic moisture exits, it produces in these men a distention and expansion of the shoulders and mouth, accompanied by a certain delectation, so that they suffer torments of yawning, and a hair-raising itching all over, because of windy matter which is warmed by friction as it passes over their sensitive members or the region of the pudenda. Such distention happens to boys who have not yet reached the age at which they are able to engage in coitus, and they take pleasure in it. And again such pleasurable distention happens to those who have reached the age at which they ought to engage in coitus, but who cease to do so because no moisture comes out of them, only windy spirit. This happens because their moisture is consumed, which can occur because frequent coitus converts all the moisture into windy spirit, due to the inflammation of the body. Or else it can occur because of illness, as in those with hectic fevers or consumption, or perhaps it happens on account of their complexion being excessively warm and dry, for this resolves the moisture into windy spirits, as happens in the case of sparrows. Although such men may perhaps not have sperm, they did have it when they were young; however, this happens to some people in the prime of life, and later, as Aristotle, Galen and Avicenna say in their books on the generation of animals. But now Aristotle says, if any of the abovementioned things should happen to anyone, either as an immature boy or as a man, so that he suffers from either of these (i.e., subtle moisture or windy moisture), and if, moved by desire or by diet, he desires to be evacuated of this material, subtle or windy, contained within him, he can find repose and enjoyment when it is evacuated and voided.

It should be noted that the statement, briefly introduced here, concerning the delectation experienced by boys who are as yet incapable of engaging in coitus, and of some men, is expressed in the first book of [Aristotle's] *The Generation of Animals* in these words: Delectation happens in coitus not only because of the emission of sperm, but because of the emission of spirit. From this spirit, when consolidated and condensed, sperm is made, and it is manifest in boys who are not yet capable of producing sperm as they approach the age at which they ought to produce sperm, and it is likewise manifest in sterile men, for in all these people, delectation arises from the release of spirit through friction.[71]

But [the naturally effeminate] . . . : He proceeds with the first part of the abovementioned division, and first he shows how in such men spermatic humor is secreted, and the consequences of this. He says that those who are naturally effeminate from the time they are first framed, or who are eunuchs, have pores constituted and fashioned in such a way that they are blocked, and no moisture can be evacuated through them, or only a small amount is expelled by them into the place in which it is expelled by those who have these pores naturally, and according to nature. Alternatively,[72] in these people, only a small amount is expelled in a place "according to nature"—their own monstrous nature, because it is expelled in a place monstrously fashioned, and because they are not constituted by nature operating in a proper manner. Anyone who wishes to ponder the cause and manner of this and other kinds of monstrosity should diligently investigate book 4 of [Aristotle's] *The Generation of Animals.*

[Though they are male this part of them . . .]: Concluding the second of the aforementioned divisions, he shows how this structural defect of the pores which transport sperm to the penis may be cured in these men. First he shows that it is not possible to cure it by surgery; secondly, he says that if such pores are so badly formed that they make people sick, they should be cured. This has to be done by cutting and by subtle division with an iron, since defects of structure are best cured thus. But it should not be done, for sometimes cutting results in the total destruction of the pores, and death; often it induces deformation and change for the worse in parts of the pores, such as not infrequently happens when wounds are cut in order to rectify scars. For this reason, it should not be done. Again, it might happen that a man could be turned into a woman, which would be a change for the worse[73]; hence it is rightly asserted that the deformation caused by such cutting damages the parts around the testicles to such a degree that a man could be made into a eunuch or an effeminate, when he had not been so previously. Nonetheless one ought not to take this to mean that a man could be changed into a woman with respect to essence, but rather, with respect to accidents, by acquiring womanly gestures and habits.[74]

So it must involve . . . : He teaches how such men may be cured. First he says that whatever spermatic moisture these men have must be evacuated away from this part, and moved to another part, and this is done with diet and drugs of a drying nature, which divert the sperm and its matter to other areas, and [transform it] into urine, sweat etc. On the other hand, Avicenna, speaking of this condition and the aforementioned one in fen 20 of book 3 [of the *Canon*] says that "the men who try to cure these people are foolish, for the cause of their illness and its therapy are not natural; if one would cure them, one must break their desire through sadness, hunger, sleeplessness, imprisonment and flogging." The Philosopher infers one of these [assertions], saying that those who are thus disposed become insatiable and insane, always craving friction to evacuate this seminal moisture. They are insatiable like women and like young girls in particular, whose passages are still narrow, so that they can only force out a small amount of liquid which has been set in motion and liquified by friction. Because the amount is small, it quickly grows cold and cannot be expelled. For this reason, they desire to be rubbed again, so that it can be expelled. And so it happens that these people's bodies are in a perpetual sweat, as was discussed in book 2, chapter 22 [of the *Problems*]. It should be noted that women are insatiable and particularly young girls of about 14 years of age: [Aristotle] discusses this in book 9 of *The History of Animals*.[75] Young girls are particularly incited to sexual acts, and when they start to have sex, they are incontinent. The reason for this is that at this time, because of the descent of spermatic and menstrual fluid,[76] their genitalia begin to swell, and the fissure of the vulva is hemmed, and the labia become tender, engorged, and covered with hair. Then they begin to have a mad longing for coitus, but they cannot gratify their desire, and the more they engage in coitus or rub themselves with their hand, the more they crave it, because such friction draws the moisture but does not expel it. Heat is drawn down with the moisture, and windiness is stirred up. But since the body is cold and the pores are closed, semen cannot readily be emitted.

   Those with whom [the semen travels to the fundament] . . . : He refers to men such as sodomites to whom the above happens because of a disgusting evil habit. And he divides [the discussion] into two parts. In the first, he repeats what he said earlier in the second part of the division, concerning those in whom the aforementioned moisture flows into the anus, so that they readily yield to those who collude in performing these vile acts. He says that some of these men in whom spermatic fluid flows down to the anus desire to play the passive role, and to be rubbed vigorously about the anus so that this moisture can be expelled, but in others this humidity flows partly to the anus and partly to the penis. These desire to rub and to be rubbed on both their parts, for they desire to rub others with their penis, and to be rubbed on the anus by another's penis. Amongst those who desire both the active and passive roles, on both parts, some prefer the passive role, by which the stimulating moisture will converge more on the penis or on the anus. One should take note of what Avicenna says in book 3 fen 20 about this kind of condition, which he calls *alguagi*: "Some say that the cause of *alguagi* is that the nerve of sensation which leads to the penis is divided into two branches, of which the delicate one continues to the root of the penis, while the coarse one bends towards the head of the penis; for this reason, the delicate [nerve] needs to be rubbed vigorously before it will feel anything, and so he debases himself to lie on top of a man, and then he experiences the fulfillment of his desire." And it seems that the Philosopher is saying this.[77] But this is not Avicenna's view: indeed, he says that "this explanation is far from the truth." Avicenna does not explain why this should be false, which puts him at odds with the Philosopher's statement; nor can I see what could impede such an inordinate and monstrous thing from being congenital (*a nativitate*), since Avicenna goes on to say as much about hermaphrodites, who appear even more monstrous with respect to nature.

In some cases [this state is the result of habit. . .]: He continues on here to the second part, concerning those who are guilty of the wicked vice of sodomy, and first he shows how this affection (*passio*) and impious deed comes about from habit, and is transformed into nature. He says that in certain men, that affection which in the men discussed above is congenital, is due to a habit—"corrupting influence" would be a better term. These men are impelled to do this by delectation, because something took place which made them enjoy and find pleasure in those who emit sperm while engaged in coitus with them, so that those to whom this happened desire to carry out this impious act for the sake of enjoyment and pleasure.

Another [possibility]: *For [men are accustomed to enjoy] what . . . :* That is, they are wholly intent on emitting sperm, that is, the seminal moisture, in order to derive enjoyment and pleasure, and this is what he says, [namely] that these men who perform these abominable acts, desire in this way. In the seventh book of the *Ethics,* Aristotle says that they will be beyond the bounds of evil.[78] The law calls for their extirpation: let the laws arise, let justice take up arms, and wield the sword of vengeance.

Hence Avicenna in book 3, fen 20: "Sexual intercourse with children is regarded as repugnant by most nations, and is forbidden by the law." But by the frequent and habitual performance of this act, custom becomes nature, as is plain from book 28, ch. 1 [of the *Problems*], and in [Aristotle's] book *On Memory and Recollection,* "Habit is like nature."[79] How habit can be converted into nature is nicely described by Hippocrates in his book on *Airs, Waters [and Places],* where he mentions people whose mothers were in the habit of elongating their heads with their hands when they were infants; eventually, the change wrought by habit became natural.[80] This raises a doubt. For it does not seem that habit can be converted into nature to the extent that nature would abandon its pristine order, because nothing in nature can be habituated now in one way, and now in another. As [Aristotle] says in the second book of the *Ethics,*[81] you can throw a stone into the air 10,000 times, but it never becomes habituated to it. It should be mentioned that there are two kinds of motion and inclination in natural things. The first is the consequence of the initial mingling of the dominant elements in the mixture, and the form bestowed by that which generates [the entity], and in this case it cannot acquire a habit which is contrary to its dominant element; this applies to inanimate things. The other motion and inclination is the consequence of the higher form resulting from the mixture of the elements, or it comes from without, and in this case something can have an inclination and motion toward what was initially contrary to it, for example by doing something repeatedly. As the second book of the *Ethics* states, from this a habit is acquired which nonetheless is often converted into nature. Aristotle's text should be understood in this [latter] sense, and not in the first, which is why the objection arose.

For this reason . . . : Here he introduces a corollary to the second point, and first he shows how those given to this act begin to perform it at the time of puberty. He says that those who are accustomed to being subjected and rubbed about the anus after puberty and the time when they are able to emit sperm, are left by this habit with a memory. This memory is caused in them by the sensations of pleasure in many parts, perceived through experience. This is how memory is generated, as [Aristotle] says in the end of the *Posterior Analytics*.[82] Because by dint of long-established habit they desire it as if these things were produced by nature; and this is possible, for frequent and lengthy habit makes it as if nature herself had established it from birth. Hence Cicero in the prologue of the *Old Rhetoric*:[83] Habit, long-established, has the force of nature. It should be noted that some men perform this wicked act of sodomy by rubbing the penis [i.e., of the male partner, presumably] with their hand, others by rubbing between the thighs of a boy, which many do these days. Others by making friction around the anus and penis by mounting [their male partner] as one would mount a vulva, and Aristotle's text appears to apply mainly to these. *If [a man happens to be] . . . :* He shows that happens to those who are subjected before puberty, saying that if this indecent lust befalls them when nature is soft and tender, those who are subjected at a time when they cannot emit sperm experience all the above more quickly, such as tremendous delectation and emission of semen into the anus and so forth, and habit is converted into nature, and especially in those who do not begin before puberty, and this is the substance of what Avicenna says in book 3, fen 20, in the chapter on *alguagi*. In the seventh book of the *Ethics*, Aristotle says that the cause of this wicked act is total bestiality and perversion of the soul, and that these men are rightly said to be beyond the bounds of evil.[84] Ptolemy in chapter 80 of the *Centiloquium* and in book 4 of the *Quadripartitum* ascribes the cause to a conjunction or aspect of evil [planets] with Venus in an evil sign, and especially in the seventh and sixth houses, with Jupiter in conjunction and its aspect remote from other [planets].

Rodrigo de Castro (1546–1623/9)

For Rodrigo de Castro, discussion of female genitals in *De universa muliebrum medicina* involves reviewing sensational sexual possibilities that are allegedly excessive, deformed, and disgraceful, including quasiphallic clitoral hypertrophy and tribadism. Son of a Jewish physician, he obtained his medical degree at Salamanca in Spain and practiced in Lisbon, his birthplace, before relocating to Hamburg around 1594 to escape religious persecution. His clients there included royalty and high nobility. After his first wife died from her third pregnancy, he married again and fathered five sons in all. The eldest, Benedict or Baruch, became personal physician to the sartorially androgynous (and perhaps hermaphroditic) Queen Christina of Sweden, and another, Daniel, was physician to the king of Denmark. Rodrigo's various Latin medical treatises include *Medicus-Politicus*, a major text of Renaissance medical ethics (1614). First published at Hamburg in 1603, his gynecological study saw many seventeenth-century editions, and conservatively advocates Galenic male-female genital homology, despite the contemporaneous challenge of*André du Laurens (1558–1609).[85]

On the Universal Medical Art of Women[86] (1603)

Part One, Book One, Chapter 3: The Parts of the Womb

... The vagina (*matricis collum*) ends in the female pudenda, also called the female genitals, the genital opening, the opening of the neck of the womb,[87] the "face," or rather the "devil-mask."[88] This neck has a skin-like epiphysis or addition, corresponding to the male foreskin,[89] and like the foreskin it exists for the sake of ornament. It is located in the vicinity of the genital cleft or opening, where hills or little mountains swell outwards, which in adult women are adorned with hairs. But on the inside, hanging down on either side, are found those fleshy growths, like a pair of lips, to which the name of "nymphs" is assigned, and which are called "the wings of the womb." Nature, it is believed, gives rise to these wings in order to protect the womb from dust, cold, and other external injuries. For just as the uvula is a bulwark for the pharynx, so also are the nymphs for the womb. They are spongy in substance, and form a longitudinal cleft, like a channel, or the letter I. At its upper end, in the thicker part of the pubic region, where these fleshy growths join together, and next to the opening from which urine passes out, they form a small, hidden protuberance, somewhat like a tiny penis, such as a rabbit has. It is spongy in substance, sinewy and full of blood. It ends in a glans, and is covered with a small foreskin. At one time I said that this [member] stops urine from flowing back into the neck of the bladder; everyone else proposes another use, and one which is not to be rejected. This member produces an exquisite itching, and for this reason it is held to be the principal seat of pleasure for women when they make love. For two oblong ligaments end at this [member]; they are sinewy and hollow, and originate on the flanks of the womb, and Columbus[90] boasts of late that he has discovered them to the principal cause of [woman's] supreme delectation. Indeed, this protuberance sometimes exceeds its natural measure, and increases to such a size that it projects outside the womb, occasioning deformity and shame. When it is continually rubbed by clothing, it is stimulated to such a degree that these women, to whom this member gives erections like men, cannot contain themselves, and fling themselves uncontrollably into love-making. They pollute themselves by coupling with incubi and succubi, as Amatus[91] relates concerning two Turkish women of Thessalonike; and we have seen some women publicly punished at Lisbon for the same crime. They are called tribades by Caelius Aurelianus, dominators (*subigatrices*) by Plautus, and Martial says of a certain Bassa, that she "Has devised a worthy demonstration of the Theban riddle: / How there can be adultery where no man is to be found."[92]

Because of this, the Egyptians used to excise [this member] in virgins, and some think that this should be carried out indiscriminately on those skin-like fleshy growths which are found before the opening of the womb. In my opinion, they are wrong, for these have their functions, which nature has bestowed upon them: they both produce great pleasure for women in intercourse, and also (as I said) protect the womb from [dangers] without. Moreover, these fleshy growths, which stand like cock's combs by the opening of the womb in the vagina, are rightly called "nymphs." For the poets say that the satyrs pursued [the nymphs] through glades and groves, because in them were those delights of sexual congress for which [the satyrs] burned. Distinct from these "nymphs" is that other member which is called "nymph," because this is a muscular skin-covered protuberance situated above the juncture of the wings of the pudendum, where the urinary passage is to be found. And I think that it is this part instead which the authorities commanded to be excised. They call this operation "nymphotomia"; nymphotomia is not the condition which Moschio[93] mistakenly records [under this name]. Mercatus[94] is of the opinion that this is the condition in which, as doctors think, women turn into men, and which is properly called a symptom of indecency. I would not be unwilling to assent to this, did I not believe that, from time to time, and in certain people, the sex is revealed rather than changed, either at puberty or on the wedding-day at the latest, for at that time nature more readily pushes the protuberant sexual members outside the body, which before that had been hidden. Many histories both of ancient times and of our own age relate this. Thus Empedocles of Agrigentum used to say, "And I was a boy myself, and once a girl."[95] Schenckius[96] has collected many stories on this subject, and I refer the reader to him. Nonetheless, when he writes on the authority of others that there are women who both conceived, and afterwards, when they had been turned into men, engendered, this is a total fabrication. Furthermore, I would not venture to affirm what Columbus claims, namely that this protuberance or "nymph" can grow to such a great size in all women. I would be more inclined to believe that this happens in those people who belong to the second species or class of hermaphrodites, as shall be explained below. Nevertheless I do not doubt that this tiny protuberance is found in all women, and that it hangs in front of the concavity of the vagina, for the purposes which we stated above, since those wings or membranes end there....

Part One, Book Three, Chapter 3: Certain Notable Facts about Coitus
... As Tertullian says in his book *To His Wife*, virginity is easier to preserve than chastity, for it is easier not to desire what we have never had, than not to desire what we once possessed.[97] Therefore virgins who have never experienced coitus do not have much desire for it, because it is only a nuisance to be gotten over with. The rest of womankind desire this activity either for this same reason, or because they recall bygone pleasure. This is even more true of those who are called tribades or "rubbers," who only love to rub one another, and thus perform a disgraceful act upon one another. As we said, some have been accused of this crime, and those convicted were sent into exile. Moreover, even when virgins desire [coitus], they fear the loss of that ornament of their nature which we called the hymen, and the pain which coincides with sexual pleasure; [sexually experienced] women have put all that behind them....

André du Laurens (1558–1609)

The discussion of female genitals in André du Laurens's compendious *Historia anatomica humani corporis* correlates the clitoris with the penis and thus broaches topics of feminine phallic potential and tribadic sex. Son of a physician at Arles in France, he obtained his first M.D. at Avignon in 1578, and his second at Montpellier in 1583, where he later gained the chair of medicine. He became a royal physician in ordinary to King Henri IV in 1596; first physician to the new queen, Marie de' Medici, in 1600; and first physician to the king in 1606. He married in 1601 and fathered one son. Du Laurens authored numerous medical treatises, and the *Historia*, apparently first published in 1593, remained a standard anatomical textbook for decades. It further contains sections called "controversies," assessing disputed questions of anatomy and physiology; *Helkiah Crooke (1576–1635) appropriated many for his *Microcosmographia*. One of these mounts apparently the first strong challenge to the Galenic theory of male and female genital homology (now often called the "one-sex model"), reprinted later here in *Crooke's version (cf. Schleiner, "One-Sex Model," 183–90).

Anatomical Account of the Human Body[98] *(1593)*

Book 7, Chapter 12: The Different Parts of the Womb

...At the upper front tip of the vulva there is a certain small member; Fallopius was the first of the moderns to describe this member, and he did so in an elegant manner. Not that it was unknown to the older writers: Avicenna calls it "albatra," that is, "the rod"[99]; Albucasis,[100] "the tumescence" (*tentiginem*); Fallopius κλητορίδα [i.e., clitoris], from the obscene verb κλητορίζειν [i.e., "to touch lasciviously"]; Columbus "love" and "the sweetness of Venus"; and we call it woman's prick and the female penis. This little member has two hollow ligaments which arise from the pelvic bone; inside, it is spongy, and full of black, thick blood, and [it has] four thin muscles. It likewise has at the tip something like a glans, which is covered by a very thin skin like a foreskin. It differs from the male penis in that it has no opening to expel semen. We acknowledge that its use is to excite the torpid potency through friction. In some women, it expands in such an untoward manner that it hangs down below the cleft like a penis, and the women who are called tribades or "rubbers" rub each other on that part. This little member is hidden in the thicker part of the pubic region, and needs to be removed by artificial section....

Helkiah Crooke (1576–1635)

An overview of medical theories and controversies about human generation, male and female genitals, differences between females and males, so-called monsters, and hermaphroditism appears in Books Four and Five of Crooke's *Microcosmographia: A Description of the Body of Man.* After entering St. John's College, Cambridge, in 1591 and obtaining his B.A. in 1596, Crooke began medical studies at Leiden in 1597, returned to Cambridge, and took further degrees, an M.B. and M.D. (1599 and 1604). Taking up medical practice in London, he became physician to King James I, to whom Crooke dedicated his lengthy *Microcosmographia* on its first publication in 1615. As the treatise seeks to survey thought on human anatomy and physiology, so the title page announces it is "Collected and Translated out of all the Best Authors of Anatomy, Especially out of Gasper Bauhinus and Andreas Laurentius" (Kaspar Bauhin, 1560–1624, and *André du Laurens). Further editions of Crooke's text were printed in 1616, 1618, and 1631. Elected fellow of the Royal College of Physicians in 1620, he became its anatomy reader in 1629.

Early modern medical discourse about sex, genitals, and sex differences was limited publicly, at least, by considerations of piety, decorum, and tactful silence, and so Crooke begins Book IV, his account of human generation, with a preface defending his publication of such material. It glorifies "the wonderful wisdom and goodness of our Creator," he insists, and uses "honest words and circumlocutions" to instruct medical practitioners and sober-minded readers in the knowledge of their bodies and sexual health. Besides, "he that listeth may separate this Book from the rest and reserve it privately unto himself." Nevertheless, on account of Books IV and V the Royal College of Physicians attempted to suppress and bowdlerize Crooke's original text, apparently because even his discreet treatment of sexual matters was deemed too provocative for publication in English.[101]

Echoing Crooke's general title, *Microcosmographia*, the preface for Book IV stresses the common early modern belief that the human body "is the Epitome of the world, containing therein whatsoever is in the large universe," and moreover that "Seed is the Epitome of the body, having in it the power and immediate possibility of all the parts." We could hold the universe in a drop of sperm. Just as "Nature" denominates the "wise administration of Almighty God" in Crooke's view, the body is God's created vehicle for the immortal soul, and sexual capacities exist to ensure the earthly continuance of the human race despite the physical mortality of individuals (Book IV, preface, ch. 9). "The Final cause ... of this pleasure which is conceived in the whole action of copulation, but especially in the emission of seed," he claims, "is only the conservation or preservation of mankind" (Book V, quest. 7). Any deliberately nonprocreative sex, including individual masturbation, would thus manifest the sinfully inordinate lust condemned in Chapter One of Book IV. In accord with the prevailing norms of medical discourse, Crooke suppresses masculine nonconformities to this reproductive teleology and concludes his account of male sexual capacities by stating that he has omitted much to avoid appealing to prurience (Book IV, ch. 8), yet discards this discretion in treating the supposedly imperfect sex. Partly to titillate male readers, he acknowledges female masturbation and "those wicked women ... called Tribades, ... in some states worthily punished" for "their mutual unnatural lusts" (Book IV, ch. 16).

Although in some ways protofeminist (Book V, ch. 1, and quest. 1), Crooke assumes males have primacy in creation as in Genesis, so that females are actually secondary, created for specifically reproductive purposes. "Nature ... made another sex of mankind, not altogether of so hot a temper or constitution, because she [i.e., woman] should have a superfluity of blood for the nourishment of the infant, as also that the parts of generation for want of heat to thrust them forth remaining within, might make a fit place to conceive, breed, and perfect the same" (Book IV, preface). Following Aristotle and Galen, Crooke considers this supposed feminine lack of heat the major constitutive difference between the sexes, and it further entails presumed imperfection relative to males (Book IV, ch. 9). In Book V, question 1, Crooke draws on *Du Laurens to review the current controversy whether males and females are genitally homologous, and argue the contrary. Despite Crooke's general claim that sex has specifically procreative ends and moral bounds, his Hippocratic account of the complexities of human gender differentiation at conception concedes that reproduction must inevitably produce many individuals whose inborn natures involve varying degrees of gender inversion (V, quest. 20). Such notions would have provided a medical basis not only for perceptions of same-sex sexual predispositions, but also for contesting interpretations of sex that denied the legitimacy of same-sex sexual unions, for they thus constitute expressions of the full natural scope of procreation.

Microcosmographia: A Description of the Body of Man[102] *(1615)*

Book Four: Of the Natural Parts Belonging to Generation, as Well in Men as in Women

CHAPTER ONE: OF THE NECESSITY OF THE PARTS OF GENERATION

...To pass by the production of other things, the generation of perfect creatures is accomplished when the male soweth his seed and the female receiveth and conceiveth it. For this purpose Nature hath framed in both sexes parts and places fit for generation; beside an instinct of lust or desire, not inordinate such as by sin is superinduced in man, but natural residing in the exquisite sense of the obscene parts. For were it not that the God of Nature hath placed herein so incredible a sting or rage of pleasure, as whereby we are transported for a time, as it were, out of ourselves, what man is there almost who hath any sense of his own divine nature that would defile himself in such impurities? What woman would admit the embracements of a man, remembering her nine months burthen, her painful and dangerous deliverance, her care, disquiet and anxiety in the nursing and education of the infant? But all these things are forgotten, and we overtaken with an ecstasy, which Hippocrates calleth a little Epilepsy or falling sickness, and the holy Scripture veileth under the name of a senselessness in Lot, who neither perceived when his daughters lay down, nor when they rose up....[103] (200)

IV, CHAPTER NINE: OF THE PROPORTION OF THESE PARTS BOTH IN MEN AND WOMEN

It was the opinion of Galen in his fourteenth Book *De usu partium*, and the eleventh Chapter, that women had all those parts belonging to generation which men have, although in these they appear outward at the *Perineum* or *interfaeminium*, in those they are for want of heat retained within.[104] For seeing a woman is begotten of a man, and perfect also in mankind (for Nature's imperfections are not so ordinary),[105] it is reasonable that the substance, yea, and the shape of the parts in both sexes should be alike, as coming from one and the same *set*, as it were, of causes....

Herein Nature hath excellently acquitted herself, that the abatement of natural heat, which in men is the only natural and necessary cause of their dissolution, should so admirably become in women the original of generation, whereby we should attain a kind of eternity even of our bodies against the destined corruption of the matter, arising from an importunate discord of contraries.[106] For so it pleased the Divine Wisdom to create for the eternal soul (the most excellent of all forms), if not an eternal habitation here, yet so absolute and admirable a structure as might so long be perpetuated below, till it come to be eternized above after an ineffable manner of recreation.... [107]

So then, in the first conception or soon after, ... the same Members are generated, but the fruit proveth male or female because of the temper of the seed and the parts of generation, either by heat thrust out, or for want or weakness of the heat retained within. [108] Wherefore a woman is so much less perfect than a man by how much her heat is less and weaker than his; yet, as I said, is this imperfection turned unto perfection, because without the woman, mankind could not have been perfected by the perfecter sex. The great Master workman therefore of set purpose made the one half of mankind imperfect for the instauration [109] of the whole kind, making the woman as a receptacle of the seed of which a new man was to be created.... (216–17)

IV, CHAPTER ELEVEN: OF THE [FEMALE] TESTICLES

The Testicles, [110] which because of the inbred coldness of women are included within the lower venter ... that they might be kept warm and be made fruitful, do lie one on either side at the sides of the matrix.... The seed of a man is the active principle of the body, that of women but the passive, or at least far less active than the other.... [111]

The use of the [female] Testicles, as say Columbus, Archangelus, Laurentius, and Bauhin, [112] is by their inbred power to make the seed fruitful. Fallopius is not of this mind, Platerus halteth betwixt both [113]; but we know assuredly that those women whose testicles are ill disposed are barren and unfruitful. For women as well as men do yield seed, but cold, though Aristotle deny it in his first book *De generatione animalium* and the twentieth chapter, who would have that humor which is avoided by the neck of the matrix not to be a seminary or seedy humor, but a proper humor of the place, to wit, an excrement of the womb, which also should be found in some, but not in others; as especially brown or swart-colored and mannish women. [114] But Hippocrates in his first Book *De diaeta* and in his book *De natura pueri*, and Galen in his fourteenth Book of *The Use of Parts* and the eleventh Chapter, have taught that to perfect generation there is required a concurrence and mixture of the seeds of both sexes, and a place wherein the form of the parts being only in power present, the seed might be brought into act, such is the womb.... [115](218–19)

IV, CHAPTER SIXTEEN: OF THE [FEMALE] LAP OR PRIVITIES

... The *Nymphae*, so called by Galen, ... of the Latins *Alae*, the wings, of others skinny caruncles, are two productions on either side.... These being joined do make a fleshy eminence, and covering the Clitoris with a foreskin ascend with a manifest rising Line to the top of the great cleft.... Sometimes they grow to so great a length on one side, more rarely on both; and not so ordinarily in maidens as in women, ... what through the affluence of humors, what through attrection,[116] that for the trouble and shame (being in many Countries a notable argument of petulancy and immodesty) they need the Chirurgeon's[117] help to cut them off (although they bleed much and are hardly cicatrised), especially among the Egyptians, amongst whom this accident (as Galen saith) is very familiar. Wherefore in Maidens before they grow too long they cut them off, and before they marry. . . .

"Clitoris" in Greek. . . cometh of an obscene word signifying contrectation,[118] but properly it is called the woman's yard. It is a small production in the upper, forward . . . and middle fatty part of the share,[119] in the top of the greater cleft where the *Nymphs* do meet, and is answerable to the member of the man, from which it differs in the length, the common passage, and the want of one pair of muscles; but agrees in situation, substance and composition. . . .

Although for the most part it hath but a small production hidden under the *Nymphs* and hard to be felt but with curiosity, yet sometimes it groweth to such a length that it hangeth without the cleft like a man's member, especially when it is fretted with the touch of the clothes, and so strutteth and groweth to a rigidity as doth the yard of a man. And this part it is which those wicked women do abuse called *Tribades* (often mentioned by many authors, and in some states worthily punished) to their mutual and unnatural lusts . . .[120] It is called *aestrum Veneris* and *dulcedo amoris*; for in it, with the ligaments inserted into it, is the especial seat of delight in [women's] venereal embracements, as Columbus imagineth he first discovered. (237–38)

IV, QUESTION EIGHT: HOW THE PARTS OF GENERATION IN MEN
AND WOMEN DO DIFFER

Concerning the parts of generation in women, it is a great and notable question whether they differ only in situation from those of men. For the ancients have thought that a woman might become a man, but not on the contrary side a man become a woman. For they say that the parts of generation in women lie hid, because the strength of their natural heat is weaker than in men, in whom it thrusteth those parts outward. Women have spermatical vessels, as well preparing as Leading vessels and testicles which boil the blood, and a kind of yard also, which they say is the neck of the womb if it be inverted. Finally, the bottom of the womb distinguished by the middle line is the very same with the cod or scrotum. This Galen often urgeth in divers of his works as before is said; so Aegineta, Avicenna, Rhazes,[121] and all of the Greek and Arabian Families, with whom all Anatomists do consent. For confirmation also hereof there are many stories current among ancient and modern writers of many women turned into men. . . .[122] The Hyena also, a cruel and subtle Beast, doth every other year change her sex. Of whom Ovid in the XV of his *Metamorphosis* saith: "The same Hyena which we saw admit the male before, / To cover now her female mate, we can but wonder sore."[123] Pontanus hath the same of Iphis in an elegant verse: "Iphis her vow benempt a Maid, / But turnèd boy her vow she paid."[124]

Of later times. Volateran,[125] a Cardinal, saith that in the time of Pope Alexander VI he saw at Rome a virgin who, on the day of her marriage, had suddenly a virile member grown out of her body. We read also that there was at Auscia in Vasconia[126] a man of above sixty years of age, grey, strong and hairy, who had been before a woman till the age of 15 years, or till within 15 years of threescore, yet at length by accident of a fall, the Ligaments (saith my Author) being broken, her privities came outward and she changed her sex; before which change she had never had her courses. Pontanus witnesseth that a Fisherman's wench of Caieta[127] of fourteen years old became suddenly a young springal.[128] The same happened to Emilia the wife of Antonie Spensa a Citizen of Ebula,[129] when she had been twelve years a married woman.

In the time of Ferdinand the first King of Naples, Carlota and Francisca, the daughters of Ludovic Quarna of Salernum, when they were 15 years old changed their sex. Amatus Lusitanus[130] testifieth in his *Centuries* that he saw the same at Conibrica a famous town of Portugal.[131] There standeth upon record in the eight section of the sixth Book of Hippocrates his *Epidemia*, an elegant History of one Phaetusa, who when her husband was banished was so overgrown with sorrow that before her time her courses utterly stopped and her body became manlike and hairy all over, and she had a beard and her voice grew stronger. The same also he recordeth to have happened to Namisia the wife of Gorgippus in Thaso.[132]

Wherefore say they, if a Woman may become a man and her parts of generation which before lay hid within may come forth and hang as men's do, then do women differ from men only in the site or position of their parts of generation. Notwithstanding all this, against this opinion there are two mighty arguments: one is taken from the αὐτοψία in dissection, another from reason, which two are the Philosopher's Bloodhounds, by which they tracked the causes of things.

For first of all (saith Laurentius) these parts in men and women differ in number. The small bladders which first Herophilus[133] found, and called *varicosos adstites*, that is, the *Parastatae*, women have not at all; nor the *Prostratae* which are placed at the root of the yard and neck of the bladder, in which seed is treasured up for the necessary uses of nature; although there be some that think that women have them but so small that they are insensible, which is (saith he) to beg the question. Again, methinks it is very absurd to say that the neck of the womb inverted is like the member of a man; for the neck of the womb hath but one cavity, and that is long and large like a sheath to receive the virile member: but the member or yard of a man consisteth of two hollow Nerves, a common passage for seed and urine, and four Muscles. Neither is the cavity of a man's yard so large and ample as that of the neck of the womb. Add to this, that the neck of the bladder in women doth not equal in length the neck of the womb, but in men it equaleth the whole length of the member or yard. Howsoever, therefore, the neck of the womb shall be inverted, yet will it never make the virile member: for three hollow bodies cannot be made of one, but the yard consisteth of three hollow bodies ... as we have before sufficiently shewed. If any man instance in the *Tentigo*[134] of the Ancients, or Fallopius his Clitoris, bearing the shape of a man's yard, as which hath two Ligaments and four Muscles, yet see how these two differ. The Clitoris is a small body, not continuated at all with the bladder, but placed in the height of the lap. The Clitoris hath no passage for the emission of seed; but the virile member is long and hath a passage in the middest by which it poureth seed into the neck of the womb.

Neither is there (saith Laurentius) any similitude between the bottom of the womb inverted, and the scrotum or cod of a man: For the cod is a rugous[135] and thin skin, the bottom of the womb is a very thick and tight membrane, all fleshy within and woven with manifold fibres.

Finally, the insertion of the spermatic vessels, the different figure of the man's and woman's Testicles, their magnitude, substance, and structure or composition do strongly gainsay this opinion.

But what shall we say to those so many stories of women changed into men? Truly, I think, saith he, all of them monstrous and some not credible. But if such a thing shall happen, it may well be answered that such parties were Hermaphrodites: that is, had the parts of both sexes, which because of the weakness of their heat in their nonage lay hid, but brake out afterward as their heat grew unto strength. Or we may safely say that there are some women so hot by nature that their Clitoris hangeth forth in the fashion of a man's member, which because it may be distended and again grow loose and flaccid, may deceive ignorant people. Again Midwives may oft be deceived because of the faulty conformation of those parts, for sometimes the member and testicles are so small and sink so deep into the body that they cannot easily be discerned.

Pinaeus[136] writeth that at Paris, in the year 1577, in the street of S. Denis, a woman travailed and brought forth a son, which because of the weakness of the infant was suddenly baptized for a daughter and was called Joanna. A few days after, in dressing the Infant, the Mother perceived it to be a manchild and so did the standers-by and they named it John.

As for the authority of Hippocrates. It followeth not that all those women whose voices turn strong or have beards and grow hairy do presently also change their parts of generation. Neither doth Hippocrates say so, but plainly the contrary, for he addeth, "When we had tried all means we could not bring down her courses, but she perished." Wherefore her parts of generation remained those of a Woman, although her body grew mannish and hairy. (249–50)

Book Five: Wherein the History of the Infant Is Accurately Described . . .

CHAPTER ONE: WHAT THINGS ARE NECESSARY TOWARD A PERFECT GENERATION

... The distinction of the Sexes is especially necessary because Generation is not accomplished but by seeds which must be sown in a fruitful ground, that is, shed into such a place as wherein their dull and sleepy faculties may be raised and roused up, which we call Conception, and afterward that which is thus conceived may be cherished, nourished, and so attain the utmost perfection of his kind. But because man was too hot to perform this office (for his heat consumeth all in him and leaveth no remainder to serve for the nourishment of the infant) it was necessary that a woman should be created (for we will insist now only in mankind)[137] which might afford not only a place wherein to cherish and conceive the seed, but also matter for the nourishment and augmentation of the same. Both these sexes of male and female do not differ in the kind, as we call it, or species (that is, essential form and perfection), but only in some accidents: to wit, in temper and in the structure and situation of the parts of Generation. For the female sex as well as the male is a perfection of mankind. Some there be that call a woman *Animal occasionatum* or *Accessorium*, barbarous words to express a barbarous conceit; as if they should say a Creature by the way, or made by mischance. Yea, some have grown to that impudency that they have denied a woman to have a soul as man hath. The truth is that, as the soul of a woman is the same divine nature with a man's, so is her body a necessary being, a first and not a second intention of Nature, her proper and absolute work, not her error or prevarication. The difference is by the Ancients in few words elegantly set down when they define a man to be a creature begetting in another, a woman a Creature begetting in herself. . . . (258)

A Dilucidation or Exposition of the Controversies Concerning the History of the Infant

V, QUESTION ONE: OF THE DIFFERENCE OF THE SEXES

Aristotle in his Books of the History and Generation of creatures doth often inculcate that the difference of Sexes is most necessary unto perfect Generation.... The Male is originally the hotter, and therefore the first principle of the work, and besides affordeth the greatest part of the formative power or faculty. The Female is the colder, and affordeth the place wherein the seed is conceived, and the matter whereby the Conception is nourished and sustained, which matter is the crude and raw remainders of her own aliment....

This difference of the Sexes do not make the essential distinctions of the creature. The reasons are: First (because as Aristotle saith in his second

Book *De generatione animalium* and the fourth Chapter, and in his fourth Book *De historia animalium* and the seventeenth chapter), in all creatures there is not this distinction or diversity of Sexes.[138] Secondly, because essential differences do make a distinction of kinds: now we know that the Male and the Female a[re] both of one kind, and only differ in certain accidents. But what these accidental differences are is not agreed upon as yet.

The Peripatetics[139] think that Nature ever intendeth the generation of a Male, and that the Female is procreated by accident out of a weaker seed which is not able to attain the perfection of the male. Wherefore Aristotle thinketh that the Woman or female is nothing else but an error or aberration of Nature, which he calleth παράβασις, by a Metaphor taken from Travellers which miss of their way and yet at length attain their journey's end. Yea, he proceedeth further and saith that the female is a by-work or prevarication, yea, the first monster in Nature.[140]

Galen in his sixth and seventh chapters of his fourteenth Book *De usu partium*, following Aristotle something too near, writeth that the formative power which is in the seed of man being but one, doth always intend the generation of one, that is, the Male; but if she err from her scope and cannot generate a male, then bringeth she forth the female which is the first and most simple imperfection of a male, which therefore he calleth a creature lame, occasional and accessory, as if she were not of the main, but made by the by.[141] Now herein he putteth the difference betwixt her and the Male, that in males the parts of generation are without the body, in Females they lie within because of the weakness of the heat, which is not able to thrust them forth. And therefore he saith that the neck of the womb is nothing else but the virile member turned inward, and the bottom of the womb nothing but the scrotum or cod inverted.

But this opinion of Galen and Aristotle we cannot approve. For we think that Nature as well intendeth the generation of female as of a male: and therefore it is unworthily said that she is an Error or Monster in Nature. For the perfection of all natural things is to be esteemed and measured by the end: now it was necessary that woman should be so formed or else Nature must have missed of her scope, because she intended a perfect generation, which without a woman cannot be accomplished.

Those things which Galen urgeth concerning the similitude, or parts of generation differing only in site and position, many men do esteem very absurd. Sure we are that they savor little of the truth of Anatomy, as we have already proved in the Book going before . . . Wherefore we must not think that the female is an imperfect male differing only in the position of the genitals.

Neither yet must we think that the Sexes do differ in essential form and perfection, but in the structure and temperament of the parts of generation.

The woman hath a womb ordained by Nature as a Field or seed-plot to receive, conceive and cherish the seed; the temper of her whole body is colder than that of a man, because she was to suggest and minister matter for the Nourishment of the Infant. And this way Aristotle in the second Chapter of his first Book *De generatione animalium* seemeth to incline, where he saith that the Male and the Female do differ as well in respect as in sense.[142] In respect, because the manner of their generation is diverse, for the Female generateth in her self, the Male not in himself but in the Female; in sense, because the parts appear other, and otherwise in the Sexes. The parts of the Female are the womb and the rest which by a general name are called *matrices;* the parts of a man are the virile member and the Testicles.... (270–72)

V, QUESTION TWENTY: WHENCE IT COMETH THAT CHILDREN
ARE LIKE THEIR PARENTS

... The similitude of the sex (that is, why a Male or Female is generated) hath for cause the Temper of the seed, his mixture and victory. For if the seed of both Parents be very hot, Males are generated, if very cold Females. If in the permixtion of the seeds the male seed have the upper hand a Male is procreated, if the Female seed a Female. This first of all Hippocrates taught in his first Book *De diaeta*, where he acknowledgeth in either sex a double seed, the one masculine hotter and stronger, the other feminine, that is colder, out of the divers permixtion of which both Males and Females are generated. He therefore thus distinguisheth a threefold Generation of Males and Females.[143] If both the Parents yield a masculine seed they breed Male children of a noble and generous disposition, ... Nobly minded and strong of body. If from the man there issue masculine seed, from the woman feminine, and the masculine prevail, a Male will be generated but less generous and strong than the former. If from the woman there issue masculine seed, from the man feminine, and the masculine overcome, a Male will be generated, but womanish, soft, base, and effeminate. The very like may be said of the Generation of Females: for if from both the Parents do issue feminine seed a Female will be procreated most weak and womanish. Which Hippocrates in the first Section of his sixth Book *Epidemion* calleth ... soft, waterish, and loose bodies.[144] If from the woman proceed a feminine seed and from the man a masculine, and yet the feminine overcome, women are begotten bold and moderate. If from the man proceed feminine seed and from the woman masculine, and the woman's seed prevail, women are begotten ... fierce and mannish. The Temper therefore of the seed and the victory in the permixtion are the causes of the similitude of the sex, that is of Males and Females; which causes are also not a little assisted by the Temper of the womb and the condition of the place, for, as I have often said, Male children are born in the right side, Females in the left.... (308–09)

V, QUESTION TWENTY-ONE: HOW TWINS OR MORE INFANTS ARE GENERATED

... Many of the Ancients refer the cause of Twins and manifold burthens to the variety of the bosoms of the womb, for they make seven bosoms in the womb of a Woman, which they call ... Cells; three in the right side of the Womb appointed for male children, and three in the left appointed for females, the seventh in the midst wherein Hermaphrodites are engendered. But these are idle conceits, next akin to Old wives' tales. For in a woman's womb there is but one bosom, as there is but one cavity in the stomach which yet may be divided into the right side and the left. ... (312)

John Marten (fl. 1704–d. 1737)

Two anecdotes about the contraction of syphilis in sex between males, one case oral, the other anal, appear in Marten's treatise on venereal disease. Though little is now known of this surgeon and medical writer, his gossipy account of venereal disease, first published in 1704, became a runaway best-seller issued in numerous revised and enlarged editions. I know of no earlier medical text that acknowledges possibilities of same-sex sexual transmission; the discussion may also discreetly evoke sex between females through the quotation of Romans 1:26. Just as various theories of syphilis' etiology and contraction had long focused on supposed characteristics of heteroerotic intercourse (*Medicine), it seems the possibility of same-sex transmission was still questioned. From the early sixteenth to nineteenth centuries, syphilis and gonorrhea were deemed aspects of the same disease,[145] and Marten's terminology conflates them. Whereas the oral case provokes Marten to stress divine punishment for putatively unnatural lust, the anal case causes him to consider denunciation to initiate charges of sodomy, in accord with its narrowly anal definition in English law.

A Treatise of All the Degrees and Symptoms of the Venereal Disease[146] *(1704)*

CHAPTER ONE: THE NATURE, CAUSES, AND SIGNS OF THE VENEREAL DISEASE ...

... I had almost forgot to acquaint the Reader, that there is yet another way of getting the Venereal Infection (which indeed I should have taken notice of in its place), and that is by one Man's conversing with, or having the Carnal use of, another Man's Body, viz., B——ry, an abominable, beastly, sodomitical, and shameful Action: an Action as it's not fit to be named, so, one would think, would not be practiced in a Christian Country, more especially since the Laws of God and Man are so directly in force against it. But, I say, by that means have we known the Distemper to have been contracted, and I am afraid is what is too commonly practiced in this dissolute Age, and the Distemper by that means very frequently gotten, as it was lately by one (as I was told) that I had in Cure.

And which is still worse, this Distemper is also gotten after another manner of Conversation, viz., by a Man's putting his erected Penis into another Person's (Man or Woman's) Mouth, using Friction, and co., between the Lips; a way so very Beastly and so much to be abhorred as to cause at the mentioning, or but thinking of it, the utmost detestation and loathing. But by that means also has it been gotten, and a Man so Infected (one that I know not, nor where to find) had I in Cure not long since, who assured me (though with seeming concern for the committing so foul a Crime) that he contracted it no other way; and that the Person from whom he got it (being a Man) had at the same time (as he has since been assured) several Pocky Ulcerations, and co., in his Mouth. But in such a woeful pickle was this Patient of mine, and indeed (as I told him) very deservedly, that I never in my Life before saw one (both for Pox[147] and Clap together) worse. And I being desirous to know the whole of this abominable Encounter (having never known, though before had heard, that such beastly Abominations were practiced), asked him if 'twas any Pleasure to him, and how he disposed of his Semen? He told me 'twas great Pleasure, and that he ejected it into the Person's Mouth he had to do with, who both willingly received it, and assisted, as he said, in this foul Act, by sucking his Penis. O monstrous! thought I, that Men, otherwise sensible Men, should so vilely debase themselves, and become so degenerate; should provoke God so highly, condemn the Laws of Man so openly, wrong their own Bodies so fearfully; and which is worse (without sincere Repentance) ruin their own Souls eternally. A Sin so heinous and aggravating, that God particularly expresses his Anger against those that commit it, as being hardened and given up by him to uncleanness, speaking of such in Romans 1, verse 4 [i.e., 1:24]: "Wherefore God also gave them up to Uncleanness, through the Lusts of their own Hearts, to dishonor their own Bodies between themselves." And again in the 26 and 27 verses: "For even their Women did change their natural Use into that which is against Nature. And likewise the Men, leaving the natural Use of the Woman, burned in their Lust one toward another, Men with Men, working that which is unseemly, and receiving in themselves that recompense of their Error which was meet." . . .

CHAPTER TWO: THE EASINESS OF CURING THE VENEREAL DISEASE . . .

[One of Marten's medical colleagues, he says, gave him this information.] . . . "I had a Letter sent me some time ago to desire my Opinion whether I thought it probable for one Man to be Clapped by the Carnal Use of another Man's Body? By way of answer, I sent word that I thought it reasonable to suspend my Judgment till I might be admitted to inspect the Person's Body who had submitted to this (Abominable) Action. The next day I had a Messenger to conduct me to a certain place where, in the Company of two Bravoes, I beheld a lovely Stripling. When he was told that he must comply with my searching of him, I first took a view of the Verge of the Anus, where discovering neither *Ficus, Thymi, Condylomata, Rhagades,* or *Papulae,* the frequent attendants on this Sodomitical Encounter,[148] I proceeded with my Finger in *Ano* to make farther inquiry. The Youth complaining, I drew back, when looking on my Finger, I found, besides the slimy Mucus of the Intestine, somewhat that seemed purulent; upon which I prayed him to put himself in the same posture, and, retaining his Breath, to bear down his Body, when with my Finger, besmeared with a bit of Butter, I got up higher than before, and could plainly perceive a couple of Fungous Caruncles.[149] But he crying out, and they fearful of being discovered, desired me to forbear. There followed my Finger several drops of Blood, which had been occasioned by the compression of the said Fungous Excrescences, together with a fresh appearance of the aforesaid purulent Matter. Upon the letting down his Shirt, I found the hind Lappet[150] stained with the same Gleet.[151] After this (out of hearing of the young Gentleman) I told his two Sparks that he was certainly Poxed, and that I thought it no more surprising, that the Person who had abused him under his present Circumstances, than if the same Virulency had been absorbed from the *Vagina Uteri* of a Woman. The Youth was quickly recommended to my Care, and whilst I was treating him with a detersive desiccating Injection (here being no place for Cathartics), I took notice of several crusty Pustules on the Scalp, likewise an Alopecia, together with a Nocturnal Hemicrane[152] which he made complaint of. All which considered, I immediately resolved upon a Salivation,[153] which he underwent for one and twenty days or thereabouts. During this, I was desired to prescribe for an unknown Person laboring with Gonorrhea.[154] I was somewhat uneasy with these People, as knowing they might, and ought indeed, to fall under the Cognizance of the Civil Magistrate; 'tis true, the poor Catamite lay much at my Mercy. But so soon as he had got his Cure, he was removed from his Lodging; and as for his Sodomitical Keeper, he kept himself Incognito, being supplied with Medicines by the Hands of one of his own Confidants. This I do affirm for certain Truth, and have too much reason to think that the Gonorrhea was got in B—ry."

And I had a Man myself, within these few Weeks, that had the like Venereal Infection in *Ano*, as he could not but confess upon my charging him with it, and asserting that it could be no otherwise, there being a Running of Matter, and co., as in a Gonorrhea. . . .

CHAPTER 4

Astrology

On being born we die, and our end depends on our beginning.
—Manilius, *Astronomica*, 4.16

Astrology afforded authoritative means to conceive of same-sex desires as innate and distinctive temperamental characteristics of particular persons. Besides potentially countering theological claims that sexual relations between males or between females are "unnatural," it could contest the authority of Christianity and the church and support sexual dissidence. For these reasons, and on account of its pervasive influence at all social levels of early modernity, this former ostensible science is important for the study of the period's sexual history and the origins of perceived sexual identities. However, astrology has as yet received little attention from historians of sexuality.[1] As many studies explain general astrological theories and practices of the Renaissance,[2] so I will outline their cultural impact and implications for understanding male and female homoeroticism instead.

Though skeptically criticized by some in Greek and Roman antiquity, such as Cicero, Favorinus, and Sextus Empiricus, "astrology . . . occupied a far more central position in any plausible map of ancient bodies of knowledge than one could anticipate from a modern perspective."[3] Sexual and amorous dispositions were a main topic of Greek and Roman astrology, and it correlated the full range of types distinguished, whether homoerotic or heteroerotic, with influences of the heavens. Perceived varieties of male and female same-sex desire (such as exclusive, nonexclusive, pederastic, generationally indifferent, "passive," "active," or both) were thus thought inscribed within particular individuals at conception or birth, along with the inclinations through which their sexual affinities would later tend to become expressed in their lives. Though many astral causes were posited, the ancients' structuring of sex and gender provided the foundations of the system, so that a so-called active role in sex appeared masculine and a passive feminine (Brooten, 116, 127). Homoerotically insertive males retained their masculinity but may well have forfeited some moral and social stature in at least the later empire, for *Firmicus Maternus assigns such lovers of boys and male youths somewhat sexually pejorative horoscopes or "genitures" (*Mathesis*, 7.15). The "passive" female partners of more assertive or masculine women received little attention, apparently because, from an androcentric viewpoint, their role did not seem to depart enough from perceived feminine sexual norms to necessitate comment. Astrologers conserved the normative two-gender hierarchy by imposing its categories and values on the apparent exceptions, thus folding them back into that structure as relatively devalued variations, while appearing to explain them.

Accordingly, a basic premise of ancient astrology was that the natal configuration of the heavens instills gendered influences, so that a male could be feminized in numerous ways and to varying extents, as Firmicus explains, and a female the contrary. The *Astronomica* of Manilius, for example, attributes generation of the cinaedus to influence of the constellation Taurus celestially rising hind-first attended by the maiden stars of the Pleiades. Both witty and pretty, such males "boast of their malady, which they call a virtue," not only giving their love but also advertising it (4.518–22, 5.140–56; trans. G. P. Goold). Though astrological theories and methods varied among the ancients as well as later, it was commonly assumed that the twelve zodiacal signs are each either masculine or feminine, and the gender of a planet or luminary shifts according to the signs traversed in crossing the heavens.[4] In *Ptolemy's view, the planets and luminaries are each gendered as well, and Mercury is both masculine and feminine; yet planetary gender still fluctuates according to the zodiacal sign occupied and other factors.

Degrees of ancient celestial determinism also varied. Firmicus and Manilius seem uncomprising (e.g., *Astronomica*, 3.56–75). Yet Ptolemy insists astrological predictions are somewhat provisional because manifold other factors are involved, including a subject's country of origin and upbringing, and the effects of stellar influences are themselves somewhat negotiable. Nonetheless, Ptolemy advocates a qualified, Stoic kind of astral fatalism. For he insists the heavens' influences are the "greatest" factors in individual temperaments, so that, as an astrologer would need to maintain, analyzing them has fundamental predictive value (*Tetrabiblos*, 1.2.8; trans. F. E. Robbins).[5] His introduction to genethlialogy (assessment of horoscopes) assumes that "the cause both of universal and particular events is the motion of the planets, sun, and moon" (*Tetrabiblos*, 3.1.104; trans. Robbins). Even in Ptolemy's theory, at nativity they inscribe some inborn erotic disposition that very powerfully affects subsequent sexual behaviors and amorous inclinations. Hence Bernadette Brooten argues that, "contrary to the view that the idea of sexual orientation did not develop until the nineteenth century, the astrological sources demonstrate the existence in the Roman world of the concept of a lifelong erotic orientation" (140). Whether or not her latter usage of "orientation" is apt, or "inclination" would better serve,[6] astrological traditions embarrass the acts paradigm that has ruled much recent sexual history (*General Introduction). As an explicatory product of human fantasy, this discipline tended to create rationalizations of observed phenomena according to existing social assumptions and apparent demand. So it would only have elaborated deterministic or essentialist conceptions of particular sexual affinities because Greek and Roman culture already accepted and manifested such

notions anyway: this pseudo-scientific etiology of personally engrained homoerotic and other sexual dispositions originated because they already appeared
and "made sense" that way.

Of course, the ancients conceived sexual relations according to the categories
of their sex/gender system, not our recent notions of "homosexuality" and
"heterosexuality." Like Greek and Roman *physiognomy, astrology too assumed
that the "femininity" of sexually receptive roles and the "masculinity" of their
insertive or at least more assertive counterparts are more important for classification than the gender of the sexual object-choice. The implied conceptualization
of sexual "nature" parallels that of some ancient medical discourse (*Medicine,
*Pseudo-Aristotle, *Caelius Aurelianus). Greek and Roman astrology assumes
that all the amorous affinities and behaviors it recognizes, including those of
same-sex desire, are equally "natural" in the broad sense that all of them more or
less result from erotic dispositions instilled by whatever heavenly configuration
prevails at nativity. Yet the extant texts nonetheless assume that at least receptive male and assertive female same-sex sexual roles and practices are "contrary
to nature." For Ptolemy, they manifest an inner "disease" in the sense excess
or deficiency of character, some disproportion, relative to a valorized mean or
norm (*Tetrabiblos*, 3.14). In effect, "nature" in Ptolemaic sexual astrology implies "normative nature," the ultimate norm being defined by reproductively
focused heteroerotic sex, as the supposed raison d'être of human sexual potential. He also thus includes perceived heteroerotic excesses in his pathology of love
(3.14.171).[7] Nevertheless, his rationale assumes that all "nonnormative" types
of sexual love are "natural deviations" from normative nature: integral parts of
sexual possibility instituted by the total natural order. Astrologers less conditioned by heteroerotic and reproductive biases would probably have elaborated
some different viewpoints for their homophile clients. Yet the surviving Greek
and Roman astrological works still assume the natural causality of the varieties
of homoeroticism, and their natal inscription in particular individual temperaments. Although the ancient astrological depreciation of sex "against nature"
might at first seem correlative to that of later Christian moralism (*Theology),
in important ways it radically differs and thus came to provide a conceptual
repertoire that offered alternatives to the latter's sexual orthodoxy, and means
of challenging it. If erotic affinities were instilled by the heavens, heteroerotic
practices would be no more individually "natural" or morally laudable than
others.

In later antiquity Christian writers such as St. Augustine increasingly attacked astrology on the grounds that its deterministic tendencies threatened
central doctrines of human free will, consequent moral responsibility, and divine providence. Perceived to challenge the authority of the church and God, it
was condemned by various early ecclesiastical councils.[8] The discipline subsequently became almost unknown or impracticable due to the loss of essential
texts and technical knowledge, and returned to the West only in the twelfth to

thirteenth centuries through reintroduction from Arabic sources and translations of them and their Greek predecessors into Latin (Tester, 113, 142, 152–53).

The subsequent cultural influence of astrology in late medieval and early modern European society was pervasive, compelling, multiform, and paradoxical. It is indeed arguable that "everybody who lived during the Renaissance believed to some extent in astrology."[9] Among the discipline's various possible subdivisions we may pragmatically distinguish two basic types, divinatory and natural. The former includes all "judicial astrology": efforts to predict the stars' influence such as genethliacal analysis of an individual's nativity to produce a horoscope or geniture, or "elections," inquiries into actions best to be taken or avoided. The natural type pursues more general meteorological, navigational, agricultural, medical ("iatromathematical"), and alchemical applications. Some accepted both types, others only the natural uses or aspects thereof, usually due to concerns about the unorthodoxy of divination.

Many celebrated Renaissance intellectuals, including major astronomers, were in different ways adherents or practitioners of astrology, such as *Marsilio Ficino (1433–1499), Copernicus (1473–1543), Girolamo Cardano (1501–1576), Tycho Brahe (1546–1601), Galileo (1564–1642), and Johannes Kepler (1571–1630).[10] It had been closely associated with medicine from the ancient Hippocratic school and Galen onward, so that courses in astrology had long been provided at medical schools such as the University of Bologna's.[11] Not only secular rulers retained astrologers for advice, as Catherine de' Medici consulted Nostradamus (1503–1566),[12] but also fifteenth- and sixteenth-century popes such as Sixtus IV, Julius II, Leo X, Clement VII, and Paul III. Astrological portents even determined the selection of Pope Julius II's coronation day. A leading Reformed enthusiast was the German Philipp Melanchthon (1497–1560), who produced a Latin translation of Ptolemy's *Tetrabiblos* published in 1553.[13] Publication of astrological texts ranged from the most learned works to popular "prophetic" broadsheets and almanacs[14]; the "formal controversy," debating the discipline's merits or demerits, was only one of its many genres active throughout Europe. Cardano launched a new vogue for gossipy anthologies of celebrity genitures with a collection of sixty-seven first printed in 1543 and increased to one hundred in subsequent editions. Official Roman Catholic reaction solidified during the Counter-Reformation, so that Pope Paul IV's index of prohibited books included divinatory astrology (1559), and it was banned by Pope Sixtus V in a 1586 decree that Pope Urban VIII reaffirmed in 1631.[15] *Calvin (1509–1564) issued his *Contre l'astrologie*, published in English as *An Admonition Against Astrology Judicial* in 1563. However, even through most of the seventeenth century, astrology retained some scientific interest, at least in theory, so that in England, for example, it received attention from Thomas Hobbes and members of the Royal Society such as Sir Christopher Wren, Robert Boyle, Nicholas Mercator, and Edmond Halley.[16]

As genethliacal astrology could be rejected, so also its account of the causes of homoerotic desires and practices, and its postulation of such innate personal dispositions. In the single most influential Renaissance critique of astrology, *Disputationes adversus astrologiam divinatricem* (A Polemic Against Astrological Divination), first published in 1495, Pico della Mirandola (1463–1494) assumes that there is a general stellar influence on the sublunary world, but comprehensively denies the possibilities of divinatory (though not natural) astrology. Since Pico's treatise includes arguments that celestial bodies and zodiacal signs have no gender, he implicitly eliminates the ostensible basis of astral influence on sex differences.[17] Adducing the case of an acquaintance who could only derive heteroerotic sexual pleasure from being whipped before sex, Pico insists that environmental conditioning influences character, not the stars, for the man's companions in youth beat rather than raped him (3.27). This argument would presumably extend to other sexual tastes astrologers ascribed to celestial alignments at nativity. Prevailing climatic conditions and not the stars, Pico also supposes, cause particular characteristics ascribed to nations, such as effeminacy or virility. And a region's legislation is important, for due laws

> can readily make fierce peoples extremely gentle. But if, on the contrary, laws are evil, they can easily enfeeble the strongest of nations, and make the best wicked. Thus is the freedom of the will demonstrated against every necessity of nature. At one time, the inhabitants of Gaul [i.e., France] were pederasts, if we believe Ptolemy and Aristotle; but now, thanks to Christian law and to the holy prince St. Louis, they abhor this vice more than any other nation under heaven. It is not necessary to restrict ourselves to the example of a single people, for the preaching of the Gospel has altered customs and ancient institutions throughout almost the entire world. (3.13)

In a chapter insisting "human morals are not fashioned by the heavens," Pico argues that, since nature is God's creation, and the stars are an especially exalted part of it, they cannot influence us to breach divine law, as in sex between males:

> ... It is absurd, this teaching of the astrologers who hold that we derive a tendency to commit burglary from such and such a position of the stars, or from another, a tendency toward incest, fraud or murder, when all of nature—and the higher reaches of nature in particular, which closely dwell in close proximity to the Divine Mind—can perhaps dispose us to observe the divine law and the law of nature, but certainly cannot prejudice or oppose it. Let them bridle their profane mouth, lest they say that Venus in conjunction with Mars summons us to commit adultery; or that, when these two [planets] are found together in "masculine" signs [of the zodiac], they drive us to disgraceful sexual congress with men; that Mars in the ninth part [i.e., ninth house] makes us irreligious, or that the other constellations incite us to other misdeeds. (4.9)

Nevertheless, despite the strictures of Pico and others, astrology's fascinations continued unabated, and it was probably the most commonly invoked early modern "scientific" means of explaining the existence and phenomena of same-sex desire. *Ficino, *Leone Ebreo (fl. 1460–1521), and *Robert Burton (1577–1640) readily turned to this discipline for such explanations. Cardano assures prospective readers that his extensive collection of genitures in the initial and expanded versions includes "the various forms of birth that yield pederasts, sodomites, whores, adulterers," among others (cit. Grafton, 80). Attributing sexual behaviors to inborn temperamental characteristics imparted by the heavens, he analyzes the horoscopes of Francesco Filelfo (1398–1481), who sexually enjoyed both boys and girls according to Cardano, and an effeminate male left anonymous (cf. Grafton, 67, 78–90, 105–07). In a competing collection, Luca Gaurico (1476–1558) concurs that the malefic influences of Mars and Venus made Filelfo burn "with wild lust for girls, and especially for boys" (cit. Grafton, 100). The biography of Michelangelo (1475–1564) published in 1553 by his pupil Ascanio Condivi (1525–1574) both assigns him a horoscope with a conjunction of Venus and Mercury, and later suggests his homophile leanings by comparing his relationships to Socrates's relations with Alcibiades.[18] "Joined with Mercury in honorable positions," Ptolemy advises, "Venus makes [the subjects] artistic, philosophical, gifted with understanding, talented, poetic, lovers of the muses, lovers of beauty, of worthy character . . . ; in affairs of love, restrained in their relations with women but more passionate for boys" (*Tetrabiblos*, 3.13.166).

Due to astrology's Renaissance intellectual prestige, the stellar etiology of same-sex love provided powerful means to question Christian sexual orthodoxy. On the issue of free will, astrology's proponents espoused a range of views from full astral determinism to moderate or variously qualified allowances for celestial influence. A common rationale of the latter sort parallels a justification of much early modern *physiognomy. Even though, in this view, the stars incline but do not compel, so that a wise man can rule them, astrological analysis nonetheless constitutes a worthy predictive science in accord with orthodoxy, because most are unwise, live according to their appetites, not reason, and hence pursue their astral inclinations. Casting a geniture could also have further value, it was said, by rendering the subject more familiar with his or her inherent flaws of character, the better to guard against them.[19] But such professed dissent from fatalistic perspectives could be a strategic genuflection to placate Christian orthodoxy while pursuing a contrary agenda, and Renaissance hermeneutics conventionally allowed for decoding the indirections imposed by official and unofficial censorships. Judicial astrologers of the period who claim to reject determinism often appear to contradict that, whether inadvertently or otherwise. Committed to making predictions of some putative value, and basing their work on more or less fatalistic ancient authorities, Renaissance astrologers tended to express themselves at least somewhat deterministically, whatever their assurances to the contrary, so that they had such habits of mind and could readily disseminate deterministic assumptions.[20] I have already shown that Ptolemy's position on this is at least ambiguous. It was rendered even more so in the Middle Ages and Renaissance by the pseudo-Ptolemaic *Centiloquium* (*Ptolemy).

Even the astrological rationales that seek to save free will raise questions awkward for orthodoxy. If the stars incline, how strongly do they do so? What if the strength of an astral inclination to a certain vice varies in different individuals according to the particular heavenly array of each nativity? If someone is more or less strongly predisposed to "unnatural vice," is not the extent of his or her alleged moral responsibility questionable? And also the justice of punishing such conduct? Moreover, if it arises from a cause in nature (the circulation of the heavens) that renders a corresponding temperament innate, are not the consequent desires and actions then natural for such a person? Would God not have authored that nature in some sense? Would he then not be responsible for it? How could it be reprehensible if God is benevolent? Although there were many official ways of countering and punishing such queries (*Theology), even knowledge of only the most elementary and nontechnical tenets of astrology could enable them to be conceived and pursued, privately or otherwise. Intensifying in the later sixteenth century, official religious condemnation of predictive astrology shows that ecclesiastical authorities had reason to be concerned about the discipline's impact on notions of moral accountability.[21] Pope Sixtus V's bull of 1586 includes condemnation of "those who dare to cast and interpret people's birth-horoscopes with a view to foretelling future events—be these contingent, successive, or fortuitous—or actions dependent on human will, even if the astrologer maintains or testifies he is not saying anything for certain" (cit. Maxwell-Stuart, 112).

Astrology further provided ways of limiting or rejecting the general authority of Christianity. The discipline's potential applications included intended pieties, as in the compendious *Christian Astrology* (1647) of William Lilly (1602–1681).[22] But Heinrich Cornelius Agrippa (1486?–1535) summarizes religion's astrological difficulties in his widely read *De incertitudine et vanitate scientiarum et artium* (On the Uncertainty and Vanity of the Arts and Sciences). Astrologers "attribute the things that belong to God unto the stars, and make us, when we were children, servants of the Stars, and whereas we know that God hath created all things, they teach that there be certain malicious Stars, the causes of mischiefs and naughty [i.e., wicked] influences, ordaining, not without exceeding great injury of God and the heavens, that in the heavenly places, in that divine Senate, mischiefs and ribaldries are determined to be done, and whatsoever willingly we commit, whatsoever through the corruption of matter doth naturally befall, they attribute it wholly to the Stars."[23]

Horoscopes could be cast for Mary and Christ, and Cardano, for example, published one for the latter that quickly became notorious.[24] If they too were subordinated to the stars, then, as Agrippa further complains, the agency of Christ as putative savior could appear compromised. The Inquisition's burning of the Bolognan university professor Cecco d'Ascoli in 1327 traditionally resulted in part from the astrologer's insistence that Christ's horoscope already epitomized his life and death.[25] Insofar as astral configurations were deemed to shape what happens here below, that could compromise the perceived scope of providential agency, though some contrarily maintained that the stars are simply instruments of providence. And according to the conjunctionist theory of ninth-century Arabic origin, major historical events are signified or caused by great planetary conjunctions, especially of Saturn, Mars, and Jupiter, which preside not only over vicissitudes and successions of cities, countries, and empires, but also religions, so that they too have their divinatory horoscopes, consequent characteristics, and inherent limitations.[26] Whereas Christianity claims to be the finally compelling religious revelation, it could thus be subjected to the stars and rendered one of a transitory series that would itself yield, in time, to some successor. Not only the significance of the religion but also that of its ecclesiastical institutions and repressions could thus be questioned, for the conjunctions further indicated or caused the advent of new prophets and sects within Christianity. Astrologers linked Martin Luther's birth to a planetary conjunction of 1484, and Cardano argued that Jupiter, Mars, and Mercury's conjunction in Aries in 1533 had precipitated England's religious breach with Rome.[27] Even the Fall itself could be attributed to a maleficent conjunction, thus jeopardizing human responsibility for original sin.[28] Astrology "taketh faith from Religion," Agrippa concludes, "it diminisheth miracles, it denieth providence: whilst that it teacheth all things to happen through the force of constellations and to depend upon the Stars with a fatal necessity. Furthermore it maintaineth vices, excusing them as though they did descend upon us from above ..." (106).

Agrippa's text further publicized astrology's challenges to conventional religion, and his actual attitude is unclear, for he himself was a famous magus and astrologer whom some thought demonically inspired. Such ideas appear in works of three writers associated with atheism and libertinism: Cardano, imprisoned by the Inquisition in 1570, condemned to abjure his heresies, and silenced; Pietro Pomponazzi (1462–1524), embroiled in controversies about his alleged subversions of religion; and Cesare Vanini (1585–1619), burnt at the stake in Toulouse after his tongue was ripped out.[29] Although the nature and extent of their heterodoxies are still controversial, it is their inherent interest in the deployment of astrological conceptions for criticizing religion that is important here. By providing means to counter the hegemony of Christian ideology and the narrowly moralistic proscriptions it entailed, these notions could support sexual dissidence and thus same-sex affiliations and behaviors. Hailed or excoriated as a godless apostle of libertinism, Vanini, for example, built his condemned texts partly on Pomponazzi's, and while in Paris evidently influenced the poet Théophile de Viau (1590–1626), a leading libertine who reportedly had sexual relationships with at least several males. (Burned in effigy in 1623, Théophile finally died from the poor conditions of his incarceration.) These particular connections exemplify some of the sexually *counterhegemonic* potential of astrological thought.

Subsequent readings mostly derive from Ptolemy and Firmicus, for they provided much of the theoretical and practical basis of the discipline in the Renaissance, and treat sexual matters more openly and expansively than seems

typical of their counterparts in the Christian era. *Ebreo in this chapter and
*Ficino and *Burton in the chapter "Love and Friendship" provide further
examples from the fifteenth through seventeenth centuries. Collectively showing
the broad impact of astrology on Renaissance conceptions of sex differences,
these early modern writers all assume that their readers will comprehend and
appreciate such observations. As sexual astrology was well known, so it was
also available for strategic applications to support homophile dissent as desired:
Unless no literate same-sex lover could make such comments as "our desire is
written in our natal stars" to an illiterate partner, and she or he in turn to others,
it must have had much popular diffusion.

Claudius Ptolemy (fl. 100–178)

Though not as astrally determinist as *Firmicus Maternus, Claudius Ptolemy
nonetheless assumes that the celestial conditions of birth powerfully instill particular sexual inclinations. An Alexandrian of Greek or hellenized descent,
Ptolemy produced definitive works in various mathematical disciplines, particularly astronomy, geography, and astrology. After his astronomical manual
the *Almagest* regained Western currency through Latin translation in the twelfth
century, it remained the preeminent text in its field until the sixteenth-century
heliocentric revolution. Ptolemy's authority underwrote astrology through his
four-book study commonly called the *Tetrabiblos* or *Quadripartitum*, and
through the pseudo-Ptolemaic collection of one hundred astrological aphorisms
known as the *Centiloquium*. Their Western recovery parallelled the *Almagest*'s
(cf. Tester, 92–93, 152–55).

Accordingly, Renaissance conceptions of Ptolemy's astrological thought are
not based on the *Tetrabiblos* alone. First printed in 1484 after much medieval
manuscript circulation in Latin, the *Centiloquium* had numerous subsequent
editions in several Latin versions and also Greek. Many aphorisms are, in themselves, bluntly determinist. Sexual affiliations thus have astral causes, and two
propositions exemplify this text's relevance to homoeroticism:

71. In the horoscopes of males, when either of the two luminaries [i.e., sun
     or moon] is in masculine signs, their effects are according to nature.
     In the horoscopes of women, their effects are intensified. Again, in the
     case of Mars and Venus: in the morning, they produce masculinity,
     and in the evening, feminity.
80. When Venus is in conjunction with Saturn, and has a certain lodger in
     the seventh house, the native will be given to perverse sexual activity
     (*sordidi coitus*).[30]

The first addresses the variance of male and female gender conformations, and
the second Saturn's sexually "queering" effects in relation to Venus. Much commentary surrounded the *Centiloquium*, and aphorism 80 occasioned discussion
of sex between males. Declaring this the sign of "infamous sexual intercourse,"

the 1493 Venice edition appends a comment attributed to Haly Abbas (al-Majūsī, c. 925–994) in Latin. Such a male thus favors "the posterior debauchery (*stuprum*) to the frontal one" and "stimulating the secretion of sperm with the hand." If Saturn is rising, the subject will "love caresses with boys... and prefer dark ones to fair." However, "if this misfortune arises from connection with Mars," such a man will "have intercourse with many boys, who will have intercourse with him and with his wife, and he will go so far as to commit fornication with his own sons."[31]

The *Tetrabiblos* was first printed in 1484, in one of the Latin translations from Arabic done in the twelfth and thirteenth centuries. At least four new translations into Latin from Greek (one partial) soon followed, first published in 1535, 1543, 1553, and 1635, respectively. Editions of the Greek text appeared in 1535, 1553, and 1581; no English translation was published until 1701. The surviving ancient commentaries were first printed in 1559, with Latin translations.[32] Aside from the major Renaissance commentary of Girolamo Cardano (1554), there were at least two others, by Agostino Nifo (1513) and Conrad Heingarten (unpublished).

Although Ptolemy recognizes various factors in an individual's development sexually and otherwise, he considers astral configurations most decisive (*Astrology). "In predictions affecting individual men," he argues, "the general characteristics of the temperament are determined [i.e., assessed] from the first starting point.... For to the seed is given once and for all at the beginning such and such qualities by the endowment of the ambient," the configuration of the heavens (3.1.105; trans. Robbins). Certain sexual tendencies are also astrally specific to the country of birth (2.1, 3; 4.10), though modified by individual celestial circumstances. Ptolemy's analysis of sexual affinities involves a certain qualified parallelism, as Brooten observes: "Heterosexually behaving men and *tribades* are produced by planetary masculinity, while heterosexually behaving women and soft men are produced by planetary femininity" (126). However, the astrologer says nothing about female partners of tribades in this sense, and the structural position and status of males who always remain homoerotically penetrative are somewhat ambiguous. Those who pursue such desire excessively, whatever that would entail from Ptolemy's viewpoint, would presumably be included in disproportions of sexual temperament, like their heteroerotic counterparts (3.14).

Tetrabiblos[33] *(c. 150)*

2.3. Of the Familiarities between Countries and the Triplicities and Stars
    ... The European quarter, situated in the north-west of the inhabited world, is in familiarity with the north-western triangle, Aries, Leo, and Sagittarius, and is governed, as one would expect, by the lords of the triangle, Jupiter and Mars, occidental. In terms of whole nations these parts consist of Britain, (Transalpine) Gaul, Germany, Bastarnia, Italy,

(Cisalpine) Gaul, Apulia, Sicily, Tyrrhenia, Celtica, and Spain....[34] However, because of the occidental aspect of Jupiter and Mars, and furthermore because the first parts of the aforesaid triangle are masculine and the latter parts feminine, they are without passion for women and look down upon the pleasures of love, but are better satisfied with and more desirous of association with men. And they do not regard the act as a disgrace to the paramour, nor indeed do they actually become effeminate and soft thereby, because their disposition is not perverted, but they retain in their souls manliness, helpfulness, good faith, love of kinsmen, and benevolence. (133–35)

Those who live in Bithynia, Phrygia, and Colchica[35] are more closely familiar to Cancer and the moon; therefore the men are in general cautious and obedient, and most of the women, through the influence of the moon's oriental and masculine aspect, are virile, commanding, and warlike, like the Amazons, who shun commerce with men, love arms, and from infancy make masculine all their female characteristics, by cutting off their right breasts for the sake of military needs and baring these parts in the line of battle, in order to display the absence of femininity in their natures. (149)

3.13. Of the Quality of the Soul

Allied with Venus in [dishonorable] positions Saturn makes his subjects... lawless in sexual relations, both active and passive, both natural and unnatural, and willing to seek them with those barred by age, station, or law, or with animals, impious, contemptuous of the gods,... rogues who will stop at nothing. (345)

3.14. Of Diseases of the Soul

One might now with propriety call "diseases" those extremes of character which either fall short of or exceed the mean. Those affections, however, which are utterly disproportionate and as it were pathological, which relate to the whole nature, and which concern both the intelligent part of the soul and its passive part,[36] are, in brief, to be discerned as follows. (363–65)

The... perversion of the [soul's] passive portion... is most apparent in excesses and deficiencies in matters of sex, male and female, as compared with what is natural,[37] and in inquiry is apprehended in the same fashion as before, though the sun is taken, together with the moon, instead of Mercury, and the relation to them of Mars, together with Venus, is observed. For when these thus fall under observation, if the luminaries are unattended in masculine signs, males exceed in the natural, and females exceed in the unnatural quality, so as merely to increase the virility and activity of the soul. But if likewise Mars or Venus as well, either one or both of them, is made masculine,[38] the males become addicted to natural sexual intercourse, and are adulterous, insatiate, and ready on every occasion for base and lawless acts of sexual passion, while the females are lustful for unnatural congresses, cast inviting glances of the eye, and are what we call *tribades;* for they deal with females and perform the functions of males. If Venus alone is constituted in a masculine manner, they do these things secretly and not openly. But if Mars likewise is so constituted, without reserve, so that sometimes they even designate the women with whom they are on such terms as their lawful "wives."

But on the other hand, when the luminaries in the aforesaid configuration are unattended in feminine signs, the females exceed in the natural, and the males in unnatural practice, with the result that their souls become soft and effeminate. If Venus too is made feminine, the women become depraved, adulterous, and lustful, with the result that they may be dealt with in the natural manner on any occasion and by any one soever, and so that they refuse absolutely no sexual act, though it be base or unlawful. The men, on the contrary, become effeminate and unsound with respect to unnatural congresses and the functions of women, and are dealt with as pathics, though privately and secretly. But if Mars also is constituted in a feminine manner, their shamelessness is outright and frank and they perform the aforesaid acts of either kind, assuming the guise of common bawds who submit to general abuse and to every baseness until they are stamped with the reproach and insult that attend such usages. And the rising and morning positions of both Mars and Venus have a contributory effect, to make them more virile and notorious, while setting and evening positions increase femininity and sedateness. Similarly, if Saturn is present, his influence joins with each of the foregoing to produce more licentiousness, impurity, and disgrace, while Jupiter aids in the direction of greater decorum, restraint, and modesty, and Mercury tends to increase notoriety, instability of the emotions, versatility, and foresight. (369–73)

4.5. Of Marriage

If Venus happens to be with Saturn, she produces merely pleasant and firm unions, but if Mercury is present, they are also beneficial. But if Mars also is present the marriage will be unstable, harmful, and full of jealousy. And if she is in the same aspect to them, she brings about marriages with equals in age; but if she is further to the east than they, marriages with younger men or women, and if she is further to the west, with older women or men. But if Venus and Saturn are also in the common signs, that is, in Capricorn or Libra, they portend marriages of kin. If the moon is present with this aforesaid combination when it is at the horoscope or at mid-heaven, she makes men wed their mothers, or with their mother's sisters, or their stepmothers, and women wed their sons, their brothers' sons, or their daughters' husbands. The sun, particularly if the planets are setting, makes men wed their daughters, daughters' sisters, or sons' wives, and the women wed their fathers, fathers' brothers, or stepfathers. But if the aforesaid aspects chance not to be composed of signs of the same gender, but are in feminine places,[39] thus they produce depraved individuals, ready in every way for both active and passive participation, and in some formations utterly obscene, as for instance in the forward and hinder parts of Aries, the Hyades, and the Pitcher, and the hind parts of Leo, and the face of Capricorn. But if the configuration is angular, on the first two angles, the eastern and mid-heaven, they make a complete display of their abnormalities and bring them forward even in public places; on the last two, that is, the western and northern, they produce spades and eunuchs or sterile women and those without passages; if Mars is present, men who have lost their genitals, or the so-called *tribades*.

In general we shall, in the case of men, investigate through Mars what will be their disposition with respect to matters of love. For if Mars is separated from Venus and Saturn, but has the testimony of Jupiter, he produces men who are cleanly and decorous in love and who aim only at its natural use. But if he is accompanied by Saturn alone, he produces men cautious, hesitant, and frigid. If Venus and Jupiter are in aspect with him, he will produce men easily roused and passionate, who are, however, continent, hold themselves in check, and avoid unseemliness. With Venus alone, or if Jupiter also is with her, but Saturn is not present, he produces lustful, careless men, who seek their pleasures from every quarter; and if one of the planets is an evening and the other a morning star, men who have relations with both males and females, but no more than moderately inclined to either. But if both are evening stars, they will be inclined toward the females alone, and if the signs of the zodiac are feminine, they themselves will be pathics. If both are morning stars, they will be infected only with love of boys, and if the signs of the zodiac are masculine, with males of any age. If Venus is further to the west, they will have to do with women of low degree, slaves, or foreigners; if Mars is further west, with superiors, or married women, or ladies of high station.

In the genitures of women one must examine Venus. For if Venus is in aspect with Jupiter or likewise with Mercury, she makes them temperate and pure in love. If Saturn is not present, but she is associated with Mercury, she makes them easily aroused and full of desire, but generally cautious, hesitant, and avoiding turpitude. But if Venus is together with Mars only, or is in some aspect to him, she makes them lustful and depraved and more heedless. If Jupiter too is present with them, and if Mars is under the sun's rays, they have commerce with slaves, men of lower classes, or foreigners; but if Venus is in this position, they consort with men of superior rank or masters, playing the part of mistresses or adulteresses; if the planets are made feminine by their places or aspects, they are inclined only to take the passive part, but if the planets are made masculine they are *so depraved as actively to have commerce with women.* However, when Saturn is brought into association with the aforesaid configurations, if he is himself made feminine, he is by himself the cause of licentiousness, but if he is rising and is in a masculine position, he makes them the objects of censure or lovers of such; but combination with Jupiter, again, always gives a more seemly appearance to those faults, and with Mercury makes them more notorious and unsafe. (401–07)

Julius Firmicus Maternus (fl. 330–354)

According to Julius Firmicus Maternus's eight-book Latin *Mathesis* (Learning), sexual affinities result from the formative imprint of astral configurations on personal character at birth. A Roman lawyer and senator apparently from Syracuse in Sicily, Firmicus compiled this text mostly from Greek sources now lost. Having become Christian at some point, he later authored a work attacking pagan mystery cults. The oldest extant manuscripts of *Mathesis* date from the eleventh century, when it began regaining Western currency. In the fifteenth century, the most influential astrological authorities were likely Firmicus and Manilius (Tester, 210); first printed in 1497, *Mathesis* was one of the fundamental Renaissance reference works in the field. However, some adepts, such as Girolamo Cardano, rejected Firmicus, seeking rather to restore an idealized ancient astrology by following *Ptolemy instead (cf. Grafton, 97–98, 124, ch. 8). While evincing a distinctive narrow moralism of his own, Firmicus's analysis of sexual dispositions typifies much ancient astrological practice by correlating perceived deviations in both sexes. Hence a given configuration of planets in masculine signs produces females who are viragos (masculine women or tribades), and in feminine signs eunuchs, hermaphrodites, or cinaedi, a word Firmicus primarily uses to denote males sexually receptive to males. Viragos and feminized men are also often astrologically comparable to prostitutes. Although his late-antique treatment of same-sex love is pejorative, "the relatively frequent occurrence of sexual deviance" in the *Mathesis* "raises the question of just what nature is when so many people are destined by the stars to live contrary to it."[40] Such elements of Firmicus's treatise could be appropriated to challenge sexual orthodoxy and justify same-sex sexual behaviors.

Mathesis[41] *(c. 335)*

3.6. Venus

4. Venus on the ascendant by day makes the natives oversexed, unchaste, of ill repute. They will be linen weavers, embroiderers, or artists in paints, dyers, innkeepers, or tavern-keepers. Saturn in aspect to Venus in any way will make the natives effeminate, [cinaedi], or engaged in sedentary activities....

6. Those who have Venus in this [i.e., second] house[42] by day will have great reverses and also late marriages.... If the Sun or Saturn are in

opposition, square aspect, or conjunction with Venus the natives will be sterile, never successful in sexual activity, will never marry, and always be lovers of boys. . . .

9. . . . If Venus is found in this sign [i.e., Aquarius] in the fourth house, with the Moon either in opposition or square aspect or conjunction with her, the natives will be sterile, not able to engender children, never enjoy conjugal life, and always prefer intercourse with boys.

14. . . . Great scandal over love affairs is indicated according to the nature of the signs. If [Venus] is in tropical, scaly, or mutable signs,[43] and Mars is with her or in opposition or square aspect, the natives are oversexed, impure, and of ill repute.

15. If Saturn is in opposition, in square aspect, or conjunction with Venus, located as we have said with Mars, women who have this combination make love [impurely and] unchastely to other women [due to lust]. These vices will be stronger if this combination occurs in Capricorn or Aries.

20. . . . If Jupiter is in square aspect or conjunction with Venus and Mercury, or if Saturn is in opposition, or if Saturn, Venus, and Mercury are together in this [i.e., ninth] house, the natives will be sterile, lovers of boys, and for this vice involved in homicides or other dangerous crimes. If a woman has this combination she will always imitate the behavior of men.

22. . . . If Venus in this [i.e., tenth] house is in a feminine sign and the waxing Moon, also in a feminine sign, is in aspect to Mars, this will make eunuchs, castrates, or hermaphrodites who do what women are accustomed to do when driven by extraordinary lust.

23. Venus in the eleventh house, if she is an evening star and aspected in any way to Mars and Saturn, will make the natives sterile, unable to engender children; only with difficulty will they attain the state of matrimony. Venus often makes them lovers of boys or of women from the stage; or they become managers of houses of prostitution, especially if she is in tropical signs. . . .

30. A woman who has Venus in this combination [i.e., in conjunction with or in square aspect to the moon, and in the twelfth house] will be involved in promiscuous sexual pleasures, an object of scandal and accused of incest. For she has intercourse either with brothers, sons, parents, nephews, sons-in-law, uncles, maternal or paternal; or she will call two brothers to her bed. Some women seek to imitate masculine behavior.

31. This effect will be stronger if Venus and the Moon are in tropical, mutable, scaly, or double signs and still more violent if Mars or Saturn are in opposition or square aspect, or together with Venus and the Moon; or if the Moon and Venus are found in the house of Saturn or Mars or in

the signs of Mercury, or if one is located in the sign of Mercury and the other in aspect as we have described.

4.13. [The Moon Moving from Venus]

5. The waning Moon moving from Venus toward Saturn in a nocturnal chart makes the natives sterile, eunuchs, castrated priests, hermaphrodites, or driven by desire to act the part of women. They will be short-lived or die a violent death.

5.2. [The Ascendant]

11. Those who have Saturn in these [i.e., ascendant] terms in a diurnal chart hate women and marriage. If it is a nocturnal chart, they will be impure, [unchaste, base, enmeshed in wretched lustful vices, and unable to approach natural coitus, but seized by preposterous raging lust against nature.] They will be in trouble from the changing nature of their plans and will be hated by all respectable people.

6.26. [Venus in Conjunction]

3. If Mars is in aspect to Mercury and Venus located together, this indicates an early marriage but connected with some scandal. For then the natives also desire to bed with boys as well as women and seek depraved pleasures beyond measure.

6.30. [Charts Showing the Influence of Venus]

16. If Venus is found with these planets [i.e., the moon and Mars] without the influence of Jupiter, all vices of impurity and unchastity are indicated. For then men are driven by heat of desire to act as women. If it is a woman's chart, she becomes a prostitute, selling her body or attaching herself to the power of a pimp, even though she appears to be of good family.

7.15. [Lovers of Boys]

1. Mercury and Mars in conjunction on the ascendant make lovers of boys. If the two are in an alien house the indication will be stronger. Also if Venus is in the house of Mercury, and Mercury is badly located, the natives are driven with [preposterous] desire to the bed of boys. To be exact: this occurs when Venus is in the house of Mercury and Mercury is on the IMC[44] or the descendant,[45] or in the sixth, eighth, ninth, or twelfth house, or on the anafora[46] of the ascendant, or in his debility.[47]

2. If the house of marriage, exactly computed, falls in the house of Mercury, and Mercury is on an angle in a masculine sign, this will make lovers of boys who never wish for intercourse with women. And if Mars and Mercury change houses so that Mars is in the house of Mercury and vice versa, this will still make lovers of boys, especially if the two thus located are in the house of Mars.

3. If Mercury is in the house of Mars and Mars is in opposition or square aspect to him, this makes lovers of boys. Likewise, if Mars is in the house of Mercury and Mercury is in opposition or square aspect to him, this indicates the same lustful vices. If the Moon is in the house or terms of Mercury, and Mercury is in the house of the Moon, this will have the same effect.

7.16. [Number of Wives]

2. Venus with Mars in the sixth house will make men and women adulterers. If they are in the house of Saturn and are in conjunction with Saturn himself in his house, in a woman's chart this makes public prostitutes; in a man's chart they either have prostitutes for wives or are joined in impure lust with [public cinaedi].[48]

7.25. [House of Sexual Desire]

1. If the Sun and Moon are in feminine signs, either together or in different houses, Venus is in a feminine sign on any angle, and the Moon and Mars are together on another angle, they will make eunuchs or hermaphrodites. If the Sun and Moon are in masculine signs and Venus is also in a masculine sign in a woman's chart, women will be born who take on a man's character and desire intercourse with women like men.

2. If Venus is in the house of Mercury and vice versa, or if they are in each other's terms, the Moon in Virgo, Capricorn, Taurus, or Leo, and the other masculine planets are in feminine signs and the feminine in masculine, hermaphrodites will be born.

4. Mars and Venus in conjunction in a morning rising and in a masculine sign make women [viragos][49] and sterile. In an evening rising in feminine signs, in a man's chart, if Saturn is in any aspect, they make [cinaedi] who serve in temple choirs. If this combination is found in Aries or Capricorn, these same afflictions are indicated. But if Venus is in opposition or square aspect and there is no influence of Jupiter, women will be born with masculine character; but men will become castrates or eunuchs or [cinaedi].

5. If the Moon is in opposition to Saturn, but Mars is so placed that he is in square aspect to them and in opposition to Venus, and all these four are in each other's houses, this combination makes women sterile and [viragos], and makes men [cinaedi]. Saturn in conjunction with the Moon will produce [cinaedi].

6. The same is true of Venus and the Moon in conjunction, also the Sun and Venus in the eighth house, Mercury and Venus in the houses of malefic planets, with Mars and Saturn in the house of Venus.

7. I shall briefly show how you may observe this more accurately: count the signs from the Moon to Venus and the same amount from the

ascendant. If the number falls in a feminine sign, and the Moon is in a feminine sign from the 25th to the 30th degree, you will find [cinaedi] who exercise their vice secretly; in a woman's chart the indication is for prostitutes.

8. But count the signs from Venus to the Moon and again from the ascendant, and if the number falls in a feminine sign, say that men will be detected in their practices. You will say the same in women's charts....

9. If Venus is not with the Moon but is in an evening rising located in the first degree of a feminine sign, aspected to the Moon also in the last degrees of a sign, this makes [men cinaedi] and women prostitutes, both of whom hide their practices. But if, with all as we have described, Saturn in a feminine sign is in square aspect to Venus or the Moon, this will make [cinaedi] who are deformed and poverty-stricken.

10. If all are located as we have said, and Mars is found with Saturn, he makes castrates. If Venus is in the last degrees of her sign and in aspect to Saturn and Mars, [this makes cinaedi with good fortune entrusted] with duties in temples; in a woman's chart they will be noblewomen involved in prostitution.

11. Mars, Mercury, Venus, and the Moon together in tropical signs, either in conjunction or in square aspect to each other, produce prostitutes, but their motivation varies according to the nature of the signs. If they are in feminine signs, this makes prostitutes, but in masculine signs, [viragos].

14. In general if the Moon, Sun, and ascendant are in the face or back of Capricorn, Aries, Taurus, or Leo, they indicate all kinds of sexual impurities together with extreme effeminization of the body. In all charts, if the Moon is found in the tail of Leo it will produce [cinaedi] who serve as tympany players to the mother of the gods.[50] But if Venus is found in the face of Leo, or of Capricorn, Aries, or Taurus, she drives both men and women to all kinds of vices.

15. If the Moon is in the signs mentioned above, Saturn and Venus in the seventh house in square aspect to the Moon, this makes [cinaedi]; also if Mars is in any aspect to the Moon, and if Mars and Saturn are in any aspect to Venus in Taurus, Leo, Virgo, or Capricorn.

18. Now I shall show you the house of sexual desire so that you may be able to find all vices and lusts. Count the signs from the Moon to Saturn, and again from the ascendant, and in whatever sign the last number falls, that is the sign of vices and the house of desire.

19. If the house of sexual desire falls in a feminine sign, if a malefic planet aspects this house in square or opposition, and if Venus is located on any angle, [cinaedi] are born but their vice is hidden. And if the house of desire has been exactly computed and found in dejected houses in a feminine sign, the native will be polluted by all impurities. But if it is located as we said and the Moon is in the first degrees of Pisces, Capricorn,

or Leo, or in the last degrees of Taurus, the natives will be involved in all vices.

20. If the house of desire is located in dejected houses and attacked by influence of malefic planets, and the Sun and Moon are in dejected houses in signs of malefic planets or in their humiliation, they make [public cinaedi (*publicos cinaedos*)] engaged in all vices. These vices grow stronger if the house of desire is in Capricorn, Aries, or Taurus.

21. If Venus is ruler of the chart and is together with Mars in a feminine sign and in dejected houses, but Saturn in a masculine sign is in trine to the ascendant in his own sign or his own terms, and the Moon is in a dejected house, [cinaedi] will be born. If the Moon, Venus, Mars, and Saturn are in feminine signs in dejected houses and are either together or in square aspect to each other, they make [public cinaedi (*publicos cinaedos*)]. But if one of these is well located the natives will exercise their vices secretly.

22. If Venus and Saturn are in feminine signs in the seventh house but the Sun, Jupiter, the Moon, and Mercury are in dejected houses, this without doubt will make [cinaedi]. And if all are located as we said and Jupiter alone is on the first angles, this will indeed make [cinaedi], but they will have the highest position, and glory and royal offices will be entrusted to them. If in this combination the Moon is found on the first angles, this will make them wealthy as well.

23. Venus and Mars in tropical signs, if they are in opposition or square aspect to each other in feminine signs, make [cinaedi], but secret ones. Located as we said, without influence of Jupiter, they make women prostitutes and men [public cinaedi (*publicos cinaedos*)].

8.25. Libra

1. Whoever has the ascendant in the first degree of Libra will be handsome, charming, and lovable. If Saturn is in that degree he will be unblemished in every part of the body. There are many stars in the second degree of Libra, some masculine, some feminine. Whoever has the ascendant in masculine stars will be noble and a writer of hymns to whom the secrets of the gods are entrusted. But if the ascendant is in feminine stars, he will be a [cinaedus] always conspicuous for charm and sophistication.

Leone Ebreo (fl. 1460–1521)

One of the more widely known books of early modernity, Leone Ebreo's *Dialoghi d'amore* ascribes the differing amorous inclinations of individuals to their particular horoscopic conditions. Also called Judah ben Isaac Abrabanel, Ebreo was born to an eminent Jewish family in Lisbon but moved to Spain and then Italy due to anti-Jewish persecution. A physician, philosopher, and minor poet, he apparently composed the *Dialoghi*, his major work, around 1502, though it was not published until 1535. This lengthy discussion between Filone and

Sofia syncretizes Florentine Neoplatonism, astrology, and cabbalistic lore. Published in Latin, French, and Spanish translations as well as Ebreo's original Italian, his treatise on love seems to have had international influence comparable to the once famous *De amore* of *Marsilio Ficino (1433–1499). However, Ebreo's treatment of Aristophanes's speech on androgynes from Plato's *Symposium* similarly suppresses its treatment of homoerotic love.[51] King Edward VI's tutor Sir John Cheke (1514–1557) signed the 1558 copy I use as source here, and Ebreo clearly influenced, for example, the poet Edmund Spenser (1552?–1599). Abraham Fraunce (c. 1560–1592/3) appropriated Ebreo's following homoerotic interpretation of the myth of Hermaphroditus for his mythography of 1592.[52]

Dialogues on Love[53] *(written c. 1502)*

Second Dialogue: Sophia and Philo on the Fellowship of Love

> Philo. Many other loves are attributed to Jove because the planet is friendly in and of itself, and brings its followers to friendship and love. Although his love is virtuous, it is by the fraternization of some of the other planets in the nativity of those born under his influence, those whom the poets call his children, that he makes them become lovers of virtuous things along with the other qualities of the followers of that planet. Sometimes he bestows an immaculate, pure, clear, sweet love, in harmony with his jovial nature.... At other times Jove gives his virtuous love not in an apparent and evident way, but in one nebulous, intimate, and clandestine. Because of this, they say he possessed and loved the daughter of Inachus in the form of a cloud. When Jupiter has intercourse with [the planet] Venus, [so to speak], he instills a love inclining to pleasure, and they suppose he possessed Europa in the form of a beautiful bull because the sign of the bull is in the tenure of Venus.... Being constituted with Mars he imparts a hot, fiery, and burning love. In this way they say Jove loved and possessed Aegina in the form of lightning. Having mingled with Saturn he produces a mixed love, virtuous and foul, partly humanly rational and partly gross and loathsome. Whence they fable that he loved and possessed Antiope in the form of a Satyr, which has the upper parts of a man and the lower ones of a goat, because the sign of Capricorn is in the house of Saturn. Further, if Jove is found in a feminine sign, he imparts feminine love (*amor feminile*), and so they say he loved and possessed Callisto in the form of a woman. And if he is found in a masculine sign, particularly in the house of Saturn, namely Aquarius, he imparts masculine love (*amor masculino*), so that they fable he loved the boy Ganymede and transformed him into Aquarius, the sign of Saturn.[54] I could tell you many more allegories of these and many more enamorments of Jove, but I won't because I wish to avoid prolixity and they are not of much importance. It is enough if you understand that all his amorous affairs indicate modes of love and friendship that depend on the influence of Jove in those whose nativities

he dominates. He sometimes imparts this influence alone and sometimes accompanied by various other celestial signs, explaining the great numbers of his diverse children and the history of those who have variously partaken of Jove's powers, and the manner of such participation. . . .

Sophia. . . . Now you must answer my question and tell me how the Hermaphrodite was born of [Mercury] and Venus.

Philo. This is what Ptolemy says in his *Centiloquium:* men in whose nativity Venus is found in the house of Mercury, and Mercury in the house of Venus—and especially if these two are in partile conjunction, conjoined bodily as it were—are inclined to foul and unnatural lust.[55] And of these there are some who love men and have no shame in being both active and passive at the same time, performing the roles not only of a man, but also of a woman. And one like that is called a Hermaphrodite, which is to say a person of one and the other sex. It is truly said these are born of the conjunction of Mercury and Venus, the reason being that these two planets do not combine together well and naturally. Mercury is wholly intellectual and Venus corporeal, so when they intermingle, their natures together produce a counterfeit and unnatural lust.

CHAPTER 5

Physiognomics

> It is possible to judge men's character from their physical appearance, if one grants that body and soul change together in all natural affections.... For if a peculiar affection applies to any individual class, e.g. courage to lions, there must be some corresponding sign of it; for it has been assumed that body and soul are affected together.
> —Aristotle, *Prior Analytics*[1]

From the ancient Greeks onward in Western culture, the physiognomical premise that human character can be deduced by assessing outer physical appearance has been pursued in the presumed cause of natural science. Sheldonian somatotypes—ectomorph, mesomorph, endomorph—are a twentieth-century example. And some recent research claims gays and lesbians can be distinguished by the relative lengths of their fingers. Although, as with *astrology, the study of early modern homoeroticism has yet to reckon with this former intellectual discipline, it too has important implications for the currently central controversies in the field. Physiognomics not only assumed different persons are characterized by distinct and abiding sexual inclinations and degrees of appetite, like astrology, but further supposed that outward physical appearances manifest the conditions of character and temperament. Hence particular erotic affinities appeared legibly inscribed in human bodies, and profoundly integral to the nature of each person, not adventitious. In addressing homoeroticism, physiognomics particularly attended to cinaedi, primarily meaning males who have receptive sex with males (exclusively or not), and it claimed to enable their ready identification by cataloguing their repertoire of behaviors and physical characteristics. Long before the advent of so-called homosexuality, physiognomics assumed the existence of particular sexual character types with correspondent morphologies, and promoted recognition of them. Though treating erotics between females much less often than the cinaedus, male effeminacy, and male homoeroticism, this discipline presupposed that personal temperament involves some distinctive interplay of masculinity and feminity, sometimes discussed masculine women, and problematized Christian moral condemnation of same-sex sexual behaviors in general by interpreting sex differences in a quasi-deterministic way.

As physiognomics had much prestige in ancient Greece and Rome, so too was the case in the Renaissance. The main surviving classical treatises on the subject are Greek: the pseudo-Aristotelian *Physiognomics*, and several versions or paraphrases of the ancient rhetorician Polemo's exposition, such as those of

Adamantius and pseudo-Apuleius, who also preserves parts of another treatise by Loxus. Not only was this apparent science endorsed by Aristotle, "the Philosopher," in the *Prior Analytics, History of Animals,* and *Parts of Animals,* as well as in the treatise formerly attributed to him, but also Galen affirmed its medical value. Whereas others designated Pythagoras physiognomy's founder, Galen named Hippocrates. To account for the significant reciprocity it assigned to mind and body, Galen applied the theory of four bodily humors of varying proportions that accordingly define physical and mental temperament. Cicero, Quintilian, Polemo, and Maximus of Tyre, among others, affirmed the rhetorical, oratorical, and thus political value of physiognomics. It could not only promise means to determine personality and predict behavior from appearance, but also to control self-presentation and influence others more effectively. In the Renaissance, then, the discipline's intellectual pedigree could appear compelling indeed.[2]

The supposed Aristotle's *Physiognomics,* on which Polemo drew heavily, argues that "dispositions follow bodily characteristics and are not in themselves unaffected by bodily impulses," so that "soul and body react on each other."[3] According to the zoological and ethnographic methods, this text explains, particular species of animals and races of humankind have certain temperamental characteristics or tendencies reflected in their typical physical appearance, and someone who outwardly looks similar shares the associated inner qualities. Alternatively, the "expressive" method notes how the human body physically manifests each passion, and assumes those who normally evince such physical traits are especially prone to it. Hence "the science of physiognomics . . . deals with the natural affections of disposition, and with such acquired ones as produce any change in the signs studied. . . . The physiognomist draws his data from movements, shapes and colours, and from habits as appearing in the face, from the growth of hair, from the smoothness of the skin, from voice, from the condition of the flesh, from parts of the body, and from the general character of the body" (806a; trans. Hett). However, some signs are more interpretively definitive than others, and these appear most of all in "the region around the eyes, forehead, and face." Chest and shoulders rank second, legs and feet third, abdominal parts last. "Generally speaking, those regions supply the clearest signs, in which there is greatest evidence of intelligence" (814b; trans. Hett). However, not any one particular sign is decisive, but rather the general impression of concurrent signs (805b–07a, 809a, 814a–b).

Following such ancient directions, physiognomical treatises proliferated in the Middle Ages and Renaissance.[4] In a census sampling seven editions of Aristotle's complete works published between 1483 and 1619 (four Latin, one Greek, two bilingual), all but the Latin edition of 1483 include the *Physiognomics,* and forty-nine sixteenth-century editions of this text have been tallied (Greek, Latin, Italian).[5] However, "Aristotle" had come to comprise further pseudepigraphic physiognomical works as well, and of these the most influential by far was the *Secretum secretorum* (Secret of Secrets), long supposed an encyclopedic epistle from Aristotle to Alexander the Great, but actually Arabic.[6] In the English version of Robert Copland (fl. 1508–1547) published in 1528 and reprinted in 1572, "Aristotle" thus admonishes Alexander, "among all other things of this world I will that thou know a noble and marvellous science that is called physiognomy by the which thou shalt know the nature and condition of people."[7]

Disciplinary subdivisions multiplied, such as chiromancy (interpretation of hands), podomancy (feet), ophthalmoscopy, pioneered by Polemo (eyes), and metoposcopy (forehead). Physiognomists could incorporate astrology in their readings of bodily features, so that the two disciplines were often intertwined. For example, physical data could be referred to the subject's astrological sign and planetary influences, as in the system of *Pietro d'Abano (c. 1250–c. 1315; cf. Thorndike, 2:910–11, 917–18). Most metoposcopy assumed that the forehead has astrological zones corresponding to the planets and interpreted its lines accordingly. "The fact that physiognomics—and more specifically metoposcopy— was assimilated to astrology underlines ... the reluctance of Renaissance scientists to accept that a phenomenon might be a random and meaningless event, not situated in the universal scheme of things."[8] Although some rejected physiognomics on various grounds, the multitude of such works published both in Latin and vernacular languages shows that it had major cultural influence.

Since identification of sex differences is fundamental to the discipline's ancient Greek sources, its medieval and Renaissance developments tend to operate likewise, and constitute a rich resource, as yet unexplored, for the study of the implications of eros and gender in early modernity. As Maud Gleason observes, Greek and Roman physiognomics interpretively assume that, as in the ancients' sex/gender system, gender is independent from anatomical sex. "You may obtain physiognomic indications of masculinity and feminity from your subject's glance, movement, and voice," Polemo advises, "and then, from among these signs, compare one with another until you determine to your satisfaction which of the two sexes prevails. For in the masculine there is something feminine to be found, and in the feminine something masculine, but the name *masculine* or *feminine* is assigned according to which of the two prevails."[9] Whether genitally male or female, then, each physiognomical subject is both masculine and feminine in some proportion displayed through the body, and those signs manifest his or her particular mental characteristics. Although a passage of Loxus indicates that feminine and masculine qualities could be understood complementarily,[10] the dominant surviving physiognomic tradition of pseudo-Aristotle and Polemo interprets them hierarchically, just as Aristotle himself associates feminity with natural imperfection. Accordingly, females "are tamer and gentler ... but less powerful," says the supposed Aristotle, "more forward and less courageous," have "a more evil disposition," and physical characteristics to match. "The males are in every respect opposite to this; their nature is as a class braver and more honest," and "speaking generally, superior to the female" (809a–b, 814a–b; trans. Hett).

In the pseudo-Aristotelian treatise, feminine features indicate weakness of character throughout, masculine ones contrary strength, and Polemo follows suit.

As a procedure for decoding character and predicting behavior from physical traits referred to perceived masculinity and feminity, ancient physiognomics had much to say about that insult to gender hierarchy, the cinaedus. In the sex/gender system of antiquity, the gender of a male's sexual object choice tended not to matter for his masculine status, so long as he remained the penetrator. Being sexually receptive was potentially disgraceful for an adult male, often concealed, and hence targeted for physiognomic decipherment, partly because, according to Aristotelian assumptions, femininity implied bad character. Also, as conformation to masculinity was physically and mentally idealized, so the cinaedus provided an admonitory "other" for disciplining male effeminacy. In the ancient texts and their Renaissance successors, there is considerable slippage between male effeminacy or "softness" and the penetrable cinaedus. In effect, the effeminate male appears a likewise deplorable counterpart of his fellow who fully consummates the imputed scandal of feminized masculinity by being sexually penetrated. Addressing the outer traits of the cinaedus in several contexts, the supposed Aristotle declares "he carries his hands palm upward and slack," his head "inclined to the right," has "two gaits, he either waggles his hips or holds them stiffly," and "casts his eyes around him." He is "weak-eyed and knock-kneed," with a voice "high-pitched, gentle and broken." The general model here is femininity, just as the author claims "the female has knock knees,"[11] and the body language connected with the cinaedus partly signals atypical male availability for sexual penetration. Polemo and pseudo-Apuleius further elaborate this inventory of fey behaviors.[12] Since the description and identification of the cinaedus was a standard topic of Greek and Roman physiognomy,[13] the attention of medieval and Renaissance practitioners was directed to that sexual category. It constituted an expected commonplace of physiognomical discourse, one of the phenomena of character conventionally treated.

Comment on female homoeroticism in this discursive domain seems relatively infrequent, just as the major ancient sources do not address it. However, an anonymous Latin physiognomic treatise of the fourth century observes that women appearing relatively feminine may seek female sexual partners of various degrees of femininity or masculinity. Fifteen known manuscripts survive, and the treatise was printed once during the Renaissance at Lyons in 1549, entitled *De diversa hominum natura*.[14] Among early modern authorities, at least the sexually frank *Bartolommeo della Rocca, often called Cocles (1467–1504), acknowledges such feminine sex differences.

As physiognomics insists that bodily characteristics and manners signify mental predispositions, so its claim that sex differences are inscribed in the body and personal deportment implies they are profoundly engrained in an individual's particular inner nature. In the case of the cinaedus, sexually receptive homoerotic inclinations entail a particular ensemble of physical characteristics manifesting this sexually defined personality type, and these are jointly evinced through both body and soul. As the discipline assumes individuals often evince diverse and contradictory sets of physiognomical signs, so each cinaedus would be assumed to differ somewhat from the collective model, but partake of its repertoire sufficiently to be identified. A cinaedus' behaviors would be arguably natural for someone formed as such, who would, in his intermediary state between masculinity and femininity, have a correspondent type of body, mind, sexual desire, and set of personal traits and affinities.

Not particularly problematic in a pagan context, such a physiognomical perspective becomes so in a Christian culture positing "unnatural vice," accursed sodomitical sin, and a loving divinity's consequent infliction of everlasting tortures allegedly justified by his human creatures' exercise of free will during their brief earthly lives. Like *astrology, this discipline offered an apparently scientific means to contest Christian sexual orthodoxy. How could a cinaedus be held morally responsible for his so-called vice if the disposition to commit it defined the joint nature and articulation of his body and soul? Moreover, how could it be unnatural in his case if it were natural to him? *Rocca assumes that personal development into a cinaedus is sufficiently determined that even a child evinces its future probability. *Giovanni Antonio Magini (1555–1617) perceives sodomitical tendencies, dispositions, and behaviors inscribed in the very lines of the forehead. In various ways a male who liked to be sexually penetrated could find physiognomical reasons to believe that is an intrinsic function of his particular nature, as his insertive homophile counterpart could also.

The discipline's potential to challenge central theological doctrines had been well understood since the Middle Ages. Assuming the body expresses predispositions of character so that behavior can be predicted accordingly, physiognomics had deterministic tendencies, impinged on divination, and appeared to compromise free will, human moral responsibility, and thus orthodox notions of sexual morality. It raised much the same moral and religious concerns as astrology, with which it was often compounded.

Medieval physiognomists such as St. Albertus Magnus (1193?–1280) and their early modern successors thus typically sought to assert their science's Christian orthodoxy by downplaying its deterministic and divinatory aspects.[15] Prefacing his adaptation of *Rocca, Thomas Hill (fl. 1556–1590) explains that physiognomy enables us to "foretell the natural aptness unto the affections ... by the outward notes of the body." However, error can occur because some may overcome these inclinations through divine "grace and wisdom." But because "men (for the more part) do live after a sensual will in themselves," unlike "the wise and godly," they live "after their affections and appetites" instead. So "the bodily notes of Physiognomating by the natural inclinations of men do procure and cause a great probability, though no necessity." Whatever some say, then, Hill urges, the science is not "wicked and detestable."[16] Such arguments drew on Cicero's *On Fate* and *Tusculan Disputations*. The physiognomist

Zopyrus found that Socrates's body evinced stupidity and lust for women, Cicero relates, and yet, just as Socrates replied he had surmounted those inclinations through reason, so an individual's particular inherent tendencies toward certain vices can be overcome.[17]

However, given Socrates's optional Renaissance role as one of the greatest patrons and exemplars of sexual love between males, this widely repeated anecdote in which he claims to have conquered inherent propensities toward lechery with females, at which his ardent young pursuer Alcibiades reportedly laughed, could well have amused sodomites in ways unintended by the enthusiasts of conventional morality. And since physiognomics would have no value if it could not identify character and predict behavior with some supposed reliability, it readily tended to involve its devotees in deterministic thinking. Whatever physiognomists said to save the orthodox appearances, and whatever they believed about that, they often wound up talking like determinists, and so their discipline tended to undermine orthodox Christian morality. Various sixteenth-century Roman Catholic indices of forbidden books incorporated works of leading physiognomists, including *Rocca and *Giambattista della Porta (1535–1615), who had difficulties with the Inquisition (Thorndike, 6:145–50). Pope Sixtus V included physiognomics in his 1586 bull against arts of divination, which was reaffirmed by Pope Urban VIII in 1631. Like astrology, this discipline had an acknowledged subversive potential that sexual dissidents could exploit.

Bartolommeo della Rocca or Cocles (1467–1504)

Topics of Bartolommeo della Rocca's *Chyromantie ac physionomie anastasis* include the outer signs of cinaedi, effeminate men, insertive sodomites, tribades, manly women, and the alleged implications for personal character. According to the formerly famous Italian mathematician, astrologer, and physician Girolamo Cardano (1501–1576), Rocca was a barber-surgeon whose dedicated physiognomical researches earned him intellectual fame and powers to foretell the time and manner of death, even his own.[18] Having finished the *Anastasis* in 1504, he was then murdered by order of its dedicatee's son, Ermete Bentivoglio, to avenge Rocca's prediction of Ermete's exile and death in battle. First published that year in Bologna, this comprehensive six-part study had many Latin editions but most are abbreviated. Also typically shortened, vernacular adaptations followed in Italian (1525), German (1516, 1519, 1530, 1537, 1544), French (1546, 1550, 1638, 1679, 1693, 1698, 1700), and English (1556, 1571, 1613).[19] The *Anastasis* first appeared with an introduction by Alessandro Achillini, a professor of medicine and philosophy, insisting "physiognomy and chiromancy do not compel human free will but act by natural causes which may be impeded, though actually they rarely are" (Thorndike, 5:43). Nevertheless, its deterministic and predictive tendencies are obvious, and Roman Catholic indices of forbidden books condemned Rocca's work in 1554 and 1559 (Thorndike, 6:146–47). Not simply reproducing ancient sources but including many case histories and personal reminiscences of contemporary personalities, the *Anastasis* has special and as yet untapped value for the history of sexuality. It seeks to engage actual conditions of current Italian society, and that no doubt contributed much to the work's substantial international vogue.

From the *Anastasis* itself I reprint a comment about feminine bodily signs that bears on tribadism, a relatively unusual topic in ancient and Renaissance physiognomics. I further add passages relevant to male homoeroticism from *The Contemplation of Mankind* (1571) by Thomas Hill (fl. 1556–1590), a work amplifying his earlier *Brief and Most Pleasant Epitome of the Whole Art of Physiognomy* (1556). Though drawn much from Rocca, whom Hill calls Cocles or "the Physiognomer," both are brief adaptations rather than translations, yet demonstrate the vernacular diffusion of Rocca's ideas.

One of the basic assumptions of Hill's *Contemplation*, deriving from ancient physiognomers, is that feminine males and masculine females are fraudulent and lustful. Their gender appears somehow double or "deceptive," and since feminity was devalued anyway, effeminacy supposedly debased a male. Although the significance of each outer sign or indicator appears absolute in its local context, Hill's chapter entitled "A Perfect Instruction in the Manner of Judging" follows the ancients in insisting "a man may not hastily pronounce judgment of any one note alone, but gather and mark diligently the testimonies of all the members, and if there happen to thee to appear divers notes, and that unto divers effects, then lean . . . unto the mightier and worthier part," such as "the eyes, the forehead, the head, and the face."[20] I retain Hill's usages of the Latin *cinaedus* as an English loanword in the form "cyned."

The Rebirth of Chiromancy and Physiognomy[21] *(1504)*

Book IV, Tenth Inquiry: What Ought to Be the Judgment if One Finds Signs of Morally Offensive Lust [Nephande Luxurie] on the Hands of a Woman?

It should be known that the qualities of a subject's hand are found to differ in two ways, depending on the subject. As a result, if signs of sodomy (*pedicationis*) are found in a female subject, there should be another indication of the deviation of the sex. For in the subject who is a young girl, it bespeaks illicit lust in both directions, even if she lacks the equipment for it. For I have nonetheless known women to sodomize (*pedicantes*) and masturbate boys, and to abuse them by rubbing their buttocks with the vulva with great fervor, avidity, and pleasure in copulation, until they emit sperm. And I saw a certain woman who was infatuated with a lad who was my servant; and I have seen many other women of this type. By "morally offensive lust" we mean the sexual congress of brothers and sisters by the same mother, and of nuns and monks, and manual pollution, and sexual union with animals, and any kind of sexual congress which falls outside the bounds of order. Note also that in women "morally offensive lust" can be understood when women come together vulva to vulva and rub one another, of which Juvenal writes in this verse: "They ride one another, turn and turn about, and disport themselves for the Moon to witness."[22] And such women are called by the ancient term *tribades*. It is said that Sappho, the Lesbian lass and poet, amused herself with this kind of lust.

The Contemplation of Mankind . . . after the Art of Physiognomy[23] *(1571)*

Chapter 12: The Dividing of Mankind into Two Forms or Natures, and a Perfect Description or Distinction of the Man from the Woman, after Physiognomy, Uttered by the Singular Conciliator[24]

The wise and skillful Physiognomers, in their examinations, do divide mankind into two forms, as into the Masculinity and Femininity, according to the property of the spirit. For man naturally, except his procreation be hindered, is perfecter than the woman both in conditions and actions. First, he is of a lively mind and courage, and unto a brunt or an attempt pressed and vehement, yet slowly moved to ire, slowly pleased, advised in businesses, in due and fit times studious, abroad liberal, stout, just, trusty, unconstant or wandering from place to place, and true of his word. Of which Avicenna . . . reporteth that man is the subtler, and that women are more pitiful and gentle than men, more convertible, lighter persuaded, sooner seduced, enviouser, fearfuller, unshamefaster, more foolish, liars, more fraudulent, more receive fraud, more esteeming trifles, slower, tenderer, weaker, and more prone, or sooner drawing into familiarity. . . . This like uttereth the Philosopher, in Book IX of *De historia animalium*, chapter one, that man in nature is perfectest. . . .[25]

But if the man possesseth the woman's properties, whose note appeareth, . . . he is unfaithful, an ill reporter, and a liar: and this rather, when he draweth near to the woman by the counterfeiting, the often shifting, and decking of parts. The like may be said of the woman's qualities, when she often exerciseth and followeth near man in the appareling and decking of her body like to him, as did that manly woman Fracassa, of whom shall fully be uttered in the proper place. The Philosopher Aristotle reporteth that the person which leaneth with the body to the right side in the going, to be effeminate, in that he is of a moist quality and soft of skin. The like of these Cocles [i.e., Rocca] noted to have a soft skin, a clear and fair throat, effeminate legs, and for the more part were slender, but the haunches were big and soft, the face white and pimpled, the voice small, low, and hoarsely, like to the common Harlot, haunting very often man's company. And these have many other notes, which for that they are more at large uttered in other places of his book, he doth here wittingly omit them. And in his time was a certain noble person imprisoned, being one of these. And another effeminate person he saw of the City of Lucca, being of sixty years, which hanged or leaned to the left side as he went, and had a red color in the face, so fair a throat as the clear[26] woman, the face pimpled, the hairs of the head trussed and finely trimmed, the voice small and soft, and to be brief, he was a very effeminate person and Cyned.....

The gelded persons become not only weak of body but in mind and courage little differ from the woman, as the Philosopher Aristotle reporteth. This worthy lesson also the Philosopher uttereth, that he wisheth to fly and eschew that woman's company when she is of composition manly, for there is a sure token in her both of luxury[27] and wickedness, but contrary, judge the courage of such men, which in composition be effeminate. (fols. 10^{c-d}, 11^{b-c}, 12^{a})

Chapter 13: The Judgment of the Color and Substance of the Hairs of the Head, and in All Other Places of the Body

By many outward signs may a man find out the qualities of the mind and courage. As when a woman is apparelled and decked in man's apparel, which doth then declare her nature to draw near to man's. As the like did that woman of courage named Fracassa, who commonly used to wear (by the report of the Physiognomer [i.e., Rocca]) man's apparel, and would upon a bravery[28] many times arm herself at all points to joust and run sundry times so armed at the ring.[29] The form of which woman... was on this wise: she had a small head, and Pineapple-like, a neck comely formed, large breasted, seemly arms, answering to the body. But in her other parts, as in the hips, buttocks, thighs, and legs, near agreeing to man's. This manly woman also walked upright in body, treading light on the ground, and bearing her head playing like to the Hart.[30] The other notes of this woman did the Physiognomer for brevity sake here omit. Yet he thus concludeth that by the sundry notes which he viewed, she was prone to come to a violent death....

Where sundry men are named to be Effeminate is understanded and meant two ways: the one, when as such be delighted to go in apparel and decked with ornaments like to women; the other, to appear lascivious and weak both of will and courage. The quality of which apparently declareth that the mind (for the more part) doth like ensue and answer to the disposition of the body. For such be noted of experience to be unfaithful and evil reporters and liars, in that they thus through their counterfeiting answer to the kind fraudulent and wily....

The hairs of the head (after the mind of the Philosopher Aristotle) very thin, do indicate an effeminate mind, for the lack of blood, through which not only a slowness but a womanly courage and dullness in conceiving is procured. (fols. 18^{a-b}, 19^{b}, 20^{b})

Chapter 15: Of the Form, Nature, and Judgment of the Forehead

The forehead appearing even and smooth doth denote such a person to be effeminate both in courage and will, according to the agreement of

Philemon, Polemo, Loxus, Aristotle, Conciliator, and the Greek author Adamantius. (fol. 38[b])

Chapter 17: The Form and Judgment of the Overbrows

The hairs of the overbrows, if they shall be stretched and lie so straight as a line in length, and these long, do demonstrate an evil, weak, and feminine mind, applied by the like to women. And these manner of eyebrows, saith the Physiognomer, do I attribute to Venus. And such he saw, for the more part, to be Cyneds, or else very luxurious.[31] (fol. 53[b])

Chapter 22: What to Be Noted and Judged of the Condition and Form
of the Nose and Nostrils

The Nostrils of the Nose do like declare the genitors[32] to be (if we may credit the Physiognomer). For if these be big and large then like are the genitors of Man judged to be big and large; but if the Nostrils appear small and narrow, then like are the genitors judged small, and co. Of which this rule seldom faileth except by accidence: as either through a sickness or by the often tractions with the hand. Which practice, as the Physiognomer reporteth, is more commonly exercised of the Cyneds or effeminate persons, which by that manner of dealing have greatly increased this member, as he of experience hath known in many. And he also uttereth of skill known, that in many persons is the right hand bigger than the left, in that the same, by his reason, cometh oftener in use. . . .

When the Nose shall be meanly small, a little dry upward, and at the end raised up, and the nether part or end turned again upward, or that his cleft be proceeding from beneath unto the part turned upward, toward the cone of the Nose, doth then indicate luxury or such an abuse of the body not here decent to be uttered, as the learned Conciliator in his Rubric of Physiognomy reporteth.

The like of this the Physiognomer Cocles observed and noted sundry times, especially in one of the Senate house of the noble city of Bologna, which for reverence unto the noble house, and honesty sake, he refuseth to name. The cause is forasmuch as such are of a moist and sanguine quality, tending unto choler, and these universally . . . are luxurious, in both the kinds, even as the same through the pricking forward of choler, which daily inflameth the blood.

And the regitive[33] nature of the whole body moveth or stirreth forward the expulsive virtue unto the sending forth of the noyous matter super-fluous, and expelleth the same unto the congruenter places by the apt passages, and sendeth the same forth unto the yard, in that it is the cause of the erection of it. So that such help forward themselves by a proper industry not decent (for honesty sake) to be here uttered [i.e., masturbation], whenas the desired subject is not at hand. And the apparent notes of these persons are that such have the nose big and blunt especially at the end, and the nostrils wide and large, through the grossness or bigness of the nose.... (fols. 94^b, 103^a–104^a)

Chapter 24: Of the Condition, Nature, and Judgment of the Mouth

The mouth... having a seemly quantity in the greatness, with the lips thin and appearing small in the closing, and to these, the eyes showing smilingly, with the rest of the face agreeable answering, doth indicate a libidinous peron, a Cyned or an effeminate creature, and a liar, as the worthy Conciliator in his Rubric of Physiognomy uttereth. (fol. 118^b)

Chapter 27: The Judgment of the Form and Condition of the Lips

The nether lip discerned loose hanging and folding downward, and that the same appeareth very red in color, doth argue, happening in the woman, to be a most sure note of the great desire unto the venereal act, and un-shamefastness in the creature. As the same the Physiognomer Cocles ob-served and noted in a famous Courtesan of Rome named Isabella di Luna. The like note seen in children signifieth that the creature in time to grow and become a Cyned or effeminate person; especially if the countenance and eyes appear smiling and the creature grown unto a ripe age,[34] as the same the Physiognomer Cocles reporteth that he noted in a certain nobleman of the like condition. (fols. 121^{a-b})

Chapter 32: The Form and Judgment of the Chin

If the chin shapeth or be formed into a round manner, doth indicate effeminate conditions and a feeble courage, in that this is a feminine note as uttereth the ancient Pythagoras. For the man's chin, after nature, ought to be formed in a square manner and not round....

The chin at the lower end seen to be divided, that the same expresseth a double form, in such manner as this be not too much or too deep dented in the middle, doth then argue, as certain report, deceitful conditions to consist in that creature. But this known to be a note of Venus in that place, after the mind of the Physiognomer Cocles, and such a person like formed shall purchase with men great favor and grace. As the like Cocles experienced in many subjects which were known to be lascivious and that haunted the company of harlots; yea, these with the Cyneds had sundry times doing and suffering. (fols. 143^b, 144^{a-b})

Chapter 36: The Condition and Judgment of the Shoulder Points

The Physiognomer Cocles reporteth that he knew and saw sundry women in his time which drew by Art and through their bestial induments[35] the shoulder points so near together that they formed in a manner the like unto Os ventris in the part behind, and they garnished or beautified these with Cosmetical waters.[36] This Cocles also noted sundry Italians and fond

Frenchmen, which he aptly nameth by that byword *Hermaphroditi*, that used and exercised the like practice with their shoulder points. A matter which seemeth in my opinion incredible to be exercised of any faithful Christian, but the Physiognomer seemeth truly to utter what he saw and knew in sundry places. (fol. 160^a)

Chapter 51: The Judgment of the Knees
The learned Conciliator reporteth that the knees appearing loose, as they were separated from the rest of the body, do denote such to be weak in their going. Such hath the Physiognomer seen and noted to have gone with the toes and knees turning toward the silvester part, that is, outward, and their knees tended unto the domestical part, that is, inward. And such persons evermore are effeminate and for the more part Cyneds, as the Physiognomer experienced in many subjects and found the same to be like. Such also are of a peevish nature, that aptly they may be attributed to women for their like. (fol. 195^b)

Chapter 54: The Judgment to Be Given of the Motions and Walkings in General
Such which go with a leaping or dancing pace and bearing out the buttock, and with the countenance borne upright, are noted to be Cyneds and womanly persons....

Such which tread on the toes in such sort going outward with them, that the heels seem to make an angle behind, are noted of a womanly nature, yea, and Cyneds, especially if the knees seem to knock together and bend in the going....

Such which for the more part go so nicely on the toes that scarcely any dirt is seen on the outsides of the rest of the shoes are argued to be of a womanly nature, and that these to be Cyneds, and such which exercise and follow the venereal conditions, especially if the feet be amiable, small, and with flat heels. (fols. 206^a–207^b)

Chapter 55: The Judgment of the Hairiness in Divers Parts of the Body
Very little or few hairs on the hands to be seen, do denote a weak body and a feminine or womanly nature. The hands quite without hairs to be seen, is a note of evil conditions and to be a presumptuous fool and an effeminate person. And this the worser if he hath no beard, for then is he compared to the gelded person and his conditions. (fol. 209^b, misnumbered 109)

A BRIEF REHEARSAL OF THE NOTES OF ALL THE MEMBERS, WITH THEIR SIGNIFICATIONS, IN THE FORM OF A TABLE
The person going with the knees and feet turning in, to be weak of strength: applied to the woman [i.e., as exemplar?].... Leaning unto the right side in the going, to be a cyned: applied to the excessive appearance. (fol. 225^a, misnumbered 125)

A BRIEF TREATISE OF THE SIGNIFICATION OF MOLES SEEN IN ANY PART
OF THE BODY, WRITTEN BY THE GREEK AUTHOR MELAMPUS[37]

If the Man shall have a Mole on the ankle of the foot, doth denote that he shall take upon him the woman's part. And the woman having a Mole the like placed, shall take upon her the man's part. (fol. 229^a, misnumbered 129)

Giambattista della Porta (1535–1615)

In *De humana physiognomonia* (1586), one of the most widely read early modern physiognomical texts, Giambattista della Porta seeks to define the identifying features of the cinaedus, and, in the expanded edition, advise how such males might become more conventionally masculine. Of wealthy noble lineage, the author was born at Vico Equense and spent most of his life in Naples, aside from travels in Italy, France, and Spain, and some years spent in Rome. Early biographies suggest he was largely an autodidact. Little is known of his marriage except that he fathered one child, a daughter, around 1579. Besides addressing many scientific topics including magic (not yet distinguished from science), his voluminous works include many once highly reputed plays. His first and most internationally famous work was *Magiae naturalis* (Natural Magic), published initially in 1558, much enlarged in 1589, often republished, and translated into Italian, French, German, and, in 1658, English. Admired by Johannes Kepler, Porta significantly contributed to the development of the telescope. His energetic physiognomical studies further yielded *Phytognomonia*, on the appearances of plants (1588); *Coelestis physiognomonia* (Heavenly Physiognomy, 1601?/1603); and *De manuum lineis* (On the Lines of the Hands), a treatise on chiromancy begun before 1581 but first published posthumously in an Italian translation as *Della chirofisonomia* (1677).[38] Enlarged in 1599 and reissued in over twenty editions and several languages (Thorndike, 5:68), *De humana physiognomonia* was Porta's most famous book aside from *Magiae naturalis*. Illustrated with delightful comparisons between the heads of animals and humans, it was largely inspired by the zoological approach associated with Aristotle on account of comments in his works and in the pseudepigraphic *Physiognomics* (*Physiognomy). In *Coelistis physiognomonia* Porta develops a predictive theory of astral signatures in the body while professing to reject judicial astrology condemned by the church. However, the author himself had cast numerous divinatory horoscopes.

At some point prior to 1580, Porta's occult studies and writings provoked investigations by the Inquisition, and his Accademia dei Segreti, an association formed to promote pursuit of occult and scientific inquiries, was disbanded by that date. From the outset of his publishing career he complained of censorship, lengthy delays and difficulties in securing printing licenses, and bans on publication. Though accused of witchcraft by Jean Bodin in *De magorum daemonomania* (The Demon-mania of Witches, 1581),[39] Porta considered his magic natural, not diabolically "black." In 1592/93, he was prohibited from publishing *De humana physiognomonia* in Italian, and from any further publication of his books without an Inquisitorial license from Rome.

Issued in 1586, the first edition of that physiognomical work includes a chapter on features of the cinaedus and male effeminacy, significantly situated between a chapter on woman and one on man. Whereas the first edition provides each of those normative gender types with a fine illustration exemplifying femininity on the one hand and masculinity on the other, the cinaedus, implicitly too ambiguous or unworthy for such notice, has no picture, but is defined rather by pictorial absence and implied interplay between the two flanking, formally depicted gender types. Largely reporting ancient physiognomers' observations, though with refinements and contributions, Porta's account of the cinaedus is, we would now say, essentialist and transhistorical. His augmented version of 1599, adding two books to the first edition's four, adds a later chapter advising that such males can lose their femininity through a tougher way of life that enhances heat, commonly deemed the definitive masculine constitutional trait, in their temperament. While thus appearing to moderate the deterministic implications of the prior chapter that posits a set character type, Porta does not endorse the corrective efficacy of reason and divine grace here, so that the cinaedus appears recalcitrant, requiring a radical change in living conditions to be reformed. Through medical intervention, in effect, he seeks to amend a condition assumed deeply rooted in personal temperament.

On Human Physiognomy[40] *(1586, 1599)*

Book Four, Chapter 11: The Face of the Cinaedus

Aristotle, discussing continent and incontinent men and the man who is capable of endurance in his *Nicomachean Ethics,* says that the soft man is the opposite of the man capable of endurance.[41] Endurance consists of withstanding, but someone who fails to withstand what others withstand is soft and delicate. Certain affected manners are a kind of softness. The man who lets his cloak drag rather than carrying it, because it is too much trouble for him, or who acts like an invalid, is wretched without knowing himself to be so. Softness is also an inherited trait, as for example with the kings of Persia. Polemo and Adamantius attribute a portrait of the cinaedus to Aristotle, and Aristotle says that such was Dionysius the Sophist.[42] [As we can see by reading Athenaeus, there were many effeminate men in the past: Sardanapalus son of Anacyndaraxes, Sagaris the Mariandynian, Xenocrates of Chalcedon, Annarus, and Ninus.][43]

Cinaedi, like women. Bloodshot (*confracti*) eyes: but Polemo and Adamantius say that [their eyes are] moist and wanton. Γονύχροτοσ: some translate this as "knock-kneed," but I would rather say it is a knee that makes a noise when it bends. Polemo writes γονὰτων χρὸτοσ. Head inclines to the right. Also, an inclined neck. Languid and dissolute movements of the hands: but here the text of Polemo is rather corrupt, and can readily be corrected from Adamantius. A double gait: one leaning backwards, the other with the hands on the hips. Likewise: the loins and all the members tremble. But all these texts are in need of emendation, because they are wrong. Roving eyes: that is, turning and surveying the scene with their eyes, as Polemo and Adamantius write, and they add: they contract the forehead and the cheeks. The eyebrows remain stationary. A voice thin, lacking in manly vigor, sharp, uneven, and quavering. Polemo describes the feet as παραχωρα, but Adamantius as παραφορὰ, which is better: that is, the feet point in different directions, as if they are walking with hips and feet turned outwards. Their necks are not particularly firm. They tremble slightly, as if maintaining stability required effort. Their lips are pulled back, and they move their lips constantly, like rabbits. [But Cocles[44] makes me laugh, because he attributes this face to the servile man and not to the effeminate man, and all the signs are changed into signs of the servile man.][45] Shrillness of the voice.[46] We add: a long chin. Cheeks contracted in a droll facial expression. Thin lips which broaden out at the incisors. A body which leans to the right. They walk with feet and hips turned out. Hair dressed in ringlets. They breathe deeply, and the breath as it issues from their nostrils is dense and rapid. They gaze with one eyelid held steady in the middle of the eye, or else they raise their eyelids up over their eyes in a soft way. They do not have steady eyelids or immobile eyebrows; rather, they tremble, and face and eyes move at the same time. Their eyes are mobile, like those of people with poor vision.

[On the island of Sicily there are many effeminate men, and I saw one in Naples who had only a few beard-hairs, with a small mouth, delicate straight eyebrows, a modest eye, like a lady's, and a weak thin voice. He could not bear much exertion, his neck was not firm, he was of a white complexion, he bit his lips, and in sum, he had the body and gestures of a woman. He preferred to stay at home, and always had a farthingale, was always occupied with cooking and spinning like a woman. He avoided the company of men, and conversed readily with women, and joked with them. He was more feminine than the women; he reasoned like a woman, and used the feminine article when referring to himself, always saying "trista me" and "amara me," and the worst of it was that he tolerated abominable sexual congress worse than a woman.][47]

Signs of cinaedi, taken from P. Africanus. P. Africanus, son of Paul, reproached P. Gallus, a delicate man, with many things, amongst which are: that he wore tunics which cover his hands completely; that he perfumed himself every day; that he adorned himself before a mirror; that he tweezed his eyebrows; that he plucked his beard; that he minced along like a woman; that as a young man he attended banquets with his lover, and that he would recline beneath him, dressed in a long-sleeved tunic; that he was not only a wine-bibber (*vinosus*), but also a man-chaser (*virosus*).

Signs of cinaedi, taken from Archesilaus. Plutarch says that Archesilaus used harsh words against a certain rich and delicate man, who was nonetheless said to be incorrupt and chaste, for he saw that the voice lacked manliness, the hair was coiffed in front, and the eyes were playful, wanton, and full of voluptuousness. "It hardly matters," he said, "with which parts [of the body] you are a cinaedus, the fore or the hind."[48]

Soft men, like women. Very plump buttocks. Fleshy knees. Straight eyebrows. Neck bent forward. Weak, disjointed shoulders. Upper back weak, thin, disjointed. Back narrow and weak. Ribs loose. Thin belly. Heels fleshy and disjointed. Feet small, slender, disjointed.

Effeminate men, like women. Sloping forehead. Nose poorly distinguished with respect to face. Small mouth; round, bare chin. Collarbone loose. Loins fleshy and soft. Walks with feet and hips turned out. Or else they move themselves with their [whole] body, shoulders, and all the limbs. Knees turned inward or knocking against one another. Eyes bulging out from the face, very small and sparkling, or else small and variegated.

Weaklings, like women. Thin eyebrows which stretch or remain in place. Speaks with a stutter or lisps. Thin neck. Forearms, upper arms, and elbows thin. Hands small, slender, and disjointed. Small, thin breasts. They shift their eyes and their eyelids are mobile, or their orbs are white and weak.

Book Six, Chapter 10: How Cinaedi Can Become Tough

In what climate sluggish men, cinaedi, and soft men are born, and also emasculated men. Hippocrates says that those who live in northern regions enjoy an atmosphere that is stable, the air being always cloudy.[49] Winter never ends in these humid locations, and the seasons are all alike, or similar, or else they vary only a little. Summer and winter, these people eat the same food and wear the same clothes. They breathe air which is watery and condensed; the water they drink comes from snow and melted ice. Their body gets no exercise, as it is not likely that a body or mind can become fit for any exercise where the changes of the weather are not pronounced. For this reason the people are thick-set, and their joints do not work well because of the softness of the humor. Hence they cannot bend a bow or wind a catapult, due to the impotence of the moisture in their shoulder. They spend most of their time slumped in wagons, and because they are always on the move, they never leave them. Their perpetual sloth makes their bodies fluid and broad, almost as fluid as a woman's. So though they desire to have sex with women, the men are little given to coitus because of their body's excessive humidity and the softness and coldness of their belly. When the men go in to their wives, and see that they have become impotent to couple with them, and when they have tried two or three more times in vain, and can accomplish nothing, they openly admit that they are outcasts, dress themselves in women's clothes, go to live in the women's quarters, perform the functions of women, act and speak in all respects like women, and are called "effeminate." The rich do this; but it is not something which affects the poor, since they do not ride about on horseback and they get exercise from their continuous labors. Those who inhabit harsh, barren lands, lacking in water, where the changes of weather are varied and frequent, have bodies which are hard, firm, and slender. Rugged of disposition and tenacious, they have well-proportioned limbs and are hairy. By nature they have a great capacity for exertion, and tend more to ferocity than mildness.

So cinaedi who wish to become tough, and to change their phlegmatic constitution for a warm one, should live in hot, harsh, windy places. They should eat hot, rustic foods, and devote themselves to exercise; so shall they emerge strong and tough, and lose their feminine demeanor.

Giovanni Antonio Magini (1555–1617)

According to *La metoposcopia*, a treatise attributed to Giovanni Antonio Magini, the forehead's lines and markings disclose an individual's temperament and future conditions in life, including sexual affinities and behaviors, such as sodomy and "unnatural vice." Focusing on males, he says nothing specifically about tribadism. Originally from Padua, Magini studied at the University of Bologna and somehow bested Galileo for a chair of mathematics there in 1588.[50] Their rivalry continued, Magini defending Ptolemaic cosmology against Galileo's Copernicanism. Lecturing also on astronomy and astrology, Magini published extensively on all these subjects as well as geography and cartography. He was additionally a court astrologer and tutor of mathematics for the Gonzagas in Mantua. The Roman Inquisition confiscated much of his library and some further unpublished writings, which disappeared. According to Angus C. Clarke, Magini's treatise on metoposcopy, composed in Italian around 1594 to 1601 on the request of a Gonzaga prince, survives in several manuscripts and also eight editions falsely attributed to Ciro Spontoni (c. 1552–1610), published between 1626 and 1654.[51] However, Clarke's reattribution may itself need modification, for at least some initial portions of this treatise are translations of the Latin metoposcopic study ascribed to Cardano. Although the Italian text's printed editions include explanatory illustrations, they omit the multitude of pictorial case studies featured in the manuscripts. Each of these pictures presents a face showing the lineaments of the forehead, with a label denoting the significance. Since both the printed discussion and the unprinted images are revealing for the early modern physiognomics of masculine love, I include samples of both.

Like the pseudo-Aristotelian *Physiognomics*, metoposcopy assumes that the bodily areas most associated with the mind are most revealing—hence the forehead has special importance. Early modern metoposcopic analysis divided the forehead into astrological zones that each reflected a planet's influence on an individual.[52] The domain of Venus had the most significance for amorous matters; reflecting heteroerotic biases, metoposcopy associated sex between males with supposedly unfavorable formations in that area. The age-old right/left distinction of the intellectual disciplines in general, whereby right was positive and left negative, provided a basic means of assessment. A mark on the left side typically appeared malign, as did a line perceived to descend from right to left. At various points this treatise and the unprinted pictorial case studies apply the terms "sodomite" or "unnatural vice" without explaining their meaning, or whether some distinction between them is implied. We may reasonably assume that at least "sodomite" and "sodomy" here involve male homoeroticism in some sense, for that was the most common or "default" sexual implication of "Sodom" and its cognates.

Figure 5 reproduces three such examples from one of the manuscripts, in which each is numbered. Number 33 bears the caption *Sodomita* (Sodomite). Number 80: *Sodomita e morira d'archibriggiata* (Sodomite and will die by a harquebus, an early portable gun). Number 156: *Sara sodomita se la linea transversale inverse ch'era la pendicolare ad Angoli retti* (Will be a sodomite if the inverse transversal line comes to intersect the perpendicular one at right angles).[53] In this case, sodomitical identity and practice would emerge from a distinctive sodomitical potential in a gradual process reflected in the evolution of facial lineaments (considered expressions of mental characteristics) through the course of life. This is not determinist, for transformation into a sodomite remains conditional here. However, it implies some individuals are distinguished by facially legible sodomitical tendencies, and that the character of the sodomite, once established, becomes quite fixed as the face itself is set in that mold.

As the pictorial case studies provide only interpretive labels for particular faces, not explanations, it is unclear why certain marks designate sodomites. But the specific rationales have far less significance for the history of sexuality than the fact that such interpretation formerly occurred. Sexual affinities were not wholly fluid and thus without implications for perceived personal identities, as some recently claim, but could be considered so particular and definitive as to be intelligibly inscribed on faces, and "scientific" techniques developed for deciphering such indicators. These are not only assumptions of the treatise's author, for they originated and "made sense" according to the prevalent cultural conditions.

Metoposcopy[54] *(written c. 1600)*

Book I, Ch. 2: Of the Number of Natural Lines on the Forehead after Taking Its Length into Account, and Those Attributed to the Seven Planets; Also, of Non-natural Lines

The lines on the forehead, after taking its length into account, do not have a set number in all men. Some have more and others less, but few men less than three. Having many lines is not in itself praiseworthy, but it is yet worse not to have any at all, because this indicates a short life, a thief's or a

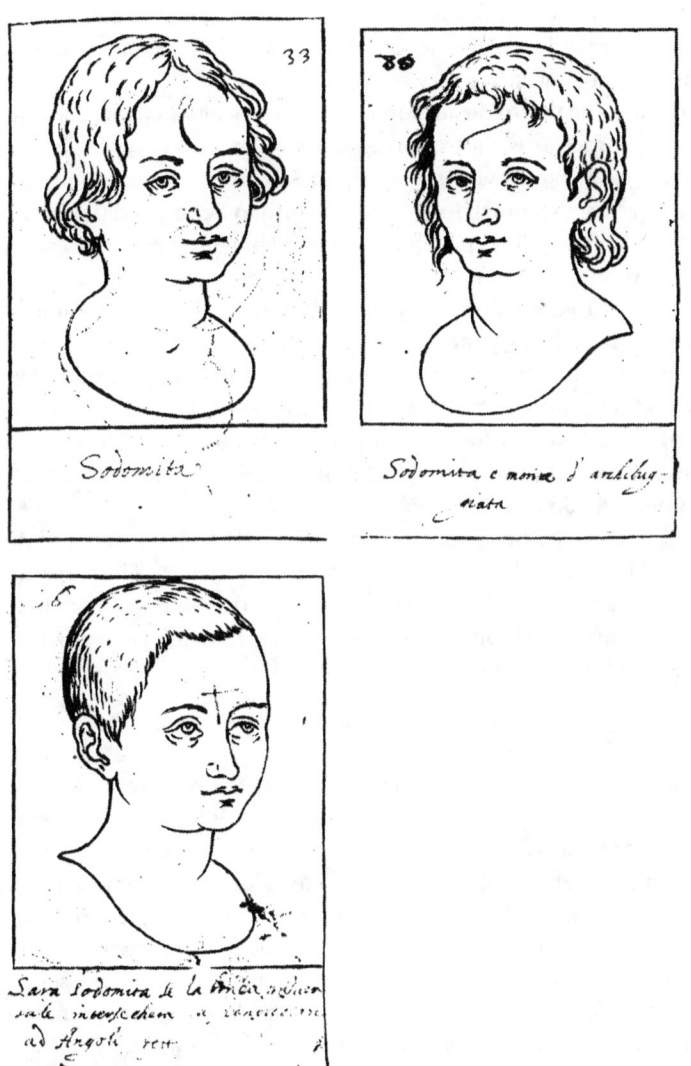

Fig. 5 Giovanni Antonio Magini (?), Sodomitical Faces, from *La metoposcopia* (c. 1600). By permission of the Biblioteca Nazionale Marciana, Venice.

murderer's death, unforeseen accidents, wretched predicaments, and falls from heights resulting in lameness. At times, they also indicate dropsy and premature death because of it. Although lines are good in some men, indicating a man of heightened intelligence, in others they are bad, indicating a great number of endeavors difficult to bring to the desired end, as well as great work and problems throughout a person's life. When there are few and simple lines along the forehead, that denotes simplicity of spirit, a man just and magnanimous, who will generally have serenity or at least worthy enterprises.

The lines on the forehead are connected with the seven planets in almost the same order as the astronomers observe in the heavens. The highest one, closest to the crown, is assigned to Saturn, the second to Jupiter, the third to Mars, the fourth to the Sun, the fifth to Venus, and those between the eyebrows to Mercury. Those directly above the eyebrows are given to the two luminaries: the one over the right eye to the Sun, and the one over the left to the Moon. If, by chance, there is a single line immediately above both eyebrows, the right-hand part is the Sun's and the left the Moon's, and this has been found to be true not only through lengthy observations, but also because it holds to reason, for the Sun dominates the right eye and the Moon the left, as the astrologers say. If there are lines between the eyebrows, at the root of the nose, it is understood that they are under the dominion of Venus....

All those other lines that are not attributed to the Planets and do not proceed in a natural order are called non-natural lines. They are the ones that traverse the forehead either ascending or descending, or are found in other eccentric positions. These non-natural lines are generally bad and foretell bad consequences.

Book I, Ch. 10: Care Must Be Taken in Judging Those Things That
Converge and Diverge at the Same Time
In determining a person's future, you must examine very carefully the things that converge and diverge at the same time. For example, if you discover that he is likely to die a bad death, and you do not perhaps know in what manner he will die, you will consider other circumstances and their consequences. If there is some sign that he is inclined to steal, then you may affirm quite rightly that he might be hanged. If you find that he is inclined to homicide, you might say that his head might be severed in the name of justice, or that he might be killed by his enemies. If there is a sign that he is a heretic or a sodomite, threaten him with the stake. In this manner temerity and a bad death go hand in hand as does disorderly living with ill health; gluttony and gambling with whoring and poverty; having little with being considered worthless; being talkative with being odious to many; being wrathful with being precipitous; and other meanings that have natural consequences. In fact, it is difficult to find an effect without a cause.

Book II, Ch. 5: On the Line of Venus
If the line of Venus is well placed and well formed, this indicates a tranquil, happy, and long life, a friend to women and they to him, also that he

will have many male friends, prosperity in his affairs, marriage, and children, earnings and acquisition of property, and a good death.... [Such a person] will be happy, festive, jocund, pleasant, agreeable, very much given to pleasures and games, and especially to the pleasures of the flesh. He will also do good, he will be devout, forgiving and somewhat jealous. If, however, the aforementioned line is in an unfortunate place, then it indicates a brief life, unhappiness in marriage and in children, and little luck with women. And if the line is weak, or thin, or barely noticeable, or broken in many places, it indicates weakness in coitus and in procreation, and that perhaps he will suffer in the genitals or in the stomach....

If, however, the line is whole, but very slanted, then it indicates nefarious lasciviousness with any type of person, infamous life. If, besides being oblique, it is intersected, it indicates, aside from the aforementioned things, that the person will suffer greatly in the genital and hidden areas from some accident, with danger of poison and perhaps of fire because of impropriety.

Book II, Ch. 10: On the Conjunction of the Martial with the Mercurial Lines
If the line of Mars were to descend into the line of Mercury, this would indicate a man of quick wit, sagacious and astute, playful, industrious and very much given to the work of smiths, and perhaps to alchemy. If the line were unfortunate and hindered, this would indicate a thief, gambler, and the worst type of spirit, and a sodomite, very contentious and inclined to fighting and to arguing.

Book II, Ch. 12: On the Conjunction of the Line of Venus with That of Mercury
If the line of Venus descends into the area of Mercury, it makes for a very ingenious person, especially in poetry and in music, someone given to pleasures and to games, someone who is also very much loved by women. If the line were wrongly placed, it would point to a person full of vice, a clown and a buffoon, someone who delights in artifice and low things.

Book II, Ch. 26: On the Conjunction of the Line of the Sun with That of Venus
If the lines of the Sun and of Venus join, this indicates a very benign and jocund man, merry and prosperous, of good manners and devout, who will gain honor in religion, if he were to look for it, who will be loved by women and by his friends beyond all bounds, and who will have a good death. But if those lines are poorly formed, they indicate a very effeminate, worthless man, given to libidinous acts and to pleasures rather than to serious undertakings.

CHAPTER 6

Encyclopedias and Reference Works

- cinaedi, why insatiable like women
- cinaedi, whence their pleasure in coitus is conjectured to originate
- masculine love, its first originator
- masculine love, its detestation and the various customs of different nations in this matter
—Lodovico Ricchieri (1469–1525), *Lectionum antiquarum*, Index[1]

Early modern Europe thronged with Neolatin and vernacular texts in manuscript and print that surveyed, organized, and digested knowledge for convenient reference, assimilation, and reuse.[2] Their conventional categories of thought, organizational patterns, and classificatory systems profoundly influenced European mentalities and structured the physical presence of apparent knowledge. The ways in which these writings represented or excluded same-sex erotics are important for understanding its implications in the period. Nevertheless, inquiries into homoeroticism in the fifteenth to seventeenth centuries have rarely engaged such texts to date, except for some dictionaries, anatomical handbooks, and legal manuals. Reference works tended either to ignore such "unspeakable" love or situate and describe it pejoratively. Yet in the latter case they gathered and publicized information that could be positively appropriated. However, aside from some handbooks on anatomy, gynecology, and continental jurisprudence, and compendia on subjects relevant to Sappho (*Medicine, *Law, *The Sapphic Renaissance), sexual relations between females seem to have received scant comment. Despite tending to document socially ascendant or orthodox perspectives, early modern reference works particular importance for sexual history at this point. Certain commonplace books and miscellaneous or encyclopedic compilations show that homoerotic sex differences were not necessarily subsumed in generalized debauchery, as some now claim, but could readily be distinguished as spheres of inquiry and knowledge distinct from other phenomena of gender, love, sex, and life.

The range of former reference works with potential relevance for the study of same-sex love in early modernity includes, among other possibilities, vernacular and Neolatin dictionaries; guides to aspects of antique culture, such as the widely used *Dictionarium historicum et poeticum* of Charles Estienne (1504–1564), which alphabetically glosses proper names from ancient Greek and Roman history, literature, mythology, and religion; miscellanies and analytic collections of readings; compendia of examples; specialized manuals; personal and printed commonplace books assembling quoted extracts under particular headings; and encyclopedias of various types, seeking to survey knowledge deemed needful, or canvass some sector. Just as "the most frequently reprinted of all Latin commonplace-books supplied . . . male contemporaries with a duly authenticated catalogue of [alleged] female defects" (Moss, *Commonplace Books*, vii), many types of reference works clarify former cultural conditions of sex differences in general. However, most directly relevant to the study of early modern homoeroticism are those that broadly survey life's scope without excluding its amorous aspects, such as the encyclopedic *Theatrum vitae humanae* of *Theodor Zwinger (1533–1588), or treat them as a main topic, such as *The Anatomy of Melancholy* by *Robert Burton (1577–1640).

A main distinction between early modern encyclopedias and texts that can be broadly called miscellanies reveals much about former intellectual assumptions affecting human life, including sex. As Neil Kenny argues, Renaissance encyclopedism sought to realize an ideal of recording a complete "circle of learning," the etymological meaning of "encyclopedia" (ch. 1). That objective entailed the presentation of a survey of knowledge deemed necessary, which was structured to reflect and expose nature's inner design as God's creation. Rather than being alphabetically ordered by topic as we would now expect, encyclopedias were schematized so as to affirm the world's conformation to some moral-theological value system that defined the universals underlying particular phenomena. Whether produced in verse like *Les semaines* of Guillaume Du Bartas (1544–1590) or in discursive or dialogic prose, and whether brief or voluminous, encyclopedias were formally characterized by this "encyclopedic order" imputed to nature. Often they were equipped with diagrams of their categorical organization and subdivisions so that relations within the areas of knowledge encompassed by the text could be visually apprehended at once. Miscellanies, on the other hand, provided a relatively heterogeneous means of learning. Some, Kenny observes, challenge the contemporaneous systematic encyclopedism by implying that knowledge involves flux, such as the *Adagia* of Erasmus (1469–1536) or *Essais* of *Montaigne (1533–1592). However, Kenny adds, many nonetheless suggest "there exists, outside the text, a broader encyclopedic structure within which their own learning comfortably sits, linked in a stable, static, and logical way with other clearly labelled areas of knowledge" (90–91).

Insofar as the universe was considered God's creation, its phenomena constituted a divinely revelatory Book of Nature supplementing the Bible, and the hierarchical, metaphysically structured perspective of early modern encyclopedism tended to dominate understanding of the world. Same-sex lovers in such a scheme were implicitly and sometimes explicitly positioned among the extremes of vice, and an encyclopedia's very structure of knowledge would appear weightily to confirm that. Similarly, many commonplace books were ordered according to the virtues and vices with their various subdivisions, thus correlating with the larger structures of encyclopedism (Moss, *Commonplace-Books*, v). Responding to pressures of burgeoning knowledge, results of changing notions of scientific method, demands for comprehensiveness, and needs for alphabetical ease of reference, a more recognizably modern encyclopedism increasingly supplanted the ideal of a significantly ordered enclosure of knowledge as the seventeenth century progressed. The 1631 edition of Zwinger's encyclopedia was alphabetically reorganized and thereby ceased to be encyclopedic in the former sense (Kenny, 40).

Yet Renaissance reference works that addressed same-sex erotics, including encyclopedias, could have effects and uses contrary to any intentional censure. One of their functions was to facilitate access to information on topics covered, and so readers interested in this subject could thus more readily find and survey commentaries on it. Depending on readers' attitudes, the encyclopedist's or compiler's citations could not only serve orthodox purposes such as the identification of examples for use in admonitions, but could also be more or less uncoupled from his pejorative assessment, and serve other ends such as the exploration of personal conflicts, quests for gossipy titillation, and development of a prohomoerotic viewpoint or agenda. Early modern writings that review exemplars of same-sex love are often citationally incestuous due to reliance, acknowledged or not, on intermediary reference compilations. However, to the extent that readers depended on these for "the truth" rather than using them to find and evaluate sources independently, they risked being misled by tendentious manipulations such as *Zwinger's. Readers most likely to be on guard would have been homophiles anyway, more used to critical reassessment of propaganda for sexual conformity. For others, encyclopedism would often have tended to reinforce homophobia by further authorizing cultural prejudices. Yet it could also have had different effects because encyclopedic codification of knowledge perhaps most acutely instantiated the crisis of heteroerotic moral orthodoxy entailed by the resurgence of Greek and Roman culture in the Renaissance. The sexual milieu revealed in the textual remains of revered antiquity could not be suppressed if the circle of knowledge were to be closed, and yet could not be acknowledged without undermining the authority of the conventional "modern" sexual morality partly structuring that enclosure. *Zwinger, for example, surveys ancient male homoeroticism with explicit pejorative intent, immediately aligning it with Sodom as a vice subverting love, yet thereby inadvertently shows it was commonplace, that ancient societies nevertheless thrived, and that diverse human endeavors from military command through statecraft, the arts, and philosophy evinced high achievers who reputedly pursued same-sex amours (such as Alexander the Great, Julius Caesar, Trajan, Hadrian, Sappho, Virgil, Socrates, Plato).

Besides acquainting us with the scope of material on same-sex erotics formerly supposed relevant for consultation and most publicized, and with revealing paradoxes of representation and reception, early modern reference works engaging this topic clarify the extent to which homoerotic sex differences could be perceived, distinguished, categorized, and thus become available for review and analysis. These texts exemplify what potential structural divisions knowledge had in this period from morally and intellectually "respectable" standpoints. Some recent accounts of sexual history assume that, until 1650 or even much later, allegedly illicit sex of all types was relegated to an undifferentiated chaos of debauchery, within "one undivided sexuality."[3] Even sex itself, some say, was not a separable or distinguishable sphere of human activity or identity formation.[4] Recognition of distinct subtypes of sexual behaviors and affinities was impossible, then, and likewise the development of same-sex sexual subcultures and subjectivities. However, analytic classifications of transgressive sex, rank-ordered for differing degrees of condemnation, much antedate the Renaissance, such as St. Thomas Aquinas's (1224/5–1274; *Theology). First published around 1503, the encyclopedic *Margarita philosophica* (Pearl of Philosophy) by Gregor Reisch (c. 1467–1525) summarizes Aquinas's analysis in Book Twelve, Chapter Forty-two, "On the Modes and Species of Lust." Sodomy is specifically "male with male or female with female," then, and constitutes the greatest sexual sin except for bestiality.[5] This is indexed under "*Sodomia.*" Despite Foucault's often-cited claim that sodomy was formerly "an utterly confused category," it is clearly not so, in this Latin reference work standard throughout sixteenth-century Europe.[6]

Some major early modern miscellanies and encyclopedic texts not only distinguish human sexual conduct as a distinct area of inquiry, but also types of illicit sexual behavior, further subtypes, and corresponding types of person. Two miscellanies or commonplace books widely used in the sixteenth century and long into the seventeenth were the Neolatin *Polyanthea* of Domenico Nani Mirabelli (fl. 1500) and *Officina* (Workshop) of Jean Tixier or Joannes Ravisius Textor, Seigneur de Ravisi (c. 1475–1524). First published in 1503 at Savona, the former presents topics in alphabetical order, and acknowledges homoeroticism only with the entry "*Sodomia,*" citing biblical and theological condemnations.[7] The *Officina,* initially published at Paris in 1520, provides curious and wideranging classified lists of facts, anecdotes, exemplars, and trivia extracted from previous texts, mostly ancient. Though the format of different editions could vary, one common arrangement treats beauty and love in a series of categories including beautiful men and beautiful women; lovers of gods; lovers of humans; female lovers of gods and of humans; cinaedi, males who penetrate males (*paedicones*), and pathics (*pathici*); weaklings (*molles*), effeminates, and dandies; male cross-dressers; female cross-dressers; prostitutes; procurers; eunuchs; incestuous persons; adulterers; wantons; lovers of animals and other things; persons loved by animals; jealous people; very chaste people.[8] Various amorous and sexual desires and behaviors could clearly be distinguished, including several types of male homoeroticism and corresponding types of person. It is highly significant that Tixier lumps male same-sex lovers into one general category, *Cinaedi, paedicones, et pathici*, indicating that these constitute aspects of a single general phenomenon of male homoeroticism distinct from other modes of amorous experience. He evinces no interest in tribadism, unlike others.

Recognition and treatment of sexual love between males as a distinct category of eros is yet clearer in the *Lectionum antiquarum* (Gleanings from Ancient Writers) by Lodovico Ricchieri or Caelius Rhodiginus (1469–1525). One of the more ambitious reference compilations of the Renaissance, it was first published in sixteen books in 1516 (Venice) and 1517 (Basel), and then in the complete thirty-book version in 1542 (Basel), of which there were at least three further editions, in 1550 (Basel), 1599 (Frankfurt), and 1620 (Cologne). In both versions an index analyzes the largely miscellaneous and digressive arrangement. And both versions extensively address sexual love between males: the first in Book Eight, Chapters Thirty and Thirty-one, the second in Book Fifteen, Chapters Nine and Ten. Though the latter, enlarged edition amplifies the discussion, the original one includes all the main points, expressed in the same language and terminology. Also, both editions index this material under the same two terms, *cinaedi* and *masculae Veneris*, as in my epigraph for this chapter. In discussing these passages, I address and cite the complete thirty-book version, but the earlier one presents much the same material in the same way. Ricchieri's views and terminology reflect social conditions of the early 1500s.

Each of Ricchieri's chapters in both versions commences with a brief italicized guide summarizing the matters treated, and in both the chapter that broaches male homoeroticism begins by stating this topic: *Masculae Veneris institutor primus* ("the first person to originate masculine love"; col. 676A). Here and subsequently, Ricchieri assumes that "masculine love" is well understood to mean sexual love between males, thus confirming its importance as a term and conceptual paradigm for male homoeroticism in the Renaissance (*General Introduction). Such love is indeed the focus of this chapter, which begins by exploring ancient traditions of its legendary originators (Orpheus, Thamyrus, Talus, Laius, or Jove), then comments on some related Greek laws and customs, and finally surveys some of its more famous or scandalous reputed exemplars, such as Achilles, Alexander the Great, Nero, and Sporus. Weaving in censures, Ricchieri calls masculine love "the most dirty thing" (*spurcissimae rei*), "this shameful practice" (*ritum hunc turpissimum*), "this most execrable love" (*Venerem execrabilem;* cols. 676D, 677C, 679B). Although we are sometimes told homophobia only arose centuries later, Ricchieri's standpoint clearly anticipates it. Thamyrus was "polluted by the wicked loves of boys and preposterous shame of that intercourse" (col. 676H). However, unlike a good many other Renaissance and later writers who thus falsely claimed that the ancient Romans outlawed male-male sex in general, Ricchieri does not betray his scholarship here, for he acknowledges that masculine love was deemed honest and just, not shameful or improper, if conducted with attractive slaves rather than free men (col. 678F). And he reports Greek laws and customs favoring male homoeroticism, though critically. Apparently seeking to avoid historical anachronism, he never explicitly applies the ideology of sodomy or uses the word, though his censures no doubt tacitly assume and appeal to antisodomitical attitudes.

Throughout this discussion, Ricchieri's general term and inclusive category for the sexual love of males is "masculine love," just as his preliminary guide for the chapter indicates at the outset. The phrase appears in it twice afterward. Thus "there was a law passed that allowed masculine love (*masculam Venerem*) in Crete" (col. 677A). Later he juxtaposes *masculam Venerem* with *muliebrum concubitem* ("intercourse with women"), so that each is a particular type of sexual pursuit that some men may or may not combine with the other. Just before, he cites Athenaeus, Aristotle, and others to note that men of certain nations tended to reject sexual relations with women and had sex with other males instead, openly accepting such love (cols. 677H–78A). Aside from substituting variants such as *masculorum coitum* ("intercourse between males") and *Venerem execrabilem* for "masculine love" (cols. 677H, 679B), Ricchieri also tacitly evokes that particular phrase and conceptual model with allusive references such as "that desire" or "this love." So a sentence addressing the origins of masculine love in the first paragraph states, "the Thracian prince Orpheus was the inventor of such a great crime, and instigator of the fact that desire would be detested and despised" (*Orpheum Thraca principem omnium tanti sceleris, et libidinis detestandae repertorem fuisse;* col. 676C).

The following chapter, Chapter Ten of Book Fifteen in the enlarged edition, continues with "other things concerning the same matter" as its prefatory guide states (col. 678G). Ricchieri misleadingly decontextualizes a passage of Plato's *Laws* so that it becomes a condemnation of sex between males in particular, just as *Zwinger does later, who used Ricchieri as a source. After reviewing further ancient exemplars, laws, and customs concerning male homoeroticism, Ricchieri then poses this now historically fascinating question: "Because we know that the cinaedi feel the greatest pleasure while they rub themselves against each other in a shameful way, should we think they are subject to some higher principle that overcomes them?" (col. 679F). In other words, we know cinaedi have such sex for pleasure, but might these behaviors result from some reason of a higher order than just desire for pleasure? And are such acts in that sense somehow involuntary? He then summarizes the anatomically essentialist theory of masculine desire for receptive anal intercourse outlined in the *pseudo-Aristotelian Problems.* Digressively flaunting breadth of knowledge as usual, Ricchieri satirically juxtaposes a discussion of puberty's relation to hircine body odor, then concludes the chapter by treating androgyny and hermaphroditism, implicitly analogous to cinaedi. *Firmicus Maternus, he notes, explains the astrological conditions producing births of hermaphrodites, eunuchs, masculine women, and emasculated priests of Cybele.

Both Ricchieri's and *Zwinger's major sixteenth-century reference works assume that sexual desires and behaviors between males constitute a distinct type of amorous affiliation or experience to be considered according to the general category "masculine love" or, in Zwinger's rendition, "masculine lust." These authoritative reference works would have further diffused and entrenched that assumption, thus inadvertently helping to enable such self-identifications for male homophiles. Also, insofar as Ricchieri and Zwinger seek to survey ancient sources, their reportage must attest to the considerable acceptance and currency of this mode of love in antiquity, and yet that potentially undermines their censures reflecting contemporary moral orthodoxy. Much information they provide is inadvertently open to prohomoerotic appropriations. Further, by inquiring whether cinaedi are overcome by factors other than desire for pleasure, and then citing the supposed Aristotle's anatomical theory and the astrologically deterministic explanations of gender deviance, Ricchieri encourages questioning of conventional moral and theological condemnations, for cinaedi would thus not be morally responsible for their sexual behaviors. As Tixier's, Ricchieri's, and Zwinger's reference works indicate, it is clear that at least male homoerotic sex differences were certainly not undistinguished and undistinguishable at this time. Immediately following his exposition in "Masculine Lust," Zwinger adds the parallel category "Tribades," and that contextualizaton tends to define sexual love between females as a distinctive pursuit likewise.

Niccolò Leonico Tomeo (1456–1531)

While surveying ancient culture in *De varia historia*, Niccolò Leonico Tomeo reports supposed origins of male homoeroticism, and the Etruscans' common public enjoyment of such sex. A Platonist of Greek descent born at Venice, he held professorships in Greek at the universities in Padua and his birthplace.[9] Besides producing scholarly editions and translations of texts by various ancient Greek authors including Ptolemy, Aristotle, and Proclus, he published a volume of philosophical and moral dialogues (1524) and an inquiry into amatory questions (1525) as well as the *Historia* (1531). The latter compendiously discusses aspects of ancient Greek and Roman antiquities, mythology, religion, philosophy, and customs. Further editions appeared in 1532 and 1555, and an Italian translation in 1544. The English learned community had special connections with Leonico, for his students from England at Padua, with whom he became friendly, included the subsequently notable scholars or churchmen Thomas Linacre (1460–1524), William Latimer (c. 1460–1545), Thomas Lupset (c. 1498–1530), and Reginald Pole (1500–1558), among others. The question of "who invented" sex between males, explored by Leonico here and also by Ricchieri (*Encyclopedias and Reference Works), is an ancient topos as in, for example, Athenaeus's *Deipnosophists* (13. 601–03). Such inquiry assumes that homoerotic sex is not a "natural" or obvious human impulse but results from some ingenious particular intervention. This would have had different implications in early modern Christian culture, with its notions of sexual "crimes against nature," than in antiquity.

Historical Miscellany[10] *(1531)*

Book Three, ch. 25

WHENCE THE ABUSE OF MASCULINE LOVE (*MASCULAE ABUSUS VENERIS*) AROSE

As to where the loves of boys and the abusive practice of sex between men first started, the explanation is doubtful, to such a degree various people have recorded various things concerning this matter. For some relate that Thamyris the Thracian, the eighth before Homer to win renown as a bard, who took Hymenaeus, son of Calliope and Magnes as his sweetheart, was the first. Others say that Rhadamantus first loved the boy Talon of Crete. Some assert that Laius carried off Chrysippus, son of Pelops, to use after this fashion. Others allege that the Itali, driven by necessity during their protracted military campaigns, abused males. All seem to agree that Cretan Jove, captivated by the beauty of the boy Ganymede, was the very first originator of masculine love (*masculae Veneris*).[11]

Book Three, ch. 96

OF THE TYRRHENIANS' UNBELIEVABLE LICENTIOUSNESS DURING THEIR
DRINKING PARTIES

... It did not seem offensive to the Tyrrhenians to do something wicked in plain view of other people, or even to be the object of some indecent act.[12] For [the historians] say that when [the Tyrrhenians], in the course of their late-night drinking parties, saw fit to set a limit to the amount of drinking and to bring the feasting to a close, at a pre-arranged moment, with many torches ablaze, servants appeared, ushering in the prettiest women and the most beautiful boys. These they would take advantage of in the vilest manner, as chance or whimsy led each individual, in some instances reaching sexual climax in plain view of everyone. At other times, with a roof overhead of hangings and curtains transforming [the hall] into a stage-set for licentiousness, male prostitutes and strapping youths were ushered in by these same servants; and these men would fondle each other in an utterly depraved way. [The Tyrrhenians], passing the time in this manner, considered that they lived in an agreeable and happy fashion. Moreover, they say that since the Tyrrhenians displayed an inclination for every species of lust, and particularly toward men, those amongst them who were notably good-looking groomed their bodies with every kind of primping. Indeed, these men resorted to public taverns, where there were usually found craftsmen skilled in this area, who among other nations are barbers; stripping every part of their body before these men without shame, they are said to have exposed themselves openly to be depilated and adorned.

Theodor Zwinger (1533–1588)

Theodor Zwinger's *Theatrum vitae humanae* reviews many examples of male homoeroticism in the section entitled "Masculine Lust" (*Libido mascula*), then some female counterparts in "Tribades." Son of a furrier in Basel, he studied printing at Lyons, philosophy at Paris, and medicine at Padua. Returning to Basel, his birthplace, he held professorships in Greek, moral and political philosophy, and medicine there. He had at least one child. Though a prolific writer in various learned fields, he did not undertake this vast encyclopedic endeavor, thirty volumes in the 1586 edition, on his own initiative. It had been begun by his stepfather Konrad Lykosthenes or Wolffhart (1518–1561), a Protestant minister best known for his apocalyptic admonitory writing on prodigies or monsters, whose dying wish was that Zwinger complete the *Theatrum*. Seeking comprehensively to expound the good and evil of human life in universal history, it gathers and classifies information and extracts under systematic headings. The *Theatrum* was first published at Basel in 1565 and, despite its costly bulk, there were at least six further editions (1571, 1572, 1586, 1604, 1631, 1661–65).

The section "On Moderation and Lack of Moderation in Sexual Matters," Book III of Volume Nine, has an extensive subsection entitled "Major Sexual Immorality with Respect to Persons," in which Zwinger canvasses types of love considered illicit, such as infatuation with statues or images, autoeroticism, bestiality, intercourse with incubi or succubi, and necrophilia. Each appears under its own distinct, capitalized heading, forming a series of chapters expounding the general topic of major sexual transgression. Situating sexual love between males in this context, he subsumes all its forms under the inclusive category *Libido mascula*. Further subdividing that into two potential modes, "active" and "passive," treated as subchapters in that order, he provides a range of examples and anecdotes for each of these two sodomitical subcategories. Although Zwinger's reportage is often pejoratively tendentious and he begins "Masculine Lust" by stressing Christian anathemas against Sodom and sodomy, his treatment of this subject is remarkably dissonant because his instances are mostly ancient, so that many are neutrally matter-of-fact or positive. The quantity of his citations demonstrates not only how integral masculine love was to Greek and Roman society, and how ordinary, but also its potential variety, intensity, and commitment. His text exemplifies the potential difficulties of reconciling the fascinations of antiquity with a morally narrowed Christian context. And this information could challenge sexual orthodoxies. By positioning the section "Tribades" after "Masculine Lust" Zwinger implies that it is a feminine counterpart of male homoerotic phenomena. As he stresses ancient exemplars of male and female same-sex sexual love, so he probably assumes, like *Agnolo

Firenzuola (1493–1543), that contemporary perpetrators can and should be condemned to obscurity, whereas records of their Greek and Roman precursors that are extant anyway can be cited for edification.

The Theater of Human Life[13] *(1565)*
Masculine Lust

I. ACTIVE: PEDICATORS, PEDERASTS, STUDS (*DRAUCI*), SODOMITES

The title—to say nothing of the examples—arouses feelings of shame. It would be preferable by far to lack examples of something so wicked. Now, since the devious mind of the habitué and the unscrupulousness of mortals have so far advanced that many examples of detestable lust can be found, we, like judges, expose the shameful deeds of villainous men. For while criminals are not condemned generically as human beings, but rather under their proper names, and with express mention of their family and nation, at the same time, since those who will be discussed here have contaminated themselves with this execrable type of lust, and have waged war against nature (their punishment is considered under the heading "Corrective Justice"), we assemble here a catalogue of these men—men, I say, who in the words of St. Paul "burned" in mutual lust, and who perverted the norms of human society, as well as the true worship of God. The one who is so far gone in madness and impiety that he prefers to imitate the indecency of these men rather than the chastity of others, him the eternal fire shall surely punish in due time, if the authority of the magistrate should decline to correct him, giving him up for lost. Consult Athenaeus, *Deipnosophists*, 13.600A–605D.[14] See the chapter, "Those who abduct cinaedi."[15]

The Sodomites, the Gomorrhans, and certain other neighboring peoples, rejoicing at this time in riches and leisure, got away with every enormity of lust, according to Moses, Josephus, and other writers on Jewish antiquities, so that men would even publicly submit to sexual intercourse like women. Everyone's mind was so overcome with this filthy lust that they did not even draw the line at raping their guests. For this they were wiped out at a single stroke by fire from heaven. Lot, a just man who was a resident alien in that place, together with his wife and children, was the only one to be spared this sword. Warned in advance by a heavenly voice, he and his people withdrew in the face of imminent peril. The conflagration fell upon Sodom in the year 3272 after the Creation, which is 1927 years before the advent of Christ the King.[16] Strabo also recalls the destruction of [Sodom], but he holds that it happened by natural causes, as at Mount Etna and the Aeolian Islands (*Geography*, 16.2.44). Thus the wily demon contrived to shroud this history in an obscurity of his own devising, lest this kind of punishment deter men from so great a crime. (Sabellico, Bk. II, Ennead I; from Genesis 18).[17]

The inhabitants of Gibeah harassed the Levite to commit this dishonorable kind of sexual intercourse (Judges 19:21–23).

The Celts, although their women were very lovely, took greater pleasure in the love of boys, so that some would often have sex on fur [rugs] with two catamites [at once] (Athenaeus, 13.603A). Aristotle attributes pederasty to the Celts; he writes that all warlike peoples are much given to women, save for the Celts (ἔξω κελτῶν) and others of their ilk, who are given to boys (*Politics*, 2.6.6). Budé in Book I of his *Pandects* translates ἔξω κελτῶν as "beyond [the territory of] the Celts," and so transfers their evil reputation to their neighbors.[18] In any event, it is probable that the Greeks once used to apply the term "Celts" to western peoples in general, since they were barely acquainted with Italy, and quite ignorant of what lay beyond it. If the things which are recounted about the Celts are true, they were to be taken to apply in particular to those who lived in the vicinity of Greece.

Amongst *the Gauls*, tradition says that this evil sometimes raged so fiercely that it was sanctioned by a disgraceful law, that no one should be allowed to take a wife who had not previously performed the office of a wife (Ricchieri, 15.10; cf. *Encyclopedias and Reference Works).

The Greeks and Romans suffered from the vice of sex with males to such a degree that the most famous philosophers of Greece openly had male lovers, and boys stood exposed to public licentiousness amongst the [male] prostitutes in the brothels at the public spectacles, until both the infidelity of all the nations and their indecency were wiped out under the Emperor Constantine (St. Jerome, *Commentary on Isaiah*, 1.2).[19]

The Cretans, it seems, were the first to take boys and young men as lovers, though they stopped short of indecency. If their circumstances permitted, they carried them off to the mountains or to their homes, and they enjoyed their company for sixty continuous days (longer was not permitted), and the lover gave gifts of clothing and other small tokens of favor, as well as an ox (Heraclides in his *Politia*, and Aristotle).[20] Strabo in Book 10 surveys their loves and the laws which were imposed against them. They call a male lover κλεινὸν φιλήτορα, "glorious lover" (*Geography*, 10.4.21).[21]

The people of Chalcis on the island of Euboea are famous in the jokes of the Old Comedy[22] for being rather stingy. Hesychius points out that this people was addressed in harsh terms because of their filthy love for boys, and hence arose the witty proverb that to be subject to a similar disease was χαλκιδίζειν, "to Chalcidize" (Erasmus, *Adagia*, 3.2.40[23]; Ricchieri, 15.9).

At *Megara*, at the beginning of spring, a kissing contest was held amongst the boys; whoever kissed his lover with greater tenderness could drink wearing a chaplet (Ricchieri, 15.[9]).

At *Thebes* there was a "Sacred Band," first established by Gorgidas, and formed of carefully selected men—as some would have it, of lovers and their male paramours. Plutarch says in *Pelopidas* that Iolaüs, Hercules' lover, participated in [their] battles and defensive campaigns. Aristotle records that in his day [male] lovers would customarily plight and confirm their troth at Iolaüs' tomb (Ricchieri, 9.22).[24] King Philip of Macedon overthrew the Sacred Band of the Thebans, which had never before suffered defeat, at Chaeroneia. Seeing the corpses of the enemy lying opposite, he said, "May the gods slay anyone who suspects such men of committing indecency, or of suffering indecency to be committed on them."[25] It is not clear how many men were in this cohort. Euphorus believed that the cohort had fifty men, Callisthenes seventy, and others—Polybius amongst them—ninety (Sabellico, Bk. II, Ennead 4; *Opera*, 1:500).[26]

The Persians invented this craze for boys (*paedomania*), some say, because in *Epigrams* 4, tit. 1 [not found], they are called ἄρρενες ἀρρενοκοίται ["male-bedding men"]. In fact, Athenaeus writes, on the authority of Herodotus, that this vice came to them from the Greeks (13.603A). Plutarch takes exception to this in his *On the Malice of Herodotus*, 857C.

Of *Bacchus*, Ovid writes in the *Fasti*: "Unshorn Ampelus, son of a satyr and a nymph, / Was loved (they say) by Bacchus upon the Ismarian hills" (3.409–10).

Laius, king of Thebes, was the first, they say, to fall passionately in love with beautiful boys, and carried off Chrysippus the son of Pelops. And thus it came about that the Thebans considered it honorable to love a handsome and graceful man (Aelian, *Historical Miscellany*, 13.5; Athenaeus, 13.602F–603A).

Orpheus of Thrace originated and discovered this detestable lust[27] for men, they say, after the loss of Euridice (Ovid, *Metamorphoses*, 10; Ricchieri, 15.9).

Hercules, in hot pursuit of his beardless companion Hyllus, abandoned the Argonauts and deserted their fleet (Plutarch, *Beasts Are Rational*, 990E).

Minos, king of the Cretans, willingly set aside his enmity with the Athenians—an enmity caused by the death of his son Androgeôs—for the sake of Theseus, whom he loved to distraction (Athenaeus, 13.601F).

There are those who say *Thamyras* was the first to be polluted by the disgraceful love for boys, and by the perverse beastliness of having sex with them, when he fell passionately in love with Hymenaeus, son of Calliope and Magnes (Ricchieri, 15.9).

Rhadamanthus the Just loved Talôs, Ibycus writes. And Diotimus states in his *Heraclea* that Eurystheus was *Hercules'* sweetheart, and that [Hercules] waged battle for his sake. It is rumored that *Agamemnon* loved Argynnus when he saw him swimming in the river Cephisos, where he perished; he erected a shrine to Venus at Argynnus' tomb. But Licymnius of Chios contends in his *Dithyrambs* that *Hymenaeus* loved Argynnus. King *Antigonus* was the lover of Aristocles, the lyre-player. *Sophocles* was devoted to young men, just as Euripedes was to women (Athenaeus, 13.603D–E).

Agamemnon entered Boeotia in pursuit of Argaeus, who had fled in secret. Falsely alleging that the winds and sea [drove him], [Argaeus] plunged his handsome self in handsome wise into Lake Copais, as if to quench his love therein, but in fact to be extricated from carnal desires (Plutarch, *Beasts Are Rational,* 990D–E).

Achilles, that great warrior, is believed to have slain Troilus upon the altar of Apollo Thymbraeus solely because he had been rejected when he offered [Troilus] his favors. Lycophron writes this in his *Alexandra* (Ricchieri, 15.9).

Gyges, king of the Lydians, so loved Magnetes of Smyrna, who was famous for his surpassing beauty, that he declared war on the Magnesians for having cut the boy's hair, which marred his looks.

Philip the Macedonian attacked Arisbas—through whom he had won Olympias, the daughter of Neoptolemus, king of the Molossi, in marriage—and ousted him from his kingdom. [Arisbas] was the king of Epirus, and cousin to Olympias, and also to Alexander, who waged war in Italy. [Philip] summoned Alexander to Macedon in Olympias' name, and coerced him into illicit sex. Later, when [Alexander] was twenty years of age, [Philip] gave to him the kingdom he had taken from Arisbas, as the unspeakable wages of his shameful deeds. Toward both men, [Philip] showed himself both indecent and unjust: he showed no regard for the laws of blood relationship toward the old man from whom he unjustly took the kingdom, and he made the man to whom he gave it first unchaste, and then a king (Sabellico, Bk. III, Ennead 4, *Opera,* 1:526–28; from Trogus, Book 8).[28]

Attalus coerced Pausanias, one of the royal bodyguard, into illicit sex by violence. When he complained of this injustice to King Philip of Macedon, Philip made fun of him; so Pausanias, when the opportunity presented itself, slew Philip (Justinus and Diodorus).[29]

Alexander the Great kissed the eunuch Bagôas of Troy in front of all the spectators in the theater. When the spectators shouted and clapped their hands, Alexander, complying immediately with their demands, leaned back and kissed him (Athenaeus, 13.603A–B). Orsinus, a Persian of the highest rank, though he heaped gifts upon Alexander and his friends, refused this honor to Bagôas alone. When asked why, he answered that he cultivated the king's friends, not his whores (Ricchieri, 15.9).

Demetrius Poliorcetes, son of Antigonus, wished to seduce Democles, a youth of praiseworthy beauty. Since the lad could in no wise escape, he threw himself into a cauldron of boiling water that was standing by, and there died (Plutarch, *Demetrius,* 24.2–3).

Pausanias the Spartan general loved Argillus, a young man of striking good looks (Ricchieri, not found).

Aristogeiton the Athenian was passionately in love with Harmodius. When [the tyrant] *Hipparchus,* son of Peisistratus, tried to seduce Harmodius, Aristogeiton stood up to him in public, abhorring the man's lust more than his tyranny (Thucydides, 6.54–59).

Cleomachus of Magnesia, a boxer, was so enamored of a certain cinaedus that he imitated the speech and manners of cinaedi (Strabo, *Geography*, 14.1.41).

Anytus, son of Anthemion, was wildly in love with Alcibiades. When he issued an invitation to a party of guests, he likewise summoned Alcibiades to dine. Alcibiades declined to come, but when he had gotten drunk on wine at home with his friends, he went to Anytus' house in a mood of revelry. Standing outside the dining room, and gazing at the tables laden with vessels of silver and gold, [Alcibiades] ordered his servants to carry off half of them, and take them to his house. He did not even deign to enter, but when he had done these things, he went his way. The revolted guests muttered that this deed perpetrated against Anytus was unworthy and insolent. Anytus, on the contrary, said it was a kindness: "He might have taken everything, but he left some for us" (Plutarch, *Alcibiades,* 4.5).

Melitus loved a rich and noble youth of Athens, Timagoras, who refused his advances and demanded of his lover many labors and deeds of daring: for example, that he should bring him good hunting dogs from abroad, and a noble and spirited horse which belonged to a certain enemy, or someone else's elegant cloak, and other things of this nature. He even ordered him to bring him someone else's fattened fowl, and slaves born of unusual stock. When he had done all these things, [Melitus] gave them to the youth. But he spurned him. Taking this contempt very deeply to heart, Melitus burst into the citadel [i.e., the Acropolis] at breakneck speed and hurled himself off the cliffs. The lad took up the birds, carrying them on his forearms. Following [Melitus'] footsteps as if he would drag his companion by force from the brink of catastrophe, he flung himself down after Melitus from the same place. A depiction of this tragic event was erected at the site: a lovely naked youth, carrying two cocks upon his forearms, and hurling himself head downwards (Suidas).[30]

Chariton of Agrigentum ardently loved Menalippus (Aelian, *Historical Miscellany,* 2.4).

Hipparinus, tyrant of Syracuse, by many promises persuaded the lad Achaeus to leave his father's house and to come to live with him. Some time later, when an enemy invasion was announced, Hipparinus left in high spirits, but ordered the lad that, should anyone try to do violence to him within the house, he should slay the assailant with the sword Hipparinus had given [the boy] as a gift. After the tyrant won his victory, drunk with much wine and ablaze with drunkenness and desire for the boy, he returned to Syracuse. He entered his house, not announcing his arrival, and putting on a Thessalian accent, shouted that he had killed Hipparinus. The indignant boy attacked Hipparinus in the dark. He survived for three days, and when he had absolved Achaeus of his murder, he departed this life (Parthenius, *Love Romances*, 24).

Ibycus, a historian and native of Rhegium, burned, they say, with an insane love of boys. *Cratinus*, the Athenian comic playwright, was notorious for the vice of pederasty (Ravisius Textor).[31]

Pindar, the first of the nine lyric poets,[32] raged with indecent love for Theoxenus (Athenaeus, 13.601C–E). The Greek records testify that he was found dead in the boy's lap in a gymnasium (Valerius Maximus, *Memorable Doings and Sayings*, 9.12.ext.7; Quintilian [not found]; and Athenaeus, *idem*).

Euripedes was summoned by King Archelaus to a banquet, and when he was deeply in his cups, he took the tragic poet Agathon into his arms (for he was seated near him) and kissed him. Agathon was about forty years old. When Agesilaus [actually Archelaus] asked him, "I don't suppose he is your sweetheart, is he," Euripedes answered, "Absolutely, by Jove! For spring is not the only ideal season for fine men; autumn is as well" (Aelian, *Historical Miscellany*, 13.4).

Plato is also said to have burned with a filthy passion for Agatho and Aster. But it seems incredible that such indecency could be compatible with a mind so exalted. In the Socratic manner, he loved the soul, not the body. For immoral men, in order to excuse their own licentiousness, do not hesitate to brand the most respectable men with this stigma. In Book VIII of the *Laws*, Plato writes: "In my view, one should abstain from males, for those who make use of them intentionally kill the human race, sowing upon stone what can never put down roots there."[33] Although Athenaeus, speaking in the person of Masurius, claims that *Socrates* also burned with indecent love for Alcibiades (5.219A–20A), the authority of a saintly philosopher carries more weight with men of intelligence than do the impudent calumnies of that grammarian, when he makes public accusations against philosophers.

Zeno the Phoenician philosopher never had relations with a woman, but only with boys, as Antigonus Carystius writes in his biography. He said on occasion that the essential thing is to love the soul, and not the body, and that one should keep one's lovers until they were twenty-eight years old (Athenaeus, 13.563E–F).

Epaminondas had as his lovers Asopichus and Caphisodorus. The latter fell with him at the battle of Mantineia and was buried at his side. Asopichus was terrible and mighty against his enemies; Eucnamus of Amphisa, the first to confront and wound him, was honored as a hero in Phocis (Plutarch, *Dialogue on Love*, 761D).

During the consulship of C. Petilius and L. Papyrius, a certain free-born youth was enslaved on account of his father's debt to *L. Papyrius.* He was very good-looking, and still of a vulnerable age. A wicked lust for illicit sex with this youth seized Papyrius. In order to take additional interest on his loan from the boy's virginity, he propositioned his prisoner with unchaste words. When the lad, more mindful of his honor than of his present condition, refused to listen to this shameful proposal, and re-mained unmoved when Papyrius resorted to threats, he was, on Papyrius' orders, stripped and flogged with many lashes. As soon as he was able, he escaped into the street, and complained of the usurer's lust and brutality before the assembly, so that he stirred up the multitude out of pity, and out of disgust at the crime. With tumult and clamor they converged on the Senate house, and helpless outrage carried more weight there than the bond of the moneylenders. The consuls were instructed to propose to the people, and the people assented, that no Roman citizen should henceforth be held in prison while awaiting punishment unless his offence deserved it. So those who were in bonds were released, and debt-slavery was in future forbidden (Sabellico, Bk. IV, Ennead 4, *Opera*, 1:552; from Livy, 8.28).

Caelius [actually *P.*] *Plotius* enslaved the youth Titus Veturius for debt, and after beating him for refusing to submit to illicit sex, killed him. When a complaint was lodged with the consuls, Plotius was thrown in prison (Valerius Maximus, *Memorable Doings and Sayings*, 6.1.9).

Lucius Quintius Flamininus was the brother of T. Quintius Flamininus, but quite unlike him in character, being given to appallingly filthy lusts, and utterly heedless of dignity. It was a habit of his that, when he was enamored of a boy, he would take him along on military expeditions, and when he should have been administering the province, he would spend all his time with his "aides-de-camp." Once when Lucius was banqueting, the boy, by way of a wanton jest, said that he loved him so ardently that he had left the gladiatorial show, and had never yet seen a man's throat being cut[34] because he gave a higher priority to serving [Lucius'] pleasure than his own. Well pleased, Lucius said, "this poses no problem, I will easily gratify your desire." And he ordered a condemned man to be brought from prison, and an attendant to behead him while the banquet was still in progress. Valerius Antias is our authority that it was not a lover-boy that Lucius so indulged, but a woman . . . (Livy, 39.42–43, Plutarch, *Titus Flamininus*, 18.2–19.4, and Cicero, *On Old Age*, 12.42).[35]

L. Cornelius Sulla, when he was a young man, pursued the actor Metrobius Lysiodius with steadfast love. With the years, his devotion grew, and he loved him still when he was an old debauchee (Plutarch, *Sulla*, 2.3–4).

Lusius, Marius' nephew by his sister, was killed by the soldier Trebonius when Lusius made a violent attack on his chastity. Marius pardoned the defendant, and on top of this, gave him a crown (Livy [not found], and Plutarch, *Sayings of Romans*, 202B–C).

Herod, king of the Jews, kept three eunuchs as his favorites because of their beauty: one was his butler, another served him at dinner, and the third was in charge of his bed-chamber. Someone informed the king that they had been corrupted with huge sums of money by his son Alexander. When questioned whether they had intimate relations with Alexander, they confessed that they had. Alexander [they said] harbored an ingrained hatred for his father; he suggested to them that Herod was in decline and already incompetent, and was trying to disguise his age and senility by dying his hair. Herod imprisoned Alexander and would have killed him, had not Archelaus, king of Cappadocia, Alexander's father-in-law, intervened (Josephus, *Jewish Antiquities*, 16.229–36, 251, 261).

Tiberius, the emperor, an utterly depraved pederast, went swimming with his "minnows"[36] (Suetonius, *Tiberius*, 44.1).

The Roman emperor *Nero* conceived so great a longing for his slain wife Sabina [i.e., Poppaea] that he ordered the freed slave-boy Sporus to be castrated, because he closely resembled her, and in every respect he treated him as his wife. For this reason, the joke went around that humanity would have been well served if [Nero's] father Domitius had such a wife. [Nero] called Sporus "Sabina," since he had been castrated because he looked so much like her. Just as Sabina before him, [Sporus] married Nero in Greece, complete with the usual contract. Tigellinus, as the law required, gave the bride away. This wedding was celebrated throughout Greece. After Nero's death, Vitellius summoned Sporus to play the role of a girl being ravished in the theater; but [Sporus], unable to bear this shame, committed suicide. At one time, Nero shared his bed with two simultaneously: Pythagoras in the role of husband (whom Nero had married, and to whom he paid out a very substantial dowry) and Sporus in the role of wife, whom he called "Lady" and "Queen." [Nero] also married the freedman Doryphorus, and he imitated the cries and shrieks of a virgin being deflowered (Suetonius, *Nero*, 28–29; Dio Cassius, epitome of Xiphilinus, 62.28.2–4, 63.13.1–3, 65.10.1; Tacitus, *Annals*, 15.37).

After Nero had been overthrown, the praetorian prefect *Nymphidius Sabinus* summoned Nero's erstwhile sweetheart Sporus from the funeral pyre while Nero's body was still burning, and took him as his wife, calling him "Poppaea"[37] (Plutarch, *Galba*, 9.3–4).

A. *Vitellius* took his pleasure with the freedman[38] Asiaticus, who shared his lusts. Often he rejected him, only to take him back; he sold him, and bought him back again, and eventually promoted him to equestrian rank (Cuspinianus, from Suetonius, *Vitellius*, 12).

Titus Vespasian was said to be very enamored of castrates. Later, as an insult to [Titus' memory], Domitian issued an edict that henceforth no one within the boundaries of the Roman Empire should be castrated (Dio Cassius, epitome of Xiphilinus, 67.2.3).[39]

The emperor *Trajan* was said to be merciful and upright by nature, except for two vices: he indulged to excess in wine, and in sex with boys (Dio Cassius, 68.7.4–5).[40]

The emperor *Hadrian* deified his lover Antinous. He built a temple for him, offered sacrifices, and set up a priesthood. A city and province of Egypt were named for him (St. Jerome, *Commentary on Isaiah*, Book I, ch. 2).[41]

Martial, concerning *Aulus:* "Aulus loves Thestylus, but burns no less for Alexis; / Perchance he loves our Hyacinthus too. / Go now: can there be any doubt that Aulus loves his poets, / Seeing that he loves his poets' darlings?" (*Epigrams*, 8.62).

Martial writes this to Auctus: "*Artemidorus* has a boy, but he has sold his land: / Calliodorus, instead of a boy, has land. / Tell me, Auctus, which of the two has got the better deal? / Artemidorus loves; Calliodorus plows" (*Epigrams*, 9.21).

Martial, on *Labienus:* "Labienus sold his orchard to buy himself some boys. / Now Labienus has nothing but—a grove of figs!"[42] (*Epigrams*, 12.33).

Martial, on *Callistratus* and *Afrus:* "Bearded Callistratus has wed rugged Afrus / Under the law by which maiden marries man. / The torches glowed, their faces were all veiled. / And no one forgot the ritual shout to Talassus.[43] / The contract for the dowry was read out. / What? You think that's not enough, O Rome? / Can it be you are waiting for me to be deflowered?" (*Epigrams*, 12.42).[44]

Libianus the sophist was driven out of Constantinople because of his shameless affairs with boys. Later Nicomedia, whither he had retreated, expelled him for the same reason.

Against *Marcus*, a seducer and pederast (*pullaria*)—for the ancients at one time called boys "chickens" (*pullos*)—Ausonius inveighs most sternly: "He has corrupted the whole boyish sex, / That rear-end rutter of perverted lust (*perversae veneris*)" (*Epigrams*, 19.77).

Sigismondo Malatesta, who ruled over much of Emilia, now the Romagna, tried to know his son Robert. But he, attacking his father with a short dagger, avenged himself of this crime (Pontano, *De immanitate*, ch. 17).[45] Marius Minerva says that in *Tunis*, where he served on a diplomatic mission, there is a solemn and holy day on which almost the entire populace gathers at a certain location outside the city to have promiscuous sexual relations with men (*idem*).

Amongst certain natives of the *New World*, particularly those who inhabit Puerto Viejo and the island of Punà,[46] pederasty is so commonplace that the most beautiful boys are kept as catamites in the temples, where they dress in women's clothes and imitate women's voice and gait.

They tend to the idols, and on feast days in honor of the demon, they prostitute themselves to princes and petty kings (Pedro de Cieza de León, *History of Peru*, I, ch. 64).[47]

Muleasses, king of Tunis, was a pederast (Giovio, bk. 35).[48]

II. PASSIVE: PATHICS, CINAEDI, CATAMITES

From an anonymous Greek epigram concerning cinaedi:

> They have denied being men yet they've not become women,
> Nor have they become men, for they've undergone women's share;
> And yet they are not women, for they're by nature men:
> They are men to women and women to men.

Eunuchs' repulsive lusts are described by Suidas in a quotation from St. Cyril, under the heading "Eunuch."

"The city of *Chios* will owe five talents because of that butt!" Aristophanes jokes these [men] are incontinent and effeminate; because of their effeminacy, they have broad rear-ends, ready to defecate (Suidas).

Although *Achilles* had already begotten a son, someone secretly wrote the inscription "Handsome is Achilles" on the temple of Apollo Proius (i.e., Ptoian Apollo; Plutarch, *Beasts Are Rational*, 990E).

Agathocles, tyrant of Sicily, had a surpassingly beautiful body, and earned his living by it, before he came to power. Accordingly, Timaeus used to call him "public slut" (Justin, *Epitome of Trogus*, bk. 22).[49]

Choerilus of Samos, exiled from there by his master, became the attendant—and the lover—of the historian Herodotus in the seventy-fifth Olympiad.

Smerdies was the beloved of Polycrates of Teos (Aelian, *Historical Miscellany*, 9.4).

Pausanias of Macedon, a member of the royal bodyguard, was loved by King Philip [of Macedon], son of Amyntas, because of his beauty. When he learned that the king had fallen in love with another *Pausanias* (who shared his name), he confronted the latter with abusive insults, accusing him of being a hermaphrodite who put himself on display for his lovers' pleasure. Unable to endure such a damnable insult, [Pausanias] held his tongue for the time being. But after he had told Attalus, one of his friends, what he ought to do, he voluntarily brought about his own death. A few days later, when Philip was fighting a battle against Pleurias king of Illyria, [Pausanias] stepped in front of the king and received in his body all the missiles aimed at the king, and so he met his death. When word of this got out, Attalus, who was quite influential with the king amongst the courtiers and prominent men, invited [the first] Pausanias to dinner. He got him dead drunk on neat wine, and handed him over to the muleteers, who abused his besotted body (Diodorus Siculus, 16.93.3–7).

Aeschines accused *Timarchus* of unchastity before the Athenians in a virulent and accusatory speech (Aulus Gellius, *Attic Nights*, 18.3).[50]

When *a certain young man* asked what he looked like, Diogenes the Cynic answered, "an Arcadian." By this Diogenes meant either that the man was stupid or, as some scholars prefer, that he was effeminate and a catamite, because the Arcadians were said to nourish themselves on acorns, as the epigram says: "Indeed the acorn-eating men are many in Arcadia." And "acorn" in Latin (*glans*) sometimes has an obscene meaning (Erasmus, *Apophthegmata*, Bk. 8).[51]

Pausanias the potter loved the poet *Agathon* with a sordid[52] love; their lovers' quarrels are described by Aelian, *Historical Miscellany*, 2.21.

Epicurus loved *Pythocles*, a choice young man, and used to write to him in this vein: "I waste and fade away, yielding to your loveable, your divine advances" (Diogenes Laertius, 10.5).

Phaedo of Elis was prostituted by his Athenian master, who kept a brothel and made a profit from his body. He refused to have any further dealings with his owner, and was redeemed [from slavery] by Alcibiades [sic; actually Cebes]. He attached himself to Socrates, and ended up becoming an outstanding philosopher (Aulus Gellius, *Attic Nights*, 2.18).

Alcaeus the lyric poet loved the boy *Lycus*. In Book I of the *Odes*, Horace writes of him, "[Alcaeus] is ever singing of Bacchus, and the Muses, / Of Venus, and that boy to whom he is attached: / Lovely Lycus of the black eyes and black locks" (1.32).

Galestes, the lover of king Ptolemy, was as tender-hearted as he was beautiful (Aelian, *Historical Miscellany*, 1.30).[53]

Aristodemus, tyrant of Cumae in Italy, was nicknamed "the Soft" because he was not much of a man and behaved immodestly (*pudicitiam substravisset*), records Dionysius, according to Caelius [i.e., Ricchieri, not found].

Cleaenetus, son of Cleomedon, not only disgraced himself, but did harm to the city [of Athens] when he sought remission of a fine of 50 talents owed by his father,[54] and brought letters from King Demetrius Poliorcetes to the people [of Athens], from whence Demetrius had driven Cassander. The people did indeed grant the remission to Cleomedon, but by a referendum they prohibited any citizen from receiving letters from Demetrius. Furious at this, Demetrius not only rescinded the referendum, but killed some of those who devised and advised it, and others he banished (Plutarch, *Demetrius*, 24.3–5).

In the camp of Hamilcar the Carthaginian general there was a distinguished and handsome young man named *Hasdrubal*, who some said was enjoyed in a shameful manner, and on terms of equality, by Hamilcar. But such a man was not to be brought low by slander. As public morality forbade Hasdrubal to keep company with Hamilcar, the latter gave him his daughter in marriage, because, according to [Carthaginian] custom, a son-in-law could not refuse his father-in-law anything (Probus [i.e., Cornelius Nepos], *Great Generals of Foreign Nations*, 22.3.2–3).

The [Roman] dictator *L. Sulla*, authors of the highest reputation relate, grew to manhood in the bosom of playboys from the time he first reached puberty, to the ruination of his chastity. And even though he was never mindful of his sex, and kept up the shameful deeds of the body even when advancing years made them unsuitable, and well beyond the bounds of what could be forgiven in youth, that old debauchee, a hostage to vice, advanced to supreme power in Rome. Though he never gave any of this up, he was honored by the whole senate and people with a vote of perpetual and triumphant felicity (Ricchieri, 15.10).

P. Atilius Philiscus, a boy let out for hire, was forced to sell his body by his master (Valerius Maximus, *Memorable Doings and Sayings*, 6.1.6).

Q. Opimius, a man of consular rank, who had a bad reputation in his youth, said to Aegilius, a witty man who was considered rather effeminate, "My dear Aegilia, when are you going to come over to my place with your distaff and wool?" Aegilius responded to this insult with urbanity: "I wouldn't dare to—mommy forbade me to keep company with any girl of ill repute" (Macrobius [not found]).[55]

C. Julius Caesar first did military service in Asia, where he was aide-de-camp to Marcus Thermus, the praetor. When [Thermus] sent him to meet the fleet in Bithynia, he tarried at [the court of king] Nicomedes, and rumors flew that he had surrendered his chastity to the king. The rumor grew when [Caesar] returned to Bithynia a few days later to recover some money owed to a freedman who was a client of his. Calvus Licinius called Nicomedes "the man who buggered Caesar." Dolabella called [Caesar] "the queen's decoy" and "the inside frame of the royal bed," and Curio called him "Nicomedes' whore-house" and "the Bithynian brothel." Bibulus published an edict which described his colleague [in the consulship] as "Queen of Bithynia: once he had a king as his darling, and now it's a kingdom he wants." A certain Octavius, a chatter-box and a bit soft in the head, saluted Pompey as "king" and Caesar as "queen" in the midst of a huge assembly. But C. Memmius accuses [Caesar] of acting as cupbearer to Nicomedes and other debauchees at a huge banquet at which some merchants from Rome were present. Not content to have written in some of his letters that "[Caesar] was conducted into the royal bed-chamber by attendants, and lying on a golden couch, clothed in purple, this descendent of Venus lost his virginity in Bithynia," Cicero further said, when Caesar was earnestly defending the cause of Nicomedes' daughter before the Senate, and recalling all the good that the king had done for him, "Please, enough of this! It is quite well known what he gave you, and what you gave him!" Finally, at Caesar's Gallic triumph, the soldiers, amongst other songs which they customarily sang in jest as they followed [the victor's] chariot, intoned this ribald ditty: "Caesar subjugated Gaul; Nicomedes, Caesar. / Lo! Caesar who subjugated Gaul now celebrates his triumph. / Nicomedes, who subjugated Caesar, celebrates no triumph." Curio declared in a certain speech that all the women hailed [Caesar] as husband, and all the men as wife (Suetonius, *Deified Julius*, 49, 52.3).

Bathyllus was the poet Anacreon's lover [e.g., Horace, *Epodes*, 14.9]. Likewise *Megitheus*. [Horace loved] *Ligurinus* (*Odes*, 4.1, 10). Likewise *Lyciscus*, whom [Horace mentions] in an Epode [11.24]. Valerius Flaccus Sestinus [loved] *Amazonicus*, whose beauty Martial commends. [The poet] Tibullus [loved] *Cherinthus*, and the poet Asinius Gallus, son of Asinius, a man of consular rank, *Hippolytus*.

Sporus belonged to Nero, and *Nero* himself belonged to Pythagoras. See the preceding chapter [i.e., "Active"].

Catullus mentions in his poetry *Aurelius, Furius, Iuvencius*, and *Thallus*. In Martial's epigram, *Pannychus* is castigated: "Your shanks bristle with hair, your chest is bushy too: / But your brains, Pannychus, are plucked" (*Epigrams*, 2.36).[56] Also *Hyllus, Gargilianus, Labienus, Naevolus, Charinus, Amazonicus*, and *Papilius. Didymus*, who was allowed to sit in the seats reserved for the equestrian order [in the theater], but not in the seats for married men. *Thestylus*, "Victor's torment, Voconius' delight" (*Epigrams*, 7.29).

For the lad *Antinous* (a native of Claudiopolis in Bithynia), the emperor Hadrian went so far in his disgraceful passion that he constructed a city for Antinous after his death, built a temple with an altar, and undertook to have his portrait reproduced. Spartianus says that this lad was mourned by the emperor as if he were his wife (Dio Cassius, 69.11.2–4; "Spartianus," *Hadrian*, 14.5–7).

Earinus, Domitian's eunuch, was for a time his darling; but later, when Domitian promulgated the law against castrating men, he repudiated him (Xiphilinus [i.e., Dio Cassius epitomized], 67.2.2–3).

Of *Draco* ("dragon"), Strato writes in Epigram 1: "Oh he is a dragon, this lad, though a pretty one: / But other reptiles poke into his hole!" (*Greek Anthology*, 11.22).[57]

The emperor *Elagabalus* played the part of a woman with men, and would seek out studs (*Draucos*) to gratify his lust. He would paint his eyes and cheeks, and pose naked before the men whom he used for this filthy service in the posture of the Venus of Paros, one hand pressed to his breast and another covering his private parts. He considered that the cup of life's pleasure was full if he appeared worthy and fitted for the lust of many (Sabellico, Bk. VI, Ennead 7; *Opera*, 2:257).

Tribades

Here we say nothing which has not been said before, and collect only a few items. Although there are not laws against it, this indecency deserves to be denounced so that good people will be deterred from imitating it. Those who were ruined readily made examples of themselves, that they might be held up as examples.

Amythone, Telesippa, Megara, Atthys, and *Cydno* were Sappho's handmaids, whom she used to gratify her lusts. Thus she writes in her letter to Phaon: "Amythone is worthless, white Cydno is nothing to me, / Atthys wins no favor in my eyes, as once she did."[58]

Erynna was Sappho's bedfellow according to Suidas and Tacianus. See the chapter "Poetesses."

Milesian women, tribades and lewd women, made use of the dildo (Suidas).

Under the heading "Eunuchs," Suidas describes in the words of St. Cyril the horrible lust of *eunuchs* who guard women.

Martial in Book I of the *Epigrams* inveighs against the tribade *Bassa,* who in his words "Has devised a worthy demonstration of the Theban riddle: / How can there be adultery where no man is to be found" (1.90).

Philaenis, another tribade, is castigated in an indecent poem by Martial (*Epigrams,* 7.67).

A certain *Galla* who disguised herself as a stableboy worked for an innkeeper in Blois for seven years. She married the daughter of a citizen, and had tribadic relations with her for two years. When the crime came to light, she was burned alive (*Henri Estienne, *Apologie pour Hérodote,* I, ch. 13).

CHAPTER 7

Prodigious Monstrosities

> A monstrosity, of course, belongs to the class of "things contrary to Nature," although it is contrary not to Nature in her entirety but only to Nature *in the generality of cases.*
>
> —Aristotle, *Generation of Animals*[1]

A main topic of early modern teratology, the study or discussion of monsters, was hermaphroditism, and that was commonly thought analogous to at least penetrative same-sex sexual relations. Also, as monsters were considered "contrary to nature" in some traditions, so sexual "sins against nature" could render their practitioners monstrous.[2] From a Christian Aristotelian viewpoint they could appear hypermonstrous, insofar as sodomitical sex appeared to violate God's entire natural order (*Theology). The Levitical rhetoric of "*ab*-homination" subsumed sex between males in the transgression of the perceived norms of humanity. Comparing females to males, Aristotle found the former incipiently monstrous, redeemed only by the natural reproductive utility of the womb.[3] From Aristotelian viewpoints, then, sexual affiliations between females would seem to revoke that exemption, while males sexually receptive to other males would perpetrate the redoubled monstrosity of degrading their "superior" manhood to assume the sexual position and imputed status of a female, but in a nonreproductive semblance. The perspectives and media of teratological discourse were manifold, involving vernacular broadsides and pamphlets, religious and political polemics, portions of Latin medical texts, popular and learned miscellanies of marvels, and modulations within other discourses and genres, as in *The Mooncalf* of Michael Drayton (1563–1631), a poem partly satirizing sexual inversions. Teratology's pejorative applications to same-sex desire helped to fuel and sustain homophobia by evoking and exploiting superstitious fears.

As Lorraine Daston and Katharine Park observe, we may distinguish three general and sometimes overlapping patterns of early modern interpretive response to monstrosity: horror, appreciation, and repugnance.[4] Insofar as same-sex lovers appeared monstrous, I infer that they were subsumed in these patterns to varying extents. The early modern reaction of horror revived and adapted some ancient divinatory precedents to interpret monstrous births as portentous signs of God's wrath and retribution for human sins through imminent calamities or even apocalypse. Such manifestations, called "prodigies," denoted sinful abrogation of moral norms through a "demonstrative" divine intervention signally rupturing the expected order of nature. As Augustine observes in

225

Fig. 6 Konrad Lykosthenes, The Monster of Ravenna, two alternative views, from *Prodigiorum ac ostentorum chronicon* (Basel, 1557). By permission of the Blacker-Wood Biology Library, McGill University.

The City of God, the words *monstra* and *prodigia* were thus thought to be derived from *monstrare*, "to show," and *porro dicere*, "to say hereafter," or predict the future (21.8). Partly on account of the utility of prodigies for propaganda in the conflicted political, religious, and military circumstances of late fifteenth- and sixteenth-century Europe, their ostensible appearances and meanings gained special cultural importance at that time.[5] Probably the most famous was the putative "Monster of Ravenna" whose numerous deformities were interpreted as signs, each rebuking a specific sin and threatening Italy's ruin if those sins were not forsaken through Christian repentance (figure 6). Its hermaphroditism, for example, purportedly signified the threat of "filthy Sodomy" (*Jakob Rüff). A pamphlet issued by the Reformers Martin Luther (1483–1546) and Philipp Melanchthon (1497–1560) in 1523 allegorizes two monsters' features for anti-Catholic polemic. One of them, the "Popish Ass," has a naked feminine belly said to symbolize sexual abominations of Roman Catholicism, implicitly evoking same-sex sexual practices, among others.[6] By association, prodigies would have tended to invest the perception of monstrosity in general with a reflex of superstitious horror, and the supercharged rhetoric of sodomitical abomination would have played to some extent on such responses.

One major cultural function of prodigies was the enforcement of moral and sexual conformity. As Arnold Davidson has argued, the early modern reaction of horror was occasioned by the appearance of contrariety to nature, by the seeming violation of a "natural norm," and thus also by the transgression of an ostensible moral norm deemed "natural" (41–51). In the latter senses, the

monstrous prodigy could horribly manifest human will countering and thwart-
ing God's, and divine judgment of such offense. Monstrous births could not
only provide ostensible tokens of forthcoming judgment to provoke fear of God
and motivate repentance for sexual and other sins, but were also ascribed to
ostensible sexual excesses or misdeeds, whether through natural causes, divine
intervention to reveal and humiliate parental sin, or both (*Rüff, *Ambroise
Paré). Even if a monster were explicable by natural means, it could nonetheless constitute a divinely admonitory prodigy, for supernatural causes could
also be involved.[7] Sexual behaviors that could supposedly produce prodigious
monstrosities were heteroerotic coitus during menstruation[8]; lustful conduct
affecting quality and quantity of seed; bestiality; and, presumably through supernatural causes thought visited on female partners, sodomy (*Rüff, *Paré).
Although, according to one tradition of moral theology, heteroerotic anal intercourse was not in itself deemed sinful if ejaculation occurred in the vagina
and the couple were married (*Theology), anal intercourse was otherwise the
sexual "sin against nature" par excellence, aside from bestiality.

Yet monsters could also appear marvels, objects of delight or intrigue, products of a nature so superabundantly replete with natural and supernatural causes
that it reveals itself in exuberant play or vagaries. In this sense, the etymology
from *monstrare* ("to show") was said to befit the wondrous novelty of monsters,
to be shown to all.[9] Physical and textual collections of natural wonders were
the chief formal expressions of this viewpoint in early modernity. The intellectually amphibian physician Sir Thomas Browne (1605–1682) observes in his
Religio medici (A Doctor's Religion, 1643), "there is no *Grotesco* in nature," and
"no deformity but in monstrosity, wherein notwithstanding there is a kind of
beauty, Nature so ingen[i]ously contriving the irregular parts, as they become
sometimes more remarkable than the principal fabric." And we ourselves "carry
with us the wonders we seek without us: there is all *Africa*, and all her prodigies
within us."[10]

Such perspectives have ancient and medieval filiations perhaps most influ-
entially epitomized in St. Augustine's discussion of monstrous births and races
in *The City of God*, where he rejects the interpretation of monsters as prodigies
"against nature," objects for terrible prognostications. "Whoever is born anywhere as a human being, that is, as a rational mortal creature," Augustine insists,
"however strange he may appear to our senses in bodily form or color or motion
or utterance, or in any faculty, part or quality of his nature whatsoever, let no
true believer have any doubt that such an individual is descended from the one
man who was first created." Such differences from the usual course of nature
are "marvelous by . . . very rarity," and divinely ordained: "God is the creator of
all things, and he himself knows at what place and time a given creature should
be created, or have been created, selecting in his wisdom the various elements
from whose likenesses and diversities he contrives the beautiful fabric of the
universe. But one who cannot see the whole clearly is offended by the apparent

deformity of a single part, since he does not know with what it conforms or how to classify it.... [God] whose works no one has the right to censure knows what he has done" (16.8; trans. William M. Green).

This relatively appreciative Augustinian interpretation of apparent exceptional beings could also have been appropriated (as Augustine would not have wished) for the understanding of same-sex lovers. Ancient, later medieval, and early modern *medicine, *astrology, and *physiognomy afforded means of assigning such sexual desires and behaviors to inborn natural causes. Augustine contextually mentions individual hermaphrodites and a race "bisexual by nature, ... who in their intercourse with each other alternately beget and conceive" (16.8; trans. Green). Despite his condemnation of sodomy in other contexts, Augustine's comment on perceived monsters can inadvertently suggest applications to other sexual possibilities that vary from conventional gender roles. Such notions of nature as divinely intelligible plenitude—and, in a further early modern development, playfulness—more readily accommodate male and female homoeroticism than restrictive models in which perceived differences or anomalies are immediately branded deformities "against nature," outside its approved order. *Joseph Hall (1574–1656) may evince some such traces of appreciation in his imaginative treatment of natural and artificial hermaphrodites.

However, from the later sixteenth century into the Enlightenment, horrified and appreciative responses to monsters could be increasingly supplemented by repugnance or distaste at seeming errors of nature that appeared to violate natural and social decorum. Monsters' ostensible failure to fulfill the natural telos of their species rendered them ugly, then: not divine portents nor wonders of natural creativity either, but deformities. In this way, the monster may well have become a less lurid analogue for the sodomite or tribade, yet lost some possibilities of bemusement and reconciliation with a nature formerly assigned more creative richness and versatility.

The hermaphroditic type of monster was most obviously correlative to same-sex lovers, for it afforded the prospect of interchanging conventional gender roles in sex, and thus appeared to confound masculine and feminine functions, upset assumptions of clear gender distinction, and challenge the restriction of coitus to encounters of opposite sexes. The Monster of Ravenna's hermaphroditism notoriously betokened sodomy (figure 6; *Rüff). "They that are given to that abominable sin of *Sodomy*, and are both active and passive in it," observes Alexander Ross (1591–1654) "may be truly termed *Hermaphrodites*."[11] Thomas Artus's *Les hermaphrodites* (1605), a satiric fantasy about a traveler's experiences in a land where everyone is both male and female, partly targets masculine love and its association with the court of King Henri III (1551–1589). It features an emblematic frontispiece that depicts a male wearing fashions of both sexes, entitled "Accords with All" or "One for All" (figure 7). "I'm neither male nor female," the epigram declares, "and so I'm on the look-out for which of those two I must choose. But what does it matter which someone resembles? Better to have them both together, for that provides a doubled pleasure."[12] The early modern

Fig. 7 Frontispiece, from Thomas Artus, *Les hermaphrodites* (Paris, c. 1605). By permission of the Osler Library for the History of Science and Medicine, McGill University.

figurative meanings of hermaphroditism were diverse and variable, including ideal conjugal union; sensual corruption; bisexuality; spiritual exaltation; the "effeminacy" of males who intensely pursue females; and males or females who appear similar to their opposite sex.[13] But the term was also pejoratively deployed against male and female homoeroticism and any apparent mixing of genders, so that to be publicly called a hermaphrodite was defamatory,[14] probably because it implied sodomitical opprobrium. Medical writings after 1550 evince a surge of interest in hermaphroditism, partly due to reassessments of sex difference and the relative status of males and females, and hermaphrodites were thus increasingly associated with sodomy, tribadism, cross-dressing, and transformations of sex.[15] Yet Plato had provided a nonhermaphroditic account of same-sex love in the well-known *Symposium*, where male-female love results from the primal division of double-personed hermaphrodites, and the homoerotic counterpart from the division of doubly male and doubly female beings (*General Introduction). Lovers of their own sex could thus reject hermaphroditic interpretations of their desires, if they wished, and tell detractors that males who love females are hermaphroditically "effeminate."

Although hermaphroditism in itself does not seem to have been considered prodigious in early modernity,[16] hermaphrodites commonly appeared in catalogues of monsters and monstrous births, and the attributes of prodigies included such sexual doubleness. Also, "prodigy" had considerable metaphoric elasticity, as in the sixteenth-century *Histoires prodigeuses* (*Claude de Tesserant). Medical explanations of the causes of hermaphroditism "ranged from a surfeit of maternal matter . . . to the positioning of the sperm in the seven cells of the uterus at conception (three produce girls, three produce boys; the middle one produces hermaphrodites), to the proportion of male to female 'seed' to astral influences."[17] From an Aristotelian viewpoint, there was no such thing as a sexually intermediate being, only the possibility of doubled genitals that did not both function, so that such a being remained either male or female in bodily complexion. Yet the Hippocratic corpus and Galen considered hermaphrodites genuinely intermediate, so that sex difference was thus problematized, and these disparate views could be counterposed or uneasily compounded.[18]

The legal and social situations of hermaphrodites differed across Europe, so that the variations comparatively reveal crosscultural shifts in early modern notions of sex and gender.[19] However, it seems they were typically pressured to live unisexually, and contrary possibilities and behaviors tended to evoke homophobia.[20] In early modern France, for example, hermaphrodites were legally obligated to live in accord with their predominant sex assigned by medical assessment, and could thus marry. But they committed sodomy if they had sex contrary to conventional roles of their nominal gender. The recourse to medical adjudication may reflect rising sixteenth-century anxieties about sexual transgression that followed from the moral prescriptiveness of the Reformation and Counter-Reformation. In 1601 at Rouen, when a hermaphrodite raised as a female asked permission to wed a woman with whom she or he was having a sexual relationship, medical controversy about his or her predominant sex narrowly averted execution for sodomy.[21] In 1603 an officially male hermaphrodite was hung and burned in Paris for having assumed a feminine sexual role.[22] Spanish laws seem to have been similar. In a particularly protean case of the late 1580s, the magistrates found that Eleno or Elena de Céspedes had lived as a married, child-bearing woman, then as a hermaphrodite deemed male, with a wife and surgical practice, but determined Eleno to be female. "I have quite naturally been a man and a woman," she or he declared, "and even though this may seem like a prodigious and rare thing that is seldom seen, hermaphrodites, as I have been one myself, are not against nature."[23] In England, the legal authority *Sir Edward Coke (1552–1634) apparently expected hermaphrodites to behave according to their prevalent sex,[24] but no such court cases or public scandals appear to have occurred there until the late seventeenth century. Insofar as it addressed the possibilities of sex among humans, the much more narrowly Levitical sodomy law in England targeted anal sex between males, without any accepted application to female homoeroticism, and, lacking investigative recourse to torture, unlike continental jurisdictions, it was comparatively difficult to enforce anyway (*Law).

Current attitudes toward homosexuality are probably still somewhat affected by cultural echoes of the early modern reception history of monsters. Defining perceived sex differences as occasions for repulsion and amazement, the discourse of monstrosity could readily support homophobia. However, since monsters appear to be exceptions to the presumed course of nature, they may also unsettle and revise assumptions about what nature's scope legitimately includes. As each sodomite and tribade lived "against nature" as it was officially defined, so that experience would likely have provoked reconceptualizations of both self and nature in contrast to conventional views, stimulating the formation of distinctive sexual self-conceptions.

Jakob Rüff (1500–1558)

In the illustrated chapter on monstrous births, including hermaphrodites, in Jakob Rüff's *De conceptu et generatione hominis*, sodomy is both a putative cause of monsters and a grievous sin signally rebuked by the manifestation of prodigies. Though what he means by "sodomy" is unclear, it most likely focuses on sex between males, particularly anal. Born at Rhytal or Wurtemburg, Rüff (also known as Rueff) practiced surgery in Zurich, and his diverse writings include not only medical treatises but also anti-Catholic biblical dramas.[25] First published in 1544, his obstetrical and embryological study *De conceptu* had many subsequent Latin editions, was translated into various languages including German, Dutch, and English, and continued to be printed far into the seventeenth century. It was a common source for other early modern teratological writers, including Konrad Lykosthenes (1518–1561) and *Ambroise Paré (c. 1510–1590).

The Generation and Birth of Man[26] *(1544)*

Book 5, ch. 3: Of Unperfect Children, Also of Monstrous Births

We see that it cometh to pass in divers manners, by experience of matters, and testimony of the times, that many monsters and imperfect or misshapen children are born. But whenas that thing is specially to be attributed and ascribed to the Judgments of God, yet afterward also the corruption and fault of the seed is to be acknowledged, to wit, which was either too much, or too little, or corrupted, from whence those monsters are engendered. But we will hereafter give you some Figures of those shapes, not to the intent to handle all things to the full perfection, but that by a few of them we may propound some knowledge of the Judgments of God by divers monsters against Nature, as it were prognosticating things to come, and that we may see how much the fault and corruption of seed availeth in this case....

But if it be demanded of the cause of such conceptions and births, we must know before all things that they come not to pass without the providence of the Almighty and Omnipotent God; but also that they are permitted oftentimes by his just judgment for to punish and admonish men for their sins. Likewise we allege the immoderate desire of lust to be a cause, whereby it cometh to pass that the seeds of men and women are caused to be very feeble and imperfect, whereby of necessity a feeble and imperfect Feature must ensue. For the defect of seed going before, the consequence is that a defect of the Feature doth follow; and contrariwise, if the seed shall be superfluous, it is easily collected and concluded that superfluous things are engendered of a superfluous matter....

It happeneth also that some are engendered, and do grow and increase until some time, that he that vieweth them cannot determine and be resolved of what sex or kind they may be of. The more unskillful do suppose them to be of both kinds, but they are far deceived. For it falleth out by some chance that the seed gathereth some corruption about these members. For example sake, it happened that such a child was brought before us, concerning whom it was not apparent of what sex or kind he should be. The testicles or stones did appear outwardly, but no privy member besides; under the testicles there was a rupture and division from which the water did issue forth. But because by reason of the defect of the yard, or urine-pipe standing outwardly (for it was not altogether wanting, but turned inwardly toward the rupture even n[o]w spoken of), Nature had given this way to the urine, it seemed good that it should not be baptized for a maiden-child, nor for such a one as is both Male and Female, but for a man-child. And the mother did confess that she was greatly affrighted and terrified by a certain thing she had seen, so that she did conjecture that by that means, that was so contracted and shrunk unto the child. But because such things are rather perceived by the understanding than the eyes, we would not frame any Figure peculiar to such a birth. But now let us return to another Figure.

In the year 1547 at Krakow, a very strange Monster was born, which lived three days. His head did somewhat resemble the shape of a man's, but that his eyes flamed like fire; his Nose was long and hooked and stood like the shin-bone of the leg, or trunk of an Elephant. In the joints of his members, near the shoulders, upon the elbows and the knees, there appeared dogs' heads; his hands and feet were like unto the feet of a Goose. He had two eyes above his Navel, a tail behind like a beast's, having a hook at the end. In sex he was a male. The cause of this misshapen Monster we ascribe to God alone; yet notwithstanding, through the insight of our reason, we may perceive also the detestable sin of Sodomy in this Monster.[27]

That of brutes such various shapes are born, it is less wonder therefore, whenas Pliny reports of living creatures in Africa that have such various forms and shapes, seeing their coupling and conception is of divers creatures.[28]

In the year 1512 at Ravenna, a City in Italy, a Monster was born which had a horn on his head, two wings, no arms, a crooked foot with talons, like a ravenous bird, an eye on his knee, of both sex [compare figure 6]. In the midst of his breast he had the form of the Greek letter Upsilon [i.e., Υ] and the Figure of a Cross. Some interpreted this thing after this manner: that the horn did signify pride, the wings fickleness and inconstancy, the want of arms to signify a defect of good works, the ravenous foot, rapine, usury, and all kind of covetousness, the eye on his knee, to portend a respect and regard alone to earthly things, and that he was of both sex, to signify filthy Sodomy. Moreover, that at that time Italy was so afflicted with the ruins and miseries of war because of these sins. But they interpreted the greek Letter Υ to be a sign of Virtue, and the cross to be a sign of Salvation. Wherefore, if these vices being forsaken they would have recourse to virtues and the Cross of Christ, that is to say, his only merit, that then they should find again ease from their warlike broils and have calm peace. These things came to pass, Ludovicus King of France, under Julius the eleventh Bishop [sic], wasting and spoiling Italy.[29]

Rabbi Moses in his *Aphorisms*, Particle 25, writeth thus: in Sicily there happened a great Eclipse of the Sun, and in that year women brought forth very many deformed and double-headed children.[30] It may be demanded here whether beasts may conceive by men, or in like sort women of beasts.[31] We affirm this may come to pass for three reasons: First, by natural appetite. Secondly, by the provocation of Nature by delight. Thirdly, by the attractive virtue of the Matrix, which in beasts and women is alike. Examples are at hand, for Plutarch in his lesser *Parallels* hath these words.[32] Aristonymus Ephesius the son of Demostratus, when he hated women, had carnal company with an Ass, which in process of time brought forth a most beautiful Maiden-child, named Onoscelin, Aristotle [sic] being author of it in the second of his Paradoxes. And again, whenas Fulvius Stellus did disdain and hate women, he had carnal company with a Mare, which, the Months of bearing being passed over, brought forth a very beautiful Maiden-child, which he named Epona (peradventure

Hippona). And indeed there is a goddess of this name, which taketh care of Horses, as Agesilaus writeth in his third book of the affairs of Italy. Again, of one Fulvius and a Mare, the Maiden-child Hippo is said to be born as we read in Plutarch.

Ambroise Paré (c. 1510–1590)

Ambroise Paré's formerly well-known *Des monstres et prodiges* addresses hermaphrodites, supposed genital indications or predispositions of tribadism, transformations of females into males, and alleged relations of sodomy, bestiality, and atheism to monstrous progeny. An artisan's son born near Laval in Mayenne, Paré became a barber-surgeon through apprenticeship, without a university education. At some points his practice was military, and he became famous for his reforms in treating gunshot wounds, publicized through a treatise issued in 1545. Based mainly in Paris, he was appointed surgeon in ordinary to King Henri II, and became chief surgeon for King Charles IX and King Henri III. In the course of two marriages he fathered nine children. Lacking knowledge of Latin as well as Greek, Paré composed his many medical works in French, provoking scorn from academically trained rivals; yet his texts circulated widely in both vernacular and Latin translations throughout Europe.[33] Having first published *Des monstres* in 1573 as the second part of *Deux livres de chirurgie*, he revised it several times in subsequent editions. An English version first appeared within Paré's *Works* in 1634, with four seventeenth-century republications.

Irked by the successes of this nonacademic interloper, the Parisian medical faculty attacked Paré legally and otherwise for his writings such as *Des monstres* for some years, beginning in 1575. Their criticisms targeted his use of French, which divulged professional knowledge to those relatively uneducated, and his inclusion of allegedly immoral content and illustrations in his volumes, which women and children could read in French and see. Some further claimed that the extensive discussion of monsters was indecorous in a medical treatise such as *Deux livres*. One of the ostensibly scandalous passages in Paré's works was his discussion of female genitalia, particularly the "nymphs" or *labia minora* of the vulva, in the 1573, 1575, and 1579 French editions of *Des monstres*.[34] Significantly situated, this material ends the chapter on hermaphrodites and introduces the following chapter on spontaneous changes of sex. Paré's assumption that these can only proceed from female to male, not the reverse, was conventional. His organization implies that females are incipiently hermaphroditic, indeed just provisionally female, and thus in a sense monstrous relative to males, rather as Aristotle had assumed (*Prodigious Monstrosities). *Des monstres* includes no parallel discussion of male genitalia. Hermaphroditic by implication, female genitals can even imitate the penis through the swelling of the nymphs, Paré claims, and they inspire female homoeroticism if substantial, so that such tissues must be surgically excised. Paré was criticized for this not because it was deemed false, misogynist, or sadistic, but because it was published in French, thus becoming accessible to a much wider readership that included females. In the three French editions of this text issued from 1573 to 1579, Paré expands and contracts the passage, and the 1579 edition adds a legal reference to two women burnt for having sex together.[35]

When Paré turns to discuss monsters thought to be produced by the copulation of different species, he links sodomites and atheists with bestiality, as alleged progenitors of these prodigious manifestations. Apparently, he assumes sodomites are so sexually unnatural, so averse to divine order, that they appear prime suspects for this further sexual "crime against nature," and correlative with atheists. Based on the 1582 Latin edition of Paré's works, the English version of 1634, my main textual source here, lacks Paré's teratological comments on feminine genitalia and on sodomy, and so I interpolate translations of those passages, as subsequently noted.

Of Monsters and Prodigies[36] *(1573, 1575)*

The Preface

We call Monsters what things soever are brought forth contrary to the common decree and order of nature. So we term that infant monstrous which is born with one arm alone, or with two heads. But we define Prodigies those things which happen contrary to the whole course of nature, that is, altogether differing and dissenting from nature: as if a woman should be delivered of a Snake or a Dog. Of the first sort are thought all those in which any of those things which ought and are accustomed to be, according to nature, is wanting or doth abound, is changed, worn, covered or defended, hurt, or not put in his right place. For sometimes some are born with more fingers than they should, othersome but with one finger; some with those parts divided which should be joined, others with those parts joined which should be divided. Some are born with the privities of both sexes, male and female.... Some women also have had their privities closed and not perforated, the membranous obstacle, which they call the Hymen, hindering. And men are sometimes born with their fundaments, ears, noses, and the rest of the passages shut, and are accounted monstrous, nature erring from its intended scope. But to conclude, those Monsters are thought to portend some ill, which are much differing from their nature.

Ch. 1: Of the Cause of Monsters, and First of Those Monsters Which Appear for the Glory of God and the Punishment of Men's Wickedness

There are reckoned up many causes of monsters. The first whereof is the glory of God, that his immense power may be manifested to those which are ignorant of it, by the sending of those things which happen contrary to nature. For thus our Savior Christ answered the Disciples (asking whether he or his parents had offended, who, being born blind, received his sight from him), that neither he nor his parents had committed any fault so great, but this to have happened only that the glory and majesty of God should be divulged by that miracle, and such great works [John 9:1–3].

Another cause is, [so] that God may either punish men's wickedness or show signs of punishment at hand (because parents sometimes lie and join themselves together without law and measure, or luxuriously and beastly, or at such times as they ought to forbear by the command of God and the Church), such monstrous, horrid and unnatural births do happen. . . .

The third cause is an abundance of seed and overflowing matter. The fourth, the same in too little quantity, and deficient. The fifth, the force and efficacy of imagination.[37] The sixth, the straitness of the womb. The seventh, the disorderly site[38] of the party with child, and the position of the parts of the body. The eighth, a fall, strain, or stroke, especially upon the belly of a woman with child. The ninth, hereditary diseases, or affects[39] by any other accident. The tenth, the confusion and mingling together of the seed. The eleventh, the craft and wickedness of the devil. There are some others which are accounted for monsters, because they have their original or essence full of admiration, or do assume a certain prodigious form by the craft of some begging companions; therefore we will speak briefly of them in their place in this our treatise of monsters.

Ch. 4: Of Hermaphrodites or Scrats

And here also we must speak of Hermaphrodites, because they draw the cause of their generation and conformation from the plenty and abundance of seed, and are called so because they are of both sexes, the woman yielding as much seed as the man.[40] For hereupon it cometh to pass that the forming faculty (which always endeavors to produce something like itself) doth labor both the matters almost with equal force, and is the cause that one body is of both sexes.

Yet some make four differences of Hermaphrodites. The first of which is the male Hermaphrodite, who is a perfect and absolute male, and hath only a slit in the Perineum not perforated, and from which neither urine nor seed doth flow. The second is the female, which, besides her natural privity, hath a fleshy and skinny similitude of a man's yard, but unapt for erection and ejaculation of seed, and wanteth the cod and stones.[41] The third difference is of those which, albeit they bear the express figures of members belonging to both sexes, commonly set the one against the other, yet are found unapt for generation, the one of them only serving for making of water. The fourth difference is of those who are able in both sexes, and thoroughly perform the part both of man and woman, because they have the genitals of both sexes complete and perfect, and also the right breast like a man and the left like a woman. The laws command those to choose the sex which they will use, and in which they will remain and live, judging them to death if they be found to have departed from the sex they made choice of, for some are thought to have abused both, and promiscuously to have had their pleasure with men and women.[42] There are signs by which the Physicians may discern whether the Hermaphrodites are able in the male or female sex, or whether they are impotent in both. These signs are most apparent in the privities and face. For if the matrix be exact in all its dimensions and so perforated that it may admit a man's yard; if the courses[43] flow that way; if the hair of the head be long, slender, and soft; and to conclude, if to this tender habit of the body a timid and weak condition of the mind be added: the female sex is predominant and they are plainly to be judged women. But if they have the Perineum and fundament full of hairs (the which in women are commonly without any); if they have a yard of a convenient largeness; if it stand well and readily, and yield seed: the male sex hath the preeminence and they are to be judged men. But if the conformation of both the genitals be alike in figure, quantity, and efficacy, it is thought to be equally able in both sexes. Although by the opinion of Aristotle, those who have double genitals, the one of the male, the other of the female, the one of them is always perfect, the other imperfect. . . .[44]

[After some pictured hermaphroditic births with brief descriptions, included also in the 1634 English version, French editions of the 1570s end the chapter on hermaphrodites with variants of this following passage not in the English text.[45]]

At the beginning of the neck of the womb is the entrance and slit of woman's nature, called *Pecten* in Latin. The sides, which are covered with hair, are called *Pterigomata* in Greek: that is to say "wings," or the lips of woman's coronation. Between them are two outgrowths of muscular flesh, one on each side, which cover the exit of the urinal duct, and contract themselves after the woman has pissed. The Greeks call them *nymphs*, which hang and, in some women, even pass outside the neck of their womb, and lengthen or shorten like the crest of a turkey cock, principally when they desire coitus. And when their husbands want to approach them, [the nymphs] rear up like the virile rod, so much that [such women can] thus pleasure themselves with other women.[46] Hence [their nymphs] make them very shameful and deformed when seen naked, and with these women we must tie them and cut off what is superfluous, for they can abuse them; provided that the surgeon takes care not to cut too deeply, for fear of great outflow of blood, or of cutting the bladder's neck. For then they would not be able to hold their urine, but it would trickle out drop by drop.

Now, that there are women who by means of these caruncles or nymphs abuse one another is a thing as true as monstrous and difficult to believe, yet nevertheless confirmed by a memorable story from the *History of*

Africa by Leo of Africa.[47] He says in Book III that among the diviners of Fez, the principal city of Mauritania in Africa, there are certain women who, leading people to believe they are familiar with demons, perfume themselves with fragrances, feigning the spirit has entered their body, and by an alteration of their voice pretend that it is the spirit who speaks from their throat. Then in great reverence the people leave them a gift for the demon. The learned Africans call such women *Sahacat*, corresponding to the Latin *Fricatrices*, because they rub one another for pleasure, and truly they are stricken with this wicked vice of using each other carnally. Hence if some beautiful woman goes to consult them, in the name of the spirit they ask her for carnal copulation as payment. Now of those are found some [wives] who, having gotten a taste for this game and allured by the sweet pleasure that they receive from it, feign to be sick, and send to fetch these divinatrices, and most often send the message by their husbands themselves. But the better to conceal her wickedness, [such a wife] pretends to her husband that a spirit has entered into her body, whose health being at issue, he must give her leave to go amongst them. Whereat the good husband, consenting to it, prepares a sumptuous feast for all this venerable band, at the end of which they dance, then the wife may go wherever seems good to her. But some husbands are found who, shrewdly perceiving this ruse, make the spirit leave their wives' bodies with some good clubbings. Also some others, giving the divinatrices to understand that their wives are detained by the spirits, deceive the former by the same means that those did the wives. That is what Leo the African wrote of it. Asserting elsewhere that there are people in Africa who go through the city in the manner of our spayers and gelders, and make a living by cutting off these caruncles [i.e., nymphs], as we have shown previously on surgical operations.

Ch. 5: Of the Changing of Sex

Amatus Lusitanus[48] reports that in the village [Esgueira], there was a maid named Maria Pateca, who at the appointed age for her courses to flow, had instead of them a man's yard, lying before that time hid and covered, so that of a woman she became a man, and therefore laying aside her woman's habit, was clothed in man's, and changing her name, was called Emanuel. Who when he had got much wealth by many and great negotiations and commerce in India, returned into his country, and married a wife. But Lusitanus saith he did not certainly know whether he had any children, but that he was certain he remained always beardless.

Anthony Loqueneux, the King's keeper or receiver of his rents of St. Quentin at Vermandois, lately affirmed to me that he saw a man at Reims, at the Inn having the sign of the swan, in the year 1560, who was taken for a woman until the fourteenth year of his age. For then it happened as he played somewhat wantonly with a maid which lay in the same bed with him, his members (hitherto lying hid) started forth and unfolded themselves. Which when his parents knew (by help of the Ecclesiastic power) they changed his name from Joanne to John, and put him in man's apparel.

Some years ago, being in the train of King Charles the ninth, in Vitry-le-François, I was showed a man called Germane Garnierus, but by some Germane Maria (because in former times when he was a woman he was called Mary). He was of an indifferent stature and well set body, with a thick and red beard. He was taken for a girl until the fifteenth year of his age, because there was no sign of being a man seen in his body, and for that amongst women, he in like attire did those things which pertain to women. In the fifteenth year of his age, whilst he somewhat earnestly pursued hogs given into his charge to be kept, who running into the corn, he leaped violently over a ditch, whereby it came to pass that the stays and foldings being broken, his hidden members suddenly broke forth, but not without pain; going home, he weeping complained to his mother that his guts came forth. With which his mother amazed, calling Physicians and Surgeons to counsel, heard he was turned into a man; therefore the whole business being brought to the Cardinal the Bishop of Lenoncort, an assembly being called, he received the name and habit of a man.[49]

Pliny reports that the son of Cassinus of a girl became a boy, living with his parents; but by the command of the Soothsayers he was carried into a desert Isle, because they thought such monsters did always show or portend some monstrous thing.[50] Certainly women have so many and like parts lying in their womb as men have hanging forth; only a strong and lively heat seems to be wanting, which may drive forth that which lies hid within. Therefore, in process of time, the heat being increased and flourishing, and the humidity (which is predominant in childhood) overcome, it is not impossible that the virile members, which hitherto sluggish by defect of heat, lay hid, may be put forth, especially if to that strength of the growing heat some vehement concussion or jactation[51] of the body be joined. Therefore I think it manifest by these experiments and reasons, that it is not fabulous that some women have been changed into men. But you shall find in no history men that have degenerated into women, for nature always intends and goes from the imperfect to the more perfect, but not basely from the more perfect to the imperfect.

Ch. 12: Of Monsters by the Confusion of Seed of Divers Kinds

That which followeth is a horrid thing to be spoken. But the chaste mind of the Reader will give me pardon, and conceive (that which not only the Stoics but all the Philosophers who are busied about the search of the causes of things must hold) that there is nothing obscene or filthy to be spoken. Those things that are accounted obscene may be spoken without blame, but they cannot be acted or perpetrated without great wickedness, fury, and madness. Therefore that ill which is in obscenity consists not in word but wholly in the act. Therefore in times past there have been some who, nothing fearing the Deity, neither Law, nor themselves (that is, their soul), have so abjected and prostrated themselves that they have thought themselves nothing different from beasts. Wherefore Atheists, Sodomites,[52] Outlaws, forgetful of their own excellency and divinity, and transformed by filthy lust, have not doubted to have filthy and abominable copulation with beasts. This so great, so horrid a crime, for whose expiation all the fires in the world are not sufficient, though they, too maliciously crafty, have concealed, and the conscious beasts could not utter: yet the generated misshapen issue hath abundantly spoken and declared, by the unspeakable power of God, the revenger and punisher of such impious and horrible actions. For of this various and promiscuous confusion of seeds of a different kind, monsters have been generated and born, who have been partly men and partly beasts.

The like deformity of issue is produced if beasts of a different species do copulate together, nature always affecting to generate something which may be like itself. . . .

[After some pictures and descriptions of monstrous progeny supposedly resulting from bestiality, also included in the 1634 English version, the French editions of 1573 and 1575, at least, end the corresponding chapter with the following comment not in the English text.[53]]

As Boaistuau says, after having recited various sacred and profane accounts all full of grievous punishments for those who are lustful, what must atheists and sodomites hope for, who encouple themselves, in disgrace of God and of nature (as I said before), with brute beasts? About this St. Augustine says the punishment of the lustful is to fall into blindness and become crazed with passion after forsaking God, and not perceive their blindness at all, being unable to listen to good advice, provoking the wrath of God against them.

Claude de Tesserant (fl. 1566–1572)

Two of Claude de Tesserant's fourteen discussions added to the original *Histoires prodigeuses* by Pierre Boaistuau (1517–1566) address the putative monstrosities of hermaphrodites, cross-dressing, natural and artificial changes of sex, and sex between males. Although little currently seems known about Tesserant, he provided the first supplement for the *Histoires*, which sufficiently enthralled readers after its intial publication in 1560 to accumulate a total of six enlargements by various writers. Publishers added these to Boaistuau's original text, the whole assemblage furnishing a conspectus of supposedly actual marvels and peculiarities culled from many sources. Tesserant includes hermaphrodites among instances of so-called monstrous births, "natural monsters." Those who change gender following birth, he says, are either "natural" or "artificial" monsters: the former include females who change into males, the latter males who have receptive sex with males, like females, or who are thus surgically modified. While the natural capability of some hermaphrodites to alternate sexual roles alarms Tesserant, he finds the "artificial" innovations of anatomically normal males horrifying. Boaistuau's initial text was translated into English and published in 1569,[54] but not the supplements. Tesserant's sources were well known to readers of Latin throughout Europe.

Fourteen Prodigious Accounts[55] *(c. 1568)*

II. The Story of Two Hermaphrodite Children United Together, and the Cause of Such Conjunctions

But what we have discussed briefly, monsters where either a great abundance or lack of semen has caused the birth of a being with either less or more limbs than a normal and perfect man requires, brings us to the story of some monsters, some contemporaneous, others from centuries ago, who were born with more or less parts than normal men....

In the time of Augustus, a woman named Fausta gave birth in Ostia to two males and two females, who were the forewarning of famine.[56] But when a Hermaphrodite happened to come out of a woman, it was taken for a monster and the sign of great calamity. So much so that, formerly, as soon as such monsters were born, the Romans as much as the Greeks threw them in the sea or fed them differently, like Pliny and Eutropius have said.[57] Since then, however, as Pliny says, they became objects of pleasure and delight to the Ancients,[58] who, slowly becoming accustomed to them, eventually just asked them to choose their sex while prohibiting the use of their other sexual part on threat of death, on account of the difficulties that could occur. Because formerly, as Saint Augustine ... says, many of them abused their sexual doubleness in such a way that they mutually fornicated, being now female, now male, both having that double nature[59]; and as Aristotle says, having their right breast masculine, and their left one feminine. Calliphanes reports, as well as Pliny, that near Nasamones and Machlyes we find people of that sort.[60] These persons have been accurately named "Androgynes" in Greek, and "Arsenotelies" by Aristotle, which signifies in one word men-women.[61] They were also called "Hermaphrodites" in that language, for the Poets claimed that the first being who was half man and half woman was son of Mercury, whom the Greeks call Hermes, and of Venus, whom they call in their language Aphrodite. But that tale is properly directed against those who have all the bodily parts of a man, but, even if they were Mars himself, haven't a more virile nor less feeble heart than a woman, being slaves to delight and pleasure. Some accounts say that not only men but also wild beasts are born with that double nature, which was observed to begin during the reign of Nero. In fact, the chroniclers report that this Prince, not wanting his lustfulness to be less than his cruelty, greatly enjoyed being drawn in his chariot by Hermaphrodite mares which were found in some Gallic field named Trevere, as if it were a great honor for the greatest Prince on earth to be hauled by prodigious beasts.[62] These histories are worthy of memory, even though they do not bring great pleasure, for they show that those who enjoyed using these monsters were no less prodigious.

But what we read in German and Italian histories is very peculiar, both stories having happened in the same year. In 1486, a year still in our memory and to which many can still bear witness, only eighty years having gone by, two twin children were born in the Palatinate near Heidelberg, in a village called Robarchie, holding each other and joined together back to back, both Hermaphrodites, having the double nature of man and woman, as we can see in the preceding picture.[63] This story, remarkable indeed for its rarity, has very few parallels. During that year the chroniclers do not report any disaster on the German side, and there is almost nothing worthy of memory, except the fact that Albert, duke of Bavaria, seized hold of Rastisbon, a powerful city on the Danube, and that Maximilian, Archduke of Austria, son of Frederick, was crowned King of the Romans in Frankfurt that year. But it might have been linked with the birth of monsters the following year in Padua and Venice. These heraldings of calamity and tumults were very important in Italy, which was very afflicted at that time, in fact more than she ever had been in four or five hundred years.... Those monsters were not only signs of civil dissensions... but also of plagues which were almost universal, especially in Flanders, in the cities of Brussels and Louvain, where many died of plague, as much as twenty thousand men in Louvain and thirty-two thousand in Brussels, in less than a few months.

As for the monster of Padua, he had two heads, but the rest of his body very well shaped, naturally like all other men. But records say that upon his birth there was a great earthquake which completely destroyed the church of the convent of Carmelites. The monster of Venice, besides the fact that he had two heads and a gaping mouth, was born with his masculine part erected and attached to his belly, and on that account the signory did not allow him to be viewed publicly. According to the sources (but I let my reader judge of the superstition), rumor had it that as soon as the monster was born, a hen screamed loudly over the Church of the Apostles, and immediately after, the owner of the hen, although he seemed in good health, died. It is added that some killed the hen, and found some time after, near the hen, an egg which seemed to contain a Basilisk.... But enough of these monsters, which can cause amazement, and also of the Hermaphrodites, since I believe that many people have seen at the Court or in this city a young man aged twenty-eight or thirty, still alive today, who goes around dressed either as a man or as a woman; and that the story about the Hermaphrodites discovered in the country of Arbigeris[64] in the past seven years is common enough.

III. The Story of a Man with Women's Hair

If monsters born fortuitously have some affinity with those made artificially, we can find no story more closely related to the Hermaphrodites than what Livy, Pliny, Aulus Gellius, and others have described and enriched with various examples of women who suddenly transform themselves into men, as if by their own nature.[65] And after reading that some men, in order to satisfy their horrible lusts, have made themselves women, we should not look any further for a story more prodigious.

Livy writes that, during the fourth consulate of L. Fabius Maximus and the third consulate of M. Claudius, in the five hundred and fortieth year of Rome, many wonders occurred: for example, an ox talked in Sicily, a child still in the womb announced a triumph, and in Spoleto some saw a woman become a man.[66] We similarly read in the Roman Histories that, during the consulate of P. Licinius Crassus and C. Cassius Longinus, in the five hundred and eighty-third year of Rome, a young girl became a boy and was sent to a deserted island by edict of the Haruspices, for the horror of the case. Licinius Mucianus swears he saw in Argos a woman named Arescusa who, though at first married, then became a man, let her beard grow, married a woman, and changed her name to Arescon. The same author says he saw the same thing happen to a young man in Smyrna. Pliny says he saw someone called L. Cossitius transform himself in that way the very day he was supposed to marry.[67]

But as for those men who seem to have wanted to accuse nature of not having made these prodigious cases happen in their own time, or of not having made them monsters by birth, they should be considered even more prodigious. For in all the cases we have seen, nature alone with no other artifice was responsible, and what happened with them can be explained by many ancient philosophers, in whose opinion accidents which occur from nature, such as being deaf, mute, blind, or lame from the womb of the mother, should not be the source of insults or remonstrations against those who suffer these accidents. But to force nature to make out of a man, for whom it is proper to command armies, hold high positions in the state, and die virtuously for his country, a woman, for whom it was anciently the greatest honor, as the tomb of Claudia indicates, to love her husband and her children, spin wool, and keep the household: this is not only the deed but also the story and memory that is the most prodigious. Principally when we read that such ignominious and abominable acts were committed, so memorably, by Monarchs and Emperors, who on the contrary should have brought light to the people by the example of their good life. The poet has well said, "All vice seems much greater / When its Author himself is great." For neither are the faults nor the virtues of the common people, unlike those of the great, ever compiled in chronicles and histories; they are filled rather with the cruelties and monstrous lasciviousness of such men as Domitius Nero, fifth Emperor of Rome, and Avitus Varius, commonly called Elagabalus[68] and the false Antoninus, whom we know for two prodigious stories, different from the previous examples in two ways. First, these faults were the result of artifice, but those previous ones were caused by nature; second, whereas previous examples concerned cases of girls or women who became men, these stories concern cases of men who became women. And so I won't discuss any longer the ways of their rising to the imperial throne and how they were both sons of whores, and how cruel they were, for I do not want to seem to rehearse Suetonius, Cassius Dio, Tacitus, Spartianus, Lampridius, Herodian, Eutropius, and the others who have written much about them.[69] I will only discuss the parts of their lives that concern our subject.

As both Suetonius and Cassius Dio (in his Life according to the Greek Epitome left by Xiphilinus)[70] have written, Nero married Sabina Poppea, whom he loved exclusively, only twelve days after having repudiated Octavia, but nevertheless killed Sabina either deliberately or accidentally while she was pregnant with his child. For as Suetonius reports, she made some insulting remarks to him one day as he came back late from the horse-races. Nevertheless, because she was so very beautiful, after she died Nero missed her so much that he had the genitals of one of his young libertine lovers named Sporus cut off to make a woman out of him (for he resembled Sabina closely, says Cassius Dio), and thereafter loved him so shamelessly that Nero used Sporus as his wife.[71] So much so that Nero forgot the dignity of his title, Emperor of the greatest people ever (but by then conceited and cowardly), and soon after married Sporus publicly with the nuptial veil, celebrated the wedding lavishly, assigned him a dowry as usual in marriage contracts, and after having installed him in the palace, considered Sporus his wife. Suetonius reports a taunt inspired by the situation saying that a great deed would have been accomplished for humanity should Nero's father, Domitius, have married such a "woman." In short, Nero was accompanied everywhere by Sporus, his new wife, adorned with the jewels of an empress and carried in a litter to all official events, markets, and Greek fairs, and kissed him publicly with such affection that Nero would not have done it any differently had he been married to the daughter of Augustus or of any other Emperor.

But it was not enough for Nero to have made a boy into a woman, as he did for Sporus, or to exhibit his dual sex: for Nero did not want to let so much excellence escape to someone else without himself taking his part.

And so he wanted his own body to be androgynous, man and woman; if not by nature (for nature had denied it to him), then at least by the turpitude of his life. For like Sporus had served him abominably as a wife, so did he want to offer himself to a libertine lover of his, whom Suetonius calls Doryphorus, and Cassius Dio calls Pythagoras, to whom Nero brought a dowry, like all women do to their husbands for supporting the household expenses. To mock Nero and display his foolishness, Suetonius reports that on the nuptial night Nero feigned the plaints and moans made by virgins when deflowered.[72] In brief he took such great pleasure in all lustfulness that he pardoned all the other crimes of those who confessed frankly to him their detestable lusts and debaucheries.

But Elagabalus, not willing to let Nero win the prize, showed he was willing to hazard upon his own body the changes that had been risked on Sporus'. In doing so, he was following in the footsteps of his mother Symiamira, as Lampridius calls her (or Symiasera, as Eutropius, or Soaemis, as Herodian), who was a good whore and worthy of her son, as Lampridius suggests, and who, having committed adultery with [the Emperor] Caracalla, bore his child.[73] At the young age of thirteen or fourteen, Elagabalus ordered the massacre of Emperor Macrinus and his son Diadumenus, and didn't omit any kind of lust, without any reservations.[74] Ordering the killing of innumerable innocent and respectable men, even his closest friends if they dared a reproach; mocking the Roman senators by calling them lackeys in long dresses; selling the judicial and constabulary offices, as writes Lampridius; immolating children for sacrifices to his Syrian god, Elagabalus, from whom he took his name and the one of "Assyrian"; debauching a Vestal virgin, as Lampridius, Herodian, and Cassius Dio have written: these were the least of his pleasures and pastimes.[75] He could have swum in the ocean to be in the presence of Hierocles or Zoticus, and had pleasure only when submerged in debauchery, so that his holiest observance was, for example, to go nightly (just like Nero)[76] from tavern to tavern, disguised with a wig, pretending to be a cook, then from there to the most notorious brothels, and chased away the whores so he could have a wider choice. But then he got a room in the Palace and exposed himself at its door, naked just like a whore, inviting passers-by with a voice soft and low, until he had procurers whose only duty was to bring him clients, from whom he demanded payment after having received pleasure. In his lucrative success he took such pride that he derided his prostitute colleagues, for they did not attract as many lovers nor earn as much money.[77]

Besides all this, he was so blinded that, not satisfied to pursue his vices in private, he wanted to make them public for everyone to see them. He decided to marry a lackey and carter named Hierocles, or Herodes as in Lampridius, and asked everyone to call himself Lady and Queen; Elagabalus even started to thread and weave wool, occasionally wore a headdress, put on make-up, colored his eyelids, shaved his facial hair, and removed the hair over all his body so his skin would have the feel of a woman. He enjoyed so much to be called one that, on one occasion, when Zoticus was brought to him as a lover and greeted him as "Sire," he at once replied, "don't ever call me Sire, because I am a Lady as I have been married to Hierocles." He wanted to name an important man of his entourage, a lover of his, Caesar, for he considered him a husband.

But I am ashamed to go on with the rest that has been recorded, and for that reason I shall be very brief. That miserable Elagabalus, in order to conform his body to his monstrous mind (even though he was quite attractive), and in order not only to have the name of woman but also the complete physical being, had his masculine parts removed, and let the barber-surgeons cut him the way they wanted, as long as they made him entirely woman, and able to have sex with men as women do naturally.[78] This is the prodigy and monster he wanted to make appear in his body, for nature had denied it to him, so that Nero could not brag to be the only one to have executed, through the body of Sporus, such a difficult and unheard-of operation, but one so shameful that it would incite horror even if executed on a brute beast.

Also the ends of both lives resembled each other for both were unhappy. For the first one, after reigning for thirteen years and eight months, was declared enemy of the state by the Senate and condemned to an ancient sentence, according to which the neck of the condemned man was to be inserted in a pitchfork, and his naked body beaten until death, as described by Suetonius.[79] Thus despairing, and finding nobody who would have been so considerate as to kill him, Nero said, almost crying, as Suetonius and Cassius Dio relate, that he had neither friend nor enemy, and had to cut his own throat with the assistance of Epaphroditus, for he did not die easily.[80] Such was the end of Nero after living thirty years and nine months. As for Elagabalus, to whom the Syrian Priests had predicted a violent death, he stocked up a great quantity of silk halter, as Lampridius reports, so he could hang himself in case of necessity. He also had a great supply of golden daggers, and kept poisons in vessels ornamented with jacinths, emeralds, and other precious stones. He had a high tower built, paved all around with gold tablets and covered with gems, from which he could throw himself down, saying that his death, in conformity with his libidinous life, should be exquisite, so that no one could say anybody else had died like him. Nevertheless he did not get so much honor or glory (if one can speak of honor and glory concerning him) as to die so marvellously surrounded by such riches. For he was killed by his own soldiers in the latrines where he had escaped, says Lampridius, with his mother holding him in her arms, says Cassius Dio. Both their heads were cut off, and their naked bodies were first ignominiously dragged around the city, until the mother's body was ejected on one side, and the son's thrown in a sewer with all the city's filth. But because the opening of the sewer was too narrow for the body to go through, he was dragged to the Tiber where his body was thrown with a weight so he would not float on the surface, and he was called "the Tiberian" and "the Dragged": a dishonor which had never happened to an Emperor before. That is how, at the tender age of sixteen, as most historians claim, or eighteen, as Cassius Dio says, he ended his days as prodigiously as he had lived as a true monster, and so strangely against nature that one would be horrified to see executed upon a slave, were slavery still in practice amongst Christians, or even upon a brute beast, that which, being a man, that is to say born with reason, and what is more a Roman Emperor, who must serve as an example of virtue to millions of people as every Prince must, he dared undertake and in fact execute upon his own body.

Joseph Hall (1574–1656)

The Isle of Hermaphrodites in Joseph Hall's *Mundus alter idem* mocks sexual indeterminacies yet turns conventional heteroerotic assumptions topsy-turvy with double-edged satire. A younger son of an earl's bailiff, he pursued an ecclesiastical career through his studies at Emmanuel College, Cambridge, from 1589 to 1610, culminating in a doctorate of divinity. He married in 1603, fathered eight children, and successively held the bishoprics of Exeter and Norwich. His prolific and once influential writings range from verse and prose satires through Theophrastan character studies, moral epistles, devotional and autobiographical texts, and pamphlets of religious controversy. A satiric imaginary voyage in Latin prose, *Mundus* appeared in 1605 under the pseudonym Mercurius Britannicus, with a false imprint of Frankfurt substituting for London. Various satires had been called in and burnt by order of ecclesiastical authorities in 1599, and Hall, apparently concerned that *Mundus* could compromise his religious vocation, never acknowledged authorship. Further Latin editions appeared in 1607 and 1643, a free English translation in 1609 (republished in 1613–14), and a German version in 1613. Adjacent to the fictional kingdom of Viraginia or New Gynia, where females rule, is Hall's Isle of Hermaphrodites.

Another World Yet the Same[81] *(1605)*

Book 2, Chapter 6: Of Double-Sex Isle, Otherwise Called Skrat or Hermaphrodite Island

Not far from Guaon, the last Isle of the Moluccas, between Cape Hermose and Cape Beach, lies Double-sex Isle, much like unto our Isle of Man on the coast of Lancashire. In this Isle nature hath so orderly disposed all things to one form that I could find no one plant in all the soil but was of a double kind. No tree, but bear two kinds of fruits or one fruit of two several kinds and names: there was your Pear-apple, your Cherry-damson, your

Date-almond, your Chestnut-filbert, and a thousand of these conclusions[82] of nature. Yea, insomuch that the very inhabitants of the whole
Island wore all their habits as Indices of a coaptation of both sexes in one.
Those that bore the most man about them wore spurs, boots, and breeches
from the heels to the haunches; and bodies, rebatos and periwigs from the
crupper to the crown.[83] And for those that were the better sharers in womankind, they wore doublets to the rump and skirts to the remainder. Nay,
their very names bore notes of their participations of either side: There
was Mary-philip, Peter-alice, Jane-andrew, and George-audrey, and many
more that I remember not. All of their own nation that have not shown
themselves perfect both in begetting and bringing forth are made slaves to
the rest. And when they take any that are but simply of one sex, Lord what
a coil they keep about them, showing them as prodigies and monsters, as
we do those that are born double-headed, or other such deformed births.
Their only glory which they esteem most is that, in their conceit,[84] they
have the perfection of nature amongst them alone, of all the world besides
them. "For seeing nature," say they, "hath bestowed two hands, two feet,
two eyes, two ears, and two nostrils to every meaner perfect body, why
should not the most excellent creature of all be perfect in two sexes also?"
And again: "the ancient sacrificers to Cybele and the Pathics of old Rome
were fain to use forced means for that which we have given us by nature."
Thus are they wont to protect their deformities.[85] And truly you may observe in them all, besides their shapes, both a man's wit, and a woman's
craft. They have no Cattle in this country but Mules nor any wild beasts
but Hares.[86] They live most upon shellfish for that is their best and most
ordinary sustenance.[87]

Helkiah Crooke (1576–1635)

A brief discussion of monsters and hermaphrodites from a medical standpoint
appears in Helkiah Crooke's synoptic *Microcosmographia: A Description of the
Body of Man.* The prior entry for this same author in the Medicine chapter
includes a brief biography and provides an introduction to this text.

Microcosmographia: A Description of the Body of Man[88] *(1615)*

V, Question Fourteen: Of Monsters and Hermaphrodites

To depraved and illegitimate Conceptions must Monsters be referred,
concerning which, it shall not be out of our way to give you some brief
Notice. Monsters Aristotle calleth Excursions and Digressions of Nature,
taking his Metaphor from Travellers, who wander out of their way yet go
still on their intended journey. For when Nature cannot accomplish and
bring to perfection that she intendeth, lest she should be idle, which is a
thing incompetent to her disposition, she doth what she can. And in the
second Book of his *Physics*, he defineth a Monster to be a fault, or error, or

prevarication of Nature working for some end of which she is frustrated because of some principle corrupted.[89]

Monsters happen many ways, and there are of them innumerable differences. We will only handle the chief in this place, because haply in another work we may be in this kind more particular. Monsters happen either when the sex is vitiated or when the Conformation is unlawful. In the sex, when they are of an uncertain sex, so that you may doubt whether it be a male or a female or both, as Hermaphrodites. Bisexed Hermaphrodites they call "Androgynes." ... In males that cometh to pass three manner of ways. When in the *Perineum* or *Interfaeminium*, that is, the place between the cod and the fundament, there appeareth a small woman's privity; again, when the same happeneth in the cod but without any avoiding of excrement[90] by it; and thirdly, when in the same place the urine issueth. In females there is but one manner, when a yard or virile member beareth out in the bottom of the share-bone above the top of the genital in the place of the Clitoris. Some add in men, when there appeareth a small privity of a woman above the root of the yard. In women, when a yard appeareth at the Lisk[91] or in the *Perineum*. In conformation Monsters are more ordinary. To Conformation we refer Figure, Magnitude, Situation and Number. In Figure Monsters happen if a man have a prone or declining Figure like a brute beast, if he have the face of a Dog, ... or such like. ...

Concerning the causes of Monsters, diverse men are of diverse minds. The Divine refers it to the judgment of God, the Astrologers to the Stars: Alcabitius[92] saith there are certain degrees in which, if the Moon be when a child is conceived, the birth becometh monstrous. We list not to exclude the just vengeance of Almighty God, which no doubt hath a great stroke in these things; but to speak as a Physician or Natural Philosopher, it must be granted that all these aberrations of Nature are to be referred unto the Material and Efficient causes of generation. The Matter is the seed, the Efficient or Agent is either Primary or Secondary. The Primary or principal cause is double, the formative Faculty and the Imagination. The Secondary is the instrument, to wit, the Place and certain qualities as heat. The matter is in fault three ways. For it is either Deficient or Abundant, or is diversly mixed. If there be want of Spermatical matter, then the Monster is deficient either in Magnitude or in Number. If there be overplus of Seed, they become double-headed, with four arms, etc. If there be a confused permixtion of the seed, then are Monsters generated of divers kinds: as upon Sodomy and unnatural copulations of men and beasts horrible Monsters have been brought into the world; so Aristotle saith that in Egypt and Africa, where Beasts of divers kinds meet at the waters of Nilus or in the Desert-places and mismatch themselves, there are often many Monsters generated. And thus come monsters arising from the Matter. From the Agent or Efficient monsters may happen divers ways. The Primary Agent, as we said, was either the Formative Faculty or the Imagination. The power of the Imagination we shall show a little after in a fitter place; here it shall be sufficient to show out of the learning of the Arabians that a strong Imagination is able to produce forms, even as say they the superior Intelligences in the Heavens[93] do produce the forms of Metals, Plants, and creatures. . . .

CHAPTER 8

Love and Friendship

Love shook my heart like a wind falling on oaks on a mountain.
—Sappho[1]

Renaissance endeavors to revive classical literature and philosophy also revitalized antique ideals of love and friendship, and these, much to the embarrassment of Christian sexual orthodoxy, encouraged passionately romantic same-sex attachments.[2] Some ancient accounts particularly celebrated love between males, even privileging it over heteroerotic love. The Renaissance is definitively characterized in part by a new cultural impetus toward male homoeroticism inspired by the recovery and dissemination of the Platonic dialogues on love, and reflected, for example, in the marvelous representations of masculine physical beauty in the visual arts of the time. Although the central repertoire of texts on same-sex bonding that survived antiquity almost wholly addresses males, testimonies to the power of female same-sex desire, typically adducing Sappho, could suggest, enable, or endorse feminine appropriations of the masculine ideals. Both male and female homophiles thus gained forceful means to rationalize expressions of desires ranging from passionate "Platonic love" involving physical intimacy that excluded genital expression, to the most avid sexual adventuring.

I divide the most relevant ancient accounts into three somewhat overlapping and historically interconnecting categories: discourses on friendship; Platonic dialogues on love; and comparative evaluations of opposite-sex and male same-sex loves, which I designate "the formal controversy." Sharing a certain set of themes and approaches, the *loci classici* for discussion of friendship are Aristotle's *Eudemian Ethics* (Book VII) and *Nicomachean Ethics* (Books VIII and IX); Cicero's *On Friendship;* Lucian's *Toxaris or Friendship;* and Plutarch's *On Having Many Friends* and *How to Tell a Flatterer from a Friend*. These texts idealize the potential of friendship between males so much that it may appear romanticized, valorized over opposite-sex attachments, and thus opened to masculine homoeroticism. As Aristotle sees how alike friendship and love can be, so he argues that notions of one can readily inform and inspire the other: "Love seems to resemble friendship, for the lover is eager to share the life of the loved one, although not in the most proper way but in a sensuous manner." Even if the sexual attraction between a lover and his beloved ceases, "many do remain friends if as a result of their intimacy they have come to love each other's characters, both being alike in character."[3] Except wisdom, Cicero insists, "no better thing has been given to man by the immortal gods" than friendship, and the word *amicitia* ("friendship") derives from *amor* ("love"). A friend's "love, and his love alone, . . . gives us delight," and we find "pleasure" especially when his reciprocations are "inspired by ardent zeal."[4] Plutarch stresses the importance of friends' full mutual intimacy (*On Having Many Friends*, 95B). All these foregoing accounts exalt relations between males alone. In the *Eudemian Ethics*, Aristotle assumes that males rather than females are suited to the highest form of friendship, which he bases on goodness more than mutual pleasure or practical advantage (7.2.16–28). Some other common principles are that the bond of genuine friendship is so close as to allow only one real friend, or a few at most; and a true friend is, as Cicero puts it, "another self" formed in a mingling of souls that makes almost "one out of two."[5] Hence in the Renaissance, Sir Thomas Elyot (1490?–1546) observes, "A friend is properly named of philosophers the other I."[6]

The Platonic dialogues constitute a different category of discourse on male bonding because Plato interprets it much more amorously in an ambience of startling homoeroticism. Whereas only a few of Plato's writings were known in medieval Europe, and none of those on love, his complete works again became accessible in the late fifteenth century, both in Greek and in Latin translation. Defining love as the desire for beauty, Platonic love theory became a new European vogue (*Marsilio Ficino). Plato's dialogues take for granted that any male youth is much courted by male lovers both around his own age and older, and the central texts on love, the *Phaedrus* and *Symposium*, treat it primarily as a relation between males. The latter concludes with handsome young Alcibiades's frank account of his ardent (though avowedly unsuccessful) sexual pursuit of Socrates. Plato begins the *Charmides* with the eponymous character's looks astonishing males both young and old, and Socrates declares, "I caught a sight of the inwards of his garment, and took the flame. Then I could no longer contain myself. . . . I felt that I had been overcome by a sort of wild-beast appetite."[7] The setting of *Erastai* (The Lovers) features such handsome youths with young male lovers that Socrates declares himself ever staggered by such beauty (133A). In the *Lysis*, the youth Hippothales blushes with infatuation for his peer Lysis. In the *Phaedrus*, Socrates notes that many male suitors pursue Phaedrus, including Lysias, whose approaches occasion this dialogue on love (237B).

However, Plato's asceticism devalues the body so that the philosopher should free his soul from bodily pleasures as much as possible, and male lovers should seek to remain sexually chaste despite the emotional intensity and physical intimacy of their bond.[8] At best, in Plato's view, the amorous rapture inspired by physical beauty should motivate growth of the lovers' souls in regaining awareness of the ideals obscured through human embodiment.[9] Socrates nevertheless allows in the *Phaedrus* that male lovers who have sex moderately will experience the same fulfillment in the afterlife as those who have none (256C–E). Love, contextually between males, is "the best of all forms of divine possession."[10]

Despite Socrates's advocacy of sexual restraint in the *Symposium*, it provides a storehouse of arguments for sexual love between males, and, together with some other Platonic dialogues, epitomizes a culture where that was an ordinary part of everyday life. Pausanias declares, "wherever the law enacts that it is wrong [for a young male] to yield to the [male] lover, you may be sure that the fault lies with the legislators—that is to say, it is due to the oppression of the rulers and the servility of the subjects." Distinguishing between earthly or vulgar love and its heavenly counterpart, an opposition called "the two Venuses," he maintains that those governed by the former focus on sexual pleasure and thus have sex with women or with boys, whereas those inspired by the latter exclusively love males who at least show the beard's first growth, thus "preferring the more vigorous and intellectual bent." They tend to remain devoted lovers.[11] In Aristophanes's famous speech, the gods originally created three types of humans so that, according to each person's inborn characteristics, he or she seeks one of three corresponding modes of love: male-female, female-female, or male-male (189C–93E). The latter, he says, "have no natural inclination to marry and beget children. Indeed, they only do so in deference to the usage of society, for they would just as soon renounce marriage altogether and spend their lives with one another" (*General Introduction).[12] Yet in the *Gorgias*, to argue against the claim that pleasure, no matter the type, yields happiness, Socrates adduces the case of a catamite whose sexual desires are abundantly fulfilled, and assumes such a life appears miserably disgraceful (494E). In Plato's last work, the *Laws*, the Athenian seeks to outlaw female and especially male homogenital acts along with extramarital sex in general (1.636B–D, 8.836B–42A), and early modern homophobes dishonestly claimed Plato's support by suppressing the latter point and ignoring the prior dialogues. Nevertheless, the *Phaedrus* and *Symposium* have inspired innumerable male same-sex lovers. And the *Timaeus* provides an argument that the so-called intemperate pursuit of sexual pleasures cannot justly be reproached, for such behavior is caused involuntarily by excess seed (86B–E).

Although Plato focuses on love between males, the crucial role of wise Diotima in the *Symposium* gives females strong implicit leverage (201D–E). Since Socrates declares that his understanding of love and beauty derives from her feminine insight, the Platonic exaltation of eros can readily apply to females, as *Agnolo Firenzuola (1493-1543) indicates.

The ancients' formal controversy on the relative merits of opposite-sex and male same-sex loves furnished additional sources for specifically prohomoerotic arguments in the Renaissance, while further encouraging revaluations of sexual morality. Along with other kinds of classical sources, these writings showed how ordinary amorous relations between males, intergenerational in their contexts, could appear in antiquity. In Plutarch's *Dialogue on Love*, Protogenes argues that love's function is "holy..., nor is there any contest or competition more fitting for a god to preside over...than the pursuit and tendance by [male] lovers of handsome young men."[13] In the course of defending heteroerotic love, his antagonist insists that feminine intelligence and virtue ensure suitability for love and friendship, and such observations could potentially be used to support protofeminist and sapphic positions. Other extant exemplars of the formal controversy are the pseudo-Lucianic treatise *Erotes* (Affairs of the Heart), which valorizes intergenerational love between males over male-female relations, and a similar part of Achilles Tatius's romance *Clitophon and Leucippe* (2.35–38). The former's speaker who depreciates sex between males notes that approval would imply females should freely do likewise (28). In 1597 *Clitophon and Leucippe* was published in English, including its advocacy of male-male love,[14] and likewise Plutarch's *Dialogue* shortly thereafter. Lucian's *Dialogues of the Courtesans* affords a tribadic version of the formal controversy, for a section on an encounter between women is implicitly comparable to the heteroerotic liaisons treated in the rest (5.289–92).

Each of these three somewhat interrelated modes of discourse had Renaissance counterparts that drew on their antique precursors, themselves quite current in educated circles. Treatises on friendship were common, as were Platonistic dialogues on love (*Marsilio Ficino). Some writers advocated sex between males in print, such as Antonio Vignali (1500/1–1559), Richard Barnfield (1574–1626?), and *Antonio Rocco (1586–1652; *Erotica). Fiction and the visual arts variously reflected these discourses, topics, and ideas. Ancient authorities' views on love and friendship were also mediated by compilers of printed commonplace books, who gathered choice extracts on selected topics (*Encyclopedias and Reference Works).[15] Sir Philip Sidney (1554–1586) splendidly expresses Renaissance ideals of loving male amity, even somewhat engaging the homoerotic potential, through the relations of Musidorus and Pyrocles in his prose romances the *Arcadias*.[16]

As Renaissance male bonding largely took its bearings from classical precedents, with, we may assume, considerable oral diffusions into illiterate milieus, so also was the case for much female bonding as well. Sappho's exemplary importance paralleled that of Socrates in both prestige and notoriety, just as Maximus of Tyre anciently exclaims, "they seem to me to have practiced love after their own fashion, she the love of women, he of men. For they said they loved many, and were captivated by all things beautiful."[17] Yet direct early modern feminine encounters with Sappho's ancient writings and reception would have been rare, for Latin and especially Greek were almost masculine preserves. Among women, then, Sappho would have tended to be a figure of mythic speculation emerging from male-mediated sources, yet nonetheless inspirationally iconic for mutual feminine love, accomplishment, and community (*The Sapphic Renaissance).

Partly on account of the socially enforced inhibitions of female public discourse and the related early modern rarity of feminine publishing, printed texts addressing female homosocial, sapphic, and tribadic relations long remained relatively anomalous, and were usually authored by males such as *Firenzuola and *Brantôme (1540?–1614). Female writings of this kind primarily appeared in private, relatively ephemeral contexts such as personal letters and diaries, through which women expressed mutual support and love. As in the *anonymous poem "As Phoebus in His Sphere's Height" from one of the Maitland manuscripts, and in the poetry of *Laudomia Forteguerri (1515–1555?) and Katherine Philips (1632–1664), females could appropriate Renaissance exaltations of male homosociality and redevelop them for promoting love and affection between women. As Harriette Andreadis argues, feminine friendship was "the primary social framework that provided both erotic opportunities and discursive camouflage for women in the sixteenth and seventeenth centuries," and its genital expressions might be characterized by an "erotics of unnaming" to occlude or avoid socially imputed transgression (12–13).

In Valerie Traub's similar historiography of female homoeroticism, "eroticization of female friendship" was "conventional, even routine," but only according to a model she designates "femme-femme" (181). "The chaste female friend ... was interpreted largely through the lenses of behavioral and bodily femininity; her chastity and innocence generally were regarded as unimpeachable, and her affection for women was judged a temporary, natural phase. Kisses and caresses, rather than penetration, were the forms of intimacy associated with her, and they were imagined to be experienced under the covers of a shared bed or under the shade of a pastoral bower." Such a friend, Traub argues, is to be sharply distinguished from the tribade associated with "somatic and moral monstrosity" and "unnatural" behaviors. "Over the course of the seventeenth century, ... what previously seemed to be two mutually exclusive modes of embodiment, the tribade and the friend," collapsed into the new eighteenth-century model of "sapphism" (Traub, 231; cf. 277–78).

However, while Traub's categories are helpful, I would define and apply them more loosely, for they were highly interpenetrable much before the seventeenth century, and their scope shifted according to viewpoint, just as male friendship and sodomy could also be mutually anamorphic. We may assume that, prior to 1600, outwardly "chaste" femme-femme friends could privately have had relations that at least some outsiders would have considered tribadic or "unnatural." And we may assume that not all such female couples would have been ignorant of the social possibilities of condemnation. Conversely, female friends who wished to appear chaste (whether or not they were) could be accused of tribadism before the seventeenth century, as *Brantôme reports in the case of Forteguerri. From some viewpoints, not only penetrative sexual behaviors between females constituted tribadism, but even mutual erotic rubbing, just as "tribade" was often equated with "rubster." Presumably nonpenetrative (because lightly punished) erotics on a bed were found objectionably "lewd" in the case of *Sarah White Norman and Mary Vincent Hammon in 1648, not at all chaste. Such perceptions would also have occurred earlier because moral theologians had long argued over the gravity and classification of a wide range of female homoerotic practices variously deemed sinful and unnatural (*Theology). Sappho had been commonly associated with both tribadism and erotic relations between females in general from at least the early 1500s (*Bartolommeo della Rocca).

By attacking the misogyny and patriarchy endemic in early modern society, some female writings of the time advance alternate conceptions of superior feminine community, such as *Jane Anger, Her Protection for Women* (1589) and *The Women's Sharp Revenge* (1640), both pseudonymous, and *Salve Deux Rex Judaeorum* by Aemylia Lanyer (1570?–1640?). The *anonymous "Phoebus" insists that the amity of females can eclipse the most celebrated masculine exemplars. Some male writers contributed to these protofeminist developments, such as *Firenzuola, Heinrich Cornelius Agrippa (1486?–1535) in *Declamatio de nobilitate et praecellentia foeminei sexus* (Declamation on the Nobility and Preeminence of the Female Sex),[18] and Baldassarre Castiglione (1478–1579) in *Il libro del cortegiano* (The Courtier). Sidney presents a fictional ideal of feminine mutuality and personal potential through the sisters Philoclea and Pamela, and Philoclea finds herself reckoning also with tribadic attractions.[19] In *Rosalind* by Thomas Lodge (1558?–1625), female Alinda assures Rosalind, "as we have been bedfellows in royalty, we will be fellow mates in poverty: I will ever be thy Alinda, and thou shalt ever rest to me Rosalind. So shall the world canonize our friendship, and speak of Rosalind and Alinda as they did of Pylades and Orestes."[20]

Applications of classical ideas about eros and friendship to same-sex love in the Renaissance ranged from homophobic censure to homoerotic advocacy. From sexually orthodox Christian viewpoints, for example, Aristotelian and Ciceronian models of masculine friendship would likely seem to preclude any physical consummation. "Friendship cannot exist except among good men," says Cicero, and without virtue "friendship cannot exist."[21] Likewise, Aristotle celebrates friendship founded on goodness, and "the only real friend is one loved on account of goodness."[22] For early moderns who considered same-sex sexual behaviors gravely sinful, such lovers would seem excluded from worthy friendship, and included in Aristotle's condemnation of false friends. Virtuous friends, he argues, "neither request nor render services that are morally degrading. Indeed they may be said actually to restrain each other from evil. . . . Bad men . . . can be friends for a short time, while they take pleasure in each other's wickedness."[23] Yet the male homoeroticism of many Platonic dialogues, for example, could enable the accommodation of masculine love to virtue and pursuit of the good. One of pseudo-Lucian's spokesmen in *Affairs of the Heart* argues that male-male love most befits dedication to philosophy and virtue, a claim that appears also in Plutarch's *Dialogue on Love*. From some early modern homophile viewpoints there could seem, as Bruce R. Smith says, a "continuity between 'spiritual' and 'sexual,' not a distinction," in male homosocial bonds (39).

Nevertheless, many Renaissance writers strove to negate the ancients' "most vile and abominable" homoerotic enthusiasms, like Philemon Holland

(1552–1637) when introducing his translation of Plutarch's *Dialogue on Love:*

> This Dialogue is more dangerous to be read by young men than any other Treatise of Plutarch, for that there be certain glances here and there against honest marriage, to uphold, indirectly and underhand, the cursed and detestable filthiness covertly couched under the name of Love of young boys. But minds guarded and armed with true chastity and the fear of God may see evidently in this discourse the miserable estate of the world, in that there be found patrons and advocates of so detestable a course. . . . Meanwhile they may perceive likewise in the combat of matrimonial love against unnatural Pederasty not to be named, that honesty hath always means sufficient to defend itself for being vanquished, yea, and in the end to go away with victory.

Actually, the "pederasty" of Plutarch's prohomoerotic spokesmen focuses not on "young boys" but on older youths and young men, such as Bacchon, whom Holland himself calls "a young man" even in this context.[24] And in a further slippage Holland inclusively calls such attractions "love of males," a designation that assumes no characteristic extreme age difference or pedophilia. To provoke antipathy, early modern homophobic polemic sometimes sought to jumble the seduction of young boys together with masculine love in general.[25]

Just as Platonic love theory was particularly provocative and influential for Renaissance conceptions of love and sex, its usages in the period were extremely diverse. In *De amore,* *Ficino strives to promote male same-sex love avowedly divorced from sexual behaviors, yet manifests profound excitement by masculine beauty. But many other Renaissance treatises on love that use Platonic theory silently expunge its homoeroticism and substitute heteroerotic attractions.[26] Conversely, as in the sonnet sequences of Michelangelo (1475–1564) and Barnfield, homophile writers appropriated the primarily heteroerotic vogue of Petrarchan love, involving the lover's amorous frustration in pursuing an elusive beloved, by merging it somewhat with Platonic love. Inadvertently or otherwise, Ficino's intensely homophile approach could so readily conduce sexual interest and genital expression that, as Giovanni Dall' Orto explains, "Socratic love" between males, explicitly chaste in Ficino's much read account, quickly became in various ways a possible code, synonym, disguise, or perceived endorsement for their fully sexual love (33–65). It not only infused male homosociality in general with strong potential for romantic passion and heady idealization, and became widely appropriated for investing heteroeroticism with such significance, but also became an alternate identity for male same-sex sexual desires and practices, contrary to Christian notions of sodomy's debasement. The ancients themselves disputed whether or not Socrates loved youths sexually,[27] and for their own different ends both Renaissance homophobes and sodomites often asserted that he did.

In any case, on account of the deeply amorous investments of the models of friendship conventionally approved in the Renaissance, that cultural ideal often exalted in the cause of virtue tended to undermine the predominant social taboos against homogenital relations. Early modern friendship's emotional union and privileged physical intimacies, such as bedsharing, produced an inadvertent homology between it and sexually coupled male and female same-sex love. That could readily constitute an unofficial covert link, a possible means of personal reconciliation, between authorized male or female homosociality, homoerotic desire, however much anathematized, and its genital enaction. For example, in Sidney's treatment of the princess Philoclea's psychology of emergent sexual attraction to the apparently female Zelmane in the *New Arcadia*, Philoclea's conception of their relationship begins with ideal friendship, but that perspective finally helps facilitate her recognition and acceptance of their mutual sexual desire, and her determination to act on it (144–49). Early modern same-sex lovers could thus be highly anamorphic: So long as their genital interaction remained private, their relationship could publicly reflect the esteemed paradigm of impassioned yet chaste amity. Renaissance ideals of homophile friendship could provide a conventionally acceptable social image for a more or less concealed sexual bond. Nevertheless, it appears any apparent male homoerotic possibilities or behaviors, however ambiguous or favorably conceived by those involved or their sympathetic associates, risked exciting socially damaging or dangerous rumors of sodomy. A social superior's unusual favor to a younger attractive retainer or subordinate would most readily have provoked comment. However, since merely retaining a boy or young man as a personal servant could spark gossip alleging sodomy, as Sir Thomas Wilson observes in an early-seventeenth-century manuscript (*Law), relations of close friends, even if social equals, would not have been immune.

Early modern friendship's homoerotic possibilities were further promoted by radical contradictions in the culture's ideologies of sex, gender, friendship, love, and marriage that resulted from the acute devaluation of females. Citing the "closed all-male societies" of the Elizabethan elite educational system, Smith points out that "structures of power in early modern England fostered the homosexual potentiality in male bonding, yet society gave official sanction only to matrimony. Likewise with the structures of ideology" (72–73). Continental conditions were similar. Based partly on Aristotelian definitions of femininity as a defect of nature (*Medicine), assumptions of female inferiority tended to privilege classically informed ideals of loving masculine friendship. Insofar as females appeared the primary human locus of unruly passion, sensuality, and inconstancy, relationships between males were deemed stronger and superior, as *Montaigne (1533–1592) assumes in his following essay on friendship, whereas those between males and females could seem relatively improper, "effeminate" for a man, or weak. The humanist premium on the intellectual qualities of love, suppositions of masculine mental superiority, and far greater male access to education would have further reinforced male homosociality and homoeroticism. Masculine expectations of finding a soul mate, another self, would most readily have focused on another male, as in Montaigne's case, and that cultural dynamic deeply dividing males from females would have reinforced feminine homosociality as well.

Yet, although male bonding in the Renaissance differed much less from sexual love than at present, due to its formerly greater emotional intensity and physical intimacy, sex between males was all the more proscribed and forbidden according to moral, legal, and religious strictures. So many cultural factors promoted masculine homosociality that a central early modern function of "sodomy" was to manifest a taboo that could appear radically to dissociate "appropriate" kinds of male-male interaction from sexual intimacy, and thus discourage and police such genital relations. On social developments well after the Renaissance, Eve Kosofsky Sedgwick says, "it had for a long time been true... that the schism in the male-homosocial spectrum created by homophobia was a schism based on minimal difference. It was all the more virulently fortified for that."[28] This diagnosis can be backdated to Renaissance society with a redoubled vengeance instantiated in its official penalties of death and invocations of purgative divine fire.

A striking contradiction central to *Montaigne's essay epitomizes the profound incoherence of the early modern sex/gender system and its impact on same- and opposite-sex bonding. Besides approving his own culture's customary abhorrence for male-male sex, Montaigne further rejects ancient intergenerational male homoeroticism because, he says, the full interpersonal exchanges of love are only possible between those who can conceive themselves as equals. Here Montaigne chooses to ignore Aristotle's and Cicero's arguments that same-sex friendships between those who appear unequals, socially or otherwise, can undergo a positive equalization through their reciprocal exchanges.[29] Renaissance same-sex lovers could do likewise if they wished. But Montaigne's objection particularly founders on his yet more revealing refusal to allow himself to recognize, at least in print, that male same-sex lovers could at least assure themselves of equality of gender, as it was then typically conceived, however many categories of age and social rank they crossed otherwise. Males who pursued heteroerotic love could not do so, except by successfully rejecting the socially prevalent gender ideology, on which Montaigne himself based his essay. Many of his own assumptions would logically require him to privilege sexual love between males over any male-female relations. But his culture forbade this very conclusion that its depreciation of feminine capacities promoted.

Although the gradual coalescence of a companionate ideal of marriage was changing the conditions of male and female bonding, male writings of the later seventeenth century such as *Paradise Lost* still evince much ambivalence toward femininity and hence the substantial persistence of the former male homosocial model. Despite having urged in his tracts on divorce that its legal grounds should be liberalized to include failure of marital companionship, John Milton (1608–1674) populates that poem's heaven with apparently masculine angels who amorously unite without any "natural" reproductive purpose, and his fallen Adam, blaming Eve, wishes God had created the world likewise.[30]

Much as the former ideology of friendship stressed the friend's importance as a revelatory "other I" sharing and disclosing distinctive personal affinities, and also as perceived difference from others is a major stimulus toward self-definition, so early modern modes of male and female homosociality may well have further promoted the differentiation and self-recognition of same-sex sexual subjectivities. "A friend really means as it were a separate self," Aristotle observes, and "to perceive and to know a friend, therefore, is necessarily in a manner to perceive and... to know oneself."[31] Or as Cicero says, "he who looks upon a true friend looks, as it were, upon a sort of image of himself."[32] And friendship, many said, is "prompted by similarity of some sort."[33] These notions had much currency in the Renaissance and would have affected passionately sexual same-sex relationships as well as those that were physically chaste. In *Euphues: The Anatomy of Wit* by John Lyly (1554?–1606), Euphues has precisely such expectations when initiating a friendship of the latter kind: "sympathy of manners" makes "conjunction of minds," he thinks, and in the prospective friend Philautus will be found "an other I," the "express image of mine own person," in whom Euphues can "view... the lively image of Euphues."[34] Every time a sodomite, tribade, or sapphist found a same-sex partner who, more or less unlike others, fully and ardently reciprocated sexual desire, he or she could perceive in that nominal "other" an instructive difference from others scandalized or relatively disinterested by such possibilities: the revelation of an "other-same" who reflected and defined a distinct sexual selfhood transgressively enjoyed in common and mirrored one to another most immediately in the exchanges of their sex. Much as Charles Taylor argues "one cannot be a self on one's own" but "only in relation to certain interlocutors" within "webs of interlocution,"[35] homoerotic sexual subjectivities could well arise from same-sex amorous reciprocations. Various former intellectual disciplines such as *astrology, *physiognomy, and *medicine provided complementary means to conceive of such sex differences according to personally formative inborn causes, as Aristophanes's myth of creation in Plato's *Symposium*, among other classical sources, also appeared to propose.

Marsilio Ficino (1433–1499)

A central document for the study of early modern notions of male same-sex love and desire is Marsilio Ficino's *De amore*. Though he was originally groomed for a medical career by his father, a physician to Cosimo de' Medici, ancient Platonic philosophy (or was it male beauty?) inspired him to become a philosopher, hermetic magus, theologian, priest, classical philologist, and translator. With few exceptions, such as part of the *Timaeus*, Plato's writings had been unknown in Europe for many centuries. But during the quattrocento the Platonic corpus became newly available in Greek manuscripts from Byzantium. Since it was thus accessible only to those few scholars who knew Greek, or in unreliable humanist Latin translations of some dialogues, the Medicis commissioned

Ficino to produce new Latin renderings of the texts of Plato and his followers. Revivifying Platonic knowledge, Ficino and his Florentine associates launched a redevelopment of European thought and culture that ensured his intellectual celebrity and continued to flower through the seventeenth century. Entering the priesthood in 1473, he garnered some ecclesiastical livings and was appointed a canon of Florence's cathedral. His original work that had the broadest cultural impact was probably *De amore*, which influenced ideas and representations of love and beauty in the visual arts, literature, pageants, and drama; the popular literary and philosophical genre of the *trattato d'amore* or dialogue on love; and hence, at least among literate classes, amorous pursuits and courtship. Composed in Latin in 1469, it circulated widely in manuscript, was first printed in 1484, and thereafter not only in many Latin editions but also in Italian and French translations.

Not just a casual reflection of the Platonic dialogues, Ficino's promotion of love between males in *De amore* is clearly Ficinian. Though nominally a commentary on Plato's *Symposium*, and likewise presented as seven speeches on love following a banquet, *De amore* provides little comment on specific passages of Plato's dialogue and instead seeks to interpret and coordinate ideas about love drawn from various authorities including Plato, Lucretius, Plotinus, Proclus, and Aquinas, among others. Ficino's reference to Plato's dialogue provides a pretext for creating a work of his own validated by that philosopher's prestige, yet nonetheless new and distinctive. Many other Platonizing Renaissance treatises on love, including ones informed by *De amore*, efface the male same-sex focus of Ficino's text and Plato's dialogues on love so as to extoll love between opposite sexes (Kraye 76–85). Moreover, whereas many Renaissance writers deplored the male homoeroticism in Plato's texts and prior translators of the quattrocento bowdlerized it, Ficino's Latin translations appear to avoid intentional bowdlerization except for one instance in the *Charmides*. In this way too Ficino became a major agent for the dissemination of positive ancient Greek understandings of male same-sex love throughout early modern Europe.[36] His concentration on love between males in *De amore* was deliberate and personally congenial. As the body is "the shadow and image of the soul," he says, so "we assume that in a beautiful body there is a beautiful soul. That is why we prefer to teach men who are handsome" (VI.1).[37]

Beauty and love, defined in the Platonic way as desire for beauty, are central in Ficino's philosophy, and *De amore* assumes the male body's beauty is paradigmatic for physical beauty in general, and the corporeal goal of human amorous desire. All Ficino's examples of compelling physical beauty are male, and he either assumes the awestruck onlooker is male or subsumes males in the admiration. "We are attracted to a certain man as part of the world order," he says, "especially when the spark of the divine beauty shines brightly in him," for "the image of the paternal countenance [i.e., God's] pleases us," and "the appearance and figure of a well-constructed man correspond most closely with that Reason of Mankind which our soul received from the author of all things and still retains" (V.5; cf. VI.2, 6, 10). Ficino's own examples of amorous attractions are between males (II.8, 9; V.5; VI.10; VII.4–6). Having been originally written in Latin, *De amore* presupposes a predominantly masculine community of reception. For Ficino, physical beauty is, though not an end in itself, the primary earthly revelation of divinity: "Beauty is a certain lively and spiritual grace infused by the shining ray of God … in the souls of men, the shapes of bodies, and sounds," which inflames souls with "burning love" that should be directed back to its ultimate source as love of God (V.7).

As in Plato's *Symposium* (180D–81D), Ficino further posits two kinds of love corresponding to two Venuses: one heavenly and intellectual, the other earthly, procreative, and infused in matter (II.7). Just as Ficino, like Plato, valorizes the former over the latter concerned with generation, so he follows some Platonic precedents in privileging the "intellectual begetting" of male same-sex love (*Symposium* 181B–D), rather than its physically reproductive male-female counterpart (VI.11, 14). Hence love between males is also central to Ficino's epistemology and notions of creativity. His assumption that meaningful intellectual exchanges are primarily masculine was endemic in early modern culture and appears much later, for example, in *Montaigne (1533–1592).

As Ficino condemns sex between males, so he misrepresents the *Symposium* to that end, most obviously in his summary and interpretation of Aristophanes's myth of human origins that appears to posit three modes of inborn sexual desire: male-female, female-female, and male-male (189D–93D). Omitting passages that comment indulgently on male-male sex, Ficino allegorizes this Platonic fable so that it pertains not to the varieties of sexual love, but to the fulfillment of different capacities for virtue in pursuit of God (IV.1–2).

However, Ficino's rapturous accounts of masculine beauty and homoerotic desire would inadvertently have encouraged physical consummation in some cases, and some of his arguments could have been decontextualized to rationalize it. Just as opposite-sex lovers appropriated *De amore* by substituting feminine beauty and heteroerotic attractions for Ficino's homophile ecstasies, and even amended his theories to allow for plenty of sex, as in Book IV of *Il cortegiano* by Castiglione (1478–1579), so same-sex lovers had their own options in dealing with this text. Whether or not Ficino, vowed to chastity as a priest, found his own homoerotic enthusiasms problematic, *De amore* would have been provocative and malleable for readers who shared such desire, and alarming to many homophobes.

On Love [38] (1469)

Marsilio Ficino to Giovanni Cavalcanti, best of friends: Eu prattein!

A long time ago, dear Giovanni, I learned from Orpheus that love existed, and it held the keys to the whole world[39]; then from Plato I learned the definition of love and its nature. But what power and influence this god has, had lain hidden from me until I was thirty-four years old, when a certain divine hero,[40] glancing at me with heavenly eyes, showed me, by a certain wonderful nod, how great the power of love is. Being in that way fully informed, as it seems to me, about amatory things, I have composed a book *On Love*. This book, written in my own hand, I have decided to dedicate exclusively to you, so that I may return to you what belongs to you. Farewell.[41]

Speech II[42]

II, CHAPTER 7: ON THE TWO ORIGINS OF LOVE AND THE DOUBLE VENUS
... If anyone, through being more desirous of procreation, neglects contemplation or attends to procreation beyond measure with women, or against the order of nature with men, or prefers the form of the body to the beauty of the soul, he certainly abuses the dignity of love. This abuse of love Pausanias censures. He who properly uses love certainly praises the form of the body, but through that contemplates the higher beauty of the Soul, the Mind, and God, and admires and loves that more strongly. And he uses the office of procreation and intercourse only as much as the natural order and the civil laws laid down by the prudent prescribe....

II, CHAPTER 8: ON SIMPLE AND RECIPROCAL LOVE. EXHORTATION TO LOVE
... Whenever two men embrace each other in mutual affection, this one lives in that; that one, in this. Such men exchange themselves with each other; and each gives himself to the other in order to receive the other. How they give themselves up while they forget themselves, I see. But how they receive each other I do not understand. For he who does not have himself will much less possess another. Rather each has himself and has the other. Certainly this one has himself, but *in* that one. That one also possesses himself, but in this one. Certainly while I love you loving me, I find myself in you thinking about me, and I recover myself, lost by myself through my own negligence, in you, preserving me. You do the same in me.

And this again seems amazing. For after I have lost myself, if I recover myself through you, I have myself through you; if I have myself through you, I have you before and more than I have myself, and I am closer to you than to myself, since I approach myself in no other way than through you as an intermediary.

In this certainly, the power of Cupid differs from the violence of Mars. Certainly dominion and love differ thus. The ruler possesses others through himself; the lover recovers himself through another, and the further each of the two lovers is from himself, the nearer he is to the other, and dead in himself, revives in the other. But in reciprocal love there is only one death, a double resurrection. For he who loves dies in himself once, when he neglects himself. He revives immediately in the beloved when the beloved receives him in loving thought. He revives again when he finally recognizes himself in the beloved, and does not doubt that he is loved. O happy death which two lives follow! O wondrous contract in which he who gives himself up for another has the other, and does not cease to have himself! O inestimable gain, when two become one in such a way that each of the two, instead of being only one, becomes two, and, as if he were doubled, he who had one life, with only one death intervening, now has two lives. For a man who dies once and revives twice has acquired for a single life a double, for a single self two selves. . . .

Each man by loving gives up his own soul, and by loving in return restores the foreign soul through his own. Therefore, out of justice itself, whoever is loved ought to love in return. But he who does not love his lover must be held answerable for murder. No, rather a thief, murderer, desecrator. Money is possessed by the body, the body by the soul. Therefore he who steals a soul, by which the body as well as the money are possessed, steals at the same time the soul, the body, and the money. Hence it happens that like a thief, murderer, and desecrator, he is punishable by a triple death, and being completely abominable and impious, he can be killed by anyone with impunity, unless he himself should, of his own accord, carry out that law, namely, that he love his lover. . . .

The astrologers think that there is a special reciprocity of love between those at whose birth there was an interchange of the lights, that is, of the sun and the moon. That is, if at my birth the sun were in Aries and the Moon in Libra, and at yours the sun were in Libra and the moon in Aries. Or those for whom the same or similar sign and the same or similar planet was in the ascendant. Or those for whom favorable planets looked on the angle of ascendance in the same way. Or those for whom Venus was situated in the same house of birth and in the same grade.

The Platonists add, or those whose life the same or certainly a similar daemon governs.[43] The natural and moral philosophers say that likeness of complexion, nourishment, education, habit, or opinion is the cause of like affection. Finally where several of these causes occur together, there the interchange of love is found to be very strong. Where they all occur together, there the passion of Damon and Pythias, or Orestes and Pylades, rises up again.[44]

II, CHAPTER 9: WHAT LOVERS SEEK

In conclusion, what do they seek when they love reciprocally? They seek beauty. For love is the desire of enjoying beauty. But beauty is a certain splendor attracting the human soul to it. Certainly beauty of the body is nothing other than splendor itself in the ornament of colors and lines. Beauty of the soul also is a splendor in the harmony of doctrine and customs. Not the ears, not smell, not taste, not touch, but the eye perceives that light of the body. If the eye alone recognizes, it alone enjoys. Therefore the eye alone enjoys the beauty of the body. But since love is nothing else except the desire of enjoying beauty, and this is perceived by the eyes alone, the lover of the body is content with sight alone.[45] Thus the desire to touch is not a part of love, nor is it a passion of the lover, but rather a kind of lust and perturbation of a man who is servile. Moreover, that light and beauty of the soul we comprehend with the Intellect alone. Therefore he who loves the beauty of the soul is content with the perceiving of the Intellect alone. Finally, among lovers beauty is exchanged for beauty. A man enjoys the beauty of a beloved youth with his eyes. The youth enjoys the beauty of the man with his Intellect. And he who is beautiful in body only, by this association becomes beautiful also in soul. He who is only beautiful in soul fills the eyes of the body with the beauty of the body. Truly this is a wonderful exchange to both. Virtuous, useful, and pleasant to both. The virtue certainly is equal to both. For it is equally virtuous to learn and to teach. The pleasure is greater in the older man, who is pleased in both sight and intellect. But in the younger man the usefulness is greater. For as superior as the soul is to the body, so is the acquisition of beauty of the soul superior to that of the body. . . .

Speech VI[46]

VI, CHAPTER 2: LOVE IS MIDWAY BETWEEN BEAUTY AND UGLINESS, AND BETWEEN GOD AND MAN

. . . A man's appearance, which is often very beautiful to see, on account of an interior goodness fortunately given him by God, can send a ray of its splendor through the eyes of those who see him and into their soul. Drawn by this spark as if by a kind of hook, the soul hastens toward the drawer. Because this drawing, which is love, derives from the beautiful, good, and blessed, and is directed toward the same, we do not hesitate to call it the beautiful, the good, the blessed, and a god, following the opinion of Agathon and the others above.[47] But because it is in a soul already kindled by the presence of that beautiful ray, we are forced to call it an emotion which is halfway between the beautiful and the not beautiful. For obviously a soul which up to now has received no image at all of a beautiful thing does not yet love that thing, because it is unknown. On the other hand he who possesses a beauty entirely is not bothered by the pangs of love. For who longs for something that he already possesses? It follows that the soul catches fire with burning love only when it has found some attractive image of a beautiful thing and is incited by that foretaste to full possession of that beauty. . . .

VI, CHAPTER 6: HOW WE ARE CAUGHT BY LOVE

. . . At the same time that the soul is perceiving a certain man in sensation, and conceiving him in the imagination, it can contemplate, by means of the intellect, the reason and definition common to all men through its innate

Idea of humanity; and what it has contemplated, it preserves. Therefore, since the soul can preserve in the memory the image of a handsome man once it has conceived and reformed that image within itself, the soul would be satisfied to have seen the beloved only once. But the eye and the spirit, which, like mirrors, can receive images of a body only in its presence, and lose them when it is absent, need the continuous presence of a beautiful body in order to shine continuously with its illumination, and be comforted and pleased.[48] Therefore, on account of their poverty, the eye and the spirit require the presence of the body, and the soul, which is usually dominated by them, is forced to desire the same thing.

VI, CHAPTER 10: WHAT ARE THE GIFTS OF LOVERS ON ACCOUNT OF [PLENTY], THE FATHER OF LOVE

These [i.e., needs or deficiencies of Love] follow the mother of Love, Poverty; but the opposite, his father, Plenty. . . .[49] The same love which makes a lover careless and indolent in other affairs makes him clever and *crafty* in affairs of love, so that in marvelous ways he goes bird-catching for the beloved's favor, whether he snares him with traps, or captures him with attentions, or appeases him with eloquence, or soothes him with song. The same madness which had made him flattering in his attention, the same madness, I say, supplies arms: ferocity to those incensed against the beloved, and confidence and invincible strength to those fighting for him.

Love, as we have said, takes its origins from sight. Sight is midway between intellect and touch; hence the soul of the lover is always being pulled in opposite directions, and thrown alternately backwards and forwards. Sometimes a desire for caressing arises, but sometimes a chaste desire for heavenly beauty, and now that and now this conquers and leads him. In those who have been brought up virtuously and are strong in sharpness of intelligence, the latter wins; in others, more often the former. Those who debase themselves in the excrements [*feces;* i.e., dregs, impurities] of the body are rightly considered to be *dry, naked, humble,* unarmed, and dull. *Dry* because they are always consuming but never filled. *Naked,* because, being rash, they are subject to all dangers, and being shameless and unrefined, they are held in disrepute. *Humble* because they think about nothing high, nothing great. *Unarmed* because they succumb to shameful desire. *Dull* because they are so stupid that they do not know where love is leading them, and they remain *on the road,* and do not arrive at the goal.[50]

But the opposite seem oppositely afflicted, for since they feed on solid goods of the soul, they are better satisfied; and since they love more quietly, they preserve their modesty. They neglect the shadowy beauty of the body and are raised higher: protected as if by armament, they drive vain lusts away from themselves, and they subject the senses to reason. Since they are the cleverest and most prudent of all, they philosophize in such a way as to walk among the shapes of bodies very cautiously as if they were footprints or odors; by following these they wisely track down the sacred beauty of the soul, and of the divine things, and by hunting thus prudently they happily attain what they desire.

Certainly this great reward of Love derives from his father, Plenty, since the ray of beauty which is both Plenty and the father of love, has the power to be reflected back to what it came from, and it draws the lover with it. But it descends first from God, and passes through the Angel and the Soul[51] as if they were made of glass; and from the Soul it easily emanates into the body prepared to receive it. Then from that body of a younger man it shines out, especially through the eyes, the transparent windows of the soul. It flies onward, through the air, and penetrating the eyes of an older man, pierces his soul, kindles his appetite, then leads the wounded soul and the kindled appetite to their healing and cooling, respectively, while it carries them with it to the same place from which it had itself descended, step-by-step indeed, first to the body of the beloved, second, to the Soul, third, to the Angel, and finally to God, the first origin of this splendor. This is the useful hunt; this is the happy bird-catching of lovers. This is certainly the kind of hunting which a certain familiar of our Socrates attributed to him in Plato in the *Protagoras*. For he asks, "Where have you been, O Socrates? I suppose of course that you are returning from that hunting to which the virtuous character of Alcibiades always excites you?"[52]

... Neither animal nor human love can ever exist without hate. Who would not hate one who took his soul away from him? For as liberty is more pleasant than anything else, so servitude is more unpleasant. And so you hate and love beautiful men at the same time; you hate them as thieves and murderers; you are also forced to love and revere them as mirrors sparkling with the heavenly glow. What can you do, O wretch? Where to turn, you do not know; alas, O lost soul, you do not know. You would not want to be with this murderer of yourself, but you would not want to live without his blessed sight. You cannot be with this man who destroys you, who tortures you. You cannot live without him, who, with wonderful enticements, steals you from yourself, who claims all of you for himself. You want to flee him who scorches you with his flames. You also want to cling to him, in order that by being very near him who possesses you, you may also be near yourself. You seek yourself outside yourself, O wretch, and you cling to your captor in order that you may sometime ransom your captive self. You would certainly not want to love, O madman, because you would not want to die. You would also certainly not want not to love since you think that service must be rendered to an image of heavenly things. Therefore, through this alternation it happens that love is at every moment drying up and growing green again, so to speak. . . .

VI, CHAPTER 14: WHENCE COMES LOVE FOR MALES, WHENCE FOR FEMALES

Just as the human body is pregnant, according to Plato, so the soul is pregnant, and both are stimulated to childbearing by the incitements of love.[53] But some, either by nature or by education, are better fitted for progeny of the soul than of the body, and others, certainly the majority, the opposite. The former follow heavenly love, the latter, vulgar. For this reason the former naturally love males and certainly those already almost adult rather than women or boys, since in them [i.e., males, verging on adulthood] sharpness of intellect flourishes more completely, which, on account of its more excellent beauty, is most suitable for receiving the learning which they [i.e., heavenly lovers] wish to procreate. The others [i.e., vulgar lovers] the opposite, motivated by the pleasure of sexual intercourse, and the achievement of corporeal reproduction.[54] But since the reproductive drive of the soul, being without cognition, makes no distinction between the sexes, nevertheless, it is naturally aroused for copulation whenever we judge any body to be beautiful; and it often happens that those who associate with males, in order to satisfy the demands of the genital part, copulate with them. Especially those at whose birth Venus was in a masculine sign and either in conjunction with Saturn, or in the house of Saturn, or in opposition to Saturn. But it should have been noticed that the purpose of erections of the genital part is not the useless act of ejaculation, but the function of fertilizing and procreating; the part should have been redirected from males to females.

We think that it was by some error of this kind that that wicked crime arose which Plato in his *Laws* roundly curses as a form of murder.[55] Certainly a person who snatches away a man about to be born must be considered a murderer no less than one who takes from our midst a man already born. He who destroys a present life may be bolder, but he who begrudges light to the unborn and kills his own unborn sons is more cruel.

Speech VII[56]

VII, CHAPTER 4: VULGAR LOVE IS A CERTAIN ENCHANTMENT

And now direct the attention of your ears and intellect to some things that must be said. In youth, the blood is *thin, clear, warm,* and *sweet.* For with increasing age, as the thinner parts of the blood are dissipated, the blood becomes thicker and on that account it becomes darker. Certainly that which is *thin* and rare is *clear* and transparent; but the opposite, the opposite. Why *warm* and *sweet?* Because life and the beginning of living, that is, procreation itself, consists in warmth and moisture, and semen, the first begetting of living things, is moist and *warm.* Such a nature flourishes in boyhood and youth. In later ages, it is necessarily changed, little by little, into the opposite qualities, dryness and cold. . . .

Why am I saying these things? Certainly in order that you may understand that the *spirits* at this age are *thin* and *clear, warm* and *sweet.*[57] For since these are generated from the purer blood by the heat of the heart, they are always the same in us as the humor of the blood. But, just as this vapor of the spirits is produced from the blood, so also it itself sends out rays like itself through the eyes, which are like glass windows. And also just as the heart of the world, the sun, from its circuit sends down light, and through the light sends down its own powers to lower things, so the heart of our body, through a certain perpetual motion of its own, stirring the blood nearest to it, spreads sparks of lights through all the parts certainly, but especially through the eyes. Certainly the spirit, since it is very light, flies out most to the highest parts of the body, and its light shines out more copiously through the eyes since they themselves are transparent and the most shining of all the parts. . . .

Therefore, what wonder is it if the eye, wide open and fixed upon someone, shoots the darts of its own rays into the eyes of the bystander, and along with those darts, which are the vehicles of the spirits, aims that sanguine vapor which we call spirit?[58] Hence the poisoned dart pierces through the eyes, and since it is shot from the heart of the shooter, it seeks again the heart of the man being shot, as its proper home; it wounds the heart, but in the heart's hard back wall it is blunted and turns back into blood. This foreign blood, being somewhat foreign to the nature of the wounded man, infects his blood. The infected blood becomes sick. Hence follows a double bewitchment. The sight of a stinking old man or a woman suffering her period bewitches a boy.[59] The sight of a young man bewitches an older man. But since the humor of an older man is cold and very slow, it hardly reaches the back of the heart in the boy, and ill-fitted for passing across, moves the heart entirely too little, unless on account of infancy it is very tender. Therefore this is a light bewitchment.

But that bewitchment is very heavy by which a young man transfixes the heart of an older man. It is this, distinguished friends, which the Platonist Apuleius complains about: "For me," he says, "you yourself are alone the whole cause and origin of my present pain, but also the cure itself and my only health. For those eyes of yours gliding down through my eyes into my inmost heart, are producing a furious fire in my marrow. Therefore have mercy on him who is dying because of you."[60]

Put before your eyes, I beg of you, Phaedrus the Myrrhinusian, and that Theban who was seized by love of him, Lysias the orator.[61] Lysias gapes at the face of Phaedrus. Phaedrus aims into the eyes of Lysias sparks of his own eyes, and along with those sparks transmits also a spirit. The ray of Phaedrus is easily joined to the ray of Lysias, and spirit is easily joined to spirit. This vapor produced by the heart of Phaedrus immediately seeks the heart of Lysias, through the hardness of which it is condensed and turns back into the blood of Phaedrus as before, so that now the blood of Phaedrus, amazing though it seems, is in the heart of Lysias. Hence each immediately breaks out into shouting: Lysias to Phaedrus: "O, my heart, Phaedrus, dearest viscera." Phaedrus to Lysias: "O, my spirit, my blood, Lysias." Phaedrus pursues Lysias because his heart demands its humor back. Lysias pursues Phaedrus because the sanguine humor requests its proper vessel, demands its own seat. But Lysias pursues Phaedrus more ardently. For the heart can more easily do without a very small particle of its humor than the humor itself can do without its proper heart. The stream needs the spring more than the spring needs the stream. Therefore, just as iron having received the quality of the lodestone is certainly drawn toward this stone, but does not attract the lodestone, so Lysias pursues Phaedrus more than Phaedrus pursues Lysias.

VII, CHAPTER 6: ON A CERTAIN STRANGE EFFECT OF VULGAR LOVE

Shall I say what follows, chaste gentlemen, or shall I rather omit it? I shall certainly say it, since the subject requires it, even if it seems out of place to say. For who can say offensive things inoffensively?[62]

The great transformation which occurs in an older man who is inclined toward the likeness of a younger causes him to want to transfer his whole body into the youth, and to draw the whole of the youth into himself, in order that either the young humor may obtain young arteries, or the younger arteries may obtain younger blood.[63] Hence they are driven to do many sinful things together. For since the genital semen flows down from the whole body, they believe that merely by ejaculating or receiving this, they can give or receive the whole body. The Epicurean philosopher, Lucretius, the most unhappy of all lovers,[64] perceived this very thing: "Thus, therefore, he who receives wounds from the arrows of Venus, whether it is a boy with girlish limbs who shoots him or a woman sending out love from her whole body, tends thither whence he is wounded and longs to come together; and to send out the humor drawn from his body into its body.... They hungrily form a body, and join salivas, and pressing lips with teeth, they breathe from each other's mouths, but in vain, since they can rub off nothing thence, nor penetrate and pass over into its body with the whole body, for they sometimes seem to wish and to be struggling to do this. They cling passionately in the couplings of Venus up to the point where their parts, violently shaken for a moment by the force of ecstasy, melt." ...[65]

VII, CHAPTER 9: BY WHOM ESPECIALLY WE ARE ENSNARED

Perhaps someone will ask, by whom especially, and in what way, lovers are ensnared, and how they are freed. Women, of course, catch men easily, and even more easily women who display a certain masculine character. Men catch men still more easily, since they are more like men than women are, and they have blood and spirit which is clearer, warmer, and thinner, which is the basis of erotic entrapment. But among males those attract men or women most quickly who are predominantly sanguine but partly choleric, and who have large eyes, blue and shining; and especially if they live chastely, and have not, through coitus, exhausting the clear sap of the humors, disfigured their serene faces. For these qualities are required in order for the arrows themselves which wound the heart to be sent out properly, as we have explained above.[66]

In addition they are quickly ensnared at whose birth Venus was in Leo, or Luna looked vehemently on Venus, and those who are endowed with the same complexion....

VII, CHAPTER 16: HOW USEFUL THE TRUE LOVER IS

You ask what good Socratic Love does? First, certainly, it benefits Socrates himself for recovering the wings by which to fly back to his homeland[67]; next, it benefits his state greatly, for living virtuously and happily. Certainly, not stones but men make a state. But men from a tender age, like plants from their younger years, must be cared for and directed toward the best fruit. The care of boys, parents and teachers look after. Young men do not transgress the rules of their parents and teachers until they are corrupted by ... the association and intercourse of wicked men, especially of those who flatter them.... There remains a single way of safety for the young, the companionship of Socrates. Therefore, devoted to this through love, that wisest of the Greeks mingles everywhere, and he walks with a great crowd of youths accompanying him.

Thus the true lover, like a shepherd, protects his flock of lambs from the abyss and plague of false lovers, or wolves. But since equals associate most easily with equals, he makes himself equal to the younger men in purity of life, simplicity of words, games, jokes, and jests.... When they are thus snared, he warns them, then a little more severely, and finally he chastises them with stricter censure. In this way he saved Phaedo, a very young man, who was a prostitute in a public brothel, from this calamity and made him into a philosopher....

Angelo Poliziano (1454–1494)

Early modern biographers typically claimed this poet and classical philologist died of infatuation for a boy, having exhausted himself in a fever by declaiming poetic endearments to his beloved.[68] After gaining Lorenzo de' Medici's patronage by translating the *Iliad* into Latin hexameters, Angelo Poliziano became Lorenzo's private secretary and tutor to his sons Piero and Giovanni (later Pope Leo X) in 1475. Despite losing these positions in 1479 when Lorenzo's wife Clarice expelled him from her household, apparently due to disputes about the boys' education, the poet was appointed professor of rhetoric and poetics and the Medici's librarian. Also garnering ecclesiastical appointments, he became a priest by 1486, and in the 1490s vainly sought to become Vatican librarian, and later a cardinal. He was implicated twice in Florentine sodomy investigations.[69]

Although some deny Poliziano actually loved males sexually, he at least assumed such postures in his writings. While his use of Greek for epigrams in which male speakers celebrate beloved youths could suggest mere classical imitation, that could also constitute a convenient alibi, and most Renaissance writers chose to efface the homoeroticism of classical models, or substitute male-female attractions. His "Love Song for Chrysokomos" pointedly eschews chastity, contrary to Ficino: "vanquished between my arms," "you hold my tongue intertwined in your mouth, O my boy."[70]

Poliziano's *Favola di Orfeo*, a brief Italian verse drama commissioned by Cardinal Francesco Gonzaga and performed at Mantua around 1480,[71] invokes Orphic authority to advocate masculine love. The story of Orpheus's loss of Euridice in Hades and subsequent life had many nonhomoerotic versions, and the Ovidian account, in which, after losing Euridice, Orpheus espouses and proselytizes sexual love between males (defined intergenerationally), is the extant *locus classicus* for Orphic homoeroticism (*Metamorphoses*, 10.79–85, 152–219). Whereas Renaissance writers ordinarily shunned that treatment of the myth, Poliziano makes it the basis of his *Orfeo* (Borris, 339–47). Although the poet's commission may have influenced his choices here, his development of the homoerotic theme is much more than dutifully enthusiastic. Poliziano amplifies Ovid's cursory treatment of Orpheus's abandonment of females for males (10.79–85) into a long speech in which the latter claims all males should flee women to enjoy instead the "holy love" of "the superior sex," like Greek and Roman gods and heroes. By juxtaposing this argument for "the more gentle and more sweet" or "holy" love between males with Orpheus's murder by dementedly drunken female killers, the Bacchantes, the poet also contextualizes Orpheus's homophile advocacy in a way that provides apparent corroboration. Poliziano's ending aligns masculinity and masculine love with mind and virtue; feminity and heteroerotic love with wanton appetite, unreason, Bacchic indulgence, and repellent vice. Such misogynous notions were quite commonly approved, and this text indicates their potential impact on amorous relations between males, somewhat like *Montaigne (1533–1592) on friendship. Since Orpheus was one of the most venerated civilizing exemplars of the Renaissance, and yet an apostle of male homoeroticism in Ovid, the evocation of his latter potential could provide strategic means to advocate such love and claim its centrality for civilization, contrary to its conventional censure. Orpheus thus provided a central authorizing archetype for male homoerotic affiliations, advocacy, and sexual subjectivities (see Borris 339–60).

The Fable of Orpheus[72] (c. 1480)

[Fleeing from the ardent shepherd Aristaeus, Orpheus' beloved Euridice dies when a serpent bites her. Orpheus descends into Hades and persuades its lord Pluto to release her. But Pluto decrees that until she returns to the living, Orpheus must restrain his desire to see her face, or else she must remain in Hades. Orpheus thus loses her again, and the drama concludes as follows.]

Orpheus laments his fortune.

Can there ever be such a woeful song as will equal the pain of my great misfortune? How could I equal my mortal pain with my cries? As long as the Heavens keep me alive, I shall forever be sad and heartbroken. And as my fortune is so cruel, I will never love another woman.

From now on I shall only pluck new flowers, the springtime of the superior sex, when they are comely and lithe, for this is the sweetest and mildest love. Let there never be another person who talks to me of women, for the one who held my heart is dead. Never must anyone who wishes to speak with me mention love for a woman.

How miserable is the man that changes for love of a woman, or ever delights or suffers for her. Like the man that foregoes his liberty for her, or believes in her wiles or words. Woman is always flighty as a leaf borne in the wind, and a thousand times a day wants and wants no longer. Hiding from her pursuers, she follows her scorner, and comes and goes like tide to a river.

Jove took this as his credo, for he enjoys Ganymede's wiles in the heavens, tied in his sweet amorous knot. And Phoebus Apollo enjoyed Hyacinth. To this holy love did Hercules surrender, he who conquered the world and was himself conquered by beautiful Hylas. I entreat all married men to divorce their wives and run from feminine company.

An indignant Bacchante invites her companions to slay Orpheus.

Behold the one who despises our love! O sisters! Let us give him death! You throw the thyrsus, and you break off that tree limb; you take a stone or fire and throw it with all your strength. You run, and break that limb over him. O, let us make that wretch pay the penalty, let us rip his heart from his chest! Die, villain, die!

The Bacchante comes back with the head of Orpheus and declares what follows.

O! O! The villain is dead! Evoè, Bacchus, I thank you! We ripped him apart throughout the forest, so every bush is full of his blood—we ripped him apart limb from limb with cruel torture, in many pieces. Now go and blame the righteous wedding torch![73] Evoè, Bacchus, accept this victim!

The Bacchantes sacrifice in honor of Bacchus.

Let everyone follow you, Bacchus! Bacchus, Bacchus, eù, oè! Whoever wants drink, come drink, come here! Fill yourselves like casks. I want to drink more! There's still more wine for you, but let me drink first!

Let everyone follow you, Bacchus! I've drained my horn, give the flask here. This mount dances round me, and my brain goes. Everyone runs here and there, as they see me do.

Let everyone follow you, Bacchus! Already I die for sleep. Am I drunk, yes or no? My feet cannot stay straight any longer. As far as I know, you are drunk. Everyone do as I do, everyone drink like me.

Let everyone follow you, Bacchus! Let everyone yell "Bacchus, Bacchus," and drink the wine down—then with our noise we'll shatter the kegs. You drink, and you, and you. I can no longer dance. Let everyone shout eù, oè–

Let everyone follow you, Bacchus! Bacchus, Bacchus, eù, oè![74]

Agnolo Firenzuola (1493–1543)

Citing Plato's Aristophanes in the *Symposium*, Agnolo Firenzuola's *Dialogo delle bellezze delle donne* defines both male and female same-sex love as a fundamental and seemingly innate characteristic of some persons. Though modifying Platonic love theory to serve heteroerotic perspectives, like most other early modern commentators on love who draw on Plato (Kraye 76–85), he further advances a proto-feminist defense of women. As his father, a notary, urged, Agnolo pursued a legal career, and in 1518 he became attorney of the Vallambrosian monastic order in Rome. His circle there included *Pietro Aretino (1492–1556) and Giovanni della Casa (1503–1556). Despising legal work, he meanwhile pursued scholarly and literary studies, and composed a diverse assortment of writings from 1524 onward, all but one published posthumously. These include two comedies, beast fables, treatises, translations and the *Ragionamenti d'amore* (Discourses on Love), an unfinished imitation of Boccaccio's *Decameron*. Many of these, Firenzuola declares, were inspired by an unidentified woman. In the *Ragionamenti*, written earlier than the *Dialogo delle bellezze*, female characters debate whether a woman should love a woman rather than a man, to avoid risking her chastity, but conclude that the beauty of the opposite sex arouses the strongest desire. Also, both a wife and a husband separately seek to initiate sex with their housemaid, neither knowing that the latter is actually a cross-dressed male. He fends off the husband's advances by claiming to have recently sprouted a penis in hermaphroditic transformation.[75] After contracting syphilis, Firenzuola left public life in 1526, but became a Vallambrosian abbot at Prato in 1538. Completed in 1541, Firenzuola's dialogue on feminine beauty was first printed in 1548; there were several sixteenth-century Italian editions, and a French translation used by *Brantôme (1540?–1614) was published in 1578. No English translation was published until 1892.

"A beautiful woman is the most beautiful object one can admire," Firenzuola's main speaker, the young gentleman Celso, tells his four female interlocutors, "and beauty is the greatest gift God bestowed on his creatures." While her virtue directs souls to contemplative desire for heavenly things, her appearance immediately arouses sweats and shudders in a man.[76] However, Firenzuola uses Neoplatonic philosophy not only to define and extol the nature, attractions, and effects of feminine beauty, but also to maintain, contrary to Aristotle, the equality of genders at least in virtue and capacity for learning. By assigning four female characters and only one male to this dialogue, Firenzuola produces an ambience starkly differing from *Ficino's De amore*, where the participants are exclusively male as in Plato's *Symposium*. While making one man the flirtatious center of quadrupled female attentions, Firenzuola incorporates females into intellectual discourse and enhances the scope of women.

He promotes feminine equality partly according to Aristophanes's proposal in Plato's *Symposium* that humans were first created as doubled beings of three types: male/female, female/female, and male/male. Envious and wary of their power, the gods divided them into single beings, and human love thus sprang from desire and pursuit of the original whole. As descendents of the primal androgynes amorously seek an opposite-sex counterpart, so those arising from the others seek the same (189C–93E). In expounding this myth, Firenzuola takes for granted that there are three corresponding distinct categories of amorous inclination, thus allowing for same-sex sexual subjectivities. Hence there is a "type of woman by nature" amorously attracted to her own sex, who "spurns marriage and flees from intimate conversation"—sexual relations—with men. Presenting both ancient and contemporary exemplars of such women, his account is essentialist or transhistorical. He approaches male same-sex love likewise, but much more censoriously refuses to name current names in that case, and thus condemns these lovers to oblivion.

Nevertheless, just as Plato's myth implies the equality of gender among descendents of the primal androgynes, insofar as they are halves of the same original creature, so also it suggests that the roots of homoerotic desire are as profoundly deep and "natural" for its devotees as for their opposite-sex counterparts. In Firenzuola's version of Aristophanes's argument, his heavy editorial interventions against sexual expression of same-sex love show that he recognized how readily Plato's myth could authorize its advocacy. Ficino strives to efface such possibilities through allegorization. Yet readers were not necessarily bound to share Firenzuola and Ficino's views or anxieties, and their divergences from this Platonic source could highlight its contrary implications. Unlike Firenzuola, Plato's Aristophanes devotes most space to sexual love between males, primarily a dedicated mutual pursuit of youths and men in his account, and treats it very lightly (191B–92D).

On the Beauty of Women[77] *(written 1541)*

First Dialogue

    Mona Lampiada: Forgive me if I should sometimes bother you with a question, but I am one of those women who, granted that they be ignorant, nonetheless wish to learn something every time they are given the opportunity. When you speak of beauty in general, are you referring to men or to women, or are you speaking of one and the other interchangeably?

Celso: It is a great sign of knowledge to begin to realize that one does not know and wishes to know. Thus Socrates, who was declared a wise man by the Oracle of Apollo, used to say that, for all his great pains and studies, he had learned nothing else than the realization that he did not know.[78] However, you do not say this because you do not know, but rather on account of your natural modesty. And you ask not so that I might teach you, for you know more than I do, but for the sake of these other ladies who, being a little younger, have less experience than you.

I say, therefore, in answer to your question, that if you had read the oration Aristophanes recited in Plato's *Symposium*,[79] there would be no need for me now to clarify this matter. . . .

When Jove created the first men and the first women, he made them with duplicate sets of limbs, that is, with four arms, four legs, two heads. And thus, being double, they had twice the strength. And there were three types of persons: some were male on both sides, some were female, and these were few, and the rest, which were the majority, were male on one side and female on the other.[80] Now it happened that these people thus formed were unappreciative of the gifts received from Jove and even considered taking over Paradise from him. Hearing about this, Jove set aside all other advice and, unwilling to destroy completely the human race lest there should then be no one left to adore him and thus deprive him of his position, decided to cleave them all in half through the middle and to make two people out of each one, for he thought that by thus dividing them in two their strength and daring would also be divided. So, without further ado, Jove carried out his decision and arranged matters so that we were left as you see us nowadays. Mercury was the sawyer, and Aesculapius the master encharged with repairing us and healing our breast,[81] which suffered more than any of our other parts (and which, for you, Selvaggia, he certainly fixed far too well), and with mending all the other parts the saw had damaged. And so, as you see, everyone is left either male or female, except for a few individuals who escaped and ran so much they completely ruined themselves and were never again good for anything and were called Hermaphrodites, which derives from Hermes, that is, Mercury, and means "escaped from Mercury."[82]

Those who were male in both halves, or are descended from those who were, wishing to return to their original state, seek their other half, which was another male. They thus love and admire each other's beauty, some virtuously, as Socrates loved the handsome Alcibiades, or as Achilles loved Patroclus, or Nisus loved Euryalus[83]; and some unchastely, as certain wicked men, more unworthy of any name or fame than that man who, in order to gain fame, set fire to the temple of the Ephesian goddess.[84] And all these men, both the virtuous and the wicked, generally flee the company of you ladies. And I know very well that you are familiar with some of these even in our own day.

Those who were female in both halves, or are descended from those who were, love each other's beauty, some in purity and holiness, as the elegant Laudomia Forteguerra loves the most illustrious Margaret of Austria [*Laudomia Forteguerri], some lasciviously, as in ancient times Sappho from Lesbos and in our own times in Rome the great prostitute Cecilia Venetiana. This type of woman by nature spurns marriage and flees from intimate conversation with us men. And, we must believe, these women are those who willingly become nuns and willingly remain so, and they are few, because the majority of women are kept in monasteries by force and live there in despair.[85]

The third type, those who were male and female, and who were the majority, are those from whom you are descended, you who have a husband and hold him dear, as Alcestis, the wife of King Admetus, and others who would not refuse to die for their husbands' sake.[86] In short, they are all those women who look upon the face of a man eagerly but chastely and as sacred law allows. And it is we men who either have a wife or are looking for one.[87] In short, it is those who like nothing more than the beautiful face of you ladies, those who, in order to be reunited with their other half and rejoice in its beauty, would not spurn any danger, as Orpheus for his dear Eurydice[88] and the Roman nobleman Caius Gracchus for his beloved Cornelia,[89] and as I would do for that cruel lady who, unwilling to admit she is my other half and I am hers, flees from me as if I were a strange creature....

Let us now return to the several men and divided women; unfortunately, we have wandered away from home. We will say that there is no need to discuss the first type, nor the second since they either contemplate the beauty of their own kind divinely and in virtue or wickedly and in vice. We cannot speak of the first because our intellect, while it resides in this prison [i.e., of the body], is scarcely able to consider divine things. About the wicked and depraved, God forbid that one should talk of such dreary offspring[90] in the company of chaste and virtuous women such as yourselves. We are left, then, to talk about you and about us, that is, about men who love women and women who love men, but who do so courteously and chastely and who are enflamed and enlightened by a virtuous ray, as has been said several times. But it seems to me Selvaggia is making fun of this.

Selvaggia: I am not making fun of this; on the contrary, I am eager to see what conclusion you will draw from all this.

Celso: I wish to draw this conclusion, that, since each of us desires with a natural instinct and appetite to rejoin and be reunited with his other half and become complete once again, it is inevitable that she should appear beautiful to us and, since she appears beautiful, it is inevitable that we love her, because true love, according to what the entire Platonist school claims, is nothing else but a desire for beauty. Loving her, it is inevitable that we should seek her out; seeking her, that we should find her (who could hide anything from the eyes of a true lover?); finding her, that we should contemplate her; contemplating her, that we should rejoice in her; rejoicing in her, that we should receive from her an incomprehensible pleasure, for pleasure is the end of all human action. In fact, it is that highest good so sought after by philosophers. In my opinion, speaking of earthly things, it is not found anywhere else but here. Therefore, it will no longer seem so remarkable that a gentle lady and a worthy man, burning with the fire of love (which is the only light that, through the eyes, opens our intellect and shows us our other half), should undertake any labor, should expose themselves to any danger, in order to find oneself again in someone else, and someone else in oneself. And so, in conclusion, so as not to hold you in suspense any longer, we must say that it is appropriate for a lady to contemplate the beauty of a man, and for a man that of a lady. And so, when we speak of beauty in general, we mean both yours and ours. Nevertheless, since a more delicate and particular beauty resides more in you, diffuses itself more in you, and in you is more discernible on account of your complexion, which is much more delicate and softer than ours, and, as many sages rightly claim, it has been made by Nature so gentle, so soft, so sweet, so lovable, so desirable, so admirable and so delightful, so that it would be a rest, a refreshment, even a harbor and a destination and a refuge in the course of all human labors, for this reason, leaving behind today all talk of male beauty, my entire discussion, my entire discourse, all my thoughts will be devoted to the beauty of you ladies. And if anyone wants to reproach me for it, let him do so, for I profess, not on my own, but in line with the conclusions not only of natural philosophers, but also of some theologians, that your beauty is evidence of heavenly things, an image and a semblance of the treasures of Heaven. How could earthly man ever be satisfied with the idea that our blessedness, which ought to consist above all in always contemplating the omnipotent essence of God and to rejoice in our vision of His divinity, could be continual blessedness without any hint of satiety, if he could not see that to contemplate the gracefulness of a beautiful woman, to rejoice in her elegance, to feast his eyes on her pleasant beauty, is an incomprehensible pleasure, an indescribable blessedness, a sweetness which, when it is over, would like to begin again, a happiness that makes him forget himself and transcend himself? And so, my dear men of Prato, if sometimes I look upon these women of yours a little too attentively, do not take it badly....

And to prove to you, my dear ladies, that what I have promised you in words I will attain in deeds, I say that from the previous discussion which concluded that we are the other half of each other, one draws the irrefutable conclusion that you women are as noble as we men, as wise, as apt in learning, be it moral or speculative, as skilled in mechanical arts and knowledge as we, and those same powers and possibilities that are in our spirit are also in yours, because, when a complete whole is divided into two parts equally, it is inevitable that one part be equal to the other, as good as the other, as beautiful as the other. And so, with this argument and this conclusion, I will boldly say to your and my enemies who, when they are in front of you seem to die for you and then, behind your back, speak badly about you, that you are in all things and at all times our equals, even though sometimes this is not universally apparent on account of the domestic duties and household management which you have modestly assumed in caring for the family. And in the same way we see that between the philosopher and the craftsman, the doctor and the merchant, there is a very great difference with respect to the operations of the intellect. But there is no need to discuss this at the moment, for we have wandered far too far from our subject.

Still, I wanted to warn you about something. If someone should say to you that that story about splitting in two is a campfire story, you should answer that Plato told it and that it is a story that was narrated one night by a wise philosopher at one of Plato's parties. If they be intelligent men, this answer will refute them; if they be ignorant men, they will be malicious anyway, and you should think very little of them, for a malicious spirit is incapable of wisdom. To say that it is one of Plato's stories indicates that it is full of high and divine mysteries and that it is meant to symbolize what I have told you, that is, that we are one and the same thing, one and the same perfection, and that you must seek us and love us, and we must seek and love you, and you are nothing without us, and we are nothing without you, our perfection is in you, and yours in us, to say nothing of the thousands of other beautiful mysteries which, for the moment, we need not go into. Do not forget to say that it was Plato; keep that well in mind.

Laudomia Forteguerri (1515–1555?)

Laudomia Forteguerri's six Italian sonnets published in the cinquecento, her only extant writings as yet known, all declare love to women while praising their physical beauty and other accomplishments. Very few such early modern feminine declarations survive. Partly through published comments of male writers, Forteguerri became one of the century's most widely known contemporary exemplars of love between females.[91] Although she "was born into the Sienese nobility, married twice, both times into two of the most important families of her city," and had three children, male writers of her time "presented her as a woman outside the the the norm—dogmatically suspect, sexually liberated, intellectually curious" (Eisenbichler, 281–82, 292). She impressed the eminent humanist Alessandro Piccolomini (1508–1578) so much that he dedicated several works to her and wrote poems in her praise, while another male writer declared her one of Italy's twelve most beautiful women and an emblem of heavenly fame

(Eisenbichler, 282). Together with two other women, she reputedly organized and led three thousand of her sex to defend Siena in the siege of 1555.

The first five sonnets, addressed to Margaret of Austria (1522–1586), the illegitimate daughter of Emperor Charles V, commemorate the poet's relationship with her. In a work published in 1541, Piccolomini says this female couple originally met in 1535 when Margaret, on her way from Rome, passed through Siena to marry Duke Alessandro de' Medici in Florence. "As soon as Laudomia saw Madama, and was seen by her," Piccolomini declares, "suddenly with the most ardent flames of Love each burned for the other, and the most manifest sign of this was that they went to visit each other many times" (cit. Eisenbichler, 282–83). In 1538, after Margaret's husband was assassinated, she returned to Rome through Siena to marry Duke Ottavio Farnese of Parma and Piacenza. According to Piccolomini, she and Laudomia then "renewed most happily their sweet Loves, and today more than ever, with notes from one to the other they warmly maintain them" (cit. Eisenbichler, 283). Piccolomini contextually urges that "the aim of the most perfect love ... consists in nothing else but the possession of the virtuous spirit of one's beloved, that is, in being loved by her." "Nor, may it please God, is the Love which I will speak about today with the reverence that is appropriate to it, the same as that love that we have in common with the beasts and leads us and pushes us to procreate.... To support my view, I will give you an example of a most ardent Love that exists in our time, not between a man and a woman, no, but between two most unique and divine women" (cit. Eisenbichler, 283–84). Piccolomini then proceeds to discuss Forteguerri's sonnet to Margaret, "Now you go proudly." Their ardent love is especially admirable in his view because, he assumes, it has not been physically consummated, and thus excels any sexual love between opposite sexes. Piccolomini's assessment depends on the Platonic distinction between Venus Urania and Venus Pandemos, the heavenly and procreative modes of love, that privileges amorous relations supposedly transcending genital expression, much as in the *De amore* of *Marsilio Ficino (1433–1499). However, Piccolomini had just previously dedicated to Forteguerri a dialogue about sex arguing that young wives should have secret lovers (Eisenbichler, 295), and so his testimony to her chastity with Margaret is not as convincing as it would be otherwise.

This female couple's love is again celebrated by *Agnolo Firenzuola (1493–1543) in his *Dialoghi delle bellezze delle donne* written in 1541, the same year Piccolomini's comments were published. Firenzuola's Forteguerri exemplifies women innately committed to love other women, not men. He allows that such women can love unchastely, but insists like Piccolomini that, in their steadfast purity, Forteguerri and Margaret exemplify heavenly same-sex love. When commenting on Firenzuola's remarks in *Les vies des dames galantes*, written around the end of the century, *Brantôme (1540?–1614) says his friend Louis-Bérenger Du Guast denied this couple's ostensible chastity, for Margaret's amorous adherence to a particular woman implies a sexual bond concealed by hypocritically avowed purity. Brantôme does not appear to know of the sonnets. Whether or not this female couple had sex, their public relationship could still serve as a tribadic exemplar.

Although Forteguerri's sonnets to Margaret do not show their relationship was physically consummated, that is only to be expected since the poems were deemed publishable. The sonnets insist on the power of her attraction to Margaret's beauty, and revolve around the poet's bereavement because of Margaret's move to Rome, which has thus become the poet's rival. Yet the imagery and diction are not physically sensual. Whereas Forteguerri stresses the relation of her eyes, typically considered the least carnal and most spiritual sense, to Margaret in the first sonnet, the sequence tends to avoid relating the poet's other senses to her beloved, especially touch. The most directly concrete evocation of Margaret's corporeal presence is just "the hem" of her "noble gown" in the fourth. Rather than blazoning the lovely attributes of Margaret's body, the poet renders it luminous or profoundly clothed. Suggestions of physical contact remain subtly indirect, as where the feminine "brow and breast" of Forteguerri's Sienese river, Arbia, would wear emeralds and rubies if Margaret returned from Rome.

However, the final sonnet to Margaret demands, resonantly enough from the viewpoint of any same-sex lover who has ever confronted obstacles of heteroerotic hegemony, "Ah cruel fortune, why do you not arrange it / For my body to go where my heart goes?" This demand most obviously refers to the geographical distance ("where") now separating the female lovers, but may further constitute a veiled tribadic allusion. Ovid's story of two mutually loving females in the *Metamorphoses*, Iphis and Ianthe, was very well known, and Iphis analogously protests her fate, referring to her frustrated sexual desire (9.724–66). This Ovidian episode was a main basis for literary portrayal of sapphic love throughout the Renaissance. A similar context based on Iphis's complaint is female Fiordespina's conscious same-sex infatuation with Bradamante in the *Orlando furioso* (25.33–37) by Lodovico Ariosto (1474–1533). Since Margaret had gone from nearby Florence to Rome specifically in order to marry, Forteguerri's complaints about Rome's rivalry and Fortune's cruel opposition may well figure complaints about marriage and her gender as obstacles to her love. Forteguerri ends the extant sequence by imploring Fortune to keep Margaret physically "close" to her.

If, as Piccolomini attests, this female couple met and became mutually enthralled in 1535, Forteguerri would have been 20 and Margaret only 13. Most or all of the sonnet sequence would have been written between 1538, when Margaret left Florence for Rome, and 1540, when Piccolomini publicly lectured on "Now you go proudly." If there were no sexual attraction, what shared interests could likely have motivated the relatively mature poet's ongoing amorous fascination with a girl who had only just entered adolescence?

Though the love expressed in these sonnets would necessarily have been coded if it had physically sexual aims or aspects, assessment of that potential is very problematic because the sequence is short and its biographical context obscure. The poet's domestic circumstances are unknown. However, as Eisenbichler explains, Margaret herself was clearly reluctant to leave Florence for Rome in 1538 to marry her new fourteen-year-old husband, refused to consummate the marriage, and provoked gossip. Some Roman Pasquinades suggested she was tribadic and her husband, his father, and grandfather Pope Paul III (both much rumored for sodomy) were sodomitically incestuous. Apparently, the marriage was not consummated until 1543. Margaret bore twins in 1545, but then lived away from her husband and seemingly lacked sexual interest in men. She twice became governor of the Netherlands for King Philip of Spain (1559–1567, 1580–1583), thus assuming a political role that was ordinarily male.[92]

Unlike the five sonnets to Margaret, the sixth, addressed to Alda Lunata of Pavia, a fellow poet, laments Forteguerri's inability ever to meet her. Others' descriptions of Alda, the poet avers, have excited her desire to enjoy Alda's beautiful presence, but can provide some consolation if held within her heart. However, Forteguerri's initial argument may involve strategic advocacy of female same-sex desire, as if to say, "beauty is the gift of God and nature, and we are to delight in what is good, so that Alda Lunata's beauty should be delightful, as it is to me too, a female." As early modern male writers who mention Forteguerri's love for Margaret always assume some explanation is necessary, because it is, from their viewpoint, unusual, so the poet would reasonably anticipate and seek to shape such reactions herself in articulating her same-sex desire.

The Sonnets of Laudomia Forteguerri[93] *(c. 1535–1540)*

To Madam Margaret of Austria

SONNET ONE

> Happy plant, so cherished in heaven,
> Where nature placed all its ideals
> When it set out to create so much beauty,
> I speak of my goddess Marguerite of Austria.
>
> I know well that she departed from heaven,   5
> Only in order to show us divine things;
> God sculpted her and with his own hand crafted
> This woman so beloved by him, and favored:
>
> If God was so generous to us with his gift,
> With showing us the glory of his kingdom,   10
> Do not disdain to show her somehow to me.
>
> And if I have left you a token of my heart,
> In return send a portrait of yourself,
> Skillfully made, here to me, where my eyes are.

SONNET TWO

    Why does your Phoebus contest with my sun,
    Proud heaven, if it has stolen its first glory?[94]
    Let it go back in the woods or stay buried
    In the sea while mine shines bright with finer rays.

    A little cloud can injure your great light,   5
    A little fog obscures its lovely face,
    But mine, in clouds (alas) and wrapped in fogs,
    Shines with more brightness and with greater light.

    When yours brings forth the day out from the waves,
    Unless it tear the veil that dims the air,   10
    It does not grace the world with its appearance.

    Mine does not part the veil or clear the air,
    But, turning what surrounds it to its image,
    It makes the clouds burn bright and darkness shine.

SONNET THREE

    Triumphant now, and more than ever proud,
    Ancient Rome proceeds along, possessing
    All the good Nature and Heaven gave us:
    She gathers it to herself and keeps it.[95]

    But were my foe, who keeps me underfoot,   5
    To be kind to me and bitter to you,
    To take it from you and grant it to me,
    Your flowers and grass would cease to smile for you.[96]

    No longer with emeralds and rubies
    Would the rich banks of the Tiber be dressed: 10
    For Arbia would have them on her brow and breast.[97]

    You would no longer have divine examples,
    Nor would angelic beauty then delight you.
    Were this to happen, I would be full of joy.

SONNET FOUR

    Now you go proudly, now you run haughtily
    Coloring both your riverbanks with flowers,
    Ancient Tiber; now well purged your waves reflect
    The image of a brighter and truer sun;

    Now you hold the sceptre, now you command   5
    Over more famous ones; now you have what makes
    Your beautiful banks more verdantly happy
    And fecund; now you are completely fulfilled,

For my fair and spotless sun is now with you,
Not distant now, or near, but always next to you;   10
And you flow past the hem of that noble gown;

For art, nature, and heaven wish it, and He
Who can do all—today they clearly show that
An immortal woman can dwell in this world.

SONNET FIVE

Alas, for my beautiful Sun will not turn
Its holy rays toward me. Must I therefore
Live without my treasure? May it not please God
That I should ever live on earth without it.

Ah, cruel Fortune, why do you not arrange it   5
For my body to go where my heart goes?
Why do you keep me in this wretched state
With no hope ever that my woes will end?

Turn, at last, happy and benign, your face
Toward me; for it is not a glorious deed   10
To cut down someone of the feminine sex.

Listen to my words, how they are ready
To beseech you; for I want nothing else
But that you keep me close to my Goddess.

TO THE SIGNORA ALDA TORELLA LUNATA

The greatest gift that God and Nature gave
To us on earth to beautify the world,
And let us find delight in what is good,
Is the shape and form of Signora Alda.

Whoever her angelic figure sees   5
Can truly say he has been richly blessed;
Whoever her judicious words can hear,
Seeks nothing else but to listen to her.

Alas, why am I not allowed this much,
By cruel destiny, by my evil fate,   10
That I may look on this angelic face?

It will not let me, yet in my heart I hold
Her divine appearance as described to me,
And this will never be taken from me.

Michel Eyquem de Montaigne (1533–1592)

Modeled on Michel Eyquem de Montaigne's own friendship with Étienne de La
Boétie (1530–1563), the great love of his life whom he met in 1557, his essay

"*De l'amitié*" exemplifies the classically influenced Renaissance idealization of masculine amity. The eldest son in a family of minor French nobility, he studied law, entered the regional parliament of Bordeaux, and inherited his father's title and estates in 1568. In 1570 he retired to the Château de Montaigne to devote himself to studies and writing. Thereafter he began composing the first two books of his *Essais*, published in 1580, in which he largely created the discursive form of the familiar or personally informal literary essay. The term itself apparently derives from his use of *essai*—a testing, probing, trial, or attempt—to designate his exploratory text. After serving as mayor of Bordeaux between 1581 and 1585, he completed the third book in 1587, but continued to revise and add new passages until his death. By turns Stoic, skeptical, and Epicurean, yet avowedly Roman Catholic, Montaigne sought truth through intellectual eclecticism and introspective self-study. Adopting *que sais-je?* ("what do I know?") as his motto, he declared himself his own central subject, yet considered his condition representative of humankind. His early modern English readers included Sir Francis Bacon (1561–1626) and Shakespeare (1564–1616).

It has been said Montaigne finally turned to writing to alleviate his profound sense of bereavement after La Boétie died in 1563. All editions of the *Essais* published in Montaigne's lifetime are memorials to his friend, for La Boétie not only appears as the author's ideal companion and audience, but also the chapter directly following "*De l'amitié*" consists of twenty-nine love sonnets by Montaigne's great friend. The *Essais* thus manifested La Boétie's authorial presence conjointly with Montaigne's, and effected a physical reunion. Two years after his friend's death, Montaigne married, apparently not for love but familial duty, and fathered six children, of whom five died in infancy.

Assessing the various types of interpersonal relationships, including familial, marital, and extramaritally sexual bonds, "*De l'amitié*" most highly valorizes the potential of friendship between two males. Like many men of his time (*Love and Friendship), Montaigne considers females constitutionally incapable of sustaining such a bond, in mind, soul, and temperament. In his view, women are either sexual outlets for males, or companions acquired in the practical bargain of marriage. If "a genuine and voluntary acquaintance might be contracted where not only minds had . . . entire jouissance, but also bodies a share of the alliance, and where man might wholly be engaged, it is certain," he declares, "that friendship would thereby be more complete and full." Nevertheless, Montaigne assumes that sexual love between males is justly abhorrent to contemporary customs, and rejects its classical norms and celebrations. His own beliefs exclude him from ever experiencing a love that would wholly engage him with another, uniting both bodies and minds in mutual *jouissance*.

Although Montaigne is otherwise often an exponent of tolerance and cultural relativism, here he seems just as incapable of applying those perspectives to a revaluation of same-sex sexual love as to the status of women. To the former he would better have applied his own conclusion on perceived queerness in "*D'un enfant monstrueux*" (Of a Monstrous Child, Book II, Chapter 30): "We call that against nature, which cometh against custom. There is nothing, whatsoever it be, that is not according to her [i.e., nature]. Let therefore this universal and natural reason chase from us the error and expell the astonishment which novelty breedeth, and strangeness causeth in us."[98] The relativistic and skeptical currents of Montaigne's thought would inadvertently have helped others to contest orthodoxies of sex and gender. Though focusing on relations between opposite sexes, his essay that most addresses sex, "*Sur des vers de Vergile*" (On Some Verses of Virgil, Book III, Chapter 5), includes some ancient male-male examples without explicit adverse judgment, and condemns sexual hypocrisies.

Essays[99] *(1580)*

Of Friendship

Considering the proceeding of a Painter's work I have, a desire hath possessed me to imitate him. He maketh a choice of the most convenient place and middle of every wall, there to place a picture, labored with all his skill and sufficiency; and all void places about it he filleth up with antique Boscage or *grotesco* works,[100] which are fantastical pictures, having no grace but in the variety and strangeness of them. And what are these my compositions, in truth, other than antique works and monstrous bodies, patched and huddled up together of divers members, without any certain or well ordered figure, having neither order, dependency, or proportion, but casual and framed by chance? "A woman fair for parts superior, / Ends in a fish for part inferior."[101]

Touching this second point I go as far as my Painter, but for the other and better part I am far behind: for my sufficiency reacheth not so far as that I dare undertake a rich, a polished, and according to true skill, and art-like table.[102] I have advised myself to borrow one of Etienne de La Boétie, who with this kind of work shall honor all the world. It is a discourse he entitled *Voluntary Servitude*, but those who have not known him have since very properly rebaptized the same, *The Against One*. In his first youth he wrote, by way of Essay, in honor of liberty against Tyrants. It hath long since been dispersed amongst men of understanding, not without great and well deserved commendations, for it is full of wit and containeth as much learning as may be. Yet doth it differ much from the best he can do. And if in the age I knew him in, he would have undergone my design to set his fantasies down in writing, we should doubtless see many rare things and which would very nearly approach the honor of antiquity: for especially touching that part of nature's gifts, I know none may be compared to him. But it was not long of him that ever this Treatise came to man's view, and I believe he never saw it since it first escaped his hands, with certain other notes concerning the edict of January, famous by reason of our intestine wars, which haply may in other places find their deserved praise.[103] It is all I could ever recover of his relics (whom when death seized, he by his last will and testament left with so kind remembrance, heir and executor of his library and writings) besides the little book I since caused to be published. To which his pamphlet I am particularly most bounden, for so much as it was the instrumental mean of our first acquaintance. For it was showed me a long time before I saw him, and gave me the first knowledge of his name, addressing and thus nourishing that unspotted friendship which we (so long as it pleased God) have so sincerely, so entire and inviolably maintained between us, that truly a man shall not commonly hear of the like. And among our modern men no sign of any such is seen. So many parts are required to the erecting of such a one, that it may be counted a wonder if fortune once in three ages contract the like.

There is nothing to which Nature hath more addressed us than to society. And Aristotle saith that perfect Lawgivers have had more regardful care of friendship than of justice.[104] And the utmost drift of its perfection is this. For generally, all those amities which are forged and nourished by voluptuousness or profit, public or private need, are thereby so much the less fair and generous, and so much the less true amities, in that they intermeddle other causes, scope, and fruit with friendship than it self alone. Nor do those four ancient kinds of natural friendships, *Natural, social, hospitable*, and *venerian*,[105] either particularly or conjointly beseem the same.

That from children to parents may rather be termed respect. Friendship is nourished by communication, which by reason of the over-great disparity cannot be found in them, and would haply offend the duties of nature: for neither all the secret thoughts of parents can be communicated unto children, unless it might engender an unbeseeming familiarity between them, nor the admonitions and corrections (which are the chiefest offices of friendship) could be exercised from children to parents. There have nations been found where, by custom, children killed their parents, and others where parents slew their children, thereby to avoid the hindrance of enterbearing[106] one another in after-times: for naturally one dependeth from the ruin of another. There have Philosophers been found disdaining this natural conjunction. Witness Aristippus, who being urged with the affection he ought his children as proceeding from his loins, began to speak and spit, saying that also that excrement proceeded from him, and that also we engendered worms and lice.[107] And that other man, whom Plutarch would have persuaded to agree with his brother, answered, "I care not a straw the more for him, though he came out of the same womb I did."[108]

Verily the name of Brother is a glorious name and full of loving kindness, and therefore did he and I term one another sworn brother. But this commixture, dividence, and sharing of goods, this joining wealth to wealth, and that the riches of one shall be the poverty of another, doth exceedingly distemper and distract all brotherly alliance and lovely conjunction. If brothers should conduct the progress of their advancement and thrift in one same path and course, they must necessarily oftentimes hinder and cross one another. Moreover, the correspondence and relation that begetteth these true and mutually perfect amities, why shall it be found in these? The father and the son may very well be of a far differing complexion, and so may brothers. He is my son, he is my kinsman; but he may be a fool, a bad, or a peevish-minded man. And then according as they are friendships which the law and duty of nature doth command us, so much the less of our own voluntary choice and liberty is there required unto it. And our genuine liberty hath no production more properly her own than that of affection and amity. Sure I am that concerning the same I have assayed all that might be, having had the best and most indulgent father that ever was, even unto his extremest old age, and who from father to son was descended of a famous house, and touching this rare-seen virtue of brotherly concord very exemplary: "To his brothers known so kind, / As to bear a father's mind."[109]

To compare the affection toward women unto it, although it proceeds from our own free choice, a man cannot, nor may it be placed in this rank. Her fire, I confess it ("Nor is that Goddess ignorant of me, / Whose bitter sweets with my cares mixèd be")[110] to be more active, more fervent, and more sharp. But it is a rash and wavering fire, waving and diverse: the fire of an ague subject to fits and stints, and that hath but slender holdfast of us. In true friendship, it is a general and universal heat, and equally tempered, a constant and settled heat, all pleasure and smoothness, that hath no pricking or stinging in it, which the more it is in lustful love, the more is it but a ranging and mad desire in following that which flies us,

> Ev'n as the huntsman doth the hare pursue,
> In cold, in heat, on mountains, on the shore,
> But cares no more, when he her ta'n espies,
> Speeding his pace only at that which flies.[111]

As soon as it creepeth into terms of friendship, that is to say, in the agreement of wills, it languisheth and vanisheth away: enjoying doth lose it, as having a corporeal end, and subject to satiety. On the other side, friendship is enjoyed according as it is desired, it is neither bred, nor nourished, nor increaseth but in jouissance,[112] as being spiritual, and the mind being refined by use and custom. Under this chief amity, these fading affections have sometimes found place in me, lest I should speak of him who in his verses speaks but too much of it.[113] So are these two passions entered into me in knowledge one of another, but in comparison never: the first flying a high, and keeping a proud pitch, disdainfully beholding the other to pass her points far under it.

Concerning marriage, besides that it is a covenant which hath nothing free but the entrance, the continuance being forced and constrained, depending elsewhere than from our will, and a match ordinarily concluded to other ends, a thousand strange knots are therein commonly to be unknit, able to break the web, and trouble the whole course of a lively affection. Whereas in friendship there is no commerce or business depending on the same, but itself. Seeing (to speak truly) that the ordinary sufficiency of women cannot answer this conference and communication, the nurse of this sacred bond; nor seem their minds strong enough to endure the pulling of a knot so hard, so fast and durable. And truly, if without that, such a genuine and voluntary acquaintance might be contracted where not only minds had this entire jouissance, but also bodies a share of the alliance, and where man might wholly be engaged, it is certain that friendship would thereby be more complete and full. But this sex could never yet by any example attain unto it and is by ancient schools rejected thence.

And this other Greek license is justly abhorred by our customs. Which notwithstanding, because according to use it had so necessary a disparity of ages and difference of offices between lovers, did no more sufficiently answer the perfect union and agreement which here we require: "For what love is this of friendship? Why doth no man love either a deformed young man or a beautiful old man?"[114] For even the picture the Academy[115] makes of it will not (as I suppose) disavow me to say thus in her behalf: That this first fury, inspired by the son of Venus in the lover's heart, upon the object of tender youth's flower, to which they allow all insolent and passionate violences an immoderate heat may produce, was simply grounded upon an external beauty, a false image of corporal imagination, for in the spirit it had no power. The sight whereof was yet concealed, which was but in his infancy and before the age of budding. For if this fury did seize upon a base-minded courage, the means of its pursuit were riches, gifts, favor to the advancement of dignities, and suchlike vile merchandise, which they reprove. If it fell into a more generous mind, the interpositions were likewise generous: Philosophical instructions, documents to reverence religion, to obey the laws, to die for the good of his country: examples of valor, wisdom and justice. The lover endeavoring and studying to make himself acceptable by the good grace and beauty of his mind (that of his body being long since decayed), hoping by this mental society to establish a more firm and permanent bargain.

When this pursuit attained the effect in his due season (for by not requiring in a lover he should bring leisure and discretion in his enterprise, they require it exactly in the beloved; for as much as he was to judge of an internal beauty, of a difficult knowledge, and abstruse discovery), then by the interposition of a spiritual beauty was the desire of a spiritual conception engendered in the beloved. The latter was here chiefest; the corporal, accidental and second: altogether contrary to the lover. And therefore do they prefer the beloved and verify that the Gods likewise prefer the same, and greatly blame the Poet Aeschylus, who in the love between Achilles and Patroclus ascribeth the lover's part unto Achilles, who was in the first and beardless youth of his adolescency and the fairest of the Grecians.[116]

After this, general community[117]: the mistress and worthiest part of it, predominant and exercising her offices. They say the most available[118] commodity did thereby redound both to the private and public, that it was the force of countries received the use of it, and the principal defense of equity and liberty: witness the comfortable loves of Harmodius and Aristogiton.[119] Therefore name they it sacred and divine, and it concerns not them whether the violence of tyrants or the demissness[120] of the people be against them. To conclude, all can be alleged in favor of the Academy is to say that it was a love ending in friendship, a thing which hath no bad reference unto the Stoical definition of love: "That love is an endeavor of making friendship by the show of beauty."[121]

I return to my description in a more equitable and equal manner. "Clearly friendships are to be judged by wits and ages already strengthened and confirmed."[122] As for the rest, those we ordinarily call friends and amities are but acquaintances and familiarities tied together by some occasion or commodities by means whereof our minds are entertained. In the amity I speak of, they intermix and confound themselves one in the other with so universal a commixture that they wear out, and can no more find the seam that hath conjoined them together. If a man urge me to tell wherefore I loved him, I feel it can not be expressed but by answering, because it was he, because it was myself.

There is beyond all my discourse and besides what I can particularly report of it, I know not what inexplicable and fatal power, a mean and Mediatrix of this indissoluble union. We sought one another before ever we had seen one another, and by the reports we heard one of another; which wrought a greater violence in us than the reason of reports may well bear: I think by some secret ordinance of the heavens we embraced one another by our names. And at our first meeting, which was by chance at a great feast and solemn meeting of a whole township, we found ourselves so surprised, so known, so acquainted, and so combinedly bound together, that from thenceforward nothing was so near unto us as one unto another. He wrote an excellent Latin Satire, since published, by which he excuseth and expoundeth the precipitation of our acquaintance, so suddenly come to her perfection. Sithence[123] it must continue so short a time, and begun so late (for we were both grown men, and he some years older then myself), there was no time to be lost. And it was not to be modeled or directed by the pattern of regular and remiss friendship wherein so many precautions of a long and preallable conversation[124] are required. This hath no other *Idea* than of itself and can have no reference but to itself. It is not one especial consideration, nor two, nor three, nor four, nor a thousand: It is I wot not what kind of quintessence of all this commixture, which having seized all my will, induced the same to plunge and loose itself in his, which likewise having seized all his will, brought it to loose and plunge itself in mine, with a mutual greediness and with a semblable concurrence. I may truly say "loose," reserving nothing unto us that might properly be called our own, nor that was either his or mine.

When Laelius in the presence of the Roman Consuls, who after the condemnation of Tiberius Gracchus pursued all those that had been of his acquaintance, came to inquire of Caius Blossius (who was one of his chiefest friends) what he would have done for [Gracchus], and that he answered, "All things." "What? All things?" replied [Laelius], "And what if he had willed thee to burn our Temples?" Blossius answered, "He would never have commanded such a thing." "But what if he had done it?" replied Laelius. The other answered, "I would have obeyed him." If he were so perfect a friend to Gracchus as Histories report, he needed not offend the Consuls with this last and bold confession and should not have departed from the assurance he had of Gracchus his mind. But yet those who accuse this answer as seditious understand not well this mystery, and do not presuppose in what terms he stood, and that he held Gracchus his will in his sleeve both by power and knowledge. They were rather friends than citizens, rather friends than enemies of their country, or friends of ambition and trouble. Having absolutely committed themselves one to another, they perfectly held the reins of one another's inclination: and let this yoke be guided by virtue and conduct of reason (because without them it is altogether impossible to combine and proportion the same). The answer of Blossius was such as it should be. If their actions miscarried, according to my meaning, they were neither friends one to another, nor friends to themselves.[125]

As for the rest, this answer sounds no more than mine would do, to him that would in such sort inquire of me, "if your will should command you to kill your daughter, would you do it?" and that I should consent unto it. For that beareth no witness of consent to do it, because I am not in doubt of my will, and as little of such a friend's will. It is not in the power of the world's discourse to remove me from the certainty I have of his intentions and judgments of mine: no one of its actions might be presented unto me, under what shape soever, but I would presently find the spring and motion of it. Our minds have jumped so unitedly together, they have with so fervent an affection considered of each other, and with like affection so discovered and sounded, even to the very bottom of each other's heart and entrails, that I did not only know his as well as mine own, but I would (verily) rather have trusted him concerning any matter of mine than myself.

Let no man compare any of the other common friendships to this. I have as much knowledge of them as another, yea, of the most perfect of their kind: yet will I not persuade any man to confound their rules, for so a man might be deceived. In these other strict friendships a man must march with the bridle of wisdom and precaution in his hand: the bond is not so strictly tied but a man may in some sort distrust the same. "Love him," said Chilon, "as if you should one day hate him again. Hate him as if you should love him again."[126] This precept, so abominable in this sovereign and mistress Amity, is necessary and wholesome in the use of vulgar and customary friendships, toward which a man must employ the saying Aristotle was wont so often to repeat, "Oh you my friends, there is no perfect friend."[127]

In this noble commerce, offices and benefits (nurses of other amities) deserve not so much as to be accompted of. This confusion so full of our wills is cause of it. For even as the friendship I bear unto myself admits no accrease[128] by any succor I give myself in any time of need, whatsoever the Stoics allege; and as I acknowledge no thanks unto myself for any service I do unto myself; so the union of such friends, being truly perfect, makes them lose the feelings of such duties, and hate and expel from one another these words of division, and difference, benefit, good deed, duty, obligation, acknowledgment, prayer, thanks, and such their like. All things being by effect common between them: wills, thoughts, judgments, goods, wives, children, honor, and life. And their mutual agreement being no other than one soul in two bodies, according to the fit definition of Aristotle,[129] they can neither lend or give aught to each other. See here the reason why Lawmakers, to honor marriage with some imaginary resemblance of this divine bond, inhibit donations between husband and wife; meaning thereby to infer that all things should peculiarly be proper to each of them, and that they have nothing to divide and share together.

If in the friendship whereof I speak, one might give unto another, the receiver of the benefit should bind his fellow. For each seeking more than any other thing to do each other good, he who yields both matter and occasion is the man showeth himself liberal, giving his friend that contentment to effect toward him what he desireth most. When the Philosopher Diogenes wanted money, he was wont to say that he redemanded the same of his friends, and not that he demanded it.[130]

And to show how that is practiced by effect, I will relate an ancient singular example. Eudamidas the Corinthian had two friends, Charixenus a Sycionian and Aretaeus a Corinthian. Being upon his deathbed and very poor, and his two friends very rich, thus made his last will and testament. "To Aretaeus, I bequeath the keeping of my mother, and to maintain her when she shall be old. To Charixenus the marrying of my daughter and to give her as great a dowry as he may. And in case one of them shall chance to die before, I appoint the survivor to substitute his charge and supply his place." Those that first saw this testament laughed and mocked at the same; but his heirs being advertised thereof were very well pleased, and received it with singular contentment. And Charixenus one of them, dying five days after Eudamidas, the substitution being declared in favor of Aretaeus, he carefully and very kindly kept and maintained his mother, and of five talents that he was worth, he gave two and a half in marriage to one only daughter he had, and the other two and a half to the daughter of Eudamidas, whom he married both in one day.[131]

This example is very ample, if one thing were not, which is the multitude of friends. For this perfect amity I speak of is indivisible. Each man doth so wholly give himself unto his friend that he hath nothing left him to divide elsewhere; moreover he is grieved that he is [not][132] double, triple, or quadruple, and hath not many souls, or sundry wills, that he might confer them all upon this subject. Common friendships may be divided; a man may love beauty in one, facility of customs in another, liberality in one, and wisdom in another, paternity in this, fraternity in that man, and so forth. But this amity which possesseth the soul and sways it in all sovereignty, it is impossible it should be double. If two at one instant should require help, to which would you run? Should they crave contrary offices of you, what order would you follow? Should one commit a matter to your silence, which if the other knew would greatly profit him, what course would you take? Or how would you discharge yourself? A singular and principal friendship dissolveth all other duties and freeth all other obligations. The secret I have sworn not to reveal to another, I may without perjury impart it unto him who is no other but myself. It is a great and strange wonder for a man to double himself, and those that talk of tripling know not nor cannot reach unto the height of it. Nothing is extreme that hath his Like. And he who shall presuppose that of two I love the one as well as the other, and that they enterlove[133] one another, and love me as much as I love them, he multiplieth in brotherhood, a thing most singular and alonely[134] one, and than which one alone is also the rarest to be found in the world.

The remainder of this History agreeth very well with what I said. For Eudamidas giveth as a grace and favor to his friends to employ them in his need; he leaveth them as his heirs of his liberality, which consisteth in putting the means into their hands to do him good. And doubtless the force of friendship is much more richly shown in his deed than in Aretaeus'.

To conclude, they are unimaginable effects to him that hath not tasted them. And which makes me wonderfully to honor the answer of that young Soldier to Cyrus, who inquiring of him what he would take for a horse, with which he had lately gained the prize of a race, and whether he would change him for a Kingdom? "No surely, my Liege," said he, "yet would I willingly forego him to gain a true friend, could I but find a man worthy of so precious an alliance."[135] He said not ill in saying, "could I but find." For a man shall easily find men fit for a superficial acquaintance; but in this, wherein men negotiate from the very center of their hearts and make no spare of anything, it is most requisite all the wards and springs be sincerely wrought and perfectly true.

In confederacies which hold but by one end, men have nothing to provide for but for the imperfections which particularly do interest and concern that end and respect. It is no great matter what religion my Physician and Lawyer is of: this consideration hath nothing common with the offices of that friendship they owe me. So do I in the familiar acquaintances, that those who serve me contract with me. I am nothing inquisitive whether a Lackey[136] be chaste or no, but whether he be diligent. I fear not a gaming Muleteer so much as if he be weak; nor a hot-swearing Cook, as one that is ignorant and unskillful. I never meddle with saying what a man should do in the world—there are over-many others that do it—but what myself do in the world. "So is it requisite for me; / Do thou as needful is for thee."[137]

Concerning familiar table talk, I rather acquaint myself with and follow a merry conceited humor than a wise man.[138] And in bed I rather prefer beauty than goodness, and in society or conversation of familiar discourse I respect rather sufficiency, though without *Prud'homie*,[139] and so of all things else. Even as he that was found riding upon an hobby-horse, playing with his children, besought him who thus surprised him not to speak of it until he were a father himself, supposing the tender fondness and fatherly passion which then would possess his mind should make him an impartial judge of such an action.[140] So would I wish to speak to such as had tried what I speak of. But knowing how far such an amity is from the common use, and how seldom seen and rarely found, I look not to find a competent judge. For even the discourses which stern antiquity hath left us concerning this subject seem to me but faint and forceless in respect of the feeling I have of it. And in that point the effects exceed the very precepts of Philosophy. "For me, be I well in my wit, / Nought as a merry friend so fit."[141]

Ancient Menander accompted him happy that had but met the shadow of a true friend[142]: verily he had reason to say so, especially if he had tasted of any. For truly, if I compare all the rest of my forepassed life (which although I have by the mere mercy of God passed at rest and ease, and except the loss of so dear a friend, free from all grievous affliction, with an ever-quietness of mind, as one that has taken my natural and original commodities in good payment, without searching any others)—if, as I say, I compare it all unto the four years I so happily enjoyed the sweet company and dear, dear society of that worthy man—it is nought but a vapor, nought but a dark and irksome light. Since the time I lost him, "Which I shall ever hold a bitter day, / Yet ever honored (so my God t'obey),"[143] I do but languish, I do but sorrow. And even those pleasures all things present me with, instead of yielding me comfort do but redouble the grief of his loss. We were copartners in all things. All things were with us at half; methinks I have stolen his part from him. "I have set down, no joy enjoy I may, / As long as he my partner is away."[144] I was so accustomed to be ever two and so inured to be never single that methinks I am but half myself.

Since that part of my soul riper fate reft me,
Why stay I here, the other part he left me?
Nor so dear, nor entire, while here I rest:
That day has in one ruin both oppressed.[145]

There is no action can betide me or imagination possess me, but I hear him saying, as indeed he would have done to me. For even as he did excel me by an infinite distance in all other sufficiencies and virtues, so did he in all offices and duties of friendship. "What modesty or measure may I bear / In want and wish of him that was so dear?"[146]

O brother reft from miserable me,
All our delights are perishèd with thee,
Which thy sweet love did nourish in thy breath.
Thou all my good hast spoilèd in thy death:
With thee my soul is all and whole enshrined,
At whose death I have cast out of mind
All my mind's sweet meats, studies of this kind;
Never shall I hear thee speak, speak with thee?
Thee brother than life dearer, never see?
Yet shalt thou ever be beloved of me.[147]

But let us a little hear this young man speak, being but sixteen years of age.

[Here Montaigne announces he has revoked his intention to close this essay with La Boétie's *Voluntary Servitude*, because Protestants, he claims, have misappropriated it. So he ends instead by briefly defending his friend to introduce the next chapter: La Boétie's twenty-nine sonnets.]

Anonymous, in Maitland Quarto Manuscript (c. 1586)

A poem in which the speaker wishes she could be transformed into a male to marry her beloved female friend appears without attribution in a manuscript collection dated 1586, and signed twice on the title page by Mary Maitland. She was one of the seven children of Sir Richard Maitland, Lord Lethington (1498–1586), and the collection, which gathers her father's poems as well as others, was probably compiled for her. Mary wed Alexander Lauder of Hatton, but little else is yet known of her life, even the dates of her birth and death. The author of this text could be either female or male, for Renaissance male poets fashionably assumed such female personas, like *Pontus de Tyard (1521–1605), *Pierre de Ronsard (1524–1585), and *John Donne (1572–1631). Nevertheless, the poem's composition, circulation, and association with Mary evince current interest in the more passionate possibilities of female bonding, and in using classical ideals of male same-sex relationships to authorize feminine counterparts. Although nature, Fortune, and Hymen (god of marriage) all oppose this female couple, the speaker maintains that their amity will triumph through virtue and constancy. A main intertext here, as for most Renaissance literary treatments of female homoeroticism, is Ovid's story of the young women Iphis and Ianthe in the *Metamorphoses*, in which Iphis wishes to become male to marry Ianthe, and does (9.666–797).

As Phoebus in His Sphere's Height [148] *(c. 1586)*

As Phoebus in his sphere's height[149]
Excells the cope crepusculine[150]
And Phoebe[151] all the starry light,
Your splendor so, madam, I ween,[152]
Does solely pass all feminine   5
In sapience superlative,
Endued with virtues so divine
As learnèd Pallas[153] does revive.

And as by hid virtue unknown
The adamant[154] draws iron thereto,   10
Your court'ous nature so has drawn
My heart, yours to continue still;
So great Joy does my soul fulfill
Contempl'ing your perfection
You hold me wholly at your will   15
And ravish my affection.

Your peerless Virtue does provoke
And loving kindness so does move
My Mind to friendship reciproc',
That truth shall prove so far above   20
The ancient heroic love
As shall be thought prodigious,
And plain experience shall prove
More holy and religious.

In amity Perithöus   25
And Theseus had not such trust,
Nor with Achilles Patroclus,
Nor Pylades with true Orest',
Nor yet Achates' love so laced

To good Aenee', nor such friendship   30
David to Jonathan professed,
Nor Titus true to kind Gisipp'.[155]

Nor yet Penelope, I wis,[156]
So loved Ulysses in her days,
Nor Ruth the kind Moabitess   35
Naomi as the Scripture says,
Nor Portia whose worthy praise
In Roman histories we read,
Who did devour a fiery blaze
To follow Brutus to the dead.[157]   40

Would mighty Jove grant me the hap
With you to have your Brutus' part,[158]
And metamorphosing our shape
My sex unto his would[159] convert,
No Brutus then should cause us smart   45
As we fare[160] now, unhappy women,
Then should we both with Joyful heart
Honor and bless the band of Hymen.

Yea, certainly we should efface
Pollux and Castor's memory,   50
And if that they deservèd place
Among the stars for loyalty,[161]
Then our more perfect amity
More worthy recompense should merit,
In heaven eternal deity   55
Among the gods so to Inherit.

And as we are, though, to our woe,
Nature and fortune do conjure,[162]
And Hymen also be our foe,
Yet love of virtue does procure   60
Friendship and amity so sure
With so great fervency and force,
So constantly that shall endure
That naught but death shall us divorce.

And though adversity us vex   65
Yet by our friendship shall be seen
There is more constancy in our sex
Than ever among men has been,
No trouble, torment, grief, or teen,[163]
Nor earthly thing shall us dissever   70
Such constancy shall us maintain
In perfect amity forever.

Pierre de Bourdeille, Abbé and Seigneur de Brantôme (1540?–1614)

One of the most extensive early modern accounts of tribadism, including some of the earliest known uses of "lesbian" to denote a female who sexually loves females,[164] appears in this writer's *Les vies des dames galantes*. He further discusses both opposite-sex and male same-sex anal intercourse. Commonly known as Brantôme, Pierre de Bourdeille was nobly born, well-traveled in Europe, and a courtier, soldier, and writer at different points of his life. When about sixteen, he received his abbacy and its income from King Henri II, and enjoyed various further ecclesiastical livings without taking holy orders. Yet by the mid-1580s his ambitions for courtly advancement had been frustrated. After a serious riding accident he retired from the court to his estates, where he composed a variety of biographical and anecdotal memoirs published posthumously in 1665–66.

A gossipy collection of anecdotes on amorous themes told from an avidly heteroerotic male standpoint, *Les vies* presents its main treatments of sodomy and tribadism when addressing cuckoldry or adultery in the First Discourse, and that context much delimits the appropriate applications of these passages in the study of early modern sex differences. Yet marriage as Brantôme depicts it could clearly accommodate extramarital same-sex love for both partners. His usages of "lesbian" in a sense comparable to its present one logically emerge, in context, from his association of tribadism with Sappho and Lesbos according to ancient sources such as Lucian. This logic and usage could have been repeated throughout early modern Europe among those versed in Latin or Greek, and their social circles. Since Brantôme obviously knew much about sexual discourse and gossip among the contemporary elite, his use of "lesbian" in this way is likely reportage, not idiosyncratic. He assumes it has a sense similar to "tribade" that requires no explanation. Compared with more enlightened men of his time, such as Baldassare Castiglione (1478–1529) or Sir Philip Sidney (1554–1586), he evinces little or no sensitivity to feminine concerns or aspirations in this text. Since the original dedication of *Les vies* addresses the living duc d'Alençon or d'Anjou, it was likely well under way by 1584, when that dedicatee died. From the first English translation of 1902 (A. R. Allinson) to the most recent of 1961 (Alec Brown), all but one anonymous version published in 1930 are bowdlerized in various ways, often without indicating omissions, especially in sections on sodomites and tribades.[165]

Lives of Fair and Gallant Ladies[166] *(written c. 1585)*

First Discourse: On Women Who Make Love and Cuckold Their Husbands

In a gallery of the Comte de Châteauvilain, known as the Seigneur Adjacet, a company of ladies with their lovers having come to visit the said fair mansion, they fell to contemplating sundry rare and beautiful pictures. . . . Among these they beheld a very beautiful picture, wherein were portrayed a number of fair ladies naked and at the bath, which did touch and feel and handle and stroke one the other, and intertwine and fondle with each other, and so enticingly and prettily and featly did show all their hidden beauties and secret places that the coldest recluse or hermit had been warmed and stirred thereat [compare figure 11]. Wherefore did a certain great lady, as I have heard it told—and indeed I do know her well—losing all restraint of herself before this picture, say to her lover, turning toward him maddened as it were at the madness of love she beheld painted: "Too long have we tarried here. Let us now straightway take coach and so to my lodging, for that no more can I hold in the ardor that is in me. Needs must away and quench it; too sore do I burn." And so she did haste away, and went with her swain to enjoy that good liquor that is so sweet without sugar, the which her faithful lover did give her from out his little phial. Suchlike pictures and portrayals do bring more hurt to a weak soul than men think for. (26–27)

There is yet another sort of cuckolds, one that of a surety is utterly abominable and hateful before God and man alike: they who, enamored of some handsome Adonis, do abandon their wives to men of this kind in order to enjoy their favor in return.

The first time ever I was in Italy I did hear of an example of this at Ferrara, the tale being told me of one who, captivated by a certain handsome youth, did persuade his wife to accord her favors to the said young man, who was in love with her, and to appoint a day and consent to do all he should bid her. The lady was willing enough, for truly she did desire no better venison to regale herself withal than this. At length was the day fixed, and the hour being come when the young lover and the lady were at their pleasant game and entertainment, lo! the husband, who was hid near at hand, according to the compact betwixt him and his wife, did rush in. So catching them in the very act, he did put his dagger to the lover's throat, deeming him worthy of death for such offense in accordance with the laws of Italy, which herein be something more rigorous than in France. So was he constrained to grant the husband what he did desire, and they made exchange one with the other. The young man did prostitute himself to the husband, and the husband did abandon his wife to the young man. Thus was the husband cuckold after an exceeding foul fashion.

I have heard tell how in a certain spot in the world (I had rather not name it) there was an husband, and one of high quality to boot, which was desperately enamored of a young man, who himself was deep in love with the former's wife, and she likewise with him. Now, whether it was that the husband had won over the wife, or that it was a pure surprise quite unexpected, at any rate he did catch the pair abed and coupled up together. Whereon, threatening the young man if he would not consent to his will, he did enter him lying just as he was, and coupled up and glued to his wife, and did take his will of him. And thus was the problem solved how three lovers could enjoy and be contented all at the same time together.[167]

I have heard tell of a lady which, being desperately in love with an honorable gentleman whom she had taken for lover and chief favorite, and this latter fearing the husband would do him or her some ill turn, did comfort him, saying, "Nay! have no fear, for he would in no wise dare do aught, for dread I should accuse him of having wished to practice the backdoor Venus,[168] which might well bring about his death if I were to breathe the least word thereof and denounce him to justice. But in this way I do hold him in check and in terror, so that for fear of my accusation he dares not say one word to me." Without a doubt such accusation would have involved the poor husband in naught less than peril of his life, for the legists declare that sodomy is punishable for the mere wish to commit the same. [But perhaps the lady did not want to say the whole truth, and her husband all along did not stop at the mere intent.][169]

I have been told how in one of these latter years a young French gentleman, a handsome gallant that had been seen many a day at Court, being gone to Rome for instruction in manly exercises, like others his contemporaries, was in that city regarded with so favorable an eye, and did meet with such great admiration of his beauty, as well of men as of women, that folk were ready almost to force him to their will. And so whenever they were ware of his going to Mass or other place of public assemblage, they would never fail, either men or women, to be there likewise for to see him. Nay, more, several husbands did suffer their wives to give him love assignations in their houses to the end that, being come thither and then surprised, they might effect an exchange, the one of his wife, the other of him. For which cause he was advised never to yield to the love and wishes of these ladies, seeing the whole matter had been contrived and arranged merely to entrap him. And herein he did show himself wise and did set his honor and good conscience above all such detestable pleasures, winning thereby a high and worthy repute. Yet at the last his squire did kill him. Divers reasons are given therefor. At any rate 'twas a sore pity, for that he was a very honorable young man, of good station, and one that did promise well of his nature as well by reason of his noble actions as of the fine and noble character he did manifest herein. For indeed, as I have heard a very gallant man of my time say, and as is most true, never yet was bugger or catamite[170] a brave, valiant and generous man but only the great Julius Caesar, seeing that by divine permission and ordinance all such abominable folk are brought low and reduced to shame. And this doth make me wonder how sundry whom I have seen stained by this horrid vice have yet prospered under Heaven in high good fortune; yet doth God wait for them, and at the last we shall surely see them meet their proper fate.

Verily, speaking of this abominable practice, I have further heard say that some husbands have been attainted thereby to the very quick. For, unhappy that they be and abominable, they have accustomed themselves to deal with their wives more by the rear than by the front and have used the latter only for the making of children. And thus do they treat their poor wives, which have all their heat in the fair parts that are in front. Are these not excusable if they do make their husbands cuckolds, who do thus prefer their foul and filthy backward parts?

How many women there be in the world, which if they were examined by midwives and doctors and expert surgeons, would be found no more virgin behind than before, and which could at any moment bring action against their husbands. Yet do they dissimulate it and dare not discover the matter for fear of bringing scandal on themselves and their husbands, or perhaps because they do find therein some greater pleasure than we can suppose. Or it may be for the purpose I have above named—to keep their husbands in such subjection if they do make love in other quarters, which indeed some husbands do on these terms allow them to do. Yet are none of these reasons really sufficient to account for the thing.

The *Summa Benedicti* saith: "If the husband chooseth thus to take his part contrary to the order of Nature, he commits a mortal sin; and if he maintain that he may dispose of his own wife as he please, he doth fall into a detestable and foul heresy of sundry Jews and evil Rabbis, which are cited as saying thus: 'Two women were denounced before the synagogue on the grounds that they had been known by their husbands after the manner of sodomites. Their reply to the rabbis was this: The husband is the lord of the wife, and so he may use her as he pleases. It is no different from a man who buys a fish, for he may eat the front part or the back part, as he wills.'"[171] This have I quoted only in Latin forasmuch as it soundeth ill to honorable and modest ears. Abominable wretches that they be—thus to desert a fair, pure and lawful part to adopt instead one that is foul, dirty, filthy and forbid, and disgraceful to boot.

But if the man will take the woman so it is lawful for her to separate from him, if there is no other means to cure him. And yet, it is stated again, such women as fear God ought never to consent thereto, but rather cry out for help, regardless of the scandal which might so arise, and of dishonor and the fear of death; for 'tis better, saith the law, to die than to consent to evil. The same book doth say another thing which I deem very strange: that whatsoever way a husband know his wife, provided she may conceive thereby, herein is no mortal sin, but only a venial one. Yet are there modes for this that be exceeding filthy and base, according to Aretino's representations thereof in his figures.[172] Nor do these same smack at all of marital purity, albeit, as I have before said, it may be permissible in case of pregnant women, as well as such as have a strong and stinking breath, whether from the mouth or nose. Thus have I known and heard speak of several women to kiss whom and scent their breath was as bad as smelling at a privy-hole; or to put it another way, I have heard it said of a certain great lady, a very great one indeed I mean, that once one of her ladies declared her breath stank more than a brass piss-pot. These are the very words she used. One of this lady's men friends, admitted to the greatest intimacy, and who had the closest access to her, did likewise confirm the fact to me, though to be sure 'tis true she was then something getting on in age.

In such case what can a husband or lover do, unless he have recourse to some extravagant mode of intercourse? But anyhow let this not go so far as the backside Venus.[173]

I would say more of this, but in truth I have a horror of speaking thereof at all. It hath vexed me to have said so much as I have; but 'tis needful sometimes to lay open public vices in order to reform the same. (99–102)

Now will I further ask this one question only, and never another, one which mayhap hath never yet been inquired into of any, or possibly even thought of—to wit, whether two ladies that be in love one with the other, as hath been seen aforetime, and is often seen nowadays, sleeping together in one bed and doing what is called *donna con donna* (lady with lady), imitating in fact that learned poetess Sappho, of Lesbos, whether these can commit adultery and between them make their husbands cuckold.

Of a surety do they commit this crime, if we are to believe Martial in Epigram 119 of his First Book. Therein doth he introduce and speak of a woman by name Bassa, a tribade, reproaching the same greatly in that men were never seen to visit her, in such wise that folk deemed her a second Lucretia[174] for chasteness. But presently she came to be discovered, for that she was observed to be constantly welcoming at her house beautiful women and girls; and 'twas found that she herself did serve these and counterfeit a man and the act of adultery and have intercourse with them. And the poet, to describe this, doth use the words *geminos committere cunnos* (to bring together two cunts). And further on, protesting against the thing, he doth signify the riddle and give it out to be guessed and imagined in this Latin line: *Hic, ubi vir non est, ut sit adulterium*—a strange thing, that is, that where no man is, yet is adultery done.[175]

I knew once a courtesan of Rome, old and wily if ever there was one, that was named Isabella de Luna, a Spanish woman, which did take in this sort of friendship another courtesan named Pandora. This latter was eventually married to a butler in the Cardinal d'Armagnac's household, but without abandoning her first calling. Now this same Isabella did keep her, and commonly slept with her; and, extravagant and ill-ordered as she was in speech, I have oft-times heard her say how that she did make her more whorish, and cause her to give her husbands more horns than all the wild fellows she had ever had. I know not in what sense she did intend this, unless she did follow the meaning of the epigram of Martial just referred to.

'Tis said how that Sappho the Lesbian was a very high mistress in this art, or even, so they say, the inventress of the thing, and that in after times the Lesbian dames have copied her therein, and continued the practice to the present day. So Lucian saith: Such is the character of the Lesbian women, which will not suffer men at all, but do go with other women like actual men.[176] Now such women as love this practice will not suffer men, but devote themselves to other women like actual men, and are called "tribades," a Greek word derived, as I have learned of the Greeks, from τρίβω, τρίβειν, that is to say *fricare*, to frig or rub together. These tribades are called in Latin *fricatrices*, and in French the same, that is, women who do the rubbing or frigging in the way of *donne con donne* (ladies with ladies), as it is still found at the present day. Juvenal again speaks of these women when he saith *frictum Grissantis adorat*, talking of such a tribade, who adored and loved the frigging of one Grissas.[177]

The excellent and diverting Lucian hath a chapter on this subject, and saith therein how that women do come mutually to conjoin like men, bringing together lascivious, obscure and monstrous organs, framed in barren wise. Moreover, this name of tribade, which doth elsewhere occur but rarely as applied to these frictionists, is freely employed by him throughout, and he saith that the female sex must needs be like the notorious Philaenis,[178] who was used to parody the actions of manly love. At the same time he doth add, 'tis better far for a woman to be given up to a lustful affection for playing the male than it is for a man to be womanish; so utterly lacking in all courage and nobility of character doth such an one show himself. Thus the woman, according to this, which doth counterfeit the man may well be reputed to be more valorous and courageous than another, as in truth I have known some such to be, as well in body as in spirit.[179]

In yet another passage Lucian doth introduce two ladies discoursing of this form of love. One asketh the other if such and such a woman had been in love with her, and if she had slept with her, and what she had done to her. To these questions the other answers freely: "First of all, she did kiss me as men do, not merely uniting the lips, but opening the mouth to boot"—that is, billing, or pigeon-kissing, with the tongue in the other's mouth—"and albeit she had no virile member, but was like other women, yet did she declare she had the heart and affection of a man and all the rest appertaining to the male. Then I embrace and kiss her like a man, and she did the like to me, kissing me and filling me with delight. And she seemed to find an extraordinary pleasure therein; and so did cohabit with me in a fashion much more agreeable than with a man." Such is Lucian's account.[180]

Well, by what I have heard say, there be in many regions and lands plenty of such dames and [lesbians][181]—in France, in Italy, in Spain, Turkey,

Greece and other places. And wherever the women are kept secluded and have not their entire liberty this practice doth greatly prevail. For such women, burning with desire as they be in body, must needs, as themselves say, have recourse to this remedy, for to refresh them a little, that they burn not away altogether.

The Turkish women go to the baths more for this naughtiness than for any other reason, and are greatly devoted thereto. Even the courtesans, which have men at their wish and at all times, still do employ this pleasant friction, seeking out and loving the one the other, as I have heard of sundry doing in Italy and in Spain. In my native France women of the sort are common enow; yet is it said to be no long time since they first began to meddle therewith, in fact that the fashion was imported from Italy by a certain lady of quality, whom I will not name.

I have heard a tale told by the late M. de Clermont Tallard, the younger, who died at La Rochelle, how that as a boy he had the honour to be comrade with M. d'Anjou, since King Henri III of France, in his study and to study regularly with him, under the tutorship of M. de Gournay. Well, one day at Toulouse, studying with his master as aforesaid in his private closet,[182] and being seated in a corner apart, he saw by a little crevice (for the closets and chambers were of wood and had been made suddenly and in haste by the pains of the Cardinal d'Armagnac, Archbishop of that See, the better to receive and accommodate the King and all his Court), in another adjoining closet, two very great ladies, with petticoats all tucked up and drawers down, lying one atop of the other and kissing like doves, rubbing and frigging one another; in a word, making great ado wantoning and imitating men. And this their pastime did last well nigh a whole hour, so that at the end they were exceeding hot and tired out, and were left so red and wet with exertion that they could no more and were constrained to rest them somewhat. And he said he did see this same game played several other days, so long as the Court tarried there, in the same fashion. But never after did he get opportunity to see the like pastime, seeing that particular spot did favor him, but nowhere else could he manage it.

He went on to tell me yet more, which I dare not write down, and did name me the ladies concerned. I know not if it be true; but he did swear it was and affirm it an hundred times by good sound oaths. And in very deed 'tis very likely; for these same two ladies have ever had this repute of making and alway practicing love in this fashion, and of passing their time therein.

Several others have I known which have given account of the same manner of loves, amongst whom I have heard tell of a noble lady of the great world who was superlatively given this way, and who did love many ladies, courting the same and serving them as men are wont, and would make love to them as a man doth to his mistress. So would she take them and keep them at bed and board, and give them whatever they would. Her husband was right glad and well content thereat, as were many other husbands I have known, all of whom were right glad their wives did follow after this sort of love rather than that of men, deeming them to be thus less wild and whorish. But indeed I think they were much deceived; for by what I have heard said this little exercise is but an apprenticeship, to come later to the greater one with men; forasmuch as being heated and put in high rut the one by the other, but their heat meanwhile being no wise diminished thereby, they must needs bathe them in clear and running water, the which doth refresh them far better than stagnant water. So do I learn of good surgeons, and have seen the same myself, that, if a man will treat a wound well and cure it, it is no use his playing at washing and anointing of the parts round it and the edges thereof. But he must probe it to the bottom, and push his probe or sound well in to do any good.

How many of these [lesbians][183] have I seen who, for all their friggings and mutual frictions, yet fail not at the last to go after men! Even Sappho herself, the mistress of them all, did she not end by loving her fond favorite Phaon, for whose sake she died?[184] For after all, as I have heard many fair ladies declare, there is nothing like men; and all they do get of other women, 'tis but appetizers to whet them to go feed a full meal with men. All these friggings serve them but in the lack of men. And if they but find a chance and opportunity free from scandal, they will straight quit their lady comrades and go throw their arms round some good man's neck.

I have known in my time two very fair and honorable damsels of a noble house, cousins of one another, which, having been used to lie together in one bed for the space of three years, did grow so well accustomed to this habit of frigging that at the last, getting the idea the said pleasure was but a meager and imperfect one compared with that to be had with men, they did determine to try the latter, and soon became downright harlots. These did after confess to their lovers that naught had done so much to debauch them and break them in to lewdness as this same practice, saying they did hate it as the sole cause of their disorderly life. Yet for all this, when they should meet, they would ever take a taste of this repast, and with other women as well, by way of whetting of their appetite for the other or better sort with men. And this was the answer a very honorable damsel I knew did once make to her lover, when he asked her if she did never follow this way with her lady friend—"No, no!" she replied, "I like men too well"—yet in sooth she did really practice both one mode and the other.

I have heard of an honorable gentleman who, desiring one day at Court to seek in marriage a certain very honorable damsel, did consult one of her kinswomen thereon, she told him frankly he would but be wasting his time; for, as she did herself tell me, such and such a lady—naming her ('twas one I had already heard talk of)—will never suffer her to marry. Instantly I did recognize the hang of it, for I was well aware how she did keep this damsel at bed and board for her delight, and did guard her carefully for her own eating. The gentleman did thank the said cousin for her good advice and warning, not without a merry gibe or two at herself the while, saying she did herein put in a word or two for herself as well as for the other, for that she did take her little pleasures now and again with her too under the rose. But this she did stoutly deny to me.

This doth remind me of certain which do thus keep harlots for themselves, and actually love these so dearly they would not share them for all the wealth in the world, neither with prince nor great noble, with comrade or friend. They are as jealous of them as a beggarman of his drinking barrel; yet even he will offer this to any that would drink. But this lady was fain to keep the damsel all to herself, without giving one scrap to others. Yet for all this did the girl make her cuckold on the sly with some of her own comrades.

'Tis said how that weasels are touched with this sort of love, and delight female with female to unite and dwell together. And so in hieroglyphic signs women loving one another with this kind of affection were represented of yore by weasels.[185] I have heard tell of a lady which was used alway to keep some of these animals, for that she had dealings with this mode of love and so did take pleasure in watching her little pets in their intercourse together.

Here is another point to be considered. For these loves can be worked in two fashions, one by frigging, or as the poet puts it, *geminos committere cunnos* (bringing two cunts together).[186] This fashion doth no injury, as sundry authorities declare, whereas 'tis not so with the other, where recourse is had to artificial instruments imitating the male organ, and which have been named *godemiches*.[187]

I have heard a tale related how a great Prince, suspecting two ladies of his Court who did so gratify one another, had the same watched. This did so well succeed that one of them was surprised in the act and was found to be fitted with a great big one between her legs, fastened so prettily with little straps round her body that it seemed like a natural member. She was caught so suddenly she had no time to take it off, so that the Prince did actually constrain her to show him how the pair of them did the thing betwixt them.

'Tis said that many women have died therefrom by reason of creating abscesses in their wombs due to unnatural movements and artificial friction. I certainly do know of some which have suffered in this way, of whom 'twas great pity, for that they were very fair and honorable dames and damsels. Surely it had been much better had they gone in company of some honorable gentleman instead, for these do in no wise cause their death, but rather do cause them to live and flourish more than afore, as I do hope to tell in another place. Nay! even for the cure of such ills, as I have heard sundry surgeons declare, there is naught more fitting than to get them well swept out inside by men's natural members, which are far better than all the pessaries[188] doctors and surgeons do use with lotions compounded for this end. Nevertheless, in despite of the inconveniences they do often see arise therefrom, women must needs have these artificial instruments.

I have heard a story related, myself being at the Court at that time, how that the Queen-Mother having given order to visit one day the chambers and chests of all such as were lodged in the Louvre, without sparing either dame or damsel, to see there were no arms or perhaps mayhap pistols concealed therein at the time of the civil troubles, one lady was surprised by the Captain of the Guard and found to have in her chest, no pistols indeed, but four great *godemiches*, cunningly made. This did give folk much cause for laughter and great confusion to the lady. I know the dame in question, and I think she is yet alive; but she was never well to look upon. Well, truly all such instruments are exceeding dangerous.

I will relate further this story of two ladies of the Court which did love each other mutually so fondly and were so hot at their trade that, in whatsoever place they might be, they could never refrain from making at the least some signs of love and indulging in a kiss or two. This was cause of great scandal to them and afforded men much food for thought. One was a widow, the other married. Now one day the married one, on a great fête day, was exceeding richly tricked out and clad in a dress of cloth of silver. Well, their mistress having betaken herself to vespers, the twain did go into her privy closet and, seated on her night-stool, did begin their frigging, and this so roughly and with such ardor that it brake down under them. Then did the married one, who was underneath, fall backward with her fine dress of cloth of silver right flat upon the ordure in the basin below. Thus did she spoil the same and befoul herself so sadly she had naught to do but wipe herself down the best she could, tuck up her skirts and away in all haste to change her frock in her own chamber—yet not without having been seen, as well as traced by the smell, she stank so vilely. Much merriment was caused hereby among some which did hear the story; nay! even their mistress did hear of it and, though she did sometime resort to the same means herself, did laugh her fill at them. Verily their ardor must have strangely mastered them that they did not wait a place and time more suitable, so as not to bring such scandal on them!

Still excuse may be made for maids and widows for loving these frivolous and empty pleasures, preferring to devote themselves to these and herein relieve their heat of blood than to go with men and get themselves pregnant and come to dishonor, or else to lose their pains altogether, as some have done and do every day. Moreover, they deem they do not so much offend God and are not such great harlots as if they had to do with men, maintaining there is a great difference betwixt throwing water in a vessel and merely watering about it and round the rim. However, I refer me to them; I am neither their judge nor their husband. These last may find it ill, but generally I have never seen any but were right glad their wives should fall in love with their lady friends, and fain they should never commit worse adultery than after this fashion. And in very deed this kind of cohabitation is a very different thing from that with men, and, let Martial say what he please, this alone will make no man cuckold. 'Tis no Gospel text, this word of a foolish poet. In this at any rate he saith true, that 'tis much better for a woman to be masculine and a very Amazon and lewd after this fashion, than for a man to be feminine, like Sardanapalus or Elagabalus and many another their fellows in sin.[189] For the more manlike she is the braver is she. But concerning all this I must refer me to the decision of wiser heads.

Monsieur du Guast and I were reading one day in a little Italian book, called the *Book of Beauty*, writ in the form of a dialogue by the Signor Agnolo Firenzuola, a Florentine, and fell upon a passage wherein he saith that women were originally made by Jupiter and created of such nature that some are set to love men, but others the beauty of one another.[190] But of these last, some purely and holily, and as an ensample of this the author doth cite the very illustrious Margaret of Austria, which did love the fair Laudomia Forteguerri, but others again wantonly and lasciviously, like Sappho the Lesbian, and in our own time at Rome the famous courtesan Cecilia of Venice. Now this sort do of their nature hate to marry, and fly the conversation of men all ever they can.

Hereupon did Monsieur du Guast criticize the author, saying 'twas a falsehood that the said fair lady, Margeret of Austria, did love the other fair dame of a pure and holy love. For, seeing she had taken up her rather than others which might well be equally fair and virtuous as she, 'twas to be supposed it was to use her for her pleasures, neither more nor less than other women that do the like. Only to cover up her naughtiness she did say and publish abroad how that her love for her was a pure and holy love, as we see many of her fellows do, which do dissemble their lewdness with suchlike words. This was what Monsieur du Guast did remark thereanent; and if any man doth wish to discuss the matter farther, well! he is at liberty to do so [*Laudomia Forteguerri].

This same fair Margeret was the fairest princess was ever in all Christendom in her day. Now beauty and beauty will ever feel mutual love of one sort or another, but wanton love more often than the other. She was married three times, having at her first wedlock espoused King Charles VIII of France; secondly John, son of the King of Aragon; and thirdly the Duke of Savoy, surnamed the Handsome.[191] And men spake of them as the handsomest pair and fairest couple of the time in all the world. However, the Princess did have little profit of this union, for that he died very young and at the height of his beauty, for the which she had very deep sorrow and regret, and for that cause would never marry again. She it was had that fair church built which lieth near Bourg en Bresse, one of the most beautiful and noble edifices in Christendom. She was aunt to the Emperor Charles V, and did greatly help her nephew; for she was ever eager to allay all differences, as she and the Queen Regent did at the treaty of Cambrai, whereunto both of them did assemble and met together there. And I have heard tell from old folk, men and women, how it was a beauteous sight there to see these two great princesses together. Cornelius Agrippa hath writ a brief treatise on the virtue of women, and all in panegyric of this same Margeret.[192] The book is a right good one, as it could not but be on so fair a subject and considering its author, who was a very notable personage.

I have heard a tale of a certain great lady, a princess, which among all her maids of honor did love one above all and more than the rest. At first were folk greatly surprised at this, for there were plenty of others did surpass her in all respects. But eventually 'twas discovered she was a hermaphrodite, which did give her the means of pleasure without any sort of inconvenience or scandal. 'Twas quite a different thing than with the tribades; the enjoyment was deeper and keener altogether.

I have heard a certain great lady also named as being hermaphrodite. She hath a virile member, but very tiny; yet hath she more of the woman's complexion, and I know by having seen her she is very fair. I have heard sundry famous doctors say they have seen plenty such, and found them especially lecherous. (109–17)

Second Discourse: On Which Pleases More in Love, Touching, Seeing, or Speaking
Others have the labia long and drooping more than is a Turkey-cock's comb when he is angry. This is the case with not a few women I have heard of—and not only mature women, but maids also.... As to these same exaggerated labia, I did once ask the reason thereof of an excellent physician, who did tell me this. Whenas maids or women are in rut, they will be for ever touching these parts, handling, twisting, twining and dragging out and pulling down the same, because being brought in contact they will so afford them much greater pleasure.

Maids and women of this sort would be very well in Persia, but not in Turkey, seeing that in Persia the women are circumcized, because their natural organ doth in some manner which I scarce understand, resemble the virile member, or so they say. But on the other hand, in Turkey, the women are never so treated; and for this cause the Persians do call them heretics, for not being circumcized, and seeing their affair, so they allege, hath no shape at all; nor do they find any pleasure in looking at these parts as the Christians do. This is what travellers who have journeyed in the East tell us. Women and girls of this sort, according to what this same physician was used to say, are very like to do the frigging trick, the *donna con donna*—lady with lady. (152–53)

Sixth Discourse: On How We Should Never Speak Badly of Women, and the Consequences of Doing So

Indeed I have heard a very great nobleman and soldier say, how that there be three things a wise man ought never to make public, . . . if he be wronged therein. Rather should he hold his tongue on the matter, or better still invent some other pretext to fight upon and get his revenge–unless that is the thing was so clear and manifest, and so public to many persons, as that he could not possibly put off his action onto any other motive but the true one. The first is, when 'tis brought up against a man that he is cuckold and his wife unfaithful; another, when he is taxed with buggery and sodomy; the third, when 'tis stated of him that he is a coward, and that he hath basely run away from a fight or a battle. All three charges be most shameful, when a man's name is mentioned in connexion therewith; so he doth fight the accusation, and will sometimes suppose he can well clear himself and prove his name to have been falsely smirched. But the matter being thus made public, doth cause only the greater scandal; and the more 'tis stirred, the more doth it stink, exactly as a vile stench waxeth worse, the more it is disturbed. And this is why 'tis alway best, if a man can with honor, to hold his tongue, and contrive and invent some new motive to account for his punishment of the old offence; for such like grievances should ever be ignored so far as may be, and never brought into court, or made subjects of discussion or contention. Many examples could I bring of this truth. (272)

Robert Burton (1577–1640)

In *The Anatomy of Melancholy*, an originary text for psychology, Robert Burton includes same-sex sexual behaviors in the range of "nasty sins" or "evils" of lust, whereby sexual desires overpower so-called natural bounds. Yet his strong interests in *astrology tend to subvert restrictive definitions of amorous "nature." The second son of gentry, Burton obtained several degrees including Bachelor of Divinity (1614) from Christ Church College at Oxford, and until his death he remained there as a Student or appointed scholar in residence (a position requiring celibacy), while also holding various ecclesiastical livings. His strangely delightful *Anatomy*, first published in 1621 and progressively enlarged through five subsequent revised editions, made him famous. Though revolving around causes, implications, and cures of the melancholic state, it also generally satirizes human frailties, and draws broadly on many disciplines including literary studies, history, theology, moral philosophy, astrology, and medicine. Burton describes his work as a macaronic cento, a compilation of citations from others' books, but both its style and thought are distinctive.

Since Burton's desired readership had an extensive knowledge of Latin, his *Anatomy* mixes that language with English and not only quotes both ancient and contemporary Latin sources without translation but also shifts to Latin for sections he considered unsuitable for easy general access—particularly commentary on sex. He most fully addresses homoeroticism in the section "How Love Tyrannizeth over Men" in Partition Three, which deals with amorous and religious melancholy. Burton uses Latin for the whole passage involving same-sex relations to betoken his disgust and ensure that only those who are relatively learned (presumed more disciplined and stable) can understand it. He significantly reverts to English for a discussion of love between opposite sexes, even in forms he considers deplorably lustful. Wherever Burton uses Latin here, I have substituted English; where he uses Latin mainly to restrict uneducated access to extensive passages, I enclose them in square brackets.

Although Burton considers marriage sacrosanct, he nonetheless acknowledges that sexual passions readily exceed any intentions or attempts to limit them. Is it really in love's nature, his account implicitly asks, to have "natural" bounds? According to sexual orthodoxy of the time, God created and defined nature, and thus established amorous norms by which all must rightly abide; any difficulties in doing so culpably arise from the Fall and human sin, particularly the species of lust. However, Burton's own view seems not to have been so settled, for he was also a committed astrologer. In the next section, "Causes of Heroical Love," he immediately explains that the stars powerfully influence amorous inclinations. Those at whose birth Venus and Saturn are in certain celestial positions thus innately tend toward male same-sex desire; the nature of nature may vary, and love itself has different natures in different persons. As this material could challenge sexual orthodoxies, so Burton presents it in Latin, then reverts again to English.

The Anatomy of Melancholy[193] *(1621)*

How Love Tyrannizeth over Men. Love, or Heroical Melancholy, His Definition, Part Affected

You have heard how this tyrant Love rageth with brute beasts and spirits; now let us consider what passions it causeth amongst men.

"Outrageous Love, to what do you not compel mortal hearts?"[194] How it tickles the hearts of mortal men, "I quake to tell of it,"[195] I am almost afraid to relate, amazed, and ashamed,[196] it hath wrought such stupend and prodigious effects, such foul offenses. Love indeed (I may not deny) first united provinces, built Cities, and by a perpetual generation makes and preserves mankind, propagates the Church; but if it rage, it is no more Love but burning Lust, a Disease, Frenzy, Madness, Hell. "'Tis death, 'tis an incurable compulsion, 'tis a mad rage."[197] 'Tis no virtuous habit this, but a vehement perturbation of the mind, a monster of nature, wit, and art, as Alexis in Athenaeus sets it out: "masculinely bold, femininely timid, furiously impetuous, with trouble diminished, a honey of gall, a delectable beating," and co.[198] It subverts kingdoms, overthrows cities, towns, families; mars, corrupts, and makes a massacre of men; thunder and lightning, wars, fires, plagues, have not done that mischief to mankind as this burning lust, this brutish passion. Let Sodom and Gomorrah, Troy (which Dares Phrygius and Dictys Cretensis will make good),[199] and I know not how many cities bear record. "For it happened before Helen,"and co.,[200] all succeeding ages will subscribe: Joan of Naples in Italy,[201] Fredegunde and Brunhalt in France,[202] all histories are full of these Basilisks. Besides those daily monomachies,[203] murders, effusion of blood, rapes, riot, and immoderate expense, to satisfy their lust, beggary, shame, loss, torture, punishment, disgrace, loathsome diseases that proceed from thence, worse than calentures[204] and pestilent fevers, those often Gouts, Pox,[205] Arthritis, palsies, cramps, Sciatica, convulsions, aches, combustions, and co., which torment the body, that feral melancholy which crucifies the Soul in this life, and everlasting torments in the world to come.

Notwithstanding they know these and many such miseries, threats, tortures, will surely come upon them, rewards, exhortations, to the contrary; yet either out of their own weakness, a depraved nature, or love's tyranny which so furiously rageth, they suffer themselves to be led like an ox to the slaughter [Prov. 7:22]. "The descent to the underworld is easy."[206] They go down headlong to their own perdition, they will commit folly with beasts, men "leaving the natural use of women," as Paul saith, "burned in lust one toward another, and man with man wrought filthiness" [Rom. 1:27].

[Semiramis with a stallion, Pasiphae with a bull, Aristo Ephesius meddled with a she-ass, Fulvius with a mare, others with dogs, goats, and co., from which cause monsters were born sometimes, Centaurs, Silvanuses, and, to the terror of men, prodigious specters. And not only with animals, but men have amongst themselves this business, which sin is commonly called Sodomy. And in former times this vice was frequent among Orientals, the Greeks obviously, the Italians, Africans, Asians. Hercules had Hylas, Polycletus, Dion, Pirithous, Abderus, and the Phrygian; and others relate that Eurystheus was loved by Hercules.[207] Socrates used to visit the crowded Gymnasium on account of the beautiful young men, and he feasted his eyes on the disgraceful spectacle, as the *Philebus, Phaedo, Rivals, Charmides,* and remaining Dialogues of Plato testify with abundant evidence.[208] Indeed, about that same Socrates Alcibiades says, "I fall silent willingly, but I am also averse; he presents such a stimulus to lust."[209] But Theodoret censured this in the last chapter of *Graecarum affectionum curatio.*[210] And indeed Plato himself marvels at his Agathon, Xenophon at

Clinias, Virgil at Alexis,[211] Anacreon at Bathyllus. However, about Nero, Claudius, and the portentous lusts of others of published memory, I might choose examples from Petronius, Suetonius, and others; you may expect such examples here, whenas they would exceed all belief; "but I complain of ancient ills."[212] Among the Asians, Turks, Italians, the vice never more frequent than at this present day[213]; Sodomy the Diana of the Romans[214]; shops of these things everywhere among the Turks, "who sow their seed among the rocks,"[215] ploughing the desert. And frequent complaints about this business even in the married state, unlawful copulations in the part opposite to the one which the magistrates approve, reversing the shoe, so to speak.[216] Nothing a more familiar sin among the Italians, who, following both Lucian and Tatius,[217] defend themselves in written volumes. Giovanni della Casa, Bishop of Benevento, calls it a divine labor, an agreeable sin, and glories in the practice, even with Venus not to be otherwise used.[218] Nothing more familiar among monks, Cardinals, priests, than this rage even to death and madness.[219] Because of the love of boys Angelo Poliziano laid violent hands on himself.[220] And admittedly, the extent to which this detestable sin has raged among us, within our fathers' memory, is horrible to relate! When indeed, in the year 1538, "the most prudent King Henry VIII had the venerable Doctors of Laws, Thomas Lee and Richard Layton, visit the cloisters of cowls, colleges of priests, of votaries, and co., among them were discovered so many whore-hunters, catamites, debauchees, buggers, boy-things, pederasts, Sodomites" (I use the words of Bale), "Ganymedes, and co., that in every one of them you may be sure of a new Gomorrah."[221] But see, if you will, the catalogue of these things in Bale: "girls" (he saith) "are not able to sleep in their beds on account of the necromantic Friars." If it is thus among votaries, monks, puny holy men, what deed, I ask you, should you suspect in the market, in the palace? What among nobles, what in brothels, how much foulness, how much filth! I do not speak, meanwhile, of those obscenities, the truly scarce-nameable self-defilements of the monks, those masturbators.[222] Rodrigo de Castro proclaims that, to be excited to Venus, they take turns scourging each other with whips, and then they have those Spintrians, Succubae, dancing girls,[223] and those foolish little women with wanton loins, Tribades, that mutually rub themselves, and even Eunuchs besides, to fulfill Venus, they have those artificial masculine members.[224] Indeed (what might amaze you more), a woman of Constantinople, desperately in love with another woman, not so long ago, dared a thing frankly incredible: with altered countenance she impersonated a man, entered into talk of marriage, and soon was married. But consult the author himself, Busbecq.[225] I omit those Egyptian Salinarios that lie with the cadavers of beautiful women; and their mad lust, who desperately love even idols and images.[226] The fable of Pygmalion in Ovid is well known.[227] In Hegesippus on the Jewish

Wars, Paulina and Mundus[228]; Pontius, legate of Caesar (consult Pliny), who is, I infer, the same one that crucified Christ, so inflamed with lust by the pictures of Atalanta and Helena that he would have stolen them away, if the nature of the wall on which they were painted had allowed it.[229] Another madly loved the statue of Good Fortune, saith Aelian[230]; another that of Bona Dea.[231] And no part free from disgrace, but rather "given over to shame" (as Seneca says), "no orifice excepted from lust."[232] Elagabalus admitted lust through all the openings of his body, saith Lampridius.[233] Hostius made certain looking glasses, and arranged them in such a way that, when he would submit to a man, Hostius could see all his partner's movements from behind, and the falsely magnified size of the member would delight him just as much as if it had been genuine. And Hostius experienced a man and a woman at the same time, which to speak of is a filthiness and detestable.[234] What Plutarch's Gryllus saith in countering Ulysses is plain truth: "To this day among us neither has male loved male, nor female loved female, as many among your memorable and famous heroes have done: as Hercules (I shall make vile utterances), following a beardless comrade, forsook his friends, and co. Your lusts cannot be restrained within their natural boundaries; indeed, like overflowing rivers, they produce fierce foulness, tumult, and confusion of nature in the matter of Venus. For men have entered goats, swine, and mares, and women have been inflamed with a mad love of beasts, whence Minotaurs, Centaurs, Silvanuses, Sphinxes," and co.[235] But so that I may not teach by means of that which is to be confuted, or put forth things which it is not fitting for all to know (truly, not unlike Rodrigo,[236] I would wish to have written these things for the learned only); and so that I should not write of foul sin, and co., for light wits and depraved minds: prepare you to speak, to sully whomever with sordid matters—I no longer wish to do so.][237]

I come at last to that Heroical Love, which is proper to men and women, is a frequent cause of melancholy, and deserves much rather to be called burning lust than by such an honorable title. There is an honest love, I confess, which is natural, "a secret snare, captivating the hearts of men, so that they are not able to be without women," as Christopher Fonseca proves,[238] a strong allurement, of a most attractive, occult, adamantine property, and powerful virtue, and no man living can avoid it. "And he who hath not felt the power of love is either a stone or a beast;" he is not a man, but a block, a very stone, "either a God or a Nebuchadnezzar," he hath a gourd for his head, a pepon[239] for his heart, that hath not felt the power of it,[240] and a rare creature to be found, one in an age, "whom no girl's beauty ever affected,"[241] for "we have all been mad once,"[242] dote we either young or old, as he [i.e., Chaucer] said,[243] and none are excepted but Minerva and the Muses: so Cupid in Lucian complains to his Mother Venus that, amongst all the rest, his arrows could not pierce them.[244] But this nuptial love is a common passion, and honest, for men to love in the way of marriage; as matter seeks form, so woman man.[245] You know marriage is honorable, a blessed calling, appointed by God himself in Paradise, it breeds true peace, tranquillity, content and happiness, than which no holier union exists, or ever did, as Daphnaeus in Plutarch could well prove, and which gives immortality to the human race,[246] when they live without jarring, scolding, lovingly, as they should do.

> Thrice happy they, and more than that,
>   Whom bond of love so firmly ties,
> That without brawls till death them part,
>   'Tis undissolved and never dies.[247]

[Burton further says the husband should rule the wife as her head; she should mirror her spouse's moods.]

... But this love of ours is immoderate, inordinate, and not to be comprehended in any bounds. It will not contain itself within the union of marriage or apply to one object, but is a wandering, extravagant, a domineering, a boundless, an irrefragable, a destructive passion: sometimes this burning lust rageth after marriage, and then it is properly called Jealousy; sometimes before, and then it is called Heroical Melancholy. It extends sometimes to corrivals, and co., begets rapes, incests, murders: Marc Antony ravished his sister Faustina, Caracalla his stepmother Julia, Nero his mother, Caligula his sisters, Cinyras his daughter Myrrha, and co.[248] But it is confined within no terms of blood, years, sex, or whatsoever else.... [Burton recites cases of amorous excesses, almost all heteroerotic.]

But to enlarge or illustrate this power and effects of love is to set a candle in the Sun. It rageth with all sorts and conditions of men, yet is most evident among such as are young and lusty, in the flower of their years, nobly descended, high fed, such as live idly, and at ease; and for that cause (which our Divines call burning lust) this mad and beastly passion,[249] as I have said, is named by our Physicians Heroical Love, and a more honorable title put upon it, "noble love," as Savanarola styles it, because Noble men and women make a common practice of it, and are so ordinarily affected with it....[250] [Burton finally reviews authorities on the nature of heteroerotic amorous passion and its origins within the body, defining it primarily as a malady of the imagination and reason.]

Causes of Heroical Love, Temperature, Full Diet, Idleness, Place, Climate, and Co.
Of all causes the remotest are stars. Ficino saith they are most prone to this burning lust that have Venus in Leo in their Horoscope, when the Moon and Venus be mutually aspected, or such as be of Venus' complexion.[251] Plutarch interprets Astrologically that tale of Mars and Venus[252]; in whose genitures Mars and Venus are in conjunction, they are commonly

lascivious, and if women, queans,[253] as the good wife of Bath confessed in Chaucer: "I followed aye my inclination / By virtue of my constellation."[254]

But of all those Astrological Aphorisms which I have ever read, that of Cardano is most memorable, for which, howsoever he be bitterly censured by Marin Marsenne, a malapert Friar,[255] and some others (which he himself suspected),[256] yet methinks it is free, downright, plain and ingenuous. In his eighth Geniture or example, he hath these words of himself: ["When Venus, Saturn, and Mercury are in conjunction, with Saturn's influence exalted by Mercury, continual thoughts of lecheries so prevail with me that I never rest." And somewhat later: "lecherous thoughts torment me perpetually, and in that it is not permissible to fulfill my thoughts in deed, or would be shameful, by means of continual thought I was deceived into pleasure." And in another place he saith: "because of the dominion of the Moon and Mercury, and commingling of the rays of Saturn, my wit was profound but lascivious, and I was foul and given to shameful lust."] So far Cardano of himself,[257] who confesses this in order to be useful to students of this subject, and for this he is traduced by Mersenne, whenas in effect he saith no more than what Gregory Nazianzen[258] of old to Chilo his scholar: ["women to be wondered and marvelled at offered themselves to me, the soundness of my chastity was tested by their surpassing elegance and manifest grace. And indeed I avoided the sin of fornication, but I defiled the virgin flower of my pure heart in my secret thoughts." But to the point. Those at whose birth Venus is in a masculine sign, and within the house of Saturn or in opposition, and co., are more prone to masculine venery.[259] Ptolemy in his *Tetrabiblos* has very many and special aphorisms about these matters, far away strengthened through long uncertain use and from experience much perfected, saith his commentator Cardano. In his book on astrology Thomas Campanella heapeth up many excellent aphorisms in his remonstrances against amatory madness,[260] which any who will may consult. The chiromancers conjecture much from the girdle and mount of Venus; for their comments you may consult, if you wish, Joannes Taisnier, Joannes Indagine, Rudolph Göckel the younger, and others.][261]

[Reviewing factors conducive to amorous passion, including those of body, mind, age, location, climate, class, and diet, Burton concludes "adultery, incest, sodomy, and buggery" are "prodigious lusts" especially indulged by those "young, fortunate, rich, high fed, and idle."]

CHAPTER 9

The Sapphic Renaissance

> When I look at you for a moment, then it is no longer possible for me to speak; my tongue has snapped, at once a subtle fire has stolen beneath my flesh, I see nothing with my eyes, my ears hum, sweat pours from me, a trembling seizes me all over, I am greener than grass, and it seems to me that I am little short of dying.
>
> —Sappho, Fragment 31[1]

The revival of classical culture in the Renaissance also effected the rebirth of Sapphic and thus sexually sapphic knowledge. For many she seems to have been as iconic for love between women as she is today. So often do printed texts of the period make this connection that it seems to have been almost automatic for Latin and even to some extent vernacular readerships throughout Europe. Sir Philip Sidney (1554–1586) modeled Amazonian Zelmane's apparently same-sex lyrical adorations of beautiful Philoclea on both prosodic "sapphics" and Sappho's poem most obviously avowing sexual passion for a woman, sampled in this chapter's epigraph.[2] And *John Donne (1572–1631) composed "Sappho to Philaenis." Nevertheless, some contested sapphic understanding of Sappho, apparently because they found it too embarrassing or threatening when linked to high cultural achievement and feminine creative excellence. Yet as Renaissance enthusiasms for revivifying the classical past tended to discourage drastic misrepresentation or erasure of the ancient commentators, so Sappho's sapphism was acknowledged to an extent unrivaled until far into the nineteenth century.[3]

Sappho confronted male humanists with a poetic genius revered throughout antiquity and hence inescapably important; yet not only female (contrary to formerly common assumptions of masculine superiority), but also a renowned exemplar, at least traditionally, of sexual love between women. Particularly important for Sappho's Renaissance reception was the epistolary poem "Sappho to Phaon" apparently rediscovered in the early fifteenth century, controversially associated with Ovid as translator or author, and usually included in his *Heroides* since the sixteenth century (Greer, 125–33). Since that collection consists of likewise epistolary poems in which distraught legendary women address their absent male lovers, it readily subsumed "Sappho to Phaon." As represented in that poem, the poetess renounces her avowedly numerous sexual affairs with females to proclaim her devotion to handsome male Phaon instead, but despairs of his requital and commits suicide by hurling herself from an ancient lovers' leap, the Leucadian cliffs. Ovid's poetry had much early modern literary currency, and so this epistle obliged confrontation with her reputed same-sex affairs. Whereas it now appears to be Ovid's own composition inspired by some almost certainly fictitious Greek dramatic sources now lost, in the Renaissance "Sappho to Phaon" was widely considered his Latin rendering of a lost autobiographical poem by Sappho herself, addressing Phaon just before she jumped to her death (*Lilio Gregorio Giraldi). I suspect that former assumption was to some extent based on Catullus's known revision of Sappho's Fragment 31 into a lyric of his own (poem 51). When *Angelo Poliziano (1454–1494) lectured on "Sappho to Phaon" at the Florentine Academy in 1481, he reviewed ancient tribadic lore and frankly though censoriously acknowledged Sappho's reputed sapphism, while suggesting that the poem freely renders one she herself authored (Mueller, 188–89, Greer 128–29). Neolatin commentaries on Ovid's *Heroides* would have been standard printed sources of information on Sappho in the early Renaissance, and at least some significant editions of the late fifteenth and sixteenth centuries acknowledge her classical associations with sexual love between females (Mueller, 187–88, Andreadis, 29–30).

From the 1540s onward scholars began identifying, compiling, and publishing Sappho's extant texts and fragments, so that editions, Latin translations, and substantial biographical accounts canvassing ancient comment all came to circulate in print.[4] Though chiefly undertaken by males in the predominantly masculine languages of Latin and Greek, these enterprises raised Sappho's cultural profile and that of her reputed sapphism. Although no manuscript of her poems, written in the latter seventh century B.C.E., was discovered, the rhetorician Dionysius Halicarnassus had quoted one whole poem, "Longinus" and Plutarch most of another, and other ancient writers lines of many more. The source of my epigraph for this chapter, the passage reproduced by the latter two writers has particular sapphic importance because it voices the female speaker's urgent sexual desire for a certain woman.

Nevertheless, many writers sought to subject Sappho to sexual orthodoxy, and such maneuvers most often depended on Ovid's supposedly veracious epistle. By acknowledging her loves of women, Ovid's fiction at least enhanced Sappho's currency as an archetype of female homoeroticism. But it made even her turn out to want a male lover most, thus enabling early modern males to reconcile sapphic desires and practices with formerly common masculine suppositions that women need phallic penetration for full sexual satisfaction (*Brantôme). And as the sordid pleasures of inflicting poetic (in)justice might tempt, the appropriation of Ovid's tale could enable the narrower Renaissance moralists to bring her perceived sexual transgressions to the requisite "bad end." Her untrammeled erotic appetites thus appeared to precipitate a disaster admonishing all, especially women, against the violation of conventional morality. Likewise, after the earliest Renaissance editions of Ovid's "Sappho to Phaon," his Sappho's comment that her loves of females were "without blame" (*sine* *crimine*) was editorially amended to affirm the contrary: "Them have I loved, not without blame."[5] Vernacular translations followed suit. Including Sappho in *Gunaikeion*, a survey of feminine lives designed to furnish edifying examples of virtue and vice, Thomas Heywood (1573/4?–1641) summarizes the traditional biographical details and translates Ovid's entire verse epistle including "Sappho's" comments on her affairs with female lovers. Introducing Ovid's text, he urges its truth to life: before Sappho leaped, "she first in an Epistle thought by all the allurements of a woman's wit to call [Phaon] back again, . . . which Ovid in her behalf most feelingly hath expressed." "From that Rock she cast herself headlong into the sea and so perished," Heywood concludes. "For preposterous [i.e., unnatural] and forbidden Luxuries [i.e., lustfulnesses] which were imputed unto her, Horace calls her *Mascula Sappho;* yet many are of opinion this to be the same whom Plato terms the wise."[6]

However, to bolster moral conformity, some rejected even Ovidian Sapphic biography, for they insisted that such a poetic genius would epitomize conventional feminine virtue and must have been chaste, or at least took only male lovers, and only after her husband's death (*André Thevet). In deference to moral orthodoxy, ancient but probably spurious traditions of "the other Sappho," another woman from Lesbos who was a courtesan, poet-musician, or both,[7] could be used to detach the great poet from suicidal infatuation with Phaon, from tribadism, or from putative sexual misbehaviors generally. They became the deeds of her evil twin.

Despite such "antisapphic" deployments of Sappho, she remained the most famous exemplar of female same-sex love throughout the Renaissance. In sixteenth-century France, male and female poets who imitated her surviving poetry often followed Catullus by transferring her amorous standpoint to a masculine speaker, or rendered it heteroerotic in some other way (DeJean, 29–41). Yet Ovid among other classical authors told a well-known different story, endorsed in various early modern Sapphic biographies. Together with the new circulation of Sappho's poems and fragments, that tradition inspired a contrary sixteenth-century imitative vogue that was sapphic as well as Sapphic, for some leading male poets such as *Pontus de Tyard (1521–1605), *Pierre de Ronsard (1524–1585), and *Donne adopted feminine personas to evoke the lyrical energies of "the Tenth Muse" in avowing female same-sex love. Although Sappho's tribadism was often criticized or condemned, the very eagerness of some to appropriate her for moral warning or to dissociate her from same-sex sexual behaviors demonstrates her perceived power to authorize such love through her acknowledged genius, despite attempts of condemnation, and to challenge sexual orthodoxy. The latter potential of classical Sapphic doxology, so to speak, could facilitate the rejection of Ovid's and other dismissive or adverse portrayals of her sapphism, much as *Donne has her abandon Phaon to return fervently to women, depreciating male love. And in some ancient and Renaissance accounts her desperate love of Phaon was induced by his possession of a rare herbal talisman or by Venus's miraculous intervention, so that it did not imply any deliberate turn against loving women (*Giraldi).

In both ancient and early modern Latin texts, Sappho's sapphism was often so frankly asserted that it would have been very widely assumed in the sixteenth century even if it had not been further diffused in vernacular writings. Despite the disparities of Latin and vernacular literacies and illiteracies in the Renaissance according to rank and gender, we must also allow for oral exchanges, for these, as in the case of prostitutes and their clients, could readily cut across social categories in sexual connections. Ovid's much-read "Sappho to Phaon" would in itself have sufficed to ensure Sappho's sapphic reputation among Latinists and their social circles, and George Turberville's English translation of the *Heroides*, for example, was published in seven editions between 1567 and 1600. When Sappho tells Phaon she has abandoned her feminine loves, Turberville makes clear they were amorously serious and many, much as in Ovid:

> Pyrino is forgot,
>   ne Dryads do delight
> My fancy: Lesbian lasses eke
>   are now forgotten quite.
> Not Amython I force,
>   nor Cydno passing fine:
> Nor Atthis, as she did of yore,
>   allures these eyes of mine.
> Ne yet a hundred mo
>   whom (shame ylaid aside)[8]
> I fancied erst: thou all that love
>   from them to thee hast wried.[9]

Sappho's archetypal sapphism entered printed vernacular sixteenth-century writings at least as early as *Agnolo Firenzuola (1493–1543). For *Brantôme (1540?–1614), an expert witness on late-sixteenth-century French courtly discourses of sex, the association of Sappho and Lesbos with women loving women is so strong that he refers to all such women, of whatever time, as "lesbians."

Subsequent readings sample Renaissance portrayals and effects of Sappho's reputation and literary significance. Poems of *Tyard, *Ronsard, and *Donne epitomize her sapphic impact on literature. The Neolatin Sapphic biography by *Lilio Gregorio Giraldi (1479–1552) was probably the most learned, comprehensive, and influential of the period. Indicating how challenging indeed her reputed sapphism and sexual freedoms could seem, *André Thevet (1502/4?–1590) reclaims her life for heteroerotic norms and devoted marital domesticity. Yet *Tanguy Le Fèvre (1615–1672) biographically reports her same-sex amours with an indulgence comparable to Tyard's, Ronsard's, and Donne's earlier poetic sapphisms. Le Fèvre's relatively positive attitude seems chronologically accidental, not indicative of any trend, for Sappho's sexual love of females appears to have been more openly and less pejoratively treated in the sixteenth century than the seventeenth, and further repressions ensued (cf. Andreadis, 31–37;

DeJean, 23). Women too could find Sappho's association with sapphism prob-lematic: Le Fèvre's own daughter Anne Le Fèvre Dacier (1654–1720), also a noted Hellenist, quickly reconfigured her father's Sappho so that the ancient role-model of feminine literary creativity pursued only heteroerotic loves, thus becoming more conventionally respectable (DeJean, 57–58).

Lilio Gregorio Giraldi (1479–1552)

Sappho's most authoritative Renaissance biography appeared in Lilio Gregorio Giraldi's collection of ancient Greek and Roman literary lives, *De historia po-etarum* (1545). A scholar-poet expert in Greek as well as Latin, he resided at various times in Ferrara (his birthplace), Naples, Milan, Bologna, Modena, and Rome. In 1514 he was appointed an apostolic protonotary or chief custodian of papal records at Rome, but fled in 1527 when the city was sacked, reportedly losing his library. He gained an international reputation for profound classical learning through his prolific publications such as a major mythography first published in 1548, *De deis gentium* (On the Gods of the Pagans), and *De historia poetarum*, among others. Issued in 1551, his *De poetis nostrorum temporum* (On the Poets of Our Times) remains an important reference source on sixteenth-century Neolatin poets. When Sappho's major sixteenth-century editor, Henri Estienne, gathered all her known texts in his edition of the nine Greek lyric poets (published in many editions after the first in 1560), he included an abbreviated version of Giraldi's account of her: the first three paragraphs as presented here, and some of the ensuing comments on her works, meters, and ancient literary reputation.[10]

Taking Sappho's amours with females almost for granted, mainly on the au-thority of Horace and Ovid, Giraldi rejects a competing claim that Horace's Sapphic epithet "masculine" (*mascula*) refers not to her sexual behavior but literary prowess. As Giraldi reports here, Ovid's portrayal of Sappho in his verse epistle "Sappho to Phaon" (almost certainly fictional) was commonly thought based on a lost poem by Sappho herself, addressing Phaon, and thus strongly influenced conceptions of her throughout the Renaissance. As Ovid's text as-signs her extensive sexual affairs with females, so such love appeared almost unavoidably Sapphic. And in a context about sexual indulgence in the *Tristia* Ovid demands, "What did Lesbian Sappho teach the girls if not love?"[11] The various biographies in *De historia poetarum* appear as dialogues between Giraldi himself and an interlocutor named Piso, and despite Giraldi's own disapproving remarks about Sappho's love life, he makes Piso conclude that all women should take pride in her. And yet from these males' androcentric viewpoint, Sappho is a great woman because she is "comparable to men."

Chronicles of Poets Both Greek and Roman[12] *(1545)*

Now let us speak of Sappho, whom Strabo praises to the extent of asserting that when it came to the art of poetry, no woman was ever in the slightest degree her peer; and Eustathius in his commentaries affirms the same.[13]

She was the daughter of Scamandronymus by his wife Cleïs. Others, such as Suidas, declare [that she was the daughter] of Simon; still others of Euminus or Eumenes; others, of Erygius or Eucrytus; others, of Semus; others, of Camon; and others (that I might convey everyone's opinion to you) of Etarchus.[14] Nonetheless it was generally held, and believed by most, that [she was the daughter] of Scamandronymus, and Herodotus in his *Histories* agrees with this.[15] She had three brothers: Larychus, Eurigion and Charaxus. Of these, she celebrated Larychus in her poetry as one who served wine in the town-hall of Mytilene, which Athenaeus also describes.[16] But she took to berating Charaxus because he shamelessly loved the courtesan Rhodopis (who was once the fellow-slave of Aesop of Phrygia, the author of the fables) and so passionately that he squandered almost his entire inheritance on her. Herodotus, Pliny, Strabo and many others extol this courtesan's pyramid.[17] And so on account of this little whore, Sappho attacked her brother Charaxus with hatred, and in verse. Athenaeus criticized Herodotus [on this point], but you should be aware that Strabo plainly agrees with Herodotus that Rhodopis and Doricha were one and the same courtesan beloved by Charaxus.[18] Yet they were in fact two people: Rhodopis was of Thressan stock, and Doricha was from Naucratis. Nor was it Rhodopis that sent the spits to Delphi, but rather Doricha: Athenaeus demonstrated this by means of the epigram of Poseidippus.[19]

But let us set aside these matters and return to Sappho herself, who married a man called Cercolas. Some incorrectly call him Cercyllas, and if the Greek authors are right, he was a very wealthy man from the island of Andros. She had a daughter by him, named Cleïs; but after his death, Sappho acquired an unsavory reputation on account of her various love-affairs, so that she was commonly called a tribade (*tribas*).[20] She consorted shamelessly with lads and young girls, so that she is believed by some to have even been called a he-woman (*mascula*), and by Horace and Ausonius to have even performed the office of a man, turn and turn about, with girls.[21] However, there are some, Porphyrio amongst them,[22] who hold that this name was ascribed to her because of her devotion to poetry, in which she conducted herself as a man—as if there were not an almost countless number of other women who had practiced this art with great distinction! Others are of the opinion that she was called a he-woman because she boldly tackled the Leucadian Leap, which was reserved for men.[23] They say that Papinianus[24] proclaimed in the funeral ode for his father: "Fearless, dauntless Sappho / Dared the manly leap from the Leucadian cliff."

Suidas names three students of Sappho: Anagora of Miletus, Gongyla of Colophon, and Euneica of Salamis. And he says that she loved three young girls: Atthis, Telesilla and Megara.[25] But I have heard of numerous others, whose names are Pyrino, Mnais, Anactorie, Cydno, and Cyrene. And after these [she loved] Phaon, a young man of Lesbos who (Pliny relates) was beloved because of the root of the herb which we call *centumcapita*, and which resembles the [genitalia] of either sex. If the male form [of the herb] comes into the possession of men, they become loveable, and it was thus (he says) that Phaon of Lesbos was loved by Sappho.[26] After he sailed to Sicily, this Phaon was honored by Sappho with a most delightful poem, which the poet Ovid is believed to have imitated in the epistle which bears her name.[27]

Despairing of the love of Phaon, Sappho launched herself, I say, from the Leucadian Cliff into the sea. And we read that others had undertaken this Leucadian leap. . . .[28] Strabo writes in the tenth book of his *Geography* that there is a temple of Apollo near Leucada, where the leap is made which extinguishes the burning heat of love.[29] Ovid sings that Deucalion was the first to hurl himself from this place, driven by his love for Pyrrha: "This place obeys this law," he says.[30] But Menander writes that Sappho, raving with frenzied love, was the first to fling herself from the high rock at the god's behest.[31] However Charon of Lampsacus and Plutarch relate that Probus of Phocas, of the race of Codrus, was the first to make the leap.[32] Some authors of antiquity, and Strabo amongst them, say that Cephalus was the first to attempt this, impelled by his love for Pterela, daughter of Deioneus.[33]

Pi[s]o asks, "But did not all these people who flung themselves from that place perish?" To him I reply with a smile (for the question seems a childish one): Not at all! For we do not read that either Deucalion or Cephalus perished. But the women—Sappho and Calyce (of whom we shall speak in [the context of] the image of Stesichorus)—died; and therefore many consider that they dared to make the leap as men and not as women.[34] And they explained it in this way in the case of Statius' Sappho, whom we mentioned earlier; however, scholars cannot sufficiently agree concerning her.[35]

These matters concerning the Leucadian Leap are briefly relayed to you so that we may proceed with the discourse as planned, and first we shall repeat what Palaephatus relates about Phaon in *On Incredible Matters*.[36] "Phaon's business," he says, "was navigation. It befell one day that Venus, disguised as an old woman, asked Phaon whether he would carry her over the ferry. He agreed, and took her across immediately without asking any fee. As a reward, the goddess turned him from an old man into a youth, and indeed, into the fairest youth of all; and it is said that on account of this, Sappho afterwards loved him passionately." Aelian says virtually the same thing in his *Historical Miscellany*, and adds that Phaon was given a container full of ointment by the goddess. When he made use of this, he became extremely beautiful in the eyes of all. Therefore he was loved by the women of Lesbos to an astounding degree, and by Sappho most of all. But when in the end he was caught in the act of adultery, he paid the penalty.[37] But observe, I beseech you, with what deceits the demon treated the human race as his plaything before the Word became flesh, so that he could compel it to self-destruction. Lucian also recalls the fable of this Phaon in *The Dialogues of the Dead.*[38] And some turn what we have said about the container full of ointment into an allegory, as they do with Psyche's jar.[39] I believe that this passage from Plautus' *Braggart Warrior* alludes more plainly to the myth of Phaon than has been hitherto realized by the critics. He says, "For I know of no mortal save two— yourself and Phaon of Lesbos—who has been loved as much as you."[40] Others say that when Venus fell in love with Phaon, she hid him among the lettuces; so Callimachus and Cratinus declare, according to Athenaeus.[41] Others have turned this into an allegory, that those who dine on lettuce are rendered weaker in the work of Venus, and for this reason lettuce is called "the eunuch" by the Pythagoreans, as we reported to you, Pi[s]o, in our symbols of Pythagoras.[42] Some think that it was another Sappho who loved Phaon.[43] There are also some who write that she invented the plectrum.[44] Indeed, Menaechmus of Sicyon says that she invented the *pectis* (the same name as the musical instrument), which Athenaeus describes at length.[45]

But now let us say something about Sappho's writings. In the first place, she composed nine books of lyrics, epigrams, an elegy, iambics, monodes, and epithalamia, and some other works, and she employed the Aeolian manner of speech. The "Sapphic" meter is derived from her, as Hephaestion, Terentianus, Atilius and Diomedes observe; and further- more, the Aeolian meter and the antipaestichon were introduced by her, as Atilius and Terentianus write.[46] Moreover, Aristoxenus states that the Mixolydian mode was discovered by Sappho, and Plutarch, in his *On Music,* agrees.[47] However, some ascribe it to the pipe-player Pythoclei- des, and Lysis [ascribes it] to Lamprocles of Athens.[48] But truly does Demetrius of Phalerum write that Sappho possessed exceptional grace in her verse from the trope of parallelism and replication, which the Greeks call "anadiplosis," some examples of which he presents.[49] But Hermogenes too, when he speaks of sweetness of expression, gives her high praise, but especially when she addresses questions to her lyre, and it replies.[50] In his *Rhetoric,* Aristotle writes that when Alcaeus said, "I would like to say some- thing to you, Sappho, but modesty prevents me," she immediately replied, "Alcaeus, if you intend to say virtuous and honest things, and not something indecent or obscene, you will not offend against modesty."[51] Aristotle likewise ascribes this statement to Sappho: "Death is utterly evil, for had the gods not come to this conclusion, even they would die."[52] According to this argument, we [contrarily] say that death is good by "antistrophon," that is, by inversion of the argument, because God wished man to be subject to [death], in the way that Paul, the teacher of the gentiles, said that he longed for death.[53] But this is not relevant to our discourse, and so we would do better to attend to our poets.

Literary history relates that Sappho wrote to a wealthy, extravagant, but quite uneducated and ignorant woman that she [ie., the woman] would soon perish utterly because she had left no memorial of herself to posterity, nor any offspring (as Sappho put it) from the rose-gardens of the Muse.[54] Without question, this statement has merit, and it is applicable to everyone, not just to one particular woman. Didymus Chalcenterus,[55] a highly reputed Greek author, entertains doubts about [the existence of] Sappho, and would call her a sibyl, or rather, poetry [itself].

When I mention this, Piso declares, "O eminent woman! How greatly does that sex deserve by right to take pride in her, for who can doubt that she is comparable to men? And what do the lasses of our day have, save flabby habits and loose tongues. I do not say this of all of them, for I hear that even today some have won praise in this divine skill [of poetry] and in other good arts. But Lilio, if anything more about Sappho remains, please pass it on to us." I say that I will do this, in order that I may more swiftly pass on to the other lyric poets.

To begin with: at Mitylene they put the image of Sappho on their coins, as Pollux says.[56] As I mentioned earlier, the Greeks have ascertained that there are two women of this name, both of Lesbos: one was from Eresus and the other from Mitylene, and both were poets.[57] Athenaeus reproaches Hermesianax for holding that Sappho was a contemporary of Anacreon, when (Athenaeus says) she flourished in the time of Alyattes, the father of Croesus, whereas [Anacreon] lived in the time of Cyrus and Polycrates.[58] Then Piso asks, "And so is Sappho somewhat older than Anacreon?" Yes indeed, say I, if Athenaeus relates the truth, although in what he wrote concerning Sappho, Chamaeleon seems to think otherwise.[59] In his fictional work about Sappho, the comic poet Diphilus says that she was the lover of Archilochus and Hipponax.[60] However, Eusebius agrees with Athenaeus.[61] And this is what we say concerning Alcaeus and Sappho.[62]

André Thevet (1502/4?–1590)

*Giraldi's talk of Sappho's "shameful" loves seems relatively mild compared to André Thevet's account scandalized by tribadism. A younger son, Thevet was parentally consigned to a Franciscan monastery in Angoulême, his birthplace, at age ten, and later studied at the University of Poitiers. After travels in Spain, Italy, and Africa, he journeyed to the Levant from 1549 to 1552, then spent several months in Brazil between 1555 and 1556. Out of these experiences he launched a series of geographical works and travel narratives that produced considerable fame and controversy; after being released from monastic vows in

1559, he was appointed royal chamberlain and cosmographer (responsible for describing and mapping the earth's features). The account of Sappho appears in his collection of famous lives, *Les vrais portraits et vies des hommes illustres* (1584), selectively reissued in English in 1657, including a section on the great Lesbian. Thevet's attempt to "exonerate" Sappho from sapphism results from homophobic conviction that her tremendous literary achievement, which he ranks second only to Homer's, is incompatible with the debasement he imputes to female homoerotic behaviors. Noting the ancient story of another Sappho who was "very unchaste," Thevet implies that her reputation was confused with the major poet's.

True Portraits and Lives of Illustrious Men[63] *(1584)*

The Life of Sappho, the Lesbian Poetess

   Poetry was in such a height of esteem amongst the Ancients as that divers accounted the Poets to have been the first who have written concerning Divine, Natural, Moral, Political, and Military Affairs. Such a one was David the Royal Prophet, who ordained those which were under his obedience to celebrate the praises of God in Verses and Hymns and to sing such Psalms as he had composed. Such were Linus, Musaeus, and Orpheus among the Greeks. And if Poetry hath been so highly honored and valued as that Virgil himself accounted Musaeus to have been a Prophet and terms him a most signal Poet in a sublime degree,[64] I would willingly demand of those who endeavor to obscure that resplendency which themselves cannot behold, why the Poets were formerly called Diviners? Was it not by reason that it is manifest such an Art doth add unto man's intellects a more than ordinary wit? The interpretation which was formerly made of this word "Poet" (which in the Greek doth signify an Artist or expert Workman), what can it be but "skillful" or "advised"? And truly, a good Poet doth in all places deserve to be acknowledged for a very wise man. No one Science almost being a stranger unto him; wherefore Divine Plato calleth the Poets God's Interpreters.[65] Strabo himself, admiring this Science, saith that all the Philosophers, Law-Makers, and Historiographers have taken their fundamentals from Homer the Poet.[66]

   However, the effects of Poetry have not only by the Muses been infused into men (whereof France more than any other Country seems to abound, as Dorat, Ronsard, Baïf, Desportes, and several others) but also unto women, several of that Sex having most ingeniously employed themselves in that Art. And to avoid prolixity, I shall only give you the names of some of them who may serve as a precious ornament to that Sex. Among such as have therefore excelled in that Art we may well give Proba the first rank, wife to the Roman Consul, who being as Beautiful as Learned, did in the year of our Lord 424 couch in Heroic Verses the contents both of the Old and New Testament as far as the coming down of the Holy Ghost. Secondly

Corinna, who was Ovid's beloved. Elpis the wife of Boethius. Polla, wife to Lucan the Poet, who often helped her husband in his composure of his *Pharsalia*. Lesbia, Mistress to Catullus. Cornificia the Roman Poetess. Thesbia, who was named the compositress of Epigrams; and the other famous Poetess Corinna, who five times had the advantage of Pindar the Poet, who in the City of Thebes had publicly challenged her to contend in the Poetical Art, upon which and the other liberal Arts and Sciences once a year there was a solemnity of representations and prizes.

But why should we stand to extend this discourse by a Catalogue of so many worthy women? Since Sappho the Lesbianite (so surnamed from the place of her birth, viz. the Island of Lesbos, called Mitylene, seated in the Archipelagus or Mediterranean Sea, and usurped on the Venetians some fifty years since, by the Turks) may justly pretend to the second best place amongst those who have been versed in this Science. And whereby in her days she attained to so great a renown as that the Romans erected a Statue of Porphyry most richly ordained to eternize her memory; and Strabo himself had so good an opinion of her as that he deemeth no one woman may be compared unto her as to the Art of Poetry; which Eustathius doth also confirm in his Commentaries on Dionysius.[67] And indeed there are very few sorts of verses in which she excelled not, which caused me to insert her Picture in this place, which I ordered to be drawn after an old Medal of hers which I did purchase and bring from the said Island.[68] The like whereof was given (together with several others) unto the Baron de la Guard, at that time Ambassador for the King of France at Constantinople by Sultan Suleiman's chief Physician. She was very expert in the compounding of Lyric verses which she evidenced in several Epigrams, Elegies and other pieces, which were translated out of Greek into Latin; besides many others which were lost by the neglect of our Ancestors or by the destruction of the Cities and Towns of Italy, and specially of the Isle of Lesbos. She also did invent a certain kind of verses which are called Sapphics by her name. As to her Father, Authors do vary who he was; some say Scamandronymus, others Simon, others Eunonimus, or Eumenus, others Eerigyius, or Ecrytus, others Semus, others Camon, and others Etarchus.[69]

But for all these supposed Fathers, we must not therefore be induced to believe that she was a Bastard, nor that Cleis (who without doubt was her Mother) had miserably prostituted her Chastity to so many several men, it being only the uncertainty of Writers which hath caused these various suppositions concerning her Father. She had three brothers, viz. Larichus, Eurygius, and Charaxus; who although they were her brothers, yet our Poetess had several sentiments of them, for by how much she loved and cherished Larichus, by so much did she hate Charaxus, against whom she wrote several Invectives because he had associated himself with

Rhodopis the Thracian Whore, and with her had spent the greatest part of his Patrimony. Which is the ruin of all those who do suffer themselves to be inveigled by such infernal Hags who like Horse-leeches suck them dry, and are the cause that they are constrained to abandon all Amity, Concord, and brothership with their friends and Allies, to cleave unto such a kind of vermin. Sappho then was constrained to estrange herself from her brother by reason of a Whore. And those who read in Horace and Ausonius that Sappho was surnamed *mascula*[70] were mistaken in their most injuriously and calumniously laying to her charge that she abandoned herself too much unto men and women. Nor can I likewise bespeak her over-chaste or untainted, since she was too much surprised with the love of Phaon (though some believe it was the other Sappho called Erenea).[71]

However, I think it very unreasonable to suppose that she should have perpetrated that crime which will be better concealed than mentioned in this place; and those Authors assuredly were to blame when they gave her the surname of *mascula* and did not specify the reason why, seeming thereby only to imply that her Actions were more becoming a man than a woman. Or whether it was by reason of the rare verses which she composed; or for that she adventured to enter into those fair walks of Leucades unto which none but men durst ever approach.[72] But that which gave the greatest cause of this suspicion was that we read she had certain women who were her constant friends and companions, viz. Anagora, Milesiania, Gongyla of Colophon, Eunica of Salamis, Erymna, and several others. But and if upon that account we should suppose her guilty of that horrid crime which is laid to her charge, we might as well conclude that the other Sappho who was a company keeper as well as this our Lesbian should be as guilty as herself, and likewise all women in general who frequent company. Wherefore it is a great injury done to our Sappho to asperse her in this manner without any lawful reason or occasion, whereas the Divine Philosopher Plato did highly admire the dexterity and vivacity of her wit, as well as the profound knowledge wherewithal she was endowed and whereby she excelled all men and women how eminently learned soever they were.[73]

And to return to our Sappho again, we find that she was joined in Marriage unto an honest considerable man, abounding in wealth, named Cercola, or as others Cercylas, by whom she had one only daughter named Cleis, by her Grandmother's name. And during her husband's life there was not the least speech of any misdemeanor at all in her; but when she became a Widow some say (as we have already hinted) that she fell in love with a certain man called Phaon, who being gone into Sicily, and she mistrusting that he bore her not a reciprocal love equal to hers, fell into such a rage and impatiency that for to free herself from so disordinate a passion, she cast herself headlong from the top of a Rock into the Sea. And thus our famous Poetess did end her days, who lived in the year of the world 4684 and before our Saviour 515 years. At which time there flourished Xenophanes the Philosopher, Theognis and Pindar the Grecian Poets, and the choice Roman Matron Lucretia. This said Isle of Lesbos did breed a second Sappho called Erexcea, famous in the Art of Poetry, who invented the Cithern or Rebec and composed many Lyric verses, though she was very unchaste as several Writers have noted, and co.[74]

Pontus de Tyard (1521/2–1605)

In 1573 Pontus de Tyard published a poem in which he assumes the sapphic persona of a woman imploring her female beloved to return and requite her passion. The poet was the third son of a well-connected Roman Catholic family of old Burgundian nobility with a château at Bissy-sur-Fley, and studied in Paris. Groomed for an ecclesiastical career, he ultimately became bishop of Chalon-sur-Saône nearby, in 1578. Much influenced by the Neoplatonism of *Marsilio Ficino (1433–1499), Tyard published a diverse oeuvre from 1549 onward, including collections of poetry; philosophical treatises on poetry, music, the universe, and astrology; commentaries on the Bible; and in 1552 a translation of the *Dialoghi d'amore* by *Leone Ebreo (fl. 1460–1521). He was peripherally involved with the Pléiade, a variously constituted group of French poetic innovators active between 1549 and the late 1580s, focused on *Pierre de Ronsard (1524–1585). Tyard's love poetry apparently celebrates actual romances with women, especially one he names Pasithée, Pernette du Guillet. When residing in Paris in the late 1560s and for some time in the 1570s, he frequented the artistic and socially prestigious salon of the maréchale de Retz. The sapphic poem was first published in these circumstances in Paris, in Tyard's *Oeuvres poétiques* (1573). A royalist, he became a counselor to King Henri III, and after the latter's death in 1589, supported King Henri IV.

This amorous elegy of meditative melancholy features a speaker who conceives her same-sex mode of love as one more moral, more honorable, than the opposite-sex alternative. Early modern culture stressed feminine "honor," in the sense of chastity, as the female virtue par excellence, and Tyard's speaker reacts against the relentless sexual pressures of male lovers, ironically for them, by opting for a female. Although this feminine beloved turns out to be fickle, in accord with stereotypical early modern male views of females, the speaker's amorous devotion implicitly rebukes the stereotype so that her own principled example validates her same-sex desire. The speaker's passionate intensity indicates their love has been fully sexual. Although *Brantôme (1540?–1614) assumes sex between females is not dishonorable nor even potentially adulterous because, from his viewpoint, it is not really sex, Tyard's speaker associates the violation of feminine honor with loving males, and so her linkage of amorous honor with female same-sex love does not depend on Brantôme's rationale.

Elegy for One Woman Enamored with Another[75] *(1573)*

I had always thought that both Love and honor,[76] the two sole ardors that burn my heart, were able to kindle such a pretty flame, brighter than the brightness of the inner Soul. But I could not impress upon myself how those two fires should be aroused together: no matter how much beauty is the cause of Love, and in entire honor beauty be entire, it did not seem at all to me that one same beauty should serve both Love and honesty. I was saying: the beauty of my honor is within me, but not the beauty I must seek through Love, because the sole beauty to value from myself would only be to love my honor. But a Mistress must seek beyond herself the conquest of beauty given her by Love. So in me only the ardor of honor will have place; should I then flee the other God's ardor?[77]

Alas! Beauty of Love, should I seek thee amongst men? Oh no, I know our times too well. A man loves beauty but despises honor: the more beauty pleases him, the faster honor dies. And so, carefully cherishing honor alone, free, I disdained all amorous flame, until Love, offended too much by my freedom, set a subtle trap for me.

He enriches thy Spirit, he sweetens thy mouth and graces thy speech; in thine eyes he reposes, in thine hair he laces a knot never seen. And so he ties me to thee, he makes a fire kindle (oh, who will believe me!) of such new flame that, alas, Love enthralls me, woman, with woman.

Never before has Love slipped into another heart so softly, because intact honor retained her beauty not marked in the least, and the Lover was enjoying the beloved beauty in a subject the same. O what pleasure, if thou, so fickle, hadst not wished to love lightly! But cruel Love, having wounded me deeply, has fled and left me all empty, emptied of Love, and of affection. But, as he fills my heart with sad passion and just despite, indeed I must beg thee, ingrate, and thy freedom mocks me. Where is thy promised faith, thy vows of love? Where are the beautiful words thou hast invented, like those of a Pitho,[78] false and persuasive, which have enchained me, captive, by the ear?

Alas! How I have spoken in vain! How I have vainly fled all other Loves! How vainly I chose thee alone (contemptuous) as the sole pleasure of my most sweet life! How vainly I thought that times to come would consider us miraculous for centuries at length, and that, as an example unique in French history,[79] our Love would serve for eternal memory to prove Love of woman for enamored woman would seize the prize from male Loves! A Damon to Pythias, Aeneas to Achates, Hercules to Nestor, Chaerephon to Socrates, Hopleus to Dymas,[80] have certainly shown that true Love from man to man has been seen. For man and woman's Love there is such ample proof that I do not need to offer any example; but of woman and woman is not yet to be found such a rich treasure under Love's empire, and shall not be found, so frivolous one. Compared to my faith thine is deceitful, for never was there greater purity in Sky, greater ardor in fire, greater sweetness in honey, greater kindness present in the rest of nature, than in my heart, where Love fed his fill. But thine heart is harder than a Rock of the sea; more than a barbarous Scythian it is cruel. And the she-bear Callisto[81] does not see as much ice as thou hast in thy bosom; nor the changing face of Nocturnal Morpheus[82] has as many forms as the various thoughts of thine inconstant soul.

Alas! Let frustration sweep me far from myself! Open to Love, ingrate, open the door to Love! Suffer the sweet arrow that has pierced our hearts to lance once again thine too lightly touched; search in thy courses the passion that's passed, tighten the sweet knot that entwined the affection common to thee and to me, and let us rejoin those hands that swore faith: faith in my mind so assured, that it shall not in the least be betrayed by death. But if new Love kindles thee another flame, I beg Anteros, Anteros,[83] avenging God, that before the pain enclosed within my heart might transform me, and make me something other that I now am— either that my sad voice alone remains, wandering in the woods, or that my tearful sorrow soon distills me into a river or pours me in a spring— and while I tell to Stags and Deer, alone in this thick forest, ingrate, thy disdains—that thou might, consumed by desire for someone unworthy, languish in love and be loved not at all!

Pierre de Ronsard (1524–1585)

Pierre de Ronsard favorably presents love between women in an epistolary poem and its appended envoy, a sonnet, and so does another poem ascribed to him. Expressions of the Sapphic revival of the mid-sixteenth century, these writings evoke "the Tenth Muse" through their sapphic persona, subject matter, or both. The fourth or perhaps fifth son in a Roman Catholic family of minor nobility, Ronsard was born at the Château de la Possonière in the Vendôme, a household imbued with Italian Renaissance culture and values. After a brief schooling in Paris when he was nine, Ronsard became a page to various royal progeny beginning in 1536, and traveled to Scotland, England, and Alsace in French retinues and diplomatic missions between 1537 and 1540. Having become arthritic and partly deaf in 1543, he forsook an anticipated military career to pursue ecclesiastical advancement; his numerous benefices garnered later through patronage included the royal chaplaincy for King Henri II and King Charles IX. In the mid-1540s Ronsard resumed his studies, guided by the humanist scholar-poet Jean Dorat, and attended the Collège de Coqueret in Paris. After first publishing a collection of odes in 1550, the poet ranged through many genres, producing elegies, an unfinished epic, erudite cosmological and seasonal hymns, pastorals, anti-Huguenot polemics, and amorous sonnet sequences extolling particular women. A leading member of the Pléiade, a loose group of French humanist poetic reformers that originated in the late 1540s, Ronsard was the most celebrated French poet of the century, with significant literary influence in other countries. Despite having become unfashionable in the seventeenth and eighteenth centuries, he now appears to be one of the foremost poets of the French canon.

Ronsard first published his paired epistle and envoy treating sapphic love in his *Elegies, mascarades, et bergerie* (Elegies, Masquerades, and Pastorals) of 1565 and again in subsequent collections, but finally omitted them from his 1584 *Oeuvres*, whether because of the topic or stylistic reservations. Nevertheless, these two poems were reprinted posthumously in 1609 and thereafter. The longer poem commencing the pair is an erotic or love elegy, a poem of amorous lament or meditation, and also epistolary, somewhat along the lines of Ovid's *Heroides*. In a notional letter, Diane addresses her friend Anne, commenting on an enclosed medal that incorporates Diane's portrait. Protesting their separation, Diane vows that Anne is so much "mistress of my body, and of the spirit that will never leave you," that they have "only one common body," much as "Diane" both contextually suggests "double Anne" and symbolically incorporates "Anne." An envoy in the form of a sonnet follows, summing up the situation of the two female lovers. Although Diane, namesake of the goddess of chastity, insists their love is chaste, the poem's passionate emphasis on mutual interpenetrations suggests the contrary, and *Brantôme (1540?–1614) indicates one means of arguing that sex between females is not unchaste. The poem's speaker could possibly have such a viewpoint. Along with three related sonnets by Étienne Jodelle (1532–1573) published posthumously in 1574, these poems may address a particular sapphic affair at the French court in the mid-1560s. Following Plato's *Symposium*, like Ronsard in his linked epistle and envoy, Jodelle's sonnets assume that love has three modes: between male and female, two males, or two females.[84]

Ronsard may well have authored a further untitled elegy of sapphic love that appears in a seventeenth-century manuscript, the third poem in this selection. An apparently male speaker sympathizes with a woman's impending loss of her female beloved, and thus of their "amorous heat, games, and pleasure," due to the latter's marriage to a husband who will take his new wife far away. The speaker is unfazed by the lady's tribadic relationship.

Elegy[85] *(1565)*

To show you I wish wholly to serve you all my life, I beg you, please, accept from me this gift, a witness to my faith, given you with the deepest feeling, together with my heart, my portrait, and myself.

The present I give you is of metal that gleams like my faith, kindled purely by the brightness of your holy fire, and so lives in your friendship that nobody but you has a part in it, or half.

The gold is engraved: the love that imprints on me your virtue, which all the world esteems, has to the life engraved on me both your grace and your lovely portrait, made so to the life that I cannot live without seeing your presence everywhere before my face, for the farther your eyes are from me the closer I see them in spirit. On each side is engraved a temple, faithful examples of love: art must portray what can make us both happy.[86]

The temple of Apollo shows beautiful Coroebus and the violent passion for Cassandra with which Love so wounded him that at length he died for his lady.[87]

Oh happy death! May I die yours, as long as I remain yours: I would think myself happy when I died from loving you, for I serve you with such affection it will be forever immortal.

And so not time, nor separation, nor tempest, war, or the exertions of the jealous, whatever their rigor and strength, will efface that friendship I hold sacred.[88] Hence I have also placed around the temple this Latin verse that means: "My love and yours so chaste, / Shall overgo loves past."

In the other temple, dedicated to Diana (where Scythia has so often praised the love of two so uncommonly united), Orestes and his Pylades appear,[89] two companions who were such firm friends that blood poured out one for the other a hundred times, as prodigals, each wishing to consecrate his life to the other—noble hearts, and worthy of renown, who have made their name[90] famous through love.

Such friendship, whatever its perfection, is nowadays surpassed by my own, for I would die for you a hundred and a hundred thousand times. So I have used a Latin verse showing that such love cannot be found here, and these two should yield place to our faith which can outdo them.

Below the temple is the altar where the Greeks, aiming to kill the youth of Troy, swore not to slacken but to die for each other in battle.

On this altar I swear to serve you, Mistress, and if I am forsworn, may Heaven, scourge of shaken faith, strike me with lightning. The Roman verse makes clear I wish to be faithful on your behalf, and would pour out my blood for you on the altar in immortal sacrifice.

In the raised roundel[91] is depicted my image: pale, mute, and sad, that too painfully endures our separation, lacking the only good I want.

Ah! Would that the artist, to help me, had not made it mute! It could, at leisure and privately, tell you of my extreme distress at seeing myself sundered from you, my all, living apart from so much good that once used to come to me, now living only on memory and on the good name you bear, Madame, written in my soul.

But what need is there to give a dead portrait that cannot satisfy, when you are the Mistress of my body, and of the spirit that never leaves you?

Alas, so that seeing it you will at least grieve for me, who languish in grief for being unable to see your face before me any more; greater good[92] I could not have than to serve you in your presence and see you.

Since I wish to be within you so much I have no wish to notice others, the Roman verse around the portrait well expresses my perfect desire: "Anne lives fervently in her Diane, Diane in Anne: Time, which breaks walls and castles[93] and makes all yield, cannot untie two such lovely names."

The greatest good that God can give us here below is friendship that effaces all else.

Without friendship anyone would die, unable to live whole in the world, and so it is the good we must follow in the world, for neither blood makes us live as much, nor heart or spirit, as friendship does, once one has found her other half.[94]

Such, Mistress, you have felt in me, finding me sure in your love—for you and I are naught but one, and if we have only one common body, then your thought is mine and all my life follows yours. We have but one heart, one soul, one faith; I am in you and you are in me with a knot so tightly tied you can never forget me without forgetting yourself. So I have no fear or dread or care, as wholly in you I find myself, Madame, for my soul is entirely in your soul.

This good comes to me, as I acknowledge, without illusion, from the favor it has pleased you to show me, knowing myself to be much less than you. For you deign to join your greatness to me, most lowly, so that this bliss might make me equal to you through favor[95]: that is why I dedicate to you my blood, my heart, my portrait, and my life.

Envoy

> For me Anne's made of her lovely image
> A handsome gift that I hold full dear—
> Dear, for no one could ever hope to find
> Any that excelled such lovely portraiture.
>
> Diane in return herewith gives her picture   5
> To her mistress Anne, not to requite
> The gift, but always[96] to pledge
> That her service to her Soul will long endure.
>
> Upon each side the portrait is engraved
> With many an example of proven friends: 10
> With Coroebus, Pylades, and Orestes,
>
> And with an altar sacred to Friendship,
> As witness that so heavenly a love
> Has made of twin half-hearts a single whole.[97]

Elegy[98] *(written c. 1565)*

Thus the widowed turtle-dove is seen holding forth in sad song all alone, from tree to tree and bush to bush, in the loveliest month of the new season, accompanied by such grief for the loss of her dear companion that the amorous presents of Spring—grass, streams, flowers, greenery— are to her no longer welcome or pleasant. Lamenting in a muffled murmur and filling the woods and fields around, complaining of fortune and love at break of day when the sun awakes, when at night he sleeps beneath the waves, and at noon when extreme heat makes flowers lose their vigor and tint: on a dry tree, in all weather and at all times, comfortless she weeps for her companion, whom in early spring a fowler has netted to imprison and hold as a slave in the darkness of a cage, far from brooks, flowers, and underbrush.[99]

"No more brooks, flowers, and groves! No more," says the sorrowing bird, "as we used to do in the time of renewal, will we walk on the green field, nor on the borders of a flowery bank, nor by woods bristling with leaves, by streams carpeted by moss, where the chattering gravel moves, rolled by the waves of a clear spring. Everything displeases me. Green is no longer green to me, Spring is covered by black darkness. All the flowers are tainted by griefs, and the streams attune themselves to my laments. Since the day thou didst leave all is changed to tears and care, all is darkened by utter sorrow and nothing lives but grief itself. Day is night to me, the night seems day, and in this forest Love no longer reigns. Alas, I die! The same day that thou didst lose thy liberty I should have been captured, for I no longer live in myself. Or if I had been prisoner with thee, at least we would live prisoners together, and the grief that seems to me harder than death, far from my love, would be sweeter if shared by halves."

So lamented the widowed dove, complaining at length throughout the forest. And I grieve that you so soon lost her who is your happiness, indeed your all. For through mutual love you have but one heart and you have but one soul. So each living in mutual thought, your two bodies are but one, and thought so unites you that your two bodies make one same thing.[100] On the sad day of departure,[101] Heaven will wish to change the sky lest it see your loving tears and hear your grieving plaints. You would make a hard rock crack when saying the farewell that you will thus say:

"Dear Companion, nay my dear life, my blood, my heart, what cruel enmity thus removes and parts me from you and from the tie that was to us so sweet, no more nor less than if some forcing pincers drew forth my entrails, liver, lungs, blood, arteries, and heart, and left my whole body lifeless. I no longer live—I am but a mass, a mass of lead, a burden to the place, feeling nothing, for movement is frozen by this parting. Farewell thoughts! Farewell sweet words, and farewell speeches. Alas, Love, thou fly swifter than I, thou speed away and I cannot follow thy flight, so weak am I. Alas, halted in cruel anguish, I have wings above to fly with but lead below restrains me.[102] Memory alone supports me. In whatever part thou goest, my friend, thou hast me neither doubtfully nor by halves, but entire. And if I can travel such long roads by dint of thought, the victor who drags you by force will have nothing more than the body and husk, a cold mouth and a very cold kiss—coal without fire. For through our thoughts our amorous heat, games and pleasure, words and delights, will always do their office between us. And thought is worth more than a heavy body wearisome to itself. The gods, who have only thoughts, cannot see their joys injured. The body is nothing but a sleepy burden; the spirit is lively, active, noble. In losing you I am left without power; I have my being in you, you are my essence; I live in you, I no longer live in me. You are all my good and my sorrow, and your soul is so enclosed in my body[103] that of two bodies there is but one same thing. Every night when the sun goes to hide the day in shadow, your noble and gracious image will come by night to rejoice my spirit, and despite shadow and wind and that wretch,[104] often will I hold you in my arms, a little comforted by your loving, empty image. If the true cannot be there, at least the false can content me.[105] And so adieu! May hail and tempest, thunder and lightning, attend the head of this wretch who drags you so far away. May rocks, pebbles, brigands, and care dog his steps, and every hard thing, to avenge the torment I endure, so that, my Heart, you can return and the body forget its loss."[106]

Thus you will speak. When I see you weeping, grieving, sad, faint, loving, and your lovely tearful eyes turned aside, I will feel pity—not because of this departure, nor because of the farewell that robs us[107] of your soul—but because, Madame, I see you in such sorrow: lonely, pensive, and unable to think of anything but to dream of that good that is no longer a good and flies toward the frosty Alps like a long wind-driven flock of clouds. I would wish to drink, in a delicious draught, a small tear falling from your eyes down your lovely face, and in my breathing to make room in my heart for the sighs you spread on the air. When they have fallen before me, I will have some slight[108] part of you, changed despite yourself; and such part will eventually be worth so much that time will bring the whole.

To conclude: Madame, as I lament the loss of your dear companion, you will gain, if you please, a gallant servant[109] who, in seeking your friendship with an unfeigned love, will assuage your sad lament.

John Donne (1572–1631)

In the poem "Sappho to Philaenis" John Donne assumes Sappho's persona as she extolls sexual love between females, specifically with her beloved Philaenis. And some of his youthful verse correspondence seems homophile. Son of a prosperous London iron merchant and a great-niece of the Roman Catholic martyr Sir Thomas More, Donne proceeded to study at Hart Hall in Oxford in 1584, but took no degree, since that would have required pledging monarchical allegiance contrary to his recusant family's Catholic beliefs. He may then have traveled on the continent in the earl of Derby's entourage. After preparation at Thavies Inn, Donne entered Lincoln's Inn, one of the Inns of Court, in 1592. Though nominally for training lawyers, the Inns served mostly as gentlemanly finishing schools and means for seeking patronage. During the 1590s Donne abandoned Catholicism for the Church of England; advancement quickly followed, for he became secretary to Thomas Egerton, lord keeper of the great seal, in 1598, and a member of parliament in 1601. But by eloping that year with Ann More, seventeen-year-old daughter of Egerton's brother-in-law, Donne ruined his prospects. Though impoverished for many years thereafter, the couple meanwhile had twelve children, including two who were stillborn. After years of avoiding an ecclesiastical career, Donne became an Anglican priest in 1615 and rose rapidly within the church. He was appointed chaplain to King James I, and then dean of St. Paul's in 1621. At the time of his death Donne was awaiting promotion to a bishopric.

Aside from Donne's now famous love lyrics, mostly written between the 1590s and 1610, his poetry includes satires, epigrams, verse epistles, poetic meditations, and devotional lyrics. His voluminous prose includes paradoxical treatises, anti-Catholic polemics, and 160 extant sermons. Although his poetry had much literary influence in England from the 1590s through most of the seventeenth century, Donne's reputation collapsed thereafter, only to be canonized in the twentieth century. Since he did not write poetry for publication, most of it was known only from manuscript circulation until the first collected edition appeared in 1633.

Although *Pontus de Tyard (1521/2–1605) and *Pierre de Ronsard (1524–1585) may have made sapphism seem poetically fashionable, Donne's main intertextual model for "Sappho to Philaenis" was the poem "Sappho to Phaon" associated with Ovid and usually included in his *Heroides*, as discussed more fully in the introduction to this chapter. The latter poem's Sappho declares that she has abandoned her love of females to love the male Phaon; in a desperate plea for his return, she threatens to throw herself from a cliff into the sea. Although early modern accounts of the poetess often assumed that she thus died from frustrated love for a male, Donne refashions Sappho's Phaon or Phao into an amorous fling she discarded to regain the much greater (as Donne's Sappho insists) erotic delights of women. If she were fully coupled with Philaenis, Donne's Sappho implies, their union would reconstitute the wondrous state of the doubled female beings whose division by envious gods originated love between females as the desire and pursuit of their former wholes, according to Plato's Aristophanes in the *Symposium* (*General Introduction). Although recent queer-positive reactions have been divided, this poem documents the cultural possibilities, circa 1600, of favorably conceiving such love, advocating it, and hypothesizing a correlative sapphic sexual subjectivity.[110]

Even though "Sappho to Philaenis" appears in many manuscript collections of Donne's poetry and in the first edition of 1633, so that its links to the poet are as strong as central undisputed poems, some editors reject its authenticity.[111] But an untitled epigram that rebukes intergenerational sex between males and appears in only two manuscripts has been eagerly institutionalized within Donne's canon. It now routinely appears with the title "Manliness," although that was first affixed only in 1942: "Thou call'st me effeminate, for I love women's joys; / I call not thee manly, though thou follow boys."[112] Such "manly" sentiments appear unquestionably canonical. Donne married an adolescent eleven years his junior.

Some incidental slurs involving prostitute boys and sodomy appear in Donne's *Satires*,[113] and his amorous elegy "On His Mistress" (perhaps addressing his young wife) persuades her to stay home rather than disguise herself as his page to accompany his forthcoming travels. In Italy's "warm land," men would thus "haunt" her "with such lust and hideous rage/As Lot's fair guests were vexed."[114] Yet Donne's youthful verse letters to T. W., a male friend thought to be a Thomas Woodward christened in 1576, and likely written between 1592 and 1594, are very warm indeed, and Donne declares in the last that he pines to death in T. W.'s absence. One of this correspondent's replies imagines their respective muses as intertwining tribades "spending their pith" together in mutual frottage, so that Donne's muse begets T. W.'s verse epistle upon him.[115]

Sappho to Philaenis[116] *(c. 1600)*

> Where is that holy fire which Verse is said
>> To have? Is that enchanting force decayed?
> Verse that draws[117] Nature's works from Nature's law,
>> Thee, her best work, to her work cannot draw.[118]
> Have my tears quenched my old Poetic fire;   5
>> Why quenched they not, as well, that of desire?
> Thoughts, my mind's creatures, often are with thee,
>> But I, their maker, want[119] their liberty.
> Only thine image in my heart doth sit,
>> But that is wax and fires environ it.   10
> My fires have driven, thine have drawn it hence;
>> And I am robbed of Picture, Heart, and Sense.
> Dwells with me still mine irksome Memory,
>> Which both to keep and lose grieves equally.
> That tells me how fair thou art: Thou art so fair,   15
>> As gods, when gods to thee I do compare,
> Are graced thereby; and to make blind men see
>> What things gods are, I say they're like to thee.
> For if we justly call each silly[120] man
>> A little world,[121] what shall we call thee then?   20
> Thou art not soft, and clear, and straight, and fair,
>> As Down, as Stars, Cedars, and Lilies are,
> But thy right hand, and cheek, and eye, only
>> Are like thy other hand, and cheek, and eye.
> Such was my Phao[122] awhile, but shall be never,   25
>> As thou wast, art, and, oh, may'st be ever.
> Here lovers swear in their Idolatry
>> That I am such; but Grief discolors me.
> And yet I grieve the less, lest Grief remove
>> My beauty, and make me unworthy of thy love.   30
> Plays some soft boy with thee, oh there wants yet
>> A mutual feeling which should sweeten it.
> His chin, a thorny hairy unevenness
>> Doth threaten, and some daily change[123] possess.

Thy body is a natural Paradise, 35
    In whose self, unmanured,[124] all pleasure lies,
Nor needs perfection; why shouldst thou then
    Admit the tillage of a harsh rough man?
Men leave behind them that which their sin shows[125]
    And are as thieves traced, which rob when it snows. 40
But of our dalliance no more signs there are
    Than fishes leave in streams, or Birds in air.
And between us all sweetness may be had;
    All, all that Nature yields, or Art can add.
My two lips, eyes, thighs, differ from thy two, 45
    But so, as thine from one another do;
And, oh, no more; the likeness being such,
    Why should they not alike in all parts touch?
Hand to strange hand, lip to lip none denies;
    Why should they breast to breast, or thighs to thighs? 50
Likeness begets such strange self flattery,
    That touching my self, all seems done to thee.
My self I embrace, and mine own hands I kiss,
    And amorously thank my self for this.
Me, in my glass, I call thee; But alas, 55
    When I would kiss, tears dim mine eyes, and glass.
O cure this loving madness, and restore
    Me to me; thee,[126] my half, my all, my more,[127]
So may thy cheeks red outwear scarlet dye,
    And their white, whiteness of the Galaxy,[128] 60
So may thy mighty amazing beauty move
    Envy in all women, and in all men love,
And so be change, and sickness, far from thee,
    As thou by coming near, keep'st them from me.

Tanguy Le Fèvre (1615–1672)

Assigning Sappho's sapphism to her "highly amorous temperament," Tanguy Le Fèvre outlines her life and reputation with refreshing urbanity. Born at Caen, he was educated by Jesuits. On his arrival in Paris in 1630, Cardinal Richelieu helped him pursue a career in classical scholarship. Converting to Protestantism in 1647, Le Fèvre reestablished himself at Saumur, where he became professor of Greek at the Protestant Academy in 1665. Partly due to his enlightened views on feminine education, his daughter Anne (later Madame Dacier) became one of the foremost Hellenic authorities in Europe, thus overcoming conventional gender biases. Besides translating Lucian, Anacreon, and "Longinus," her father issued a Greek edition of Sappho with Latin translations and commentary in 1660. He outlines Sappho's life and reputation in *Les poètes Grecs*, first published in 1664 and addressed to the twelve-year-old comte de Limoges. Whereas Le Fèvre's account ignores the husband conventionally ascribed to the poet in her sixteenth- and seventeenth-century biographies, it openly acknowledges her love of women, citing the evidence of a surviving ode (now often designated Fragment 31). Though recommending Ovid's "Sappho to Phaon," Le Fèvre does not mention Phaon as a Sapphic male lover, and avoids according Ovid any biographical authority. Whereas Le Fèvre finds female same-sex love accountable as a matter of personal "temperament" and "taste," in 1712 the Sapphic translator François Gacon attacked him "as a bad Christian who 'deserved to be publicly chastised by the Calvinists for having tried to excuse [Sappho] in spite of St. Paul's condemnation of her shameful passion'" (DeJean, 132).

The Greek Poets[129] (1664)

Sappho

The one in bygone days who named Sappho the Tenth Muse undoubtedly gave her a glorious and marvelous name[130]; but that name is still nowadays the most appropriate that could be given her. Therefore the greatest authors in Antiquity have recognized her as the most knowing in Apollo's art: I am not saying the most among Greek ladies, for that would mean too little for Sappho, the one whose knowledge surpassed that of the most excellent poets. It is important not to doubt the sincerity of the authors I will invoke, since neither personal interest, nor love, nor kindness interfere with their judgment, and their testimony sticks to the truth. You will not disagree with me, Sir, once you know the names and qualities of those who have praised her. And if there were only Socrates, wouldn't that be enough? But Aristotle and Strabo say the same as Socrates. That is not all: will Dionysius of Halicarnassus, Plutarch, Longinus, and the emperor Julian be accounted authors of little worth?[131]

So there was nothing more beautiful than the Poems of Sappho, and one could hardly doubt the statements of such enlightened persons. But all those graces, all those beauties, that secret and admirable art of penetrating hearts, of speaking and vanquishing at once, to touch the most tender passions—for it is thus that she acquired such a singular esteem—all of these treasures, I say, never reached us. They were lost in many ways: the barbarity and ignorance of past centuries have ravished them from us, and without Dionysius of Halicarnassus and the Great Rhetorician whom I just named,[132] we would possess of that incomparable personage only a few little fragments which we find in the ancient Scholiasts. But the happy Destiny of Great Literature has allowed that these two great Authors have saved for us one hymn she dedicated to Venus, and a certain ode of sixteen verses addressed to a girl with whom she was in love. As for the rest, Sappho lived in the time of Stesichorus and Alcaeus, which is to say 610 years before Jesus Christ. The isle of Lesbos was her birthplace, and the Mitylenians had her poetry in such high esteem that they engraved the image of this Heroine on their coinage, and in this way showed her the honor reserved to a Queen, after her death. This story might perhaps seem a little apocryphal to you, but it comes from too good a source to be doubted, and those who wrote it are too trustworthy to have invented it. However, some will tell you there is no appearance of truth in this Account, and that sophisticated gentlemen would not believe it. But I shall say, Sir, that the Greeks had undoubtedly great wits, and that those who are so reluctant to believe extraordinary cases prove themselves witless, or at least don't well know the value of great art.

But to avoid becoming further annoyed, let's leave behind those sophisticates. We shall rather explain the word I let slip when I mentioned that Ode of sixteen verses. I mean, Sir, that Sappho had a highly amorous temperament,[133] and so, not being satisfied with what other women encounter in the company of men not unattractive to them, she sought to have mistresses as well as male lovers.[134] Here is another story than that of the Mitylenian coinage, as you see, but not less true; and I shall tell you more, for Giovanni Leo of Africa, who lived around 140 years ago, says that, in his time, many women of his country had the same taste as Sappho.[135]

This is nearly enough on Sappho, if I don't mislead myself; nonetheless I will tell you one more thing I've forgotten that deserves to be known. It is, Sir, that some consider Ovid's Elegy assuming Sappho's character more exquisite than many of his other compositions, for he took all that was sweetest and most passionate from her poetry and put it in this beautiful Poem. And they add that this Roman Poet wrote only what the Tenth Muse dictated to him. That may well be false, but I wish it were true.

CHAPTER **10**

Erotica

> Both the ancient and modern sculptors have sometimes written or carved lascivious things to disport their genius, like the marble satyr in the Chigi Palace who attempts to violate a boy.... Hypocrites to the contrary, I despair of the thievish judgment and filthy habit which forbid the eyes what delights them most. What harm is there in seeing a man mount a woman? Indeed, should the beasts be freer than us?
>
> —*Pietro Aretino (1492–1556), Letter[1]

A genre of explicit sexual representation, the forerunner of pornography, coalesced during the Renaissance. "Pornography" itself derives from an ancient Greek word literally meaning "painters of whores" that had come to include writing by at least the second century, as in Athenaeus.[2] However, this term is now fraught with meanings that render it too anachronistic for early modern application. Yet "eroticism" and "erotic writing" are too diffuse, too modal, to register formalized sexual specificity. I will use "erotica" for this purpose, and "homoerotica" for its male and female same-sex variant.[3] Though a recent term, "erotica" at least remains relatively neutral in its connotations while suggesting materials categorized according to a deliberate, distinctive, and constitutive focus on sexual or sexually charged activity. On account of official constraints on printing increasingly enforced from the early sixteenth century onward, much erotica (as opposed to relatively diffuse eroticism) would have circulated only in manuscript, among like-minded coteries. Unfortunately, little such early modern homoerotica currently seems to have survived the purges of centuries, and so this chapter and its readings revolve around printed texts and the implications of censorship. Just as the visual arts and literature in general were produced primarily by and for males, homoerotica addressing sexual relations between females seems to have been relatively rare from the fifteenth well into the seventeenth centuries, and tended to serve male heteroerotic appetites anyway. Although no such manuscripts by women are presently known, it is not unlikely that some, at least on a small scale within notes or letters, were likely created.

Three main differences of Renaissance erotica from current pornography are the former's strong affinities with social satire and with philosophizing, and its tendency, despite any authorial claims of originality, to evoke classical precedents as pretexts and as esthetic and formal inspirations. Early modern conceptions of satire encouraged its modal convergence with erotica. As "satire" was thought to be derived from "satyr" in the Renaissance, that genre appeared a definitively rough mode of expression that, among other options, allowed for much frank comment on sex and contemporary sexual mores.[4] Verbal erotica readily assimilated "satyric" modulations, and in one motif of its visual counterpart satyrs have sex mutually or with humans (figure 8). Philosophizing afforded a means to contest sexual repression, and erotica positively involving sex between males seems to have stressed philosophical and satiric elements to a greater extent than its more heteroerotically aligned counterparts. Such further efforts of justification and social criticism presumably responded to stronger felt taboos and social pressures. Like pornography, early modern verbal erotica such as *Aretino's often involves conventionally "obscene" words; a survey of sexual positions, possibilities, and partners; and characters whose sexual desires appear boundless. Inventory of postures also characterizes central exemplars of Renaissance visual erotica, though even this turns out to have originated from classical precedent. Following ancient Lucian's *Dialogues of the Courtesans* and Aretino's correlative *Ragionamenti*, dialogic presentation, voiced through female prostitutes and thus involving male authorial transvestism, became common. Also typical were anticlericalism; an instructional format "educationally" disseminating sexual knowledge; androcentric discussion of how to please men sexually; and, as Ian Moulton observes, some acknowledgment of female sexual autonomy and resultant male anxieties, unlike the feminine passivity conventional in much modern pornography (12, 15–16).

Renaissance erotica focusing on male-female relations further diverges from its modern counterparts in that, as some main exemplars show, not only female but also male same-sex behaviors could be at least somewhat included in a subordinated way. Conditions of reception entailed a further difference. Since females were linked with the senses, appetites, and pleasure, as opposed to the so-called masculinity of mind and reason, one meaning of male "effeminacy" was allegedly excessive sexual pursuit of women, and thus some claimed even erotica catering to heteroerotic tastes emasculated its male audience.

Despite the currency in the period of idealizing ideologies that sought to exalt mind and soul, much of its erotica insists on the corporeal and sexual nature of humanity, most obviously in vernacular writings but also in the priapic lucubrations of learned humanists. Prompted by tumescent Priapus himself, Greco-Roman god of sex and the phallus, this most phallocentric early modern genre is to some extent carnivalesque in Mikhail Bakhtin's sense, reveling in that antique divinity's earthiness and bodily grotesqueries, and thus also in the "satyric" inversion of conventional moral hierarchies.

Although Moulton has proposed that the normative social and political engagements of early modern erotic representation show "sexuality does not seem to have constituted a separate sphere of identity formation,"[5] we may readily conclude the contrary. Partly on account of the formerly prevalent literary

Fig. 8   Joseph Heinz the Elder, *Pan and Daphnis,* modeled after an ancient Roman sculptural type (c. 1592). By permission of Grafische Sammlung Albertina, Vienna.

theory, social and political engagements are quite common to the period's fictional genres in general.[6] So, unless we suppose our forebears had difficulty in making any distinctions, the appearance of that cultural trait in erotic creations would not necessarily imply inability to conceive of sex differences as a notionally separable sphere, or to develop distinct notions of self arising from perceptions of those differences. The very linkage of a particular transgressive representation of sex to social and philosophical comment in former erotica suggests that sexual desires and experience could serve as a stimulus, locus, or basis for elaboration of an ensemble of personally characteristic insights and attitudes addressing life's full scope. This is particularly clear in sixteenth- and seventeenth-century homoerotica such as that of Antonio Vignali (1500/01–1559) and *Antonio Rocco (1586–1652), discussed subsequently, in which social and philosophical analysis serves the promotion of masculine love, contrary to conventional norms. These texts have a different sexual agenda of their own, deliberately framed and pursued.

As Italy led the rest of Europe in many cultural innovations of the Renaissance, so also was the case in the development of verbal and visual erotic representation. Despite native traditions of erotic writing in England, Italian exemplars provided much inspiration for English verbal eroticism at this time, and Roger Ascham (1515–1568) among others represented Italy as the source of lewd books conducing moral corruption (Frantz, ch. 5; Moulton, 113–18). Two strains of Italian erotic writing can be distinguished: the "popular" mode, vernacular and deliberately "low" or "vulgar" in diction and style, as in the transgressive carnivalesque realism of Domenico di Giovanni or Burchiello (1404–1449); and its "academic" counterpart, flaunting humanistic, classicizing elegance, and based in learned academies or societies (Frantz, chs. 1–2). The humanist program to recuperate Greek and Roman culture provided much stimulus and authorization. Excavation of material remains, such as ubiquitous statues of the ithyphallic god Priapus, physically disclosed the relative sexual frankness of life in antiquity, contrary to Christian moral strictures. Many much-esteemed classical writers such as Martial, Ovid, Catullus, Horace, and Lucian had written bawdily; Virgil appeared to have done so in the ancient *Priapeia*, commonly attributed to him *through* much of the sixteenth century, and included in numerous editions of his complete works.[7] As the poems collected in the *Priapeia* focus on sex, so that text inspired a vogue for "priapic poems" and probably gave much impetus to the formalization of sexual depiction in early modernity. Surviving ancient sources further record the currency in antiquity of sex manuals, some illustrated, and of treasured paintings of sexual activities. Contrary to the antisodomitical homophobia endemic in Christian culture, the presence of much casual and celebratory treatment of male same-sex love in Greek and Roman writings endorsed its pursuit and advocacy in the Renaissance. As Paula Findlen explains, the classical revival conjoined with printing's advent to disseminate and commodify transgressive depictions and conceptions of sex, and conduce formation of erotica with its various subgenres (52–86).

Two significant quattrocento verbal exemplars of male homoerotica are the Latin *Hermaphroditus* of Antonio Beccadelli (1394–1471) and *Hecatelegium* (One Hundred Elegies) of Pacifica Massimo (c. 1400–c. 1500). Published in manuscript in 1425 and dedicated to Cosimo de' Medici, Beccadelli's collection gathers eighty-one sexually pointed epigrams, some positively indulging masculine love. The book itself is hermaphroditic, he advises, the first part corresponding to the penis, the second to the vagina, and yet the whole might also suggest being named for its lyrical paeans to the anus.[8] After initial praise, burgeoning condemnation resulted in public burnings of the text in Mantua, Bologna, and Ferrara, to rebuke the author and discourage further such classicizing challenges to official Christian morality. Probably as a result, Beccadelli's *Hermaphroditus* did not appear in print until 1791. The homoerotic poems of Massimo's *Hecatelegium*, first published in 1489 and dedicated to the Bishop of Volterra, adumbrate the erotic intrigues of a vibrant sodomitical subculture, ranging through seductions of male youths, love affairs, unrequited love, amorous rivalries, and involvements with male prostitutes.[9]

However, as the subversive potential of printing became manifest, disciplinary reactions followed. The religious rivalries of the Reformation strongly stimulated efforts to regulate the publication and transmission of theological ideas, and heightened restrictions soon extended to political and erotic writings. Whereas sexually explicit materials could circulate in relatively private, limited, and unregulated ways in manuscript, their dissemination in print was far more disturbing to early modern moralists. Throughout sixteenth-century Europe, civil and ecclesiastical authorities elaborated controls such as the requirement of official approval before printing; listings of interdicted books for expurgation or suppression; and restraints on imports.[10] Although catalogues of forbidden texts dated back to antiquity, the papal Tridentine Index of 1564 was the first explicitly to identify perceived obscenity or immorality as a reason for prohibition, and its rules remained in force until 1966. Authors were thus pressured to practice self-censorship. In England, for example, a complex array of press controls developed through the sixteenth century, and in 1551 King Edward VI introduced mandatory licensing for all works to be printed. Both books and presses could be confiscated or destroyed for transgressive publication. In 1599 Archbishop Whitgift and Bishop Bancroft of London proscribed and burned a range of books including sexually provocative English satires and amorous poems.[11] Countermeasures by political, religious, and sexual dissidents included illegal presses; clandestine printings; authorial anonymity or false attribution; false imprints (stating a false publisher and place of publication, typically abroad); and book smuggling. This chapter's readings were published and circulated in such illicit ways: Aretino's erotica after Pope Paul IV's enduring inclusion of his entire *oeuvre* in the papal index of 1558–59, *Rocco's from the outset. But even though Aretino's could be legally printed in Venice during his life, due to the relative freedom of the Venetian book trade at that time, import restrictions of many states would have sought to exclude it.

Various landmarks of sexual representation, subversion, and censorship were established at Rome in 1524. Introducing a new means to market erotica in print media, Giulio Romano (1499–1546) produced a series of sixteen drawings of explicit heteroerotic couplings (some possibly anal), Marcantonio Raimondi (c. 1480–c. 1534) engraved them, and they were published under the title *I modi* (Positions). But papal agents soon confiscated the prints, jailed Raimondi, and required destruction of the plates to prevent further printings. Giulio had designed the series partly on the classical model of "spintriae," Roman medals or tokens depicting sexual acts, issued in sets of sixteen, and incorrectly associated in the Renaissance with the notorious pansexual choreographies of the Roman emperor Tiberius, anciently reported by Suetonius among others (Talvacchia, ch. 3). Unfortunately, none of Giulio's drawings survives, and only the first engraving of Raimondi's published set, but numerous inferior versions proliferated (many also now lost).

Ironically, this papal prudery aroused *Aretino's seminal debauching of print to propagate encoupled visual and verbal representations of sex. After helping to secure Raimondi's release, Aretino composed sixteen heteroerotically explicit poems, the *Sonetti lussuriosi* (Lascivious Sonnets), to accompany the banned pictures, and thus revenge himself on the papal court, censorship, and sexual hypocrisy.[12] Or so his epistolary comment on this affair, the source of my introductory epigraph here, suggests. Joint publication ensued at Venice in 1527. Each of the sonnets comments on a corresponding visual image, and Aretino devised the former to magnify the latter's offense to conventional morality. Whereas the pictures evoke male-female anal sodomy ambiguously, Aretino makes it central to his representation of heteroerotic pleasure. Although his epilogue declares that these sonnets honor "pricks who serve asses *and* pussies" (emphasis mine), the females in the second and eighth sonnets declare "there isn't a man who isn't a bugger," and "Fuck me and do with me what you will both in my pussy and my behind.... If I were a man, I wouldn't want pussy" (cit. Talvacchia, 201, 209). Aretino brusquely discards conventional sonnet sequences' elevated diction and frustration of amorous desire for an icon of virtuous beauty. By combining verbal and visual materials to create such a book, he introduced a new and heightened means to compose and disseminate erotica and contest restrictive concepts of sex. Numerous editions and verbal-visual imitations by others followed. This text and some others made "Aretino" a byword for scandalous erotica throughout Europe for centuries, and some of his writings, such as the *Sonetti* and *Il marescalco* (The Stablemaster), would have tended to liberalize attitudes toward male homoeroticism.

The crackdown on *I modi* in 1524 ensured that subsequent new series of erotic engravings were much toned down. Giulio and Aretino's naturalism that eschewed pretexts and excuses was supplanted by clearly mythological contextualization distancing the scenes from present reality. And the depicted sexual situations were confined to foreplay, or to sexual positions that could not appear unorthodox or "unnatural" (Talvacchia, ch. 7). The next set published in Rome, *Gli amori degli dei* (The Loves of the Gods), was drawn accordingly by Rosso Fiorentino (1494–1540) and Perino del Vaga (1500/01–1547), and published in a series of probably twenty engravings by Jacopo Caraglio (1505–1565) in the late 1520s (cf. Talvacchia, 140–57). Though predominantly heteroerotic, it includes an *Apollo and Hyacinth* analogous to a superior drawing of Giulio's on a similar theme (figure 9). Instead of depicting outright sex, like *I modi*, both these visual images use the iconographical convention of the slung leg, discreetly signifying prospective sexual consummation through the intertwining of limbs.[13] Many copies and versions of the *Amori* were produced. Agostino Carracci (1557–1602) published an also much copied series of twenty heteroerotic prints in the 1580s recuperating some of Giulio's more transgressive approach (cf. Frantz, figures 14–20).

Though some unknown quantity of Renaissance visual depiction of homoerotic sexual behaviors has been lost (particularly drawings), presumably such material was usually treated with much more caution, which the *Modi* affair would only have increased. The portrayal of figures from Greek and Roman myth often furnished the necessary pretexts and alibis.[14] Main subjects that could readily display masculine beauty in muscled or other aspects, and thus appeal to male homophiles, were Apollo, Narcissus, Bacchus, Ganymede, and pictorial or sculptured telamones; sapphists might turn to Amazons and especially to Diana and her nymphs bathing. If need be, all these could be rationalized as antique conventions or high-minded allegories, however sensually portrayed. Nevertheless, some genre scenes, particularly same-sex communal bathing, could afford considerable license for depicting contemporaneous homoeroticism, if somewhat coded. When Albrecht Dürer (1471–1528) envisioned a male bathhouse, he incorporated much anamorphic visual punning on penises, including an impressive horizontal erection in the bottom right foreground, constituted by some collectively phallic ground-lines culminating in a stone shaped like a glans. That is best perceived by turning the picture sideways, so the man drinking appears at the bottom edge (figure 10). The poses of bathing women drawn by Luca Penni (1500/4–1557) and engraved by Jean Mignon (fl. 1535–1555) at Fontainebleau involve the "slung leg" motif (figure 11). Further options of imagistically coded eroticism included, for example, the adjacent depiction of sensually evocative fruit and vegetables, as in a series of paintings of young males by Caravaggio (1573–1610); or situations involving prospects of fingered arpeggios on musical instruments

Fig. 9 Giulio Romano, *Apollo with a Lover* (c. 1525). By permission of the Nationalmuseum, Stockholm, Sweden.

together with physical intimacies such as some exposure of flesh (cf. Talvacchia, 261n.11). An engraving of a soldier adjusting his leggings further instances the tendency toward formalization of ambiguity in homoerotic depiction (figure 12). In one sense a homage to revered Michelangelo (1475–1564), it is modeled on a figure from his lost cartoon for a fresco never executed, *The Battle of Cascina* (1504–1507). Yet, intentionally or otherwise, that composition was

Fig. 10 Albrecht Dürer, *Men's Bathhouse* (c. 1498). By permission of Giraudon/Art Resource, New York.

Fig. 11   Jean Mignon, *Women Bathing,* after Luca Penni (c. 1540). By permission of Grafische Sammlung Albertina, Vienna.

homoerotically provocative: a dense arrangement of muscular soldiers in various states of undress or nude. Relative to the range of figures now known through surviving copies, this engraving imitates the one with the most specifically sodomitical potential, displaying shapely buttocks, and seems to have accentuated the cleavage. This image appears partly addressed to a sodomitical clientele, but could also have other appeals.

Since the depiction of religious subjects allowed male nudity or near-nudity, that afforded further scope for imputed or artistically intentional male homoeroticism, whether through portrayal of ancillary or background figures or the main subject. Male saints and biblical personages that were often pictured more or less erotically nude or seminude include St. Laurence, David, St. Sebastian, John the Baptist (as in some of Caravaggio's renderings), and Jesus himself in certain traditional representative aspects, such as the transfigured state of bodily glorification in which he supposedly appeared after the crucifixion. Such religious images were not only commissioned for private collections of the elite, but also to adorn Italian religious communities and public churches (though some works considered indecorous were rejected or removed). In 1552 the Roman Catholic archbishop Lancelletto de' Politi (1484–1553) complained, "The most disgusting aspect of this age is the fact you come across pictures of gross

Fig. 12   School of Agostino Veneziano, *Soldier Adjusting Leggings,* after a figure in Michelangelo's lost cartoon, *The Battle of Cascina* (c. 1517). Collection of Kenneth Borris, by permission.

indecency in the greatest churches and chapels, . . . all the bodily shows that nature has concealed, with the effect of arousing not devotion but every lust of the corrupt flesh."[15]

With the notable exception of the pre-Tridentine Venetian book trade, verbal erotica in late-sixteenth- and seventeenth-century Europe was driven as underground as *I modi*, to appear either somehow illegally, if printed, or configured in symbolic code. Richard Barnfield (1574–1626?) favorably encodes anal sex between males in his poem of homoerotic advocacy, "The Affectionate Shepherd."[16] Among the erotica produced by "the Aretines" (Aretino's Venetian associates and imitators), the prose *Puttana errante* (Wandering Whore), long falsely attributed to Aretino himself, includes some episodes with tribadic sex and males having anal coitus. Now sometimes called "perhaps the single most influential piece of early modern European erotic writing," it circulated very widely in diverse versions (often deleting the homogenital activities), and anticipates pornography by focusing almost wholly on sex.[17]

But much more significant for male homoeroticism, at least, is *La cazzaria* (The Book of the Prick, in Moulton's rendering) by the Sienese academician Vignali.[18] Composed around 1525, his dialogue circulated in manuscript and through more or less clandestine printings. Arsiccio inducts relatively innocent Sodo (obviously predestined for sodomy, lucky fellow) into a knowledge of sexual organs and pleasures as the basis of natural philosophy, including justification of anal sodomy between males through brilliant mockery of the theological claims condemning it, climaxing with Sodo's implied seduction. The dialogue concludes with Arsiccio's fable of the rivalries and mutual negotiations of Big Pricks, Pretty Cunts, Pricks, Cunts, Balls, and Asses. While Vignali's recent editor and translator Ian Moulton emphasizes that this satirizes political foibles in Siena, from my viewpoint the fable primarily analyses and critiques human sexual arrangements through a mock etiology of their origins. In that way it seems a ribald parody of the etiological myth of the varieties of love recounted by Aristophanes in Plato's *Symposium*. Reducing the competition of social, political, and other interests to interactions of synechdochal genitals, Vignali insists on the bodily and sexual basis of human relations, mocks pretensions to the contrary, and implicitly promotes erotic pleasure as a more honest and worthwhile focus. Of the cinquecento editions, three are currently known, two Venetian and one Neapolitan, and the dialogue's reputation, at least, extended to sixteenth-century London.[19] Focusing instead on male pederasty in particular, *Rocco's *L'Alcibiade fanciullo a scola* written around a hundred years later is otherwise similar in seeking to propound and reinforce a libertine philosophy advocating sex between males. Another apparently pederastic text, now unidentifiable, was attributed to Aretino by Gabriel and Richard Harvey in the 1590s (Moulton, 145–47). Just as prints themselves could serve as "a forum for unofficial, unsanctioned, moderately aberrant ideas,"[20] prohomoerotic works could be wholly visual rather than verbal, informing and seducing the mind by immediate apprehension through the enraptured eye.

Unfortunately, for verbal exemplars of Renaissance female homoerotica we must at present rely wholly on male writers such as *Aretino.[21] Though we thus possess notional accounts of early modern tribadic sexual encounters and discussions, they are rendered from masculine viewpoints and largely aimed at titillating men who desire women. However much these females pleasure each other, then, their enjoyments serve only to intensify their sexual longings for phallic penetration. Rather than revealing "what eros between females was like," these texts indicate how such sexually adventurous males might accommodate it into their personal panoramas of erotic perspectives, desires, and practices, or into the normative androcentric sex/gender system.

During the seventeenth century the Italians forfeited their preeminence in publication of erotica to the French. The sexual writing of Nicolas Chorier (1612–1692) has been called the "most advanced pornographically" for its century (Thompson, 21), yet nonetheless displays formal traits of prior early modern erotica. A bizarre English exemplar likewise somewhat beyond my chronological scope is the burlesque tragedy *Sodom, or the Quintessence of Debauchery*, printed several times in the 1680s, but suppressed. Though it has often been attributed to the sodomitical poet-rake John Wilmot, earl of Rochester (1647–1680), its style, wit, and resources do not meet his standard. Having tired of vaginas, Bolloxinian, the King of Sodom, decrees reversal of the conventional status of heteroerotic vaginal intercourse and buggering between males, and after assorted interludes involving opposite- and same-sex conjunctions, including tribadism, and his entire army's recourse to buggering each other, nature revolts and demons arrive to inflict punishment. But Bolloxinian, refusing to change, tells his trusty minion Pockenello, "Let Heavens descend and set the world on fire! / We to some darker Cavern will retire; / There on thy Buggered Arse I will Expire."[22] *Sodom* ridicules threats of divine retribution, and early modern erotica promoting transgressive sex dismisses such bugbears implicitly or otherwise.

Pietro Aretino (1492–1556)

Addressing sexual topics freely in various publications, Pietro Aretino became almost synonomous throughout Europe with scandalous representations of sex. His notorious *Sonetti lussuriosi* (Lascivious Sonnets) are heteroerotic yet sodomitical; his comedy *Il marescalco* (The Stablemaster) features a hero who openly loves male youths; and though his *Ragionamenti* (Dialogues) mostly focuses on heteroerotic sex, it deals frankly with same-sex sexual behaviors, and with masculine desires for insertive anal intercourse, whether with males or females. Since the *Sonetti* are mainly heteroerotic and *Il marescalco* is not erotica, I comment briefly on these and provide readings from the *Ragionamenti*. Although no early modern English translations of these sexually transgressive texts were published, John Wolfe printed the first collected Italian edition of the *Ragionamenti* in London in 1585 and issued a second in 1597. In England Aretino quickly became a legendary epitome of Italianate sexual and political disorder, yet also an imitated archetype of authorial power (Moulton, chs. 3–4). Ben Jonson (1573?–1637) based his play *Epicoene* (1609) partly on *Il marescalco* (Moulton, 211–19).

Born in Arezzo, this cobbler's son or noble's bastard arrived in Rome around 1517 to seek courtly advancement. Having become notorious for satiric pasquinades attacking current notables, including a cardinal who became Pope Adrian VI, Aretino fled Rome when nearly assassinated in 1525. After seeking patronage from Federico Gonzaga, duke of Mantua, the fugitive established himself in Venice's relative freedom in 1527, when he published his *Sonetti* together with illustrations based on Giulio Romano's sixteen drawings of heteroerotic sexual positions (*Erotica). Until his final years Aretino then resided on one level of a substantial house on the Grand Canal near the Rialto (where Jacopo Tintoretto decorated his bedroom ceiling), and meanwhile prospered greatly as a political and cultural commentator and extortionist. Many eminent patrons, including the French and English kings François I and Henry VIII, richly paid Aretino to ensure favorable press. His elite Venetian circle included the painter Titian and sculptor-architect Jacopo Sansovino. Although Aretino's varied publications encompass sonnets, plays, satiric dialogues and prophecies, erotica, an incomplete epic, devotional works, and saints' lives, his wide fame and influence mostly arose from his printed collections of letters (1538–1557). He was unsuccessfully charged with blasphemy (and perhaps sodomy) in 1538 (Moulton, 140). Although some enemies publicly accused him of having oral and anal sex with males both insertively and receptively, these claims may be unfounded, for he was very much sexually attracted to women, despite remaining unmarried, and had two illegitimate daughters.[23] However, his casual and extensive treatment of anal intercourse in both the *Sonetti* and *Ragionamenti* indicate he had actively enjoyed that at least with females. From his libertine viewpoint, informed by classical precedent, the gender of the receiving end might not have been much of an issue.

Although Aretino seriously aspired to become a cardinal, all his works were papally forbidden in Paul IV's Index of Prohibited Books promulgated in 1558–59, and remained so. Provocations would have included Aretino's frank treatment of sex, extensive satire of sexual and ecclesiastical hypocrisies, and subversion of officially approved sexual ideology. Contrary to Christian orthodoxy, Petrarchism, and Neoplatonic representations of love, he focused on the bodily pressures and diverse physical possibilities of enacting sexual desire, including acts conventionally thought transgressive, while acknowledging the realities of homoerotic attractions.

Written for the duke of Mantua around 1526 and first published in 1533, Aretino's *Il marescalco* assumes that male same-sex desire can be a determining characteristic of personal identity and promotes its social acceptance. As the prologue relates, the duke has a stablemaster "as backward with women as usurers are with spending" (he has never even seen a woman's nightgown, we find), yet orders him to marry a certain beautiful young maiden with a lavish dowry.[24] Instead of being overjoyed at this advantageous match evincing high ducal favor, the stablemaster, who has no wish to marry, must be dragged to his wedding. But the duke has actually provided a cross-dressed handsome page as the bride, and after the ceremony and conjugal kiss, in which the page has been instructed to use his tongue, the stablemaster discovers the duke's prank, whereupon he is "happier to find out that she was a boy than he had been sorry to believe that she was a girl" (37).

Although the stablemaster meanwhile endures much teasing pressure to marry and forego masculine love, as his interlocutors cite supposed divine law, he steadfastly maintains his homoerotic commitment despite the blandishments of riches and ducal favor. When advised to "leave the ways of shame and sin," referring to his sex with males, the stablemaster demands, "What shame? What sin?" (46–47). He insists, "I want to live in my own way, sleep with whoever I please" (65). On the stablemaster's final delight in his bride's revealed masculinity, the nurse comments, "you never get the frog out of the marsh" (108), and her metaphor implies that his particular homoerotic inclinations render him an exemplar of a distinct species with a way of life appropriate to him. Same-sex love suits the stablemaster, and that happy union cannot be severed even by the most attractive contrary inducements possible. No more has he considered marrying, he insists, than he has "thought of flying": The former would be as unnatural to him as the latter (52). Aretino treats this character's sexual difference in a matter-of-fact way, and it is not only at last accepted by his social milieu, but even reaffirmed by the fictional duke of Mantua, who corresponds to the actual duke for whom the play was written and first performed. "I've known the Marescalco for a long time," the respectable married courtier Jacopo declares, and "he's a fine fellow and deserves to be loved" (92). While presumably reflecting attitudes current in Federico Gonzaga's court, some characters may correspond to specific personalities in his entourage.

Aretino originally published the *Ragionamenti*, indebted to ancient Lucian's *Dialogues of the Courtesans*, in two parts, the first in 1534 and the second in 1536. While chiefly addressing heteroerotic sexual appetites, this text canvasses a range of topics and social issues satirically and otherwise. The main interlocutor, Nana, is an experienced prostitute. In Part One, dedicated to a monkey, she and a younger prostitute discuss potential female roles in three dialogues, sequentially on the lives of nuns, wives, and prostitutes. In the three further dialogues of Part Two, women including Nana discuss the arts of female prostitution, male treacheries, and how to become a procuress. The fictionally feminine viewpoint and milieu of the *Ragionamenti* offer male readers the pleasures of evesdropping on a group of women talking openly about sex and their attitudes toward men as lovers and sexual clients. Female readers might enjoy evaluating Aretino's authorial transvestism that seeks to express intimately feminine sexual perspectives; on the *Sonetti*, Talvacchia claims that he presents "sexually empowered, authoritative, and sometimes dominant female voices" (96). By situating most of these dialogues in an implicitly Bacchic vineyard under a luscious fig tree, in implicit contrast to the relatively austere plane tree of Plato's amorous dialogue *Phaedrus*,

Aretino mocks fashionable Neoplatonic love philosophy, which urged restraint of physical desire. Figs were strongly associated with both vaginal and anal sex.

As the implied primary audience of the *Ragionamenti* is fascinated by the relations of female prostitutes with their male clients, so same-sex sexual acts, attitudes, and ways of life are relatively incidental in this text. Aretino mainly addresses homoeroticism in the first dialogue of Part One, where Nanna recounts her experiences within a secretly orgiastic nunnery. By exposing the contradictions between sanctimonious repression and ecclesiastical hypocrisy, he satirizes the church's sexual positions, so to speak. As well as vaginal couplings, there is much delighted tribadism, and both opposite- and same-sex anal intercourse. No one has or seeks same-sex sexual pleasures exclusively in these sex scenes, for that social phenomenon is not of interest to Aretino in this particular work, unlike *Il marescalco*. Instead, to these participants, such sexual acts seem further opportunities for sensual enjoyment. Much like *Brantôme (1540?–1614) on sapphism, Aretino makes his nuns abandon their sex together in quest of supposedly greater phallic fulfillment. The *Ragionamenti*'s linkage of same-sex desire to ecclesiastics is just pragmatically satiric, for it is not particularly ecclesiastical in *Il marescalco*. Tribadism disappears after the first dialogue; mentions of males who seek their own sex are brief and pejorative, for the female narrators resent their sexual disinterest and competition.

Although Aretino's references to oral sex now seem surprisingly sparse, males eagerly want insertive anal sex throughout the *Ragionamenti,* and that textually appears to be what men most crave from females when they have the freedom of dealing with prostitutes.[25] For their clients' pleasure, the latter may even masquerade as male youths and have anal intercourse in that guise (147–49, 186). Yet, whereas women in the *Sonetti* lust for anal penetration, in the *Ragionamenti* their interest in such sex is wholly mercenary. The latter text implies that masculine sexual desires are anally insertive and thus, from a sexually orthodox viewpoint, perverse: dedicated to seeking a most transgressive pleasure. Such male appetites are so prevalent, the experienced prostitute Nanna concedes, that "the sodomites," whom she calls wretches whose doings are too shocking to be heard, "steal three thirds of our trade" (286–87). Anal intercourse appears such a common desire and pleasure in the *Ragionamenti* that the author seems concerned to subvert taboos on sodomy in that particular sense.

A remark in the second dialogue of Part One, devoted to discussion of wives, epitomizes both Aretino's delight in affronting conventional sexual morality, and the satiric thrust of the *Ragionamenti*'s titillations. A wife has both anal and vaginal intercourse with many men in a row, a consensual *trentuna* or thirty-one, then goes to the toilet, loosens her sphincters, and, "like an engorged Abbot discharges soup from his belly," thus restores "twenty-seven unborn souls... to the earthly Limbo" (86). As sexual orthodoxy maintained that sperm must be carefully conserved for deposit in the right orifice in the right way, sanctified by marriage (itself a sacrament for Roman Catholics), so this casual disposal is deliberately outrageous, while also indicating the multitude of the world's gratuitous and so-called transgressive spermatic emissions. Yet, despite Aretino's emphasis on the joys of sex including anathematized varieties, his eroticism not only appeals to sexual appetites but also, having provoked them, satirizes their urgencies and extent.

The Dialogues[26] (1534, 1536)

Part One, First Dialogue

Nanna. I saw four sisters, the General, and three milk-white and ruddy young friars in the cell pulling off the Reverend Father's cassock and dressing him in a velvet coat. Hiding his tonsure was a small gold skullcap covered with a velvet one adorned with drops of crystal and a long white feather. They girded him with a sword, and then the blessèd General, just between you and me, started swaggering around like a Bartolomeo Coglioni.[27] Meanwhile, the sisters and friars having taken off their habits, three sisters put on the friars', who in turn put on the sisters'. Wrapping herself in the General's cassock and seating herself pontifically, the other nun began to mimic a superior dictating the laws for the convent.

Antonia. What lovely tricks!

Nanna. It only gets better.

Antonia. How so?

Nanna. Because Reverend Father called the three friars and, leaning on the shoulders of one of them, a long thin person who'd prematurely sprouted, he had the other ones take the sparrow out of the nest where it was resting. The most cunning and attractive one of the lot palmed and started petting it on the back, as one would caress the tail of a cat that starts purring and stirring, and soon the sparrow lifted its crest. The splendid General grasped the most gracious and girlish sister, tossed her tunic over her head, and made her prop her forehead against the bedstead. His hands delicately opening her anal missal, he lost himself in its contemplation: its face was neither caved to the bone for leanness, nor was it pushing itself outward for its plumpness—it was just right. The tremulous fissure in the midst shone like a living thing of ivory. And those little dimples we see on the chins and cheeks of pretty women adorned her fetching buttocks (to speak like Florentines).[28] Its softness would have put to shame that of a mouse born in a mill-house and raised on flour. So smooth were all the limbs of that sister that no sooner would a hand have touched her loins than it would have slipped to her calves, quicker than your foot upon ice. On her skin no hair dared grow, no more than on an egg.

Antonia. So the father General spent his day in meditation, eh?

Nanna. It wasn't that he spent. While putting his paintbrush in the sister's little cup of color submitted first to his spit, he made her squirm like women in pangs of birth or pregnancy. To drive the spike more firmly into her crack, he gave a sign to his young calf to pull down his pants. The lad, after dropping them to his ankles, inserted his clyster[29] in the Reverend's *visibilium*, while the latter fixed his eyes on the other two young lads who had gently and comfortably arranged the sisters on the bed and were pounding sauce into their mortars, causing the fourth little sister to despair. She was a squinty, dark-skinned lass, deserted by all and left to her own devices. Filling her glass tool of a Bernard with the heated water[30] used to wash the good sirs' hands, she sat upon a pillow on the floor, planted her feet against the wall, and came down hard on that enormous pastoral staff, sheathing it within her body as a sword in a scabbard. By the odor of their pleasure I was more overcome than pawned pledges are consumed by usury, and rubbed my little monkey with my hand like cats rub their rumps on rooftops in January.

Antonia. Ha ha! And how ended the game?

Nanna. When they had been wiggling and waggling for more than half an hour, the General declared, "All together now, and kiss me now boys, and you do the same too, my dove." With one hand in the angel's box and the other fussing over the cherub's buttocks, kissing first one and then the other, he made the same wry face that the marble figure in the Vatican belvedere makes at the serpents strangling him between his sons.[31] At last, the sisters on the bed, the young lads, the General and the sister under him, and the novice behind him, as well as the nun with the Murano parsnip, all agreed to cry out with one voice, like choristers harmonize, or more truly, as blacksmiths pound hammers. As each took care to finish off, all to be heard was "ah, ah," "hug me," "turn me over," "my sweet tongue," "give it to me," "take it," "push harder," "wait till I do it," "do it now," "hold me," "help!" With voices murmuring and moaning aloud, it seemed like musical runs of *sol, fa, re, mi, do.* The widened eyes, the panting, the spanking, the bouncing of the chests, beds, chairs, and bedposts made everything shake and rattle as if there were an earthquake.

Antonia. Fire!

Nanna. Eight long sighs arose at once from the liver, lungs, heart, and soul of the Reverend *et cetera*, from the sisters and from the little friars, that made a wind so great it would have blown out eight torches. Breathlessly they fell about the room from fatigue like drunks falling from wine. And I, who had been nearly unstrung from the frustration of gazing, suitably withdrew, and sitting down, took a look at that suchness of glass.[32] (1:25–28)

Nanna. I returned to the chink, where light gleamed through from a lamp the sisters had lit upon nightfall. And gazing anew, I saw them all naked. And certainly, if the General, the nuns, and little friars had been old, I would have compared them to Adam, Eve, and the other souls in Limbo—but leave the comparisons to the Sybils. The General got his calf, the long slender friar, to mount upon a small square table where the four Christianettes of the Antichrist were eating. Proclaiming the joust, the lad held up a stick instead of a trumpet, as trumpeters do their instruments. After a "tarantara," he declared: "The grand Sultan of Babylon notifies all the gallant jousters to take the field with lances at the ready, and to the one that breaches the most targets will be given a hairless ring with which he may amuse himself all night long, *et amen*."[33]

Antonia. What a fine proclamation. His master must have composed a draft for him. Go on, Nanna.

Nanna. And now the jousters are in order. They made themselves a quintain with the backside of that dim-sighted little negress[34] that was previously consuming glass with great gusto, and drew lots. The first stroke fell to the trumpeter. While one of his friends continued blowing his horn, he spurred himself onward with his fingers up his ass as he buried his spear to the hilt in the shield of his sweetheart. Since that thrust was worth three, he was much applauded.

Antonia. Ha ha ha!

Nanna. The General's turn was next by lot, and he ran with his lance at ready to stuff the hole of the one who had filled the sister. So they were fixed and rigid as the bounds between two fields. The third stroke went to one of the nuns, and not having a lance of fir, she took one of glass and at the first stroke embedded it in the General's behind while, just to be on the safe side, placing the balls inside her.

Antonia. Hers must have been big!

Nanna. Then came the turn of the second friar, who drove his arrow smack into the target of the first pretty. The other nun, copying her sister with the lance of the two balls, assaulted the rear of the young lad who, upon receiving the thrust, began squirming like an eel. Then came the last female and male, and there was reason for laughter because the girl buried her glass ring-cake,[35] on which she had breakfasted that morning, in her friend's bumhole. Remaining hindmost of all, the last friar planted his spear in her behind and so they all seemed like a skewer of damned souls, ready for Satan to roast on the fire at Lucifer's carnival.

Antonia. Ha ha ha! What a feast!

Nanna. The squinty sister was a very funny one indeed, for as everyone was pushing and shoving, she was saying the most delightful nonsense in the world. Hearing them I let out a laugh and was overheard, so I pulled myself back, knowing that they had heard me. Some started squabbling, and a short while later, when I returned to the spy hole, it was covered with a bed sheet, so I could not see the rest of the joust nor to whom was awarded the prize. (1:30–31)

Antonia. The holes in those walls would put a sieve to shame.

Nanna. I think that they couldn't care less about stopping them up, and enjoyed watching each other. Whatever the case may be, I overheard a huffing, sighing, grunting, and snuffling that sounded as though it came from ten people in their dreams, groaning. Paying attention, I heard whispering, at the partition on the opposite side of the one where the joust was carried out. I put my eye to the chink and saw two fresh, fleshy sisters with four white legs in the air, showing off their white, round, quivering thighs. You would have thought of milk. Each held in hand her carrot of glass. Said one to the other, "What stupidity to believe that our appetites can be satisfied with these dirty daubers that have neither kisses nor tongue nor hands to play upon our keys. And if we get all this pleasure from these cold instruments, imagine the pleasure from real flesh and blood. We are right to be called foolish if we waste our best time with pieces of glass." "You know, Sister," replied the other one, "I suggest you come with me." "And where are you going," she asked. "At nightfall I wish to forsake this order and go away with a young man to Naples. He has a friend, a blood brother, who'd be just right for you. Let's leave this cave, this sepulchre, and feel our ages like young women are supposed to." The friend needed little convincing for she was halfway up. To accept the invitation they at once hurled the glass fruit-trees against the wall, covering the shattering din by yelling "Cats! Cats!"—pretending these animals had broken their pitchers and other things. Jumping off the bed they made a parcel of their best clothing and left their cell while I remained. (1:32)

Nanna. While the good and charitable Abbess played with her phallic idol,[36] there was a soft tapping at the door of their cell that surprised both of them. Hearing another sound, they realized it was the confessor's acolyte, whom they immediately admitted. The boy knew what they were really like, so they did not hide their game from him. The treacherous Abbess, deserting the chaffinch of the father to grab the son's goldfinch by the wings, longing to rub the youngster's bow on her lyre, entreated the monk, "My love, do me a favor?" "I'm happy to do whatever you require," that nasty brother answered. "I want to grate this cheese on my grater," she told him, "but you must put your harpoon in the drum of your spiritual son. And if it pleases you, we'll give the horses the go to gallop. If not, we'll keep trying something else, because we're sure to find something that pleases us." After Friar Galasso had hauled the sails from the boy's behind, her ladyship lay down on her back, threw open her bird-cage, popped the nightingale inside, and pulled all the weight on top of her to the delight of all concerned. And I don't have to tell you that she endured some distress with such a great globe of the hemispheres upon her belly, which she kneaded as a piece of cloth is scrunched and rubbed at a fuller's. Finally she discharged her load and they their crossbows, thus ending the game. I could never tell you how much wine they swilled and pastry they devoured. (1:35)

Nanna. Having read the letter, I kissed it and hid it in my bosom. I removed the covering from the parcel and noticed it was a very nice prayer book that my friend sent me. That's what I thought at first. It was bound in green velvet, signifying love, with ribbons of silk. I picked it up smiling, regarding it fondly, and kissed it all over, declaring it the most beautiful prayer book I had ever seen, and dismissed the courier, instructing him to kiss his master for me. Alone, I opened the book to read the *Magnificat* and noticed it was full of pictures of people diverting themselves in the same manner as the learned nuns. While looking at one of the pictures of a woman letting her private parts hang out of a bottomless basket hung on a rope, to fall upon an immense member, I laughed so loudly that a sister who'd become a close friend came running, and demanded "What's so funny?" Without keeping anything from her, I told her, and showed her the prayer book. We got so much pleasure from looking at it that we got the urge to try some of the positions depicted, and so we turned to the glass handle. My friend placed it so admirably between her legs that one would have thought it was a man's organ facing its temptation. I lay on my back like one of those women on the bridge of Santa Maria, and placed my legs on her shoulders. Poking me now in the good side and now in the bad one, she quickly made me do what I was there for. Then, after she took the position I'd been in, I returned blood pudding for cake. (1:53–54)

Part Two, Dialogue One

Nanna. The monks are calling me and urging me to tell you that in this day and age, women smell of mould, and it all comes from the priests, generals, priors, ministers, provincials, and the other rabble leagued with the reverends and the most reverends. When they sleep with a woman they waste her like someone treats food who's already eaten to bursting just before. And even though you sing the song of old men to them—

> Slug and snail
>> Bring forth your three little horns,
> Three and four
>> And those of the Stablemaster—

they don't get a rise until their husbands come to bed with them.

Pippa. Friars and priests have husbands?
Nanna. In the same way they have wives!
Pippa. Fire!
Nanna. I would like to tell you and at the same time not tell you.
Pippa. Why not?
Nanna. Because telling the truth crucifies Christ. I've said it already, it's a nice piece of work too. Telling lies gets a kind reception, and telling truth a bad one. It's a wretched tongue that calls me an old whore and thieving go-between. And so I tell you that the big fish of the friary and priesthood sleep with courtesans so they can see them get screwed by their male whores (*bardassoni*)—yes, male whores. And they whet their appetite by seeing them drilled *per alia via,* as the epistle says. And you must account them good friends and go when they summon you. Understand me properly, if they can have their lovers do what they wish with you, then they fall in love with you and throw all the money of the bishopric, the abbey, the chapter house and the order after you.

Pippa. By following your advice and selling myself to them, I hope to get everything out of this, right down to the bell in the belfry.

Nanna. It's only your duty to do it. (2:66–67)

Part Two, Dialogue Two
Nanna. Those who say the first one who used us like males (*maschi*) the very first time did not have to force us to take his peg in our rears, is a liar and a damned liar at that. And it's also true that cursed money is to blame for bewitching the first woman to turn to that side. I, having been one of the most wicked of women and received my share of it, never used to consent to that unless the pleadings of my client became so overwhelming that I would turn and stick my ass in his stomach and ask him, "What's next after this?"

Pippa. Indeed, what'll be next?

Nanna. And the laughter that comes from their throats when they see it enter and when they see it exit. And when they push hard to the side, or thrust in certain weak spots, they are in ecstasy for hurting us. Sometimes they take a really big mirror and after making us strip nude, make us stay in the most indecent postures they can dream up. They devour our face, our bosom, breasts, nipples, shoulders, bodies, slits, and thighs with their eyes, and I cannot tell you how much pleasure they derive from them. And how many times do you think they put their husbands and their young studs at peepholes so they too can gawk?

Pippa. Really?

Nanna. I wish it were not so. And how many times do you think that they satisfy three at once, in the priestly fashion? O Abyss, from now on don't just open, throw wide your gates if you wish! (2:122–23)

Antonio Rocco (1586–1652)

A brief dialogue on male homoerotic pedagogy and seduction, Rocco's *L'Alcibiade fanciullo a scola* counters conventional moral and religious claims to advocate such intergenerational relations according to classical precedent. Many of his rationales could have been used to justify and promote same-sex love in general. Although little is currently known about this Venetian philosopher, priest, and libertine, he was a member of the Accademia degli Incogniti, along with Ferrante Pallavicino (1615–1644). The latter authored one of the most widely known exemplars of early modern erotica, *La retorica delle puttane* (Whore's Rhetoric, 1642), and was beheaded for his anticlerical satires. Between 1635 and 1652 Rocco was denounced five times for various heterodoxies, including praise of sex as nature's means for pleasure and delight whether pursued "naturally" or "against nature." His *Alcibiade* similarly argues that it is natural to use all bodily means of sexual pleasure, for nature provided them all. Rocco's two speakers are the pederastic pedagogue Philotimus ("love of honor," "honorable love," or "honored love")[37] and his pupil Alcibiades. Philotimus thus correlates with Socrates, often invoked as an authority warranting male same-sex love: according to Plato's *Symposium*, Socrates's famously handsome student Alcibiades found the philosopher irresistibly attractive. In response to his teacher's seductive propositions, Rocco's Alcibiades voices the conventional objections, and as he changes his mind, that expresses the strength of Philotimus's arguments and furnishes erotic intrigue.

Probably published in Venice around 1651, the first edition bears a false imprint, Juann Wart, Oranges 1652, to dodge legal sanctions, and also a false attribution on the title page: "D. P. A.," presumably to suggest "the divine" *Pietro Aretino, as he was sometimes called, but punning on "di Padre Antonio." Although this text does not seem to have been published again until the nineteenth century, it records attitudes and ideas circulating much beyond Rocco and his circle in Venice, or even Italy, as Giovanni Dall' Orto has shown,[38] and seems to recall Antonio Vignali's much earlier *La cazzaria*, which had a wider circulation (*Erotica; Turner, *Schooling Sex* 93). As few early modern texts advocating homoeroticism in an extended and programmatic way survive, such writings as Rocco's are important for the history of sex differences and for related cultural and theoretical debates. Letters by the Venetian Giovàn Francèsco Loredàn state that he had a manuscript of this dialogue around 1630, and that Rocco might have written it much earlier.[39] Aside from the much more readily censored medium of print, prohomoerotic texts and arguments had a significant manuscript circulation, as in this case.

The Boy Alcibiades at School [40] *(1651?, written before 1630)*

"I shall fill the vessel of your mind," said Philotimus, "with the seed of doctrines plentiful and pleasant, such doctrines as will seem to you supernatural. You shalt not encounter the stern rigor I am accustomed to use with the other children to gain their respect; nay, our first interviews will brim over with pleasure and sweet trust. Indeed, as a gage of my affection, and to seal the equality of our intercourse, let me bestow this, need I say honorable, kiss on your young lips." (42)

At this renewed attack the child, quivering and growing suddenly pale, took a hasty step backwards.

"Fear not, my son," said the master, "no man's tongue will harm you, save when its brash impudence offends the bounds of Justice. That eloquence you wish to learn from me, which your first instructors pursued so zealously, my devotion will impart to you, but you shall not possess it truly until your tongue be joined to mine. For the hand helps the hand, the mind assists the mind, the tongue aids the tongue. Come here, come here, my ruby...," and folding him against his bosom, he punctuated each word he spoke with a lingering kiss. (44)

The child turned away a little, and looked scornful, but it was only one of those coy rebuffs which but kindle lust and add spice to wantonness. Indeed Alcibiades rebelled not and even suffered his master to fondle the shapely, small and velvet globes of his apples. Therefore the latter was feverishly visiting the lad's garden of Eden, and, in the futile transports of unsatisfied desire, nevertheless, upon touching the delicious entry with his finger, he apprehended the surpassing felicity of the blessed. This delightful play continued a short while before Philotimus was called away upon some pressing affair; but his senses having been moved to such rapture, the merest thought of that bliss he had just quit obliged him to interrupt his business. (45)

[Having returned, Philotimus continues Alcibiades' instruction.]

But let's come now to the point," urged Philotimus. "In which of our gods do we have faith? In Jupiter, king of the gods and of men. Didn't he kidnap Ganymede? Or if the deeds of the gods are for the example and imitation of men, why are we prohibited from that which they teach with their deeds? Jupiter was allowed to use force, he was a god, his divine will is the measure of justice for our deeds, since we don't have the sovereign ruling power; let prayers be in place of force, let it be that the desires of the deaf bend to uniform consent. Apollo didn't enjoy Cyparissus and Hyacinth? Hercules of Hylas? And is not Cupid, moreover, man and boy in order to show the principal love to be of boys; and for the feminine love there is Venus, who has no weapons nor fire, if she does not borrow them from her son.

"Boys then have the first scepter in love, the women have delegated and dependent authority; therefore, so very far it is from the truth that this sovereign delight is abhorred by the gods, that they prepare atrocious punishments, as it is far from right that a servant should be punished for executing the orders and the examples of his master; and to you it will be believable exactly as if you heard it said that the sun at night shuts itself up in a cocoon of the moon. (57–58)

"If God is always God, immutable and very wise in works of justice and clemency, why is it that now he doesn't punish that fault? Is he perhaps different from what he was? Has he changed his opinion? Is he perhaps afraid of us? Or is he destroying the work of the world he has made? If a watch has motion from wheels and counterweights that its maker has given it, is it a defect of this watch that it tells the hours in this way or in another? Inclinations are counterweights given us by nature and God; whosoever follows these doesn't stray from his own origins, he does not go against his maker. (59)

"And it is ... a notable thing that of all the very diligent, famous, and universal writers of our Greeks, there is not even one that made mention of [the punishment of Sodom as described in the Bible]. . . ."

"Perhaps," responded Alcibiades, "perhaps being of your view, they didn't, for their self-interest, want to take away this pleasure from men by frightening them."

"It isn't likely, son, that which you propose, if they had believed it to be a divine scourge, this pleasure prohibited and punished by God to whose rule everything is subject, [so] as to not fall into his disdain and not be esteemed guilty of a tacit offense. Or at least if they were so obstinate, keeping it only for themselves by frightening the others at the same time, [they] would have had themselves judged as pious and would have put themselves in secure possession of this power, so that they would have filled up volumes, as well as papers and sheets. This is easier to believe because some of them preferred life to the truth, and they had the utmost integrity and were very observant of justice; so that they did not write of it because there was no foundation of truth upon which they could base their writing.

"In fact, the author of this invention [i.e., sanctions against sex between males], [since] it seemed to him that it was too severe to put into action and what he had invented by amplification and by terror in his written laws, does not say that through the simple use of young boys the aforementioned cities [i.e., Sodom and Gomorrah] were submerged, but because they were impious, cruel, miserly, greedy, violent, and that their final ruin was the violence they directed against those angels. And thus ... violence, therefore, was punished, not pleasure; cruelty, not love; inhumanity, not embraces. I say this, however, alluding to the tale, not to what happened. . . . [T]here is stated a decree in which one of the very excellent ones, who extolled and was believed to have dealings with God, threatened punishments for the crimes of the people: and when it came to the use of young boys, did not complain of this, but reproached those who left the young boys of their nation for foreigners. . . . If it is a crime to leave them, it is therefore praiseworthy and a virtuous act to take care of them; and owing love in the first place to one's own rather than to foreigners, abandoning those for these is against the laws of nature. So that, by reproaching the mingling with others, he wants us to get together with our own. But if the human laws, made by whoever wants to, become the universals, the infallible ones of nature, you will find the use of young boys ordained rather than prohibited by them. And here I come to the proof.

"I call laws of nature ... those that by the light of the intellect are in every man, of whatever sect or nation, naturally, without artifice, and approved by universal consensus, by the wisest and by the most just. They are divided into two principal parts: one concerns the honor of God, the other the benevolence and equity of the neighbor. ...

"To love God above everything; [and one's] neighbor as oneself; or not to offend God or the neighbor. Now these two precepts, if in effect they are different, should not be confused with one another, because if they were contained in one another and confused they would not be distinct, so that there would be only one. And if not offending God or the neighbor were the same, it would be enough to say not offending God: they are then indubitably distinct, neither the one depends nor belongs to the other. Now I ask you: if your neighbor is happy about what you want, has pleasure and is satisfied, and sometimes benefited, could one call him offended? Would the precept be transgressed? Could we call him insulted? Would he summon you to justice?"

"On the contrary," responded Alcibiades, "the precept will have been fulfilled, and will be rewarded; and I consider calling him offended as different as giving would be from robbing."

"You conclude well," answered the teacher, "but if it is so, that a young boy is happy to give of himself to whoever desires him, and he takes delight and use from it, is the neighbor offended here? Who would say this nonsense? And if from free will, the royal gift of God, comes the will and the power to do what pleases him, why can't he do it? If one can lend a house, a horse, a dog, why not his own limbs? Who is a tyrant so wicked that, giving liberty to a servant of his, he prohibits him the use? Therefore, did God make us free so that we are slaves of our passions and the reckless excesses of them? He, thus, in the tempering that He gave to our fragility, will see the causes weaken, will take again that which is His? Or perhaps he pities our well-being? Does he envy our pleasure? If one does not give solace with pleasures to human calamity, the inhabitants of the world will be prisoners of Pluto. Man would not be king of the animals, but the epilogue of sorrows and torments. These foolish beliefs should not disturb the gloriousness of your soul."

"Why then is it that the young boys that submit to the pleasures of men are despised and considered infamous under the disgraceful name of *bardassi*? And if what you say is true, perhaps the common way of men has not transformed reality into language. Relieve me of this doubt," said Alcibiades.

"This name of *bardassa*," responded the teacher, "is not suitable nor should be given, and in effect is not given, to boys who through affection and courtesy graciously give themselves to respectable and worthy lovers. As one does not give the title of prostitute to that fair amorous damsel who kindly gives in to her lover to satisfy the laws of love: on the contrary, it is so far from reasonable and just, that in place of these unworthy epithets, by wise and discreet people, they are called *divi* and *dive*, redeemers of human afflictions, restorers of falling and afflicted spirits. And by many great princes altars and temples have been erected to them, priests have been dedicated to them and sacrifices and incense have been offered to them. Of these things the history of the Greeks and of the Roman writers is full. *Bardassa* really means mercenary and venal boy, who only for simple recompense, almost by measurement, sells himself, nor is concerned with other than his servile earnings. An amorous young boy is as different from the mercenary as a venerable priest would be from a vituperous simoniac; each is a priest, each administers the same sacerdotal offices: but the first in the ministry seeks excellent works, the greatness of his office, the spiritual gratification of the people, the due of divine laws; the other, the useful, self-interest and earnings. So that the first is sacrosanct and detestable the second. Things of high value must not be exposed to the baseness of a price: and what thing is more valuable and more worthy than amorous young boys? Glorious and divine boy, who, without a mercenary goal, blesses men on earth; vile infamous mercenary, who sells himself for a price, who from being gardener and treasurer of the joys of love becomes vile butcher of his own flesh."

"Isn't it perhaps reasonable," answered Alcibiades, "that whoever does things for others receives benefits? That he who is ready to serve others is relieved in his needs? Why, therefore, can't a boy, without falling from the glorious into the foul, receive money from whoever receives such sweetness from him?"

"My beautiful boy," responded the teacher, "markets are one thing and courtesies are another. A man is never so rich nor so powerful that at a certain time he doesn't need another man; and whoever gives benefits expects them too. The beloved boy, then, should be remembered and given gifts by his kind lover; he should be to him very liberal and kind, but far from the terms of convention and wages, neither tacit nor expressed.

"Love makes rules in these cases; he develops and works it out honorably and in a worthwhile manner; gifts and kindness and favors are not prohibited, only sordid merchandising." (60–65)

[Alcibiades questions his teacher: "Pray tell me the pleasure is keener with lads or with the women, and why."]

"There is something offensive in the mingling of juices," observed Philotimus. "It is like an untimely and unseasonable downpour which wearies and enfeebles the senses. So vast is the cunt's capacity it's frightening. It is a labyrinth inviting one to lose oneself in its passages rather than to tarry and take one's pleasure there. Mark, on the contrary, that pretty declivity leading to the flowered garden of a boy. Does it not enclose all the delights? Doesn't the motion of those two fresh, rounded, velvety little cushions gamboling between your thighs incline one to the pitch of wantonness? Doesn't it surpass all the pleasures, real and imagined, in women? Doesn't it seem to you that Nature, in giving you these happy, happy cheeks, that plump form and dainty softness, expressly intended to teach us her purpose, which is to fill the concavity of our body when it presses against them?[41] It is the opposite with women. In congress the convexity of the two stomachs joining together leaves a gap between the parts and hinders the perfect harmony necessary to extreme bliss. Whereas taking one's pleasure of a boy one is neither deprived of the sweetness of his kiss, nor of the delight in breathing in the perfumed breeze that escapes between his passionate lips. Here too the agreement is complete and the rapture entirely shared, so long as the beloved lies in such a way that he can turn his visage and bring it close to his lover's; meanwhile, depending on the charming stripling's fancy, the spring onion is planted in his garden or quivers in his hand. (65–67)

"As to know why some youths discharge more frequently and plentifully than others, the reason is that, in them, the parts of their 'garden' are connected to their little 'finch' with subtler nerves, which improves the circulation of the spirits; so that the wanton agitation of the 'bird' accompanies and sometimes even precedes the transports of the 'garden.' Certain lads find such delight in being mounted that they become mad with desire, begging and praying and even forcing their lovers to do the thing to them. These children are keener and quicker than all others because the abundance of lascivious spirits in them makes their motions nimble and causes them to be hotter in action; and therefore their body constantly betrays the goal to which it tends, not to mention the wanton movements of their hips and a certain lascivious to-and-fro which is produced in them by the circulation of the spirits. There are other boys who are tranquil and modest, and have not the same immoderate urge to 'chime,' but notwithstanding how feebly the amorous inclination common to all creatures in them dwells, they are nevertheless as readily inclined as the others to yield to tender toyings, which they like though they'll never admit to it." (82–83)

"I'll submit to your urgings," Alcibiades declared. "It is the desire to learn above all which decides me. Look, I am ready to satisfy you. . . ."

Thereupon he lifted his gown and modestly took the posture the circumstances required. The master assisted him with his hand, and before long the lad's arse displayed its glorious love treasures which put the sky and the stars to shame. The sun himself, vanquished by those more than celestial glories, hastened to veil his visage. What poet could ever describe the wonders richly scattered through that epitome of the marvels of the universe. The two hemispheres, like unto two celestial spheres, with coursing blood tinted, were starred with sprightly tufts of hyacinths and privet. They quivered at the slightest touch, darkened with a thousand rubies that sparkled on a bed of milk and cinnabar. All was but delightful meadows, flowered gardens, many-hued rainbows, white beams of light and twinkling stars. Their constant, slow, and amorous motions would have roused a statue of marble or bronze; ah, the majestic and beauteous spectacle of that little bud, whose folds were tight and dainty like a rose before it blossoms, a lovely floweret tinted with a thousand mottled tones among which the purest snow disputed with gorgeous purple. (85)

How they continued their pleasant frolics, their amorous toyings, shall be related in the second part, which will be more wanton still.[42] (87)

Endnotes

Introduction

1. Marlowe, *Edward II*, 1.4.391–97, in *Complete Works*, ed. Fredson Bowers, 2 vols. (Cambridge, UK: Cambridge University Press, 1973), 2:35.
2. DiGangi, *The Homoerotics of Early Modern Drama* (Cambridge, UK: Cambridge University Press, 1997), 2; also cited in text hereafter.
3. Smith, *Homosexual Desire in Shakespeare's England: A Cultural Poetics* (Chicago: University of Chicago Press, 1991), 18; Alan Bray, *Homosexuality in Renaissance England*, 2nd ed. (New York: Columbia University Press, 1995). Both also cited in text hereafter.
4. Bishop, *Beautiful Blossoms* (London: 1577), STC 3091, fol. 51[b].
5. Digangi, ix-x, 10–19, 22. In my view, he underestimates the importance of theological discourse and the role of continental influences in assessing the status of sex between males in early modern English culture. See Kenneth Borris, "'Ile hang a bag and a bottle at thy back': Barnfield's Homoerotic Advocacy and the Construction of Homosexuality," in Borris and George Klawitter, eds., *The Affectionate Shepherd: Celebrating Richard Barnfield* (Selinsgrove, Ky.: Susquehanna-Associated University Presses, 2001), 196–202. Also cited in text hereafter.
6. Bret Hinsch, *Passions of the Cut Sleeve: The Male Homosexual Tradition in China* (Berkeley: University of California Press, 1990); Jonathan D. Spence, *The Memory Palace of Matteo Ricci* (New York: Viking-Sifton, 1984), ch. 7.
7. Janet E. Halley, "*Bowers v. Hardwick* in the Renaissance," in Jonathan Goldberg, ed., *Queering the Renaissance* (Durham, S. C.: Duke University Press, 1994), 17, 19.
8. See Bernadette J. Brooten's comment in "The *GLQ* Forum: Lesbian Historiography before the Name?" *GLQ* 4 (1998): 612–13.
9. See, e.g., J. W. Binns, *Intellectual Culture in Elizabethan and Jacobean England: The Latin Writings of the Age* (Leeds, UK: Cairns, 1990).
10. Traub, *The Renaissance of Lesbianism in Early Modern England* (Cambridge, UK: Cambridge University Press, 2002), 12; hereafter cited in text.
11. Andreadis, *Sappho in Early Modern Europe: Female Same-Sex Literary Erotics 1550–1714* (Chicago: University of Chicago Press, 2001), ch. 1; also cited in text hereafter.
12. Craig A. Williams, *Roman Homosexuality: Ideologies of Masculinity in Classical Antiquity* (Oxford: Oxford University Press, 1999), 7; hereafter cited in text.
13. My treatment of such issues here draws on but supersedes Borris 236–44 (an earlier discussion that focuses on more local problems in study of Barnfield and remains useful for that purpose), whereas I now seek to address historiography of early modern homoeroticism more generally. The terminology I use here thus also supersedes that earlier discussion's.

14. For example, Francis Barker, *The Tremulous Private Body* (London: Methuen, 1984); Andreadis, 2–3.
15. See David Aers, "A Whisper in the Ear of Early Modernists; or, Reflections on Literary Critics Writing the 'History of the Subject,'" in Aers, ed., *Culture and History 1350–1600: Essays on English Communities, Identities, and Writing* (Detroit: Wayne State University Press, 1992), 177–202; hereafter cited in text.
16. Halperin, *How to Do the History of Homosexuality* (Chicago: University of Chicago Press, 2002), ch. 1 (quoting 29, 46); also cited in text hereafter. The volume collects revised versions of various essays Halperin published on this topic between 1992 and 2000 (listed ix–x). For further critiques of the acts paradigm in early modern applications, see Borris 236–44, and Stephen O. Murray, *Homosexualities* (Chicago: University of Chicago Press, 2000), 139–61.
17. For Morlino, see Cecile Beurdeley, *L'amour bleu* (New York: Rizzoli, 1978), 92–93. For another example, see David F. Greenberg, *The Construction of Homosexuality* (Chicago: University of Chicago Press, 1988), 309.
18. Fradenburg and Freccero, "Preface" and "Introduction," in Fradenburg and Freccero, eds., *Premodern Sexualities* (New York and London: Routledge, 1996), xi, xx.
19. Bredbeck, *Sodomy and Interpretation: Marlowe to Milton* (Ithaca: Cornell University Press, 1991), ch. 4.
20. Sinfield, *The Wilde Century: Effeminacy, Oscar Wilde and the Queer Movement* (New York: Columbia University Press, 1994), 13, 31. Hereafter cited in text.
21. Jordan, *The Invention of Sodomy in Christian Theology* (Chicago: University of Chicago Press, 1997), 164. Frantzen, *Before the Closet: Same-Sex Love from "Beowulf" to "Angels in America"* (Chicago: University of Chicago Press, 1998), 167, 171, 174. Compare Francesca Canadé Sautman and Pamela Sheingorn, "Introduction: Charting the Field," in Sautman and Sheingorn, eds., *Same Sex Love and Desire Among Women in the Middle Ages* (New York: Palgrave, 2001), 1–47. Jordan and the latter cited hereafter in text.
22. Brooten, *Love Between Women: Early Christian Responses to Female Homoeroticism* (Chicago: University of Chicago Press, 1996). Halperin debates Brooten in "Lesbian Historiography," 557–630. Richlin, "Not Before Homosexuality: The Materiality of the *Cinaedus* and the Roman Law against Love between Men," *Journal of the History of Sexuality* 3 (1992–93): 523–73.
23. See Cady, "'Masculine Love,' Renaissance Writing, and the 'New Invention' of Homosexuality," *Journal of Homosexuality* 23.1–2 (1992): 9–40; his "The 'Masculine Love' of the 'Princes of Sodom' 'Practising the Art of Ganymede' at Henri III's Court: The Homosexuality of Henri III and His *Mignons* in Pierre de L'Estoile's *Mémoires-Journaux*," in Jacqueline Murray and Konrad Eisenbichler, eds., *Desire and Discipline: Sex and Sexuality in the Premodern West* (Toronto: University of Toronto Press, 1996), 123–54.
24. Halperin, ch. 4; a revision of "How to Do the History of Male Homosexuality," *GLQ* 6 (2000): 67–123.
25. See Giovanni Dall' Orto, "'Socratic Love' as a Disguise for Same-sex Love in the Italian Renaissance," *Journal of Homosexuality* 16.1–2 (1988): 35–65.
26. See Cady, "Renaissance Awareness and Language for Heterosexuality: 'Love' and 'Feminine Love,'" in Claude J. Summers and Ted-Larry Pebworth, eds., *Renaissance Discourses of Desire* (Columbia: University of Missouri Press, 1993), 43–158.
27. See Charles R. Forker, "'Masculine Love,' Renaissance Writing, and the 'New Invention' of Homosexuality: An Addendum," *Journal of Homosexuality* 31.3 (1996): 85–93.
28. On Ricchieri, *Encyclopedias and Reference Works. On Holland, *Love and Friendship.
29. Aristotle, *Nicomachean Ethics*, 8.7.2, 8.8.5; Cicero, *On Friendship*, 19.69, 20.71–73.
30. See William W. Chiang, *"We Two Know the Script; We Have Become Good Friends": Linguistic and Social Aspects of the Women's Script Literacy in Southern Hunan, China* (Lanham, Md.: University Press of America, 1995); Cathy Silber, "From Daughter to Daughter-in-Law in the Women's Script of Southern Hunan," in Christina K. Gilmartin et al., eds., *Engendering China: Women, Culture, and the State* (Cambridge, Mass.: Harvard University Press, 1994), 47–68.
31. See Alan K. Smith, "Fraudomy: Reading Sexuality and Politics in Burchiello," in *Queering the Renaissance*, 84–106; Mary Bly, *Queer Virgins and Virgin Queens on the Early Modern Stage* (Oxford: Oxford University Press, 2000), also cited in text hereafter.
32. Michael Rocke, *Forbidden Friendships: Homosexuality and Male Culture in Renaissance Florence* (Oxford: Oxford University Press, 1996), 148–51, citing studies of further European

cities. Later, Rocke oddly backtracks: "There was no truly autonomous and distinctive 'sodomitical subculture'" in Florence, only "*a single male sexual culture* with prominent homoerotic character" (191, my emphasis). But theology, moral philosophy, and law clearly demarcated the perceived transgressive difference of male-male *versus* male-female sex, while many types of such homoerotic contact were prosecuted as Rocke himself shows (91–93). Leonardo Bruni (1369–1444), for example, "seems to have had a particular horror of homosexual behavior." Ficino calls sex between males a "wicked crime" comparable to "murder," and, unlike male-female copulation, specifically "against the order of nature" (see *Ficino, *De amore*, Speech II, chapter 7, and Speech VI, chapter 14, both reprinted subsequently). While calling for human "pity and compassion" for this "pestiferous and poisonous" "evil," Giovanni Pico della Mirandola (1463–1494) assumes it clearly deserves divine punishment. Benvenuto Cellini (1500–1571) takes for granted that being publicly called a sodomite (*soddomitaccio;* contextually a male who has sex with male youths, as Cellini's reply makes clear) is to be considered a horrible, infuriating injury (*scelleratamente, sporco, ingiuria*). Many other Florentines made such comments as these. Not single but diverse, *pace* Rocke, Florentine male sexual culture provided that necessary precondition of sodomitical community or nascent subculture. On Bruni, quoting James Hankins, *Plato in the Italian Renaissance*, 2 vols (Leiden: Brill, 1990), 2:396–97. Pico, *Commentary on a Canzone of Benivieni*, trans. Sears Jayne (New York: Peter Lang, 1984), 167. Cellini, *La vita*, in *Opere*, ed. Bruno Maier (Milan: Rizzoli, 1968), Book II, lxxi (530–32).

33. We may compare, e.g., how gays and lesbians in Israel became much more assertively public after the sodomy law's repeal in 1988. See Lee Walzer, *Between Sodom and Eden: A Gay Journey through Today's Changing Israel* (New York: Columbia University Press, 2000), ch. 5.

34. D'Ewes, *Diary*, ed. Elisabeth Bourcier (Paris: Didier, 1974), 92–93.

35. See, e.g., Judith M. Bennett and Amy M. Froide, eds., *Singlewomen in the European Past, 1250–1500* (Philadelphia: University of Pennsylvania Press, 1999).

36. Wahl, *Invisible Relations: Representations of Female Intimacy in the Age of Enlightenment* (Stanford: Stanford University Press, 1999). Her temporal scope is mainly after mine.

37. Helmut Puff, "Female Sodomy: The Trial of Katherina Hetzeldorfer (1477)," *Journal of Medieval and Early Modern Studies* 30 (2000): 41–61.

38. See *Giovanni della Porta, Thomas Middleton's poem "Ingling Pyander," or ancient *physiognomics. Also Rugh Mazo Karras and David Lorenzo Boyd, "'Ut cum muliere': A Male Transvestite Prostitute in Fourteenth-Century London," in *Premodern Sexualities*, 101–16.

39. As in, e.g., Bray, ch. 1; Traub, "Recent Studies in Homoeroticism," *English Literary Renaissance* 30 (2000): 284; Greenberg, 278. Subsequent citations of Traub in my General Introduction refer to her *Renaissance of Lesbianism*.

40. For discussion of such historiographical issues, cf. Aers, 196–97, Traub, 28–29.

41. On Jodelle, see *Ronsard. For probably allusive Shakespearean contexts, see, e.g., *A Midsummer Night's Dream*, 3.2.204–17; *Twelfth Night*, 5.1.215–22. *Complete Works*, ed. Stanley Wells et al. (Oxford: Clarendon, 1986).

42. Pasolini, Interview with Tommaso Anzoino, in his *Pier Paolo Pasolini, Il Castoro*, No. 51, p. 7.

43. A promising new resource now in press is Gilbert Herdt and Catharine R. Stimpson, eds., *Critical Terms for Gender Studies*, forthcoming from University of Chicago Press (2003?).

44. See, e.g., Winfried Schleiner, "'That Matter Which Ought Not to Be Heard Of': Homophobic Slurs in Renaissance Cultural Politics," *Journal of Homosexuality* 26.4 (1994): 41–75.

45. Du Bartas, *The Vocation, The Second Week*, in *The Divine Weeks and Works*, ed. Susan Snyder, trans. Josuah Sylvester, 2 vols. (Oxford: Clarendon, 1979), 2:525, 527 (lines 1301–06, 1365–70).

46. Anonymous, *The Legend of Orpheus and Euridice*, in his *[?], o[r] Loves Complai[nts]* (London: 1597), STC 16857, sigs. E6ᵇ–E8ᵇ.

47. Foucault, *An Introduction*, Vol. 1 of *The History of Sexuality*, trans. Robert Hurley (New York: Pantheon, 1978), 38, 101.

48. See Borris, 196–202; Bly, 143, 148n. 19, 186n. 134; Randy Conner, "Les Molles et les chausses: Mapping the Isle of Hermaphrodites in Premodern France," in Anna Livia and Kira Hall, eds., *Queerly Phrased: Language, Gender, and Sexuality* (Oxford: Oxford University Press, 1997), 129–33. On "sodomy" as sex either "male with male or female with female" in Gregor Reisch's encyclopedia widely used in the sixteenth century, see *Encyclopedias and Reference Works.

49. See Gordon Williams, *A Dictionary of Sexual Language and Imagery in Shakespearean and Stuart Literature*, 3 vols. (London: Athlone, 1997), s.v. "cynede."

Chapter 1

1. Jordan, *The Invention of Sodomy in Christian Theology* (Chicago: University of Chicago Press, 1997), 33; also cited hereafter in text.
2. Willet, *Hexapla in Genesin: That Is, a Sixfold Commentary upon Genesis* (London: 1608), STC 25683, 212–13. Arnold Williams surveys commentaries on Genesis from 1527 to 1633 in *The Common Expositor* (Chapel Hill: University of North Carolina Press, 1948).
3. Antonio de Corro, *A Theological Dialogue Wherein the Epistle to the Romans Is Expounded* (London: 1575), STC 5786, fols. 8^b–9^a. A Spanish Catholic, then a Protestant minister in London.
4. Judith C. Brown, *Immodest Acts: The Life of a Lesbian Nun in Renaissance Italy* (Oxford: Oxford University Press, 1986), 6–7; also cited hereafter in text.
5. David F. Greenberg, *The Construction of Homosexuality* (Chicago: University of Chicago Press, 1988), 141; also cited hereafter in text. Compare Saul M. Olyan, "'And with a Male You Shall Not Lie the Lying Down of a Woman': On the Meaning and Significance of Leviticus 18:22 and 20:13," *Journal of the History of Sexuality* 5 (1994): 179–206.
6. J. F. Harvey, "Homosexuality," *New Catholic Encyclopedia*, first edition, 118. However, J. Keefe's corresponding homophobic article in the second edition reinstates the alleged authority of Sodom's biblical destruction for condemnation of homosexuality (66–7).
7. See Bernadette J. Brooten, *Love Between Women: Early Christian Responses to Female Homoeroticism* (Chicago: University of Chicago Press, 1996), 244–53, 353; also cited hereafter in text.
8. See James A. Brundage, *Law, Sex, and Christian Society in Medieval Europe* (Chicago: University of Chicago Press, 1987); Thomas N. Tentler, *Sin and Confession on the Eve of the Reformation* (Princeton: Princeton University Press, 1977), 162–232.
9. See Greenberg, 218–34; Merry E. Weisner-Hanks, *Christianity and Sexuality in the Early Modern World: Regulating Desire, Reforming Practice* (London and New York: Routledge, 2000), 28–43, 49 (also cited hereafter in text); Brooten, ch. 11.
10. Greenberg, 261–70; Brown, 6–9, 12–16. Damian, *Book of Gomorrah: An Eleventh-Century Treatise against Clerical Homosexual Practices*, trans. Pierre J. Payer (Waterloo, Ont.: Wilfrid Laurier University Press, 1982).
11. Franco Mormando, *The Preacher's Demons: Bernardino of Siena and the Social Underworld of Early Renaissance Italy* (Chicago: University of Chicago Press, 1999), 127; hereafter cited in text.
12. Anne Lake Prescott, "English Writers and Beza's Latin Epigrams: The Uses and Abuses of Poetry," *Studies in the Renaissance* 21 (1974): 83–117; Winfried Schleiner, "'That Matter Which Ought Not to Be Heard Of': Homophobic Slurs in Renaissance Cultural Politics," *Journal of Homosexuality* 26.4 (1994): 63, 73n.39. The Benedictine priest Augustine Baker (1575–1641) claims Protestantism increased male-male sex at Oxford and Cambridge. *Memorials of Father Augustine Baker*, ed. Justin McCann and Hugh Connolly (London: Catholic Record Society, 1933), 34–35.
13. John Bale, *The Acts of English Votaries* (London: 1560), STC 1274, First Part, sig. M5^a; Second Part, sig. A2^a; hereafter cited in text.
14. See, e.g., St. Thomas Aquinas, *Summa contra gentiles, Book Three: Providence*, trans. Vernon J. Bourke, 2 vols. (Notre Dame: University of Notre Dame Press, 1975), 3.122; and Aquinas, *Summa theologiae*, 61 vols. (Cambridge, UK: Blackfriars, 1963–81), 1a2ae.31, 2a2ae.151–54. See also Nicholas Davidson, "Theology, Nature, and the Law: Sexual Sin and Sexual Crime in Italy from the Fourteenth to the Seventeenth Century," in Trevor Dean and K. J. P. Lowe, eds., *Crime, Society and the Law in Renaissance Italy* (Cambridge, UK: Cambridge University Press, 1994), 74–98; Bette Talvacchia, *Taking Positions: On the Erotic in Renaissance Culture* (Princeton: Princeton University Press, 1999), 114–24; Tentler, 162–232.
15. Heinrich Bullinger, *Fifty Godly and Learned Sermons*, trans. H. I. (London: 1577), STC 4056, 222, 236–37.
16. "Of the State of Matrimony," in *Sermons or Homilies to Be Read in Churches in the Time of Queen Elizabeth* (London: 1828), 551.

17. Compare, e.g., the Elizabethan homily "Of Whoredom and Uncleanness," in Ronald B. Bond, ed., *Certain Sermons or Homilies (1547) and A Homily against Disobedience and Wilful Rebellion (1570)* (Toronto: University of Toronto Press, 1987), 178–84.

18. *Geneva Bible*, introd. Lloyd E. Berry (Geneva: 1560; facsim. rpt. Madison: University of Wisconsin Press, 1969).

19. Thomas Wilson, *A Commentary upon the Most Divine Epistle of S. Paul to the Romans* (London: 1614), STC 25791, 93. Compare Brundage, 555–58.

20. As in, e.g., Aquinas, *Summa contra gentiles*, 3.16, and *Summa theologiae*, 2a2ae, Questions 153–54. See Brown, 7, 16; Jordan, chs. 6–7.

21. Aquinas, *Summa theologiae*, 2a2ae.154, Articles 11, 12; trans. Gilby.

22. Davidson, 77–78; Talvacchia, 114–24.

23. Aquinas, *Summa theologiae*, 2a2ae.154, Articles 11, 12, trans. Gilby. Compare Jordan, chs. 6–7.

24. Denis R. Janz, "Thomism," *Oxford Encyclopedia of the Reformation*.

25. See, e.g., Lactantius, *Divine Institutes*, trans. Sister Mary Francis McDonald (Washington: Catholic University of America Press, 1964), 6.23 (458); *John Marten.

26. Bray, *Homosexuality in Renaissance England*, 2nd ed. (New York: Columbia University Press, 1995), 16–17, 25–26, 31.

27. "The Thirty-nine Articles, 1563," in David Cressy and Lori Anne Ferrell, eds., *Religion and Society in Early Modern England: A Sourcebook* (London: Routledge, 1996), 67.

28. *Book of Common Prayer*, 1559, in Rev. William Keatinge Clay, ed., *Liturgies and Occasional Forms of Prayer Set Forth in the Reign of Queen Elizabeth*, Parker Society, vol. 30 (Cambridge, UK: 1847), 241–45.

29. "Of Whoredom," in Bond, ed., *Certain Sermons or Homilies*, quoting 178, 184.

30. The official English *Paraphrases* gathered the Acts and Gospels in the first volume, the Epistles in the second. Not specifically required by the *Injunctions*, the latter's circulation was much lower, though still in the thousands, not counting Latin editions. See E. J. Devereux, *Renaissance English Translations of Erasmus: A Bibliography to 1700* (Toronto: University of Toronto Press, 1983), 13–15, 14–52.

31. Erasmus, *The Second Tome or Volume of the Paraphrases*, ed. Miles Coverdale, trans. Coverdale et al. (London, 1552), STC 2866, fol. 3^a; cited hereafter in text.

32. See A. D. Wraight and Virginia F. Stern, *In Search of Christopher Marlowe: A Pictorial Biography* (London: 1965; rpt. Chichester: Hart, 1993), 309, 316.

33. See Raymond-Jean Frontain, "'An Affectionate Shepheard sicke for Love': Barnfield's Homoerotic Appropriation of the Song of Solomon," and Kenneth Borris, "'Ile hang a bag and a bottle at thy back': Barnfield's Homoerotic Advocacy and the Construction of Homosexuality," both in Kenneth Borris and George Klawitter, eds., *The Affectionate Shepherd: Celebrating Richard Barnfield* (Selinsgrove, Ky.: Susquehanna-Associated University Presses, 2001), 99–114, 220–23.

34. Wilson, *A Christian Dictionary* (London: 1616), STC 25787, s.v. "Libertines" (345).

35. For point one (and comment similar to point two): *Summa contra gentiles*, 3.122, trans. Bourke. Otherwise, *Summa theologiae*, 2a2a3.153, Articles 3, 12; trans. Gilby.

36. Tempier and Bacon cit. Joan Cadden, "'Nothing Natural Is Shameful': Vestiges of a Debate about Sex and Science in a Group of Late-Medieval Manuscripts," *Speculum* 76 (2001): 72–73.

37. John T. Noonan, Jr., *Contraception: A History of Its Treatment by the Catholic Theologians and Canonists*, enl. ed. (Cambridge, Mass.: Harvard University Press, 1986), 357n.34.

38. See Don Cameron Allen, *Doubt's Boundless Sea: Skepticism and Faith in the Renaissance* (Baltimore: Johns Hopkins, 1964); Michael Hunter, "The Problem of 'Atheism' in Early Modern England," *Royal Historical Society Transactions*, Fifth Series, 35 (1985): 135–57; Hunter and David Wootton, eds., *Atheism from the Reformation to the Enlightenment* (Oxford: Clarendon, 1992).

39. Aquinas, *Summa theologiae*, 2a2ae.153, Articles 4–5.

40. La Primaudaye, *French Academy*, trans. T. Bowes et al. (London: 1618), STC 15241, 81.

41. See Wraight and Stern, 306–16.

42. Giovanni Dall' Orto, "Antonio Rocco and the Background of his *L'Alcibiade fanciullo a scola* (1652)," in Mattias Duyves et al., eds.,*Among Men, Among Women: Sociological and Historical Recognition of Homosocial Arrangements* (Amsterdam: Sociologisch Instituut, 1983?), 230–31.

43. Winthrop, *History of New England*, ed. James Savage, 2 vols. (Boston: 1825), 2:265.

44. Cited in Michael Rocke, *Forbidden Friendships: Homosexuality and Male Culture in Renaissance Florence* (Oxford: Oxford University Press, 1996), 205; cf. 204–5, 221–23, 228–29.

45. William Monter, *Frontiers of Heresy: The Spanish Inquisition from the Basque Lands to Sicily* (Cambridge, UK: Cambridge University Press, 1990), 173–76; Weisner-Hanks, 123–24.

46. On early modern French and English translations of Bandello, see Frank S. Hook, ed., *The French Bandello*, by Matteo Bandello (Columbia: University of Missouri, 1948), 9–51.

47. On the story's dating, the historical Porcellio, and discrepancies between his life and the anecdote, see Delmo Maestri, ed., *La primo parte de le novelle*, by Matteo Bandello (Alessandria: Edizioni dell'orso, 1992), 67n.12.

48. Part One, Tale Six, in *Le novelle*. From *The Novels of Matteo Bandello*, trans. John Payne, 6 vols. (London: Villon Society, 1890), 1:90–100, revised by Kenneth Borris and Nicola Martino to eliminate Payne's interventions and pseudo-Elizabethan diction. We compared Bandello, *Le novelle*, ed. Gioachino Brognoligo, 5 vols. (Bari: Laterza, 1911–31), 1:94–100.

49. **the flesh of young goats always pleased him far more:** metaphor for Porcellio's strong sexual preference for young males. **go in overshoes through the dry:** overshoes are for wet weather; hence a metaphor for Porcellio's unconventional same-sex sexual behavior.

50. **going on ship through the wet:** metaphor for "appropriate" sex—male with female.

51. The friar laments allowing an unrepentant sodomite to ingest the eucharist: supposedly Christ's body.

52. Xenophon, *Symposium*, 8.30–31, citing Homer, either erroneously or referring to writings now lost. Following Xenophon, Alciato's epigram also invokes Homer. See James M. Saslow, *Ganymede in the Renaissance: Homosexuality in Art and Society* (New Haven: Yale University Press, 1986).

53. Compare, e.g., Sir Thomas Palmer (1540–1626), *Emblems*, ed. John Manning (New York: AMS, 1988), 11; Thynne, *Emblems and Epigrams*, ed. F. J. Furnivall (London: EETS, 1876), Emblem 45 (36); Henry Peacham (1576–1643?), *Minerva Britannia* (London: 1612), STC 19511, 48; and his MS Royal 12A LXVI, in Alan R. Young, ed., *Henry Peacham's Manuscript Emblem Books* (Toronto: University of Toronto Press, 1998), 188.

54. Translated by Kenneth Borris. Literally: "It is disgraceful to say, but a dishonest thing to do, / If someone excretes the burden of his belly into a choinix [i.e., vessel used for duly measuring the daily ration of food]. / This means to exceed the measure and decorum of sacred law / Such as it would be to be polluted by incestuous adultery" (trans. Dorota Dutsch). As the motto's generality indicates, *incesto* here has its figurative or transferred senses "sinful," "polluted," "criminal," and *adulterio* the senses pollution, defilement, illicit sex. Compare W. D. Heckscher, "Pearls from a Dungheap: Andrea Alciati's 'Offensive' Emblem, 'Adversus naturam peccantes,'" in Moshe Barasch and Lucy Freedman, eds., *Art the Ape of Nature: Studies in Honor of H. W. Janson* (New York: Abrams, 1981), 293–94.

55. Alciato, *Andreas Alciatus: Index Emblematicus*, ed. Peter M. Daly with Virginia W. Callahan, 2 vols. (Toronto: University of Toronto Press), 2: Emblem 80.

56. Compare Heckscher, 291–311; John Manning, "The Dungheap Revisited: Some Further Reflections on Alciato's Emblem LXXX and the Nature of Its 'Obscenity,'" in Peter M. Daly and Daniel S. Russell, eds., *Emblematic Perceptions* (Baden-Baden: Koerner, 1997), 123–34.

57. Cited in Heckscher, 294–95.

58. Translated by Faith Wallis, from Thuilius's commentary, in Alciato, *Emblemata cum commentariis* (Padua: Petrus Paulus Tozzi, 1621), 354–56. Her notes are parenthetically designated "(Wallis)."

59. Martial, *Epigrams*, 1.37. In a later epigram (1.90) Bassa is a tribade and prostitute.

60. **hysteron proteron:** reversal of conventional or causal order; a rhetorical term.

61. The *Authentica* are the collected imperial edicts or *Novellae*, a portion of Justinian's grand compilation of Roman laws and legal commentary, the *Corpus juris civilis*.

62. Actually, the *Lex Scantinia* (149 B. C. E.) apparently sought to discourage sexual harassment of freeborn male and female adolescents, while exempting young slaves from such protection (*Law). **Laetus:** Giulio Pomponio Leto, 1428–1497.

63. Referring to the *Codex* of Justinian's *Corpus juris civilis*, and its citation of the Augustan *Lex Julia*. Outlawed in 342, this crime actually pertains to husbands and wives having sex in any manner other than phallic penetration of the vagina.

64. Thuilius's three examples (Cornelius, Mergus, Lusius) are from Valerius Maximus, *Memorable Doings*, 6.1.10–12 (I silently normalize the names as in Loeb). But Valerius condemns disregard for freeborn status, not male-male sex. Compare Craig A. Williams, *Roman*

Homosexuality: Ideologies of Masculinity in Classical Antiquity (Oxford: Oxford University Press, 1999), 101–3.

65. That is, his case could not be heard in court. *The Digest of Justinian*, trans. Alan Watson, 4 vols. (Philadelphia: University of Pennsylvania Press, 1985), 3.1.1. **Ulpian:** Domitius Ulpianus (fl. 202–223), who became the major ancient authority on Roman law.

66. Plato, *Laws*, 836B–C. But the Athenian actually claims that, before Laius's reign (Oedipus's mythic father), sex between a male and a youth was illegal, without indicating gravity or type of punishment.

67. **Ausonius:** Roman writer and politician, c. 350. His current concordance has no such phrase.

68. So says Plato's Athenian, *Laws*, 838E–839B, while advocating men also avoid sex with women unless pregnancy is desired (a point Thuilius suppresses).

69. Maximus of Tyre (a second-century Middle Platonist), *The Philosophical Orations*, trans. M. B. Trapp (Oxford: Clarendon, 1997), Oration 20.9 (p. 180), drawing on Plato, *Laws*, 838E–39B.

70. Emending *particidas* to *patricidas* (Wallis).

71. See *Claude de Tesserant.

72. **carrying out:** *patrare*, i.e., to accomplish; perhaps also, to reach sexual climax (Wallis).

73. Probably part of Justinian's *Corpus juris civilis*, most likely the *Digest;* but not found. **Paulus:** Julius Paulus, early-third-century Roman legal authority, extensively excerpted in Justinian's *Digest.*

74. Thuilius cites two legal authorities and an encyclopedist. In *Liber quintus receptarum sententiarum integer*, Giulio Claro (1525–1575) discusses crimes in alphabetical order, including *Sodomia* (e.g., Frankfurt: Richter, 1604, 81–82). The 1587 Cologne edition of *De arbitraris judicum quaestionibus et causis*, by Giacomo Menochio (1532–1607), treats sex between males in section 2.2.286 (404–6). **Rhodiginus:** Ludovico Ricchieri (1469–1525); *Encyclopedias and Reference Works.

75. From Calvin, *A Commentary of John Calvin upon the First Book of Moses Called Genesis*, trans. Thomas Tymme (London: 1578), STC 4393, 399–402, 404–6, 409, 420–21.

76. **preposterous:** against nature, monstrous; confounding the right order of things, so "pre-post."

77. Compare Willet, *Commentary upon Genesis*, 209: the Sodomites "were come to that impudency that they were not ashamed publicly to proclaim their wickedness: but the scripture setteth down an unhonest thing by an honest name."

78. Compare Willet, *Commentary upon Genesis*, 213: God destroyed all the Sodomites including their infants. The latter "to increase . . . sorrow and torment in seeing the destruction of their children"; "to show his perfect detestation of that wicked nation, whose very seed was accursed"; and "to chastise the children for their fathers' sins." All the Sodomites were condemned to "everlasting damnation" according to "the sentence of Saint Jude" (Jude 1:6–7).

79. From Calvin, *A Commentary upon the Epistle of Saint Paul to the Romans*, trans. Christopher Rosdell (London: 1583), STC 4399, fols. 15^a, 16^b–17^a.

80. **the horrible sin of preposterous lust:** primarily referring to male-male coitus. Calvin might assume that Paul's reference to feminine "unnatural" sex refers to nonvaginal heteroerotic coitus, or to tribadism, or to both (Rom. 1:26–27). **preposterous:** against nature, monstrous.

81. **that filthiness . . . which the brute beasts abhor:** i.e., male-male sex, Calvin claims. **vulgar:** customary, ordinary.

82. **that one execrable example:** i.e., sex between males, Rom. 1:27.

83. From Calvin, *A Commentary upon S. Paul's Epistles to the Corinthians*, trans. Thomas Timme (London: 1577), STC 4400, fols. 65^a–67^a.

84. **The fourth:** i.e., "abusers of themselves with mankind," male same-sex lovers.

85. Canisius, *A Sum of Christian Doctrine*, trans. H. Garnet (London?: 1592–96), STC 4571.5, 251–67; also cited hereafter in text.

86. From Canisius's *A Sum of Christian Doctrine*, trans. H. Garnet (London?: 1592–96), STC 4571.5, 287–89, 296–98, 312–14, 324–29. I omit most of the plethora of marginal references citing ostensible biblical and theological (mainly patristic) corroborations. Canisius's biblical citations correspond to Roman Catholic versions, such as the Vulgate and early modern Douay English text.

87. **certes:** certainly.

88. Introducing this section, "Of Sins against the Holy Ghost," Canisius declares "the worst kind of sinning of all others without comparison, is when a man sinneth against the Holy Ghost."

89. "Thou shalt not lie with mankind as with womankind, because it is an abomination. Thou shalt not copulate with any beast, neither shalt thou be defiled with it" (Douay Bible). To convey especial condemnation at this point, the translator atypically preserves the Latin here, from the Vulgate, Lev. 18:22–23. Canisius marginally invokes the patristic authorities Tertullian, St. Augustine, and the especially homophobic St. John Chrysostom.

90. Henri Estienne, *A World of Wonders*, trans. R. C[arew?] (London: 1607), STC 10553, 358; also cited hereafter in text.

91. Coryate, *Coryats Crudities* (London: 1611), STC 5807, 264–65, 270–71.

92. From Estienne's *A World of Wonders*, trans. R. C[arew?] (London: 1607), STC 10553, 53–55, 68–69. Though the Genevan consistory forced Estienne to cut allegedly objectionable materal after the first edition, that did not affect the passages relevant here and reprinted. Estienne's original edition, now very rare, was reprinted by Isidore Liseux in 1879.

93. **then:** i.e., the later fifteenth century, the time of Olivier Maillard and Menot.

94. In Chapter Eleven, Estienne claims that the number of vices has increased in his time because of increased "traffic and commerce with other countries, a thing more common at this day than ever it was in former times, to whom an hundred miles seemed longer than five hundred to us" (57).

95. Athenaeus, *Deipnosophists*, 13.603A. Celtic men sexually enjoyed boys so much more than women, he says, that some often slept with two at once.

96. "But I was not allowed to be a boy in Rome." The English translation says "third," not fourth, because *bardasse* is listed third in the Italian verse on Siena. **Pasquin:** Pasquino, the ancient Roman torso on which early modern Romans publicized satiric poems or "Pasquinades." See Valerio Marucci et al., eds., *Pasquinate romane del Cinquecento*, 2 vols. (Rome: Salerno Editrice, 1983).

97. Chapter Twelve expounds how "whoredom [i.e., debauchery] is greater, and more notorious at this day, than ever it was."

98. Early modern anti-Catholic polemicists often excoriated Giovanni della Casa, responsible for enforcing Catholic theological conformity, for advocating sodomy (typically implying anal sex between males) in a published book. According to subsequent scholars, they exaggerated and distorted his early publication of a poem that includes apparently positive comment on heteroerotic anal sex as *questo mestier divino*, "this divine work" (Schleiner, 49–54). However, Thomas Coryate claims he saw an entire book of sodomitical advocacy by Della Casa, 390–91.

99. **our M. Maillard:** here Estienne means Jean Maillard (flourished 1560s), not, as elsewhere, Olivier Maillard, according to P. Ristelhuber, ed., *Apologie pour Hérodote*, 2 vols. (Paris: Liseux, 1879), 1:175–76n.

100. **fry a faggot:** be burned alive, as heretics. The current sense is relatively recent.

101. Anti-Catholic polemicists frequently recounted this story of Pier Luigi Farnese, son of Pope Paul III, and Cosimo Gheri. Its veracity has never been confirmed (Schleiner, 55–57).

102. **brute beasts do condemn us herein:** i.e., animals set an example superior to humans in these sexual matters, Estienne claims.

103. Estienne's distinction between the Frenchwoman's so-called crime and the ancient tribades claims that her crossdressing and posing as a husband are new developments in female same-sex love.

104. From Willet, *Hexapla in Leviticum: That Is, a Sixfold Commentary* (London: 1631), STC 25688, 433–34, 504–5. I silently adjust Willet's modes of citation, inserting marginal biblical references parenthetically, expanding abbreviations, and transferring some references to endnotes. In most cases I silently ellide Willet's usages of Latin, Greek, and Hebrew where he translates them into English himself.

105. Solon was a famous Athenian lawgiver; there were several notable philosophers named Zeno. Minos and Rhadamanthys were mythic brothers who gave humankind its first laws, then became judges of the living and dead.

106. **Chrysostom:** St. John Chrysostom, early Patriarch of Constantinople, an especially homophobic patristic authority. See John Boswell, *Christianity, Social Tolerance, and Homosexuality: Gay People in Western Europe from the Beginning of the Christian Era to the Fourteenth Century* (Chicago and London: University of Chicago Press, 1980), 359–63.

107. The judgment of Sodom was held to prefigure the Last Judgment, as in Jude 1:7.

108. **Rupertus:** Rupert of Dutz, a leading medieval biblical exegete.

109. **Tostatus:** Alonzo Tostado (1400?–1455), theologian and exegete.

110. **Pseudo-Christian Idolaters of these times:** i.e., Roman Catholics, from Willet's viewpoint.

111. Pliny, *Natural History*, 36.4.21.
112. **Ravisius:** Jean Tixier, seigneur de Ravisy (1480?–1524), *Officina* (1520).
113. Ancient Roman Varro discusses *nefas* in *On the Latin Language*, 6.29–30, 53, but interprets it in relation to unspeakability, and this has nothing to do with same-sex love in his contexts.
114. Piously Christian, Theodosius was Roman emperor in the later fourth century, and Arcadius his eastern successor. Willet notes the Augustan *Lex Julia de adulteriis coercendis*, a law promoting procreation and marriage, but its treatment of same-sex sexual love is actually unknown. The sanctions, if any, were not enforced, so that public pursuit of such love continued. The Theodosian law appears not to have had much practical significance. Compare Greenberg, 159–60, 229–30.
115. Willet misrepresents Aeschines, *Against Timarchus*, 16, 19–20. Aeschines actually cites the death penalty for male-male rape, and notes male prostitutes are barred from public office under Athenian law.
116. **Petrus Crinitus:** Pietro Crinito, 1475–1507.
117. Cicero (Tully), *On Behalf of Milo*, 9. Actually the young man is not named.
118. That is, Pausanias slew Philip. Compare Diodorus Siculus, 16.93.3–94.3.
119. **Lorinus:** Jean de Lorin (1559–1634), Jesuit theologian.
120. An apparently corrupt quote. Emending *honorandae* to *honorando*: "The sacred field for dandies, the venerable altar of the Cinaedi, it is in service of worshipping the gods, the temple for Ganymedes" (trans. Dorota Dutsch). Source not found. **Mantuan:** Mantuanus, or Baptista Spagnuoli (1448–1516), prolific poet and religious author, finally head of the Carmelite order.
121. Bale (1495–1563), *Acta Romanorum Pontificum* (1558); John Jewel (1522–1571), *Defense of the Apology of the Church of England* (1567), in *Works*, ed. Rev. John Ayre, 4 vols. (Cambridge, UK: 1845–50), 4: 657–62. See n. 101 above.
122. Giovanni della Casa (1503–1556). On this allegation, see n.98.
123. **Borrhaeus:** Martin Borrhaus (1499–1564), German Reformed theologian.
124. **Suidas:** supposed author of the eponymous tenth-century Byzantine lexicographical compendium.
125. St. Bernard of Clairvaux (1090–1153), *Sermones in cantica*.
126. Again misrepresenting Aeschines, *Against Timarchus*, 16, 19–20.
127. From Willet, *Hexapla: That Is, a Sixfold Commentary upon the Most Divine Epistle of the Holy Apostle S. Paul to the Romans* (Cambridge, UK: 1611), STC 25689.7, 76–77, 79. I silently adjust Willet's modes of citation as for his previously excerpted Levitical commentary.
128. **Aretius:** Martin Bucer (1491–1551); major German Reformer who lived in England after 1549.
129. **Faius:** Antoine de La Faye (1540–1615), Protestant theologian at Geneva.
130. **Pareus:** David Wängler (1548–1622), Calvinist theologian.
131. **Tolet:** i.e., Toletus, Francisco de Toledo (1532–1596), Jesuit theologian and cardinal.
132. **Theophylact:** Theophylactus of Ochryda (c. 1050–c. 1108), Byzantine exegete.
133. **Lyranus:** Nicholas of Lyra (1270?–1349?), exegete and theologian.
134. **Osiander:** Lucas Osiander (1571–1638), Lutheran theologian and controversialist.
135. Some authorities apply the passage to tribadic sex, Willet says, others, more rightly in his view, to "unnatural" (i.e., nonprocreative) heteroerotic sex.
136. Plato's dialogues take different positions on male homoeroticism. The two main negative contexts are *Laws* 1.636C–D, 8.836C–E. Willet suppresses Plato's favorable treatments.
137. For Chrysostom's homophobic commentary on Romans, cf. Boswell, 359–62.
138. **Beza:** Théodore de Bèze (1516–1605); led the Genevan church after Calvin's death.
139. **Bucer:** Martin Bucer (1491–1551), major German Reformer who resided in England after 1549.
140. **Gryneus:** Johann Jacob Grynaeus (1540–1617), Swiss Reformed theologian and exegete.
141. **Haymo:** Haymo of Halberstadt, medieval exegete and theologian, whose formerly attributed works are mostly now considered pseudepigraphic.
142. From Wilson, *A Commentary upon the Most Divine Epistle of S. Paul to the Romans* (London: 1614), STC 25791, 83–84, 87–88, 107–10.
143. **Fathers:** Hebrew patriarchs of the Old Testament.
144. From Beard, *The Theater of God's Judgments* (London: 1597), STC 1659, 359–63. Although Beard expanded the *Theater* in subsequent editions, this section remained unchanged.
145. Cicero, *Tusculan Disputations*, 5.35.101–2 (marginal gloss). Cicero's context actually stresses

the value of the simple life of prudence and temperance. Beard also marginally cites "Frog. lib. 1" (unidentified).

146. Marginally citing (pseudo-) Lampridius. Compare *Commodus* and *Heliogabalus*, in *Lives of the Later Emperors* (or *The Augustan History*). **jakes:** latrine.

147. **inhabitable:** uninhabitable.

148. Josephus, *Jewish Antiquities*, 1.169–206; *Jewish War*, 4.484–85.

149. Protestant anti-Catholic polemic often accused Pope Julius III and Giovanni della Casa of sodomy; compare n.98. By "holy father" Beard means Julius III, who died of gout according to Beard's earlier chapter on atheism (142–43).

150. Lev. 20 (marginal gloss). Beard further invokes Augustus' *Lex Julia de adulteriis coercendis*, but its relation, if any, to same-sex sexual love is unknown. See n.63; also *Law.

151. Lev. 18, 20; Exod. 22; Deut 27 (marginal gloss).

152. **Caelius:** Lodovico Ricchieri (1469–1525); *Encyclopedias and Reference Works. **Volaterranus:** probably Raffaele Maffei (1455–1522).

153. In Numbers 22:21–35, God inspires Balaam's ass to resist him because his "way is perverse," i.e., contrary to God's will. In 2 Kings 17:25–26, God sends lions to harrass settlers displacing Hebrews in Samaria. **strange:** foreign.

Chapter 2

1. Cited in Michael Rocke, *Forbidden Friendships: Homosexuality and Male Culture in Renaissance Florence* (New York: Oxford University Press, 1996), 59; hereafter cited in text.

2. See James A. Brundage, *Law, Sex, and Christian Society in Medieval Europe* (Chicago: University of Chicago Press, 1987), 48–49, 121–22; David F. Greenberg, *The Construction of Homosexuality* (Chicago: University of Chicago Press, 1988), 152–60, 228–34 (also cited in text hereafter).

3. See Derrick Sherwin Bailey, *Homosexuality and the Western Christian Tradition* (London: Longmans, 1955), 73–78.

4. See Louis Crompton, "The Myth of Lesbian Impunity: Capital Laws from 1270 to 1791," *Journal of Homosexuality* 6.1–2 (1980–81): 15–16; Judith Brown, *Immodest Acts: The Life of a Lesbian Nun in Renaissance Italy* (Oxford: Oxford University Press, 1986), 8–9, 13 (also cited in text hereafter).

5. See Michael Goodich, *The Unmentionable Vice: Homosexuality in the Later Medieval Period* (Oxford: ABC-Clio, 1979); Greenberg, 272–74.

6. See Rocke; E. William Monter, "Sodomy and Heresy in Early Modern Switzerland," *Journal of Homosexuality* 6.1–2 (1980–81): 41–55; Louis Crompton, "Homosexuals and the Death Penalty in Colonial America," *Journal of Homosexuality* 1.3 (1974–76): 277–93; Jonathan Ned Katz, *Gay/Lesbian Almanac* (New York: Harper and Row, 1983), 23–133; Colin L. Talley, "Gender and Male Same-Sex Erotic Behavior in British North America in the Seventeenth Century," *Journal of the History of Sexuality* 6 (1995–96): 385–408.

7. Imperial edict cited in Greenberg, 302–3. On Venetian impunity of sapphism, see Guido Ruggiero, *The Boundaries of Eros: Sex Crime and Sexuality in Renaissance Venice* (New York: Oxford University Press, 1985), 189n.21; cited hereafter in text.

8. See Kenneth Borris, "'Ile hang a bag and bottle at thy back': Barnfield's Homoerotic Advocacy and the Construction of Homosexuality," in Kenneth Borris and George Klawitter, eds., *The Affectionate Shepherd: Celebrating Richard Barnfield* (Selinsgrove, Ky.: Susquehanna-Associated University Presses, 2001), 196–202; Robert F. Oaks, "Defining Sodomy in Seventeenth-century Massachusetts," *Journal of Homosexuality* 6.1–2 (1980–81): 80–81; Rocke, 46.

9. *R. v. Wiseman* (1718), 92 ER 774 (with learned citations of authorities).

10. Dirk Jaap Noordam, "Sodomy in the Dutch Republic, 1600–1725," *Journal of Homosexuality* 16.1–2 (1988): 207–28.

11. William Monter, *Frontiers of Heresy: The Spanish Inquisition from the Basque Lands to Sicily* (Cambridge, UK: Cambridge University Press, 1990), 280, 295. Also André Fernandez, "The Repression of Sexual Behavior by the Aragonese Inquisition between 1560 and 1700," *Journal of the History of Sexuality* 7 (1996–97): 469–501; Francisco Guerra, *The Pre-Columbian Mind* (London: Seminar, 1971), 222–23; Mary Elizabeth Perry, "The 'Nefarious Sin' in Early Modern Seville," *Journal of Homosexuality* 16.1–2 (1988): 67–89.

12. I thank William Naphy for this information.
13. Alan Bray, *Homosexuality in Renaissance England*, 2nd, rev. ed. (New York: Columbia University Press, 1995), 38–42, 70–80, 120n.12, also cited in text hereafter; J. A. Sharpe, *Crime in Early Modern England 1550–1750*, 2nd, rev. ed. (London: Longman, 1999), 51–58, 77–79.
14. Bruce R. Smith, *Homosexual Desire in Shakespeare's England: A Cultural Poetics* (Chicago: University of Chicago Press, 1991), 48; also cited in text hereafter.
15. Monter, *Frontiers of Heresy*, 288.
16. Ruggiero, 128. See also Patricia H. Labalme, "Sodomy and Venetian Justice in the Renaissance," *Legal History Review* 52 (1984): 217–54.
17. Monter, "Early Modern Switzerland," 54–55.
18. See Brown, Introduction; Helmut Puff, "Female Sodomy: The Trial of Katherina Hetzeldorfer (1477)," *Journal of Medieval and Early Modern Studies* 30 (2000): 41–61; Valerie Traub, *The Renaissance of Lesbianism in Early Modern England* (Cambridge, UK: Cambridge University Press, 2002), 42–45 (also cited in text hereafter).
19. Monter, "Early Modern Switzerland," 46–47.
20. Katz, *Almanac*, 101–2.
21. Crompton, "Lesbian Impunity," 16.
22. Monter, "Early Modern Switzerland," 46.
23. See *Henri Estienne; *Montaigne in this chapter. Also Traub, 164–69, 182; Patricia Crawford and Sara Mendelson, "Sexual Identities in Early Modern England: The Marriage of Two Women in 1680," *Gender and History* 7 (1995): 362–77.
24. See Cynthia B. Herrup, *A House in Gross Disorder: Sex, Law, and the 2nd Earl of Castlehaven* (New York: Oxford University Press, 1999), 26–38; also cited in text hereafter.
25. Likewise, the Henrician statute on marital consanguinity was referred to Leviticus (32 Henry VIII, ch. 38). Compare *Harrison* v. *Burwell* (1668), 124 ER 1039 (CP).
26. *R.* v. *Samuel Jacobs* (1817), 168 ER 830.
27. For a contrary view that some sexual relations between males were socially "orderly," in early modern England, thus normative, see Mario Digangi, *The Homoerotics of Early Modern Drama* (Cambridge, UK: Cambridge University Press, 1997). Compare Borris, "Barnfield's Homoerotic Advocacy," 196–202, and *Theology.
28. Fitzherbert, *The New Book of Justices of the Peace* (London: 1538), STC 10969, fol. 23^b; Lambarde, *Eirenarcha, or of the Office of the Justices of Peace* (London: 1610), STC 15172, 422 (compare 255–56); Dalton, *The Country Justice: Containing the Practice of the Justices of the Peace*, (London: 1666), Wing D146, 319 (first published in 1618).
29. Cited in Alan Stewart, *Close Readers: Humanism and Sodomy in Early Modern England* (Princeton: Princeton University Press, 1997), xv.
30. D'Ewes, *Autobiography*, British Library, Harleian MS 646, fol. 59^b.
31. See Frank McLynn, *Crime and Punishment in Eighteenth-century England* (London: Routledge, 1989), 282–85.
32. See Lawrence Stone, "Interpersonal Violence in English Society 1300–1980," *Past and Present* 101 (1983): 22–33; Keith Wrightson, *English Society 1580–1680* (London: Hutchinson, 1982), 159–62.
33. See Nathaniel Shurtleff, ed., *Records of the Colony of New Plymouth*, 2 vols. in 1 (Boston: 1855), 1:64, 2:35.
34. See *New Haven Town Records 1649–1662*, ed. Franklin Bowditch Dexter (New Haven.: New Haven Historical Society, 1917), 178–79; Katz, *Almanac*, 101–2.
35. For their informative texts, see William Bradford (1588–1657), *Of Plymouth Plantation, 1620–1647*, ed. Samuel Eliot Morison (New York: Knopf, 1952), 404–13.
36. Trumbach, "Sodomitical Subcultures, Sodomitical Roles, and the Gender Revolution of the Eighteenth Century: The Recent Historiography," *Eighteenth Century Life* 9, n.s. 3 (1985): 113, 118.
37. Compare Nazife Bashar, "Rape in England Between 1550 and 1700," in London Feminist History Group, ed., *The Sexual Dynamics of History* (London: Pluto, 1983), 33–40.
38. D'Ewes, *Diary*, ed. Elisabeth Bourcier (Paris: Didier, 1974), 92–93.
39. According to Giles Jacob, "in every Indictment for this offense, there must be the words, *Rem habuit veneream & carnaliter cognovit, & co.;* and of consequence some kind of [anal] Penetration and Emission must be proved; but any the least Degree is sufficient." *A New Law Dictionary*, 4th, enl. ed. (London, 1739), s.v. "Buggery." See further Herrup, 28, 174n.9, 12.

40. *Between 1540 and 1640* in England, official warrants authorized torture in a small number of cases mostly involving alleged political or politico-religious crimes such as treason or sedition. None involved sexual offenses. See John H. Langbein, *Torture and the Law of Proof: Europe and England in the Ancien Régime* (Chicago: University of Chicago Press, 1976); Malise Ruthven, *Torture: The Grand Conspiracy* (London: Weidenfeld and Nicolson, 1978), ch. 3.

41. Monter, *Frontiers of Heresy*, 74–75, 140, 279.

42. See J. H. Baker, "Criminal Courts and Procedure at Common Law 1550–1800," in J. S. Cockburn, ed., *Crime in England 1550–1800* (London: Methuen, 1977), 15–48.

43. English prosecution of sodomy further differed from some parts of the continent, such as Lucca and Geneva, in that such cases there could include forensic examination of those accused, for signs of prior anal intercourse (so doctors could check, e.g., how difficult an anus was to penetrate). On a seventeenth-century continental forensic manual's discussion of this issue, see George Rousseau, "'Homoplatonic, Homodepressed, Homomorbid': Some Further Genealogies of Same-Sex Attraction in Western Civilization," in Katherine O'Donnell and Michael O'Rourke, eds., *Love, Sex, Intimacy and Friendship Between Men, 1550–1800* (Houndmills, UK: Palgrave–Macmillan, 2003), 17–18, 41.

44. See Bradford, 404–13.

45. Martin Ingram discusses parliamentary efforts to criminalize fornication and adultery, without comment on implications for sodomites and tribades, in *Church Courts, Sex and Marriage in England, 1570–1640* (Cambridge, UK: Cambridge University Press, 1987), 152–54. According to Giles Jacob, s.v. "Fornication," the Rump's act mandated "three months imprisonment for the first offense, and the second 'tis said was made Felony." Fornication and adultery were otherwise regulated by ecclesiastical courts in England. When the secular sodomy law was in force, same-sex sexual behaviors other than anal sex could still presumably have been treated as fornication. But English church courts very rarely prosecuted such homoerotic liaisons in the sixteenth and seventeenth centuries. The reasons for that are as yet obscure, but no doubt faith in divine retribution contributed. Compurgation would have been one technical problem: If an accused could find a few witnesses to testify to his or her good character, charges were necessarily dropped in church courts, unlike secular ones. And an accuser would have had to reckon with possible vengeance by the accused. See John Addy, *Sin and Society in the Seventeenth Century* (London and New York: Routledge, 1989), ch. 9; F. G. Emmison, *Elizabethan Life: Morals and the Church Courts* (Chelmsford: Essex County Council, 1973), 36–37, 47.

46. Brundage, 313, 468.

47. Sharpe, 220–23, Greenberg, 337–41.

48. See Alex K. Gigeroff, *Sexual Deviations in the Criminal Law: Homosexual, Exhibitionistic, and Pedophilic Offences in Canada* (Toronto: University of Toronto Press, 1968), 16–17.

49. See Joan R. Kent, "Attitudes of Members of the House of Commons to the Regulation of 'Personal Conduct' in Late Elizabethan and Early Stuart England," *Bulletin of the Institute of Historical Research* 46 (1973): 43.

50. See Gigeroff, chs. 1–2; Herrup, 34–36; François Lafitte, "Homosexuality and the Law," *The British Journal of Delinquency* 9 (1958–59): 8–19; Smith, 43–49.

51. Ingram, 151–54.

52. Sharpe, 95–96.

53. G. R. Elton, *The Parliament of England 1559–1581* (Cambridge, UK: Cambridge University Press, 1986), 110–11.

54. From *The Whole Volume of Statutes at Large*, 2 Parts in 1 Vol. (London: 1587), STC 9316, 1:637 (Henry VIII); 2:72–73 (Edward VI); 2:199–200 (Mary); 2:449 (Elizabeth I).

55. **Praemunire:** i.e., under royal jurisdiction, rather than the papacy's through ecclesiastical courts.

56. Cited in Alessandro d'Ancona, ed., *L'Italia alla fine del secolo XVI: Giornale del viaggio di Michele de Montaigne in Italia nel 1580 e 1581* (Città di Castello: 1889), 293n.1, trans. Nicola Martino and Kenneth Borris.

57. Translated by Kenneth Borris, from Montaigne, *Journal du voyage en Italie*, ed. Meunier de Querlon, 2 vols. (Paris: Le Jay, 1774), 1:12–13, 2:31–32.

58. For discussion, see Marie-Jo Bonnet, *Un choix sans équivoque: Recherches historiques sur les relations amoureuses entre les femmes XVIᵉ–XXᵉ siècle* (Paris: Denoël, 1981), 53–58.

59. King Philip II of Spain had recently succeeded to the throne of Portugal, so that the Portuguese ambassador had to transfer his former allegiance to Philip.

60. The joke is that they suffered in doing so, because of the foregoing political circumstances.

61. Hogenberg, *Engravings of Scenes from the History of France and the Netherlands, 1559–1582* (Cologne, 1570?–1582?), leaf 117. Figures 3 and 4 are leaves 121, 119. Hogenberg produced hundreds of prints in this series, and apparently no two collections include all the same ones, so that pagination and contents vary greatly. This volume is at the New York Public Library, Spenser Collection German 1570. I thank Louis Mirando, Josef Schmidt, and Horst Richter for assisting in the translation.

62. Coke, *The Third Part of the Institutes* (London: 1644), Wing C4960, sig. B2^a.

63. Translated by Faith Wallis, from Coke, *A Book of Entries: Containing Perfect and Approved Precedents of Counts, Declarations, Informations, Plaints* (London: 1614), STC 5488, 351^b–52^a. Ellipses indicate the omission of some formulaic Latin legal abbreviations. Though Coke does not mention rape, this case seems to have been treated as such, for the youth he names was over the age of discretion and yet apparently not charged with sodomy in Coke's account. Compare *The Stafford Scandal.

64. From Coke, *The Third Part of the Institutes of the Laws of England* (London: 1644), Wing C4960, 58–59. I silently replace Latin (trans. Faith Wallis) and French phrases with English.

65. **Praemunire:** i.e., under royal jurisdiction, rather than the papacy's through ecclesiastical courts.

66. Coke implies the crime's origin is Italian. However, "buggery" derives from the French *bougre*, apparently of eleventh-century origin. It first applied to heretics, then became antisodomitical by extension. Compare Goodich, 8–9.

67. Marginal reference: parliamentary rolls, 50 Edward III. In 1376 parliament petitioned the king to banish Lombard moneychangers for alleged evils and usury: "Some among them . . . have lately practiced in this land a very horrible vice which should not be named. By which the Kingdom cannot fail shortly to be destroyed, if stiff punishment be not speedily ordained" (cit. Katz, *Almanac*, 36).

68. Marginal references: Britton, ch. 9; Gen. 19:9; Rom. 1:[2]7; F.N.B. 269A. In Britton, a late thirteenth-century legal compilation of uncertain authorship, Chapter Ten, "Of Arsons," requires arsonists to be burnt, and "the same sentence shall be passed upon sorcerors, sorceresses, renegades, sodomites, and heretics." Coke cites Chapter Nine, "Of Treasons," which broadly defines treason as "any mischief, which a man knowingly does, or procures to be done, to one to whom he pretends to be a friend." Treason may thus subsume arson and the other crimes listed in Chapter Ten. "F.N.B." abbreviates "Fitzherbert's *Natura Brevium*," and Fitzherbert (1470–1538) cites Britton. *Britton*, ed., trans. Francis Morgan Nichols (Washington, D.C.: Byrne, 1901), Book I, chs. 9–10; Sir Anthony Fitzherbert, *The New Natura Brevium*, trans. anon., 2 vols. (London: 1794), 2:269B.

69. Marginal reference: Fleta, I, ch. 35. Like Britton, this late-thirteenth-century legal work of unknown authorship condemns sodomy in its chapter "Of Arson." "Those who have connexion with Jews and Jewesses or are guilty of bestiality or sodomy shall be buried alive in the ground, provided they be taken in the act and convicted. . . ." *Fleta*, ed., trans. H. G. Richardson and G. O. Sayles (London: Quaritch, 1955), Vol. 2, Book I, ch. 35.

70. Marginal reference: *Mirror*, several passages. Having supposed this work records ancient British law dating from King Arthur, Coke thought it particularly authoritative. It is actually of uncertain authorship, c. 1300. The *Mirror* classifies sodomy as a "crime of *laesa majestas*," offense against the sovereign, and thus mortal sin. "The crime of laesa majestas is a horrible sin committed against the king, and this may be against the king of heaven or earth. Against the king of heaven in three ways: by heresy, apostasy [these include sorcery], and sodomy." "Because of the scandal of sodomy our ancient fathers would not suffer that there should be any actions, accusations, indictments, or audience of any kind concerning so abominable a sin, but ordained that those notoriously guilty should be judged without respite and the judgments executed, and in cases that were not notorious every tongue should hold its peace." *The Mirror of Justices*, ed. William Joseph Whittaker (London: Quaritch, 1895), 15, 53.

71. Marginal comment: "This is grounded upon the Word of God," citing Gen. 19:4–5, Judg. 19:22. "*Ut cognoscamus eos*" (i.e., so that we may recognize them).

72. Marginal reference: Coke cites the account in his *Book of Entries*, reprinted above.

73. Marginal references: Ezek. 16:49; Gen. 18:29; Deut. 29:23; Isa. 13:9; Jer. 23:14, 49:18, 50:4; Luke 17:28–29; 2 Pet. 2:6; Jude 7; Rom. 1:26–27; Wisdom 10:6–7.

74. Coke gives marginal references on the legal status of accessories.

75. In this theological tradition, these four sins especially "cry out" to God for punishment. See *St. Peter Canisius, and Goodich, 80–81. **voice of lamentation:** oppression of widows and orphans. **voice of blood:** homicide.

76. From Coke, *The Twelfth Part of the Reports* (London: 1656), Wing C4969, 36. I silently replace Latin phrases with English (trans. Faith Wallis). The preceding entry, *The Third Part of the Institutes*, annotates Coke's references significant for sodomy.

77. **drawn:** dragged to the place of execution, behind a horse or upon a hurdle, in disgrace.

78. Fogossa's case concerns import duties and contested seizure of goods, not any sexual matters. See Edmund Plowden (1518–1585), *The Commentaries*, trans. Bromley (London: 1816), 1–20a.

79. Sir William Stanford (1509–1558), *Les plees del Coron divisees in plusiours titles*. The 1583 edition (London, STC 23223) discusses rape, fols. 21ᵃ–24ᵃ.

80. Anonymous, *The Arraignment, Judgment, Confession, and Execution of Humphrey Stafford, Gentleman* (London: 1607), STC 23131, sig. B3ᵇ; also referenced parenthetically in my text hereafter.

81. From *Execution of Humphrey Stafford* as above, sigs. B1ᵃ–B2ᵃ.

82. **fact:** evil deed.

83. In the multitude of documents for this case, in manuscripts and print, "each editor seems to have added, suppressed, embroidered, and, in some cases, created information to suit his or her own purposes" (Herrup, 5). Herrup analyzes differences and agendas of surviving accounts, ch. 5.

84. *Complete Collection of State Trials*, 4 vols. (London: T. Goodwin, 1719–30), 1:269; also cited in text hereafter.

85. Hutton, *The Reports* (London: 1656), Wing H3843, 116; published posthumously.

86. *The Case of Sodomy in the Trial of Mervin, Lord Audley* (London: 1707/08), 34. In another account, Fitzpatrick only acknowledged mutual masturbation, and in yet another avowed mutual anal penetration (Herrup, 61, 96). Whereas Herrup gives the earl's denial of anal sex with Fitzpatrick much credence, this sexually transgressive earl was not likely to observe such conventional boundaries. I am thankful to Cynthia Herrup for informing me that there is no extant documentary evidence that either confirms or disproves Fitzpatrick's final admission of mutual buggery according to *The Case of Sodomy*. However, if someone wished to invent a confession by Fitzpatrick to justify Castlehaven's execution, the servant would most obviously confirm he was penetrated "like a woman," as his lord's younger minion. Since mutual buggery by males seems to have been most difficult to imagine from a sexually conventional standpoint, Fitzpatrick's putative confession prior to execution seems unlikely to have been invented, and most likely to have been suppressed (which would explain why it does not appear in more sources).

87. *The Trial and Condemnation of Mervin, Lord Audley* (London: 1699), Wing T2144, 7.

88. *The Case of Sodomy* (1707/8), 25–27.

89. *The Arraignment and Conviction* (London: 1642), Wing A3743, 9–10.

90. From *A Complete Collection of State Trials*, 4 vols. (London: T. Goodwin, 1719–30), 1:264–71.

91. Suetonius, *Lives of the Caesars*.

92. *The Trial and Condemnation* (1699) is more specifically antisodomitical here: "This is a Crime, to the Honor of our Nation be it spoken, that is scarcely to be heard of in an Age, and whenever it happens calls aloud for timely punishment, that the Infection spread no farther, nor provoke Divine Vengeance . . . upon the whole Kingdom"—i.e., as a new Sodom to be destroyed (9).

93. That is, "no time limit obstructs the king."

94. That is, "sodomitical crime without penetration."

95. According to *The Trial of the Lord Audley* (1679), the prosecutor further discussed sodomy as the "sin which should not be named amongst Christians, and a strange sin in this Land, brought hither by strangers," concluding that "every Breach of this filthy sin" is "within the compass of Felony," whether or not penetration occurs (4–5). In *The Trial and Condemnation* (1699), the prosecutor insisted that sodomy "is of so abominable and Vile a Nature that . . . it is a Crime not to be named among Christians. And by the Law of God as well as the Ancient Laws of England it was punished with Death," so that sodomites were "buried alive in the Earth" or "set deep and alive into a Pit . . . with their heads above ground, till . . . famished to Death" (11–12).

96. That is, "no one becomes most wicked suddenly."

97. According to *The Trial of Lord Audley* (1679), the prosecutor added "the Earl's Filthiness with his Maid Blandina, . . . how the Earl's House was a common Brothel-house, the Earl himself delighting to be not only an Actor, but a continued Spectator of Filthiness. And also Blandina was abused by himself and his Servants for the space of seven hours together, until she had the French Pox . . ." (5). Similarly, *The Trial and Condemnation* (1699), 19.

98. Since Fitzpatrick was Roman Catholic, the earl attempted to disqualify his testimony. Considering the pope supreme head of all Christians, recusants refused to acknowledge the king's supremacy and thus refused the Oath of Allegiance.

99. In one account of the trial, Fitpatrick says he and the earl interchanged receptive and insertive sexual roles (Herrup, 61). But the jury's widely attested split verdict on the sodomy charge shows Fitzpatrick denied penetration at the trial.

100. I reprint Fitzpatrick's full testimony according to my source, and omit following examinations of two further servants of the earl, Scott and Fry, which repeat other testimony. According to *The Trial and Condemnation* (1699), Fitzpatrick said, "my Lord made me lie with him at Fonthill and Salisbury, and once spent his Seed, but did not penetrate my Body, and I understood he had *often* done the like with others" (my emphasis). He saw Skipwith "lie with" the countess and Elizabeth "several times, it being done in my Lord's sight also." On Blandina, he putatively said much the same as the prosecutor in *The Trial of Lord Audley* (1679), quoted in note 97 (18–19).

101. *The Trial of Lord Audley* (1679) assigns the earl some additional arguments: (1) Fitzpatrick is a recusant and therefore cannot act as a witness; (2) Fitzpatrick's testimony is unreliable because the earl "for his Knavery . . . had oftentimes beaten him and turned him away," and the earl's son has now bribed him; (3) Broadway ejaculated after he had struggled with the countess, and did not penetrate her (6–7). Other issues mentioned there in the 1679 text are treated subsequently in my copy text. These first two points also appear in *The Trial and Condemnation* (1699), which adds that the earl said "my Wife has been a Whore, and has had a Child which I concealed to save her Honor" (21–23).

102. Considering whether nonpenetrative sex between males constitutes sodomy in *The Arraignment and Conviction* (1642), the judges answered "it may, the use of the body to spend seed doth it," i.e., makes it felonious buggery, even without penetration (10). According to *The Trial of the Lord Audley* (1679), the earl asked "whether the Statute did intend that all kind of pollution (man with man) were Buggery or not, seeing by their [i.e., the witnesses'] Confession, there was no Penetration. To this the Judges . . . answered it was Buggery by the Law, and that the Law of this Land made no distinction of Buggery, if there be *Emissio Seminis*" (7). *The Trial and Condemnation* (1699) assigns that answer to the Lord Chief Justice, Sir Nicholas Hyde (24). But this appears to have been a uniquely exceptional interpretation of the English sodomy statute, advanced to enable the Crown to convict the earl in particular.

103. In both *The Trial of Lord Audley* (1679) and *The Trial and Condemnation* (1699), the earl protested his innocency of the charges here (9, 27).

104. From *A Complete Collection of State Trials*, 4 vols. (London: T. Goodwin, 1719–30), 1:271–72. This account is virtually identical with the corresponding part of the 1707/08 *Case of Sodomy* (except the latter omits the judges' letter to the Lord Keeper), and probably derives from the same manuscript source. Fitzpatrick and Broadway were perceived to matter so little that the prior published accounts of the Castlehaven case (1642, 1679, 1699) do not even mention their fates.

105. From *The Case of Sodomy* (1707/8), 33–38, apparently based on a ms. eyewitness account.

106. **Whoring:** whereas "whore" and its cognates now connote female prostitution, that was not necessarily so c.1630. "Whoredom," e.g., could mean illicit sexual intercourse in general, including homophile possibilities.

107. **Ghostly father:** father confessor; **Ghostly** has the former sense "spiritual."

108. Fitzpatrick claims he was so sorry for his confessed sins, especially sodomy, that he resolved to leave the earl's service, but due to weakness and dependence on the earl's employment did not.

109. See J. R. Roberts, "'leude behauior each with other vpon a bed': The Case of Sarah Norman and Mary Hammond," *Sinister Wisdom* 14 (1980): 57–62. My biographical account follows Roberts.

110. I reprint legal records pertaining to this case from Shurtleff, 2:137, 148, 163.

111. **vild:** vile.

Chapter 3

1. Caelius, *On Acute Diseases and On Chronic Diseases*, ed., trans. I. E. Drabkin (Chicago: University of Chicago Press, 1950), 903. Aristotle, *Nicomachean Ethics*, 7.5.3–4; trans. H. Rackham.

2. On the foregoing points, see Joan Cadden, *Meanings of Sex Difference in the Middle Ages: Medicine, Science, and Culture* (Cambridge, UK: Cambridge University Press, 1993);

Lawrence I. Conrad, et al., *The Western Medical Tradition, 800 BC to AD 1800* (Cambridge, UK: Cambridge University Press, 1995); Danielle Jacquart and Claude Thomasset, *Sexuality and Medicine in the Middle Ages*, trans. Matthew Adamson (Cambridge, UK: Polity, 1988); Ian Maclean, *The Renaissance Notion of Woman* (Cambridge, UK: Cambridge University Press, 1980), ch. 3; Nancy G. Siraisi, *Medieval and Early Renaissance Medicine: An Introduction to Knowledge and Practice* (Chicago: University of Chicago Press, 1990). On relief of uterine suffocation, cf. Rachel P. Maines, *The Technology of Orgasm: "Hysteria," the Vibrator, and Women's Sexual Satisfaction* (Baltimore: Johns Hopkins University Press, 1999), ch. 2; Winfried Schleiner, *Medical Ethics in the Renaissance* (Washington, D.C.: Georgetown University Press, 1995), 107–29.

3. See Katherine Park, "The Rediscovery of the Clitoris: French Medicine and the Tribade, 1570–1620," in David Hillman and Carla Mazzio, eds., *The Body in Parts: Fantasies of Corporeality in Early Modern Europe* (New York and London: Routledge, 1997), 180. See further Cadden, *Sex Difference*, 201–14; Jacquart and Thomasset, 139–43; Maclean, 36. According to Lorraine Daston and Katharine Park, "Aristotelian interpretation of sexual difference . . . presented male and female less as points on a spectrum, in the Hippocratic manner, than as polar opposites," so that the "Hippocratic model . . . posed a potential challenge to the male-female dichotomy, and to the whole social and sexual order based on that dichotomy." "The Hermaphrodite and the Orders of Nature: Sexual Ambiguity in Early Modern France," in Louise Fradenburg and Carla Freccero, eds., *Premodern Sexualities* (New York and London: Routledge, 1996), 119–20.

4. See Fridolf Kudlien, "The Seven Cells of the Uterus: The Doctrine and Its Roots," *Bulletin of the History of Medicine* 39 (1965): 415–23; Cadden, *Sex Difference*, 93, 131, 199–200; Jacquart and Thomasset, 34–35; Siraisi, *Medicine*, 95–96.

5. Mark D. Jordan, *The Invention of Sodomy in Christian Theology* (Chicago: University of Chicago Press, 1997), 123.

6. These generalizations about early modern medical treatises and sex between males may need some future revision in light of George Rousseau's recent discovery that a mid-seventeenth-century forensic manual's discussion of sodomy cites some Renaissance anatomical treatises. I have not been able to investigate them because his essay mentioning this was published while this book was in production. I thank George Rousseau for discussing this with me. See his "'Homoplatonic, Homodepressed, Homomorbid': Some Further Genealogies of Same-Sex Attraction in Western Civilization," in Katherine O'Donnell and Michael O'Rourke, eds., *Love, Sex, Intimacy, and Friendship Between Men, 1550–1800* (Houndmills, UK: Palgrave–Macmillan, 2003), 17–18, 41.

7. Bartholin, *Bartholinus Anatomy*, trans. anon. (London: 1668), Wing B977, 76; cited hereafter in text.

8. See Valerie Traub, *The Renaissance of Lesbianism in Early Modern England* (Cambridge, UK: Cambridge University Press, 2002), ch. 2; cited hereafter in text.

9. See Judith Brown, *Immodest Acts: The Life of a Lesbian Nun in Renaissance Italy* (Oxford: Oxford University Press, 1986), 12.

10. Craig A. Williams, *Roman Homosexuality: Ideologies of Masculinity in Classical Antiquity* (Oxford: Oxford University Press, 1999), 180–81. On antiquity, sex, and "nature," see 231–44.

11. See Jacquart and Thomasset, 45–46; Park, "Rediscovery of the Clitoris," 173, 176–77.

12. Falloppio, *Observationes anatomicae* (Paris: apud J. Kerver, 1562), fol. 116^b, trans. Faith Wallis.

13. Park, "Rediscovery of the Clitoris," 170–83. Up to this point in this paragraph, I largely follow Park, who cites Vesalius, 177.

14. Brooten, *Love Between Women: Early Christian Responses to Female Homoeroticism* (Chicago: University of Chicago Press, 1996), ch. 5; also cited hereafter in text.

15. See Patricia Crawford, "Attitudes to Menstruation in Seventeenth-Century England," *Past and Present* 91 (1981): 47–73.

16. See McLean, 29–33; Thomas Laqueur, *Making Sex: Body and Gender from the Greeks to Freud* (Cambridge, Mass.: Harvard University Press, 1990), chs. 2–3; Helen Rodnite Lemay, "Masculinity and Femininity in Early Renaissance Treatises on Human Reproduction," *Clio Medica* 18 (1983): 21–31; Park, "Rediscovery of the Clitoris," 189n.19, 190n.31, 187; Cadden, *Sex Difference*, 3, 24, 281.

17. Winfried Schleiner, "Early Modern Controversies about the One-Sex Model," *Renaissance Quarterly* 53 (2000): 180–91.

18. See Thomas Laqueur, "Amor veneris, vel Dulcedo Appeletur," in Michel Fehrer, ed., with Ramona Naddaff and Nadia Tazi, *Fragments for a History of the Human Body*, 3 vols. (New York: Zone, 1989), 3:103–5, 113; Laqueur, *Making Sex*, 52–53.

19. See Jon Arrizabalaga, John Henderson, and Roger French, *The Great Pox: The French Disease in Renaissance Europe* (New Haven: Yale University Press, 1997); Bruce Thomas Boehrer, "Early Modern Syphilis," *Journal of the History of Sexuality* 1 (1990–91): 197–214; Richard Davenport-Hines, *Sex, Death, and Punishment: Attitudes to Sex and Sexuality in Britain Since the Renaissance* (London: Collins, 1990), ch. 2; Ann Foa, "The New and the Old: The Spread of Syphilis (1494–1530)," in Edward Muir and Guido Ruggiero, eds., *Sex and Gender in Historical Perspective* (Baltimore: Johns Hopkins University Press, 1990), 26–45. Seventeenth-century surveys of prior theories include Daniel Sennert, *Of the Venereal Pox*, in *Two Treatises* (London: 1660), Wing S2547; and Gideon Harvey, *Great Venus Unmasked* (London: 1672), Wing H1067.

20. See Francisco Guerra, *The Pre-Columbian Mind* (London: Seminar, 1971), 56–57.

21. Roch le Baillif (1540–1605), physician to King Henri III, thus etymologizes "gonorrhea" while attacking Sodom and sodomy in his *Premier traité de l'homme et son essentielle anatomie* (Paris: Abel l'Angelier, 1580), fol. 33^b. Jacquart and Thomasset cite an early fifteenth-century example, 153.

22. On former gynephobic interpretation of the origins and transmission of syphilis, see Schleiner, *Medical Ethics*, ch. 6; Harvey, 23–28.

23. Cited in Cecile Beurdeley, *L'amour bleu*, trans. Michael Taylor (New York: Rizzoli, 1978), 122.

24. Andrew Wear, "Medicine in Early Modern Europe, 1500–1700," in Conrad et al., 215–17.

25. See Brian Lawn, *The Salernitan Questions: An Introduction to the History of Medieval and Renaissance Problem Literature* (Oxford: Clarendon, 1963); Ann Blair, "The *Problemata* as a Natural Philosophical Genre," in Anthony Grafton and Nancy Siraisi, eds., *Natural Particulars: Nature and the Disciplines in Renaissance Europe* (Cambridge, Mass.: MIT, 1999), 171–204 (also cited in text hereafter).

26. See E. S. Forster, "The Pseudo-Aristotelian *Problems*: Their Nature and Composition," *Classical Quarterly* 22 (1928): 163–65. On its early modern Aristotelian attribution, see Blair, 179–80.

27. William A. Wallace, "Aristotle and Aristotelianism," *Encyclopedia of the Renaissance*, 110.

28. Edward Cranz, *A Bibliography of Aristotle Editions 1501–1600*, 2nd, rev. ed., rev. Charles B. Schmitt (Baden-Baden: Valentin Koerner, 1984), 219; Lawn, ch. 7.

29. For the ostensible vernacular "translations," see Cranz, 219. At least for the English ones, he did not verify their relation to the ancient pseudo-Aristotelian work. Compiled in the later thirteenth century, the spurious version of the supposed Aristotle's *Problems* had many editions in Latin and vernacular languages, and Cranz might confuse the former as well as the latter with the ancient text. See Lawn, 99–103; Blair, 181–82.

30. Charles B. Schmitt, *John Case and Aristotelianism in Renaissance England* (Kingston and Montreal: McGill-Queen's University Press, 1983), 52.

31. From pseudo-Aristotle, *Problems*, trans. W. S. Hett, Loeb series (London and Cambridge, Mass.: Heineman and Harvard University Press, 1926), 127–31.

32. **this region:** i.e., the anus.

33. On "nature" and sex in antiquity, see *Medicine, and Williams, 180–81, 231–44.

34. On the reception history, see I. E. Drabkin, ed., "Introduction," *On Acute Diseases and On Chronic Diseases*, by Caelius Aurelianus, trans. I. E. Drabkin (Chicago: University of Chicago Press, 1950), xii–xvi. Also Williams, 212–15.

35. "In treating satyriasis have the patient lie in a warm room and rest in silence without sleeping.... Do not admit visitors and particularly young women and boys. For the attractiveness of such visitors would again kindle the feeling of desire in the patient. Indeed, even healthy persons, seeing them, would in many cases seek sexual gratification" (*On Chronic Diseases*, 3.18.180–81, trans. Drabkin).

36. From Caelius Aurelianus, *On Acute Diseases and On Chronic Diseases*, ed., trans. I. E. Drabkin (Chicago: University of Chicago Press, 1950), 901–05.

37. Possibly one of Caelius's fifth-century interpolations, reflecting Christian influence by distancing the topic as much as possible (cf. Brooten, 148n.16). Or perhaps a hyperbolic way of saying such desires might seem so incomprehensible as to appear incredible.

38. Drabkin's ellipses: "text and meaning are unclear." He proposes "in (*or* to overcome) their degradation they seek to blame others for their affliction; then plagued by double sexuality,"

but adds the text "may refer to renewed (heterosexual?) promiscuity." Brooten proposes, from "jealousy" onward: "and, when they are freed from the disease or temporarily relieved, they seek to accuse others of that from which they are known to suffer, then, in their baseness of spirit, worn out by their two-fold sexuality, as though often ravished by drunkenness, they, bursting forth into new forms of lust that have been nourished by shameful custom, rejoice in the outrage to their own sex" (152).

39. Drabkin alternatively proposes, "'in general, any pain or affliction that was relieved must have come from some other source,' i.e., other than unnatural desire" (903n.8).

40. On Parmenides's theory, see Brooten, 156–57.

41. Drabkin's ellipses, showing that "the text is uncertain." He proposes "the point may have been that the affliction under discussion becomes even worse as the person grows older" (905n.13).

42. See Nancy G. Siraisi, *Avicenna in Renaissance Italy: The "Canon" and Medical Teaching in Italian Universities after 1500* (Princeton: Princeton University Press, 1987), 128, 359–76.

43. See Jacquart and Thomasset, 156–59; Siraisi, *Avicenna*, chs. 5–6.

44. Siraisi outlines the *Canon*'s contents in *Avicenna*, ch. 1.

45. See Aristotle, "On Length and Shortness of Life," in *Parva Naturalia*, 466B.

46. Translated by Faith Wallis, from Avicenna, *Liber canonis*, trans. Gerard of Cremona (Venice: per Paganium de Paganinis, 1507), Book III, fen 20, tr. 1, chs. 11, 42–44. Wallis informs me these chapters are so numbered in almost all early modern editions, but appear as chapters 6, 36–38 in the Venice (Giunta) edition of 1523. Wallis's notes are ascribed to her parenthetically. See Jacquart and Thomasset, 156–60; Jordan, 115–25; Bassem Nathan, "Medieval Arabic Views on Male Homosexuality," *Journal of Homosexuality* 26.4 (1994): 37–39.

47. The obscurity of this sentence was notorious among medieval and Renaissance commentators (cf. Jordan, 118n.19). I am not convinced by Jordan's attempt to translate it: "It is not so much attended by self-consciousness as is copulation in the vulva" (Wallis).

48. A Latinized form of the Arabic *al-ûbnah*, as it appears in the 1507 edition. There are numerous variant versions: the 1608 edition lists *alabone* and *alabene*; Pietro d'Abano renders it *alguagi* (Wallis). See Jordan, 119.

49. An extremely obscure phrase that I have rendered in accord with Jacques Despars's gloss (Wallis). Alternatively, "knowledge" here might refer to experience, i.e., habit, as in pseudo-Aristotle.

50. In the 1507 edition, the relative pronoun is masculine (*quem*), which can refer to either men or women. Although the 1523 edition substitutes the feminine *quam*, Jacques Despars's commentary printed in the same volume glosses it as *iuuenum uel iuuenculam*, "a young man or woman." Avicenna may mean that sexually unsatisfied women will either copulate with any available man, or mutually masturbate with a woman, or both (Wallis). Despars, in *Praesens maximus codex est totius scientie medicine principis Aboali Ainsene cum expositionibus* (Venice: Philippo Lincio, 1523).

51. See Lynn Thorndike, "Peter of Abano and Another Commentary on the Problems of Aristotle," *Bulletin of the History of Medicine* 29 (1955): 517–23. Blair mentions three new commentaries first published in the early seventeenth century, 179, 186.

52. See Lynn Thorndike, *A History of Magic and Experimental Science*, 8 vols. (New York: Columbia University Press, 1923–58), 2:938–47; and his "Relations of the Inquisition to Peter of Abano and Cecco d'Ascoli," *Speculum* 1 (1926): 338–43.

53. Charles H. Lohr, "Medieval Latin Aristotle Commentaries, Authors: Narcissus–Richardus," *Traditio* 28 (1972): 329–32.

54. Joan Cadden, "Sciences / Silences: The Natures and Languages of 'Sodomy' in Peter of Abano's *Problemata* Commentary," in Karma Lochrie, Peggy McCracken, and James A. Schultz, eds., *Constructing Medieval Sexuality* (Minneapolis: University of Minnesota Press, 1997), 40–43; Cadden, "'Nothing Natural Is Shameful': Vestiges of a Debate about Sex and Science in a Group of Late-Medieval Manuscripts," *Speculum* 76 (2001): 66–89.

55. Translated by Faith Wallis, from Pietro d'Abano, *Expositio problematum Aristotelis* (Mantua: Paul of Butzbach, 1475). Wallis's notes are ascribed to her parenthetically. See Cadden, "Sciences / Silences," and "Nothing Natural Is Shameful."

56. For example, in vomiting, or in the production of swellings that burst, thereby expelling the morbid matter (Wallis).

57. Ancient and medieval physiology divided digestion into three stages: the first broke down the food in the stomach, and its waste was feces; the second transformed aliment into blood in the liver, and its by-product was urine; the third digestion was the processing of blood into

specific body parts, and it produced various waste products, including earwax, sweat, etc. (Wallis).

58. Ancient and medieval anatomy held that the brain contained three chambers or ventricles, one behind another. Each ventricle housed a different cognitive faculty: "imagination" in the first, foremost ventricle; reason in the middle; and memory in the rear (Wallis).

59. Corresponding to what modern anatomists call the cribriform ("sievelike") plate, the opening for the olfactory nerves between the brain and the nose (Wallis).

60. The arteries were understood to be primarily for the conveyance of air or spirit, though it was acknowledged that they also contained blood (Wallis).

61. Women, whose supposedly natural cold and moisture did not permit them to fully digest food, eliminated the surplus in the form of mentrual blood, which was considered a waste product. Because they collect around the anus, hemorrhoids were also deemed repositories of waste blood (Wallis).

62. It should be recalled that Pietro did not know of the capillaries that connect the venous and arterial systems. For him, veins come to an end at the extremities of the body (Wallis).

63. Galenic physiology posited that bodily functions were directed by three spirits or virtues: the natural spirit in the liver, responsible for growth, nutrition and reproduction; the vital spirit in the heart, responsible for warmth (in both the physical and psychological senses); and the animal (from *anima*) spirit in the brain. The animal spirit in turn had two aspects: sensation and motion (Wallis).

64. Apparently referring to Book IV of Aristotle's *Nicomachean Ethics*, but not found there.

65. Emending *qui* to *quia* (Wallis).

66. That is, the second of the three parts of the *Tegni* or *Art of Medicine*.

67. The 1475 edition used here consistently reads *menstruosum* ("menstruous"). As Cadden notes ("Sciences / Silences," 55n.30), this reading also appears in the 1484 ed., but the 1501 ed. reads *monstruosum*, which would appear to be correct (Wallis).

68. Aristotle, *On the Soul*, 3.10.

69. Aristotle, *On the Movement of Animals*, 6.

70. The "natural things" comprised the body and its parts; the "nonnatural things" were the environmental and behavioral factors affecting health; the "contra-natural things" were diseases and their causes. The sixth of the "natural things" was the "operations," i.e., body functions (Wallis).

71. Aristotle, *Generation of Animals*, 1.20.10–18.

72. That is, an alternative reading of the meaning of the phrase "according to nature" (*secundum naturam*) in Aristotle's text (Wallis).

73. Conventionally following Aristotle's claim that females are a "defect of nature" relative to males. See Maclean, 7–9, 30–32.

74. This is the Aristotelian distinction between essence or substance—the underlying substrate of being—and "accidents," or properties and qualities (Wallis).

75. Aristotle, *History of Animals*, 9.581a33–581b23.

76. The ovaries were considered the female homologue of the testes, and in one view produced female spermatic fluid or seed that contributed to conception, like male sperm, though inferior in quality and strength. Both this and menstrual fluid could be considered sexual stimulants for women.

77. Though different in its specifics, the supposed Aristotle's account likewise posits a congenital cause, and that is what Pietro presumably means here.

78. In *Nicomachean Ethics*, 7.5.1–9, Aristotle argues that practices resulting from personal nature, engrained habit, or disease do not properly "fall within the limits of Vice," for "when nature is responsible, no one would describe such persons as showing Unrestraint, any more than one would apply that term to women because they are passive and not active in sexual intercourse" (trans. H. Rackham). But Pietro seems to interpret that context as condemnation, not exculpation, especially in his subsequent conclusion. For another view, cf. Cadden, "Sciences / Silences," 49–50.

79. Aristotle, *On Memory and Recollection*, 452a27–30.

80. Hippocrates, *Airs, Waters, and Places*, 14.

81. Aristotle, *Nicomachean Ethics*, 2.1.2.

82. Aristotle, *Posterior Analytics*, 2.19.

83. Cicero, *On Invention*, 1.2.3.

84. Again Pietro misrepresents Aristotle, *Nicomachean Ethics*, 7.5.1–9, for condemnation. Compare n. 78 above.

85. See Schleiner, "One-Sex Model," 181–90; Harry Friedenwald, *The Jews and Medicine: Essays*, vol. 2 (Baltimore: Johns Hopkins, 1944), 448–52.
86. Translated by Faith Wallis, from Rodrigo de Castro, *De universa mulierum medicina . . . opus* (Hamburg: Froben, 1603), 6–7, 65. Wallis's notes are ascribed to her parenthetically.
87. *Cervicis uteri*, "neck of the womb," is another term for the vagina, and is not to be confused with the modern "cervix" (Wallis).
88. *Lavra* means both "demon" and "a frightening theater-mask." Since Castro juxtaposes *lavra* to *facies*, "face," I assume he is referring to the mask. However, to convey the specific character of this mask, I have translated *lavra* as "devil-mask" (Wallis).
89. Castro is thinking of Galen's description of the female sexual organs as male genitalia turned inside out. The vagina/uterus complex corresponds to the penis, so the ring of tissue around the vaginal orifice corresponds to the foreskin (Wallis).
90. **Columbus:** Realdo Colombo, 1510–1559.
91. **Amatus:** Amato Lusitano, or João Rodrigues, 1511–1568.
92. See *Caelius Aurelianus. On Plautus, cf. Brooten, 4n.5. Martial, *Epigrams*, 1.90.9–10.
93. **Moschio:** Moschion, also known as Mustio or Muscio, fifth- or sixth-century Latin translator of Soranus's treatise on gynecology (*Caelius Aurelianus).
94. **Mercatus:** Luis Mercado, 1520–1606.
95. "For before now I have been at some time boy and girl, bush, bird, and a mute fish in the sea." *Katharmoi*, Fragment 108 (117), in *Empedocles: The Extant Fragments*, ed., trans. M. R. Wright (New Haven: Yale University Press, 1981), 275.
96. **Schenkius:** Johann Georg Schenk, fl. 1584–1620?
97. Tertullian (c. 160–c. 240), *To His Wife*, 6, in his *Treatises on Marriage and Remarriage*, trans. William P. Le Saint (Westminster, Md.: Newman, 1956), 18.
98. Translated by Faith Wallis, from André du Laurens, *Historia anatomica humani corporis* (Paris: Marc Orry, 1600), 356–57.
99. **the rod:** *virgam*, i.e., "rod" as euphemism for penis.
100. **Albucasis:** Abū al-Qāsim, c. 936–c. 1013.
101. See K. F. Russell, *British Anatomy 1525–1800: A Bibliography*, 2nd ed. (Winchester: St. Paul's Bibliographies, 1987), 88.
102. From Crooke, *Microcosmographia: A Description of the Body of Man* (London: 1615), STC 6062, Books IV–V. Since the numbers for chapters and questions that I reprint indicate those that I omit, I use ellipses in this case only to show omissions within the numbered sections selected. Page references appear parenthetically at the end of each excerpted chapter or question.
103. Thus allegorizing Lot's drunken stupor (Gen. 20:32–35) as sexual ecstasy.
104. See Galen, *On the Usefulness of the Parts of the Body*, trans. Margaret Tallmadge May, 2 vols. (Ithaca: Cornell University Press, 1968), 14.6 (not 14.11).
105. **perfect also in mankind (for Nature's imperfections are not so ordinary):** i.e., fully integral to or part of humankind (for Nature's imperfections would not be so general as to preclude that for one entire gender of a species).
106. Marginal gloss: "The wonderful providence and wisdom of God."
107. Marginal gloss: "To bring a kind of eternity out of imperfection."
108. Crooke has just reviewed the supposed genital homologies between males and females, whereby female genitals are unextruded male ones, as for Galen. In Book IV, question 8 (reprinted here subsequently), Crooke further reviews and rejects such claims.
109. **instauration:** institution, renewal.
110. **Testicles:** i.e., ovaries.
111. Compare Crooke, Book IV, ch. 4: "The Testicles in men are larger and of a hotter nature than in women; not so much by reason of their situation, as because of the temperament of the whole body, which in women is colder, in men hotter. Wherefore heat abounding in men thrusts them forth of the body, whereas in women they remain within, because their dull and sluggish heat is not sufficient to thrust them out. . . . They add also to the body much strength and heat, as appeareth by Eunuchs, whose temperament, substance, habit, and dispositions are all altered" (204, 207).
112. **Columbus, Archangelus, Laurentius, and Bauhin:** Realdo Colombo, 1510–1559; Archangelo Piccolomini, 1526–1605; *Du Laurens; Kaspar Bauhin, 1560–1624.
113. **Fallopius:** Gabriele Falloppio, 1523–1562. **Platerus:** probably Felix Platter, 1536–1614.
114. Aristotle, *Generation of Animals*, 1.20.
115. Hippocrates, *Regimen*, 1.26–29. And *Nature of the Child*, 12, in *The Hippocratic Treatises*, ed. Iain M. Lonie (Berlin: de Gruyter, 1981). Galen, *Usefulness of the Parts*, 14.11.

116. **attrectation:** touching, handling; i.e., as in masturbation.
117. **Chirurgeon's:** surgeon's.
118. **contrectation:** handling, touching, fingering; i.e., as in masturbation.
119. **share:** pubic region, groin.
120. Marginal gloss: "*Tribades odiosae feminae.* Leo Africanus, Caelius Aurelianus."
121. **Aegineta:** Paulus Aegineta, 625–690. **Rhazes:** al-Rāzī, 865–925?
122. Crooke rehearses Pliny's examples, *Natural History*, 7.4.36, also cited by *Claude de Tesserant.
123. Ovid, *Metamorphoses*, 15.409–10.
124. **Pontanus:** Giovanni Pontano, 1426–1503, following Ovid's myth of the female lovers Iphis and Ianthe, *Metamorphoses*, 9.666–794. **benempt:** benamed.
125. **Volateran:** probably Raffaele Maffei, 1455–1522, not a cardinal.
126. **Auscia in Vasconia:** Auch, in Gascony.
127. **Caieta:** Gaeta, in Italy.
128. **springal:** male youth.
129. **Ebula:** Yèbles, in France?
130. **Amatus Lusitanus:** Amato Lusitano, or João Rodrigues, 1511–1568.
131. **Conibrica... of Portugal:** Coimbra.
132. Hippocrates, *Epidemics*, 6.8.32.
133. **Herophilus:** Herophilus of Chalcedon, c. 330–260 B.C.E.
134. **Tentigo:** ancient Roman term for the tip or head of the clitoris, Crooke says (IV, ch. 16).
135. **rugous:** wrinkled.
136. **Pinaeus:** Séverin Pineau, d. 1619.
137. **for we will insist only in mankind:** i.e., we speak here only of humans, not all creatures.
138. Aristotle, *Generation of Animals*, 2.4; *History of Animals*, 4.11 (not 4.17).
139. **Peripatetics:** Aristotelians.
140. See Maclean, 7–9, 30–32.
141. Galen, *Usefulness of the Parts*, 14.6–7.
142. Aristotle, *Generation of Animals*, 1.2.
143. Hippocrates, *Regimen*, 1.28–29. Crooke's explanation of Hippocrates's view ignores his advice that a person's degree of masculinity (and presumably feminity too) depends not only on factors of conception, but also somewhat "upon nourishment, education, and habits" (trans. W. H. S. Jones).
144. Not found in that book of Hippocrates's *Epidemics*, Loeb edition.
145. See Davenport-Hines, 24.
146. From Marten, *A Treatise of All the Degrees and Symptoms of the Venereal Disease* (London: 1708), 68–69, 150–51.
147. **Pox:** implying pustules.
148. Through this Latin catalogue Marten or his correspondent (invented?) warns readers against sodomitical desires and affirms expertise in venereal infections. His implication that this sexual act necessarily entails unpleasant medical problems, or more of them, is homophobic propaganda.
149. **Fungous Caruncles:** spongy, fleshy excrescences.
150. **Lappet:** flap, shirt-tail.
151. **Gleet:** discharge.
152. **Hemicrane:** headache on one side of the head.
153. **Salivation:** course of mercury treatment producing much saliva; a torturous ordeal.
154. **Gonorrhea:** not distinguishing gonorrhea from the French disease or syphilis, Marten probably means urethral inflammation and discharge.

Chapter 4

1. Exceptions include Bernadette J. Brooten, *Love between Women: Early Christian Responses to Female Homoeroticism* (Chicago: University of Chicago Press, 1996), ch. 4 (also cited hereafter in text); Helen Rodnite Lemay, "Human Sexuality in Twelfth- through Fifteenth-Century Scientific Writings," in Vern L. Bullough and James Brundage, eds., *Sexual Practices and the Medieval Church* (Buffalo: Prometheus, 1982), 187–205; and her "The Stars and Human Sexuality: Some Medieval Views," *Isis* 71 (1980): 127–37.
2. The best single introduction is Eugenio Garin, *Astrology in the Renaissance: The Zodiac of Life*, trans. Carolyn Jackson, June Allen, with Clare Robertson (London: Routledge,

1983). See also Daniel Bini, ed., *Astrologia: Art and Culture in the Renaissance* (Modena: Bulina, 1996); J. C. Eade, *The Forgotten Sky: A Guide to Astrology in English Literature* (Oxford: Clarendon, 1984); Anthony Grafton, *Cardano's Cosmos: The Worlds and Works of a Renaissance Astrologer* (Cambridge, Mass.: Harvard University Press, 1999), also cited hereafter in text; P. G. Maxwell-Smith, ed. and trans., *The Occult in Early Modern Europe: A Documentary History* (London: Macmillan, 1999), also cited hereafter in text; Keith Thomas, *Religion and the Decline of Magic* (New York: Scribners, 1971), chs. 10–12; Lynn Thorndike, *A History of Magic and Experimental Science*, 8 vols. (New York: Columbia University Press, 1923–58).

3. Tamsyn S. Barton, *Power and Knowledge: Astrology, Physiognomics and Medicine under the Roman Empire* (Ann Arbor: University of Michigan Press, 1994), 33. See also her *Ancient Astrology* (London and New York: Routledge, 1994).

4. Prior to the telescope's invention, the five known planets were Mercury, Venus, Mars, Jupiter, Saturn. The two luminaries are the sun and moon.

5. See S. J. Tester, *A History of Western Astrology* (Woodbridge, UK: Boydell, 1987), 2–3, 68–71, also cited hereafter in text; Barton, *Power and Knowledge*, 69–71.

6. Brooten and David Halperin debate ancient astrology's homoerotic implications in "The GLQ Forum: Lesbian Historiography Before the Name?" *GLQ* 4 (1998): 564–66, 617–18, 625.

7. On "nature" and sex in antiquity, cf. Craig A. Williams, *Roman Homosexuality: Ideologies of Masculinity in Classical Antiquity* (Oxford: Oxford University Press, 1999), 180–81, 231–44.

8. See Barton, *Power and Knowledge*, 62–71; *Ancient Astrology*, ch. 3.

9. Don Cameron Allen, *The Star-Crossed Renaissance: The Quarrel about Astrology and Its Influence in England* (Durham, N.C.: Duke University Press, 1941), viii.

10. See, e.g., Sheila J. Rubin, "Kepler's Attitude Toward Pico and the Anti-astrology Polemic," *Renaissance Quarterly* 50 (1997): 750–70.

11. See Lemay; Tester, 186–87, 223–24; Nancy G. Siraisi, *Medieval and Early Renaissance Medicine: An Introduction to Knowledge and Practice* (Chicago: University of Chicago Press, 1990), Index, s.v. "Astrology."

12. See, e.g., C. A. J. Armstrong, "An Italian Astrologer at the Court of Henry VII," in E. F. Jacob, ed., *Italian Renaissance Studies* (London: Faber, 1960), 433–54.

13. See Thorndike, *History*, 5: ch. 17; Stefano Caroti, "Melanchthon's Astrology," in Paola Zambelli ed., *"Astrologi hallucinati": Stars and the End of the World in Luther's Time* (Berlin and New York: de Gruyter, 1986), 109–21.

14. See, e.g., Bernard Capp, *Astrology and the Popular Press: English Almanacs 1500–1800* (London: Faber, 1979).

15. Thorndike, *History*, 6:34.

16. See J. D. North, *Horoscopes and History* (London: Warburg-University of London, 1986), 181–82; Mary Ellen Bowden, "The Scientific Revolution in Astrology: The English Reformers, 1558–1686," Ph.D. diss. Yale University, 1974, 139–40.

17. Pico, *Disputationes adversus astrologiam divinatricem*, ed., trans. Eugenio Garin, 2 vols. (Florence: Vallecchi, 1946–52), 6.6, 15; hereafter cited in text. English translations of Pico appear here courtesy of Faith Wallis.

18. Condivi, *The Life of Michelangelo*, ed. Hellmut Wohl, trans. Alice Sedgwick Wohl, 2nd ed. (University Park: Pennsylvania University Press, 1999), 6, 105. I thank Wayne Dynes for this observation. On the artist's horoscope in general, see Don Riggs, "Was Michelangelo Born under Saturn," *Sixteenth Century Journal* 26 (1995): 99–121.

19. Compare St. Thomas Aquinas (1224/5–1274), e.g., in *Summa Theologica*, 1a.115, Article 4.

20. Cardano, e.g., makes both antideterminist and determinist pronouncements. Grafton assumes "Cardano, like most specialist astrologers before and after him was no determinist. He followed Ptolemy in insisting that environment and other factors modified and sometimes reversed the judgment of the stars" (85). But contrast Cardano's comment, "it is clear beyond a doubt that all who are born, when they are in a soft and malleable condition, and newly born, receive the influence of the stars like wax, when it is taken off the fire, or lead, when it is first poured and forced into a mold" (cit. Grafton, 108). Ptolemy's position approximates Stoic fatalism, as we have seen. While publicly disavowing astral determinism in *A Defence of Judicial Astrology* (Cambridge, UK: 1603), STC 13266, Christopher Heydon, e.g., says the contrary in a private letter (cf. Bowden, 139–40).

21. See Ugo Baldini, "The Roman Inquisition's Condemnation of Astrology: Antecedents, Reasons and Consequences," in Gigliola Fragnito, ed., *Church, Censorship and Culture in*

Early Modern Italy, trans. Adrian Belton (Cambridge, UK: Cambridge University Press, 2001), 79–110.

22. Reformers, e.g., used astrology for anti-Catholic polemics and eschatological research. See Robin Bruce Barnes, *Prophecy and Gnosis: Apocalypticism in the Wake of the Lutheran Reformation* (Stanford: Stanford University Press, 1988), chs. 4–5.

23. Agrippa, *Of the Vanity and Uncertainty of Arts and Sciences*, ed. Catherine M. Dunn, trans. James Sanford (Northridge: California State University Press, 1974), 104–05, a translation first printed in 1569; cited hereafter in text.

24. See North, *Horoscopes and History*, 163–73; Wayne Shumaker, *Renaissance Curiosa* (Binghamton, N.Y.: Medieval and Renaissance Texts and Studies, 1982), ch. 2.

25. North, *Horoscopes and History*, 163–64.

26. See Garin, *Astrology*, ch. 1; J. D. North, "Astrology and the Fortunes of Churches," *Centaurus* 24 (1980): 181–211.

27. See Grafton, 75–77; Don Cameron Allen, *Doubt's Boundless Sea: Skepticism and Faith in the Renaissance* (Baltimore, Md.: Johns Hopkins Press, 1964), 51.

28. Allen, *Star-Crossed Renaissance*, 61–62.

29. See Thorndike, *History*, 6: ch. 47; Garin, *Astrology*, 96–105; Allen, *Doubt's Boundless Sea*, ch. 2.

30. Translated by Faith Wallis, from pseudo-Ptolemy, *Centiloquium*, trans. Giovanni Pontano (1426–1503), in Ptolemy, *De praedictionibus astronomicis* (Basel: Joannes Oporinus, 1553), 263, 265.

31. Translated by Dorota Dutsch, from Ptolemy, *Quadripartitum. Centiloquium cum commento Hali*, ed. Hieronymus Salius (Venice: Bonetus Locatellys, 1493), fol. 114va.

32. See F. E. Robbins, "Introduction," in Ptolemy, *Tetrabiblos* (Loeb), x–xv.

33. From Ptolemy, *Tetrabiblos*, ed., trans. F. E. Robbins. Page references appear parenthetically after each extract, and I indicate ellision only within an excerpted section (from title onward), not before or after, in this case.

34. **Bastarnia:** southern Poland and southwestern Russia. **Apulia:** southeastern Italy. **Tyrrhenia:** Tuscany. **Celtica:** western Spain?

35. **Bithynia, Phrygia, and Colchica:** i.e., in the area of Asia Minor.

36. **passive part:** affective, irrational; the passions, in contrast to the soul's "active" or rational part.

37. On Ptolemy's complex usage of "nature," see *Astrology.

38. Ptolemy assumes the planets and two luminaries (sun and moon) are each inherently gendered (Venus feminine, Mars masculine, e.g.), yet also that planets fluctuate in gender as they pass through the heavens, according to various factors. Compare *Tetrabiblos*, 1.6.

39. According to Ptolemy's principles for feminization of planetary influences, *Tetrabiblos*, 1.6.

40. Brooten, 137; cf. 132–37. Also Barton, *Ancient Astrology*, 163–65; Maude W. Gleason, *Making Men: Sophists and Self-Presentation in Ancient Rome* (Princeton: Princeton University Press, 1995), 66–67.

41. From Firmicus Maternus, *Ancient Astrology, Theory and Practice: "Matheseos Libri VIII,"* trans. Jean Rhys Bram (Park Ridge, N.J.: Noyes, 1975). Chapter headings in square brackets are Bram's additions, as in Bram's published translation. However, I have clarified and revised Bram's translation, especially the sexual terminology, in square brackets within my text, with reference to *Firmici Materni Matheseos Libri VIII*, ed. W. Kroll, F. Skutsch, K Ziegler, 2 vols. (Leipzig: Teubner, 1897, 1913). Whereas Bram translates *cinaedus*, e.g., as "male prostitute," "homosexual," "degenerate," and "pervert," I have restored the Latin term, difficult to translate and used as a loanword in Renaissance English. Likewise, where Bram translates *virago* (usually a masculine woman, in Firmicus's usage typically meaning assertive tribade) as "shrew," I restore "virago." I use ellipses here only to indicate omissions within numbered sections, not between them. On Firmicus's technical terms, see further *Mathesis*, Book II; Bram's apparatus; and Barton, *Power and Knowledge*, 71–82.

42. **house:** division of horoscope, usually twelve in total, relating to some aspect of life, such as marriage (seventh house).

43. **tropical:** Aries, Cancer, Libra, Capricorn. **scaly:** e.g., Pisces. **mutable:** Gemini, Virgo, Sagittarius, Pisces.

44. **IMC:** *Imum Caelum*, the nadir, as opposed to the MC, the *Medium Caelum* or midheaven of a horoscope.

45. **descendent:** opposite to the ascendant, the degree on the horizon of the horoscope.

46. **anafora:** second house from the ascendant, thus rising.

47. **debility:** fall, as opposed to planetary exaltation; the planet thus supposedly loses power.
48. **public cinaedi:** throughout the *Mathesis*, Firmicus opposes covert, discreet cinaedi to those who make themselves publicly known as such, whom he considers worse, and shameless. By this he may sometimes mean male prostitutes, exclusively or otherwise. However, analogous passages in the *Astronomica* of Manilius do not imply male prostitutes, but rather a community of cinaedi with a value system approving their sexual behaviors and publicly advocating them (4.518–22, 5.140–56).
49. **virago:** typically meaning tribade, in Firmicus's usage, so that he imagines females who sexually desire their own sex are masculine. Compare Brooten, 133–34.
50. Thus accompanying the festive rites of Cybele.
51. Compare Ebreo, *The Philosophy of Love*, trans. F. Friedeberg-Seeley and Jean H. Barnes (London: Soncino, 1937), 343–65.
52. Fraunce, *The Third Part of the Countess of Pembroke's Ivychurch* (London: 1592), STC 11341, fols. 48ᵇ–50ᵃ.
53. From Ebreo, *Dialoghi d'amore* (Venice: Domenico Giglio, 1558), fols. 79ᵇ–80ᵇ, 86ᵇ–87ᵃ, trans. Nicola Martino and Kenneth Borris (Sir John Cheke's copy, Thomas Fisher Rare Books Library, University of Toronto).
54. "Feminine love": i.e., male-female; "masculine love": i.e., male-male (*General Introduction), just as the paradigmatic agent in both cases here is male (Jove). Ebreo's context here assumes the astrological subject is male, just as "masculine love" always implied a male agent.
55. Not in Pontano's Latin version. Ebreo may use a different one, or mean *Tetrabiblos*.

Chapter 5

1. Aristotle, *Prior Analytics*, 2.27.70b, trans. Hugh Tredennick.
2. See A. MacC. Armstrong, "The Methods of the Greek Physiognomists," *Greece and Rome* 5 (1958): 52–56; Tamsyn S. Barton, *Power and Knowledge: Astrology, Physiognomics, and Medicine under the Roman Empire* (Ann Arbor: University of Michigan Press, 1994), ch. 2; Jan Bremmer, "Walking, Standing, and Sitting in Ancient Greek Culture," in Jan Bremmer and Herman Roodenburg, eds., *A Cultural History of Gesture: From Antiquity to the Present Day* (Cambridge, UK: Polity, 1991), 15–35; H. MacL. Currie, "Aristotle and Quintilian: Physiognomical Reflections," in Allan Gotthelf, ed., *Aristotle on Nature and Living Things* (Pittsburgh: Mathesis, 1985), 359–66; Elizabeth C. Evans, *Physiognomics in the Ancient World* (Philadelphia: American Philosophical Society, 1969), *Transactions of the American Philosophical Society* 59 (1969); Maud W. Gleason, *Making Men: Sophists and Self-Presentation in Ancient Rome* (Princeton: Princeton University Press, 1995), chs. 2–5; Maria Michela Sassi, *The Science of Man in Ancient Greece*, trans. Paul Tucker (Chicago: University of Chicago Press, 2001), ch. 2.
3. Pseudo-Aristotle, *Physiognomics*, 805a, 808b; trans. W. S. Hett. The treatise consists of two peripatetic works spliced together.
4. See Lynn Thorndike, *A History of Magic and Experimental Science*, 8 vols. (New York: Columbia University Press, 1927–58); also cited hereafter in text. Also Carroll Camden, "The Mind's Construction in the Face," in Baldwin Maxwell et al., eds., *Renaissance Studies in Honor of Hardin Craig* (Stanford: Stanford University Press, 1941), 208–20; Joan Cadden, *Meanings of Sex Difference in the Middle Ages: Medicine, Science, and Culture* (Cambridge, UK: Cambridge University Press, 1993), Index, s.v. "physiognomy"; Angus G. Clarke, "Metoposcopy: An Art to Find the Mind's Construction in the Forehead," in Patrick Curry, ed., *Astrology, Science, and Society: Historical Essays* (Woodbridge, UK: Boydell, 1987), 171–95; Danielle Jacquart and Claude Thomasset, *Sexuality and Medicine in the Middle Ages*, trans. Matthew Adamson (Cambridge, UK: Polity, 1988), 143–45; P. G. Maxwell-Stuart, ed. and trans., *The Occult in Early Modern Europe: A Documentary History* (London: Macmillan, 1999), 22–29.
5. William A. Wallace, "Aristotle and Aristotelianism," *Encyclopedia of the Renaissance*, 110; Edward Cranz, *A Bibliography of Aristotle Editions 1501–1600*, 2nd, rev. ed., rev. Charles B. Schmitt (Baden-Baden: Koerner, 1984), 215.
6. See Charles B. Schmitt, "Francesco Storella and the Last Printed Edition of the Latin *Secretum secretorum* (1555)," in W. F. Ryan and Charles B. Schmitt, *Pseudo-Aristotle, the Secret of Secrets: Sources and Influences* (London: Warburg Institute, 1982), 124–31. See further Charles

B. Schmitt and Dilwyn Knox, *Pseudo-Aristoteles Latinus: A Guide to Latin Works Falsely Attributed to Aristotle before 1500* (London: Warburg Institute, 1985), 21–24, 45–50, 54–76; Cranz, 222. M. A. Manzaloui, ed., *Secretum Secretorum: Nine English Versions*, Early English Text Society, No. 276 (Oxford: EETS, 1977); Robert Steele, ed., *Three Prose Versions of the Secreta Secretorum*, Early English Text Society, E.S. 74 (London: EETS, 1898).

7. *The Secret of Secrets*, trans. Robert Copland (London: 1528), STC 770, sig. H3^b.
8. Quoting Clarke, 189.
9. See Gleason, 58–60. Polemo, *Physiognomy*, 2.1.192F, cit. Gleason, 58.
10. Gleason, 59.
11. *Physiognomics*, 808a, 813a, 809b; trans. Hett. Throughout, Hett's bowdlerizing, homophobic code-word for cinaedus (in the Greek equivalent) is "morbid."
12. See Gleason, 62–64. On characteristics of ancient cinaedi, see Amy Richlin, "Not Before Homosexuality: The Materiality of the *Cinaedus* and the Roman Law against Love between Men," *Journal of the History of Sexuality* 3 (1992–93): 523–73; John Winkler, *The Constraints of Desire: The Anthropology of Sex and Gender in Ancient Greece* (London and New York: Routledge, 1990), ch. 2.
13. See Gleason, 62–67; Barton, *Power and Knowledge*, 115–18.
14. See Jacques André, ed., trans., *Anonyme Latin: Traité de physiognomie* (Paris: Belles Lettres, 1981), 39–42, 47, 118; Bernadette J. Brooten, *Love Between Women: Early Christian Responses to Female Homoeroticism* (Chicago: University of Chicago Press, 1996), 56–57.
15. On Albertus Magnus, see Thorndike, *History*, 2:575.
16. Hill, *The Contemplation of Mankind* (London: 1571), STC 13482, fols. 1^b, 3^b–4^a, sig. ¶¶3^a.
17. *De Fato*, 5.10–11; *Tusculan Disputations*, 4.37.80–81. A similar tale was often told about Hippocrates, as in versions of the pseudo-Aristotelian *Secretum secretorum*.
18. On Rocca's biography, now obscure, see Thorndike, *History*, 5:42–43, 50–65, my source here.
19. This partial inventory derives from Thorndike, *History*, 5:63–65, and *NUC* pre-1956.
20. Hill, *Contemplation*, fols. 214^a–215^a (misnumbered 114–115).
21. Translated by Faith Wallis, from Rocco, *Chyromantie ac physionomie anastasis* (Bologna: per Joannem Antonium Platonidem Benedictorum, 1504).
22. Juvenal, *Satires*, 6.311.
23. From Hill, *Contemplation of Mankind* (London: 1571), STC 13482. I parenthetically note the corresponding pages of the source after each chapter excerpt, and dispense with introductory and terminal ellipses before and after the whole selection from each chapter.
24. **Conciliator:** *Pietro d'Abano (1257–1315/6).
25. Aristotle, *History of Animals*, 9 (8 in Loeb edition). 608a–b.
26. **clear:** self-evident (vs. the pseudofeminine male).
27. **luxury:** lust.
28. **upon a bravery:** in defiance.
29. **ring:** suspended metal circle that riders competed to bear off on their lances.
30. **like to the Hart:** with "eyes rolling and turning here and there, still turning the head," and denoting "especial unstableness and an insatiable luxury," i.e., lust (fol. 19^b).
31. **luxurious:** lustful.
32. **genitors:** i.e., male genitals.
33. **regitive:** ruling, governing.
34. **grown unto a ripe age:** i.e., old enough that these youthful features seem prospectively adult.
35. **induments:** clothing; or enduements.
36. The ladies pulled their shoulder blades together by exercise ("art") or by corsetting ("induments") to look like the lips of the vulva (*Os ventris*), and presumably wore dresses cut low in the back to display this allusion. I thank Faith Wallis for this explanation.
37. **Melampus:** Greek author of two divinatory works, third century B.C.E.
38. On the chiromantic study, see Thorndike, *History*, 6:163–64. On Porta's life and these works, see Louise George Clubb, *Giambattista Della Porta: Dramatist* (Princeton: Princeton University Press, 1965), ch. 1; Miller Howard Rienstra, "Giovanni Battista della Porta and Renaissance Science," Diss. University of Michigan, 1963, 43–44, 61–72.
39. Clubb, 28.
40. Translated by Faith Wallis, from the first, four-book edition of *De humana physiognomonia* (Vico Equense: apud Iosephum Cacchium, 1586), for Book Four, ch. 11; from the 1602 edition (Naples: apud Tarquinium Longum) of the expanded, six-book version first published in 1599, for Book Six, ch. 10. Porta's Italian translation, first published in 1598, adds further

material interpolated here between square brackets, trans. Faith Wallis from *Della fisonomia dell'uomo* (Venice: Combi, 1652), 508–10. Greek words appear as in the *editio princeps*.

41. Aristotle, *Nicomachean Ethics*, 7.1.6, 7.7.4.
42. Pseudo-Aristotle, *Physiognomics*, 808a.
43. Sentence added in the Italian version. Athenaeus, *Deipnosophists*, 12.528–31.
44. **Cocles:** i.e., *Bartolommeo della Rocca, 1467–1504.
45. Sentence added in the Italian version.
46. Sentence omitted in the Italian version.
47. The Italian version adds the anecdote of the Sicilian transvestite.
48. Plutarch, Fragment 181.
49. Porta paraphrases the paragraph's following material from Hippocrates on the Scythians, *Airs, Waters, and Places*, 18–23, and concludes by applying this information to the general case of the cinaedus, deemed constitutionally analogous to females (thought colder and moister than males).
50. See Luigi Campedelli, "Magini, Giovanni Antonio," in *Dictionary of Scientific Biography*.
51. Clarke, 178–79.
52. See further Clarke, 180–89.
53. I thank Nicola Martino for consultation on these rubrics.
54. Translated by Konrad Eisenbichler and Nicola Martino, from Ciro Spontoni, i.e., Magini (?), *La metoposcopia overo commensuratione delle linee della fronte* (Venice: Evangelista Deuchino, 1626), 20–31, 61–63, 83–85, 96–97, 99–100, 121.

Chapter 6

1. Sampled index entries for "cinaedi" and "masculine love," from the original sixteen-book version and its thirty-book successor. Not all these index headings appear in both. Ricchieri, *Lectionum antiquarum libri XVI* (Basel: apud Ioannem Frobenium, 1517); *Lectionium antiquarum libri triginta* (Frankfurt: apud heredes A. Wecheli, C. Marnium, I. Aubrium, 1599). I also cite the latter edition hereafter in text; all translations of Ricchieri appear courtesy of Dorota Dutsch.
2. See Ann Moss, "Commonplace Books" and "Dictionaries and Encyclopedias" in *Encyclopedia of the Renaissance*, 6 vols. (New York: Scribners, 1999). See further Neil Kenny, *The Palace of Secrets: Béroalde de Verville and Renaissance Conceptions of Knowledge* (Oxford: Clarendon, 1991); A. H. T. Levi, "Ethics and the Encyclopedia in the Sixteenth Century," in Peter Sharratt, ed., *French Renaissance Studies 1540–70: Humanism and the Encyclopedia* (Edinburgh: Edinburgh University Press, 1976), 170–84; Ann Moss, *Printed Commonplace-Books and the Structuring of Renaissance Thought* (Oxford: Clarendon, 1996); Walter J. Ong, "Commonplace Rhapsody: Ravisius Textor, Zwinger, and Shakespeare," in R. R. Bolgar, ed., *Classical Influences on European Culture A.D. 1500–1700* (Cambridge, UK: Cambridge University Press, 1976), 91–126; Richard Yeo, *Encyclopedic Visions: Scientific Dictionaries and Enlightenment Culture* (Cambridge, UK: Cambridge University Press, 2001). I follow Kenny's formal distinction between early modern encyclopedias and miscellanies, and cite Kenny and Moss in text hereafter.
3. For example, Alan Bray sees 1650 to 1700 as the turning point in *Homosexuality in Renaissance England*, 2nd ed. (New York: Columbia University Press, 1995), ch. 1 (quoting 25).
4. For example, Ian Frederick Moulton, *Before Pornography: Erotic Writing in Early Modern England* (Oxford: Oxford University Press, 2000), 12, 38–40.
5. Reisch, *Margarita philosophica* (Basel: J. Schottus, 1508), sig. 2O4^b.
6. Foucault, *An Introduction*, Vol. 1 of *The History of Sexuality*, trans. Robert Hurley (New York: Pantheon, 1978), 38, 101.
7. Mirabelli, *Polyanthea* (Strasbourg: Apud Matthiam Schurerium, 1517), fol. 201^a.
8. Tixier, *Officina*, 2 vols. (Venice: Giovanni Griffio, 1574), 1: fols. 103^a–33^b.
9. See M. J. C. Lowry, "Niccolò Leonico Tomeo," in Peter G. Bietenholz and Thomas B. Deutscher, eds., *Contemporaries of Erasmus: A Biographical Register of the Renaissance and Reformation*, 3 vols. (Toronto: University of Toronto Press, 1985–87), 2: 323–24.
10. Translated by Faith Wallis, from Leonico, *De varia historia libri tres* (Lyons: apud Gryphium, 1532), pp. 273, 326–27.
11. Orpheus was another supposed originator of male homoeroticism according to an apparently Hellenistic variant of the Orphic legends featured in Ovid's *Metamorphoses*, Books 10 to 11.

12. **nequitur agere, aut etiam turpissime pati:** the verbs *agere* and *pati* are euphemisms for taking insertive and receptive roles in sexual intercourse (Wallis). Leonico's preceding account of Tyrrhenian sexual indulgences says, e.g., they did not find public nudity shocking, and their women exercised naked in public gymnasia, even wrestling with men. **Tyrrhenians:** Etruscans.

13. Translated by Faith Wallis and, for Greek verse, Jack Mitchell, from Zwinger, *Theatrum vitae humanae*, 30 vols. in 6 (Basel: Eusebius Episcopius, 1586–87), vol. 9, Book III, 2301–4. Wallis's notes are parenthetically attributed to her. I normalize some proper names as in Loeb editions. When Zwinger discusses Greek terms, I reproduce their rendering in that Basel edition. I retain Zwinger's system of concluding each example with its reference, but give further information in a note where needed.

14. Contrary to Zwinger's pejorative purpose and contextual implication, Athenaeus provides a lengthy entertaining survey of the prevalence of intergenerational and other homoerotic loves in Greek antiquity, noting their opposition to tyranny because of male lovers' code of honor.

15. That is, "Puerorum, Pathicorum," Zwinger, *Theatrum*, Vol. 9, Book III, 2282–83; a category in discussion of rape.

16. This would put Christ's birth at *anno mundi* 5199, the date St. Jerome proposed in his *Chronicon*, a translation and expansion of Eusebius's world chronicle. This chronology was widely accepted in the medieval West (Wallis).

17. Marcantonio Sabellico (1436?–1506), *Enneads*, in *Opera*, 2 vols. (Basel: ex officina Hervagiana, 1538), 1:17.

18. Guillaume Budé (1468–1540); not found.

19. St. Jerome, *Commentariorum in Esaiam*, ed. Marcus Adriaen, vol. 73 of *Corpus Christianorum*, Series Latina (Turnhout: Brepols, 1963), I.ii.5–6 (31–32).

20. Heraclides Lembus, *Excerpta Politiarum*, ed., trans. Mervin R. Ditts (Durham, N.C.: Duke University Press, 1971), 19. The text collects excerpts from Aristotle's now fragmentary *Politiae*. Despite Zwinger, it actually insists the Cretans "seem to have been the first to engage in pederasty, and this is not shameful among them." And the boys "to a great extent go to bed with one another" (trans. Dilts).

21. Strabo positively describes these Cretan customs honoring homoeroticism. In claiming "they stopped short of indecency" and emphasizing contrary "laws," Zwinger also misrepresents Strabo.

22. **Old Comedy:** Athenian comedy of the fifth century B.C.E.

23. Zwinger's entry closely follows Erasmus (1469–1536). *Adages II vii 1 to III iii 100*, trans. R. A. B. Mynors, Vol. 33 of *Collected Works of Erasmus* (Toronto: University of Toronto Press, 1991), 240.

24. Zwinger follows Plutarch, *Pelopidas*, 18.1–19.4 (including the citation of Aristotle), which discusses the amorous basis of the Band's fellowship. However, Plutarch adduces Iolaüs and Hercules to exemplify male lovers who are also valiant comrades-in-arms, like the Theban Sacred Band, not as former members of it. Compare Plutarch, *Dialogue on Love*, 761D–E: "Believing Iolaüs to have been beloved by [Hercules], to this very day [male] lovers worship and honor Iolaüs, exchanging vows and pledges with their beloved at his tomb" (trans. W. C. Hembold).

25. Probably drawing on Plutarch, *Pelopidas*, 18.1–19.4. However, whereas Zwinger implies Philip was thus anticipating others' adverse comment on the moral status of male same-sex love, in Plutarch he probably comments on the status of their personal honor in their valiant defeat. Philip had various male lovers, as did his son Alexander the Great.

26. Zwinger suppresses Plutarch's much higher figure of three hundred, *Pelopidas*, 18.1.

27. **detestable lust:** not Ovidian; Zwinger's and Ricchieri's early modern homophobic viewpoint.

28. That is, from Justin's epitome of Pompeius Trogus's lost history. Compare Justin, *History of Trogus*, trans. Robert Codrington (London: 1682), Wing J1274, 80.

29. Zwinger tells the full story below in the following subchapter, "Passive," s.v. "Pausanias."

30. Suidas is a tenth-century Byzantine lexicographical encyclopedia.

31. Textor, i.e., Tixier, *Officina*, 1: fol. 113[b].

32. Pindar, Alcman, Sappho, Ibycus, Anacreon, Bacchylides, Stesichorus, Alcaeus, Simonides; 650–450 B.C.E.

33. The better to attack masculine love, Zwinger misrepresents Plato's context, *Laws*, 8.838E–39A. Plato's Athenian Stranger actually proposes curtailing extramarital sex in general, including sex between males, while allowing for others' skepticism about the practicality of this. In

reviewing ancient sources, Zwinger suppresses positive representations of male same-sex love in some other Platonic dialogues (and elsewhere).

34. That is, the boy had never stayed till a contest ended, when the loser's throat was cut (Wallis).

35. Zwinger further explains that Lusius and his brother were thus politically attacked by Cato and dishonored, but regained popular sympathy.

36. **minnows:** young boys Tiberius trained to swim between his legs and nibble his genitals.

37. I amend *Poppaeum* (the masculine form) in Zwinger's text to *Poppaeam* (the feminine form), which agrees with Plutarch (Wallis).

38. **freedman:** *liberto.* Asiaticus was a slave, as the anecdote indicates; presumably, *liberto* ("freedman") acknowledges his ultimate social position (Wallis).

39. Roman emperor Titus Vespasian and his successor Domitian were the sons of Vespasian. The following subchapter, "Passive," states that Domitian himself loved the eunuch Earinus.

40. Dio's comment differs from what Zwinger makes of it. Trajan "was devoted to boys and to wine, but if he had ever committed or endured any base or wicked deed as the result of this, he would have incurred censure; as it was, however, he drank all the wine he wanted, yet remained sober, and in his relation with boys he harmed no one" (trans. Earnest Cary).

41. St. Jerome, *Commentariorum in Esaiam,* I.ii.5–6 (32).

42. *Ficus* ("fig") is slang for anus, or for a sore on the anus. If Martial's joke is malicious, the boys have contracted a venereal disease from anal intercourse, whether from Labienus or otherwise. If not (Martial liked such sex too), it plays on *ficus* in the sense of anus, so that Labienus exchanged one bunch of figs for another.

43. **Talassus:** Roman god of marriage.

44. **to be deflowered:** *patior,* i.e., to undergo penetration. Loeb has *pariat,* i.e., for him to give birth.

45. Giovanni Gioviano Pontano (1426–1503), *De immanitate,* ch. 17, in Vol. I of *Opera omnia* (Venice: In aedibus Aldi, et Andreae soceri, 1518), fols. 321^b–22^b

46. **Puerto Viejo and . . . Punà:** now in Chile and Ecuador, respectively.

47. Compare Cieza de León (1518–1554), *The Incas,* ed. Victor Wolfgang von Hagen, trans. Harriet de Onis (Norman: University of Oklahoma Press, 1959), 313–15.

48. Paolo Giovio, 1483–1552 (not found).

49. See *History of Justin,* 181.

50. Zwinger's citation of Aulus Gellius is coy, for he gives no information on the accusations. According to Aeschines, Timarchus had been a notorious male prostitute. Compare *Against Timarchus.*

51. Erasmus, *Opera omnia,* ed. Jean Leclerc, 10 vols. in 11 (Leiden: Vander Aa, 1703–06), 4: col. 361. Similarly Nicolas Udall, *Apophthegms* (London: 1542), STC 10443, fols. 137^b–38^a.

52. **sordid:** Zwinger's interpolation. Aelian's account is positive.

53. Aelian tells how Ptolemy's lover pitied some men about to be executed, and obtained their release (Wallis).

54. In Plutarch, this episode directly follows that of the boy Democles, who plunged into a cauldron of boiling water to escape Demetrius's sexual harassment (see above). Plutarch implies Cleaenetus contrarily submitted to Demetrius's desires to gain his support for remission of the fine.

55. Opimius uses the feminine form of *Aegilius* (Wallis).

56. Zwinger suppresses Martial's further comment here: "I don't want too much of a man, Pannychus, and I don't want too little" (trans. D. R. Shackleton Bailey).

57. Or in Jack Mitchell's fantasia upon a printer's smudge in Zwinger's quotation: So there goes the lad they call Dragon, / A beautiful youth beyond braggin': / Now shan't we extol / His luverly hole, / Which a mightier Snake should be shaggin'?

58. Actually Ovid, *Heroides,* 15.17–18. It was commonly assumed that Ovid based this fictional verse epistle on an autobiographical poem by Sappho, subsequently lost (*The Sapphic Renaissance).

Chapter 7

1. Aristotle, *Generation of Animals,* 4.4770b; trans. A. L. Peck.

2. Augustine differently argues that prodigies and monsters are contrary only to what is known of nature, for they happen according to God's will, and God's will constitutes nature (*City of*

God, 21.8). On sodomy and monsters, cf. Arnold I. Davidson, "The Horror of Monsters," in James J. Sheehan and Morton Sosna, eds., *The Boundaries of Humanity: Humans, Animals, Machines* (Berkeley and Los Angeles: University of California Press, 1991), 36–67 (also cited in text hereafter).

3. Aristotle, *Generation of Animals*, 4.3.767b.

4. Daston and Park, *Wonders and the Order of Nature, 1150–1750* (New York: Zone, 1998), ch. 5. Adapting Daston and Park's analysis of these interpretive patterns, I reapply them to consider teratological implications of homoeroticism. See also Dudley Wilson, *Signs and Portents: Monstrous Births from the Middle Ages to the Enlightenment* (London and New York: Routledge, 1993).

5. See Ottavia Niccoli, *Prophecy and People in Renaissance Italy*, trans. Lydia G. Cochrane (Princeton: Princeton University Press, 1990), ch. 2; Philip M. Soergel, "The Afterlives of Monstrous Infants in Reformation Germany," in Bruce Gordon and Peter Marshall, eds., *The Place of the Dead: Death and Remembrance in Late Medieval and Early Modern Europe* (Cambridge, UK: Cambridge University Press, 2000), 288–309.

6. Luther and Melancthon, *Of Two Wonderful Popish Monsters*, trans. John Brooke (London: 1579), STC 17797.

7. Daston and Park, *Wonders*, 197–98.

8. See Ottavia Niccoli, "'Menstruum Quasi Monstruum': Monstrous Births and Menstrual Taboo in the Sixteenth Century," in Edward Muir and Guido Ruggiero, eds., *Sex and Gender in Historical Perspective* (Baltimore: Johns Hopkins University Press, 1990), 1–25.

9. Daston and Park, *Wonders*, 200.

10. Browne, *Religio medici* (London: 1642), Wing B5166, 24–29.

11. Ross, *Mystagogus Poeticus, or the Muses Interpreter* (London: 1648), Wing R1965, 171.

12. Translated by Mawy Bouchard and Kenneth Borris. See Donald Stone, Jr., "The Sexual Outlaw in France, 1605," *Journal of the History of Sexuality* 2 (1991–92): 597–608.

13. See Ann Rosalind Jones and Peter Stallybrass, "Fetishizing Gender: Constructing the Hermaphrodite in Renaissance Europe," in Julia Epstein and Kristina Straub, eds., *Body Guards: The Cultural Politics of Gender Ambiguity* (New York and London: Routledge, 1991), 94–100; Lauren Silberman, "Mythographic Transformations of Ovid's Hermaphrodite," *Sixteenth Century Journal* 19 (1988): 643–52.

14. See Lorraine Daston and Katharine Park, "Hermaphrodites in Renaissance France," *Critical Matrix* 1, No. 5 (1985): 10–11; Jones and Stallybrass, 91, 100–4.

15. Lorraine Daston and Katharine Park, "The Hermaphrodite and the Orders of Nature: Sexual Ambiguity in Early Modern France," in Louise Fradenburg and Carla Freccero, eds., *Premodern Sexualities* (New York and London: Routledge, 1996), 117–36.

16. Daston and Park, "Hermaphrodites," 5–6.

17. Quoting Daston and Park, "Hermaphrodites," 4.

18. Daston and Park, "Hermaphrodite and the Orders of Nature," 118–20.

19. See, e.g., Daston and Park, "Hermphrodite and the Orders of Nature," passim; Jones and Stallybrass, passim; Kathleen Perry Long, "Sexual Dissonance: Early Modern Scientific Accounts of Hermaphrodites," in Peter G. Platt, ed., *Wonders, Marvels and Monsters in Early Modern Culture* (Newark, N.J.: Delaware–Associated University Presses, 1999), 145–63.

20. On homophobic reactions, see Daston and Park, "Hermaphrodites," 7–8.

21. Daston and Park, "Hermaphrodites," 1–3.

22. Daston and Park, "Hermaphrodites," 8.

23. Cited in Israel Burshatin, "Elena Alias Eleno: Gender, Sexualities, and 'Race' in the Mirror of Natural History in Sixteenth-Century Spain," in Sabrina Petra Ramet, ed., *Gender Reversals and Gender Cultures: Anthropological and Historical Perspectives* (London and New York: Routledge, 1996), 105–22 (quoting 112).

24. Jones and Stallybrass, 104–5.

25. See Richard Anthony Leonardo, *Lives of Master Surgeons: Supplement I* (New York: Froben, 1949), 508.

26. From Rüff, *The Expert Midwife, or... Treatise of the Generation and Birth of Man*, trans. anon. (London: 1637), STC 21442, 151–61.

27. Implying that this is a divinely originated prodigy symbolically rebuking the sin of sodomy in general, and/or such sexual sins of one or both parents. Or that its unnatural deformity symbolizes sodomy's.

28. Pliny, *Natural History*, 17.42.
29. Referring to King Louis XII and Pope Julius II. On the Monster of Ravenna, see Niccoli, 35–52.
30. Moses Maimonides (1135–1204), *The Medical Aphorisms*, ed., trans. Fred Rosner and Suessman Munter, 2 vols. (New York: Yeshiva University Press, 1970–71), 24.1 (2:154).
31. See Marie–Hélène Hunt, *Monstrous Imagination* (Cambridge, Mass.: Harvard University Press, 1993), 21.
32. Rüff's subsequent comment, including the reference to Agesilaus, derives from Plutarch, *Greek and Roman Parallel Stories* (in *Moral Essays*), 29, but substitutes Aristotle for Plutarch's Aristocles.
33. See Janet Doe, *A Bibliography of the Works of Ambroise Paré* (Chicago: University of Chicago Press, 1937).
34. See Jean Céard, "Introduction," in Ambroise Paré, *Des monstres et prodiges*, ed. Jean Céard (Geneva: Droz, 1971), xiv–xix.
35. For the successive French texts of this passage, see Paré, *Des monstres*, ed. Céard, 26–27.
36. From Ambroise Paré, *Works*, trans. Thomas Johnson (London: 1634), STC 19189, Book 25, 961–63, 972–75. Compare Paré, *On Monsters and Marvels*, trans. Janis L. Pallister (Chicago: University of Chicago Press, 1982).
37. Disorders of maternal imagination could supposedly cause monstrous progeny. See Hunt.
38. **site:** posture.
39. **affects:** bodily dispositions, distempers.
40. Paré previously rejects the theory that the womb has seven cells, "three on the right side for males, three on the left side for females, and one in the midst for Hermaphrodites" (972). On early modern causal theories of hermaphroditism, see Daston and Park, "Hermaphrodites," 4–5.
41. **cod and stones:** scrotum and testicles.
42. Hermaphrodites in France had long been obligated to live according to their dominant sex assigned by medical judgment. See Daston and Park, "Hermaphrodites."
43. **courses:** menstrual discharge.
44. Aristotle, *Generation of Animals*, 4.4.772b.
45. First paragraph trans. Mawy Bouchard and Kenneth Borris, from Ambroise Paré, *Deux livres de chirurgie* (Paris: André Wechel, 1573), 416–17. Second paragraph, added to the 1575 edition, trans. Kenneth Borris, from Paré, *Oeuvres* (Paris: Gabriel Buon, 1575), 813–14. For the successive French versions, see Paré, *Des monstres*, ed. Céard, 26–27. Paré finally transferred discussion of the topic from *Des monstres* to his treatise on human anatomy. Hence a chastened version appears in the 1634 English translation of Paré's works, Book III, ch. 34, "Of the Womb" (130). It ignores tribadic sex, but adds conventional comment on the clitoris, much as in *Rodrigo de Castro and *André du Laurens.
46. Marginal gloss: "A most monstrous thing that is done with the nymphs of some women."
47. Compare Leo Africanus (c. 1490–c. 1554), *A Geographical History of Africa*, trans. John Pory (London: 1600), STC 15841, 148–49, 317.
48. **Amatus Lusitanus:** Amato Lusitano, 1511–1568.
49. *Montaigne (1533–1592) includes this apparent sex-change in both his *Essais* and *Journal de voyage*. See his *Complete Works*, trans. Donald M. Frame (Stanford: Stanford University Press, 1948), 69, 870.
50. Pliny, *Natural History*, 7.4. Pliny cites no "Cassinus" but situates these events at "Casinum." **of a girl:** i.e., from being female.
51. **jactation:** tossing, swinging.
52. **Sodomites:** in this very vague context, Paré may generally mean sexual libertines, or specifically males and females who enjoy anal intercourse, or same-sex lovers (in that case probably male). He apparently assumes that sodomites are so depraved they would stop at nothing.
53. Translated by Mawy Bouchard and Kenneth Borris, from Paré, *Deux livres* (1573), 485–86. Derived from Pierre Boaistuau (1517–1566), *Histoires prodigeuses*, ch. 37. Paré confuses Boaistuau's citation of St. Paul (Eph. 4:17–19; compare Rom. 1:18–32) with Augustine (Céard, 172n.120).
54. Boaistuau, *Certain Secret Wonders of Nature*, trans. Edward Fenton (London: 1569), STC 3164.5.
55. Translated by Kenneth Borris and Mawy Bouchard, from Tesserant, *Quatorze histoires*

prodigeuses, in Pierre Boaistuau, *Histoires prodigeuses* (Paris: I. de Bordeaux, 1568), fols. 222^b–33^b.

56. Pliny, *Natural History*, 7.3.33.
57. See Bruce MacBain, *Prodigy and Expiation* (Brussels: Latomus, 1982), 127–35.
58. Pliny, *Natural History*, 7.3.34.
59. Augustine, *City of God*, 16.8.
60. Tesserant's immediately previous references to Aristotle, Calliphanes, and Pliny are all from Pliny, *Natural History*, 7.2.15–16.
61. **Arsenotelies:** transliterates the Greek ἀρσενοθηλυς. I have not found this Aristotelian context.
62. Pliny, *Natural History*, 11.109.262.
63. The chapter begins with this illustration, as described here, including double genitalia.
64. **Arbigeris:** an apparently anomalous term, but probably referring to the area of Florida that the French explored and colonized beginning in 1560. They reported that the native peoples included many hermaphrodites (actually berdaches, males dressed as females).
65. **as if by their own nature:** *de leur propre naturel.*
66. Livy, *From the Founding of the City*, 24.10.6–13.
67. After the reference to Livy, Tesserant's source for the paragraph is Pliny, *Natural History*, 7.4.36.
68. **Elagabalus:** formerly known as "Heliogabalus," as in Tesserant.
69. The ancient historians cited are not equally reliable. "Spartianus" and "Lampridius" are now considered false personae of a late-fourth-century author.
70. Much of Cassius Dio's history of Rome survives only in Xiphilinus's condensed version.
71. On Nero and Sporus, cf. Suetonius, *Nero*, 28.1, and Cassius Dio, 62.28.2–3. Suetonius says Nero "castrated the boy Sporus and actually tried to make a woman of him" (trans. J. C. Rolfe). According to Cassius Dio, Nero "caused a boy, . . . Sporus, to be castrated, . . . and he used him in every way like a wife" (trans. Earnest Cary). As Tesserant's subsequent comments show, especially on Elagabalus, he wrongly thinks Sporus was not merely castrated, but underwent a complete sex-change, gaining an artificial vagina.
72. Suetonius, *Nero*, 29.
73. **bore his child:** i.e., bore Elagabalus, Tesserant means, following various classical historians.
74. Young Elagabalus's mother and grandmother used him as a figurehead for their political ambitions and decisions. **didn't omit any kind of lust, without any reservations:** *n'oublia aucune espece de luxure de laquelle il ne voulust scavoir parler.*
75. Extant ancient sources on Elagabalus's brief reign were much influenced by the self-justificatory propaganda of his victorious political opponents. Like Nero, he became one of the favorite whipping boys for the more disciplinarian moralists in Western culture, and attracted a wondrous elaboration of legendary decadence.
76. Suetonius, *Nero*, 26.1.
77. Much of the foregoing paraphrases Cassius Dio, 80.13.2–4.
78. Neither "Lampridius" nor Herodian say Elagabalus wanted or underwent any such operations. Cassius Dio claims this emperor "carried his lewdness to such a point that he asked the physicians to contrive a woman's vagina in his body by means of an incision," but was nevertheless just circumcised (itself scandalous to Romans) as his priestly service of his eponymous Syrian god required (80.16.7, 11.1; trans. Earnest Cary). Tesserant seems naively to have assumed that young Elagabalus's reputed delight in assuming receptive roles in sex with well-endowed athletes means he had an artificial vagina.
79. Suetonius, *Nero*, 49.
80. Tesserant effaces Sporus's loyalty; Suetonius and Cassius Dio say he attended Nero to the end.
81. From Hall, *The Discovery of a New World*, trans. John Healey (London: 1609), STC 12686, 110–12. Compare Hall, *Another World and Yet the Same*, ed., trans. John Millar Wands (New Haven: Yale University Press, 1981).
82. **conclusions:** experiments.
83. **bodies:** the torsos of women's dresses. **rebatos:** stiff collars worn by either sex from around 1590 to 1630. **crupper:** rump.
84. **conceit:** conception.
85. Or more literally from Hall's Latin: "Furthermore, should anyone inquire into the little women of olden days as they worship their Cybele (with perfectly chaste rites, indeed!), or the notorious pedicators of ancient, and indeed modern, Rome, he will ascertain they

embrace in a wicked manner, and this we readily admit. Men not entirely immature are wont to protect themselves with these or other utterly vile schemes." ("Pedicators" anally penetrate other males.) Translated by Faith Wallis, from Hall, *Mundus alter idem* (Frankfurt, i.e., London: 1605), STC 12385a, 104.

86. Marginal gloss: "The Mule is held both to conceive and to beget, in Syria, Arist[otle] and some hold the like of the Hare." Being the issue of a male ass and a mare, a mule is double-natured. Pliny says hares are hermaphroditic (*Natural History*, 8.81.218–19). **Cattle:** livestock in general.

87. Shellfish were commonly considered aphrodisiacs.

88. From Crooke, *Microcosmographia* (London: 1615), STC 6062, 299–300.

89. Aristotle, *Physics*, 2.8.

90. **avoiding of excrement:** voiding, emptying of superfluous matter.

91. **Lisk:** groin.

92. **Alcabitius:** al-Qabīsī, fl. 950.

93. **superior Intelligences in the Heavens:** spirits, such as the angelic intelligences thought to inspirit heavenly bodies including the planets and sun, like Uriel in *Paradise Lost*.

Chapter 8

1. Sappho, Fragment 47, in Loeb *Greek Lyric*, 1:47; trans. David A. Campbell.

2. See John Charles Nelson, *The Renaissance Theory of Love: The Context of Giordano Bruno's "Eroici Furori"* (New York: Columbia University Press, 1958); Giovanni Dall' Orto, "'Socratic Love' as a Disguise for Same-Sex Love in the Italian Renaissance," *Journal of Homosexuality* 16.1–2 (1988): 33–65. On male bonding, see Alan Bray, "Homosexuality and the Signs of Male Friendship in Elizabethan England," in Jonathan Goldberg, ed., *Queering the Renaissance* (Durham, N.C.: Duke University Press, 1994), 40–61; Laurens J. Mills, *One Soul in Bodies Twain: Friendship in Tudor Literature and Stuart Drama* (Bloomingon, Ind.: Principia, 1937); Katherine O'Donnell and Michael O'Rourke, eds., *Love, Sex, Intimacy, and Friendship Between Men, 1550–1800* (Houndmills, UK: Palgrave Macmillan, 2003); Bruce R. Smith, *Homosexual Desire in Shakespeare's England* (Chicago: University of Chicago Press, 1991), 35–41, 72–77. On female bonding, see Harriette Andreadis, *Sappho in Early Modern England: Female Same-Sex Literary Erotics, 1550–1714* (Chicago: University of Chicago Press, 2001); Janel Mueller, "Troping Utopia: Donne's Brief for Lesbianism," in James Grantham Turner, ed., *Sexuality and Gender in Early Modern Europe: Institutions, Texts, Images* (New York: Cambridge University Press, 1993), 192–95; Valerie Traub, *The Renaissance of Lesbianism in Early Modern England* (Cambridge, UK: Cambridge University Press, 2002); Elizabeth Wahl, *Invisible Relations: Representations of Female Intimacy in the Age of Enlightenment* (Stanford: Stanford University Press, 1999). I cite Smith, Andreadis, and Traub hereafter in text.

3. *Eudemian Ethics*, 7.12.11; *Nicomachean Ethics*, 7.4.1–2; trans. H. Rackham.

4. *On Friendship*, 6.20, 8.26, 14.51; trans. William Armistead Falconer.

5. *On Friendship*, 21.80; trans. Falconer.

6. Elyot, *The Book Named the Governor*, ed. S. E. Lehmberg (London: Dent, 1962), 134.

7. *Charmides*, 155E; trans. Benjamin Jowett, in Edith Hamilton and Huntington Cairns, eds., *The Collected Dialogues* (Princeton: Bollingen-Princeton University Press, 1961). On Platonic homoeroticism and Renaissance translations of Plato, see *Ficino.

8. See, e.g., *Phaedo*, 64E–65A; *Phaedrus*, 253C–56E.

9. See, e.g., *Phaedrus*, 246A–56E.

10. *Phaedrus*, 249D; trans. R. Hackforth, in *Collected Dialogues*.

11. *Symposium*, 182C–D, 181B–C; trans. Joyce, in *Collected Dialogues*.

12. *Symposium*, 192A–B, trans. Joyce, in *Collected Dialogues*.

13. *Dialogue on Love*, 758B; trans. W. C. Helmbold.

14. Achilles Tatius, *The Most Delectable and Pleasant History of Clitophon and Leucippe*, trans. W. Burton (London: 1597), STC 90.

15. On Renaissance disseminations of classically derived ideas of friendship, see Mills, chs. 3–6. Common classically derived motifs, he says, include "the joining of two souls in one; community of joys and sorrows; friendship tends toward virtue; equality and likeness in

manners are the conditions of friendship; friends delight in service; to wrong a friend is a foul deed; steadfast friends should be cherished; ... friends share person, counsel, comfort, and goods; a friend is another self" (244).

16. See Casey Charles, "Heroes as Lovers: Erotic Attraction Between Men in Sidney's *New Arcadia*," *Criticism* 34 (1992): 467–96.

17. "Sappho," in Loeb *Greek Lyric*, 1:21; trans. Campbell.

18. See Agrippa, *Declamation on the Nobility and Preeminence of the Female Sex*, ed., trans. Albert Rabil, Jr. (Chicago: University of Chicago Press, 1996).

19. Sidney, *The Countess of Pembroke's Arcadia (The New Arcadia)*, ed. Victor Skretkowicz (Oxford: Clarendon, 1987), 144–49; also cited hereafter in text.

20. Lodge, *Rosalind*, in *Complete Works*, vol. I (Glasgow: Hunterian Club, 1883), 35.

21. *On Friendship*, 5.18, 27.104; trans. Falconer.

22. *Eudemian Ethics*, 7.2.53, 12.4; trans. Rackham.

23. *Nicomachean Ethics*, 8.8.5; trans. Rackham. Compare Elyot, 133: "Since friendship cannot be but in good men, nor may not be without virtue, we may be assured that thereof none evil may proceed, or therewith any evil thing may participate."

24. Plutarch, *The Philosophy Commonly Called the Morals*, trans. Philemon Holland (London: 1603), STC 20063, fol. 1130.

25. Like William Caxton (1422–1491). See Kenneth Borris, "R[ichard] B[arnfield]'s Homosocial Engineering in *Orpheus His Journey to Hell*," in Borris and George Klawitter, eds., *The Affectionate Shepherd: Celebrating Richard Barnfield* (Selinsgrove, Ky.: Susquehanna-Associated University Presses, 2001), 345–46. Cited hereafter in text.

26. See Jill Kraye, "The Transformation of Platonic Love in the Italian Renaissance," in Anna Baldwin and Sarah Hutton, eds., *Platonism and the English Imagination* (Cambridge, UK: Cambridge University Press, 1994), 76–85; also cited hereafter in text.

27. See, e.g., pseudo-Lucian, *Affairs of the Heart*, 54. Also Dall' Orto, 60.

28. Sedgwick, *Between Men: English Literature and Male Homosocial Desire* (New York: Columbia University Press, 1985), 201.

29. Aristotle, *Nicomachean Ethics*, 8.7.2, 8.8.5; Cicero, *On Friendship*, 19.69, 20.71–73.

30. *Paradise Lost*, ed. Alastair Fowler, 2nd ed. (London: Longman, 1998), 8.618–29, 10.888–908. On companionate marriage, see Lawrence Stone, *The Family, Sex and Marriage in England 1500–1800* (New York: Harper and Row, 1977), 102–05, 135–38, chs. 7–8.

31. Aristotle, *Eudemian Ethics*, 7.12.14–15; trans. Rackham.

32. Cicero, *On Friendship*, 7.23; trans. Falconer.

33. Aristotle, *Nicomachean Ethics*, 8.3.7; trans. Rackham.

34. Lyly, *Euphues: The Anatomy of Wit*, in *Complete Works*, ed. R. Warwick Bond, vol. I (Oxford: Clarendon, 1902), 197.

35. Taylor, *Sources of the Self: The Making of the Modern Identity* (Cambridge, Mass.: Harvard University Press, 1989), 36.

36. See Kraye 76–85; James Hankins, *Plato in the Italian Renaissance*, 2 vols. (Leiden: Brill, 1990), 1:313–14.

37. Ficino, *Commentary on Plato's "Symposium on Love" (De amore)*, trans. Sears Jayne (Dallas, Tx.: Spring Publications, 1985). A Neoplatonic text comparable in its homoeroticism to *De amore* is the *Commento* of Ficino's renegade disciple Giovanni Pico della Mirandola (1463–1494). See Pico, *Commentary on a Canzone of Benivieni*, trans. Sears Jayne (New York: Peter Lang, 1984). In *De vita libri tres*, Ficino recommends sucking "an ounce or two" of blood from a youth as a tonic for advanced age. See Ficino, *Three Books on Life*, ed., trans. Carol V. Kaske and John R. Clark (Binghamton, N.Y.: Medieval & Renaissance Texts & Studies, 1989), II.11.

38. From Ficino, *Commentary on Plato's "Symposium on Love" (De amore)*, trans. Jayne. Numbers for speeches and chapters show omissions of them; I use ellipses to show omissions within chapters. On Renaissance interpretations of "Socratic love" as sexual love between males, see Dall' Orto.

39. Referring to Orpheus's audacious mythic descent to the underworld to regain his lost love, Euridice; or to the extant hymns and theogonies formerly ascribed to "Orpheus." Yet in Ovid's *Metamorphoses*, Books 10–11, Orpheus was the originator of sexual love between males.

40. Playing on "eros," a Platonic etymology of "hero." Plato, *Cratylus*, 398C–D.

41. This amorous dedicatory letter prefaces Ficino's own handwritten manuscript copy of *De amore*, dated July 1469. Probably born in 1448, Cavalcanti would thus have been nineteen

when Ficino was thirty-four, and twenty-one when chosen as dedicatee. Ficino cautiously dedicated the Italian translation of 1474 to Bernard del Nero and Antonio Manetti, exhorting them to explain his love "to anyone who might presume to read this book carelessly or with malice." See *De amore*, 3, 8, 27n.1, 178–81.

42. Ficino assigns his beloved Giovanni Cavalcanti this speech, addressing the portion of Plato's *Symposium* spoken by Pausanias.

43. Ficino later defines daemons as the rational beings inhabiting the sublunar regions of ethereal fire and pure or humid air. They are immortal yet subject to passions causing them to approve good men and dislike bad ones. Whether or not evil daemons exist, good daemons act as guardian spirits or angels (VI.3). Aside from Plato himself, Platonic commentators on daemons include Chalcidius, Iamblichus, Proclus, and Apuleius.

44. Proverbial exemplars of male friendship. The Syracusan tyrant Dionysius I condemned Pythias to death for conspiring against him. So that Pythias could go away to settle his affairs, Damon freed him by pledging his own life as bond, until Pythias's return. When Pythias honored this arrangement by returning, Dionysius pardoned him. Pylades assisted Orestes in avenging his father Agamemnon's murder; in a later adventure each offered to sacrifice himself for the other.

45. In the standard Platonic definition, love is desire for beauty. Ficino privileges sight as the highest sense, for it is most far-sensing, relatively removed from contact with matter, and informs the intellect. He depreciates smell, taste, and especially touch for their physical materiality, and links the latter sense with sexual love and lust (V.2, VI.8–9).

46. Ficino attributes Speech VI, addressing the speech of Plato's Socrates in the *Symposium*, to his friend Tommaso Benci.

47. That is, preceding speakers in Plato's *Symposium*, such as Agathon.

48. On the role of the spirit in Ficino's theory of perception, see n.57.

49. Here Ficino interprets Plato's *Symposium*, 203B–E, where Diotima says Love is born of Poverty and Plenty. As Poverty's son, Love is "dry, thin, and squalid, bare-footed, humble, without a home, without a bed, ... and finally, he is always needy" (*De amore*, VI.9). Love's riches as son of Plenty counter these needs or deficiencies.

50. Ficino lists Love's deficiencies as son of Poverty and associates them with sensual or bodily love.

51. **the Angel and the Soul:** i.e., the Angelic Mind and the World Soul. In Ficino's Christian Platonist emanationist metaphysics, there are hypostases proceeding from God (or the One) and mediating between God and matter. The Angelic Mind contains the Ideas: imprints, as it were, of the natures of all things to be created. The World Soul procreates them in the World Body, material creation or the physical world. Compare *De amore*, I.3; VI.7, 15–17.

52. Plato, *Protagoras*, 309A. "In Plato the statement is a sarcastic allusion to Socrates' homosexuality; he is said to have been hunting not Alcibiades' 'virtuous character' but his 'ripeness' (*hora*)" (Jayne, trans., *De amore*, 149n.77).

53. Plato, *Symposium*, 206C–E.

54. As in Plato, *Symposium*, 181B–D.

55. **that wicked crime:** i.e., sex between males. Hence Plato's Athenian in the *Laws* advocates outlawing it, and also extramarital male-female sex in which pregnancy is not desired, for procreative seed is thus wasted (8.838E–39D). The subject of Ficino's paragraph is not "abortion," *pace* Jayne, 151n.107 (*De amore*), but male-male sex as alleged murder worse than abortion. Ficino ignores the contrary Platonic argument in the *Timaeus* that sexual acts are often involuntarily provoked by a surplus of reproductive seed, and thus cannot be justly reproached (86B–E).

56. Ficino assigns this response to Plato's Alcibiades in the *Symposium* to another student, Cristoforo Marsuppini.

57. For Ficino, soul and body "are joined by means of the spirit, which is a certain very thin and clear vapor produced by the heat of the heart from the thinnest part of the blood." The spirits thus diffuse the soul's powers into the body and in turn image sensory percepts to the soul, thus enabling cognitive sensation (VI.6).

58. In Platonic theory, vision depends on emission of beams of light through the eyes (*Timaeus*, 45B–46C). So the eye-beams of others can also enter the body through the eyes. In this chapter Ficino uses some current medical and ocular theories to explain why eye contact can have great amorous impact.

59. Reflecting early modern menstrual taboos. See Patricia Crawford, "Attitudes to Menstruation in Seventeenth-Century England," *Past and Present* 91 (1981): 47–73.

60. Apuleius, *Metamorphoses*, 10.3, where actually a woman says this to a youth, so that Ficino substitutes homoerotic for heteroerotic love here.

61. In Plato's *Phaedrus*, handsome Phaedrus delightedly tells Socrates that Lysias talked to him most eloquently about love, and Socrates teasingly insists Lysias loves Phaedrus (227A–28C, 237B). From these hints Ficino chose to develop his full-blown example of love's onset between males.

62. In Ficino's Italian translation he "attributes the whole of the following paragraph to Lucretius, but he omits the quotation altogether" (Jayne, trans., *De amore*, 176n.56). Ficino thus became deliberately evasive here.

63. Compare Ficino's account of the ocular exchange of blood and humor between Lysias and Phaedrus, VII.4. He adds, "all the blood of the older man, when it has been converted into the nature of young blood, seeks the body of the youth in order to inhabit its own veins, and also in order that humor of the young blood may flow in equally young and tender veins" (VII.5).

64. Later Ficino states that, driven mad by love, Lucretius killed himself (VI.9).

65. Lucretius, *De rerum natura*, 4.1052–56, 1108–14.

66. Referring to *De amore*, VII.4, reprinted here.

67. Compare *De amore*, VII.14: Plato "attributes to the soul wings [*Phaedrus*, 246, 251, 255B–D] on which it is carried to the sublime;... one is that investigation by which the intellect assiduously strives toward truth; the other is the desire for the Good by which our will is always influenced." Also VII.15: "True love is nothing other than a certain effort of flying up to divine beauty, aroused by the sight of corporeal beauty. But adulterous love is a falling down from sight to touch."

68. See Alan Stewart, "The Singing Boy and the Scholar: The Various Deaths of Politian," in Ingrid de Smet and Philip Ford, eds., *Eros et Priapus: Erotisme et obscénité dans la littérature néo-latine* (Geneva: Librairie Droz, 1997), 45–63.

69. Michael Rocke, *Forbidden Friendships: Homosexuality and Male Culture in Renaissance Florence* (Oxford: Oxford University Press, 1996), 198, 202.

70. From James T. Wilhelm, ed., *Gay and Lesbian Poetry: An Anthology from Sappho to Michelangelo* (New York: Garland, 1995), 309 (trans. Wilhelm).

71. See Antonia Tissoni Benvenuti, ed., *L'Orfeo del Poliziano* (Padua: Editrice Antenore, 1986).

72. Translated by Nicola Martino and Kenneth Borris, from Angelo Poliziano, *Le stanze, l'Orfeo, e le rime*, ed. Attilio Momigliano (Turin: Editrice Torinese, 1925), 115–17.

73. A remark probably addressed to Orpheus's dismembered corpse.

74. Ovid's Bacchus then punishes the Bacchantes for murdering Orpheus, turning them into trees (11.67–88). Their well-known Ovidian fate produces dramatic irony here.

75. See Judith C. Brown, *Immodest Acts: The Life of a Lesbian Nun in Renaissance Italy* (Oxford: Oxford University Press, 1986), 10; Domenico Zanrè, "Alterity and Sexual Transgression in the Sixteenth-Century Tuscan Novella," in Gloria Allaire, ed., *The Italian Novella: A Book of Essays* (New York and London: Routledge, 2003), pp. 163–67.

76. Firenzuola, *On the Beauty of Women*, ed., trans. Konrad Eisenbichler and Jacqueline Murray (Philadelphia: University of Pennsylvania Press, 1992), 11.

77. From Firenzuola, *On the Beauty of Women*, ed., trans. Eisenbichler and Murray, 15–21.

78. Plato, *Apology*, 21A–23B.

79. Plato, *Symposium*, 189C–93E.

80. Plato's Aristophanes does not quantify the relative numbers of the three original types of human beings. To affirm the primacy of heteroerotic love, Firenzuola insists the androgynous type, which produced opposite-sex lovers, was the "majority," whereas the others were "few."

81. Plato's Aristophanes attributes these tasks to Zeus and Apollo instead.

82. Apparently Firenzuola's invention to entertain readers. "Hermaphrodite" conventionally derives from "Hermes" and "Aphrodite," combining masculine and feminine divinities.

83. In Plato's *Symposium* (219B–E), Socrates loved youthful Alcibiades chastely, but many assumed Socrates loved youths sexually (e.g., *Theodor Zwinger). Achilles's love of Patroclus appears in Homer's *Iliad* and many other ancient sources; the ancients often assumed it was sexual. Virgil devotes an episode of the *Aeneid* to the heroic male lovers Nisus and Euryalus (9.176–449). Sexual love most readily accounts for the intensity of their intergenerational relationship. Young males were Virgil's traditional sexual preference, as in his Second Eclogue (no doubt known to Firenzuola).

84. **Ephesian goddess:** Artemis or Diana, goddess of chastity. In 356 B.C.E. Herostratus burned her temple at Ephesus to immortalize his name, but the Ephesians attempted to efface his memory. Firenzuola implies sodomites so scandalously violate chastity that they deserve oblivion even more. Contrary to Firenzuola, Plato's Aristophanes treats sexual love between males very casually.

85. Though Cecilia Venetiana is now very elusive, courtesans had long been associated with tribadism; so too had nunneries. See Jacqueline Murray, "Agnolo Firenzuola on Female Sexuality and Women's Equality," *Sixteenth Century Journal* 22 (1991): 210–11; Konrad Eisenbichler, "Laudomia Forteguerri Loves Margaret of Austria," in Francesca Canadé Sautman and Pamela Sheingorn, eds., *Same Sex Love and Desire among Women in the Middle Ages* (New York: Palgrave, 2001), 280–81. Unlike Firenzuola, Plato's Aristophanes says much more on male same-sex love than female.

86. In the various versions, e.g., Apollo arranged that Admetus would never die if someone were willing to die for him, and his wife Alcestis volunteered; or Admetus was captured in battle, and Alcestis exchanged herself for him, to be sacrificed instead. Some say Hercules restored her to life.

87. Plato's Aristophanes contrarily says descendents of the primal androgynes, Firenzuola's third type of being that produces opposite-sex lovers, are adulterous (191D), probably as a provocative joke.

88. Orpheus risked descent into the underworld to regain his beloved wife Euridice. In most versions he was unsuccessful and in some, contrary to Firenzuola's application, Orpheus thus originated sexual love between males, as in Ovid and *Angelo Poliziano.

89. Confronted with an omen that, according to the soothsayers, showed either he or his wife Cornelia would die, Tiberius (Firenzuola incorrectly says Caius) chose the course supposed to result in his death, thus sparing his wife. Compare Plutarch, *Tiberius and Caius Gracchus*, 1.1–3.

90. **dreary offspring:** *trista semenza*, possibly echoing Dante's *Divina comedia* on the damned (Eisenbichler and Murray, 75n.38).

91. I thank Konrad Eisenbichler for bringing this writer and Margaret of Austria to my attention, and for his assistance here, both by translating Forteguerri's sonnets and providing a prepublication copy of his essay "Laudomia Forteguerri," in Sautman and Sheingorn, eds., *Same Sex Love and Desire*, 277–304. Hereafter cited also in text.

92. My information on Margaret derives from Eisenbichler, 282, 290–92.

93. Translated by Konrad Eisenbichler, from *Rime diverse d'alcune nobilissime, et virtuosissime donne*, ed. Lodovico Domenichi (Lucca: Vincenzo Busdragho,1559), 102–4.

94. This sonnet compares the sun or Phoebus of "Proud heaven," subsequently referred to in the second person, with the poet's sun, Margaret.

95. The third to fifth sonnets to Margaret clearly follow her move to Rome to marry her unwanted second husband, and express the poet's reaction to that. Though the first two might have been written earlier, they likely address the same circumstances.

96. The poet's foe is most probably Fortune, as in the fifth sonnet, but might be Nature; "you" refers to personified feminine Rome, enriched now by Margaret's presence.

97. That is, if Margaret were to return to the poet, she would then grace Arbia, the river that flows by Siena, rather than Rome's Tiber.

98. Montaigne, *The Essays, or Moral, Politic, and Military Discourses*, trans. John Florio (London: 1603), STC 18041, 409.

99. From Montaigne, *Essays*, trans. John Florio (London: 1603), STC 18041, 89–96. That text gives Montaigne's Latin quotations in Latin as well as Florio's English; I silently omit the former. On this essay, see further Marc D. Schachter, "'That Friendship Which Possesses The Soul': Montaigne Loves La Boétie," *Journal of Homosexuality* 41.3–4 (2001): 5–21.

100. **Boscage:** design of decorative foliage. **grotesco:** grotesque, in the ancient Roman style as in Nero's Golden House, fashionably revived in the Renaissance as in, e.g., Florence's Uffizi gallery.

101. Horace's metaphor for a multiform or mishapen book, *Art of Poetry*, lines 3–4.

102. **table:** painting; and writing tablet or inscription. Florio keeps Montaigne's wordplay (*tableau*).

103. The Royal Edict of January 1562 gave Protestantism limited tolerance and recognition within France. La Boétie had written a pro-Catholic treatise objecting that such measures would conduce civil unrest and disunity. Civil wars followed.

104. Aristotle, *Nicomachean Ethics*, 8.1.4. There, lawgivers value friendship more highly than justice for it conduces concord in the state.
105. **venerian:** subject to Venus, sexual.
106. **enterbearing:** mutually supporting.
107. Compare Diogenes Laertius, "Aristippus," *Lives of the Philosophers*, 2.81.
108. Plutarch, *On Brotherly Love*, 479E.
109. Horace, *Odes*, 2.2.6.
110. Catullus, 68.17–18.
111. Ludovico Ariosto, *Orlando furioso*, 10.7.
112. **jouissance:** enjoyment, delight.
113. Referring to La Boétie. Montaigne published his love sonnets as the following chapter.
114. Cicero, *Tusculan Disputations*, 4.33.70.
115. **Academy:** Plato's followers or philosophical school.
116. Phaedrus thus criticizes Aeschylus in Plato's *Symposium*, 180A–B.
117. That is, after courtship, the two male lovers would enjoy a mutual communion or companionship.
118. **available:** effectual, beneficial (availing).
119. In Plato's *Symposium*, Pausanias argues that despotic states consider men's courting of youths disgraceful because such love begets high thought and faithful fellowship rather than servility. He credits the relationship of Harmodius and Aristogiton with ousting tyrants in Athens (182B–C).
120. **demissness:** submissiveness, abasement; i.e., to tyranny.
121. Cicero, *Tusculan Disputations*, 4.34.72.
122. Cicero, *On Friendship*, 20.74.
123. **Sithence:** seeing that, since.
124. **preallable:** preliminary. **conversation:** social intercourse, discourse.
125. In *On Friendship* Cicero recounts the same anecdote with a different application, 11.37–39.
126. Aulus Gellius, *Attic Nights*, 1.3.30. Compare Cicero, *On Friendship*, 16.59.
127. Diogenes Laertius, "Aristotle," *Lives of the Philosophers*, 5.21.
128. **accrease:** increase.
129. Diogenes Laertius, "Aristotle," *Lives of the Philosophers*, 5.20.
130. Diogenes Laertius, "Diogenes the Cynic," *Lives of the Philosophers*, 6.46.
131. Lucian, *Toxaris, or Friendship*, 22.
132. Required by Montaigne's meaning but lacking in my source for Florio's translation.
133. **enterlove:** mutually love.
134. **alonely:** only, solely.
135. Xenophon, *Cyropaedia*, 8.3.25–26.
136. **Lackey:** footman.
137. Terence, *The Self-tormentor*, 1.1.80.
138. **merry conceited humor:** wittily ingenious or merrily resourceful disposition.
139. **Prud'homie:** wisdom, prudence, probity.
140. Plutarch, *Agesilaus*, 25.
141. Horace, *Satires*, 1.5.44.
142. Plutarch, *Of Brotherly Love*, 479C.
143. Virgil, *Aeneid*, 5.49–50. Thus Aeneas mourns and commemorates the day of his father's death.
144. Terence, *The Self-tormentor*, 1.1.149–50, on paternal affection for a son; adapted by Montaigne.
145. Horace, *Odes*, 2.17.5–9.
146. Horace, *Odes*, 1.24.1–2.
147. Catullus, 68.20–26, 65.9–11. Combined and adapted by Montaigne.
148. Translated by Kenneth Borris, from W. A. Craigie, ed., *The Maitland Quarto Manuscript*, Scottish Text Society, new ser., vol. 9 (London: Blackwood, 1920), Poem XLIX, 160–62. I render the poem's Scotticisms into English while seeking to preserve as much of its diction, meter, and rhyme as possible. Otherwise, I modernize this text like my early modern English selections, preserving former English words and usages but updating spelling etc., so that the changes are minimal. See Jane Farnsworth, "Voicing Female Desire in 'Poem XLIX,'" *SEL* 36 (1996): 57–72.
149. Referring to the concentric orbs assigned to the heavens in former astronomy.

150. **cope crepusculine:** heavenly canopy of twilight; a cope is a cloak or ecclesiastical vestment.
151. **Phoebe:** i.e., the moon, as feminine counterpart of Phoebus, the sun; a surname of Diana, as the moon's goddess.
152. **ween:** think, believe.
153. **Pallas:** Athena or Minerva, goddess of wisdom; perhaps further alluding to her "childhood friendship with the maiden, Pallas" (Farnsworth, 60).
154. **adamant:** magnet, lodestone.
155. Perithöus and Theseus, legendary archetypes of faithful male friendship, aided each other in many dangerous exploits. Often presumed lovers, Achilles and Patroclus typified devoted comradeship. Pylades assisted Orestes in avenging his father Agamemnon's murder; in a later adventure each offered to sacrifice himself for the other. Achates was a friend of Aenee' (i.e., Aeneas, legendary founder of Rome) proverbial for loyalty. The Bible claims David and Jonathan's love surpassed the love of women (2 Sam. 1:26). Titus risked his life for Gisipp' (i.e., Gisippus), who previously relinquished his bride to Titus when the latter fell in love with her.
156. **wis:** know.
157. Penelope, wife of Ulysses, famously remained loyal despite his absence of decades. Naomi and Ruth biblically typify mutual feminine devotion, for when Naomi moved from Israel to Moab, Ruth married Naomi's eldest son and loyally returned to Israel with Naomi after he died (Ruth 1:16–17). When Brutus, the conspirator against Julius Caesar, died after Caesar's murder, his wife Portia killed herself by swallowing burning coals.
158. **part:** perhaps playing on the sense "sexual organ," i.e., penis (Farnsworth, 64).
159. **would:** originally "vaill," perhaps a scribal error for "wald," meaning "would" (Craigie, 288). Or "vaill" might mean "value," referring to the male identity or type. Compare Farnsworth, 69n.19.
160. **fare:** originally "do," meaning "fare."
161. Pollux and Castor were twin brothers, sons of Jupiter by Leda. When Pollux volunteered to sacrifice his immortality to restore the life of mortal Castor after he died, Jupiter transformed them into the constellation Gemini.
162. **conjure:** command, solemnly exhort.
163. **teen:** hurt, injury, vexation.
164. For a medieval example dating from 914, cf. Bernadette J. Brooten, *Love Between Women: Early Christian Responses to Female Homoeroticism* (Chicago: University of Chicago Press, 1996), 5, 337.
165. The foreword for one edition of Allinson's bowdlerized version says "a few of Brantôme's examples... belong more in a treatise on abnormal pathology than in a book of literary or historical interest and value, so nothing of any value is lost by omitting them." *Lives of Fair and Gallant Ladies,* trans. Allinson (London and New York: Alexandrian Society, 1922), v.
166. From the only unexpurgated English translation, published in a limited edition of 1,000 copies and never reprinted: *Lives of Fair and Gallant Ladies,* trans. anon. (London: Fortune Press, 1934), stylistically updated somewhat as in my "Note on Editorial Practice." Page references to this source appear parenthetically after each excerpt; I use ellipses here to indicate omissions within an excerpt, not before or after. As noted below, I have corrected the translation at some points, with reference to *Les dames galantes,* ed. Maurice Rat (Paris: Garnier, 1960).
167. Probably derived, directly or indirectly, from Boccaccio's *Decameron,* Fifth Day, Tenth Story.
168. **the backdoor Venus:** *l'arriere Venus* (*Dames galantes,* 109).
169. Correcting my source's bowdlerization here (100); compare *Dames galantes,* 109.
170. **bugger or catamite:** *bougre ny bardasche* (*Dames galantes,* 110).
171. Referring to Jean Benoit (a Cordelier monk), *La somme des péchés et le remède d'iceux* (The Catalogue of Sins and Their Remedy), published at Paris, e.g., in 1587, and Lyons in 1584. Brantôme tells the anecdote in Latin. No prior published English version translates it. Translated by Faith Wallis.
172. Referring to the illustrated *Sonetti lussuriosi* of *Pietro Aretino (1492–1556). See *Erotica.
173. **the backside Venus:** *l'arriere Venus* (*Dames galantes,* 112).
174. **Lucretia:** legendary Roman matron famed for chastity, who committed suicide after being raped by the son of the last Tarquin king. Popular outrage supposedly led to the establishment of the republic.
175. This epigram appears in the Loeb edition of Martial's *Epigrams* as number 90 in Book I.

176. Lucian, "Leaena and Clonarium," *Dialogues of the Courtesans*, 5.2: "'She's a sort of woman for the ladies. They say there are women like that in Lesbos, with faces like men, and unwilling to consort with men, but only with women, as though they themselves were men'" (trans. M. D. MacLeod). This dialogue strongly associates tribadic love with Lesbos and thus "Lesbian" females.

177. Brantôme misquotes Juvenal, *Satires*, 6.32. *Grissantis* should be *crissantis*, a verb, and *frictum* should be *fluctum*. Juvenal's context deals with drunken lusts and sex games at women's festivals just prior to the admission of males for phallic intercourse (6.314–41).

178. **Philaenis:** a classical exemplar of tribadism often cited in the Renaissance (*John Donne).

179. Pseudo-Lucian, *Affairs of the Heart* (*Erotes*), 28.

180. Lucian, "Leaena and Clonarium," *Dialogues of the Courtesans*, 5.3.

181. **lesbians:** correcting "Lesbian devotees"; *telles dames et lesbiennes* (*Dames galantes*, 121).

182. **private closet:** personal room, bedroom; or private place of study.

183. **lesbians:** correcting "Lesbian dames"; *de ces lesbiennes* (*Dames galantes*, 123).

184. As in Ovid's *Heroides*, 15, "Sappho to Phaon" (*The Sapphic Renaissance).

185. See, e.g., Pierio Valeriano, *Hieroglyphica* (Lyons: P. Frelon, 1602), 133 (Book XIII).

186. Martial, *Epigrams*, 1.90, as formerly.

187. **godemiches:** dildos, typically fabricated from leather, horn, wood, or, as in Murano, glass.

188. **pessaries:** vaginally (or otherwise) inserted plugs or suppositories for medicating ailments.

189. Probably referring to pseudo-Lucian, *Affairs of the Heart* (*Erotes*), 28, as formerly: "And how much better that a woman should invade the provinces of male wantonness than that the nobility of the male sex should become effeminate and play the part of a woman!" (trans. M. D. MacLeod).

190. See *Agnolo Firenzuola. A French translation of Firenzuola's text was published in 1578.

191. Brantôme's biography of Margaret, including her supposed endowment of a church, confuses her with another sixteenth-century Margaret of Austria (*Laudomia Forteguerri).

192. Heinrich Agrippa of Nettesheim (1486–1539); see n.18.

193. From Burton, *The Anatomy of Melancholy*, ed. Rev. A. R. Shilleto, 3 vols. (London: Bell, 1903–04), 3: 53–65 (Part. 3; Sect. 2; Memb. 1, Subsect. 2; Memb. 2, Subsect. 1). Latin passages trans. Keira Travis. I report Burton's marginal glosses in endnotes parenthetically ascribed to him, but silently revised for more specific reference. On this part of the *Anatomy*, see further J. B. Bamborough with Martin Dodsworth, *Commentary on the Third Partition*, Vol. 6 of *The Anatomy of Melancholy* (Oxford: Clarendon Press, 2000), 32–43; Winfried Schleiner, "Burton's Use of *praeteritio* in Discussing Same-Sex Relationships," in Claude J. Summers and Ted-Larry Pebworth, eds., *Renaissance Discourses of Desire* (Columbia: University of Missouri Press, 1993), 159–78. Shilleto's text, reprinted here, is the 1651–1652 edition. According to Schleiner, Burton's long Latin passage on same-sex love, given in English transation here, remained virtually unchanged after the *Anatomy*'s third edition (1628).

194. Virgil, *Aeneid*, 4.412 (Burton).

195. Virgil, *Aeneid*, 2.204 (Burton).

196. "For it is a shame to speak of those things which are done of them in secret." Eph. 5:12 (Burton).

197. Plutarch, *Dialogue on Love*, 757A (Burton).

198. Athenaeus, *Deipnosophists*, 13.562 (Burton).

199. Dares and Dictys's supposedly eyewitness accounts of the Trojan war were much read in medieval and Renaissance Europe, but written long after the putative time of the conflict.

200. Horace, *Satires*, 1.3.107–08.

201. Thomas Fuller says the late-medieval queen Giovanna I of Naples murdered her first husband, had three more, and was openly adulterous. See *The Holy State and the Profane State* (London: 1642), Wing 2443, Book V, ch. 2.

202. Originally a servant, the early medieval Frédégond became Frankish queen by inciting the king to murder his wife and promoted further murders and assassinations. Her contemporary Brunhilda ambitiously figured in dynastic, political, and military strife.

203. **monomachies:** duels.

204. **calentures:** deliriums.

205. **Pox:** venereal disease.

206. Virgil, *Aeneid*, 6.126.

207. From Lilio Gregorio Giraldi (1479–1552), *Vita Herculis* (Burton).

208. *The Rivals* is now often called *The Lovers*. Burton notes, "he would have the love of boys restricted only to philosophers," applying to Socrates a context in Pseudo-Lucian, *Affairs of the Heart*, 51. There, in contrast to marriage, love of boys is the privilege of philosophy and the wise.

209. Paraphrasing handsome Alcibiades's account of how strongly Socrates sexually attracts him and other youths, in Plato's *Symposium*, 214A–23B. For a different view, see Schleiner, 161, 171.

210. Theodoret of Cyr, fl. 393–466, Greek patristic author.

211. Virgil's Second Eclogue traditionally expressed his own sexual desire for the youth Alexis.

212. Seneca, *Hercules Enraged*, line 19, where Juno laments Jove's numerous extramarital affairs.

213. Burton refers readers to Ogier Ghiselin de Busbecq (1522–1592), whose letters describing Turkey were widely read. They briefly mention the Turkish prevalence of sex between males.

214. That is, sodomy is the only way in which Romans exercise "chastity" in regard to the vagina; or the Romans are so libertinous that they account sodomy chastity, relative to other sexual possibilities.

215. Proverbial phrase. In Ovid's *Heroides*, 5.115, a woman so pursues a man who loves another woman. Pseudo-Lucian's *Affairs of the Heart* so describes sex between males, 20.

216. Busbecq says that, by reversing their shoes, Turkish wives testified their spouses had anally penetrated them (Bamborough with Dodsworth, 35).

217. Lucian, *Charidemus*, 5, 7–9, 24; Achilles Tatius, 2.34–38 (Burton).

218. On Della Casa (1503–1556), see Chapter One, n.98.

219. "Isn't this cock crazy," Martial, *Epigrams*, 3.76.3 (Burton).

220. Burton cites Paolo Giovio (1483–1552), *Elogia doctorum virorum*, and "Musc.," perhaps Andreas or Wolfgang Musculus. See Bamborough with Dodsworth, 35.

221. John Bale (1495–1563), Reformer; address to readers, *Acta Romanorum pontificum* (Burton).

222. Burton cites Girolamo Mercuriale (1530–1606), *Medicina practica*, 3.38; Lodovico Ricchieri (1469–1525), *Lectionum antiquarum*, Book 11, ch. 14 (*Encyclopedias and Reference Works); and Galen, *De locis affectis*, ch. 6 (cf. Bamborough with Dodsworth, 36).

223. **Spintrians: male prostitutes. Succubae:** female prostitutes; or women who sexually supplant each other; or Burton may mean devils in female form, literally or metaphorically.

224. *Rodrigo de Castro, *De universa mulierum medicina*, Part 2, 1.15, discussing masturbation (Burton; see Bamborough with Dodsworth, 36).

225. Referring to Busbecq's Turkish letters, as previously noted.

226. Burton cites Herodotus to explain that, in Egypt, bodies of socially eminent or beautiful women were not given to embalmers until three or four days after death, to discourage sexual usage (2.89).

227. Ovid, *Metamorphoses*, 10.243–97 (Burton).

228. To have sex with Paulina, who rejected him, Mundus posed as a god in a temple. "Hegesippus" is now considered a translation of Josephus. See the latter's *Jewish Antiquities*, 18.65–80.

229. Pliny, *Natural History*, 35.6.17–18 (Burton). Pliny says Caligula lusted for these frescoes. Former error in editions of Pliny substituted Pontius (Bamborough with Dodsworth, 36).

230. Aelian, *Historical Miscellany*, 9.39 (Burton).

231. **Bona Dea:** a goddess of Rome and Latium, whose rite excluded males.

232. Seneca, *On Anger*, 2.9.3–4 (Burton); then citing Clement of Alexandria, *Paedogogus* or *The Teacher*, 3.3.21 (Burton). Clement records how every orifice is used for lust, and decries both sex between males and between females, who are now, he complains, both wives and husbands to each other.

233. "Aelius Lampridius," *Elagabalus*, 5, in *Lives of the Later Emperors*, or *The Augustan History* (Burton).

234. Seneca, *Natural Questions*, 1.16.1–9 (Burton). To show lust's ingenuity and resourcefulness, Seneca recounts how Hostius arranged mirrors so that he could see all aspects of sex acts, and delight in the magnified size of his partners' penises.

235. Plutarch, *Beasts Are Rational*, 990A–91A, which lacks the remark about vile utterances. Burton uses a contemporary Latin translation here (Bamborough with Dosworth, 36).

236. *Castro, *De universa mulierum medicina*, Part Two, 1.15 (Burton).

237. Burton uses Latin for this entire foregoing paragraph.

238. Cristóbal de Fonseca (?1550–1621), *Amphitheatrum amorum*, trans. C. Curtius, ch. 4 (Burton; Bamborough with Dodsworth, 36).

239. **pepon:** pumpkin.
240. For the foregoing passage Burton cites Enea Silvio de' Piccolomini (Pope Pius II, 1405–1464) and the patristic theologian Tertullian (see Bamborough with Dodsworth, 36–37).
241. Juvenal, *Satires*, 4.114 (Burton). As here, English renderings of Burton's text traditionally alter the meaning of Juvenal's quoted phrase somewhat, to accord with Burton's context.
242. Giovanni Battista Mantuanus or Spagnuoli (1448–1516), *Eclogae*, "Faustus," 177 (Bamborough with Dodsworth, 37).
243. Chaucer, Knight's Tale, line 954, in *The Canterbury Tales*.
244. "The Muses do not burn with love," Lucian, *Dialogues of the Gods*, 23.1–2 (Burton).
245. A main basis of misogynistic assumptions of feminine inferiority in Western culture, the correlation of masculinity with form and feminity with matter originated with the ancient Greeks.
246. Plutarch, *Dialogue on Love*, 750C–52B (Burton).
247. Horace, *Odes*, 1.13.17–20 (Burton; his translation).
248. Burton confuses Marc Antony with Marcus Aurelius Antoninus (Bamborough with Dodsworth, 38). Cinyras was a legendary king whom his daughter Myrrha tricked into committing incest.
249. Burton cites Pieter van Foreest (1522–1597), *Observationum et curationum medicinalium*, 10.29; and Plato, *Phaedrus*, 265A (Bamborough with Dodsworth, 40).
250. Giovanni Michele Savonarola, Italian physician (1384–1462), *Practica major*, 6.1.4 (Bamborough with Dodsworth, 40).
251. *Ficino (1433–1499), *De Amore*, 7.9 (Burton); see also 5.8 and 6.4–5.
252. Plutarch, *How the Young Man Should Study Poetry*, 19F (Burton). There, some say the story of Apollo's disclosure of Venus's adultery with Mars expresses how the planetary conjunction of Mars and Venus indicates adulterous births that are revealed just as the sun returns to its course.
253. Burton incorrectly cites Plutarch (Bamborough with Dodsworth, 42). **queans:** prostitutes.
254. Chaucer, Wife of Bath's Prologue, lines 615–16, in *The Canterbury Tales*. Claiming joint influence of Mars and Venus, she says her horoscope has Taurus in the ascendant.
255. Mersenne (1588–1648), *Quaestiones in Genesim*, various contexts (Burton; see Bamborough with Dodsworth, 42).
256. "And if in this I will not be far enough from notorious disgrace and folly, nevertheless the love of truth prevails" (Burton). This note by Burton summarizes part of the geniture that Girolamo Cardano (1501–1576) cast for himself and appended to his published commentary on *Ptolemy's *Tetrabiblos* (Bamborough with Dodsworth, 42).
257. Burton presents Cardano's Latin analysis of his desires, from his own geniture as above. (This English translation includes editorial corrections; see Bamborough with Dodsworth, 43.)
258. **Gregory of Nazianzen:** fourth-century bishop of Constantinople and prolific patristic author.
259. Likewise *Ficino, *De Amore*, 6.14, included in this anthology. **masculine venery:** *masculinam venerem*, Burton. That is, male pursuit of sex with males, as opposed to conventional opposite-sex "venery" (*General Introduction).
260. Campanella (1568–1639), *Astrologicorum libri VI*, 4.8.4–5 (Burton).
261. Burton uses Latin for the foregoing passage, from Gregory of Nazianzen's comments onward. In chiromancy or palmistry, main areas of the hand that supposedly reflected sexual desires were the mount of Venus at the thumb's base, and the girdle of Venus, a line across the top of the palm. Taisnier, 1508–1562; Indagine (widely published and translated in the Renaissance), 1457–1537; Göckel, 1572–1621.

Chapter 9

1. Loeb *Greek Lyric*, 1:79–81 (trans. David A. Campbell).
2. Zelmane is a prince in transvestite disguise. Zelmane's choice of sapphics: Sidney, *The Countess of Pembroke's Arcadia* (London: 1590), STC 22539, fol. 97[a–b]. Zelmane's poem evoking Sappho's Fragment 31: "My Muse What Ails This Ardor," Second Eclogues of *Old Arcadia*, printed in the hybrid 1593 *Arcadia*. See *The Countess of Pembroke's Arcadia*, ed. Maurice Evans (London: Penguin, 1977), 430–31.
3. See Joan DeJean, *Fictions of Sappho 1546–1937* (Chicago: University of Chicago Press, 1989), pp. 2, 41, 123–24, 132–34; also cited hereafter in text, as are Andreadis, Greer, and Mueller

below. See further Harriette Andreadis, *Sappho in Early Modern England: Female Same-Sex Literary Erotics, 1550–1714* (Chicago: University of Chicago Press, 2001), ch. 2; Bernadette J. Brooten, *Love Between Women: Early Christian Responses to Female Homoeroticism* (Chicago: University of Chicago Press, 1996), 29–41; Germaine Greer, *Slip-Shod Sybils: Recognition, Rejection and the Woman Poet* (Harmondsworth: Viking–Penguin, 1995), ch. 4; Janel Mueller, "Troping Utopia: Donne's Brief for Lesbianism," in James Grantham Turner, ed., *Sexuality and Gender in Early Modern Europe: Institutions, Texts, Images* (New York: Cambridge University Press, 1993), 184–92. For Sappho's ancient doxography, see David A Campbell's Loeb edition, *Greek Lyric*, vol. 1. I use his numbering of Sappho's fragments.

4. See DeJean, 30–37, 313; Mueller, 185–90; Mary Morrison, "Henri Estienne and Sappho," *Bibliothèque d'Humanisme et Renaissance* 24.2 (1962): 388–91.

5. Mueller, 187. Compare Ovid, *Heroides*, 15.19.

6. Heywood, *Gunaikeion: Or, Nine Books of Various History Concerning Women* (London: 1624), STC 13326, 389, 394.

7. Campbell observes "'the other Sappho' was almost certainly the invention of a scholar [in antiquity] who wished to save Sappho's reputation." Loeb *Greek Lyric*, 1:7.

8. Presumably Turberville's Latin text of Ovid's poem was a version in which, as mentioned earlier, "Sappho" herself acknowledges that her love of women occasioned shame or blame.

9. Ovid, *The Heroical Epistles*, trans. George Turberville (London: 1567), STC 18940, fol. 109[b].

10. See, e.g., Estienne, ed., *Pindari... caeterorum octo lyricum carmina*, 2 vols. (Geneva: Henri Estienne, 1566), 2:33–35. Estienne's second, augmented edition. See Morrison, 388–91.

11. Ovid, *Tristia*, 2.365; trans. Arthur Leslie Wheeler, rev. G. P. Goold.

12. Translated by Faith Wallis, from Giraldi, *Opera omnia*, 2 vols. (Leiden: apud Hackium, Boutestyn, Vivie, Vander AA, Luchtmans, 1696), 2: cols. 456–60.

13. Strabo, *Geography*, 13.2.3. **Eustathius:** twelfth-century Byzantine literary commentator and ecclesiastic.

14. Much of Giraldi's basic biographical information appears in Suidas or Suda, a tenth-century Byzantine lexicon. Compare "Sappho: Biographies," Loeb *Greek Lyric*, 1:5–7.

15. Herodotus, *Histories*, 2.135.

16. Athenaeus, *Deipnosophists*, 10.425A.

17. Rhodopis's lovers reportedly erected a splendid pyramid for her burial, at Naucratis on the Nile delta. Herodotus, *History*, 2.134–35; Pliny, *Natural History*, 36.17.82; Strabo, *Geography*, 17.1.33.

18. Athenaeus, *Deipnosophists*, 13.596B–C; Strabo, *Geography*, 17.1.33.

19. Also following Athenaeus on the differentiation of Rhodopis and Doricha, *Deipnosophists*, 13.596B–D. **spits:** votive offerings to the shrine of Apollo. See Herodotus, *History*, 2.135.

20. Apparently following Suidas on Sappho's putative marriage, daughter, and "unsavory reputation." See "Sappho: Biographies," Loeb *Greek Lyric*, 1:5–7.

21. Horace calls her *mascula Sappho* ("manlike Sappho"), *Epistles*, 1.19.28. In Horace's *Odes*, Sappho sings passionate love songs (4.9.10–12) about girls (2.13.24–25). Ausonius, 8.24–25.

22. Pomponius Porphyrio's third-century commentary on Horace, extant in a fifth-century (?) epitome. It also notes her tribadic reputation. See "Sappho: Life," Loeb *Greek Lyric*, 1:19.

23. Leaping into the sea from the cliff of Leucas supposedly cured love. Also, a man leaped every year in rites for Apollo. See Strabo, *Geography*, 10.2.9.

24. **Papinianus:** presumably Aemilius Papinianus, a major Roman legal authority, fl. 200.

25. See "Sappho: Biographies," Loeb *Greek Lyric*, 1:5–7.

26. Pliny, *Natural History*, 21.9.20–21.

27. Ovid, "Sappho to Phaon," *Heroides*, 15; an almost certainly fictional text.

28. Omitting chatter unrelated to Sapphic biography, between Giraldi and his fictive interlocutor Piso.

29. Strabo, *Geography*, 10.2.9.

30. According to Ovid, Deucalion thus jumped, survived, and was freed from his love of Pyrrha. "Sappho to Phaon," *Heroides*, 15.165–72.

31. From Strabo, *Geography*, 10.2.9.

32. **Charon of Lampsacus:** Greek historian somewhat antedating Herodotus. **Probus of Phocas:** not found in Plutarch. **Codrus:** mythical ruler of Athens, eleventh century B.C.E.

33. Strabo, *Geography*, 10.2.9. Giraldi or his edition of Strabo gives Cephalus's beloved a sex change. The Loeb text states "Pteralas," a son, instead.

34. **Calyce:** flung herself from the Leucadian cliff as a result of unrequited love for a young man;

memorialized by Greek poet Stesichorus, sixth century B.C.E. See Athenaeus, *Deipnosophists*, 14.619D–E. **image of Stesichorus:** one of the anciently celebrated statues erected in his honor.

35. Statius refers to Sappho as bold, heroic, or virile, apparently because of her supposed leap, but there is a controversial textual crux in that passage. *Silvae*, 5.3.154–55.

36. A mythography of the late fourth century B.C.E. (?), of which only an excerpt survives. See "Sappho," Fragment 211, Loeb *Greek Lyric*, 1:193.

37. Aelian, *Historical Miscellany*, 12.18.

38. Lucian, *Dialogues of the Dead*, 361.

39. On Psyche and her Renaissance allegoresis, cf. H. David Brumble, *Classical Myths and Legends in the Middle Ages and Renaissance* (Westport, Conn.: Greenwood, 1998), 286–88.

40. Plautus, *Braggart Warrior*, 4.6.1247.

41. Aelian, *Historical Miscellany*, 12.18; Athenaeus, *Deipnosophists*, 2.69D.

42. Following Athenaeus, *Deipnosophists*, 2.69E. Giraldi refers to his own treatise, *Libelli duo... in altero Pythagorae symbola... sunt explicata.*

43. For example, Suidas. "Sappho: Biographies," Loeb *Greek Lyric*, 1:7.

44. For example, Suidas. "Sappho: Biographies," Loeb *Greek Lyric*, 1:7.

45. Athenaeus, *Deipnosophists*, 14.635A–E, citing the Greek historian Menaechmus, c. third century B.C.E.. The *pectis* is a lyre played with the fingers.

46. Hephaestion, *Handbook of Meter*, 43. See "Life of Sappho," Loeb *Lyra Graeca*, 1:181. Hephaestion, Terentianus, Atilius, Fortunatianus, and Diomedes are all metrists, rhetoricians, and grammarians who flourished in the first to fifth centuries.

47. Pseudo-Plutarch, *On Music*, 16; from which Giraldi cites Aristoxenus (commentator on music, fourth century B.C.E.).

48. Information largely derived from pseudo-Plutarch, *On Music*, 16.

49. Pseudo-Demetrius of Phalerum, *On Style*, 140.

50. Hermogenes, *On Types of Style*, trans. Cecil W. Wooten (Chapel Hill: University of North Carolina Press, 1987), 331, 334.

51. Aristotle, *Art of Rhetoric*, 1.9.20.

52. Aristotle, *Art of Rhetoric*, 2.23.12.

53. To counter Sappho, Christian Giraldi inverts her argument, claiming that death for humanity is good, because it accords with God's will.

54. Sappho, Fragment 55, Loeb *Greek Lyric*, 1:99.

55. **Didymus Chalcenterus:** prolific Alexandrian scholar of the first century B.C.E., long after Sappho.

56. Pollux, *Vocabulary*, 9.84. "Sappho: Birthplace," Loeb *Greek Lyric*, 1:13.

57. Athenaeus, *Deipnosophists*, 13.596E.

58. Athenaeus, *Deipnosophists*, 13.599C. **Hermesianax:** Greek poet, third century B.C.E.. **Anacreon:** Greek lyric poet, sixth century B.C.E..

59. Citing Chamaeleon, a literary and philosophical writer of the fourth to third centuries B.C.E., from Athenaeus, *Deipnosophists*, 13.599C.

60. From Athenaeus, *Deipnosophists*, 13.599D. The poets Archilochus and Hipponax were not Sappho's contemporaries. Only a fragment of Diphilus's comedy of the later fourth century B.C.E. survives.

61. The *Chronicle* of Eusebius, the famous third- and fourth-century ecclesiastical historian. "Sappho: Chronology," *Greek Lyric*, 1:9.

62. Giraldi's account of Alcaeus precedes that of Sappho, paired because they were the major exponents of Aeolian lyric poetry, and both associated with Mitylene on Lesbos.

63. From Thevet, *Prosopographia: Or, Some Select Portraitures and Lives of Ancient and Modern Illustrious Personages*, trans. G. Gerbier (London: 1657), Wing P2633, 26–27. See Rouben C. Cholakian, "Introduction," in Thevet, *Les vrais portraits et vies des hommes illustres (1584)*, 2 vols. (Paris: 1584; facsim. rpt. Delmar, N.Y.: Scholar's, 1973), 1:v–xv.

64. Virgil, *Aeneid*, 6.666–71.

65. Plato, *Republic*, 2.366B; *Ion*, 534A–535A.

66. See Strabo, *Geography*, 1.1.1–2.5.

67. Strabo, *Geography*, 13.2.3. **Eustathius:** eminent twelfth-century Byzantine literary commentator and ecclesiastic.

68. For the illustration, see Thevet, *Les vrais portraits* (1584), 1:fol. 55ᵃ.

69. Much as in *Giraldi, or in the Suidas or Suda (Loeb *Greek Lyric*, 1:5–7).

70. Horace, *mascula Sappho* ("manlike Sappho"), *Epistles*, 1.19.28. Ausonius, 8.24–25.

71. This hypothetical other Sappho was supposedly a courtesan from Eresus. See Athenaeus, *Deipnosophists*, 13.596E; Aelian, *Historical Miscellany*, 12.19.

72. Referring to the Leucadian lovers' leap, typically undertaken by men (*Giraldi).

73. In Plato's *Phaedrus*, the poets Sappho and Anacreon exemplify writers wise about love, 235B–C.

74. For ancient sources on this hypothetical other poetic Sappho, see Loeb *Greek Lyric*, 1:7, 23.

75. Translated by Mawy Bouchard and Kenneth Borris, from Tyard, *Oeuvres poétiques*, ed. Ch. Marty-Laveaux (Paris: Lemerre, 1875), 191–94. We use "thou," etc. to translate the French intimate second-person pronoun here.

76. **honor:** for women, almost interchangeable with chastity, in early modernity.

77. **the other God's ardor:** i.e., Love's ardor. The speaker notionally deifies both honor and love.

78. **Pitho:** Greco-Roman goddess of persuasion; also a famously charming Roman prostitute's name.

79. The speaker's insistence on the uniqueness of her tribadic love probably involves dramatic irony expressing her naiveté. *Brantôme indicates that such amours were common courtly gossip.

80. Pythias offered himself as hostage to enable his friend Damon, condemned by the tyrant Dionysius, to settle his affairs before execution. When Damon returned to redeem Pythias, Dionysius was so impressed that he pardoned the former and befriended them. Achates proverbially typified the faithful friend. Hercules spared Nestor due to his youth and enthroned him, but slew his eleven brothers. In Plato's *Apology*, 21A, Socrates says Chaerephon was his friend from boyhood onward. In Statius's *Thebaid*, 10.347–448, the soldiers Hopleus and Dymas risk their lives and die together.

81. **Callisto:** one of Jupiter's loves, transformed by his jealous wife Juno into a bear, then by Jupiter into a constellation, the Great Bear.

82. **Morpheus:** Roman god of dreams, and adept mimic.

83. **Anteros:** "against love." Cupid's brother, he presided over mutual love. The speaker invokes him to avenge betrayal by her beloved.

84. See Richard Griffiths, "'Les trois sortes d'aimer': Impersonation and Sexual Fantasy in French Renaissance Love Poetry," *Journal of the Institute of Romance Studies* 3 (1994–95): 111–27.

85. Translated by Anne Lake Prescott, with thanks to Roger Kuin and Laurie Postlethwaite, from Ronsard, *Elegies, mascarades, et bergerie* (Paris: Gabriel Buon, 1565), fols. 52ᵃ–54ᵇ. Having compared Ronsard's *Oeuvres complètes*, ed. Jean Céard, Daniel Ménager, and Michel Simonin, 2 vols. (Paris: Gallimard, 1993–94), I note significant differences. Prescott's notes are attributed to her parenthetically. Ronsard does not use the French intimate second-person pronoun in either poem.

86. Depicting on one side Apollo's temple and on the other Diana's, the medal may pointedly juxtapose them. They were twins born to Jupiter and Latona. Diana's aversion to marriage and sex with men, so that she lived only with like-minded nymphs, mythically arose when, after being born first, she saw her mother's pain in giving birth to Apollo.

87. **Coroebus:** fought for the Trojans so that Priam, their king, would reward him with marriage to Cassandra. When she prophetically advised his withdrawal from the war, he disregarded her warning and died in battle.

88. **I hold sacred:** *que sainctement je porte* (1565); *qui seule nous conforte* ("which alone strengthens us"), Céard et al., 2:422.

89. **Orestes and his Pylades:** legendary princely cousins reared and educated together, who became proverbial types of faithful friendship. The Scythians deified and worshipped them accordingly.

90. Ronsard writes "name," not "names," showing their unity as "OrestesPylades" (Prescott).

91. **roundel:** *pomme*, i.e., apple, in the French, a word with derivatives often used for something full and rounded, such as a boss, presumably in this case found at the center of the images (Prescott).

92. **greater good:** *plus grand bien* (1565); *plus grand plaisir*, Céard et al., 2:423.

93. **walls and castles:** *Murs et Chateaux* (1565); *Empire et Rois*, Céard et al., 2:423.

94. **neither blood makes us live as much, nor heart or spirit, as friendship does, once one has found her other half:** *Car ny le sang ne nous fait pas tant vivre, / Le coeur, l'esprit, comme fait l'amitié / Ayant trouvé un autre sa moitié* (1565); *Le sang, le coeur ne font les hommes vivre / Tant comme fait la fidele amitié / Quand on retrouve une fois sa moitié* ("Neither blood nor heart make anyone live as much as faithful friendship, once each has regained her

other half"), Céard et al., 2:423. Ronsard alludes to the myth of Plato's Aristophanes in the *Symposium*, whereby humans were originally doubled beings, male/female, male/male, and female/female, but split by the gods, who were jealous of their power. For humans love is thus the desire and pursuit of the lost whole, and descendents of the doubled male or doubled female beings by nature seek lovers of their own sex (189D–93D). In declaring that Anne is her lost half, Diane implies she herself loves females by nature.

95. **so that this bliss might make me equal to you through favor:** *affin que ce bonheur / Me rende egalle à vous par la faveur* (1565); *afin que tel honneur / Me rende égale a vous par le bonheur* ("so that such honor might make me equal to you through good fortune"), Céard et al., 2:424.

96. **always:** *toujours* (1565); *humble*, Céard et al., 1:514.

97. Again alluding to Plato's *Symposium*, 189D–93D.

98. Translated by Anne Lake Prescott, from Ronsard, *Oeuvres complètes*, ed. Prosper Blanchemain, 8 vols. (Paris: P. Jannet, 1857–1867), 8: 121–25. I note the substantive differences from the text in Céard et al. Prescott's notes are parenthetically attributed to her. The French original shifts between the intimate and formal second-person pronouns, and Prescott uses "thou," etc., to translate the former.

99. Though doves are the traditional lovebirds, comparable here to the female lovers, it could be relevant that according to *Brantôme, open-mouth kissing (something he quotes Lucian as saying tribades enjoy) was called kissing *en pigeonne*. See his *Recueil des dames, poésies et tombeaux*, ed. Etienne Vaucheret (Paris: Gallimard, 1991), 2:363 (Prescott).

100. Ronsard has a plural subject and a singular verb. The phrase *n'est qu'une mesme chose* recalls the bleak end of his sonnet to Hélène, written in grief at her refusal and at the death of King Charles IX: Love and Death *n'est qu'une mesme chose* (Céard et al., 1:423; Prescott).

101. **the sad day of departure:** i.e., the day when the woman beloved by the female addressee must move with her new husband to a faraway place.

102. The metaphor recalls a common emblem of ambition foiled by poverty: a figure with wings on his upstretched hand and a clog on his feet (Prescott).

103. **your soul is so enclosed in my body:** *vostre ame est en mon corps si enclose*, Blanchemain; *nostre ame est en noz corps si enclose*, Céard et al., 2:1234.

104. **that wretch:** presumably the female beloved's husband (or perhaps prospective husband) who requires her impending move to a faraway place.

105. Compare Ronsard's concluding line of *Sonnets pour Hélène*, 42, on the lady's empty nocturnal image: *S'abuser en amour n'est pas mauvaise chose* (Céard et al., 1:400). Céard cites the *Greek Anthology*, 5.2 (Prescott).

106. *Affin, mon coeur, que puissiez revenir / Et que le corps perde le souvenir*—i.e., forget the memory of loss due to separation from the beloved.

107. **us:** *nous*, Blanchemain; *vous*, Céard et al., 2:1235.

108. **slight:** *faible*, Blanchemain; *doulce*, Céard et al., 2:1235.

109. **a gallant servant:** *un servant / Qui sera brave*, Blanchemain; *ung servant / Qui sera vostre*, Céard et al., 2:1235.

110. See, e.g., Mueller, pp. 182–207. Valerie Traub summarizes the burgeoning critical commentary in "Recent Studies in Homoeroticism," *English Literary Renaissance* 30 (2000): 299–300.

111. For example, Helen Gardner, ed., *John Donne: The Elegies and the Songs and Sonnets* (Oxford: Clarendon Press, 1965), xlvi. However, with its eloquent ingenuity, paradoxical wit, and full projection of the speaker, the poem superbly evinces stylistic features most associated with Donne.

112. Donne, *Satires, Epigrams, and Verse Letters*, ed. W. Milgate (Oxford: Clarendon, 1967), 52.

113. See Satire I, line 40, Satire II, line 75, in *Satires*, ed. Milgate, 4, 9.

114. Donne, *Elegies*, ed. Gardner, 24 (lines 38–41).

115. See George Klawitter, *The Enigmatic Narrator: The Voicing of Same-Sex Love in the Poetry of John Donne* (New York: Peter Lang, 1994), ch. 1.

116. From John Donne, *Poems* (London: 1633), STC 7045, 166–68 (erroneously designated 152). **Philaenis:** a name anciently associated with tribadism and masculine feminity (Martial's *Epigrams* and pseudo-Lucian's *Affairs of the Heart*); also with authoring erotic poetry and a handbook on sex.

117. **draws:** "imitates" (with **from** in the sense "according to"); or "pulls."

118. As even the trees flocked to hear Orpheus's poetic song, so verse could mythically suspend laws of nature. Since **her** likely refers twice to Nature, **her work** would be love, which Sappho

seeks from Philaenis through her verse. Sappho would insist on the naturalness of female same-sex love.

119. **want:** both "lack" and "need"; the first *OED* example for "desire" dates from 1706.
120. **silly:** possible senses include "pitiable," "insignificant," "simple," "foolish."
121. **A little world:** each human being was considered so, hence a microcosm of the universe.
122. **Phao:** legendary ferryman of Mitylene on Lesbos, whom Venus made exceptionally handsome. He exemplifies the height of masculine beauty, which Philaenis easily surpasses.
123. **change:** formerly a token or attribute of imperfection.
124. **unmanured:** "uncultivated" (i.e., Philaenis's body is inherently replete with pleasure). In contrasting females with males, and feminine sexual pleasure with masculine here, Donne's Sappho may further contrast female same-sex love with its male counterpart, often associated with anal intercourse.
125. **that which their sin shows:** i.e., semen and pregnancies.
126. **thee:** "shee," 1633 copy text.
127. **my half, my all, my more:** alluding to Aristophanes's myth of love's origins in Plato's *Symposium* (189D–93D). Originally doubled beings, male/female, female/female, and male/male, humans were split by gods envious of their power, and hence seek their lost wholes through corresponding modes of love. Donne's Sappho argues her union with Philaenis would thus perfect both, freeing them from change and sickness, as in the poem's closing.
128. **Galaxy:** Milky Way.
129. Translated by Mawy Bouchard and Kenneth Borris, from Le Fèvre, *Les poètes Grecs* (Saumur: D. de Lerpinière, 1664), 21–24. On Le Fèvre's Sappho, cf. DeJean, Index, s.v. "Le Fèvre, Tanguy."
130. Sappho was often called this in antiquity. For Plato's context, see Loeb *Greek Lyric*, 1:49.
131. For Julian, see Loeb *Greek Lyric*, 1: Index, s.v. "Julian." For the others, see *Giraldi.
132. **Great Rhetorician:** i.e., pseudo-Longinus.
133. *Sappho fut d'une complexion fort amoureuse*, 23.
134. *Elle voulut avoir des maistresses aussi bien que des serviteurs*, 24.
135. Leo Africanus (c. 1490–c. 1554), *A Geographical History of Africa*, trans. John Pory (London: 1600), STC 15841, 148–49 (*Ambroise Paré).

Chapter 10

1. Translated by Kenneth Borris, from Aretino, Letter to Battista Zetti, 1537, in Vol. I of *Lettere*, ed. Paolo Procaccioli (Rome: Salerno, 1997), 425. Compare figure 8.
2. Betty Talvacchia, *Taking Positions: On the Erotic in Renaissance Culture* (Princeton: Princeton University Press, 1999), 102–04; also cited in text hereafter.
3. The various accounts of Renaissance erotica treat homoeroticism incidentally. See Paula Findlen, "Humanism, Politics and Pornography in Renaissance Italy," in Lynn Hunt, ed., *The Invention of Pornography: Obscenity and the Origins of Modernity, 1500–1800* (New York: Zone, 1993), 49–108; David Foxon, *Libertine Literature in England 1660–1745* (New Hyde Park, N.Y.: University Books, 1965); David O. Frantz, *"Festum Voluptatis": A Study of Renaissance Erotica* (Columbus: Ohio State University Press, 1989); Ian Frederick Moulton, *Before Pornography: Erotic Writing in Early Modern England* (Oxford: Oxford University Press, 2000); Talvacchia; Roger Thompson, *Unfit for Modest Ears: A Study of Pornographic, Obscene and Bawdy Works Written or Published in England in the Second Half of the Seventeenth Century* (Totowa, NJ: Rowman and Littlefield, 1979); James Grantham Turner, *Libertines and Radicals in Early Modern London: Sexuality, Politics, and Literary Culture, 1630–1685* (Cambridge, UK: Cambridge University Press, 2002), and his *Schooling Sex: Libertine Literature and Erotic Education in Italy, France, and England 1534–1685* (Oxford: Oxford University Press, 2003). All also cited hereafter in text, except for Turner's *Libertines*.
4. See Alastair Fowler, *Kinds of Literature: An Introduction to the Theory of Genres and Modes* (Oxford: Clarendon, 1982), 132.
5. Moulton, 12. He draws the same conclusion from the free mixture of topics in some English manuscript miscellanies (ch. 1). But as he concedes, some are entirely erotic (44). Manuscript miscellanies tend to have an additive and random structure anyway. When it was relevant to distinguish sex differences as a separate sphere, they were (*Encyclopedias and Reference Works).

6. See Kenneth Borris, *Allegory and Epic in English Renaissance Literature: Heroic Form in Sidney, Spenser, and Milton* (Cambridge, UK: Cambridge University Press, 2000), 22–25.
7. See *The Priapus Poems: Erotic Epigrams from Ancient Rome*, trans. Richard W. Hooper (Urbana: University of Illinois Press, 1999).
8. See Beccadelli, *Antonio Beccadelli and the Hermaphrodite*, ed., trans. Michael de Cossart (Liverpool: Janus, 1984), epigram 1.3 (26).
9. See Massimo, trans. James J. Wilhelm, in Wilhelm, ed., *Gay and Lesbian Poetry: An Anthology from Sappho to Michelangelo* (New York: Garland, 1995), 290–302; Massimo, *Les cent elégies: "Hecatelegium,"* Florence, 1489, ed., trans. Juliette Desjardins (Grenoble: University of Grenoble Press, 1986).
10. See Paul F. Grendler and Cyndia Susan Clegg, "Censorship," and J. M. De Bujanda, "Index of Prohibited Books," in *Encyclopedia of the Renaissance*, 6 vols. (New York: Scribners, 1999).
11. See Moulton, 103–4; Andrew Hadfield, ed., *Literature and Censorship in Renaissance England* (New York: Palgrave, 2001).
12. Talvacchia reproduces and translates the sole copy known to survive, 198–227.
13. On this iconographical convention, see Leo Steinberg, "The Metaphors of Love and Birth in Michelangelo's *Pietàs*," in Theodore Bowie and Cornelia V. Christenson, eds., *Studies in Erotic Art* (London and New York: Basic Books, 1970), 231–85.
14. See James M. Saslow, *Pictures and Passions: A History of Homosexuality in the Visual Arts* (New York: Viking-Penguin, 1999), ch. 3; Patricia Simons, "Lesbian (In)Visibility in Italian Renaissance Culture: Diana and Other Cases of *donna con donna*," *Journal of Homosexuality* 27.1–2 (1994): 81–122; Andreas Sternweiler, *Die Lüst der Götter: Homosexualität in der italienischen Kunst von Donatello zu Caravaggio* (Berlin: Rosa Winkel, 1993).
15. Cited in David Freedberg, "Johannes Molanus on Provocative Paintings: *De historia sanctarum imaginum et picturarum*, Book II, Chapter 42," in *Journal of the Warburg and Courtauld Institutes* 34 (1971): 239.
16. See Kenneth Borris, "'Ile hang a bag and a bottle at thy back': Barnfield's Homoerotic Advocacy and the Construction of Homosexuality," in Kenneth Borris and George Klawitter, eds., *The Affectionate Shepherd: Celebrating Richard Barnfield* (Selinsgrove, Ky.: Susquehanna-Associated University Presses, 2001), 193–248, esp. 209–10.
17. See Moulton, 150–52; Frantz, 92–100. A English rendering of a passage involving male-male sex appears in Cecile Beurdeley, *L'amour bleu*, trans. Michael Taylor (New York: Rizzoli, 1978), 94.
18. See Findlen, 86–94; Moulton, 147–48. For an English translation, see Vignali, *La cazzaria: The Book of the Prick*, ed., trans. Ian Frederick Moulton (New York: Routledge, 2003).
19. As Moulton comments in Vignali, 50, 55–56. See further Moulton, *Before Pornography*, 145–48, where he conjectures *La cazzaria* was the Italian apology for pederasty known to Gabriel and Richard Harvey in the 1590s. If so, they use "pederasty" broadly, as some did, to mean male-male love involving a youth or younger man (not necessarily a boy).
20. Patricia Emison, "Prologomenon to the Study of Italian Renaissance Prints," *Word and Image*, 11 (1995): 1–15 (quoting 15).
21. Beyond my chronological scope, Nicolas Chorier (1612–1692) provides an extensive portrayal of erotics between females. See Manuela Mourão, "The Representation of Female Desire in Early Modern Pornographic Texts, 1660–1745," *Signs* 24 (1998–99): 573–602; Turner, *Schooling Sex*, ch. 4.
22. *The Works of John Wilmot Earl of Rochester*, ed. Harold Love (Oxford: Oxford University Press, 1999), 332. Love discusses issues of attribution, 496–98.
23. See Frantz, 110–16; Giovanni Dall' Orto, "Aretino, Pietro," in Wayne R. Dynes, ed., *Encyclopedia of Homosexuality* (New York: Garland, 1990); Patricia H. Labalme, "Personality and Politics in Venice: Pietro Aretino," in David Rosand, ed., *Titian: His World and His Legacy* (New York: Columbia University Press, 1982), 24–25. Moulton's Aretino is bisexual, 140–41.
24. Aretino, *The Marescalco*, trans. Leonard G. Sbrocchi and J. Douglas Campbell, 2nd ed. (Ottawa, Ontario: Dovehouse, 1992), 37; hereafter cited in text.
25. *Aretino's Dialogues*, trans. Raymond Rosenthal (London: Allen & Unwin, 1971), 130, 172–73; cited hereafter in text.
26. Translated by Nicola Martino and Kenneth Borris, from Aretino, *I ragionamenti*, ed. D. Carraroli, 2 vols. (Lanciano: Carabba, 1914). I provide page references to this edition parenthetically after each section translated, and thus indicate elisions only within a section, not before or after.

27. **Bartolomeo Coglioni:** famous fifteenth-century condottiere; punning on *coglia*, "scrotum."
28. **to speak like Florentines:** Aretino exploits the Renaissance linkage of Florence with anal sex.
29. **clyster:** enema, medicine or nutriment injected into the rectum; figuring the penis. Aretino's *cristeo* ("clyster") plays blasphemously on *Cristo* ("Christ") here.
30. **Filling her glass tool … with the heated water:** a hollow glass dildo thus heated.
31. Referring to the famous ancient sculpture of Laocoön discovered at Rome in 1506, and displayed at the Vatican.
32. **took a look at that suchness of glass:** i.e., Nanna contemplated her glass dildo.
33. Tournaments often featured competitive jousting to spear and bear off a suspended ring.
34. **negress:** *negretta*. A pejorative hence racist metaphor for this Italian nun's dark complexion.
35. **glass ring-cake:** *berlingozzo*, a cake shaped like a ring; i.e., the glass dildo. In Aretino's ingenious trope, the ring of the orifice metonymically denominates the dildo, but in an aspect delectably transformed by the pleasure provided.
36. **her phallic idol:** the monk's penis that she reverently fellates.
37. Compare τιμή, "honor," and its cognates.
38. See Laura Coci, ed., *L'Alcibiade fanciullo a scola* (Rome: Salerno, 1988); Giovanni Dall' Orto, "Antonio Rocco and the Background of His *L'Alcibiade fanciullo a scola* (1652)," in Mattias Duyves et al., eds., *Among Men, Among Women: Sociological and Historical Recognition of Homosocial Arrangements* (Amsterdam: Sociologisch Instituut, 1983?), 224–32, 571–72. See further Turner, *Schooling Sex*, 88–105.
39. Dall' Orto, 225.
40. From two previously published excerpts: one translated by Michael Taylor in Cecile Beurdelay, ed., *L'Amour bleu* (New York: Rizzoli, 1978), 125–26; the other by Jill Claretta Robbins in Byrne Fone, ed., *The Columbia Anthology of Gay Literature* (New York: Columbia University Press, 1998), 153–56. Neither source states the Italian editions used. I have stylistically harmonized the translations by modernizing Taylor's most obvious archaisms, and standardized the format by using attributed quotations throughout. Both translators sometimes elide substantial passages. Where this occurs, I parenthetically state the pages in Laura Coci's edition (noted above) corresponding to the previous translated section. I mark other elisions only within, not before or after, each such section. Robbins's translation appears in the middle, corresponding to pages 57–65 in the Coci edition.
41. An argument also in Vignali's much earlier *La cazzaria*. See Findlen, 89.
42. According to a prefatory address to readers, the promised second part is *Il trionfo d'Alcibiade* (The Triumph of Alcibiades), but nothing is currently known of it otherwise.

Permissions

Abano, Pietro d'. See Pietro d'Abano.

Anonymous. Poem XLIX, from *The Maitland Quarto Manuscript*. Edited by W. A. Craigie (Scottish Text Society, new series, vol. 9 (London: Blackwood, 1920). Used as source by permission of the Scottish Text Society.

Aretino, Pietro. Selections from *Ragionamenti* (Dialogues). Translated by Nicola Martino and Kenneth Borris. Printed by permission of the translators.

Avicenna, or Ibn Sīnā. Selections from *Liber canonis* (The Canon of Medicine). Translated into Latin by Gerard of Cremona. Translated into English by Faith Wallis. Printed by permission of the translator.

Brantôme, Abbé and Seigneur de, or Pierre de Bourdeille. Selections from *Les vies des dames galantes* (Lives of Fair and Gallant Ladies). Translated by anonymous (London: Fortune Press, 1934). Reprinted by permission of Caversham Communications Ltd./ Charles Skilton Ltd.

Burton, Robert. Latin passages in selections from *The Anatomy of Melancholy*. Translated by Keira Travis. Printed by permission of the translator.

Caelius Aurelianus. Selection from *On Chronic Diseases*, in *On Acute Diseases and On Chronic Diseases*. Edited and translated by I. E. Drabkin (Chicago: University of Chicago Press, 1950). Copyright 1950 by the University of Chicago. Reprinted by permission of the publisher.

Castro, Rodrigo de. Selection from *De universa muliebrum medicina* (On the Universal Medical Art of Women). Translated by Faith Wallis. Printed by permission of the translator.

Du Laurens, André. Selection from *Historia anatomica humani corporis* (Anatomical Account of the Human Body). Translated by Faith Wallis. Printed by permission of the translator.

Ficino, Marsilio. Selections from *Commentary on Plato's Symposium on Love* (De amore). Translated by Sears Jayne (Dallas, Tx.: Spring Publications, 1985). Reprinted by permission of the publisher.

Firenzuola, Agnolo. Selection from *Dialogo delle bellezze delle donne* (On the Beauty of Women). Translated and edited by Konrad Eisenbichler and Jacqueline Murray. Copyright © 1992 University of Pennsylvania. Reprinted by permission of the publisher.

Firmicus Maternus, Julius. Selections from *Ancient Astrology: Theory and Practice* (Mathesis). Translated by Jean Rhys Bram, Noyes Classical Studies (Park Ridge, N.J.: Noyes Press, 1975). Reprinted by permission of William Andrew Publishing.

Forteguerri, Laudomia. Sonnets to Margaret of Austria and Alda Lunata. Translated by Konrad Eisenbichler. Reprinted by permission of the translator.

Giraldi, Lilio Gregorio. Selection from *De historia poetarum tam Graecorum quam Latinorum* (Chronicles of Poets Both Greek and Roman). Translated by Faith Wallis. Printed by permission of the translator.

Index of Anthologized Authors and Headings

This index locates the entries for anthologized authors or, in the rare cases where an entry is not headed by an author's name, by the heading used in the chapter. Exceptions are legal cases, where the case is located here not by my heading, but by the name of the accused.

For Product Safety Concerns and Information please contact our EU
representative GPSR@taylorandfrancis.com
Taylor & Francis Verlag GmbH, Kaufingerstraße 24, 80331 München, Germany